THE BIG RED ONE

MODERN WAR STUDIES

Theodore A. Wilson
General Editor

Raymond Callahan
Jacob W. Kipp
Allan R. Millett
Carol Reardon
Dennis Showalter
David R. Stone
James H. Willbanks
Series Editors

In collaboration with
Cantigny Military History Series
Cantigny First Division Foundation
Wheaton, Illinois

Paul H. Herbert
General Editor

THE BIG RED ONE

America's Legendary
1st Infantry Division
Centennial Edition, 1917–2017

James Scott Wheeler

University Press of Kansas

Published by the University Press of Kansas (Lawrence, Kansas 66045),
which was organized by the Kansas Board of Regents and is operated
and funded by Emporia State University, Fort Hays State University,
Kansas State University, Pittsburg State University, the University of
Kansas, and Wichita State University

Library of Congress Cataloging-in-Publication Data

Names: Wheeler, James Scott, author. | Cantigny First Division Foundation.
Title: The Big Red One : America's legendary 1st Infantry Division / James
Scott Wheeler.
Description: Centennial edition, 1917–2017. | Lawrence, Kansas : University
Press of Kansas, 2017. | Series: Modern war studies | Series: Cantigny
military history series | Published in collaboration with the Cantigny
First Division Foundation and the Cantigny military history series (edited
by Paul H. Herbert). | Includes bibliographical references and index.
Identifiers: LCCN 2017007059| ISBN 9780700624522 (cloth : alkaline paper)
| ISBN 9780700624539 (ebook)
Subjects: LCSH: United States. Army. Infantry Division, 1st—History.
| United States—History, Military—20th century. | United States—History,
Military—21st century. | BISAC: HISTORY / Military / World War I.
| HISTORY / Military / Iraq War (2003–).
Classification: LCC UA27.5 1st .W485 2017 | DDC 356/.130973—dc23
LC record available at https://lccn.loc.gov/2017007059.

British Library Cataloguing-in-Publication Data is available.

Printed in the United States of America

10 9 8 7 6 5 4 3 2 1

The paper used in this publication is recycled and contains 30 percent
postconsumer waste. It is acid free and meets the minimum
requirements of the American National Standard for Permanence of
Paper for Printed Library Materials Z39.48–1992.

TO THOSE WHO SERVED AND THEIR FAMILIES

CONTENTS

LIST OF ILLUSTRATIONS

PHOTOGRAPHS

Following page 200:

1. The first American gun fired in France, 0605, 23 October 1917
2. The 16th Infantry in first-line trenches, Gypse Hill, near Einville,
   Meurthe-et-Moselle, France, 19 November 1917
3. General John J. Pershing addressing officers of the 1st Division,
   Chaumont, France, 16 April 1918
4. The 26th Infantry training for Cantigny with French tanks at Breteuil,
   France, 11 May 1918
5. Doughboys waiting for orders to take a machine-gun nest at Berzy-le-
   Sec, France, 21 July 1918
6. A French-made Renault tank with a 37mm gun from Colonel George S.
   Patton's brigade
7. Brigadier General Frank Parker talking to Lieutenant Colonel
   Theodore Roosevelt Jr. of the 26th Infantry and Eleanor B. Roosevelt
   in Romagne, Meuse, France, 13 November 1918
8. The 1st Division circus parades past Cologne Cathedral, Rhenish
   Prussia, 4 August 1919
9. The Victory Parade of the 1st Division, New York City, Fifth Avenue,
   10 September 1919
10. Horse-drawn 75mm guns of Battery D, 6th Field Artillery, on Pulaski
    Highway from Fort Hoyle to Fort Meade, Maryland, for maneuvers in
    1938

FOREWORD

For 100 years, the quintessential element of the US Army has been the combined arms division. First among the hundreds of divisions that have been organized, deployed, and deactivated in that time is the 1st Division, today's 1st Infantry Division, the "Big Red One." Nearly alone among the storied formations that have waged our country's wars, the 1st Division has been on continuous active duty since its assembly on the docks of Hoboken, New Jersey, in June 1917. Its story is the story of the US Army and the American soldier—and in many ways the story of the United States—in the twentieth century and into the twenty-first.

The 1st Division got its name by happenstance. When the United States entered World War I in April 1917, it had no permanently organized divisions. Nevertheless, President Woodrow Wilson understood the urgency of French and British pleas for an immediate US presence in France. He promised to send a division at once, a psychological down payment on the forty-two that would follow. The regiments hastily ordered to Hoboken from duty in Texas on the Mexican Punitive Expedition were organized into the 1st Expeditionary Division, meaning just that—the first of many.

Since then, the 1st Division has been first many times—first to Europe in both world wars, and, in both, first in contact with the enemy; first ashore at Omaha Beach in 1944; first to deploy troops by jet transport from the United States to Europe; one of the first two divisions deployed simultaneously to Vietnam in 1965; first to train at the National Training Center at Fort Irwin, California. Its combat history is important and compelling, but its long list of firsts is also significant—how the United States adapted militarily to the changing strategic and domestic imperatives of the last hundred years can be traced in the story of the 1st Division.

Any division history is replete with commanders, battles, and weapons—this history is no exception. But just as important are the remarkable soldiers who have made up the 1st Division over the years. They have consistently shown an esprit de corps remarked upon by credible observers in every generation. 1st Division veterans banded together in 1919 to form the Society of the First Division, an organization that has published a newsletter and held an annual reunion ever since and is active today. Officers who have served in the division in combat have been gathering at an annual dinner since 1920. The division's soldiers and veterans have passed their legacy and traditions from generation to generation.

Recognizing the significance of this story, the First Division Museum at Cantigny Park sponsored the first edition of this book between 2003 and 2007. Dr. James S. "Scott" Wheeler proved and remains the perfect researcher and author. A combat veteran and retired army colonel, he has a passion for the subject that has carried this project through all challenges. Now, as the centennial of the Big Red One approaches and its soldiers have been at war for most of the intervening ten years, we are delighted to add this updated and revised edition to the Cantigny Military History Series. We are even more delighted to have the University Press of Kansas present it again in their distinguished Modern War Studies series.

Since we began this project, another generation of Americans has been called to service, many of them with the 1st Division. The 1st Division provided its 1st Battalion, 63rd Armor, to the 173rd Airborne Brigade's parachute assault into northern Iraq in 2003, the largest airlift of an armor unit into hostile territory in American military history. The 1st Division's 1st Brigade fought in Ramadi, Iraq, from September 2003 to September 2004. In 2004, the rest of the 1st Division deployed from Germany to Iraq as Task Force Danger. Combining Regular Army, Army Reserve, Army National Guard, US Air Force, US Marine, and Iraqi units, as well as civilian agencies, the division conducted sophisticated counterinsurgency operations in north-central Iraq for over a year, helping to make possible, in January 2005, the first free and fair election in Iraqi history. For three years, the 1st Division at Fort Riley, Kansas, oversaw the training of American military advisers to the Iraqi and Afghan security forces. After the modularization of the army in 2006, new "brigade combat teams" of the Big Red One deployed again and again to Iraq and Afghanistan, as did the division headquarters, aviation, artillery, engineers, and logistical units. The 4th Infantry Brigade Combat Team of the division was part of the "surge" of US troops to Iraq in 2007. Since the withdrawal of major US combat forces from Iraq and Afghanistan in 2011 and 2014, units of the 1st Division have been back to both countries to assist their fledgling governments and security forces in their continuing struggles against terrorist organizations such as the so-called Islamic State and the Taliban. Soldiers and units of the 1st Division have provided military assistance to friendly states throughout Africa and stand ready for deployment anywhere in the world.

We are hard at work documenting this unfolding history. In time, we will help the soldiers of today's Big Red One add their own important chapter to the story. This book offers them and all readers the story to date. We believe familiarity with our shared military past fosters responsible citizenship and the leadership, civic and military, that will help ensure our democracy for the future. It is a goal worthy of the soldiers of the last hundred years who have served under the 1st Division's long-standing motto:

"No mission too difficult, no sacrifice too great—Duty First!"

—Paul H. Herbert
Cantigny Park, April 2017

ACKNOWLEDGMENTS

I owe thanks to the many people who helped make this book possible. First and foremost to my wife, Jane Ennis Wheeler, who worked diligently to help with the research and editing. The idea for the original project came from John Votaw, former director of the First Division Museum, and the idea for the book's update came from Colonel (Ret.) Paul Herbert, current director of the museum. The editorial staff of the University Press of Kansas, led by Kelly Chrisman Jacques and Mike Briggs, did a wonderful job in getting the book into shape for publication, and Jon Howard did a superb job as copy editor.

During my years of research for this project I received invaluable help from archivists and librarians. Tim Nenninger guided me through the National Archives, and Brigadier General Hal Nelson and Con Crane helped me negotiate the materials at the Military History Institute at Carlisle Barracks. The research staff of the McCormick Research Center at the First Division Museum, and especially Eric Gillespie and Andrew Woods, helped by finding primary documents covering the period from 1990 to 2016. Gayln Piper, museum director of media, recommended photos and maps and managed many important aspects of preparing them for publication.

Paul Herbert, Roger Barber, and Jane Wheeler read multiple drafts of the new edition and corrected many errors. The McCormick Tribune Foundation funded the original book, and Major General (Ret.) David Grange, then CEO of the foundation, gave me a free hand to tell the story of the Big Red One. Generals Paul Gorman, George Joulwan, Frank Murdock, Ronald Watts, Leonard Wishart, Bill Mullen, and Monty Meigs helped shape the work for the periods of their service. Rudy Egersdorfer, Tim Reese, Bill Schustrom, and Chris Kolenda also provided me with personal insights into the division's history. My close friends Walter Groves, Charles Kirkpatrick, Major General Bill Stofft, Harry Dolton, and Layne Van Arsdale reviewed portions of the first draft and discussed various issues and ideas with me over the years.

In spite of the encouragement, help, and work of all of these people, there may be mistakes in the book. I am fully responsible for those and have done all I can to minimize them. Last, and of most importance, I want to thank and remember the thousands of soldiers, and their families, who have served with the Big Red One over the past century. They have made it their nation's premier division.

—James Scott Wheeler
Kalispell, Montana, April 2017

THE BIG RED ONE

Introduction

THIS IS THE HISTORY OF THE 1ST INFANTRY DIVISION, the quintessential organization of the US Army during the past century. The division saw action in all American wars since 1917, except the Korean, and performed magnificently in all of its service. Often the first unit of the army to deploy and to engage the enemy, the division has been characterized by an ability to learn systematically from experience and to distill this learning into techniques and methods to improve battlefield performance. Central to this learning has been the training of soldiers and the development of competent leaders at all levels. In the process, the Big Red One (so called for the red numeral that has adorned its shoulder patch since 1918) has been characterized by the remarkable esprit of those who have served in the division.

Divisions in the US Army

The military structure known as a "division" is a way to organize, command, and maneuver combat units of brigade, regiment, and battalion size. Historically, American infantry divisions have varied in size from 10,000 to 28,000 soldiers. The division headquarters is the heart of a division. The headquarters maneuvers and operates subordinate units to provide the maximum combat power on the battlefield while sustaining and training soldiers for future operations. The divisional structure has survived because it has been the critical link between the tactical and operational levels of war. Divisions have proven essential in providing "campaign quality" military forces to the nation in times of war.

Armies have organized their combat units into divisions since the beginning of the Napoleonic Wars. American armies in the Civil War adopted the division as their basic combat organization. During that war, divisions were composed of either cavalry or infantry regiments. The division headquarters maneuvered those units on the battlefield. Divisions served as parts of corps that were composed of two or more divisions supported by separate artillery battalions. After the Civil War, the US Army reverted to the regiment as its basic tactical organization.

From 1865 to 1898, the regimental organization proved suitable for the Indian Wars. However, the Spanish-American War of 1898 forced the army to create ad hoc divisions for its overseas campaigns. The army found that it was cumbersome and inefficient to have army commanders maneuver individual regiments in battle and that an intermediate division headquarters lessened the army commander's span of control and maximized the tactical power of infantry and cavalry regiments. By 1912, the US Army recognized the need to maintain modern divisions similar to those used by European military powers.

In an appendix to the Annual Report of the Secretary of War in 1912, the Army General Staff proposed a reorganization of the army into brigades and divisions that could serve in expeditionary operations. The National Defense Act of 1916 authorized the army to organize brigades and divisions. Brigades were to consist of three infantry or cavalry regiments, and divisions were to contain three brigades and other supporting organizations, including artillery and signal units.

The army's first peacetime divisions were organized along geographical lines suited to the administrative needs of a widely dispersed army. National Guard divisions also were organized on a geographical basis. In 1916, the US government ordered the US Army to deploy forces to the Mexican border to combat Mexican bandits. Since the standing army was too small to carry out this mission, the Wilson administration mobilized a number of National Guard units, using powers granted to the federal government by the National Defense Act of 1916. The Regular Army gathered its "2nd Division" for this border operation. The divisions that occupied the US-Mexican border were organized in a number of different ways, in large part because the army lacked an agreed-upon divisional structure. Roughly 16,000 of the men gathered along the border entered Mexico under the command of Brigadier General John J. Pershing in his unsuccessful attempt to run down the Mexican bandit Pancho Villa.

Fortunately, the United States and the Mexican government worked out a compromise that avoided a major war, allowing Pershing's expedition to return to the United States after a fruitless campaign. Pershing did, however, learn valuable lessons about supply, aviation, communications, and the techniques of how to command a large force.

In the spring of 1917, the United States entered World War I on the side of the Allies. It quickly became apparent that an American army was going to deploy to France. At first, the War Department planned to send one million men. Consequently, it was necessary to develop organizations to provide tactical command and control for this large force. The US Army decided to use a divisional structure as the basic building block of its expeditionary force. The army initially copied the European model, with each division consisting of about 12,000 soldiers in infantry, artillery, machine-gun, and engineer units, supported by medical, signal, and logistical troops. Hence, the 1st Expeditionary Division was created in June 1917. This division was renamed the 1st Division shortly after it arrived in France. From that date forward, the army has adapted and modified the division structure to fit its tactical needs and the changing technologies and dynamics of war.

First Born and First to Fight

The 1st Division was the first US division organized and fielded in World War I. It was the first division committed to combat in 1917 and the first to suffer casualties. It launched the first offensive of the American Expeditionary Forces (AEF) in 1918 and played a key role in all subsequent American offensives. The Fighting First, as it was sometimes known, led the way in devising tactics and practices suited to the large "Square Division" used by the US Army in World War I. The division, with over 28,000 soldiers, was so named because it contained two infantry brigades (1st and 2nd), each with two infantry regiments (16th, 18th, 26th, and 28th). The 1st Artillery Brigade, with three artillery regiments (5th, 6th, and 7th), provided artillery support. The Square Division included the 1st Engineer Regiment, the 2nd Signal Battalion, and the 1st, 2nd, and 3rd Machine Gun Battalions to provide support to the infantry units. Medical and logistical services were provided by the Trains, which included a Military Police (MP) Company, the 1st Ammunition and the 1st Supply Train, and the 1st Sanitary Train (with four hospital companies and four ambulance companies). Twice the size of a German or Allied division, the Square Division provided staying power in the tough fighting of the Western Front.

The 1st Division was General John J. Pershing's test bed for "open warfare" tactics and epitomized the AEF's use of after-action reports to shape training. During 1917 and 1918, the 1st Division was the schoolhouse for a number of remarkable officers who went on to command divisions, corps, and armies. Three of the division's officers became army chiefs of staff in the 1920s and 1930s, including the most famous, George C. Marshall. Many of the division's junior officers in World War I, such as Lesley McNair and Clarence Huebner, served at high levels of command in World War II.

The commitment of the division to the front lines in October 1917 was an important boost to French and British morale. American divisions helped stop the German offensive of 1918, and the 1st Division launched the first American offensive action in May. In July, the 1st and 2nd Divisions spearheaded the French army's counteroffensive at Soissons, cutting the Germans' lines of communications and forcing them to begin a withdrawal that stopped only when they left French soil. From May through October 1918, the 1st Division took part in four major campaigns, sustaining over 20,000 casualties. Nonetheless, after each battle, the division assessed the lessons learned and trained thousands of replacements, ensuring that the division remained combat ready. In the final offensive of the war, the Fighting First endured two weeks of heavy combat and cracked the German defenses in the Meuse Argonne.

After the Armistice, the 1st Division led the American army of occupation across the Rhine at Koblenz. It was the last American division to leave Germany in 1919. Its occupation service provided lessons used by the army in 1940 to develop its doctrine for military government. Upon its return to the United States, the division was greeted with homecoming parades in New York City and Washington, DC, before moving to posts first in Kentucky and then in New York and New Jersey.

During the interwar years of 1919 to 1939, the 1st Division was one of the few army divisions to serve continuously on active duty. In 1940, when the US Army expanded for a global war, the 1st Division was the first to train for amphibious warfare. It also was one of the first divisions to convert to the "Triangular Division" structure, and it conducted field tests that confirmed the utility of that design. The Triangular Division, with about 14,000 soldiers, contained three infantry regiments (16th, 18th, and 26th), four artillery battalions (5th, 7th, 32nd, and 33rd), and the 1st Reconnaissance Troop as its combat units. Support was provided by the 1st Engineer and the 1st Medical Battalions, the 1st Quartermaster, the 1st Signal, and the 1st Ordnance Companies. The army chief of staff, George Marshall, converted the army's infantry divisions to the new structure because tests proved that it was easier to maneuver than its predecessor in World War I. During the 1940s, the division was designated the 1st Infantry Division.

The Big Red One deployed to England in July 1942. By September, it was preparing for the first American offensive action against the Axis powers in North Africa. The division spearheaded the invasion at Oran, Algeria, on 10 November. In 1943, it played a crucial role in Allied success in Tunisia, winning significant victories at El Guettar and in northern Tunisia. During its service in North Africa, the division demonstrated the wisdom of deploying a unified division in combat, rather than frittering away its regimental combat teams and battalions piecemeal. During the heavy fighting in Africa, and later in Sicily, the Division Artillery refined practice and procedures that enabled the division to mass the fires of multiple artillery battalions rapidly against a single target. For the remainder of the war, American artillery was the envy of friends and foes.

The Big Red One led the II Corps' assault in Sicily in July 1943. Without adequate armor or air support during its first two days ashore, the division defeated the concerted efforts of the *Hermann Goering Panzer Division* to drive it into the sea. The 1st Infantry Division fought its way across Sicily and fractured the German defenses at Troina. The division refined its use of its Regimental Combat Teams to mix infantry and armor as "combined arms" teams. These combat teams were backed by the division's artillery and its organically assigned combat service support organizations. Under the leadership of Major General Terry Allen, the division set the example for night offensive operations.

Following its successes as an amphibious force in the Mediterranean theater of operations, Generals Omar Bradley and Dwight Eisenhower selected the division to lead Force O in the assault on Omaha Beach, Normandy. Starting in November 1943, the division trained for Operation Overlord under the exacting leadership of Major General Clarence Huebner. Six months later, the three combat teams were ready to face the challenges of another amphibious invasion. On 6 June 1944, the division overcame intense German resistance and, over the next six days, pushed farther inland than any other Allied division. In July, the 1st Infantry Division exploited the gap torn in the German lines by Operation Cobra. After the collapse of the German army, the division swept across France with VII Corps. Reaching the Siegfried Line near Aachen on 12 September, the Big Red One breached the German frontier defenses and captured Aachen, the first German city to fall to the Allies. For the next six months, the division served in the hottest of actions in the Hürtgen Forest, the north shoulder of the Battle of the Bulge, and the final offensive across Germany.

The Triangular Division structure was remarkably flexible and resilient in the heavy fighting of World War II. The 1st Infantry Division and its three regimental combat teams conducted three amphibious assaults, served as a motorized division, fought in the mountains of Africa, Sicily, and Germany, and captured the first major German city taken by the Allies in the war. The headquarters, staff, and signal units allowed the division commander to maneuver his combat teams and numerous attached tank and tank destroyer battalions in these varied operations. The division's support units provided efficient logistical and medical support to a combined arms team that often numbered over 20,000 soldiers. Consequently, when the war ended, the US Army decided to retain the triangular structure as its major tactical organization. From 1946 to 1950, the 1st Infantry Division was the only US division in Germany. It helped dismantle the Nazi regime and provided deterrence to Communist aggression during the early Cold War. The Big Red One remained on the ramparts of freedom in Germany until its return to the United States in 1955.

The 1st Infantry Division was the first division to take part in Operation

Gyroscope, the wholesale swap of stateside for overseas units. It was one of the first to be reorganized in the "Pentomic" fashion in the late 1950s. The Pentomic Division controlled five battle groups, each with five infantry companies. Designed for a nuclear war, the Pentomic Division was too small and had too few supporting organizations to serve in operations other than a nuclear war. It lacked staying power for long campaigns and was cumbersome for a single headquarters to maneuver and sustain effectively. During the brief Pentomic era, the army broke the traditional regimental affiliations with its divisions. By 1959, few of the regiments or battalions that had served with the Big Red One in the previous forty years remained with it.

From 1955 to 1961, the division served at Fort Riley, Kansas, where it trained recruits for the army and provided Pentomic Battle Groups for rotations to Germany. With the buildup of conventional forces in 1961–1963 under President John F. Kennedy, the Big Red One ended its basic training mission and became a full-strength division assigned to the nation's strategic reserve. In 1963, the division adopted the structure of the "ROAD" division (Reorganization Objectives Army Division). The ROAD structure was similar to the triangular structure, with three maneuver brigades to control the infantry and armor battalions assigned to the division. The division commander assigned combat battalions to the brigades for specific missions. The division artillery controlled four artillery battalions and provided support where needed.

When the United States committed major ground forces to combat in South Vietnam in 1965, the 1st Infantry Division deployed to the critical area around Saigon. For this mission, the division took nine infantry battalions, an armored cavalry squadron, and four artillery battalions overseas. For the next five years, the division operated between Saigon and the Cambodian border, the crucial region for the defense of the South Vietnamese capital and many American logistical centers and air bases. The division helped to pioneer helicopter-borne "airmobile" operations and demonstrated time and again that mechanized infantry and armored units could play a valuable role in the defeat of a heavily armed insurgency. The Big Red One did not win every battle it fought in Vietnam, but under the innovative leadership of men like Major Generals Bill DePuy and Orwin Talbott the division drove the major Communist units away from population centers and played a large role in the successful pacification efforts of 1968 to 1970.

In early 1970, the division redeployed its colors and a few of its soldiers to Fort Riley, Kansas, where it took over the troops and equipment of the 24th Infantry Division (M, for Mechanized). For the remainder of the Cold War, the division headquarters and two brigades remained at Fort Riley, while one brigade served in Germany as the 1st Infantry Division (Forward).

The division deployed frequently to Germany from Fort Riley to take part in REFORGER ("return of forces to Germany") exercises. The collapse of the Soviet empire and the Warsaw Pact was a tribute to the service of the thousands of men and women who served in the division and the rest of the American armed forces during the Cold War from 1946 to 1989.

In 1991, the 1st Infantry Division (M) deployed from Fort Riley to Saudi Arabia to serve with VII Corps in the destruction of Saddam Hussein's forces in Kuwait. After the 1991 Gulf War, the Big Red One returned to Fort Riley and then, in 1995, to Germany, where the 3rd Infantry Division (M) was redesignated as the 1st Infantry Division (M). As part of NATO, the division deployed forces repeatedly to the Balkans and Southwest Asia to maintain the peace and to help rebuild the shattered infrastructure of that strategically important region.

In late 2002, elements of the Big Red One deployed to Turkey to prepare the lines of communication across that country for the 4th Infantry Division (M) to use during the invasion of Iraq in 2003. Although the Turkish government ultimately chose not to allow American combat forces to cross its country, the division's work in Turkey diverted Iraqi forces from the main theater in southern Iraq. During the successful American invasion of 2003, the 1st Battalion, 63rd Armor, which was one of the division's battalions, deployed its tanks and Bradley Fighting Vehicles in US Air Force transports to Kirkut, in northern Iraq. The armor battalion, as part of the 173rd Airborne Brigade, secured the northern oilfields of Iraq and proved to be valuable assistance to the Kurds in the area.

Since 2003, the 1st Infantry Division (M) has deployed units repeatedly to Iraq and Afghanistan to fight terrorists and to help rebuild those nations. In 2005, the division was moved from Germany to Fort Riley, Kansas, as the United States repositioned its forces in a new global strategic environment. During the ensuing twelve years the US Army made repeated changes in the division's structure and in the organization of the battalions and brigades that make up the fighting edge of the army. From 1917 to 2017, the 1st Infantry Division (M) has played a leading role in American military operations and strategy. It has worked consistently to maintain its fighting edge through training and innovative tactical practices to meet the ever-changing challenges of combat in the twentieth and twenty-first centuries.

The 1st Infantry Division's Historical Importance

The 1st Division set the standard for the US Army in World War I for discipline, training, and tactical innovation. During the twenty years of peace after the war, it maintained a structure in which officers and noncommissioned officers (NCOs) could retain the traditions of a successful army and practice their profession. As war again approached in 1940, the Big Red One expanded, reorganized, and, in 1942, deployed overseas, where it again led the way and set the standard for tactical performance, lesson-learning, training, and caring for its soldiers. In the postwar period, the division remained deployed to a critical strategic theater, where it provided stability and deterred Communist aggression.

In spite of the erratic structural experiments of the 1950s, the 1st Infantry Division was again ready to answer duty's call in 1965 when it deployed to South Vietnam. There it pioneered a number of tactical innovations and successfully exploited the potential of army helicopters. The division structure again proved its utility and versatility in training, sustaining, and maneuvering combat units on the battlefield.

During the final three decades of the twentieth century, the 1st Infantry Division (M) continued to demonstrate the viability of the division structure. It performed superbly in the 1991 Gulf War as a mechanized infantry division. It conducted numerous expeditionary operations in the Balkans and the Middle East, with its soldiers often serving as peacekeepers, police, and nation-builders. In the Iraq War the Big Red One demonstrated the need for a divisional structure in the heavy fighting in the cities of the Sunni heartland of Iraq. After 2005, the division no longer deployed as a unified organization to the antiterrorist campaigns in Iraq and Afghanistan. Nonetheless, the Big Red One has maintained the traditions, esprit, and unit morale that are such an important part of any military organization.

This book is a history of America's first division. From the beaches of France to the difficult terrain of Iraq and Afghanistan, the men and women who are the Big Red One have lived up to its motto: No mission too difficult; no sacrifice too great. Duty First!

I

Lafayette, We Are Here
Creation of the 1st Infantry Division

THE 2ND BATTALION, 16TH INFANTRY REGIMENT, 1st Expeditionary Division, stepped out smartly from the Caserne de Reuilly for its first parade in Paris, on 4 July 1917. After a stop at Les Invalides, the battalion marched through the heart of the French capital to the Picpus Cemetery. The khaki-clad soldiers did not march as smartly as General John J. Pershing, the American commander in France, might have hoped. Nonetheless, their appearance in the streets of Paris electrified the population, giving the war-weary city and nation a badly needed sense of hope that American soldiers from the mighty industrial power across the Atlantic were coming.[1]

The American soldiers responded to their rapturous reception with pride and greater military precision than their commanders had believed possible.[2] At a ceremony in Picpus Cemetery, Colonel Charles E. Stanton gave an oration near Lafayette's grave, ending with the stirring words, "Lafayette, we are here."[3] Following their march through Paris, the soldiers of the 16th Infantry boarded a troop train bound for a training area near Gondrecourt, in eastern France. Seventeen months of hard training, brutal fighting, and heavy losses awaited them before they and another two million Americans delivered the aid promised by Colonel Stanton.

The Entry of the United States into the War to End All Wars

The 1st Division arrived in France in June 1917, the first of forty-two infantry divisions that the United States sent to serve in the American Expeditionary Forces. The European war was in its third year when the United States entered. By early 1917, the two senior German military leaders, Field Marshal Paul von Hindenburg and General Erich Ludendorff, controlled German military and political policy. They calculated that the German navy could strangle the sea lifelines of Britain and France if allowed to conduct unrestricted submarine attacks against all ships in European waters. They believed that this strategy would cut the flow of food and raw materials to the Allied populations and war efforts, bringing victory to Germany.

The German renewal of unrestricted submarine warfare, on 31 January 1917, propelled the United States into a war that Americans had done a

9

great deal to avoid. After German submarines sank four unarmed American merchant ships, and after clumsy German attempts to encourage Mexico to attack the United States, the US Congress declared war on the German empire in April. This was one of the few encouraging events of the year for the Allies.

The bad news for the Allies began in Russia, where a revolution broke out in March. The Imperial Russian Army disintegrated, allowing German forces to advance all along the front. For all intents and purposes, Russia was out of the war. In mid-April, Allied hopes for a decisive offensive in France were frustrated by strong German defenses and poor leadership by British and French senior commanders. The British, after a promising start in their offensive at Arras and Vimy Ridge, on 9 April, failed to exploit their initial gains.[4] The French fared no better. Mutinies broke out in many French divisions, and disaster was avoided only because the Germans did not learn of the French situation. For the remainder of 1917, any major Allied offensive on the Western Front would have to be carried out by the British.[5]

Hope for Allied victory henceforth depended upon the arrival of significant numbers of American troops in France before the Germans could exploit their victory against Russia by shifting troops from the Eastern to the Western Front. The British and French faced this prospect with dwindling manpower reserves, and a shortage of replacements forced them to decrease the size of their infantry divisions and to consider the disbandment of weaker divisions. If the Americans failed to field a significant number of trained units before the Allies ran out of manpower, Germany could win the war.

The Creation of the AEF

The United States was less prepared for war in April 1917 than it would ever be again in the twentieth century. The Regular Army's total strength was 127,588 soldiers, and the National Guard consisted of another 181,000.[6] A significant percentage of the Regular Army was serving overseas, making it difficult to collect a large force on short notice to send to Europe. The army lacked permanent organizations larger than regiments, even though the scattered garrisons around the nation had been organized into "divisions" in 1912 to provide opportunities to train larger formations.[7] The army's punitive expedition into Mexico in 1916 had depleted the small reserves of Quartermaster materials needed to equip an expeditionary force with basic items such as uniforms, artillery, gas masks, and machine guns. In this situation, President Woodrow Wilson and Secretary of War Newton D. Baker had to decide what America's role in the European war was to be.

In retrospect, the Wilson administration's decision to send an army to France to fight alongside the British and French appears to have been the only logical choice unless America was willing to risk a German victory. In April 1917, it did not appear so clear to most Americans, who "had no conception of the extent of the contribution they would eventually have to make. Presumably, it would largely be economic with only a token military force."[8]

At the beginning of May 1917, no one anticipated how quickly the United States would send military forces to France. In fact, the War College Division of the army's General Staff recommended that all of the Regular Army be used in the United States as cadre to train a mass army to be raised through conscription. Army divisions were to be fully trained and equipped before being sent to Europe. If the United States had adopted such a logical plan, it would have been at least a year before any significant American forces would have arrived in France and two years before an independent US Army could have been capable of fighting the German veterans.[9] But the Allies needed a morale boost and material help immediately.

The Wilson administration heeded the pleas of the French and British delegations to Washington about when to send the first army units to Europe. The chief French representative, Marshal Joseph Joffre—victor in the 1914 Battle of the Marne—asked for immediate assistance in the form of at least a division to demonstrate that help was on its way.[10] Secretary of War Baker directed the army to select a commander and identify a force to send to France as the first installment of the AEF. On 2 May, the War Department ordered Major General John J. Pershing to select and command the first units to be sent. The president expanded Pershing's mission on 24 May, when he appointed him to serve as commander in chief of all American forces in France.[11]

Pershing was the logical choice for commander. Although five other army major generals were senior to "Blackjack" Pershing, he was the only general who had commanded a force larger than a regiment in active operations. As commander of the expedition into Mexico in 1916, he led over 10,000 soldiers in the field. And he had acquired valuable understanding of the logistical and political implications of operations conducted in a foreign country.[12]

Pershing selected the 16th, 18th, 26th, and 28th Infantry Regiments and the 6th Field Artillery for assignment to what was known initially as the 1st Expeditionary Division. During the next few months, these regiments were joined with the 5th and 7th Field Artillery Regiments and numerous other organizations to form the 1st Division.[13]

The infantry regiments were units that Pershing knew well. The 16th Infantry had served in Mexico with Blackjack. The 16th traced its lineage to the Civil War, where it had served in the Army of the Potomac. It was one of twenty-four infantry regiments kept on active duty after the war. The 18th Infantry traced its history to the Civil War and had served along the Mexican border in 1916–1917. The other two regiments were newer. Congress had authorized the recruitment of the 26th and 28th Regiments in 1901. The 26th Infantry served twice in the Philippines before its assignment to the Mexican border in 1915. The 28th Infantry served in Pershing's Southern Department, with headquarters in Fort Ringgold, Texas, until its movement to France.[14]

The artillery regiments had distinguished service records. The 1st Battalion, 5th Field Artillery, had the longest continuous service of any unit in the Regular Army, tracing its lineage to Alexander Hamilton's battery of New York artillery. Hamilton's battery was incorporated into the Continental Army as John Doughty's Company of the Artillery Regiment. The 5th and 6th Field Artillery Regiments were constituted in the Regular Army on 25 January 1907 at Forts Leavenworth and Riley, Kansas, respectively. The 7th Field Artillery Regiment was established on 1 July 1916 at Fort Sam Houston, Texas. Many of the batteries in these regiments claimed a lineage to units that had served in the Civil War.[15]

When the infantry regiments received orders for movement to New Jersey, their average rifle company strength was sixty men. General Hugh Scott ordered the rifle companies expanded to 150 men each and a machine-gun company of 146 men assigned to each infantry battalion. Because many of the officers and noncommissioned officers of the infantry regiments had been transferred to other units to train conscripts, it was necessary to transfer additional officers and soldiers to the 1st Division's regiments and to fill the ranks with men who had enlisted since the declaration of war. Consequently, the 1st Division was a Regular Army division more in name than reality when it departed the Southwest.[16]

The 1st Division's officer corps was typical of most of the divisions that served in World War I. The commanding general, Major General William L. Sibert, and the two brigade commanders, Brigadier Generals Robert L. Bullard and Omar Bundy, were graduates of the United States Military Academy. All were acquaintances of Pershing. Bullard and Bundy had served with Pershing along the Mexican border, and Sibert was a well-respected Engineer officer.[17]

Pershing stamped his personal imprint on the officer corps of the expeditionary forces and, therefore, on the US Army for at least the next thirty years. He did this through his selection of division and corps commanders and through his determined efforts to dictate the doctrine that would guide army training for the next two decades. Pershing knew many of the best and brightest officers available to raise, train, and lead the mass army needed

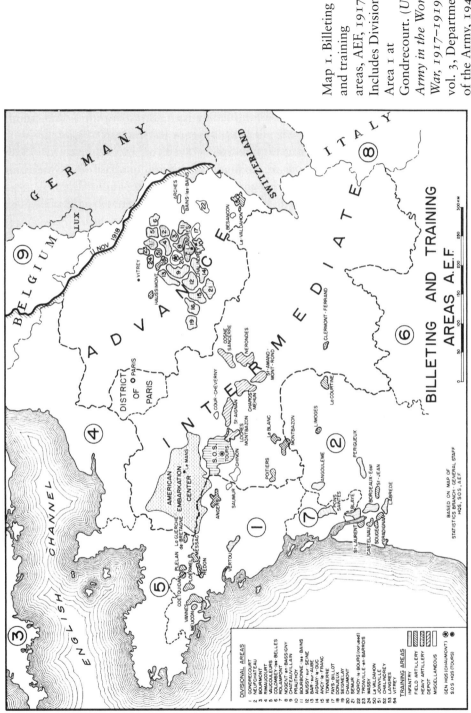

Map 1. Billeting and training areas, AEF, 1917. Includes Divisional Area 1 at Gondrecourt. (*U.S. Army in the World War, 1917–1919*, vol. 3, Department of the Army, 1948)

BILLETING AND TRAINING AREAS A.E.F.

BASED ON MAP OF STATISTICS BRANCH- GENERAL STAFF HQS, S.O.S., A.E.F

DIVISIONAL AREAS
1 GONDRECOURT
2 NEUFCHATEAU
3 BOURMONT
4 CHAUMONT
5 RIMAUCOURT
6 VAUCOULEURS
7 COLOMBEY-les-BELLES
8 NOGENT-en-BASSIGNY
9 CHATEAUVILLAIN
10 PRAUTHOY
11 BOURBONNE-les-BAINS
12 MUSSY-sur-SEINE
13 BAR-sur-AUBE
14 AIGNAY-le-DUC
15 ANCY-le-FRANC
16 TONNERRE
17 FAYS-BILLOT
18 DONJEUX
19 SEIGNELAY
20 CHAUMONT
21 SEMUR
22 NOROY-(ø-BOURG (not used)
23 TROINVILLE-en-BARROIS
24 MASSY
50 La VALDAHON
51 JOINVILLE
52 CHALLINDREY
53 LANGRES
54 VITREY

TRAINING AREAS
INFANTRY
FIELD ARTILLERY
HEAVY ARTILLERY
DEPOT
MISCELLANEOUS

GEN HQS (CHAUMONT) ⊛
SOS HQS (TOURS) ●

in France. He understood that modern warfare requires officers trained in contemporary staff procedures by the army's staff and war colleges.[18]

The men selected to fill the senior field grade positions in the 1st Division fit Pershing's vision. Most of the division's colonels and lieutenant colonels were regulars, although not necessarily West Point and Staff College graduates. Colonel Campbell King, chief of staff of the division for much of the war, enlisted in 1897 and received a commission through competitive examination in 1898. King saw combat in the Spanish-American War, attended the Staff College, and served in Mexico in 1916. Captain George C. Marshall, a Virginia Military Institute and Staff College graduate, was the operations officer (G3), although he had not served with Pershing.

Although most of the division's senior leaders were professional soldiers, there were interesting exceptions. Major Theodore Roosevelt Jr. was a reserve officer. Roosevelt received command of the 1st Battalion, 26th Infantry, shortly after the division arrived in France and ultimately commanded the 26th Infantry Regiment. The combat service of a son of a former president was not as unusual in World War I as it might appear today. Many prominent Americans in 1917 would have agreed with President Theodore Roosevelt, who observed, in a letter to the commander of the division's 2nd Brigade, that "men of prominence ask nothing for themselves or their sons except to be put in positions of service and danger."[19] Teddy Roosevelt Jr. was wounded while leading his battalion; his aviator brother was killed during the war.

The prominent journalist Major Robert McCormick was another example of successful nonprofessional officers in the AEF. McCormick, who had served with the Illinois National Guard along the Mexican border in 1916, took command of an artillery battalion in 1917. McCormick commanded his battalion successfully and was promoted to colonel. In the summer of 1918 he returned to the United States to train an artillery brigade. Without such citizen-soldiers, neither the 1st Division nor the US Army could have accomplished its missions in World War I.[20]

Few of the division's lieutenants or captains were Regular Army officers. Many junior officers earned their commissions through the Officer Training Corps (OTC), and a number of lieutenants were promoted from the enlisted ranks of the army.[21] Of the roughly 200,000 officers who served in the army during the war, fewer than 9,000 had been officers on active duty in April 1917, and only 5,791 of those were regulars. Nearly half (96,000) of the army's officers earned their commissions in the OTC; 12,000 were national guardsmen, 16,000 were commissioned from the ranks, and 68,000 officers received direct commissions.[22] Initially, most of the 1st Division's junior officers were from the OTC or promoted from the noncommissioned officer ranks.

The Condition of the US Army: June 1917

The 1st Expeditionary Division reflected the miserable readiness condition of the US Army in 1917. There was no structure for an army division beyond the tentative decision that it would contain four infantry regiments and that it would be a combined arms organization of infantry and artillery. In July, the War Department proposed a divisional structure that included 19,492 men in two brigades of two regiments each. This organization was to include an artillery brigade of seventy-two guns and a machine-gun company for each of the twelve infantry battalions.

Pershing raised the infantry strength of the division from 7,344 to 12,288 men by increasing rifle companies to 250 men each and adding a fourth rifle company to each battalion. These changes reflected Pershing's belief that infantrymen, armed with rifles and trained in long-range marksmanship, were the principal offensive weapons needed to break the tactical stalemate on the Western Front.[23] He did not ignore the power of the machine gun, however, as his divisional structure provided for fourteen machine-gun companies of twelve guns each. Pershing's "Square Division," as it was called, due to its having four infantry regiments, was supported by three regiments of field artillery and detachments of engineers, signal troops, and medical personnel, bringing it to a strength of approximately 28,000 officers and men.[24] Fewer than half of the 1st Division's soldiers arrived in France in the first convoys of June 1917. The rest joined the division during the summer.

The 1st Division received most of its weapons from the Allies in 1917, especially artillery. Although American field artillery units were equipped with a 3-inch gun in 1917, there were only 544 of them available. It was clear that American artillery units in the numbers needed for trench warfare could not be equipped with a US gun quickly enough. There was no American-made heavy howitzer available to compete with the German 150mm piece or equal to the French 155mm gun. Consequently, American artillery regiments received French-designed and -manufactured guns and howitzers. This had the added benefit of reducing the amount of equipment that had to be shipped to Europe in the all-too-scarce merchant shipping. The French provided American artillery units with over 3,000 of the 3,500 artillery weapons used by the US Army in France. The 6th and 7th Field Artillery Regiments received the French 75mm cannon, and the 5th Artillery used the French 155mm howitzer.[25]

The infantrymen of the 1st Division were armed with American rifles. Most Regular Army and National Guard units carried the superb Springfield M1903 rifle in 1917. However, only 900,000 of the 3.5 million rifles used by American troops were Springfields. The remaining rifles were Enfields modified to fire the same cartridge as the Springfield and manufactured in US factories.[26]

Far less had been done to provide machine guns for a large force. In 1912, Congress authorized four machine guns per infantry regiment; by 1919 each division had 260 machine guns and more than 700 automatic rifles.[27] The 1st Division initially carried French-designed Hotchkiss heavy machine guns and the lighter Chauchat gun. Eventually, the United States developed a heavy machine gun and an automatic rifle, both manufactured by Browning.[28] Many machine-gun crewmen saw their first machine gun after they arrived in France.

The US Army also was reliant on the French for most of the horses, trucks, wagons, and railway cars needed to transport and support the AEF. Horses remained the prime means of moving artillery. The French were short of suitable horses for their own units, and a large percentage of the animals the division received during its first year in France were in poor physical condition. The American automotive industry failed to fill the gap with trucks in sufficient numbers, due to bottlenecks in production, acquisition, and overseas shipment. Transport was a persistent problem for the division and the AEF throughout the war.

Where Is the Division to Go?

The infantry regiments had only two weeks to get organized for their railroad trip to New Jersey, which began on 3 June. This was barely time enough for the leaders to meet the new recruits and to issue uniforms, rifles, and mess kits to the roughly 14,000 men who would initially constitute the division. The troop trains arrived in Hoboken Meadows on 8 and 9 June. Major General Sibert joined his division on 10 June along with his hastily gathered staff that included Campbell King, George Marshall, Lesley McNair, and Frank McCoy. The twelve troopships, most of which were converted German merchant vessels that had been interned in American ports in 1914, were loaded by 14 June.[29]

Meanwhile, Pershing and his staff sailed to England on 28 May and then on to France. The new commander in chief and his staff faced a series of difficult questions during their voyage and first three months in France. While crossing the Atlantic, they worked feverishly to develop a plan for the mobilization and training of the large force needed to defeat Imperial Germany.

Pershing had broad power to train and command what would become an army of over two million soldiers by November 1918. He received two letters of instructions before he left Washington in May. One was drafted by Pershing and his chief of staff, James Harbord, for the signature of the army's chief of staff. The other was a letter of instruction prepared by Secretary of War Newton Baker.[30] Both documents gave Pershing the power to organize, train, and employ the AEF as he determined best to win the war. The Baker letter emphasized that Pershing was "to cooperate with the forces of the other countries employed against that enemy; but in so doing the underlying idea must be kept in view that the forces of the United States are a separate and distinct component of the combined forces, the identity of which must be preserved."[31] Pershing was to develop an army whose contributions to victory would ensure the president a place at the peace table as a full partner of the Allies.

As Pershing and his assistants tackled their challenges, the soldiers of the 1st Division crossed the Atlantic and disembarked in Saint-Nazaire, France, on 26 June. The voyage had been smooth, although there had been several U-boat alerts. With little fanfare, the soldiers marched to their temporary quarters, a cantonment recently used to house German prisoners of war (POWs). For the next few weeks, the division's leaders attempted to teach thousands of recruits how to dress, march, and salute and how to perform the hygiene tasks and household chores needed to keep soldiers healthy. This training challenge was made more difficult by the inadequacy of equipment, training areas, and living facilities near Saint-Nazaire. Probably no one complained when the division was ordered to move to a more permanent training base at Gondrecourt, in Lorraine, in early July.[32] (See Map 1.)

The 1st Division's soldiers and equipment moved to Lorraine on French trains. The officers traveled in second-class passenger coaches, and the enlisted men rode in boxcars known as "forty and eights" because their capacity was rated as forty men or eight horses. Herbert McHenry, a machine gunner in the division in 1918, described his experience of a forty and eight in his memoirs:

> [The forty and eight] was [a] freight car. When equipped for men it had seats along each wall of the car, and two seats, placed back to back ran lengthwise along the middle of the car. The toilet consisted of a running board on the outside of the car . . . running the full length of the car. A rod ran along the full length of the car, by holding which the boys could prevent themselves from falling off the train while using that wonderful open-air toilet. In that car . . . there were packed forty-five men, forty-five soldiers' packs, forty-five rifles, and rations for ten days. There was a seat for every man.[33]

McHenry remembered that "when night came we slept on the seats where we sat and exactly as we sat with the exception that each soldier, as he slept, leaned his head on the shoulder of the soldier next him."[34]

When the troops arrived in Gondrecourt, they were billeted in the surrounding villages in barns and other farm buildings rented from French farmers. For the next six months, these poorly ventilated and malodorous quarters housed the division's enlisted soldiers. Men such as Private Warren Mavity, of the 7th Artillery, found living conditions far from comfortable:

> Our sanitary system consisted of a hole dug in the ground with canvas walls on three sides; with an outhouse like this, we did not linger long in taking care of our needs. . . . Six of us were billeted in a room between [two adjacent] homes with a door at each end that fit so poorly it let the snow in and there was a constant draft. . . . We slept on bed sacks on a stone floor with full pack which meant only removing our rolled leggings, wet shoes, and socks. We put on dry socks and slept on the wet ones to dry them. Our folded jackets served as pillows. Our shoes never did dry completely.[35]

Officers fared somewhat better. Most, like George Marshall, the division's operations officer, rented small rooms in local houses. Spartan and cold, these drafty quarters were welcome relief from the rigors of winter training.

In less than three months, men such as Vern S. Baldwin, who had enlisted on 7 April 1917, went from the familiarity of rural and small-town America to an entirely different culture in a country that had been at war for over three years. It is a tribute to the American soldiers and the French population that there was little evidence of disharmony between the two groups.[36]

Training the AEF

The training challenges facing General Sibert and his leaders at all levels were daunting. A lot was at stake, since the division was the model for all subsequent divisions trained in France. If the 1st Division failed to become an effective fighting force, it would prove that the Germans and Allies were correct in their assessment that Americans were incapable of training and commanding a modern army.[37] The division's success would validate American methods of training and warfare.

No one in the AEF had served in an infantry division. Neither of the brigade commanders had led a brigade before. None of the officers or NCOs had experienced trench warfare, with its new weapons such as flamethrowers, trench mortars, and chemical munitions. No one in the division or the AEF had ever been in an army made up mostly of new enlistees and conscripts. None of the leaders knew how to train such inexperienced soldiers in such numbers, let alone how to train regiments and divisions.

Pershing addressed the issues of training head-on. He created a section of his staff dedicated to training doctrine and methods. This section, known as the G5, was an extension of the AEF commander and played a direct role in the training of the 1st Division for the next ten months. On 17 July 1917, Pershing sent a telegram to the War Department detailing his training philosophy and methods. It was evident to Pershing "that the first troops to arrive must receive their training in France." Therefore, the first four divisions to join the AEF—the 1st, 2nd, 26th, and 42nd—would be trained directly by the AEF. The training of the "later troops [of the following divisions] should not be delayed until their arrival in France."[38] Therefore, the War Department needed to develop a training system and camps in the United States in which to train all other units before they sailed to France.

Pershing determined that "in physical training, close order drills and disciplinary instruction, and musketry, the systems in vogue in the army of the United States are entirely adequate."[39] Further, AEF trainers recognized that it was vitally important for the army to create schools for the education of specialists in the new skills of trench warfare, "since we have practically no qualified instructors," and that the first priority needed to be to train instructors "who in turn must train others in schools within the organizations." French and British officers traveled to the United States to help establish the initial specialty training; the divisions in France were to train with French units.[40]

Artillery training in the United States was to focus on fundamentals. Those "artillery units arriving in France in the near future" were to train with the French at their artillery center at Valdahon, in Lorraine, "where they will receive their new material and their horses and where they will take up their preliminary training." As soon as possible, a school run by American officers was to be established at Saumar for the training of artillery battery commanders.[41] Consequently, the three artillery regiments of the 1st Division moved directly to Valdahon after their arrival in France in August. When the 1st Artillery Brigade joined the division, in October, it was ready to support the infantry in the front lines.

Pershing accepted a French offer to train staff officers for the rapidly expanding army. However, he quickly changed his mind when he became convinced that such instruction would imbue American officers with French doctrine that he believed adhered too closely to the defensive methods of trench warfare. Consequently, he ordered Brigadier General Robert Bullard to create a staff college at Langres, where Leavenworth graduates, aided initially by British and French officers, would educate the officers who would fill the staff positions in the American army.[42] The first officers to serve as instructors and students at Langres came from the 1st Division, increasing the turmoil in the regiments, especially when nine of the division's twelve infantry battalion commanders were absent in November.[43]

Measures to establish the specialty schools to prepare the AEF for combat eventually were successful. However, the first four divisions suffered the growing pains of the system and paid the price for it in a number of ways. The 1st Division provided the cadres and first groups of students for the schools and suffered the effects of the personal attention of Pershing and his staff during its training. The 2nd Division had to deploy soldiers to work on construction projects on the lines of communications, delaying its training until early 1918. The 1st Division was spared this fate in exchange for its role as the training laboratory for the AEF.

At the regimental level, Colonel George Duncan, commander of the 26th Infantry in 1917, had only seventeen officers in the regiment with more than a year of service. Duncan recalled that "among the older officers were those wholly unfitted for the responsibility of command and among the lieutenants old noncommissioned officers unaccustomed to leadership and independence of thought or action. This vanguard of the superb army that was to be developed . . . was, at this time, certainly a motley outfit."[44]

Pershing provided detailed guidance concerning the standards he expected in the training of the soldiers:

> All officers and soldiers should realize that at no time in our history has discipline been so important; therefore discipline of the highest order must be exacted at all times. The standards for the American Army will be those of West Point. The rigid attention, upright bearing, attention to detail, uncomplaining obedience to instructions required of the cadet will be required of every officer and soldier of our Armies in France.[45]

Pershing issued such strict guidelines in October 1917 because he was dissatisfied with the standards of soldier conduct he observed during his early visits to the 1st Division.[46] He particularly aimed his directives at the division commander, William Sibert. Pershing had not picked Sibert for command of the division. Sibert had been selected by General Tasker Bliss and Secretary Baker, based upon his superb performance as an engineer in the Panama Canal Zone. Sibert had little experience with infantry units, and he relied heavily on the French for training assistance. The French provided the 47th Infantry Division to instruct the 1st Division in the intricacies of trench warfare. However, by preparing the Americans for trench warfare, the French increased Pershing's belief that such training dulled the offensive spirit needed to break the stalemate on the Western Front and win the war.[47]

Sibert was caught in the middle doctrinally and lacked experience with combat training. He also did not appear to be soldierly or aggressive enough to Pershing. AEF training inspectors were quick to report to their boss any evidence that the division's training was not up to standard.[48] As George Duncan remembered, Sibert

> had commanded a Coast Artillery District. He was a most considerate, high-minded officer but was having his first military experience with combatant field troops, something entirely new to him, so he was utterly dependent upon his staff officers and no officer ever had a better educated or more dependable set of men to deal with. So it was a case of tactful education by the staff on one hand and the lack of fundamentals of tactical experience and knowledge upon which to build, on the other.[49]

By 20 October 1917, Pershing was intimating to Robert Bullard that he was going to replace Sibert.[50] In November, relations between Sibert and Pershing reached a new low when Pershing dressed down Sibert in front of the assembled officers of the division for what Pershing considered poor performance in a training exercise. That at least some of Pershing's anger against Sibert was misplaced was made clear when the division's operations officer, Lieutenant Colonel George Marshall, publicly risked his career to defend the division's performance to the commander in chief.[51] Pershing listened to Marshall's explanation of the difficulties faced by the division's leaders, but he did not change his mind about Sibert's unsuitability for command.

Pershing's dissatisfaction stemmed from more than his view that the 1st Division's soldiers were not meeting the standards of the Military Academy. The conclusion at AEF headquarters was that "the progress made by the First Division by these methods was not good, so a Training Program was prepared by the Training Section, General Staff, and issued to the division on October 6, 1917."[52]

The AEF training program was based on the belief that American soldiers needed to master the skills required of open warfare before they came to France to learn the expedient tactics of trench warfare. What the expression "open warfare" meant was not clearly spelled out, but what it was *not* was made evident in repeated messages and training directives sent from Pershing's General Headquarters (GHQ) in Chaumont to the War Department and to the divisions of the AEF.

Open warfare was not trench warfare, with its emphasis on defensive positions, machine guns, heavy use of artillery, and barbed wire. It was an offensive doctrine emphasizing open formations of infantrymen using their rifles at long ranges and maneuver by dispersed units to close with and destroy enemy machine-gun positions. It was a state of mind as much as a doctrine. It certainly did not fit the tactical situation or prepare the American army for its tactical role in World War I.[53]

The AEF training program was not available for the 1st Division and the other three divisions training in France until October 1917. Sibert had few advantages when he began to address the shortfalls in the training of his solders evident to everyone in July. Sibert candidly assessed the state of the division's training in a letter to the commanding general of the French 47th Infantry Division on 18 July 1917:

> Over fifty percent of the soldiers in the division are recruits almost entirely without training. Practically all of the officers below the grade of captain have been appointed less than six months. Some of these new officers have had service in the ranks. Few of the present noncommissioned officers have had longer service than two years. The members of the division were assembled for the first time upon landing at St. Nazaire.

Consequently, Sibert concluded that "it is essential that the training of the troops should be limited for the next four weeks, at least, to elementary work and the development of a proper disciplinary spirit."[54]

Sibert's candor may have been appropriate within the division, but it was a mistake to give such an assessment to the French, who already believed that American officers and staffs were incapable of training units larger than battalions. Most French and British leaders were convinced that the best way to train the Americans to serve successfully in the front lines was to place American companies and battalions in French or British divisions for an extended period of service. The British felt it would be even better if individual American soldiers were incorporated into British formations. Through this process of "amalgamation," the Allies believed they could fill their depleted ranks.[55]

Pershing steadfastly refused to accept amalgamation or any version of training that would slow the development of independent American divisions. He believed that the amalgamation of American battalions in Allied divisions would be a mistake for a number of reasons. As Joffre, who also opposed amalgamation, noted to Pershing, American soldiers would be commanded by foreign officers whose orders they might resent. "In case of a reverse [in battle] there would be at once the tendency to assess the blame to the command." And, as Joffre further pointed out, the British had not amalgamated Canadians, Australians, or New Zealanders in British divisions.[56]

If Pershing had accepted amalgamation, he would have ignored Baker's letter of instruction of 26 May 1917 and undermined American clout at the negotiating table at the end of the war. In this debate, any rhetorical ammunition that Sibert gave to the French to support their views on the need for amalgamation was anathema to Pershing. In the end, Pershing allowed American troops to train with the British and the French for short periods, but not to be integrated into Allied divisions.[57]

The Training of the First Division: 1917

In July, Sibert and the 1st Division staff developed a plan to conduct training eight hours a day, with Saturday afternoons and Sundays excepted. This instruction stressed physical conditioning, close order drill, bayonet practice, rifle instruction, and road marches. Special attention was given to the outward manifestations of military discipline such as saluting, personal bearing, the proper wearing of the uniform, and personal hygiene. "The casual discharge of duties or the lack of scrupulous attention to every detail of orders, instructions or work" was "rigorously checked and corrected."[58]

By 2 August 1917, Sibert believed that sufficient progress had been made in these areas to allow the division to spend half of each day, from 6 to 25 August, emphasizing bayonet combat, rifle firing at targets to a range of 300 yards, road marches with full packs, and more close order drill. During the remainder of each day, French instructors taught the Americans how to use grenades, Stokes mortars, 37mm cannons, and machine guns. The French also taught the 1st Division's junior leaders how to construct fieldworks and to perform the basic tasks of trench warfare.[59]

By 21 September, it was clear that "the time has come for the 1st Division to stand alone. Its officers must be required to solve problems in trench warfare, giving the necessary orders and executing the problems without the help of French officers."[60] As training intensified, Sibert relieved several commanders whom he felt could not get the job done. Aggressive and promising officers like Colonel John Hines joined the division as replacements. Hines, who succeeded Colonel Frank A. Wilcox as commander of the 16th Infantry Regiment, led the 16th until he was promoted to brigadier general and took over the 1st Brigade, in May 1918. Hines had served as Pershing's adjutant during the Mexican expedition and as an assistant adjutant general at GHQ until he arrived in the 1st Division in November.[61]

During this phase of training, the infantry practiced tasks related to trench warfare.[62] The 1st Engineer Regiment constructed a trench warfare training center known as Washington Center, near Gondrecourt, in which the division learned the skills needed to maintain units at the front. The 2nd Signal Battalion laid telephone lines and operated the wireless sets of the brigade and division posts of commands (PCs). The trains handled the food, water, and ammunition services that they would provide when the infantry went into the lines. The infantry regiments rotated through Washington Center from the middle of September to mid-October.

By early October, Sibert considered the division ready for a program of special instruction as a final preparation for the rotation of the infantry battalions into the front lines with a French division.[63] This next stage of training would involve the deployment of all divisional elements, to include the artillery regiments that had been training separately at Valdahon. Sibert's favorable appraisal of the progress of training pleased French leaders, who were eager to get some American soldiers into the front lines to demonstrate to their army and people that the Yanks were in the fight.

During the autumn, as the division trained for its first combat experience, the weather turned foul. As George Marshall remembered,

> The cold raw days of the French fall now descended upon us and made training in trench warfare particularly difficult, as the practice trenches filled with water, and few of our men had more than one pair of shoes. We were suffering at this time from a lack of many necessary articles of clothing. The serious deficiency in socks was finally met by large purchases near Nancy, but the shortage in shoes could not be overcome in this way.[64]

Colonel Hines noted in his diary that it was a "very hard winter. Poor fuel, poor billets, [and therefore it was] necessary to keep the troops employed."[65] The soldiers endured the miserable weather in billets that initially were in barns and farm buildings and then in hastily constructed shacks covered with tar paper.

The three artillery regiments had arrived in France in August and moved directly to the French artillery training camp in Valdahon. There the French provided the artillery units with most of their equipment, including horses and cannons. The batteries received training in the morning from French instructors and practiced their new skills in the afternoon under the direction of their own officers. This system worked well. By October, the 1st Artillery Brigade was ready to send its battalions to the front, where they could continue to hone their skills while firing in support of French and American troops.[66] This phase of training for the artillery and the rest of the division was to be conducted under the control and guidance of the French 18th Infantry Division in a sector of trenches near Sommerville, in Lorraine.

The First Combat Experience: The Sommerville Sector, Lorraine

On 8 October 1917, GHQ ordered Sibert to select the first four battalions to serve in the French trenches. Each battalion was to be supported by a machine-gun company and the appropriate engineer, signal, and medical units. The American battalions would serve three days in the French second line before replacing a French battalion in the first trench line, where they would remain for seven days. The leading battalions would be replaced by battalions of their respective regiments in the second line. After seven days, the following battalion would relieve the leading unit in the first line. This rotation and experience in the trenches would be controlled by French commanders at battalion and higher echelons, with American officers in charge of their companies and platoons. The American battalion commanders and staffs joined the French commanders and staffs to observe operations and techniques.[67]

The first battalions to go into the front lines set out from their billets near Gondrecourt by truck, on 17 October. They occupied positions in the second trench lines of the French 18th Division on the night of 20–21 October. Three days later, the Americans occupied the first line, beginning active American participation in the ground fighting of the war. The infantry was supported by French artillery units reinforced by the 1st Division's artillery battalions. Each artillery regiment sent one battalion at a time to serve with the French. Battery C, 6th Field Artillery Regiment, fired the first American artillery round of the war at 0605, 23 October 1917.[68]

The deployment of the troops to the Sommerville front went relatively well. Since the American infantry battalions of over 1,000 men were much larger than French battalions, the French truck convoys used to make the move had too few vehicles. This transportation difficulty was dealt with, but the differences in size between American and Allied units remained a challenge for rail and truck movements throughout the war.

The division commander and his staff were not allowed to do more than observe the first deployment of the division's soldiers. They visited the French division headquarters to observe French staff and command techniques while American battalion, regimental, and brigade commanders and staffs spent time in the trenches with their French counterparts. In this fashion, the 1st Division's senior leaders learned the art of command in trench warfare.[69]

The French selected the Sommerville sector for the first deployment of American units because it was a quiet sector in which the green troops would have a chance to gain combat experience without suffering demoralizing losses. The first four battalions rotated through the trenches without major incident, and the second battalions from each of the four regiments entered the front lines on the night of 2–3 November. However, as the 2nd Battalion, 16th Infantry, was settling into its miserably wet trenches, the Germans launched a raid against a position held by Company F. The attack was supported by a barrage designed to isolate the point attacked with a curtain of artillery fire. The German assault party broke into Company F's position, killed three soldiers in hand-to-hand combat, and departed with ten prisoners.[70] This action took place quickly, with the intruders gone before the battalion could respond.

When reinforcements reached Company F, they found three dead Americans: Corporal James B. Gresham and Privates Thomas F. Enright and Merle Hays. Hays's and Enright's throats had been cut, and Gresham was shot through the head. The French had their proof that the Yanks had come. More important, the division had begun the process that makes combat veterans out of trained soldiers. As Robert Bullard noted in his *Personalities and Reminiscences*, it is "astonishing sometimes how some men become warriors if not killed in the beginning."[71]

The third set of battalions finished their ten days in the front line on 20 November and were relieved by French troops. While in the line, the 3rd Battalion, 26th Infantry, repulsed a second German raid, indicating the Americans' increased combat capability. As the weary men trucked back to the billets around Gondrecourt, Sibert issued a general order telling the division that "we are now starting on the final period of training. Weather conditions will make it a peculiarly hard and trying one."[72] This uninspiring message was one of the last Sibert issued to the division.

On 14 December 1917, Pershing relieved Sibert, and Major General Robert Lee Bullard assumed command. Sibert was sent to the United States, where he established the Chemical Warfare School. Pershing relieved Sibert because he did not fit Blackjack's vision of an aggressive, loyal, and optimistic commander. Sibert had reinforced Pershing's negative view of his leadership in a series of messages to AEF headquarters in October and November that emphasized the division's difficulties and omitted the progress it was making in its training.[73] Pershing believed that the author of such pessimistic reports could not get the most out of a division destined to face far more painful and costly experiences than those inflicted by bad weather and shortages of socks.

As Duncan observed, "In General Bullard the Division got for its Commander an officer who was essentially a successful field soldier with [an] outstanding record of achievement in previous campaigns."[74] Bullard had a good feel for the readiness of the division, having accompanied Pershing on seventeen visits to the unit. He knew that the commander in chief had no patience for training deficiencies and that for a division commander to remain in command he needed to exude the optimism that was lacking in Sibert's September letter to the French commander or in his General Order Number 67 in November. Pershing, in a message to senior AEF officers in

December, made it clear that he demanded "positive attitudes, determination, and conservative firmness and faith in our cause."[75] Ironically, Bullard confided to his diary "that our General Pershing is not a fighter; he is in all his history a pacifist and, unless driven thereto by the A.E.F., will do no fighting in France for many a day."[76] He wisely kept his opinions to himself.

Bullard, who had commanded the 1st Brigade of the 1st Division in 1917, imparted to the division's senior commanders his sense of urgency and total commitment to Pershing's philosophy of training. At a meeting with his staff and the brigade and regimental commanders, he noted that "if we cannot do the job, we will be replaced." He also let them know he would not be the first to be relieved.[77] He followed these words with action when he replaced his artillery brigade commander, Brigadier General Charles McKinstry, with Charles P. Summerall. He relieved McKinstry because that engineer officer's "regimental, battalion, and even many of his battery commanders knew more about his duties than he, and the rest of the division knew it and felt it." He selected Summerall because he was a trained artilleryman whose technical competence, loyalty, and positive leadership abilities were widely appreciated in the AEF.[78] Bullard also relieved Colonel Ulysses Grant McAlexander, whom he found competent but "impervious to new techniques," and selected Colonel Frank Parker to command the 18th Infantry Regiment.[79]

The senior leaders of the 1st Division in December 1917 were an impressive group of men, nearly all of whom were later promoted to general officer. The artillery brigade commander, Charles Summerall, was to take command of the division in July, when Bullard was promoted to command a corps. Summerall later assumed command of V Corps (October 1918) and served as chief of staff of the US Army from 1926 to 1930. George Duncan, commanding general of the 1st Infantry Brigade, later commanded the 77th and 82nd Infantry Divisions. Beaumont Buck, commander of the 2nd Brigade, was promoted to major general in 1918 and commanded the 3rd Division during its successful actions in the Marne campaign of June and July 1918.

John Hines, commander of the 16th Infantry Regiment, went on to lead the division's 1st Brigade and was promoted to command the 4th Division (September 1918) and III Corps (October 1918). Hines served as army chief of staff from 1924 to 1926. Frank Parker, commander of the 18th Infantry Regiment, eventually took over 1st Brigade and then the division, in October 1918. The commander of the 26th Infantry, Hamilton Smith, was killed in July 1918, after successfully leading his regiment in the Soissons offensive. Hanson Ely, commander of the 28th Infantry, became commanding general of 2nd Brigade when Buck was promoted and then commanded the 5th Infantry Division in the Meuse Argonne campaign. These men remained with their units through the spring, giving the 1st Division stable senior leadership. Bullard was ably assisted by Colonel Campbell King, the division's chief of staff, and Lieutenant Colonel George C. Marshall, the operations officer. King and Marshall were two of the ablest of staff officers in the AEF. They served Bullard loyally and with the deference Bullard seemed to appreciate in subordinates. Marshall was to become the operations officer of First Army in September.[80]

The "Winter of Valley Forge": Final Training of the First Division

In the midst of bitterly cold winter weather, Bullard led the division on overnight maneuvers, culminating in January 1918 with a five-day field exercise. "This training was made a severe test of officers and noncommissioned officers."[81] George Marshall later wrote that "this was the gloomy and depressing period previously referred to as the Winter of Valley Forge. . . . When we were not cursed with mud, we were frozen with the cold."[82] The division's ability to cope with these harsh conditions was made more difficult by the departure of nine of the twelve infantry battalion commanders to attend AEF schools. Officers newly arrived from the United States replaced most of these experienced commanders just as a large number of new soldiers from a replacement battalion joined the division. Bullard wrote in his diary: "I have much difficulty in getting officers who know anything. All are untrained, and many of even our regular officers can never be worth anything in this war, unadaptable and immovable."[83]

While Bullard's pessimism is understandable, he was wrong about the ability of most of the officers to become competent leaders. But it would take time and experience before that process was complete. The loss of experienced leaders, coupled with shortages of shoes, blankets, and overshoes, had a demoralizing effect on the soldiers, even though "the officers labored to reduce the discomforts and hardships of their men."[84] Little wonder that Marshall observed that a "number of the officers became much depressed." News of the collapse of Imperial Russia (November) and of the massive defeat the Italians suffered at Caporetto did not help morale.[85]

The artillery units suffered extreme hardships during the training in December 1917 and January 1918. The roads were ice-covered when they were not knee-deep in mud. Even rough-shod mules found it difficult to walk, and entire horse teams with caissons and guns slid off the road into the ditch and had to be unharnessed and manhandled back onto the road. Making things worse, there was a severe shortage of forage for the draft animals, due in part to transportation difficulties caused by the movement of French and British divisions to Italy to bolster the Italians after their defeat. "The horses and mules in the First Division chewed up the woodwork of their stalls, ate their leather-and-rope halter straps, and on one maneuver so many dropped dead that the exercise had to be terminated."[86] It would be months before the division's horses fully recovered, often forcing the gunners to use double teams to haul guns and caissons, thus increasing the number of trips required to move the batteries.

As the division was undergoing its final training, Bullard received orders to prepare to move his troops to the front west of Toul, where they were to relieve the French of a section of line on 16 January 1918. The 1st Brigade and five battalions of artillery were the first to take over French positions. The commander of the French 69th Infantry Division initially commanded the Americans, with Bullard expected to assume command of his division in the line within three weeks. The 2nd Brigade remained near Gondre-court conducting rifle training and close order drill, while Duncan's brigade moved into the line.[87]

The lead elements set out on foot for the Ansauville subsector, 40 kilometers away, on 14 January, in the face of a blizzard. No motor transport was available to carry the men, and the roads were covered with smooth ice, making it difficult for the heavily laden soldiers and animals to walk without falling: "The roads were covered with ice and snow. About noon a heavy rain set in and turned into sleet. The men were drenched, increasing the weight of their load; the skirts of wet overcoats impeded progress. The distance had to be covered and a sandwich for the noon meal was all that could be provided. . . . The next day's march was a repetition of the experiences of the first."[88] The troops suffered horribly before reaching the sector between the villages of Seicheprey and Bouconville.[89] There they relieved the French over three nights, from 18 to 21 January. The 3rd Battalion, 18th Infantry, was on the right, facing north, with its headquarters in the remnants of the village of Seicheprey, and the 16th Infantry deployed its 3rd Battalion in the center and its 1st Battalion on the left of the sector, respectively. Each infantry battalion was supported by its machine-gun company and another from the 2nd Machine Gun Battalion and by elements of the divisional signal, engineer, and medical units.

Duncan's brigade headquarters was established in Ansauville. The division post of command was set up in Mesnil-la-Tour, about 16 kilometers from the infantry positions. The 2nd Signal Battalion established two wire communications nets for the division—one net for the command and control of the infantry and a second for artillery fire control. The five battalions of Summerall's artillery brigade supported the infantry from firing positions spread from Beaumont to the northern edge of the Forêt de la Reine.[90] For the next two months, the 1st Division occupied the Ansauville subsector.

Bullard and his officers understudied the officers of the 69th French Infantry Division for eighteen days before assuming control of the division, on 5 February. George Marshall observed that "the staff work during this period was exceedingly difficult" due in part to the inexperience of the commanders and staff and to the complexity of the tactical situation. The sector the 1st Division inherited was in marshy ground overlooked by a large hill known as Montsec. From positions on Montsec, the Germans could call for artillery fire against any movement in the American lines. Matters were made worse by the miserable condition of the trenches. The dugouts were poorly constructed, and little had been done to drain the water from the positions in the low ground. For the first few weeks the infantry and engineers spent a great deal of time repairing their positions. The division also modified the layout of its defensive lines to better deal with the new German assault methods. This meant that the sector was to be held in depth and organized in strongpoints rather than as a series of single trench lines.[91]

Final Examination: The Division in Action

During its stay in the Ansauville area, the 1st Division received a tremendous amount of attention and "help" from AEF headquarters, General Pershing, and visiting Allied leaders. Everyone wanted to visit the first sector of the front controlled by Americans. Marshall noted that he and his staff in Mesnil-la-Tour worked in cramped quarters with several officers from GHQ looking over their shoulders. When the division executed its first trench raid, Pershing was present, only to be disappointed by the need to cancel it due to the engineers' difficulty in getting bangalore torpedoes up to the front in time to blow a hole in the German wire emplacements.[92]

Steadily, nonetheless, Bullard and his staff developed the routines and techniques needed to command and control a division at war. In the front, the division got "settled in its duties. . . . We are losing a few men killed and wounded every day now. Three hundred or four hundred enemy shells fall upon our sector daily. We are really in the war a little at last."[93] Bullard recognized the need for an offensive attitude and encouraged his troops to fire on the enemy whenever given the opportunity. Summerall's artillery aggressively sought targets in the German lines, and artillery observers lived at the front with the infantry, connected to their guns by telephone.

By the middle of February, the division was demonstrating a better understanding of its combat tasks. For example, Marshall observed that German trench mortars were firing single rounds in a seemingly random pattern. He deduced that this behavior was typical of the German artillery units when they were registering new batteries for some sort of offensive mission. Consequently, Marshall convinced Bullard that the infantry should adjust their operations to minimize their exposure to a German barrage and infantry raid. The infantrymen were instructed to abandon their exposed first-line positions after dark each evening and not reoccupy them until after dawn the next day. By doing so, they made it difficult for a German barrage to destroy troops in the first trenches, and they denied enemy raiding parties the opportunity of using a box barrage to isolate and attack a small American unit.[94]

Marshall's precautions paid off on the morning of 1 March, when the Germans fired a heavy artillery bombardment in support of a raid by 200 men against the division's right front near Seicheprey. The trenches were demolished by the heavy German trench mortars, but few soldiers were hurt. When the German raiders reached the first American lines, Summerall's artillery unleashed preplanned fires that caught the attackers in a hail of fire. This fire and a counterattack by the 18th Infantry broke up the German attack and drove the raiders back. Unfortunately, one American platoon leader had decided to return to his frontline positions before dawn, and his platoon was caught in the heavy German artillery barrage and by the raiders. More than twenty Americans were killed and twelve were captured. Nonetheless, the division's repulse of the raid with what was considered minimal loss and its ability to inflict significant casualties on the enemy impressed everyone from the French corps commander to Georges Clemenceau, premier of France. It certainly pleased Pershing. On 2 March, Clemenceau arrived to distribute the Croix de Guerre to soldiers of the 18th Infantry. It was a splendid day for the soldiers so honored, and it was an important day for the AEF, since the 1st Division had passed its test as a combat division. As Bullard noted, "It was no great affair—probably two hundred men on each side engaged—but its inspiriting effect was one of the first things that helped to make the 1st Division what it afterwards really became, a magnificent fighting machine."[95]

The division remained in the Ansauville sector until March, when it was withdrawn so that it could be committed to face the German offensive to the west. Its casualties were 143 dead and 403 wounded. Both brigades served in the lines, and the entire division system functioned effectively. On 8 April, Pershing declared the division fully trained. The 1st Division had become America's first combat-ready division in the twentieth century.

2

Cantigny to Soissons

THE 1ST DIVISION COMPLETED ITS TRAINING NONE TOO SOON. Events on all fronts had gone from bad to worse during 1917. It is difficult to imagine how the Allies could have avoided defeat had the United States not entered the war. Because the 1st Division was ready for offensive action in April 1918, it was able to play an important role, along with the rapidly expanding AEF, in stemming the advance of the German armies in France, and then, starting in July, helping to turn the tide as part of a series of Allied offensives that broke the back of the German army.

Allied Disasters: April to November 1917

The disastrous defeat of the French army in April 1917 and its subsequent mutiny forced the British to carry the combat burden while General Henri Pétain rebuilt his army's morale. The situation remained critical through the summer of 1917.[1] The Russian Revolution in February led to the abdication of the czar and the creation of the Provisional Government, which pledged to continue the war. However, the Russian army was in no condition to do so. Consequently, American divisions were desperately needed to offset the large number of German divisions transferred to the Western Front.[2]

The US National Guard was called into federal service on 15 July 1917, and 200,000 new guardsmen brought it to its authorized strength of 435,800 men.[3] In September, the 26th Division of New England guardsmen arrived in France as the second organized division of the AEF. The 26th Division was followed to France by the 42nd Division, composed of units from twenty-six states and the District of Columbia. The 26th and 42nd Divisions were ready for their service at the front by April 1918. The 26th Division replaced the 1st Division in the Ansauville sector in April.[4]

The third AEF division to arrive in France was the 2nd Division. It was unique, with one brigade composed of two army regiments (the 9th and the 23rd) and the other containing the 5th and 6th Marine Regiments. Its soldiers were used as laborers on the lines of communication in France in the autumn, delaying training for several months. By March, the 2nd Division was concentrated for training, and by June it was ready to help stop a German offensive east of Paris.[5]

The Last German Offensives

As American soldiers began to arrive in France, the Germans massed 192 divisions against the 172 British and French divisions on the Western Front. These German units had sustained heavy losses over the past three years, but their morale was high after victories in Russia and Italy. Ludendorff used this opportunity to transfer older soldiers from units on the Western Front to the forty-three German divisions in Russia and to shift fitter soldiers from those divisions into the western army. The Germans also developed new offensive tactics to penetrate entrenched positions with storm troopers trained to bypass strongpoints and drive through the defenses.[6] By the time the German offensive, code-named Michael, commenced on 21 March 1918, there were five American divisions in France, including the 41st Division, which was dismantled to provide replacements for the others. Three more divisions, the 3rd, the 32nd, and the 5th, were arriving but would not be available for several months for offensive action.[7]

The Michael Offensive began with its main effort of seventy-six divisions aimed at the destruction of the twenty-eight divisions of the British Third and Fifth Armies and the rupture of the Allied front where the British Fifth adjoined the French Sixth Army east of Amiens. The Germans surprised the defenders and over the next three days advanced nearly 20 miles across a 50-mile front. It looked as if the Germans would drive to Amiens, 20 miles farther west, and cut the rail communications between the British and the French.[8]

Pershing recognized the dangerous situation and offered to commit American divisions wherever the Allies felt they could best help stem the German tide. The French army commander, General Pétain, initially asked that the 1st Division expand its Ansauville sector and that Pershing deploy the 2nd, 26th, and 42nd Divisions to the Heights of the Meuse near Saint-Mihiel to replace French units for service elsewhere. Pétain also suggested to Pershing that, if he deemed the 1st Division ready for offensive operations, it could move to Picardy, northwest of Paris where the main battle was raging.[9]

Although Pershing offered to commit American troops to battle, disagreement continued between the French and the Americans over the best way to use American manpower. Pétain and Pershing agreed that the training of the first four US divisions had progressed far enough to enable them to be committed to the front. The French, however, did not think that American staffs at corps level were ready to be entrusted with the operation of divisions in an American sector. The French also believed that the 1st Division, even after six months' training, was not fully ready and that "the serious deficiencies which have been observed in that division in this connection would all the more likely be found to exist in units hastily thrown into battle to meet the needs of the moment." The French concluded that American battalions and regiments ought to be amalgamated into French divisions for the foreseeable future, delaying the formation of independent US corps or an army until the winter.[10] Pershing, however, insisted that American regiments and divisions must be commanded by American commanders and that their service with the French was to be of limited duration for training.[11]

Pershing considered the 1st Division ready for full active service. As he negotiated with Pétain about the commitment of American forces, the 1st Division acted on its original orders to bring its 1st Brigade back into the line to extend the division's front. However, as Colonel John Hines, commander of the 16th Infantry, was coordinating the deployment of his regiment into the trenches near Gironville, on 29 March, these orders were cancelled. The division instead was relieved from the Ansauville sector by the 26th Division and transferred to Gisors, northwest of Paris.[12]

The relief in the sector between the 26th and 1st Divisions did not take place without a hitch. The 26th Division reported that the 1st Division had not properly policed its former positions, leaving sick and dead mules and horses, cluttered billets, and unburned classified documents in the area. Colonel Malin Craig, the I Corps chief of staff, told the AEF chief of staff that the division was guilty of "demoralization [and] lack of discipline."[13] Craig recommended to Pershing that Brigadier General Charles Summerall, who had supervised the 1st Division's clearing of the sector, be court-martialed along with the officers of the 26th Infantry and the officer in charge of Bullard's administrative section. Fortunately, Pershing and Harbord recognized that there may have been some sour grapes involved in the initial allegations by the 26th Division and that in a time of crisis it was not a good use of time to pursue such charges. When Bullard complained to Pershing about "the most irritating experience of my life," the commander in chief told Bullard to "drop it, drop it; don't spend your time on it."[14]

The 26th Division relieved the 1st Division in record time. Concentrating near Toul, the 1st Division's infantry boarded troop trains on the evening of 4 April. The trains traveled west of Paris to avoid the congestion east and north of the capital. The division assembled near Chaumont-en-Vexin and Gesors over the next two days.[15] The division staff supervised the move without Bullard's leadership, since the commanding general was in the hospital in Toul suffering from neuritis. Campbell King and George Marshall conducted the operation with few problems. Bullard rejoined the division on 12 April, retaining Pershing's faith in his ability to carry out his rigorous duties. Doubtless, with a less talented staff, Bullard would not have survived this incident without being relieved.[16]

The division's supply trains made the 310-mile journey by road, commencing on 7 April. This was the trains' first long-distance deployment. The motor vehicles took one route while the horse-drawn units took another, making it hard for commanders to control their troops. Within the motor columns, the drivers' insufficient training in road-march techniques and the varying capabilities of the twelve types of trucks in the division made it impossible to maintain steady speeds and intervals between vehicles. As a result, the units took up too much space on the congested French roads. Brakes, transmissions, and engines received excessive wear as the convoys telescoped back and forth. The trip took five days to complete rather than three as planned, but the units arrived on 12 April in time to help the division move to the front beginning on 17 April. This road-march experience for the Sanitation Train, the Ammunition Train, and the medical units proved beneficial because actions were taken to correct the deficiencies noted. When next called upon to move the division over long distances in July, the trains performed considerably better.[17]

Pétain initially assigned the 1st Division to the French Fifth Army. Bullard immediately put the infantry through exercises to hone their skills in maneuver warfare, anticipating battle in open terrain rather than in trenches. A week later, the division moved to the Montdidier sector, where it became part of the French First Army on 17 April.[18]

On 16 April, Pershing spoke to the division's officers near Chaumont-en-Vexin. John Hines likened Pershing's speech to "the talk the football coach gives his team just before they go onto the field for the championship game." Pershing told the officers that he was confident the division would do well:

> This was in the nature of an expression of confidence that our division was going to maintain the excellent record that it had made in training and in previous fighting, and that our work on this job in the greatest battle of the ages would prove a fitting example to the future American forces and would justify the confidence placed in us. . . . The General threw the whole of his forceful personality into this short talk; every officer was inspired to do his best out of personal loyalty to such a chief, even if for no other motive.[19]

Pershing understood that the division's success in its first offensive action was essential to Allied morale and to American prestige. He also felt a special affection for the division. As he wrote later, "It was a source of real regret to me not to command the division in person and this coupled with the fact that its entry into battle was of considerable moment led me to speak a word of confidence and encouragement."[20]

The infantry set out from their billets on 17 April to the assigned sector,

7 kilometers west of Montdidier. (See Map 2.) The 1st Brigade was to occupy the front, while the 2nd Brigade remained in reserve. On 20 April,
the 1st Brigade's regimental and battalion commanders reconnoitered their
4-kilometer-wide front between the French 42nd and 162nd Divisions. The
troops occupied the lines on the night of 24–25 April, with the 18th Infantry on the left (north) and the 16th Infantry on the right. The men found
the French positions to be shell holes rather than organized defenses, with
no communication trenches and no barbed wire to the front. The Germans
overlooked the positions from the higher ground around the village of Cantigny. This allowed the Germans to observe American movement, making
daytime activity deadly and restricting to the nighttime efforts to supply the
front or improve positions.[21]

The division's forward post of command was located in Mesnil-Saint-
Firman, with the second echelon post of command located farther back at
Bonvillers. The 2nd Brigade was in battalion assembly areas 5 kilometers
behind the front. Two battalions of the brigade were designated corps reserve for the French X Corps, which assumed control of the sector on 6 May.
The 1st Battalion, 1st Engineers, and uncommitted infantrymen of the 1st
Brigade set to work to improve the second and third defensive lines and to
dig communications trenches so that carrying parties could get to the first
line safely at night and the medical units could evacuate the wounded with
some protection from artillery fire.

The soldiers paid a high price for their exposed positions. German artillery fired high-explosive and chemical rounds against the lines and behind
the front. The need to improve the positions made it necessary for officers
to move about, increasing casualties.[22] American losses were significantly
heavier than those of French troops, prompting Bullard to tell his subordinates "that our men, either from ignorance or carelessness, are not taking
cover."[23]

The overall situation made life in these positions exceptionally dangerous, as the Germans remained in a position from which they could launch
further attacks, and their artillery was active.[24] The Germans also made
special efforts to demoralize what they thought were green troops, hoping
to demonstrate their superiority over all Americans.

Sadly, "danger was a better teacher than exhortation." The division suffered more than 4,700 casualties, including at least 1,000 dead, on the
Montdidier front.[25] German artillery hammered the roads and villages in
the rear. One German barrage of over 15,000 rounds of high explosives
and mustard gas hit a battalion of the 18th Infantry in Villers-Tournelle on
the night of 3–4 May. The battalion lost more than 600 gas casualties, was
forced to work for seven hours in masks, and finally had to abandon the

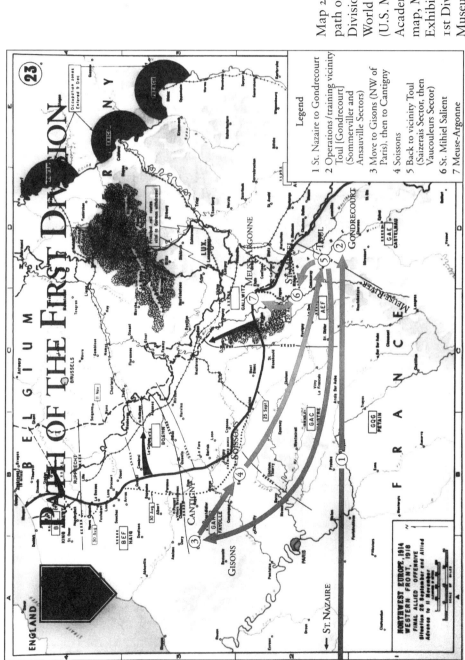

Map 2. The path of the 1st Division in World War I. (U.S. Military Academy map, Main Exhibit Hall, 1st Division Museum)

cellars of the village and dig new positions in nearby fields. Another barrage destroyed an ammunition dump near division headquarters, and the division posts of command were often under artillery fire.[26]

The troops and leaders persevered and learned how to operate in such an environment. Marshall pointed out in his *Memoirs* that he and other staff officers made their inspection tours of the front lines at night, returning just after dawn to avoid drawing enemy fire:

> During this period of our service, the most dangerous duty probably fell to the Quartermaster Sergeants and teamsters who went forward each night with the ration carts to revictual the infantry. Confined to roads and anticipated by the enemy, they had to make their way up along the most heavily beaten zones in the sector. The casualties among these men and the poor mules who hauled the carts were very heavy.[27]

The large number of wagoneers in the honor roll of men who died in the war attests to the truth of Marshall's observation.[28]

Offensive Action: Cantigny, May 1918

While the 1st Division was moving to Picardy, the Germans launched their second major offensive of the year, on 9 April. This attack was designed to divide the British armies and force them out of France. The strongest German forces struck near Armentières. Although the attackers made some progress, British Field Marshal Douglas Haig rallied his troops with his famous "backs to the wall" message, and the British stopped the Germans. This offensive achieved less than had the March attack, leading Ludendorff to conclude that his hope to drive the British into the sea was unattainable. Consequently, he shifted his strategic effort and reserves of shock troops to an attack against the French.[29]

Expecting further German attacks, the French X Corps commander proposed to the commander of the French First Army that he prepare an attack with his three divisions in case the Germans resumed their offensive in Flanders or Picardy. This attack was to secure the plateau around the village of Cantigny and to push the front lines closer to Montdidier. Bullard's 1st Division was to participate in this attack.

The commander of the French First Army, General Eugene Debeney, was receptive to the idea, but changes in the general situation led him to cancel the planning for a corps attack. In response, on 12 May, the X Corps commander proposed that a smaller attack by one regiment be launched to secure Cantigny. This idea originated with Bullard and was readily approved by Debeney.[30] The 1st Division was to conduct the assault. Bullard was pleased with the performance of the division thus far and anxious to demonstrate its offensive capability. As he informed Pershing's headquarters:

> Coming in contact with the enemy April 25, the division has been in practically a continuous engagement. The infantry has been aggressive and reasonably successful. The engineers have done very effective work. The artillery has been active day and night. Total result is [that] German prisoners report that life is very hard for them upon their front, that they no longer can have cooked or hot meals in their two front positions, that they are obliged to keep very close to shelter even far to the rear, the reliefs and evacuation of the wounded are extremely dangerous. Our officers and men are undergoing hardships and losses but sustain them[selves] in fine spirits.[31]

Planning for the limited attack was set in motion when the 1st Division was ordered to seize the Cantigny Plateau. A reinforced infantry regiment, accompanied by French tanks and flamethrowers, was to conduct the assault. On 16 May, Bullard delayed the attack from 25 to 28 May to allow more time for planning and the rehearsal of the assault troops.[32]

Bullard delegated the detailed planning for the attack to George Marshall and Charles Summerall, commander of the 1st Artillery Brigade. Bullard selected Colonel Hanson Ely's 28th Infantry to make the assault, supported by the rest of Beaumont Buck's 2nd Brigade (see Map 3).[33]

The scheme of maneuver was simple. Ely's regiment was to attack the Cantigny Plateau with its three infantry battalions on line, each organized in three waves. The assault force was to attack in open order, sweeping through Cantigny and past the village to a final objective line 400 meters east. The 1/28th Infantry had responsibility for the right (south) side of the objective. The 2/28th was to attack in the center through the village and along the ground just to its north, supported by twelve French tanks. The second and third waves of the 2nd Battalion were to clear the Germans out of the cellars and bunkers in Cantigny with the help of French flamethrowers. The 3rd Battalion was to attack on the left (north) to its portion of the objective line, where it was to defend positions in an arc around the northern and northeastern portions of Cantigny. When the assault was completed, the regiment was to defend along the objective line northeast and east of Cantigny. The French 152nd Infantry Division was to protect the left flank. Major Theodore Roosevelt's 1/26th Infantry was to protect the 28th Infantry's right flank.[34]

The French contributed a tremendous amount of artillery to support the assault. X Corps provided one artillery group of eighteen batteries of

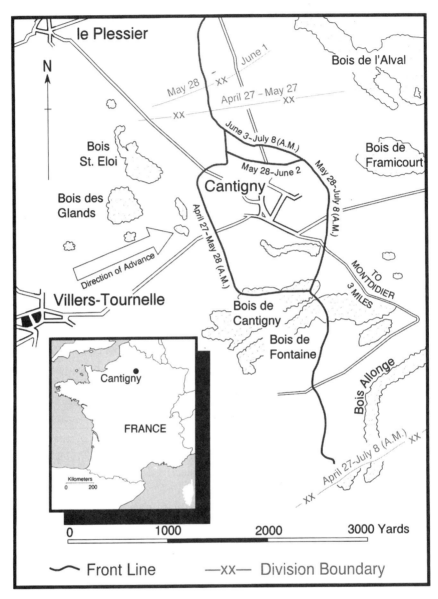

le Plessier

N

Bois de l'Alval

May 28
XX
June 1
April 27 – May 27
XX
XX

Bois
St. Eloi

June 3 – July 8 (A.M.)
May 28 – June 2

Bois de
Framicourt

Cantigny

May 28 – July 8 (A.M.)

Bois des
Glands

April 27 – May 28

Direction of Advance

April 27 – May 28 (A.M.)

TO MONTDIDIER 3 MILES

Villers-Tournelle

Bois de
Cantigny

Bois de
Fontaine

Bois Allonge

Cantigny

FRANCE

Kilometers
0   200

April 27 – July 8 (A.M.)
XX

XX

0   1000   2000   3000 Yards

⌒ Front Line   —xx— Division Boundary

Map 3. The front lines at Cantigny, 27 April to 8 July 1918. (Main Exhibit Hall, 1st Division Museum)

105mm, 120mm, 155mm, and 280mm guns. First Army established another group of seventeen batteries of 145mm, 155mm, and 160mm guns and three battalions of 240mm cannons. Summerall's three regiments of artillery provided seventy-two 75mm and 155mm guns, while the French division on the left flank was to fire in support of the attack with its seventy-two guns. An American, Lieutenant Colonel Lucius Holbrook, was to direct the sixty-eight 75mm guns providing the rolling barrage, while the remaining fifteen French batteries (four guns each) of 75mm guns were to fire to protect the flanks of the advancing infantrymen.[35]

Most of the division's machine guns were to provide direct support for the attack. Each of the assaulting infantry battalions was accompanied by a machine-gun company of twelve guns. The twenty-four guns of the Division Machine Gun Battalion, designated Barrage Group 1, eight guns from the 26th Infantry (Barrage Group 2), and twenty-four guns from the 16th Infantry (Barrage Group 3) were assigned target areas in which to fire to prevent the Germans from attacking the flanks of the assault force. The first two machine-gun targets were to be fired according to a time schedule. The remaining targets were called "SOS" targets, which the barrage units were to fire when requested by the 28th Infantry.[36]

On 22 May, the 28th Infantry was relieved from its positions by the 18th Infantry and moved to the rear of the division, where the 1st Engineers had prepared a replica of the Cantigny area. There Ely's men rehearsed the attack. On the night of 26–27 May, the 2nd Battalion moved back to the front and took over the sector of the 1/18th Infantry. The remaining battalions of the 28th were to occupy their assault positions on the evening of 27 May.[37]

The Germans now intervened by commencing a major offensive to the east against the French positions along the Chemin des Dames, near the Aisne River. In the Cantigny sector, German raiding parties struck the 1st Division's front on the morning of 27 May. One party penetrated the lines of the 26th Infantry and captured two Americans before withdrawing. A second German detachment was wiped out by rifle and machine-gun fire, and several Germans were captured. The division staff was concerned that the attack plan might have been compromised by an engineer officer who had become lost in no-man's-land several nights before, but Bullard decided to go ahead with the attack as planned.[38]

The more dangerous development was the German offensive against the French north of the Aisne. The offensive caught the French by surprise when a massive artillery barrage destroyed their forward positions. The Germans advanced 12 miles, crossing the Aisne and reaching the Vesle River by 27 May. Over the next three days, Ludendorff's storm troopers drove south to the Marne, capturing 400 guns and 45,000 British and French prisoners.[39] The German offensive threatened Paris and cut the Paris-Verdun railroad.

Pétain reacted quickly to establish a coherent front by moving the French Fifth Army into line and by transferring reserves to positions east of Paris. These reserves included the American 2nd and 3rd Divisions. Consequently, the French informed Bullard that most of the artillery units allocated to the Cantigny attack would be withdrawn, beginning on the evening of 28 May, and sent east. The 1st Division would be on its own once it had taken Cantigny. The attack now assumed greater significance because it would serve as a tangible way for Americans to relieve some of the pressure on the French, as well as to demonstrate American tactical competence.

On the afternoon of 27 May, the division order was issued, setting the time and date of the Cantigny attack for 0645 hours, 28 May. That evening, the 28th Infantry occupied attack positions without incident. German prisoners confirmed that the assault troops faced depleted battalions of the *82nd Reserve Division* and that the Germans were in the process of rotating their frontline units.

On the morning of 28 May, the 28th Infantry attacked Cantigny. As one eyewitness, Colonel W. S. Grant, reported:

> At 4:45 A.M. our artillery . . . started its neutralization fire on the hostile artillery. There was no sudden increase in the artillery fire . . . but the volume of fire gradually increased. At 5:45 our artillery started its preparation and diversion fire. At this hour the increase in volume of fire was marked, and from my O. P. I could observe the various areas and lines behind the enemy's front where this fire was being directed. . . . At 6:40 the rolling barrage started. The infantry promptly moved out. . . . The objective was taken and our men proceeded to dig in. Up to this time [about 09:20 A.M.] there were no indications of any great losses on our side.[40]

The infantry moved forward with three assault companies in each battalion. The 1/28th swept south of Cantigny toward its objectives on the road to Fontaine-sous-Montdidier, where it was to establish a blocking position on the eastern side of Cantigny. The 1/28th had just three of its four infantry companies in the attack since one was in regimental reserve. Company A received heavy fire from German machine guns after it reached the blocking position, losing its three officers and several soldiers. Company B on the right also received heavy fire as it moved through the ravine south of Cantigny. Both companies held their positions, thanks in part to support from the 1/26th in the Bois de Cantigny to their south and to the supporting artillery and machine-gun fire directed at German counterattack routes. At about 0800, Roosevelt's 1/26th helped the 1/28th repulse the first German counterattack. At the same time, the counterbattery fires of the heavy artillery prevented the Germans from bringing effective artillery fire to bear on the exposed infantrymen while they were consolidating their positions.[41]

In the center, the three assault companies of Robert Maxey's 2/28th, accompanied by French tanks, advanced through Cantigny and 400 yards farther east to their objective line (Map 3). Ely reported at 0724 that "nearly all of objective [had been] reached. Everything going fine. Hardly any casualties." Maxey's support company, assisted by French flamethrowers, rooted stunned Germans out of the cellars of Cantigny, capturing about 100 prisoners. Nonetheless, it took several days to kill or capture all of the Germans in the village. Maxey was mortally wounded as his battalion dug in east of town. Captain Clarence R. Huebner assumed command of the battalion.[42]

On the left flank, Ely's third battalion made some progress but failed to reach its objectives due to intense enemy fire. Company K was shattered by machine-gun fire and failed to get far beyond its initial positions. In the center of the battalion, Company L received punishing fire and recoiled to the south. The battalion commander, J. M. Cullison, brought his support troops forward to establish foxholes in and around the Cantigny cemetery, while Company M occupied its objective to the east. Cullison did not report his situation accurately, leaving Ely and the rest of the division in the dark as to the exposed left flank. Consequently, Ely's PC reported erroneously that the regiment had taken all objectives.[43]

Although things were not going as smoothly as Bullard thought they were, the attack had gone well. The 28th Infantry captured 175 Germans and secured Cantigny and most of its objective line, while suffering roughly 300 casualties. The 1/26th and 1/28th repulsed German counterattacks, and German artillery was unable to respond effectively to Summerall's barrages. Pershing, who visited the 1st Division PC on the morning of 28 May, was satisfied with the results thus far. Later in the day, he ordered Bullard to hold Cantigny at all cost. Pershing was right to be concerned, as the Germans prepared to use all available reserves to recapture their lost positions.[44]

Summerall's gunners effectively interdicted enemy counterattack routes. Reports from the 26th Infantry indicated that the Germans had difficulty moving and had to send troops to forward positions a few soldiers at a time. Consequently, it was late afternoon, at about 1730, before the German infantry attacked again. This attack came from the Bois de Framicourt, to the east of Cantigny. A preplanned artillery barrage smashed the assault before it reached American lines.

At about the same time, German artillery and machine-gun fire hammered the 28th Infantry's 1st and 3rd Battalions on the flanks. The battalions began to fall back, forcing Ely to commit his reserves. On the right, Company C reinforced the 1st Battalion, allowing it to retain its positions. The 1/26th Infantry and the divisional machine-gun units on that flank also contributed to the defense. On the left, north of Cantigny, 3rd Battalion fell back to more protected positions and held on until Company F, 18th Infantry, counterattacked through its lines, carrying the battalion back to its forward positions.[45]

Buck's 2nd Brigade headquarters also alerted Colonel Frank Parker's 18th Infantry that its two companies attached to the 28th Infantry had been committed and that it might be necessary to send a battalion of the 18th Infantry into the fight. Buck further told Parker that his remaining two battalions might be called on the next morning to reinforce Ely.[46]

The final German assault of the day struck at about 1845 hours. The rolling barrage supporting the attack caused heavy casualties in the 1/28th, causing Ely to recommend that the battalion be relieved by one of Parker's battalions. The German assault, however, was blown apart by Summerall's artillery before it reached Ely's lines, preserving the front. It had been a long but successful day. At the end, 1st Division reported to X Corps that its troops had taken their objectives and that the division had smashed three enemy counterattacks. At least 200 prisoners had been captured, including three officers. Six hundred Americans were killed or wounded. The 28th Infantry was holding its new positions and the division had things in hand.[47]

The Hard Part: Holding the Line, 29–31 May

The commander of the German *Eighteenth Army*, in whose sector Cantigny was situated, was concerned that the 1st Division's attack was part of an operation to capture Montdidier. Consequently, he ordered the *25th Reserve Division*, along with the remnants of the *82nd*, to launch another counterattack on 29 May. These attacks were to strike Cantigny from the southeast along the Cantigny-Fontaine Road.[48]

The 1st Division reorganized its sector early on 29 May. The boundary between the two regiments in line was moved north, making the 26th Infantry responsible for the defense of the Bois de Cantigny. The 28th Infantry's front narrowed, and Bullard ordered Buck to have Ely thin his front line to two battalions while his third battalion assumed a supporting position. Parker's 18th Infantry remained in reserve. The companies in the exposed positions also occupied more sheltered positions closer to Cantigny, while planned artillery concentrations and the direct-fire weapons of the 1/26th Infantry covered the open area between Hill 104 and the Bois de Cantigny.[49]

The Germans mounted their counterattack at about 1630, 29 May. The division's artillery, machine guns, and the 1/26th Infantry helped the tired soldiers of the 28th shatter the German attack near its jumping-off positions. Enemy artillery, in turn, pulverized Ely's positions, causing heavy casualties.

The Germans launched two more attacks on 29 May and one small probe early on 30 May. Each time, the division artillery and the infantry-men slaughtered the attackers. At times, Ely thought that his regiment was through, but the soldiers hung on. By the end of the second day of counter-attacks, the *82nd Reserve Division* had only 2,500 men fit for duty, and the *25th Reserve Division* had suffered heavy casualties. Convinced that Cantigny was not worth further losses, the Germans ended efforts to recapture the village.[50] The 1st Division had won its first offensive action.

The cost of American success was high. Losses totaled about 1,067 men, mostly from the 28th Infantry. Along with 186 enlisted soldiers, thirteen officers, including one battalion commander, were dead.[51] Nonetheless, Bullard thought it was worth it. This "was the first serious fight made by American troops in France, and it was greeted enthusiastically as a wonder-ful success. . . . The success tremendously increased the Allies' confidence in the American soldiers, and from this date the morale of the Allies steadily rose."[52]

On the nights of 30–31 May and 31 May–1 June, the 16th Infantry re-placed the 28th in the line. The 2nd and 3rd Battalions of the 16th occupied the front, and the 1st Battalion became the division reserve battalion. The Germans greeted the new troops with intensive artillery fire. Private Alfred Buhl of the 16th Infantry recalled:

> We had a rather hard time of it here as the Germans sent over gas all of the time, so when our food finally reached us, it was all green and we had to throw it away. We spent forty-eight hours here without a drink of water. . . . As our trenches here were only fifty or sixty feet from the Germans we had a lot of fun throwing hand grenades over into the German lines and they did not spare any either.[53]

While Buhl and his comrades traded grenades with the enemy, Ely's men withdrew to recuperate. They were given little time to recover before being called on first to serve as the division's reserve and then to enter the front lines again, on 3–4 June.[54]

On 1 June, newly promoted Brigadier General John Hines, who had re-placed George Duncan as 1st Brigade commander when Duncan was pro-moted to major general, received orders that his brigade was to relieve the French 152nd Infantry Division north of the 1st Division. This move al-lowed the French to shift another division to the heavy fighting east of Paris.

The division henceforth occupied a frontage equivalent to that normally assigned to two French divisions. The 16th Infantry, now commanded by Colonel Frank Bamford, replaced the French troops on the night of 3–4 June as the 28th moved into positions between the 16th and 26th Infantry regiments.[55]

For the next month, until its relief by two French divisions on 7–8 July, the 1st Division held its sector. Life in the trenches was anything but pleasant, as the Germans continued to probe the defenses with raids and artillery.[56]

The division suffered heavy casualties in the Montdidier area. The four field hospitals assigned to the division (the 2nd, 3rd, 12th, and 13th) admitted more than 4,500 patients from 26 April to 8 July. Casualties totaled 4,928 men, including 1,000 men killed. Troops in the forward positions often did not receive one warm meal a day. It was difficult to provide the men with an opportunity to change clothes, let alone get a shower or go through delousing during the seventy-two days in the line.[57] However, the division's solid defense bolstered French morale on the Picardy front, especially when French division commanders on the flanks realized that the 1st Division did not plan to withdraw if the Germans attacked again.[58]

When the last major German attack in the area came, on 9 June, the division held its positions, in spite of the withdrawal of the French division to its right. The French First Army commander was most appreciative, since the 1st Division served as an anchor for a French counterattack to restore the front.[59] The performance of the 1st Division in the Montdidier sector gave Pershing proof that amalgamation of American battalions and regiments with Allied divisions was not necessary for the training of American divisions.

Relief and Recuperation

The 1st Division left its positions in the Montdidier sector on 8 July and assembled in the villages of the Beauvais, northwest of Paris. For the next four days, the troops bathed, deloused, changed clothes, and attempted to catch up on their sleep. Nearly 2,700 replacements were needed by the division in June, in addition to the 1,892 received in May. A number of men who had been hospitalized rejoined their regiments. Many of the replacements were new soldiers, some of whom had been in the army less than ninety days. Replacement officers had been in the service for less than six months. Bullard expected the division to be assigned to a quiet sector to train the new soldiers, but this was not to be.[60]

The successful performance of duty by so many of the division's senior officers in May and June 1918 earned them promotions and positions of greater responsibility in the rapidly expanding AEF. Bullard was selected to command III Corps. Charles P. Summerall assumed command of the 1st Division on 15 July. Bullard recommended both infantry brigade commanders for promotion to major general and all four regimental commanders for promotion to brigadier general. Hanson Ely left his position as commander of the 28th Infantry to take command of the 3rd Brigade, 2nd Division. Colonel Conrad Babcock assumed command of the 28th, and Lucius Holbrook replaced Summerall as 1st Artillery Brigade commander. George Marshall moved to the operations section of GHQ. On 11 July, as the shift in divisional leaders was taking place, the 1st Division received orders to move east to join the French Tenth Army.[61] Its brief rest period was over.

The Allied Concentration for the Champagne-Marne Counteroffensive: July 1918

The 1st Division was assigned to the French GHQ reserve in early July to help meet the next anticipated German offensive. This time, Marshal Ferdinand Foch planned to meet the enemy's attack with a flexible defense along the front of the German bulge east of Paris and then to regain the initiative with an offensive against the shoulders of the German salient (Map 4). American divisions were to play a prominent role in these Allied operations.

The presence of 604,000 American soldiers in France on 1 June 1918 gave the Allies numerical superiority for the first time in the year.[62] This allowed Pétain to prepare a counteroffensive to be launched in mid-July. Although Pershing hoped that Bullard's III Corps would be able to take part in the offensive, Bullard prudently decided that his organization would not be ready to control divisions that soon. Consequently, the 1st and 2nd Divisions were assigned to General Pierre Emile Berdoulat's French XX Corps.[63] The 1st Division moved from Dammartin-en-Goële on 15 July to assembly areas east of Compiègne.[64]

Pétain planned to launch his main attack with General Charles Mangin's army against the German salient at its western shoulder near Soissons. Simultaneously, three other French armies were to attack the southern and eastern portions of the German lines from the Ourcq River to the eastern shoulder near Reims. Mangin's main thrust was to be spearheaded by Berdoulat's XX Corps, with the American 1st and 2nd Divisions and the French 1st Moroccan Division in the initial assault. During the night of 15–16 July, the 1st Division's infantry moved into final assault positions. The Moroccan division already was deployed across the sector. The 2nd Division moved forward on 16 and 17 July.[65]

Mangin's offensive was to be launched without a preparatory artillery barrage, thus achieving surprise. The artillery was brought forward at the last possible moment, and there were no registration fires by the batteries. These precautions convinced the Germans that the French deployment opposite the Soissons sector remained defensive. Consequently, the Germans continued to post battle-worn divisions along the western side of the Marne salient. These weakened units did little to improve their positions.[66]

German attention was further diverted from the point of greatest danger because Ludendorff launched his fifth offensive of the year, on 15 July, against the French near Reims and along the Marne River near Château-Thierry. The French were forewarned and took precautions to prevent a disaster similar to that of May along the Chemin des Dames. The first line was thinned to minimize the damage from German artillery fire. The main defensive positions were prepared in depth, and reserves were deployed in a third line from which they could launch immediate counterattacks. Finally, on the night of 14–15 July, the French artillery fired a massive counterpreparation barrage against the positions in which the German assault troops were massing. The results were satisfactory from a French point of view. Ludendorff's troops were unable to break the French lines or to gain appreciable amounts of ground. The French retained control of Reims and counterattacked to throw the Germans back across the Marne. The American 3rd Division soundly defeated the German *10th* and *36th Divisions* in their attempts to cross the Marne east of Château-Thierry, earning the title "Rock of the Marne" and the respect of friend and foe. Ludendorff suspended the offensive on 17 July.[67]

The Battle of Soissons: 18–23 July 1918

The Battle of Soissons was part of the Allied Aisne-Marne offensive. The main attack was to be carried out by the French Tenth Army, consisting of thirteen infantry divisions. Mangin's army had 324 tanks, with forty-eight tanks in direct support of the 1st Division.[68] Tenth Army's mission was "to break the enemy front between the Aisne and the Ourcq and push east in conjunction with the Sixth Army to its south." This move would sever the German supply lines in the Marne salient by seizing the terrain around and to the southeast of Soissons.[69] XX Corps was to seize the important area between Berzy-le-Sec and Buzancy, south of Soissons (see Map 4).

The XX Corps attack was to be led by the American 1st and 2nd Divisions and the 1st Moroccan Division.[70] If the Germans lost the use of the road and rail line from Soissons to Château-Thierry, they would be unable to supply their armies on the Marne, forcing them to retreat. The 1st Division deployed on a 2.5-kilometer front on the corps' left (north), with the

153rd Division to its left and the 1st Moroccan to its right. The 1st Division had three objective lines for the first day of the offensive. The first line ran along the road running northeast from Dommiers and La Glaue Farm to St. Amand Farm. The second objective was a line running from just west of Chaudun through Missy-aux-Bois, and the third line ran from just east of Chaudun to the division's left boundary on the Paris-Soissons Road (the N2).[71]

The soldiers of the 1st Division were as surprised about the offensive as the Germans. From their time of relief from the Montdidier sector on 8 July until they received orders on 15 July to move east from Dammartin, the men supposed they would have time to rest. In fact, a composite battalion of soldiers from all four infantry regiments and the division's band went to Paris to take part in Bastille Day celebrations on 14 July, hardly an indication of an impending offensive. On the night of 16 July, the division moved forward, with the supply trains going to Crepy-en-Valois, and the infantry moving by truck to positions 10 kilometers west of the line of departure near Cutry and Coeuvres-et-Valsery.[72]

The 6th and 7th Artillery Regiments moved their firing batteries to the zone of attack on trucks, while their horse-drawn caissons marched 90 kilometers to a linkup point with the guns at La Raperie. The artillery brigade's ammunition train arrived early on 18 July, just in time to deliver the 2,000 rounds to be fired by each battery in the initial rolling barrage. The 6th and 7th Artillery Regiments moved six guns each into the initial firing positions on the morning of 17 July, allowing each battery to have one gun in place to serve as a position marker for the remaining guns that were moved forward just before the attack. The 5th Artillery towed its 155mm guns forward with French trucks into positions from which it could provide longer-range fire against German artillery.[73] The French 253rd Artillery Regiment reinforced the 1st Artillery Brigade.[74]

Summerall deployed the division with Beaumont Buck's 2nd Brigade on the left and John Hines's 1st Brigade on the right. The infantry regiments attacked four abreast with their three battalions in column. A machine-gun company was attached to each infantry battalion. The leading battalion in each regiment served as the assault battalion. The second battalion in the regimental column was the support unit, prepared to assume the mission of or reinforce the lead battalion. The third battalion in the column was in reserve, with the exterior units in division reserve and the interior battalions in brigade reserve.[75]

The 37mm guns and the Stokes mortars of each regiment supported the assault battalion or accompanied the support battalion. One machine gun battalion

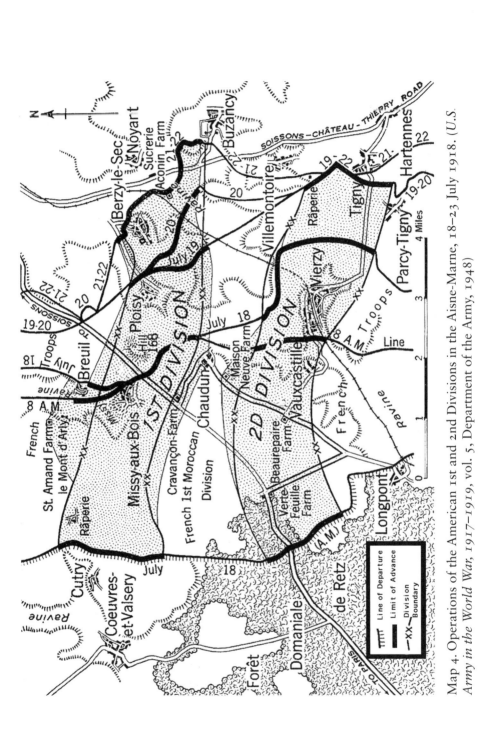

Map 4. Operations of the American 1st and 2nd Divisions in the Aisne-Marne, 18–23 July 1918. (*U.S. Army in the World War, 1917–1919*, vol. 5, Department of the Army, 1948)

was held in division reserve. The Engineer regiment was apportioned among the Infantry, Artillery, Tanks, and Division Reserve. The 6th Field Artillery (75's), supported the 1st Infantry Brigade (16th and 18th Infantry); the 7th Field Artillery (75's) supported the 2nd Infantry Brigade (26th and 28th Infantry); the 5th Artillery (155's) was held under the direct command of the Division Commander for heavy concentration fire and fire of demolition. Initial artillery positions were all west of the Coeuvres ravine.[76]

The infantry crossed the line of departure preceded by a rolling barrage at 0435 hours, on 18 July. The barrage was to move 100 meters forward every three minutes until the first objective line was reached, at which time the fire would halt for fifteen minutes to allow the infantry to reorganize before advancing. Initially this plan worked well.

By 0530 hours, both brigades had crossed fields of waist-high wheat and reached the first objective line. After a pause, the infantrymen resumed the attack. The advance of the 1st Brigade continued rapidly across the open ground east of Dommiers, assisted by French tanks. In the 2nd Brigade's zone, however, Major Willis Tack's 3/28th, advancing as the support battalion, suffered heavy casualties from German artillery as it crossed the line of departure near Cutry. German machine-gun fire from positions in the zone of the 153rd French Division caused considerable confusion and losses in Major Clarence Huebner's 2/28th Infantry. The French failed to keep pace with Huebner's flank, forcing him to send troops across the division's northern boundary to clear Germans out of the St. Amand Farm. From that point on, Buck's 2nd Brigade suffered heavy casualties, and only with difficulty was it able to reach the second objective line by the end of the day. As a result of heavy losses, the 2nd and 3rd Battalions, 28th Infantry, merged that evening for the next day's advance.[77]

The 2nd Brigade's difficult situation forced Hines to deploy 1st Brigade's reserve battalion facing to the north to maintain contact with the 26th infantry, although it did not prevent the 18th Infantry from reaching the second objective line on the Paris-Soissons Road by 0715.[78] There the 1st Brigade held while Buck's troops caught up on their left and the Moroccans came up on their right.[79] Things went relatively well in the 1st Brigade's initial attack, as Private Buhl's (of the 16th Infantry) recollection indicates:

On July 17, we started again for the front, and on the morning of the 18th of July at five AM (after a twenty mile hike) we went over the top at Soissons without any preparatory artillery barrages. It was a spectacular sight—the thousands of red lights thrown up by the Germans calling for their artillery and the American barrage playing on the Germans in the distance and the thousands of prisoners who came over in groups from twenty to two hundred, all with their hands up, calling "comrade."[80]

The 2nd Brigade faced more formidable terrain between the first and second objective lines than did the 1st Brigade. Its 28th Infantry had to protect the division's exposed left flank while the 26th Infantry crossed a wide depression known as Missy Ravine. This obstacle contained numerous caves in which Germans took shelter from American artillery fire. A stream lined with marshy terrain flowed through the middle of the ravine, making it harder for the attackers to cross. The small village of Le Mont d'Arly was on the western slope, and the larger habitation of Breuil was on the eastern slope. The stone houses in these villages afforded the Germans protected positions for machine guns and artillery observers, forcing the Americans to clear both villages. Since the ravine was unsuitable for tanks due to the steep slopes and marsh, the infantrymen were on their own.

After clearing the Germans out of St. Amand Farm, the 2/28th pushed into Missy Ravine. The fighting was fierce as Huebner's men captured Mont d'Arly, fought their way across the stream, and attacked Breuil. In the process, the battalion lost every officer except Huebner. Buck quickly lost touch with his regiments and decided to go forward in person. He then got lost and spent a considerable amount of time wandering the battlefield.[81] Meanwhile, Babcock reorganized the 28th Infantry and established contact with the French 153rd Division while Major Theodore Roosevelt Jr. pushed his 1/26th Infantry through the southern portion of Missy Ravine, by 0900.[82]

The left flank of the division was exposed to enemy fire because the French failed to keep up with the 28th Infantry's advance. The initiative to close the gap was taken by Clarence Huebner and other junior leaders, such as Second Lieutenant Samuel Parker, Company K, 28th Infantry. Observing an enemy machine-gun position in a quarry to the north, Parker "ordered his depleted platoon to follow him in an attack upon the strong point. Meeting a disorganized group of French Colonials wandering leaderlessly about, he persuaded them to join his platoon. This consolidated group followed Lieutenant Parker through direct enemy rifle fire and machine gun fire to the crest of the hill and rushing forward took the quarry by storm, capturing six machine guns and about forty prisoners."[83]

Beaumont Buck lost control of his brigade on 18 July. Nonetheless, the 2nd Brigade accomplished a great deal in a very difficult situation by clearing St. Amand Farm and fighting its way across Missy Ravine. In the process, the 28th Infantry captured 600 Germans and maintained contact with the French to the north.

Communications were difficult throughout the division during the Soissons attack:

> From division to brigade, command, communications, and control were generally adequate, at least until the brigade headquarters moved forward. Thereafter, communications were erratic for the most part. From brigade to regiment, command could be described as adequate even if communications were primarily by muscle power. But forward of regiment, command existed only on the initiative of individuals. Communications really existed only when the commander went forward in person, and only when the troops had halted long enough for someone from the rear to find them.[84]

After the troops crossed the line of departure, there was no easy way for them to keep higher headquarters informed of their situation. The radios of the time were too heavy and unreliable to be used by infantrymen during an attack. The 2nd Signal Battalion did all it could to maintain wire communications between the various posts of command, but once the brigades moved forward wire communications were vulnerable to German artillery fire and susceptible to being cut by tanks and artillery vehicles.

Once 1st Brigade reached its third objective line, Hines realigned his regiments to maintain contact with the 2nd Brigade to the north and the Moroccans to the south. The 18th Infantry maintained contact with the French and held the objective line north of Chaudun, while the 16th Infantry refused its left flank and brought its support battalion into a line facing northeast, connected with the 26th Infantry.[85] On the 2nd Brigade's front, Babcock's 28th Infantry was unable to fight its way to the third objective line on the Paris-Soissons Road. The day ended with the division's forward elements in those positions. Approximately 1,500 men had been killed or wounded, and many more wandered the battlefield in search of their units.[86] However, the attack surprised the Germans. The 1st Division captured over 2,000 prisoners and thirty field guns, most of which were taken in Missy Ravine.[87]

The machine-gun units suffered some of the heaviest casualties on 18 July. As Lieutenant John Hale, commander of Company A, 2nd Machine Gun (MG) Battalion, later wrote, "Machine guns followed too closely in the wake of the infantry [and] the majority of our casualties resulted from fire directed at the infantry to which we were attached and our guns did not prove any more effective than if they had followed up more slowly. [The riflemen who had been detailed to carry ammunition] deserted us and caused a shortage of ammunition."[88] The commander of the 2nd MG Battalion, Captain Paul Ransom, concluded that "there was a serious shortage of ammunition throughout the operation. . . . There were too many guns up forward. [Consequently] . . . the loss of material was considerable."[89]

Half of the machine gunners were casualties.[90] "At a time when needed most, during the organization of the objectives . . . , there was a vital lack of coordination of the machine gun defense, owing to the scattering of units and their depletion during the advance with the infantry."[91] The relative success of the first day's advance posed tactical problems that the AEF had not encountered. The AEF's and the division's use of after-action reports to identify problems, and then the concerted efforts made to solve them, indicate that the US Army learned from its mistakes in 1918.

Mangin ordered the attack to be continued on 19 July. Summerall anticipated this order and issued instructions to the brigades to plan to continue the advance to a line between Berzy-le-Sec and Buzancy.[92] The division headquarters received XX Corps' attack order late on 18 July and issued the division order at 0135 hours, on 19 July. The order barely reached the brigade commanders before 0400, the time the attack was supposed to have been launched.[93] The division attacked as soon as possible, again supported by French tanks and a rolling artillery barrage. The 18th Infantry on the right of 1st Brigade advanced about half the distance between Chaudun and Buzancy, taking advantage of the withdrawal of most of the Germans in its zone. "On account of the opposition met on the left of the Division it was necessary [to continue] to refuse the left flank of the 16th Infantry to join with the 26th Infantry." On the right of the brigade, the 18th Infantry was slowed by its need to maintain contact with the Moroccans.[94]

The 2nd Brigade again found itself under heavy flanking fire from the north. Buck was forced to commit the 1/28th, which had been returned to him from division reserve, in the attack on his left. The 28th Infantry then pushed up to the Soissons-Paris Road. German machine guns swept the positions along the road, pinning down the attacking infantrymen. Artillery fire destroyed the French tanks that tried to clear the way for the infantry. Buck found the situation desperate when he went forward:

> By 7:00 AM I was on my front line on the Paris-Soissons highway. My 26th Infantry was hugging this highway which was built up two feet above the open ground. Long range firing was going on when I arrived. Shrapnel and high explosive shells were bursting on the road while I talked to Colonel Hamilton A. Smith. . . . Sixty yards in front of the position two of our tanks were wrecked. They had been put out of commission by artillery fire. A battery of four field guns had been run up to the line by our men but the gunners had been driven under cover by the enemy. Gusts of machine gun bullets whistled through the

branches of the trees which lined the highway, or ricocheted from the surface of the road.[95]

The 26th Infantry suffered heavy losses getting to this position, including Major Roosevelt, who was wounded. Smith continued to push small groups of soldiers forward to locate enemy strongpoints, but the 2nd Brigade made little progress that morning. After bringing the 28th Infantry forward, Buck launched another attack, at 0530, that carried the brigade's front to the edge of Ploisy Ravine. While advancing a kilometer, the 1/28th lost all but eight of its officers. The attack was halted there for the day, short of the division's objective near Berzy-le-Sec.[96] By this point in the battle, the Germans had committed elements of four divisions against the 1st Division.

The 2nd Brigade's costly advance on 19 July was made possible by the leadership of junior officers. Lieutenant Samuel Parker, by then

> in command of the merged 2nd and 3rd Battalions [28th Infantry] was in support of the 1st Battalion. Although painfully wounded in the foot, he refused to be evacuated and continued to lead his command until the objective was reached. Seeing that the assault battalion was subjected to heavy enfilade fire . . . , Lieutenant Parker led his battalion through this heavy fire and up on line to the left of the 1st Battalion and thereby closed the gap.

During the consolidation, Parker crawled "about on his hands and knees on account of his painful wound."[97]

The division's artillery performed well during the operations of 18 and 19 July. The 6th Field Artillery maintained a rolling barrage for the 1st Brigade's attacks. By the afternoon of 19 July, the batteries of the regiment had moved to positions south of Missy-aux-Bois. From there, the 6th Artillery supported the hard-pressed 26th Infantry to the north. On the night of 19 July, the regiment moved four batteries forward to near Chazelle Ravine, east of Chaudun, to fire 6,000 rounds in a rolling barrage during the attack on 20 July. These guns fired in support of the 2nd Brigade's final attack on Berzy-le-Sec on 21 July as well. During the fighting for Berzy, the 6th Artillery noted that "the enemy's artillery fire was directed entirely by direct observation and was not of a prearranged nature. The fire was quite accurate and the range was diminished as our lines advanced."[98]

The 7th Artillery also performed well in support of the 2nd Brigade. On 18 July, as the infantry advanced, the batteries displaced to the ravine south of Missy-aux-Bois to engage German machine guns that were pinning Buck's infantrymen down. On 20 July, they moved to positions on the

Soissons-Paris Road to support the attacks on Berzy-le-Sec.[99] Warren Mavity, a wireman in Battery F, remembered the day in the following manner:

> The next move forward was to a gun position along a road. . . . Our signal detail set up our usual lines with one going over the bank, across a field where it was hooked up to a line running to headquarters. . . . The Germans set the range of one 88mm gun with shell in the breach and when any movement of ours was seen at that opening they fired about six shells rapidly. This was breaking our lines and when it was mine and my buddy's turn to repair we got caught in this fire. . . . This was one of those times for me to repeat the 23rd Psalm as it was pretty scary when you were the target being aimed at.[100]

The division did not reach all of its objectives on 19 July. In the process it lost another 3,000 men, including many officers. But Summerall considered the division capable of further offensive action. On the southern flank of XX Corps, the 2nd Division had suffered so many casualties that Harbord requested that his division be replaced that night. General Berdoulat complied with the request.[101]

The ability of the 1st Division to stay in the fight after suffering over 4,500 casualties indicates that it possessed the cohesion and discipline essential to staying power in intense combat. Summerall understood that his division was capable of continuing the offensive.[102] His appreciation of the dreadful calculus that must be made in such situations, and his ability to push tired commanders and troops, are two of the traits that made him one of the best American tactical commanders of World War I.

The plan for the attack on 20 July was simple. The 2nd Brigade was to push east across Ploisy Ravine and take Berzy-le-Sec. The 1st Brigade was to support the attack and move its front to the high ground east of the valley of the Crise, overlooking the Soissons-Villers-Cotterets rail line and the road from Soissons to Château-Thierry.[103] At 0200, after two hours of artillery preparation fires, the infantry advanced. On the left, the 3/26th made progress toward the rail line, but, as the men crested the ridge overlooking the Crise, German artillery fire plowed through their ranks, driving the troops to the ground. The regimental commander, Colonel Hamilton Smith, refused to renew the frontal assault when ordered, telling Summerall later that "the order was impossible and I did not try to obey it."[104] The 28th Infantry also failed to take Berzy-le-Sec.[105]

The 1st Brigade crossed the Chazelle Ravine and carried its attack into the valley of the Crise, cutting the rail line and reaching the Bois Gerard. Its mission now was to hold these positions. Frank Bamford's 16th Infantry maintained contact with the 2nd Brigade on its left but, in doing so, faced mostly north. On the division's right, the 18th Infantry connected with the French 87th Division. This success was costly. Private Buhl remembers that in his battalion in the 16th Infantry "all our officers had either been killed or wounded. Our first sergeant, who was an old timer, rounded up the second battalion and found after twelve hours of fighting the company had thirty seven left out of two hundred and seventy three, not including officers. Scanon was in charge of the battalion, and Corporal Mitchell was put in charge of the company."[106]

More sacrifice was required as Summerall passed on the XX Corps order to continue the drive. On the evening of 20 July, Summerall visited his units to explain the mission and his expectations. He promised the troops that they would be relieved on the night of 21 July, and "they promised him they would take Berzy-le-Sec." During this visit to the front, Summerall found Buck and his regimental commanders physically exhausted. Summerall told Buck to get some sleep so that he could lead the next attack. He and Buck evidently concluded that Babcock and Smith were incapacitated due to fatigue, forcing the brigade commander personally to organize the remaining troops of the 28th Infantry for the assault.[107]

Berdoulat's order specified that all three divisions of the corps would attack at 0445, 21 July. The French 153rd Division would move to the north of Berzy to facilitate the 1st Division's final drive. The 87th Division on the right was to push forward to catch up with the advance of the 1st Brigade. Plans were made to bring the 15th Scottish Division forward on the evening of 21 July to relieve the 1st Division.

Things did not go as planned. The commander of the brigade of the 69th Division on the left refused to attack until a three-hour artillery preparation was fired. This allowed Buck to delay his attack, giving him time to issue orders and organize his troops for the assault. The delay also allowed the division's artillery to concentrate the fires of the 6th and 7th Artillery Regiments in support of one brigade at a time, while the 5th Artillery hammered Berzy-le-Sec. The 1st Brigade attacked at 0445 behind a rolling barrage. Hines's men moved across the rail line onto the Plateau of Buzancy. The 87th Division attacked at 0600. By 0645, the French had driven the Germans across the highway south of Villemontoire and reached the edge of Buzancy, which changed hands several times during the day.[108]

Buck spent the early morning of 21 July explaining the plan to the remaining squad and platoon leaders of the 28th Infantry. He went from foxhole to foxhole giving the junior leaders sketch maps showing the line of departure and the objective. After returning briefly to his post of command for breakfast, Buck hurried forward to be with the soldiers of the 28th when they attacked at 0830. He arrived in time to launch the first of three waves of infantry, led by Lieutenant John Cleland, toward the objective. The line wavered as it reached the brow of the ridge overlooking Berzy, where Cleland was wounded, but the men resumed the advance before Buck caught up with them. As Buck remembered, "The second wave followed, and when it started down the slope I hastily gathered up every man left, mostly machine gunners, directed them on the run to the brow of the slope, where they took posts. This was scarcely finished when the fighting in the village ceased." Berzy-le-Sec was in the division's hands.[109]

The 1st Division paid a horrific price for the victory, and its ordeal was not over on 21 July. Because the 15th Scottish Division was late in arriving, Summerall was unable to relieve his exhausted infantrymen that night. "Casualties continued heavy in the front line from machine gun and increasing artillery fire. . . . On 22 July, the 26th infantry occupied the Sucrerie so as to straighten out the line at the front." During this period, the 1st Sanitation Train worked to bury the dead. The division's medical units treated casualties until 25 July, by which date the four hospital units had admitted 9,789 casualties (Allies and Germans included). The division lost over 7,200 men, including 1,714 dead.[110]

The division's heavy losses were not in vain. The Soissons offensive permanently wrested the initiative from the German army. On the evening of 22 July, the Scots relieved the division's infantry and machine-gun units. The artillery brigade stayed in position two more days to support the Scots.[111] After their relief, the soldiers marched 11 kilometers to meet trucks for the trip back to Dammartin. There they were given hot food and a chance to sleep. The division was reunited with its artillery and medical units at Dammartin before its movement to Lorraine on 28 July, where it occupied a quiet sector northeast of Toul.

The Results: The Decisive Battle of World War I

The 1st Division secured the line from Berzy-le-Sec to the edge of Buzancy, to the southeast, cutting the Soissons–Château–Thierry Road and the rail communications of the Germans on the Marne to the south. As a result, on 22 July, Ludendorff ordered his armies to begin the withdrawal from the salient to the south of the Soissons-Reims line.[112] The Allied offensive continued until 6 August, when the last Germans crossed the Aisne. The US Army had come of age, and for the first time it had deployed divisions and corps in major offensive action in Europe.

3

Victory in Alsace-Lorraine
St. Mihiel and the Meuse Argonne

THE ALLIES' DEFEAT OF THE GERMAN ARMY in July 1918 did not end the war. It did, however, firmly shift the initiative to the Western powers. On 8 August, the British launched an offensive east of Amiens, spearheaded by over 450 tanks and supported by 1,900 French and British airplanes. To the south of the British, the French attacked as well. The Allies surprised the German *Second Army* and captured 16,000 men and 200 guns in several hours. On 9 August, the French Third Army joined the offensive, capturing Montdidier and the German supply center near that town. Although these attacks ran out of steam, the impact of the attack shattered Ludendorff's and the German High Command's faith that they could win the war. Ludendorff called it the black day of the German army. From that point on, the German military leaders debated how and where to maintain a coherent defense in France as part of a strategy of exhaustion.[1]

The strength of the German armies in the west fell from 5.1 million men in March 1918 to 4.2 million in August. The Germans needed 200,000 men per month to replenish their losses, but only 300,000 new recruits were available for the year. As a result, German divisions were understrength, and many of the weakest were disbanded. Further, the continued hammering by the Allies prevented the Germans from resting their divisions adequately, decreasing morale and efficiency.[2]

The AEF Grows as the 1st Division Recovers

By August 1918, the American military contribution to the Western Front was second only to the French. The AEF had grown to over 1,169,000 soldiers, while the British army in France decreased to 543,000.[3] Pershing commanded twenty-nine divisions, with six more slated to arrive in August. Major General Hunter Liggett's I Corps took part in the Aisne-Marne offensive, and Robert Bullard's III Corps was activated at the end of July. The II Corps, commanded by Major General George W. Read, was responsible for the administration of the American divisions training with the British and would assume tactical control of two divisions (the 27th and 30th) by

59

the end of September. Two additional American corps (IV and V) were organized in August. New units and replacements poured into France at a rate
of over 230,000 men per month.[4] The American First Army was officially
activated on 10 August to command the American I and III Corps on the
Aisne front. Pershing assumed command of the army while retaining his
position as AEF commander in chief.[5]

American casualties in July exceeded 38,000 men, of whom about 20
percent were killed. The medical system returned 70 percent of the wounded
it treated to active service during the war. Replacements filled the remaining
gap. In order to keep up with the losses, Pershing asked the War Department to send 44,000 replacements in June and 56,000 in July. This was in
addition to the 166,000 combat troops sent to France in divisions.[6] The 1st
Division lost 6,500 men in May and June 1918 and was short 2,700 men
at the beginning of July. The 7,200 casualties suffered during the Soissons
offensive left the division nearly 8,900 men short at the end of July. The infantry and machine-gun units suffered most of the losses. The four infantry
regiments had an average of 2,134 men each on 21 August, well below their
authorized strength of over 3,700 men. During August, the division received
sufficient replacements and returnees from hospitals to bring its strength to
27,727 men, with over 14,000 soldiers in the rifle regiments.[7]

Following the Soissons offensive, the 1st Division moved to Gondreville,
near Toul, where it was billeted until 5 August. It then occupied a quiet portion of the front known as the Saizerais sector until 24 August. Summerall
launched a strenuous training program to integrate replacements and to
correct tactical shortcomings. This period of training was a brief but crucial
respite that allowed the division to prepare for the battles ahead. Summerall
forcefully prescribed how his soldiers were to act when off duty. "All forms
of gambling will be kept off the public street; Out of doors, all men will be
required to appear in the proper uniform with blouses buttoned; All men
will be carefully instructed to salute officers."[8]

These rules, along with stringent rules about sexual contact with French
women and the prevention of venereal diseases, are examples of the effort
made to live up to the high standards Pershing expected of the AEF. Along
with such rules came a steady stream of reports about lessons learned in
combat.

The use of after-action reports allowed Pershing's army to improve its
tactical capabilities. Summerall issued summaries of the problems identified
in after-action reports to his brigade and regimental commanders, along
with guidance on how troops were to be trained. One of the issues of greatest concern was the way in which automatic weapons were deployed at
Soissons. Automatic riflemen and machine gunners had accompanied the

infantry battalions in the assault, but due to the weight of their weapons and ammunition they had been unable to keep up. Both weapons had been scattered through the infantry formations without officers in control of their employment. Few guns were used properly. Soldiers often fired their automatic weapons needlessly, leaving them with little ammunition when they reached the objective. The machine-gun crews were easy targets for the Germans, and a large percentage were casualties. Consequently, the infantry had too little automatic-weapons support when the Germans counterattacked. Many Chauchat automatic rifles and ammunition magazines were damaged, and many were fired too rapidly, causing the parts to overheat and malfunction. To fix these problems, Summerall imposed stringent rules concerning the employment of automatic weapons:

a. All soldiers are to be taught to use the automatic rifle and how to care for it.

b. Officers are to be taught that the machine gun is a defensive weapon that has to be saved in the attack for defensive purposes "at all hazards."

c. Only the best and strongest soldiers will carry the automatic rifles.

d. Companies are to organize for an attack in four lines, with the automatic weapons generally in the rear. From there the guns will be deployed by unit commanders.

e. Every soldier in the company is to carry a magazine for the Chauchat, and spare parts are to be carried by [NCOs].

f. Machine gun company commanders are to command and control their machine guns in support of the battalion to which their company is assigned. Liaison officers will look for places where the guns can best be employed.

g. Both the Chauchats and the machine guns are to be moved from covered position to covered position as much as possible.

h. Liaison teams from the supporting machine gun company will accompany the supported battalion commanders to advise them on use of the guns and relay instructions to the machine gun company commander.[9]

Too many officers had been killed or wounded during the battle. Every infantry battalion commander in the division had been wounded, and Colonel Hamilton Smith, commander of the 26th Infantry Regiment, was killed. Of the 990 officers authorized in the division, 234 were casualties. The 2nd Brigade alone needed 135 officer replacements, along with 4,429 enlisted men.[10] Such high officer casualties were due to inexperience. Too many leaders exposed themselves needlessly to enemy fire, and many battalion commanders had not been in positions from which they could observe and control their units.

Summerall issued guidance that "the battalion commander will always occupy a position from which he can observe the movements of the battalion. . . . While it is proper to take such cover as may be found to exist, at no time will the battalion commander place himself where he cannot observe the terrain and his troops." Each battalion commander was to "reduce the number of officers accompanying him to the minimum. . . . [And] the battalion commander and his personnel will move by the safest practicable routes, and as rapidly as possible in order to conceal their movement, and to diminish losses."[11]

On 29 August, Summerall issued another memorandum detailing flaws in the movement of units in offensive operations. Since the brigade and most regiment and battalion commanders were new in their jobs, these tactical rules gave the division a standardized approach. It opened with a typical Summerall view of leadership: "All officers and men must be impressed with the necessity of enduring great fatigue, hunger, thirst and lack of sleep. These conditions do not prevent vigorous action and it must be borne in mind that they will pass away with the successful accomplishment of our mission."[12]

Summerall's memorandum described tactical methods that reflected the lessons learned from German infiltration tactics. Strongpoints and machine guns were to be bypassed by units not under their direct fire while enemy positions were "vigorously reduced by intense fire of machine guns, automatic rifles, Stokes mortars and 37mm guns, and the accompanying artillery. Under cover of this fire the infantry must advance by rushes around the flanks, in small groups or individually, accompanied by automatic rifles."[13]

There also had been major problems with the employment of infantry during the recent offensive. Combat power was weakened by the diversion of troops from the assault, while conversely, the bunching of men in their formations afforded the enemy easy targets. Pershing's "Combat Instructions for Troops of the First Army" noted that straggling and "detachments to the rear and the *wholly unnecessary reinforcement of the front line based on alarming messages or on the pessimistic reports of wounded and stragglers*" needed to be avoided. Tanks and artillery were to work with engineers and infantry to cut through the enemy's wire, trenches, and strongpoints. Assault formations generally were to follow a rolling barrage, while support and reserve battalions followed in echelon.[14]

Rigid timetables for the initial attack were to be abandoned. Battalions and companies were to have an axis of advance assigned, and "all must progress as rapidly as possible through the heart of the enemy's position.

Reinforcements must only be thrown in where 'the going is good,' and not piled up against strong resistance." All unit commanders had to be trained to understand their axis of advance and to *"act on their own initiative with resolute determination."* [15]

Pershing stressed that the fighting "depends upon individual initiative, rapidity of decision, resolute daring and driving power, [which] should afford the American officer and soldier the opportunity to display his best known national characteristics to their greatest advantage." Instead of a rolling barrage, artillery was to be directed against specific targets, "while the infantry presses through the weak points in his [the German's] line and turns him out." [16]

Training of Individual Replacements

While the division worked to correct tactical deficiencies, thousands of replacements filled its ranks. Most of these men arrived in mid-August when the division was in the quiet Saizerais sector. Private Herbert L. McHenry was representative of these new soldiers. He was drafted on 28 May 1918 in Pennsylvania and boarded a train to Camp Lee, Virginia, the next day. After six weeks of basic training that emphasized rifle marksmanship, trench warfare, and dismounted drill, McHenry sailed for France. McHenry arrived in Brest on 29 July, just two months after his induction into the army. On 2 August, he was put on a troop train consisting of forty and eights and rode for three days to St. Aignan. On 6 August, McHenry marched with a company of replacements to Nours, where they were billeted in barns and lofts for three days. During this period, he and the other replacements received no training or drill. [17]

On 11 August, McHenry boarded a train with men assigned to the 16th Infantry. After three days' travel, these men reached the 1st Division, where, as McHenry recalls,

> the train stopped at a point that was near enough to battle action to give us a view of the German airplanes as they soared over the terrain. . . . We then "fell in" and marched about five miles to a woods where there were a few barracks. . . . The few hours spent there were devoted to lectures, telling how to dig trenches and what we would find at the front. We loafed around there, eating reserve rations until dusk, when we were loaded on a flock of American trucks. . . . Around ten o'clock that night, we reached a point as near to the battle front as the trucks dared to go. There we lined up in company front. An officer, I think a colonel, walked along our front and picked out forty five of the largest men, and ordered us to fall out and form a line in the rear and out

of hearing of the company. . . . The colonel then said something to us like this: "Men you are now in the best branch of the service, the machine gun service. You are superior to the soldiers in all other troops, and will hold yourselves as superior to them." He was a smooth article and some hot air artist.[18]

McHenry joined the machine-gun company of the 16th Infantry Regiment. The company had only thirty-five of its authorized ninety-six men, due to its heavy losses at Soissons. McHenry had never handled a Hotchkiss machine gun, let alone fired, assembled, or disassembled the weapon. He was assigned as an ammunition carrier to an eight-man squad led by a Corporal Reynolds. Reynolds was one of four survivors in the squad when McHenry joined it. Reynolds's squad was in the front line for the next six days as McHenry learned his duties under the watchful eyes of his squad leader and the Germans, who were a short distance away. He survived this initial taste of combat and withdrew from the front when his unit was relieved on 24 August.[19] When McHenry's unit came out of the line, the division moved to a training area. This move commenced with a fourteen-hour hike to where the trucks were to pick the men up. Each soldier carried a pack weighing about 65 pounds:

> That pack consisted of a haversack, a pack carrier, mess equipment, a shelter half, a blanket, change of underwear, an extra olive drab shirt, six pair of socks, an extra pair of shoes, a pistol belt and holster, four extra clips of ammunition, a half gallon French canteen, a gas mask, a steel helmet, a first aid pouch, a rain coat or slicker, and an American bolo, which was sort of a short sword, made something like a cleaver.[20]

Once in the training area, the division continued to train its new men. McHenry's company joined a machine-gun battalion for three days of training on its equipment before this work was cut short by the need to conduct regiment and division exercises. McHenry's training with the French-built Hotchkiss machine gun was adequate, although not extensive. He learned how to care for and fire the weapon. "We could take that gun apart and assemble it in the darkest night without even lighting a match," he said, "as no lights were allowed on the front lines, or on any lines that were under possible German observation."[21]

Throughout the AEF, responsibility for training replacements rested on the units to which they were assigned. Men joining the 1st Division in mid-1918 were luckier than most in having a cadre of combat veterans to teach them how to fight and survive. As McHenry noted, the division's leaders did all they could to prepare the new men for battle. "Our treatment by them, from our first assignment to that Division was of the most kind and considerate nature. Their great anxiety was to teach us to be real soldiers." Small-unit training was cut short by the need to conduct division-level practice exercises for the forthcoming offensive. Nonetheless, the officers and NCOs instructed the soldiers in critical skills as they moved toward assembly areas for the St. Mihiel operation. "Our instruction in the use of the gas mask was most carefully attended to. We had much, very much gas-mask drill. . . . We were compelled to drill on that mask until we could put it on, perfectly adjusted, in six seconds."[22]

The St. Mihiel Offensive

Pershing had looked forward to the establishment of the First Army since his arrival in France. He had planned from the beginning to employ the AEF in its first independent offensive operation against the German salient across the Meuse near St. Mihiel. The American logistical system and training areas had been set up to support American forces operating in Lorraine. Pershing envisioned that the objective of the American forces would be to seize Metz after reducing the St. Mihiel salient, thus severing the Germans' supply routes through that city to their armies in northern France. The Germans then would have to rely on the rail lines from Germany to Liège, and these were inadequate to support their western armies.

In July, Pershing won acceptance from Marshal Ferdinand Foch to activate the First Army, with the intent of the American army pushing north across the Aisne River in pursuit of the German armies. The stiffened enemy resistance along the Aisne in early August, however, caused Foch to end the offensive in that sector. Pershing then convinced Foch and Pétain that the American army should launch an offensive against the St. Mihiel salient.[23] Pershing finally had achieved his goal of fielding an independent American army. It was crucial to American and Allied morale that this army's first offensive succeed. To this end, the British and French agreed to release nearly all American divisions to Pershing and to provide the artillery and support units needed by the First Army.[24]

First Army headquarters moved from La Ferte-sous-Jouarre to Neufchâteau between 11 and 16 August. There, Pershing's staff planned the offensive. The First Army had three American and one French corps available for the attack. Fourteen US divisions were to take part in a pincer movement. The difficulty of moving 3.3 million rounds of artillery ammunition, 550,000 men, and 3,000 artillery pieces into position delayed the offensive until 12 September. Pershing depended on the French for the majority of the artillery, aircraft, tanks, and transportation equipment used in the offensive.

On 2 September, Foch, Pétain, and Pershing met and agreed, after a long discussion, that the American First Army was to carry out its attack against the St. Mihiel salient and then shift twelve divisions north to conduct an offensive west of the Meuse by 25 September.[25] With this agreement in place, and therefore French troops, artillery, and planes available for the St. Mihiel operation, Pershing's chief of staff completed the plans.[26]

The Plan for St. Mihiel

On 1 September, the 1st Division began moving toward its zone of operations north of Toul for the offensive. (See Map 5.) Division headquarters established operations in Pagny-sur-Meuse by the evening of 2 September. By 6 September, the infantry and artillery regiments had reached assembly areas in the forest between the Meuse and their assault positions around Richecourt and Seicheprey. As the division moved, the brigade commanders ordered regimental and battalion commanders to leave a detail "in command of an officer, to inspect the area that has been vacated and gather up *all stragglers*. This detail will then follow in rear of the column and allow *no stragglers* to fall behind during the march."[27]

The assault troops moved into position at night to avoid detection by German aircraft. The infantry units marched along roads crammed with horse teams and trucks hauling guns, ammunition, and supplies. As McHenry noted in his memoir,

> We marched during the night until about an hour before sunrise, when we reached a woods, in which we camped all day. . . . We could not light any fires, with the exception of the field ranges for cooking purposes. . . . We had dry wood, which made little smoke, and by the time it got out over the tops of the trees it was so scattered that it was not noticeable. At nightfall we resumed our march until we reached another camping place and another woods. As we marched into that woods the road we traveled was so crowded with traffic taking munitions to the front, and the night was so dark, that we marched holding to each other to keep from getting lost and separated. . . . Of course these vehicles were driven very slowly, but with all the care possible being exercised, there were accidents. There were head-on collisions and telescope collisions and there were side-swipe variety of accident. The First Division was composed of steel-souled men . . . and anything that halted them in their work, either individually or collectively, met with the wrath of the men. Those responsible for the unauthorized halt were chastised in the language of the soldier, which consists, largely, of religious words irreligiously uttered.[28]

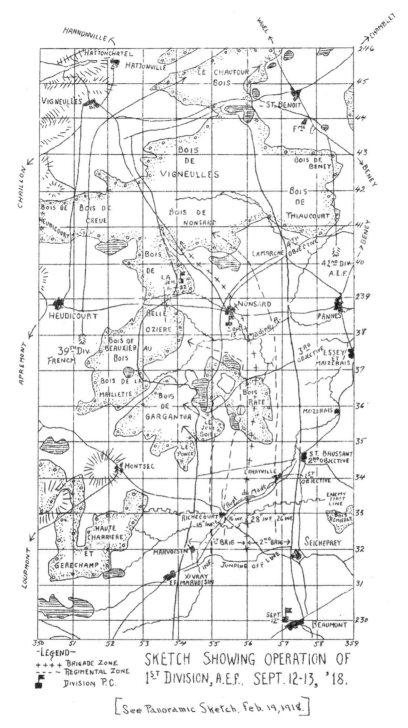

Map 5. Battle of St. Mihiel, 12–13 September 1918. (*U.S. Army in the World War, 1917–1919*, vol. 5, Department of the Army, 1948)

With a great deal of help from the French, the First Army got its divisions, supporting aviation, tanks, and artillery into position by 9 September. While the 1st Division's infantry and artillery were moving, Summerall issued the division's plan. The 1st Division was to attack as the left-hand division in IV Corps, with the French 39th Colonial Division on its left and the US 42nd Division attacking on its right. The mission was to seize four successive objective lines while protecting the left flank of the corps. The advance was aimed toward Vigneulles, where planners hoped the division would meet the 26th Division and cut off the western half of the salient. The 39th Colonial Division would launch its attack one hour after the Americans jumped off.[29] This meant that the left flank of the division would be exposed to the enemy on Montsec (Map 5).

The infantry moved to a line of departure between Xivray and Seicheprey on the night of 11–12 September. The attack was to commence at 0500 hours, 12 September, following a four-hour artillery preparation. The 1st Brigade deployed on the left, with 18th Infantry on its left and 16th Infantry on the right. The 2nd Brigade was on the division's right, with the 28th Infantry on its left and the 26th Infantry on the right. The division ordered the 18th Infantry to place two battalions in its first line and only one company in the support line. The third battalion of the 18th Regiment was to follow in the third line as a reserve. As it advanced, the 18th Infantry was to face its battalions west to protect the flank of the division until the French 39th Division caught up.[30]

The division's other three infantry regiments deployed with their battalions in three successive lines. In the first line were the assault battalions that were to drive through the enemy's main defensive belt. The second line contained the support battalions that were to pass through the leading battalions after they reached the second objective line and to carry the attack to the last two objective lines. The third battalions in each regiment were designated as reserves. A machine-gun company accompanied each infantry battalion, and the 7th Machine Gun Battalion of the 2nd Division reinforced the 18th Infantry. As an innovation, Summerall ordered the artillery brigade to provide a 75mm gun to accompany each assault battalion to knock out German bunkers.[31]

Three Engineer teams accompanied each of the leading infantry platoons. One was to cut the German barbed wire, the second was to provide bangalore torpedoes to blow holes in the wire, and the third team was to construct footbridges across the stream known as the Rupt de Mad, which ran across the division's front. An American tank battalion of forty-nine Renault tanks was attached to the division to help the infantry get through the German wire and to destroy pillboxes north of the Rupt de Mad.[32]

The Battle of St. Mihiel

The infantry movement into assault positions was covered by the artillery preparation that commenced at 0100, 12 September. By 0500, when the infantry attacked, it was clear that the German artillery was not responding vigorously. In fact, the Germans had chosen the night of 11 September to begin an evacuation of the St. Mihiel salient, having previously decided to withdraw to the shorter line at the base of the triangular bulge. The American attack caught the Germans in the midst of this move. The first line of infantry crossed the German wire with little difficulty, walking over the wire in a number of cases. Their advance was covered by a rolling artillery barrage that moved forward at a rate of 100 meters every four minutes.[33] Smoke shells were fired steadily at Montsec to the west to mask the moving infantry and to screen the engineers as they bridged the Rupt de Mad. By 0600, the infantry reached the first objective line. On the left, the 18th Infantry wheeled one battalion counterclockwise opposite the Bois de Tombois to protect the flank. The machine guns, following the lead battalions at a distance of between 150 and 400 yards, found few targets, especially after the tanks passed the infantry at the second objective line and aided the advance by destroying German pillboxes.[34]

The assault battalions reached the second objective line along the old German trenches at about 0700, collecting prisoners as they advanced. There the rolling barrage stopped to allow the infantry to reorganize and to pass the support battalions through the original assault units. The advance then resumed. By 1000 hours the infantry had reached the third objective line on the northern edge of the Bois de Rat and stopped to reorganize. On the left, the 18th Infantry deployed its second battalion along the western flank. By this time, the main German line of resistance had been breached on the southern side of the Quart de Reserve.[35]

While the infantry and machine-gun units consolidated along their third objective line, the artillery moved to positions just south of the Rupt de Mad. The 51st Pioneer Infantry, a labor unit attached to the division, and the 1st Engineers built roads through the original no-man's-land and erected bridges across the Rupt de Mad so that artillery, ambulances, and ammunition vehicles could cross.[36]

The Germans were unable to react effectively against the initial attack. McHenry, in the 16th Infantry, reported:

Our hardest work on this part of the drive was in getting over the German trenches. . . . We were compelled to sort of tumble into one side and then crawl out the other. The tanks had a difficult time in getting through. The weather

had been wet and much mud and water were in the trenches. . . . When we
reached our objective at the edge of the woods, we were totally covered with
mud. As we passed over this ground the effect of our artillery fire was apparent
all around us.

McHenry's squad lost only one of its eight men, when Corporal Reynolds
was hit in the foot by a bullet.[37]

By noon, the division had captured 600 Germans. These men confirmed
that the Germans had been expecting an offensive, "but that later there had
been [so] much nonchalant strolling about by American soldiers in this sector that some officers decided that there were no offensive intentions on our
part."[38] Once the third line was breached, the only resistance encountered
was from German machine-gun squads left behind to slow the American
advance.

The attack was resumed shortly after 1100. The 28th Infantry Regiment
cleared the village of Nonsard in the center of the zone, capturing several
large bunkers. On the right of 2nd Brigade, the 26th Infantry sent a battalion
to clear the village of Lamarche on the boundary with the 42nd Division.
This move cleared the last pocket of German resistance in the 1st Division's
sector, allowing the infantry to reach the fourth objective line around 1230.
This was the first objective planned for the second day's attack. At this point
the division paused to allow the 39th Colonial Division to the west and the
42nd Division to the east to catch up.

During the late afternoon of 12 September, Pershing realized that the attack was progressing ahead of schedule and that the corps should be ordered to push on to their second day's objectives before the Germans could
reinforce the salient. Consequently, Pershing ordered V Corps to drive a
brigade of the 26th Division forward to Hattonchattel and Vigneulles. He
also instructed IV Corps to order the 1st Division to send forces north toward Vigneulles. The 26th Division's 51st Brigade resumed its advance that
evening, securing Hattonchattel around 0300 before pushing a strong patrol
into Vigneulles.

The 1st Division, after securing the first of its second-day objectives, sent
forward the provisional cavalry squadron of the 2nd Cavalry Regiment to
reconnoiter and exploit the advantage offered. The cavalrymen captured a
number of prisoners and reported that there was little resistance. By 1945
hours, the 1st Brigade had infantry advancing through the Bois de Nonsard and into the Bois de Vigneulles. Forward units reached the Vigneulles–
St. Benoit Road at about 2200, where they paused before resuming their
advance to Vigneulles. At about 0600, 13 September, the 1st and 26th

Infantry Divisions closed the escape route for all Germans remaining south of Vigneulles.[39]

After the 1st Division broke through the last organized German positions, reconnaissance units advanced, reaching Huttonville, north of Vigneulles, at about 0630. These units had been organized after the Soissons offensive to give the infantry battalions the capability to reconnoiter once open warfare was achieved. Each battalion had about thirty men in their reconnaissance unit. During the St. Mihiel offensive, these ad hoc organizations functioned smoothly, allowing the division to maintain contact with the retreating enemy without exposing large numbers of infantry to hostile fire. The scouts were recalled once they had located the German machine-gun line near Huttonville.[40]

One of the few sour experiences of the advance took place on the afternoon of 12 September, when the 1st Battalion, 16th Infantry, was slow to advance from the fourth objective line to the Decauville Railroad and then failed to follow orders to send a company on to Vigneulles. The battalion received the first movement order at 1700 but moved out a full two hours later. When ordered to send troops to Vigneulles after dark, the battalion commander failed to comply. His regimental commander concluded that the battalion commander's "mind works too slowly to make him an efficient field commander of troops." He was relieved from his command after the offensive.[41]

The advance on the afternoon of 12 September pinched the 1st Brigade out of the line. Once the French 39th Colonial Division caught up with the brigade, fighting on the left flank ended. The 2nd Brigade consolidated its positions along the Vigneulles–St. Benoit road as planned and halted. By the afternoon of 13 September, the 39th Colonial Division on the left and the 42nd Division on the right pinched out the 2nd Brigade. This made it possible for Summerall to begin the withdrawal of the 1st Division to an assembly area in the Bois de la Belle Oziere.

Losses were light during the offensive. The division lost seventy-eight men killed and 386 wounded from 11 to 16 September; sixty men were missing or captured, of whom only ten were eventually counted as missing.[42]

On 14 September, the division withdrew from the front. The soldiers spent six days in assembly areas in the Bois de la Belle Oziere recuperating from their exertions. After three days of combat and movement in the rain and mud of the Woevre Plain, the soldiers were pleasantly surprised to be camped in an elaborately constructed German rest camp.

It was a novel sight that was presented to the tired men when they looked around them on the morning of September 14th. The extensive woods in which they found themselves had been converted into an attractive rest camp by the Germans. There were billets and recreation rooms and the most artistic cottages and bungalows elaborately furnished from the homes in the defenseless villages. Club-houses for officers and men, with pianos and moving picture machines, gave evidence of the pleasure that was afforded.[43]

The Preparations for the Meuse Argonne Offensive

As the American divisions moved into their positions for the St. Mihiel campaign, the First Army prepared plans for the Meuse Argonne offensive. Lieutenant Colonel George Marshall prepared the elaborate orders to move 600,000 soldiers to assault positions from La Harazée, in the Argonne Forest, to the Meuse River near Cumières, 12 kilometers northwest of Verdun. Marshall considered this task the most important one he performed in the war. He prepared the basic scheme in less than two days, although the hardest part of his job would be to coordinate the movements with the French transportation agencies. Simultaneously, the French Second Army had to move 220,000 French and Italian troops out of the sector on the limited rail and road networks in the area. Over 3,900 artillery pieces with 40,000 tons of ammunition had to move into firing positions. Many of the artillery units had to make this shift after the completion of the St. Mihiel offensive.[44]

The Meuse Argonne region was difficult terrain that favored the defenders. On the west, the Argonne Forest sat on a north-south ridge, providing the Germans with observation posts from which to direct artillery fire into the flank of the attackers. The forest was strewn with barbed-wire barriers and pillboxes. The Argonne dominated the terrain of the only open corridor for attack, along the Aire River Valley, east of the forest. On the eastern flank, the Heights of the Meuse overlooked the American zone of action. In the center of First Army's sector, the remnants of the village of Montfaucon sat on a hill dominating the area. The Germans had reinforced the terrain by building four belts of defenses, or *Stellungen*, along the ridges that ran roughly west to east, perpendicular to the direction of the American attack.[45]

First Army's plan called for three corps, each with three divisions, to attack online to the north. The initial objective line was 16 kilometers north of the jump-off positions, on the ridge from Brieulles sur Meuse west to Grandpre on the Aire. This advance would flank the Argonne Forest and facilitate a second advance of 16 kilometers north to a line that ran from Stenay to La Chesne. Pershing hoped his troops could reach the first objective line by the end of the second day. Time was critical since First Army estimated that the Germans could reinforce the sector with fifteen divisions within three days.[46]

The overall plan was sound, but the allocation of available forces for the initial assault was badly flawed. V Corps received the least experienced divisions for the main effort. Cameron was assigned the 37th, 79th, and 91st Divisions for his difficult pincer attack against Montfaucon. None of these divisions had its assigned artillery brigade. Thus the infantry had to work with artillery units that had been shifted from the St. Mihiel sector after 15 September. Cameron's divisions also had received little training in the front lines before their first offensive, and the 79th Division had been in France for barely seven weeks.[47] Yet these green troops were expected to attack at dawn across a forest barrier south of Montfaucon and then ascend the open fields surrounding the German positions on top of Montfaucon.

The experienced corps commanders, Liggett and Bullard, commanded veteran divisions. Only the 35th Division of I Corps had not taken part in active operations. All of Liggett's divisions were supported by their assigned artillery brigades. Bullard's three divisions had completed their training, and two of them had their own artillery. The apparent reason for the misallocation of forces for the main attack is that AEF inspectors had reported favorably on the efficiency of the three rookie divisions in Cameron's V Corps.[48]

The 1st Division's Deployment

First Army identified the 1st Division as one of the units that would be available for the offensive once the St. Mihiel operation "stabilizes."[49] The swift advance of 12–13 September allowed IV Corps to pull the division out of line on the evening of 13 September. Consequently, the division was in good shape for further operations. While the nine assault divisions for the offensive moved into positions between the Argonne Forest and the Meuse River, the 1st Division crossed the Meuse and assembled between Souilly and Benoite-Vaux. The infantry and machine-gun units moved on trucks in three nights, beginning on the evening of 20 September. The artillery, hospital units, and trains traveled on separate routes in four night moves. During the day, the soldiers slept in the wet woods, with only the kitchen units allowed to build fires.[50]

The division was a reserve of First Army, with a possible assignment to attack east of the Meuse. This mission depended upon the successful completion of the attacks to the army's objective line from Apremont to Brieulles. On 27 September, First Army ordered the division to assemble near Blercourt and Nixeville. The division post of command moved to Blercourt, where it and the brigade posts of command set up in close proximity by 2200 hours, 27 September. Summerall assembled the brigade commanders at the division post of command to await orders.[51] The division remained in place until 29 September, as Pershing assessed the first phase of the offensive.

First Army Meuse Argonne Offensive: 26–30 September 1918

The Germans anticipated Pershing's offensive, but they expected the attack to be made toward Metz, as a logical extension of the St. Mihiel operation. The majority of the German reserves in the area were near Metz, allowing First Army to outnumber the five German divisions in the Argonne sector.[52]

Pershing's attack commenced at 0530, following a three-hour artillery barrage. The troops initially met little opposition due to the German practice of maintaining few soldiers in their forward positions. Although the local commander, General Max von Gallwitz, had indicators that the attack was coming, he received them too late to change his dispositions.

On the right, the 33rd Division of Bullard's III Corps crossed its line of departure along Les Forges stream, using duckboards to span the water and chicken wire to bridge the German barbed wire. The 66th Brigade maneuvered one regiment in an arc along the north side of the Bois de Forges while its other regiment attacked the woods from the west. The brigade captured 1,400 Germans while losing about 250 men killed or wounded. By 1000 hours, the 33rd Division had accomplished its first day's mission.[53]

The other two III Corps divisions advanced as well. The 80th Division cleared the Bois Jure and captured Hill 262. The 4th Division took Septsarges, 5 miles beyond the starting line, and would have gone farther if V Corps had kept up on the left. However, the First Army order stipulated that the corps were to hold up at the first objective line until all three had caught up, so the 4th Division stopped and dug in.[54]

Liggett's I Corps also got off to a promising start, even in the dense Argonne where the 77th Division slugged its way forward for nearly a kilometer. The 28th Division seized Varennes in the center along the Aire, while the 35th Division captured Cheppy and Vauquois and pushed almost to Charpentry. Heavy German artillery fire directed from the high ground on the east slopes of the Argonne, however, forced the 35th to give ground.

Things did not go nearly so well in V Corps' attack. On the left, the 91st Division pushed through the Bois de Cheppy and across open ground to a line just short of Epinonville. There, German fire disorganized the attack, forcing the troops to ground. In the center, the 37th Division struggled through the Bois de Montfaucon but was stopped in the open ground southwest of Montfaucon. On the right, the rookie 79th Division took Malancourt and crossed the tangled woods north of that village before emerging into the open ground overlooked by the German machine guns on Montfaucon.

The division commander lost communications with his brigades, the leading infantry, and the artillery. This made it difficult to push sufficient force onto Montfaucon. By the end of 26 September, Montfaucon remained in German hands, and von Gallwitz was moving four divisions to reinforce his defenses.[55]

Although First Army failed to reach all of its objectives on 26 September, its divisions had driven through the Germans' initial line and into the forward edge of their second positions. But V Corps' failure to take Montfaucon made it impossible to drive farther north in the I and III Corps sectors. Pershing, therefore, ordered the offensive to resume on 27 September. This time the three corps were to advance as far as possible, ignoring the progress of adjacent units. The attacks, launched in a steady rain on 27 September, made progress. Cameron pushed Joseph Kuhn's 79th Division hard to capture Montfaucon. Kuhn brought both of his brigades on line and, after relieving a brigade commander, got his infantry moving. By noon, Montfaucon was in American hands, and the 37th and 91st Divisions had pushed forward as well.[56]

The two flank corps gained additional ground, but the cost was high as German reserves arrived. On I Corps' front, the 77th Division painfully inched forward in the Argonne Forest while the 28th Division pushed into Apremont. The 35th Division almost got to Exermont before the *1st Guards Division* stopped it cold. III Corps made some additional gains but was unable to break through. All three corps continued the attack on 28 September, but German counterattacks forced American troops to retreat from some advanced positions on 29 September. Losses mounted, and the 35th Division was on the verge of disintegration. After three days of heavy fighting, Pershing recognized that his gamble of launching the offensive with four unprepared divisions had failed. Pétain, ungenerously, reported that "the reasons for this momentary stabilization are to be found, less in the resistance of the enemy than in the difficulties experienced by the American General Staff in moving its troops and in supplying them."[57]

In this situation, Pershing ordered the 35th, 37th, and 79th Divisions replaced by veteran divisions. Consequently, the 1st Infantry Division moved from Nixeville to Neuvilly, behind I Corps, to replace the 35th Division. While these moves were carried out, First Army limited itself to local attacks.[58]

The 1st Division Enters the Meuse Argonne Offensive

From the beginning of the offensive, Major General Peter Traub's 35th Division had faced tough terrain and determined resistance. Nonetheless, the division made the farthest advance in the I Corps sector, capturing the Butte de Vauquois and the village of Cheppy on the first day. On 27 and 28 September, the division fought through Charpentry and Baulny and into the Montrebeau Woods south of Exermont. Traub's inexperienced infantrymen suffered heavy casualties from enemy fire.[59] The 35th Division also had serious problems with stragglers. When the troops attacked on 29 September, the German *5th Guards* and *52nd Infantry Divisions* counterattacked, shattering the cohesion of the 35th Division.[60] As the First Army inspector general reported, "The men began to filter back from this forward position and soon the entire front line became disorganized and what amounted to a panic started in which the men came back."[61]

General Traub stopped the rout near Charpentry, but only 1,600 of the 14,000 riflemen in the division remained on the line on the evening of 29 September. The casualties included one brigade commander, two regimental commanders, and nearly all of the infantry battalion commanders. Most of "these losses were due to their being in the actual front line during the advance . . . and when wounded or killed their organizations were disorganized, out of touch and were lost."[62] Pershing ordered the 1st Division to replace the 35th Division during the night of 30 September–1 October and launch a new assault.[63]

The 1st Division moved north on 29 September. Division headquarters set up in Cheppy the next morning. The infantry and artillery moved forward on the night of 30 September to occupy a front running from Baulny to Eclisfontaine, with Parker's 1st Brigade on the left and Frank Bamford's 2nd Brigade on the right.[64] The troops marched cross-country, since the roads were clogged with artillery, ambulances, and supply vehicles. Wire-cutting detachments led each battalion. McHenry remembered the division's march to Cheppy vividly:

> There was wire, tons and tons of wire all about us, through which lanes had been cut. . . . The road on which we would have traveled had been mined and blown up. Great holes were in it, in which a country school house could easily have been dropped. . . . It was evident from all about us that there had been severe fighting there as the whole surface was torn by shell holes. . . . We also passed some new crosses that marked the resting places of the American dead. . . . We marched further on . . . and came in view of what had been Cheppy, now nothing but a mass of tangled ruins and crumbing walls. . . . When we reached Cheppy, we marched on, and into the black darkness of as dark a night as I ever saw.[65]

After reaching a position near Baulny, McHenry's squad dug foxholes, which the men lined with straw and camouflaged with branches. McHenry's unit

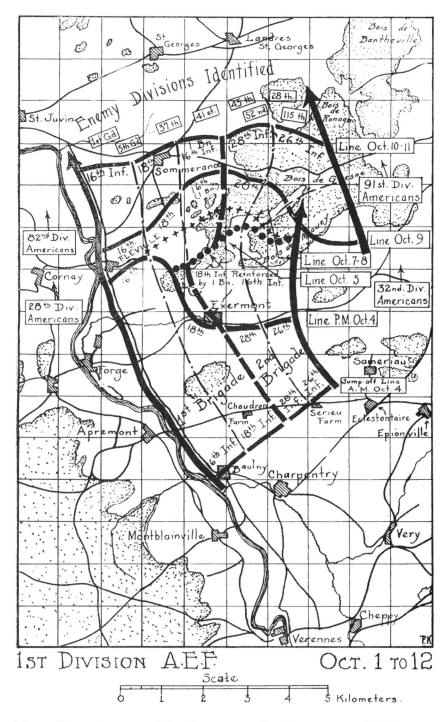

Map 6. Operation west of the Meuse, 1–12 October 1918, 1st Division, AEF. (Ben Chastaine, *History of the 18th U.S. Infantry* [Hymans, 1919])

was on the left flank of the 1st Division. The original plan had called for the division to occupy the forward positions held by the 35th Division and then attack on 1 October. But the 35th had disintegrated, and no one knew where the German positions were. As the infantry occupied three lines in depth in each regimental sector, Pershing postponed the date for the assault.[66] This postponement gave the engineers time to repair the roads in the army's zone and allowed artillery and logistics units time to struggle forward on the mud-choked roads.

The soldiers of the 1st Division remained in their positions for three days. The assault battalions were just south of the road from Esperance to Eclisfontaine. (See Map 6.) The support battalions dug in on the reverse slope of the ravine that ran northeast from Baulny, and the reserve battalions took cover in a ravine running northeast from Charpentry. German artillery observers on the eastern slope of the Argonne Forest overlooked these positions.

The Germans observed the division's arrival and anticipated an attack. In response, they opened a steady fire of high-explosive and gas shells. German artillery fire increased on 1 October, and for the next three days the 1st Division suffered heavy casualties, especially from chemical weapons. The Germans fired 3,470 rounds of phosgene and mustard gas against the division in this period. These munitions fell in small amounts spaced over time. High explosives hit the high ground, while gas shells fell in the ravines and along the slopes where the artillery and supply units were deployed.[67]

There was little the troops could do other than to mask often and remain alert for gas attacks. This was not always done. For example, on 1 October, 392 men out of a battalion of roughly 1,000 soldiers in the 18th Infantry were mustard-gas casualties "as a result of failure to recognize the presence of gas."[68] Repeatedly, American troops dug positions in ground already contaminated with mustard gas, suffering casualties before they discovered their predicament. During the campaign, the 1st Division had 1,613 gas casualties, the majority of which were lost during the first three days of October.[69]

The Americans lost contact with the Germans in the 1st Division's new sector. Consequently, the division sent reconnaissance patrols forward to locate the enemy and to identify the line of departure for the coming attack. These patrols advanced on the morning of 2 October, crossing ground littered with the bodies of men from the 35th Division. The patrols advanced about 300 yards before they came under withering machine-gun fire and suffered heavy casualties. They had located the forward edge of the German defenses.[70]

On 2 October, Summerall issued the attack order.[71] He did not designate the date, since that depended upon how long it would take First Army to reorganize its rear areas. The order designated three objective lines for the division. The first ran along the north side of the Montrebeau Woods overlooking the ravine just south of Exermont. The second objective was a line running from the southern edge of Fléville to the Ferme d'Arietal. The third objective was a line from Hill 272 west to the Aire, about 1 kilometer north of Fléville.

The artillery plan called for five minutes of preparation fires. At H-hour, the 6th and 7th Artillery Regiments were to use their eighty-four 75mm guns to fire a rolling barrage moving 100 meters every four minutes. The 155mm howitzers of the 5th Artillery were to fire at enemy artillery. Summerall also ordered two 75mm guns from the artillery to accompany each assault battalion for direct-fire support. A platoon of tanks was attached to each assault battalion. The 1st Engineer Regiment was in reserve near Very, and the 1st Machine Gun Battalion was ready to deploy "at a moment's notice." While waiting for the attack, the engineers repaired roads and constructed bridges.[72]

The division waited three days for the order to advance. During this period, the Germans inflicted 1,660 casualties of all types, or roughly 10 percent of the division's infantry strength.[73]

The assault battalions attacked at 0525 hours, 4 October, along the ridge running east-northeast from Esperance. The 1st Battalion, 26th Infantry, immediately met heavy fire from the woods on the eastern end of the Montrebeau Ridge. The infantrymen were forced to ground as artillery fire worked through their ranks. Many officers fell, making reorganization difficult. The tanks that were to accompany the infantry had not caught up, prompting Summerall to ask First Army for more tanks. The commander of the 2/26th Infantry moved forward and determined that his men needed to be committed with those of the 1st Battalion. The regiment then pushed across the eastern end of the Exermont Ravine, taking La Neuville le Comte Farm by the end of the day. This position was well short of the division's second objective line.[74]

The 28th Infantry ran into similar difficulties as its accompanying 75mm guns were destroyed and the Germans knocked out its tanks. The soldiers attacked across open ground against well-concealed positions in the Montrebeau Woods. Once the men got across the Exermont Ravine, they received heavy fire from the Montrefagne Ridge. By the end of 4 October, 2nd Brigade had gotten only to the base of the Montrefagne. In an effort to get the attack going again, Summerall shifted a company of the 1st Gas Regiment to the 2nd Brigade so that it could cover the advancing infantrymen with the smoke from its thermite rounds.[75] Even with these difficulties, the 2nd Brigade had advanced farther than the 32nd Division on its right.

Things went considerably better in the 1st Brigade's sector. The 3rd Battalion, 16th Infantry, drove through the western edge of the Montrebeau Woods and reached its first objective at 0700. After reorganizing, the battalion moved across the Les Granges–Exermont Road to the second objective line. Evidently the Germans on the Montrefagne had their hands full with the regiments to their front, allowing the 16th Infantry to drive to the third objective at Fléville at around 1300 hours. Anticipating a heavy German barrage, the 16th Infantry pulled back to more defensible terrain just south of Fléville. Summerall, realizing the importance of this advance, ordered Company F, 1st Engineer Regiment, forward to help the infantrymen fortify their positions.[76]

As the 16th Infantry made progress, the 3rd Battalion, 18th Infantry, kept pace through the first objective before becoming snarled up with the Germans in the Bois de Boyon. The 2nd Battalion advanced to fill a gap between the 16th Infantry and the 28th Infantry. By the end of the day, the 18th Infantry was facing northeast, with its lead elements in the western end of the Bois de Boyon. The 16th Infantry had advanced well ahead of the 18th Infantry to the east and of the 28th Division to the west. Although the 1st Division failed to reach its final objective line, it had advanced farther than any other division and had driven a wedge into the Germans' lines.[77] The cost was high, as the 2nd and 3rd Hospitals treated over 1,600 wounded during the day.[78] Pershing ordered the offensive continued the next day.

Summerall's plan for the attack on 5 October called for the 16th Infantry to hold its positions south of Fléville, while the 18th Infantry and 2nd Brigade seized their original objectives. The 26th Infantry was to extend its right flank to the northeast to include the western edge of the Bois de Moncy. This move would allow the division to clear the German machine guns out of the positions from which they had poured so much fire into the 2nd Brigade's right flank. The 3rd Battalion, 26th Infantry, which had been in division reserve, returned to its regiment to make this move. The artillery again planned a rolling barrage. All available tanks were to join the 2nd Brigade and to pay special attention to the woods north of Hill 212.[79]

Summerall issued special instructions to 2nd Brigade. First, the brigade was to seize the crest of Hill 240 on the Montrefagne and the woods north of Hill 212, thus bringing itself on line with the 1st Brigade. It was to use two battalions in each regiment in the normal formation, with an assault battalion followed by a support battalion. The reserve battalions in each regiment were to be held out of the attack until the leading battalions had reached the first objective line, at which time the reserve battalions were to pass through the assault battalions and assume the lead to the second and third objectives.[80] This guidance stemmed from Summerall's concern that reserves be husbanded for as long as possible and then used to carry the momentum of the attack.

The attack on 5 October got under way at 0630. The 18th and 28th Infantry Regiments pushed through the defenses on the Montrefagne before running into heavy resistance. By noon, the 18th Infantry had advanced 350 meters north of the Bois de Boyon, while the 28th Infantry had reached the Farm St. Germain. The 26th Infantry had slower going due to strong resistance from the Farm d'Arietal and along the western edge of the Bois de Moncy. The division identified four German divisions in its sector, and prisoners reported that the Germans had suffered heavy casualties. By noon, the 1st Division had captured 600 prisoners, six 77mm guns, and numerous machine guns. But the Germans continued to defend each hill and woods tenaciously. During the afternoon, the 26th Infantry captured Farm d'Arietal, allowing the 28th Infantry on its left to advance to the base of Hill 272. The division's front now ran generally from a point just south of Fléville to Hill 269. The 26th Infantry secured the western edge of the Bois de Moncy and sent a patrol to occupy Hill 269. The patrol occupied the lower spur of the hill but, through a navigation error, did not reach the crest.[81] Nonetheless, the division had driven a wedge 5 kilometers into the German positions.

While the 18th Infantry and 2nd Brigade fought their way forward to the line held by the 16th Infantry, the 16th Infantry deployed troops along the division's western flank, overlooking the Aire. The division was ahead of the neighboring 28th Division, and 1st Brigade needed to protect its flank from counterattacks. The Germans, however, lacked the necessary reserves in the Argonne to exploit the opportunity. With the division on the objective line near Fléville, the I Corps commander, Hunter Liggett, saw an opportunity for American forces to attack to the west, from behind 1st Brigade and into the Argonne Forest against the Germans' flank. Liggett convinced Pershing that the 82nd Division should move up behind the left of the 1st Division and drive across the Aire to seize Cornay and the hills around it. The 28th Division's right-hand brigade was to attack in a northwesterly direction on the left of the 82nd.[82]

On 7 October, the 1st Division consolidated its positions and moved its artillery forward. Summerall ordered all units to reorganize, collect stragglers, and mark their positions with identification panels for friendly aviation. Division headquarters also informed the regiments that "we have control of the air and that our observation planes are conducting and have conducted constantly successful photographic, reconnaissance, and special missions." The frontline troops, however, had been firing at friendly aircraft and had failed to show their identification panels.[83] The division accomplished grimmer tasks as well during the lull of 6 October. Burial parties had buried 700 dead comrades, while the medical units had dealt with 5,050 wounded and sick soldiers since the start of the operation.[84]

During the rainy night of 6–7 October, the 82nd Division moved a brigade to assault positions behind the 1st Division. Half of the 164th Brigade arrived near Les Granges in time to launch an assault at 0500 on 7 October. Duncan's men captured Hill 180 and pushed toward Cornay. To the west, the 28th Division seized Chatel Chehery and Hill 244. In two more days of heavy fighting, the 82nd and the 28th Divisions secured the ridge in the Argonne from Cornay to Chatel Chehery. Liggett's maneuver flanked the German defenses in the Argonne, allowing the 77th Division to drive north, liberate the encircled "lost battalion," and reach the Aire River just south of Grandpre on 10 October.[85]

The 1st Division Resumes the Attack

As the soldiers of the 82nd and 28th Divisions drove into the Argonne, Summerall prepared the 1st Division for another push. For this attack, the 1st Division was transferred to V Corps, since the drive was to be toward the northeast, against Hills 272 and 263 in the Bois de Romagne. This attack would flank the German positions along the Romagne Heights, allowing V Corps to move into the *Kriemhilde Stellung* at Romagne. Cameron attached the 181st Brigade, 91st Division, to the 1st Division for the operation.[86] This unit, composed of men from Montana, Idaho, and Washington, was a welcome addition to Summerall's command, especially since the 1st Division's front had widened to over 6 kilometers.

H-hour for the assault was 0830, 9 October. The artillery was to fire a fixed barrage in front of 1st Brigade for three minutes at H-hour before shifting to a rolling barrage. At H plus 15 minutes, the rolling barrage was to slow down until the first objective (Hill 272) was reached. The barrage in front of 2nd Brigade was to remain stationary until H-hour plus twenty-two minutes, and then it was to roll forward at the rate of 100 meters per six minutes. The artillery was to halt the barrage just beyond the first objectives and fire there for two hours. When the infantry resumed their attacks, the artillery again was to fire rolling barrages at different times, at a rate of 100 meters each six minutes.[87]

For this drive, Summerall committed his remaining reserves. The 1st Battalion, 16th Infantry, assembled in the woods on the north slope of Hill 240 on the night of 7–8 October and, on command, was to spearhead the drive to capture Hill 272. A battalion of the 1st Engineers joined the 2nd Brigade, along with a company from the 1st Machine Gun Battalion, to assist the drive onto Hill 263.[88] Once the attack started, Summerall planned to have the 181st Brigade move a battalion into the line west of Hill 269 to maintain contact with the 2nd Brigade.[89]

Four groups of machine guns were to be controlled by the division's machine-gun officer. These groups, with twelve guns each, were to fire a standing barrage for ten minutes, 500 meters in front of the first objectives. The machine gunners were to stockpile 20,000 rounds of ammunition at each gun during the night of 8–9 October. The 2nd Machine Gun Battalion provided seventy carts to haul the ammunition forward to the guns.[90]

The 1st Division attacked at 0830, 9 October. The assault troops of the 2nd Brigade reached their first objective (Hill 263) at 0930, "overcoming considerable machine gun resistance from their left flank." 1st Brigade overran Hill 272 at about 1000 hours "after heavy fighting." During the assault, the battalion of engineers on Hill 269 repulsed a counterattack. Roughly 230 Germans were captured as another German division entered the area in an effort to stop the 1st Division's drive.[91] The advance continued against diminishing resistance in the afternoon as the enemy fell back to a line north of the St. Juvin–Sommerance Road. By 1600, the division had secured all of its objectives. The division then halted while 1st Brigade sent patrols toward Sommerance to regain contact with the enemy.[92] A veteran of the battle remembered this advance to the final objective: "At this time came the most painful moment of the surviving soldiers. It was caused by the cries of the wounded and the moans of the dying. The ground in front of us was covered with [American] dead and wounded."[93]

The I Corps' attacks into the flank of the Argonne forced the Germans to retreat to the Hindenburg Line, running along the ridges from Grandpre to just north of Brieulles on the Meuse. This retreat opened the way for the 1st Division to advance. On 10 October, the division sent patrols forward to the line of exploitation, where they encountered light resistance. By noon, the division had reached a line running from the St. Juvin–Fléville Road to the northern edge of the Bois de Romagne. There the exhausted infantrymen ran into strong resistance. The 1st Division could go no farther, having fought continuously for eleven days and suffered over 7,000 casualties. During its last two days of action, the division captured 603 prisoners, bringing its total to 1,407 in October. The Germans had committed five divisions against the 1st Division.[94]

Out of the Line

On 11 October, the 1st Division passed control of its sector to the 42nd Division and assembled near Cheppy. The battered division was on its way to a training area to receive thousands of replacements and prepare for further combat. The relief of the infantry took place on the night of 11–12 October, but the 1st Artillery Brigade remained to support operations for the remainder of the month. One hundred men from each regiment stayed behind to bury their dead comrades.[95]

As the 1st Division turned its positions over to the Rainbow Division, the men learned that Major General Summerall was to take over V Corps. Many of the men thought Summerall "was a wonderful general," but, two weeks later, they also "were well pleased with the promotion of Brigadier General Frank Parker to succeed" Summerall as their division commander.[96] The promotion of these officers was part of a reorganization of the AEF. Pershing created the Second Army on 12 October, placing Robert Bullard in charge of the new army, while Hunter Liggett assumed command of First Army. Colonel George Marshall was to serve as Liggett's G3. Major General John Hines took command of III Corps. Pershing also established the first American army group headquarters in history. These moves were necessary because the strength of the AEF had reached nearly two million men.[97]

The primary interest of the soldiers in the 1st Division, however, was not the personnel changes in the AEF. As they pulled out of line, the men were hungry, thirsty, and tired. As McHenry remembers, "During the three days that I just described we were out of contact with our field range and company rations. It was a total impossibility for the men in charge of the slum cart to get us rations. . . . In addition to being short of food, we were . . . out of water."[98] The lack of water was more painful to the troops than was the shortage of food. The incessant rain and cold added to their misery. "Wearily and painfully, the depleted regiments made their way" to Cheppy over ground that was a sea of mud and churned by thousands of artillery rounds. Hot food and water was waiting for the survivors who, after eating, slept from exhaustion. On 13 October, the division, minus its artillery brigade, moved south to Les Islettes. The infantry walked, since all motor transport was committed to hauling troops and supplies forward to the battle raging to the north. At Les Islettes, the soldiers learned that they were to walk the 75 kilometers to Conde-en-Barrois, north of Bar-le-Duc, where they were to rest and train.[99]

During this march, the infantry showed signs of fatigue and poor march discipline. The division G1 (personnel officer), Major Paul Peabody, observed that the "general impression of the column as viewed from a little distance was that the road discipline was poor." Men tended to stray too far left on the road as they moved and to lie on the road when they rested. He also noticed that there "was considerable straggling which was largely due to the extreme fatigue of the men coming from the front and from the heavy packs carried by the large number of replacements which had just joined the division." For the most part, Peabody noted that the men cleared the road for oncoming traffic and that the transportation units of the infantry brigades "kept well to the right, were well spaced, and the general road discipline was good."[100]

The acting division commander, Frank Bamford, concluded, in his summary of operations, that the "division came out of the action very depleted in strength, but with an excellent nucleus as a fighting unit. Throughout the operation the morale of the officers and men was excellent."[101] Pershing agreed and ordered the division quickly to prepare for further operations. "Immediately, replacements began to arrive and the division set about delousing, re-equipping and training to take its place in the line of battle."[102]

Time to Rest?

The division paid a high price for its October advance, having lost 7,169 men killed or wounded. Another 1,713 men were still missing at the end of the month.[103] The division was short 7,707 men on 9 October and still short 3,753 men on 30 October.[104] The division's hospitals treated 7,079 wounded, while 1,222 men had been killed.[105] By the end of October, about 4,000 replacements had joined the remaining veterans. The AEF was short over 50,000 replacements by then, making it impossible for the division to be brought up to its authorized strength of over 28,000 men. As a result, Pershing reduced the strength of infantry companies throughout the AEF to 175 men, from 250.

The majority of the new soldiers had not been in France for long. A number of the replacements, however, were returnees from the AEF's hospitals. During the war, the army medical system in France admitted 689,179 soldiers for various diseases and another 236,766 for wounds. Pneumonia, aggravated by influenza, was the killer disease of the war for the American army. Over 18,000 of the total of 23,000 men who died from disease in Europe were its victims. Diseases of all types accounted for slightly over half of all US deaths in the war (57,460), compared to 43 percent due to battle deaths (50,280). Over 608,000 (or 88 percent) of the AEF's disease cases returned to duty, while roughly 54,000 (23 percent) of the wounded soldiers went back to units.[106] AEF's policy was to return soldiers to their original units whenever possible.[107]

New soldiers had little time to learn their jobs before the division received orders on 24 October to return to the front. At least this time, the troops were moved by truck and bus to Epinonville, west of Montfaucon.[108] The division was going to take part in First Army's next big attack in the Meuse

Argonne. This offensive was to be spearheaded by veteran divisions. Also, the main effort was going to be conducted by V Corps in the center, with I and III Corps launching supporting attacks.[109] All available artillery was to be used, and massive amounts of chemicals were going to be fired at enemy artillery and machine-gun positions.[110]

Hunter Liggett made important changes to First Army's method of attack for the next offensive. After taking command of the army on 12 October, Liggett made it clear to Pershing that he needed to rest and reorganize the army. For the remainder of October, Liggett launched only minor attacks to capture suitable jump-off positions. He rotated battered divisions out of the line, replacing them with rested formations. He instituted measures to round up the estimated 100,000 stragglers in the sector and get them back to their divisions. First Army units also trained assault teams to deal with German pillboxes and strongpoints.[111]

The Final Offensive

Liggett's offensive was slated to begin at 0530, 1 November. The 1st Division was to serve as a reserve for V Corps and was to pass through the 2nd Division once it had blown a hole in the defenses. Liggett emphasized that V and I Corps "should drive through the German center to the neighborhood of Buzancy and the high ground of the Bois de Barricourt ridge after dark of the first day," thus denying the enemy good terrain from which to launch a counterattack. Once these tasks were completed, John Hines's III Corps was to wheel east and cross the Meuse near Duns-sur-Meuse. I Corps on the left faced the strongest German positions and was to limit its initial efforts to a demonstration to tie the Germans down, rather than to make a costly frontal assault. V Corps success in the center would flank the Germans, forcing them to withdraw from in front of I Corps, which could then drive north toward Buzancy.[112]

Liggett was so confident "that we would break through as planned that at the second of two conferences of corps commanders we issued detailed orders for the pursuit."[113] While First Army planned its attack, Allied armies to the northwest blew a 35-mile-wide breach in the German lines on the Selle, capturing 20,000 prisoners and 475 guns. Ludendorff resigned in despair on 26 October, indicating the disintegration of the German High Command, as well as the progressive collapse of the German army. Tough fighting lay ahead, but the tide was clearly running with the Allies and Americans.

First Army's artillery preparation commenced at 0330, 1 November. The 1st Artillery Brigade supported the 2nd Division. Since 11 October the artillerymen had taken only one brief rest, on 23 October, when they marched back to Cheppy to bathe, eat a hot meal, and change clothes. This respite was accompanied by a ceremony to commemorate the first shot fired by an American artillery unit exactly a year earlier.[114]

The First Army deployed 608 artillery pieces in support of the V Corps attack. The preparation fires and the rolling barrages that preceded the infantry attack were designed by Summerall to cover the 8-kilometer front with a wall of shell and shrapnel 1,000 meters deep. All available machine guns added their fires to the artillery barrage. One-quarter of the 75mm rounds fired were smoke shells, providing cover for the infantry from enemy observation. Chemical munitions were used against enemy positions on the flanks.

With this support, V and III Corps drove 6 miles through the Hindenburg Line on 1 November. By nightfall, American infantrymen had passed through the German artillery positions and into the enemy's logistical areas. During the next two days, the attack continued against increasingly disorganized and fruitless resistance. These successes forced von Gallwitz to order his forces to retreat across the Meuse. There he hoped to use the river barrier to help his exhausted troops stop the Americans from driving northeast across the Sedan-Metz rail lines. On 4 November, Major General Hanson Ely's 5th Division crossed the Meuse south of Duns-sur-Meuse, while V Corps, facing strong resistance, pushed the 2nd and 89th Divisions to a line just south of Beaumont. This advance was made possible at low cost due to an advance by the two army regiments in the 2nd Division during the night of 3–4 November.[115]

The 1st Division followed V Corps' advance, ready to reinforce or replace one of the leading divisions. On 3 November, the 1st Division assembled east of Buzancy. The next day, the division was in the Bois de Belval behind the 2nd Division. During this period of pursuit, Parker ordered the 1st Artillery Brigade to provide a battery of artillery to each frontline battalion. Due to the continuing success of the 2nd and 89th Divisions, V Corps had no need to call on the 1st Division. Finally, on 5 November, Liggett ordered Parker to swing the 1st Division west, pass through the 80th Division, and attack at 0530 the next morning to seize a crossing over the Meuse at Mouzon.[116]

The infantry arrived on the jump-off line along the Stonne-Beaumont Road by 0530, 6 November. 1st Brigade attacked on the left, with the 16th and 18th Infantry Regiments on line. The 2nd Brigade attacked on the right, with only two battalions of the 26th Infantry on line. The 28th Infantry remained in reserve.[117]

What should have been the division's last assault of the war met minimal resistance. Patrols found that the Germans had destroyed the bridges over the Meuse at Mouzon. When the 1st Brigade reached that town, the

Germans laid down heavy fire to add to the destruction caused by demolitions. As the division consolidated positions along the Meuse, Summerall ordered Parker to pull the division out of the line and prepare to advance to the northwest through I Corps to capture Sedan.[118]

The Sedan Incident: 6–7 November 1918

Pershing initiated what was to become the embarrassing American lunge toward Sedan when he ordered First Army troops to seize that city. This order was a violation of an agreement with the French that their Fourth Army was to liberate Sedan. Pershing later excused his decision by claiming that he had mentioned to the French that the boundary between the French Fourth Army and the American First Army should be ignored during the pursuit of the Germans.[119] But Foch had intentionally moved the boundary between the two armies to the east, ensuring that the French would have the honor of taking Sedan and in this way make up for the defeat the French had suffered there at the hands of the Germans in 1870.

The First Army G3, George Marshall, was reluctant to issue the order in the absence of Liggett and the army chief of staff, Hugh Drum. Connor, nonetheless, convinced Marshall to prepare the following order:

1. General Pershing desires that the honor of entering Sedan should fall to the First American Army. He has every confidence that the troops of 1st Corps, assisted on their right by the 5th Corps, will enable him to realize this desire.
2. In transmitting the foregoing message, your attention is invited to the favorable opportunity now existing for pressing the advance throughout the night.[120]

Connor then added a final sentence to the order: "Boundaries will not be considered binding." When Drum returned to the headquarters, he sent the modified order to I and III Corps.[121]

First Corps was the logical choice for the mission, since it was positioned on the west of the army. Major General Joseph Dickman certainly understood the order and sent the 42nd Division north toward Sedan. Summerall, however, interpreted the order as a call for a race for the city. Consequently, he gave the mission to his favorite division.

Parker wasted no time in issuing an order for the division to march toward Sedan. To make this maneuver, the 1st Division pulled its troops out of the line facing the Meuse and marched them west, behind the 77th Division. The 1st Brigade marched on the right, with the 16th and 18th Infantry Regiments on separate roads heading to Wadelincourt and Chaumont respectively. The 2nd Brigade sent the 28th Infantry west through Chemery-sur-Bar, Cherhery, and Frénois, a village on the south side of the Meuse. The 26th Infantry followed the 28th to Chemery before turning toward Omicourt and on to St. Martin.[122]

The advance of the 1st Division was an impressive maneuver. It was also totally unnecessary and risked friendly casualties as the division crossed behind the 77th Division and in front of the 42nd Division. Summerall failed to coordinate the move of the 1st Division with I Corps or with the 77th and 42nd Divisions. Liaison officers from 1st Division did not reach I Corps headquarters until that evening, after the 1st Division was well on its way. Parker, and perhaps some of his soldiers, welcomed the chance to be the unit that captured Sedan before the French Fourth Army could catch up. "Conscious of its own high purpose and guided by a spirit of cooperation and helpfulness that had been a distinguishing quality of the Division, [it] accepted its mission with eagerness."[123] But most of the soldiers probably did not think such lofty thoughts, as the division history hints:

> The sufferings of that night march will remain one of the war's horrors. The men were already worn physically and mentally. Again rain soaked their packs and made the destroyed roads even more muddy for the weary and sore feet. . . . In the streets of the towns there was fighting at close quarters. . . . At every turn, the enemy was surprised by the appearance of the Americans during that night of wildness and stress. . . . There was violent street fighting in Allicourt, which was reached at 3:30 AM.[124]

Overcoming enemy resistance and fatigue, the 16th Infantry captured Pont Maugis. There, the regiment was surprised to encounter soldiers of the 42nd Division. At 0530, 7 November, the 18th Infantry met more men of the Rainbow Division in Bulson, where they captured Brigadier General Douglas MacArthur, thinking he was a German due to his outlandish costume. The 2nd Brigade also came upon units of the 42nd Division on its routes. At this point Parker ordered a halt, with his units generally in a line along the ridges south of the Meuse, 5 kilometers from Sedan. The regiments had covered between 50 and 70 kilometers over bad roads in about thirty hours. The 1st Division suffered roughly 500 casualties in this needless maneuver.[125] The collapse of the German defenses and the 1st Division's advance brought together the US 42nd and 1st Divisions and the 40th French Infantry Division on a narrow 8-kilometer front. It also outraged the French.

With the French sending repeated messages to First Army asking it to stop its drive, Liggett issued orders for I Corps to halt. Liggett was furious about the entire debacle and especially about Summerall's unilateral decision to assume the mission that logically belonged to I Corps. Liggett later wrote that "this was the only occasion in the war when I lost my temper completely." After soothing Dickman, who was justifiably furious with Summerall, Liggett got the army oriented northeast, with its left flank on the Meuse south of Wadelincourt.[126] After a cursory investigation, Pershing dropped the matter. For the 1st Division, the world war was over.

The 1st Division in the War

The 1st Division was the first American division organized in World War I. For seventeen months, it led the way through training and combat for the AEF. It served more time in combat than any other division and suffered 21,618 combat casualties, including 4,411 dead.[127] The division had served as the test organization for Pershing's training methods and combat doctrine. It had learned to survive in the trenches on the defense, then to launch a limited attack at Cantigny, before reaching its combat maturity in the Soissons offensive. At St. Mihiel, its leaders demonstrated their ability to combine all arms effectively on the battlefield. In the Meuse Argonne, the division made a critical attack over a period of twelve days that opened up the German defenses in the Argonne Forest to a flank attack. After quickly recovering and absorbing thousands of replacements, the division was back at the front two weeks later. The 1st Division had established an enviable reputation in its first seventeen months.

4

Between the World Wars
The Twenty-Year Peace

As the American First Army sorted out the intermingled soldiers of the 1st and 42nd Divisions south of Sedan, German representatives arrived in France to sign an armistice to end the fighting on the Western Front. The Germans agreed to a cessation of hostilities at 1100 hours on 11 November 1918. They promised to evacuate all occupied territory and to surrender most of their artillery, airplanes, and roughly half of their machine guns. The armistice did not, however, end the war between the Allies and the Central Powers. Instead, an international conference was to be convened in Versailles, France, to negotiate the treaties that would end the war.

One of the provisions of the armistice allowed the American and Allied armies to establish zones of occupation in Germany at Cologne, Koblenz, and Mainz. If the Germans did not accept the peace treaty, the Allies would be able to resume the war from within Germany. The British and French occupied the Cologne and Mainz zones, respectively, and the Americans were assigned the area on both sides of the Rhine at Koblenz. On 17 November 1918, the US Army began its advance toward Germany. On 13 December, the 1st Division crossed the Rhine. For the next eight months, the division stood guard on the Rhine.

The Occupation of Germany: 1918–1919

Four days before the armistice was signed, Pershing directed that the Third Army, commanded by Major General Joseph Dickman, was to control the occupation forces in the Koblenz bridgehead. The AEF staff selected the corps and divisions to serve in the occupation force. The 1st, 3rd, and 4th Divisions were assigned to IV Corps, and the 2nd, 32nd, and 42nd Divisions were assigned to III Corps. VII Corps rounded out Third Army with the 5th, 89th, and 90th Divisions.[1]

On 11 November, the 1st Division was in an assembly area near Montfaucon, where it had marched after its dash for Sedan.[2] The division commander, Frank Parker, was dealing with morale problems he had noticed the previous week on the march to Sedan. In a memorandum, Parker told the troops that

there are unfortunately in this Division, as in all Divisions, a certain number
of men who have to be carried along by the will and determination of the others. . . . The Division commander noted, even at the beginning of the march on
the night of November 6th-7th, a number of men who were grumbling, swear-
ing and criticizing higher authority. These men, however, were carried along by
the real members of the First Division, just as a piece of rotten wood is carried
by a strong tide.[3]

Parker called upon the veterans of the division

who have made its reputation as being the best of the American Expeditionary
Forces to carry on those newer and weaker members of the Division who have
not yet gotten the spirit of the First Division, which is to obey all orders from
proper authority with all that we have in us, never to criticize higher authority,
and to remember that it is only under painful circumstances that we get a man's
real value as a soldier.[4]

Parker was addressing an endemic problem in the AEF. Morale had not
been high during the heavy fighting in October, as indicated by the prevalence of straggling. The 1st Division had developed methods to minimize
straggling. In an attack, company first sergeants and military police followed
the advancing infantry so that they could collect stragglers and return them
to their units before the men became separated from their platoons. On the
march, each battalion designated a straggler squad with an officer in charge
to follow the battalion and collect stragglers.[5] Through such means, the division had been able to remain effective in battle longer than had units, like the
35th Division, that lacked the 1st Division's battle experience.[6]

One of the major causes of straggling was the lack of small-unit cohesion caused by high personnel turbulence. Because the 1st Division lost over
7,000 men in October, it was understandable that Parker found signs of
discontent during the forced march toward Sedan. The division had not had
sufficient time to integrate new soldiers. New soldiers did not feel the sense
of community that is an essential cement of a coherent combat unit. Morale
also suffered during the race to Sedan because the soldiers knew that the
fighting was about to end. They very likely resented being sent on an operation that would not affect the outcome of the war and yet posed a serious
risk of getting men killed.

Nonetheless, Parker was right to reinforce discipline at the war's end.
The division was to advance deep into enemy territory to establish positions
from which future offensive operations could be undertaken if necessary.
The Third Army ordered commanders to "so dispose their forces as to be

able to resume the offensive on receipt of orders from higher authority."[7] With this in mind, veteran divisions had been chosen for the Third Army.

On 13 November, Fox Connor told George Marshall to issue the orders for Third Army's move to Germany. He indicated that the 1st Division was to be one of the second-echelon divisions in IV Corps. Marshall, as a proud alumnus of the division, asked Connor "why this veteran unit was not to be permitted to lead in the triumphant march." Connor answered that the division was too far west of the line of departure to get there in time for the advance to commence on the morning of 17 November. After Marshall hung up, he called Colonel Fuqua, 1st Division's chief of staff, and asked if the division could reach a point east of Verdun by the afternoon of 16 November. Fuqua told Marshall that the distance was too great for the men to cover in time. Marshall then asked, "Is the honor of leading the advance into Germany worth the effort, or would you rather go up in the second line?"[8] Fuqua quickly changed his mind and asked only where the division needed to be by the evening of 16 November. Thus, the Big Red One was one of the divisions leading the Third Army into Germany.

The order for the division's movement from the vicinity of Montfaucon, across the Meuse at Charny, and on to the Third Army's line of departure was issued on the evening of 13 November. First Army's chief of staff, Campbell King, telephoned the division that night with its routes and staging areas. With hard marching, the troops reached the vicinity of Abaucourt, east of Verdun, in time. Third Army moved forward on 17 November with III Corps' 2nd and 32nd Divisions on the left and the 1st and 3rd Divisions of IV Corps on the right. The 42nd and 4th Divisions followed in reserve. The troops were "well echeloned in depth" to provide local security and to allow them to deploy rapidly for battle if necessary.[9]

The 1st Division moved along two routes (Map 7). An advance guard of an infantry battalion led each column, followed at a distance of 500 meters by a main body with the remaining battalions of each brigade. First Brigade marched on the left route and 2nd Brigade moved on the right-hand route. The artillery brigade followed, with battalions on both routes. The supply units followed closely behind the artillery.[10] Third Army had reached the German-Luxembourg border after marching through Luxembourg, where American soldiers were greeted as liberators.[11]

Third Army paused along the German border from 24 to 30 November to allow the German armed forces to evacuate the occupation zone. On 1 December the advance resumed. The 1st Division crossed the border near the village of Konz with 22,965 men and 5,191 horses and mules.[12] By this time, Major General E. F. McGlachlin was in command, and Brigadier General Parker had resumed command of 1st Brigade. The division advanced

northeast along the Moselle River, passing through Trier, Wittlich, and
St. Médard. McGlachlin ordered the brigades to protect local property along
the way. Military police followed each column to collect stragglers and to
guard convoys and prisoners. The Red Cross established kitchens in towns
along the route of advance to receive and feed former prisoners of war.[13]
In this manner, the division moved through the Moselle region with little
incident, arriving on the west bank of the Rhine on 10 December. The 1st
Division occupied the west bank of the Rhine from Boppard to the Moselle
River north of Koblenz.

By 12 December, a quarter of a million American soldiers stood on the
west bank of the Rhine. General Dickman selected the 1st Division to lead
the army across the river. John Hines's III Corps was to command the divisions (1st, 2nd, and 32nd) in the northern half of the bridgehead east of the
Rhine. A French corps secured the southern half of the bridgehead. The US
IV Corps established its divisions west of Koblenz. VII Corps remained farther west in army reserve. The 1st Division was reassigned to III Corps on
12 December. McGlachlin concentrated the division in Koblenz that day, in
preparation for its march over the Rhine. To the north, the British prepared
to occupy the bridgehead east of Cologne; to the south, the French army
prepared to cross the Rhine at Mainz.[14]

At 0700 hours, 13 December 1918, the US Third Army crossed the Rhine
on a pontoon bridge connecting Koblenz and Ehrenbreitstein, led by the 1st
Division. The 32nd Division followed a short time later to move into the
northern portion of the corps zone. The 1st Division entered its occupation
zone in two columns without incident. Division headquarters was established in Montabaur, "a quaint place, filled with memories of ancient days,"
and connected to Koblenz by an all-season road. The 1st Brigade occupied
the northern half of the division's sector, with its command post in Wirges.
The 2nd Brigade set up operations in the southern sector, with headquarters
in Boden.[15] For the next eight months, the 1st Division remained east of
the Rhine. By July 1919, the 2nd and 32nd Divisions had pulled out of the
bridgehead, leaving the Big Red One as the sole American division in the
bridgehead.

Occupation Duty in Germany: December 1918–July 1919

The US Army lacked the training, doctrine, and special organizations needed
to administer a region with perhaps a million German citizens. The occupation forces' primary mission was to be prepared to resume hostilities if
necessary, but their secondary mission was to administer a significant piece
of German territory that encompassed the Moselle Valley as well as the

region around Koblenz. Pershing expected the soldiers to carry out their duties in such a way as to avoid unnecessary offense to the local population while maintaining strict discipline and combat proficiency. Pershing made this clear in a message to the AEF on 28 November 1918:

> You have come not as despoilers or oppressors, but simply as the instruments of a strong, free government whose purposes toward the people of Germany are beneficent. During our occupation the civil population is under the special safeguard of the faith and honor of the American Army. . . . While you appear among them as a conquering army, you will exhibit no ill will towards the inhabitants. On the other hand, you are warned against conduct unbecoming your position as instruments of military rule. So long as a state of war continues, Germany remains enemy territory, and there must be no intimate personal associations with its inhabitants.[16]

General McGlachlin reminded his troops that the Germans remained enemies. Contacts with Germans were restricted. Soldiers were not to leave their camps in groups smaller than four men led by a noncommissioned officer. American units had the right to requisition billets, fuel, and other supplies, even against the will of the German citizens. Receipts, however, were to be given to the inhabitants for the materials provided.

The AEF organized a separate headquarters in Trier to handle civil affairs with the German population, while Third Army retained responsibility for military matters. Brigadier General H. A. Smith commanded this civil affairs organization, and Colonel I. L. Hunt served as the civil affairs liaison officer to Third Army at its forward headquarters.[17] As the 1st Division arrived in its forward positions, the brigade commanders appointed "town majors" to conduct affairs with the German inhabitants. Division commanders exercised civil authority as well as military responsibility in their areas. This system assured unity of command but ignored the opportunity to use the existing German government, which would have provided "a civil hierarchy to which a foreign military government could be adapted."[18]

The American occupation force was dispersed in roughly 300 German villages and towns. Billeting officers made special efforts to use public buildings for headquarters, logistical, and medical facilities. Most of the soldiers lived in barracks and public buildings, although many were placed in private homes. An average of 840 soldiers were in each village or town. Americans often outnumbered the locals, as the 5th Artillery did in Holler, where 500 men billeted with 400 Germans and no German man slept in a bed.[19] Inspector general reports indicate that troop accommodations were generally less than pleasant. As late as February 1919, some soldiers did not have beds, and many who did shared beds with other soldiers. Congestion in quarters and a shortage of mess halls aggravated problems with the influenza epidemic that was sweeping through the world. But the inspectors concluded that "it is believed that the soldiers of the 3d Army are as comfortable as troops could be under the circumstances and at this time of the year and conditions are constantly improving."[20]

The US Army had little expertise for dealing with the problems it faced in the occupation of Germany. The occupation zone contained 250,000 Americans and nearly 900,000 Germans. Martial law was enforced throughout the sector. The US Army had tremendous power over the German population and established special tribunals to punish Germans who violated American regulations.[21]

These judicial bodies conducted 9,699 trials from December 1918 to January 1920. The majority of the offenses were minor and included 2,317 cases of "violation of the circulation orders" and 1,580 cases of "sale or unlawful possession of U.S. property." There were 302 cases of "unlawful possession of deadly weapons" and 556 cases of "failure to obey lawful orders of military authorities." Third Army also established special "vagrancy courts" in the spring of 1919 to try prostitutes who violated the sanitation and public health orders. This move was in reaction to Pershing's concern about the rapid rise in venereal disease rates and his desire to return a "clean army" to the American people. This tribunal convicted 401 people, most of whom were local women.[22]

Maintaining discipline in the AEF was equally critical during the occupation. As early as 12 December, McGlachlin had to forbid 1st Division soldiers billeted in homes in Koblenz from damaging or deranging their quarters or from making "unreasonable demands on the occupants."[23] There were, however, far greater chances that the soldiers would violate the antifraternization rules than those prohibiting illegal requisitioning. The AEF generally handled serious crimes through general courts-martial during and after the war. The nature of offenses committed against the articles of war by members of the 1st Division during the occupation differed little from those committed during the war.

The AEF general court-martial records indicate that from June 1917 to July 1919 there were at least 190 general court-martial convictions involving members of the Big Red One. Absence without leave was the most frequent offense, with twenty-four cases tried in 1917–1918 and twenty cases tried in 1919. Larceny was the next most frequent offense, with about ten cases tried each year. There were four cases of disloyal language in 1917, but none thereafter. Twenty-seven soldiers were convicted of running away in battle, abandonment of their post, or sleeping on duty. All but six of these offenses

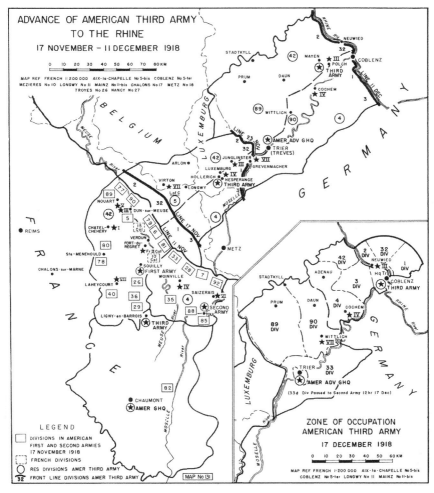

Map 7. Advance to the Rhine, November–December 1918. (*World War Records,* vol. 11, 1st Division AEF, 1930)

were committed in 1918. Six men were convicted of murder, and four were found guilty of sodomy. The murderers received dishonorable discharges and between five and twenty-five years' confinement with hard labor. The penalty for sodomy was dishonorable discharge and five years' confinement. Disloyal speech in 1917 brought dishonorable discharges. No soldier in the 1st Division was executed, and the longest confinement adjudged by the AEF general courts-martial evidently was twenty-five years.[24]

Third Army maintained separate records for the general courts-martial of American soldiers accused of committing offenses against the

German population. Germans filed 800 complaints against US personnel for serious offenses up to 1 October 1919. These ranged from murder and rape to a variety of felony thefts. The commanding officers of the soldiers involved were responsible for the investigation of each complaint and the trial and punishment of the suspected offenders if warranted. Army general courts-martial tried eleven soldiers for murder and eight for rape. The courts convicted six men for murder and five for rape. Of the 256 complaints of felonies, 118 resulted in general courts-martial. Additional minor offenses were investigated and punished by company commanders. There are no records of how many minor offenses were reported or of how many men were punished. But discipline was maintained by the 1st Division and the other units of Third Army.[25]

Maintaining the Occupation Force: Disease, Rations, and Entertainment

Germany's infrastructure was highly developed, allowing the Allied armies to use railways and public facilities to sustain the occupation forces. The German food distribution system in the area, however, lacked the capacity to provide rations for an additional 250,000 Americans. Consequently, Third Army relied on the Supply of Services for logistical support from its warehouses, bakeries, and slaughterhouses in France. Often, due to distance and poor quality control, bread shipped from the AEF's bakery in Is-sur-Tille, France, arrived at the 1st Division's railhead in Montabaur moldy and unfit for human consumption. In response, a division bakery was established in Montabaur capable of baking 31,000 pounds of bread daily. In operation by 23 January 1919, this facility required 600,000 pounds of flour and 34,500 pounds of other ingredients monthly. The ovens consumed 75 tons of coal in the same period. As a result, the soldiers of the Big Red One received fresh bread.[26]

Health problems were among the greatest challenges facing the Third Army. The German population's resistance to disease had been lowered by wartime rationing, with the average number of calories consumed daily falling from 3,500 in 1914 to no more than 1,400 in 1917–1918.[27] American soldiers also were susceptible to disease, having been exhausted by the final battles of the war and the long advance into Germany. Wet fall and winter weather and the shortage of overcoats and shoes aggravated these problems. The 1st Division established its four hospitals where they could serve the dispersed troops. On 22 November 1918, the AEF issued instructions to all units to identify sick and wounded soldiers so that they could be promptly sent to the United States. Once in Germany, the division suffered a steady loss from disease, as high as 3 percent per month in some outfits.[28]

On 1 December 1918, Third Army notified its units that "influenza has become so widely prevalent in Europe that it has grown to be a problem of considerable military importance. . . . It may and often does become dangerous to life by paving the way for pneumonia." Crowding in billets was to be avoided. Men with colds were to be excluded from common sleeping quarters, and commanders were to ensure that soldiers washed their mess kits in boiling water after meals.[29] This was great advice but impossible to comply with completely during the first few months of the occupation.

Influenza and pneumonia killed millions worldwide in 1918–1919. Remarkably, the AEF suffered a significantly lower loss rate than that of the army in the United States. Within the AEF, 23,000 died due to the effects of disease from July 1917 to June 1919. Of these, 18,047 men succumbed to pneumonia, in most cases brought on by influenza. The influenza epidemic peaked in the AEF in October 1918. Another surge in the disease rate occurred in February 1919. The peak rate of loss per 1,000 soldiers in the United States was 207, while it was 45 per 1,000 among the troops in France.[30] In spite of the uncomfortable living conditions and the prevalence of influenza, the 1st Division remained at nearly full combat strength, with over 25,000 men present for duty during the winter of 1918–1919.[31]

Venereal disease was less deadly but more prevalent than influenza in the AEF during the war. Pershing recognized the importance of preventing venereal disease "from the purely practical standpoint of difficulty in replacing men." He expected commanders to encourage high moral standards among the men, and he issued stringent regulations to deter soldiers from sexual contact. He attempted to have the licensed prostitution houses of the British and French forces placed off-limits. The other Allies were amazed at what they thought were prudish views toward one of their soldiers' favorite extracurricular activities, but the AEF's losses due to venereal diseases were lower than those of their allies, with an annual rate of about 40 cases per 1,000 men. With two million men in France, Pershing was justified in worrying about 80,000 cases of venereal disease per year.[32]

When the Third Army reached Koblenz, it established venereal disease prophylactic stations and enforced the antifraternization rules as rigidly as possible. In one case, two officers were reprimanded and sent to the replacement depot at Gondrecourt because they were seen having lunch with two German civilians. In the 1st Division, McGlachlin decreed that any soldier who contracted a venereal disease was to be court-martialed. He forbade the medical evacuation of any such soldier from the division until after his court-martial.[33]

Threats of punishment failed to prevent a threefold increase in the division's venereal disease rate from January to February 1919. In frustration, McGlachlin wrote a letter to the division pointing out that "the only way to avoid venereal disease is by abstaining from sexual intercourse." Unfortunately, he noted, "some men with minds benumbed by intoxicants and others not amenable to reason are willing to take the chance." In a final appeal, the division commander asked, "Are you going home with the Division? [If so,] let us get together, with every company, every regiment, and the entire division, physically pure; every man in the Division clean physically and morally."[34] This appeal may have had some positive effect.

Commanders at all levels established as many wholesome recreational activities as possible. The division created a circus, and the artillery and trains units held regular horse shows. Commanders organized a rigorous athletic program, to include divisional-level championships in baseball, football, and track. Soldiers were allowed to take leave and visit Britain, France, and Belgium.[35] In spite of the recreational and educational opportunities available by the spring, many of the soldiers wanted to go home. By February 1919, a steady stream of officers and men departed the 1st Division and returned to the States. Soldiers from other divisions of the AEF that were due to be disbanded reenlisted to fill the gaps as the army resumed Regular Army enlistments. In this manner, the division's strength was maintained. Low morale remained a problem nonetheless, prompting McGlachlin to order commanders and entertainment officers "to eliminate 'want to go home' songs, recitations, etc., not only from soldier entertainments but [also] from overseas shows."[36]

To maintain esprit and cohesion and to remember fallen comrades, the 1st Division's officers established the Society of the First Division, holding their inaugural meeting in Montabaur on 11 February 1919. The society was open to any soldier who served with the division. Its principal object was "the good of the military service and the American people." One of the organization's first projects was to commemorate those who fell in defense of their nation by erecting monuments on each of the division's five major battlefields. The names of the dead were inscribed on each monument and the shaft was surmounted by an eagle perched on a granite shell. The Society of the First Division held its first reunion in Montabaur on 6 June 1919, culminating the event with a show put on by the division's circus.[37]

Preparation and Training for War

Following the armistice, Pershing insisted that all divisions remain ready for combat until the final peace was signed. Once the 1st Division was east of the Rhine, McGlachlin initiated a training program to keep the troops ready for the possible resumption of hostilities. This training stressed marksmanship and artillery practice. The division turned in its Hotchkiss machine guns and Chauchat automatic rifles and received Browning weapons in their place. The 5th Artillery Regiment was motorized as well, easing a severe shortage of horses. The soldiers grumbled about the monotony of training in the cold winter weather, but such activities helped to maintain discipline and combat efficiency.

In February, it became clear to Pershing that the leaders of the victorious powers were preparing a harsh peace treaty that the German government might not accept. Consequently, the AEF's operations officer, Colonel George C. Marshall, prepared options for a possible advance by the Third Army into the heart of Germany. Marshall found the task daunting, especially since so many men had already been demobilized. He concluded that a broad front advance by the American and Allied armies moving from the Rhineland northeastward toward Berlin was feasible, although the American occupation zone was too small to serve as a suitable base of departure.

Marshall recommended that the zone be expanded to a 60-kilometer front along the Rhine and that an American army of ten divisions be given a 100-kilometer-wide zone of action if an advance was launched. This sector included two railroads for logistical support and would provide a corridor to the Elbe River just south of Magdeburg. From there, further operations could be conducted toward Berlin. Marshall believed that, based on intelligence estimates, "it appears reasonable to conclude that, in proportion to the frontage and assuming prompt replacements, a moderate sized force equipped with a few heavy guns and a full allotment of light guns, airships, and transport, should be able to break down and through the enemies' most determined resistance."[38]

Pershing and Marshall nearly got their chance to advance into Germany. On 7 May 1919, the Germans received the draft peace treaty. Its terms were harsh and humiliating. The German government was split over whether or not to accept it. The Western Powers refused to change the terms that reduced the German army to 100,000 men and eliminated any significant air and naval forces. When the final treaty reached Weimar on 17 June, a significant portion of the government and most of the German generals favored rejecting the treaty. For several days, a debate was conducted among the generals and politicians concerning resistance or acceptance. On 18 June, Pershing ordered Third Army, now commanded by Robert Bullard, to deploy to its battle positions and prepare to advance into Germany on 23 June. In Weimar, however, General Wilhelm Groener, quartermaster general of the

German General Staff, convinced the other generals and the government to accept the treaty, ending the crisis.[39]

German acceptance of the Treaty of Versailles ended the need for the United States to maintain the AEF in Europe. The treaty established a permanently demilitarized Rhineland, to include a 50-kilometer belt on the east side of the Rhine. The Western Powers retained bridgeheads over the Rhine. In the American zone, the Third Army ended its occupation in August 1919 and turned its bridgehead over to a constabulary force. The 1st Division was the last American combat division to leave Europe, in mid-August. Pershing and his staff, including George Marshall, sailed with some of the divisions' units aboard the passenger liner *Leviathan*, arriving in New York harbor on 8 September, in time to take part in the final victory parades of the war.

Upon its arrival in Hoboken, New Jersey, the Big Red One received a complete set of organizational equipment for the victory parade in New York City on 10 September and another in the nation's capital on 17 September. In less than a week, the soldiers repainted and serviced hundreds of artillery carriages, transport wagons, trucks, and machine-gun carts for the parade down Fifth Avenue. Over a million New Yorkers lined the route to welcome home the 1st Infantry Division. Pershing and his staff led the parade, just as they had led the American troops in the celebrations in Paris and London. Following the New York parade, the division boarded trains for Camp Meade, Maryland, where it prepared for the victory march through the nation's capital.

After participating in the parades, the Big Red One returned to Camp Meade, where most of the soldiers were demobilized. Men who reenlisted received one month's leave to visit their homes before resuming service. By 30 September, the demobilization process was complete, and the reconstituted regiments had set out for Camp Zachary Taylor, Kentucky, the first stateside home of the division.[40] At Camp Meade, Major General McGlachlin said farewell to the troops, as Charles P. Summerall resumed command. By the end of October 1919, the division had settled into new quarters. The future of the division, however, was uncertain, since Congress had yet to decide how to provide for the common defense in peacetime.

The New Army: The National Defense Act of 1920

The US Army was in flux and turmoil in 1919–1920. Most of the four million men of the wartime army had resumed civilian life. Only the Regular Army divisions remained in federal service. The National Guard divisions did not automatically return to their previous status of states' militias.

Instead, the soldiers of the Guard were demobilized on the East Coast and returned home as individuals. In some cases, National Guard regiments voluntarily reunited for victory celebrations in their home states, but there was no certitude that the National Guard would be retained as part of America's defense establishment.[41] In fact, the War Department had other plans.

Believing that the nation needed to retain a robust military establishment in peacetime so as to avoid the lack of preparedness it had faced in 1917, Secretary of War Newton Baker and Army Chief of Staff Peyton March submitted a military organization bill to Congress in January 1919. This bill called for a Regular Army of 500,000 men, organized in five corps. This army was to serve as an expandable force that could be filled by 500,000 trained reservists at the start of a war. The Baker-March bill proposed that a peacetime draft be established to provide the men that the Regulars would train for the Reserve force. There was no mention of the National Guard or Reserve divisions in the bill.[42] The Baker-March bill was based on the assumptions of Emory Upton and his disciples, who believed that there was no place in modern war for the citizen-soldier militias and National Guard units that had fought in the Civil War and in World War I. These Uptonians believed that modern warfare was too complex for militiamen to master quickly and that a large expansible Regular Army was the proper institution in which men could receive the intensive professional training needed for war.[43]

Although the Baker-March bill was based on solid Uptonian logic, it ignored political reality. The majority of Americans believed that citizen-soldier armies had won the nation's wars. They conceded the point that professional cadres were an essential part of the military system, but there was strong sentiment in the nation and the Congress that the expansible professional armies of Europe were dangerous to democracy and had played a prominent role in the origins and outbreak of the recent war. The War Department's bill went nowhere. All that could be accomplished in early 1919 was to get Congress to allow the resumption of enlistments in the active army. Otherwise, a deadlock ensued, leaving the army in limbo.[44]

In October 1919, Pershing testified before a congressional committee about the future organization of the army. Pershing praised the National Guard divisions' performance in the war. Colonel John McAuley Palmer, one of the brightest army officers of his generation, also testified that the National Guard soldiers had done well and that the Baker-March bill was flawed in its assumptions that Guard units could not be trained quickly enough to meet a national emergency. Palmer recommended an organization of Regulars, guardsmen, and trained reservists. This Army of the United States could provide the forces needed in the beginning of a war. Reservists, provided by a system of universal military service (conscription), would be able to fill the Regular, Guard, and Reserve divisions.[45]

The Senate was so impressed with Palmer's approach that it asked the War Department to detail him to the committee to prepare the legislation. Palmer provided the Senate committee with an organizational structure that fit political and financial realities and allowed for the continuation of the national tradition of citizen-soldiers.[46] The result of the Senate's work was the Defense Act of June 1920.

The National Defense Act of 1920 provided for a Regular Army of 280,000 enlisted men and 13,000 officers. The National Guard was to consist of no more than 435,000 soldiers. Congress rejected universal military service, relying instead on volunteers to fill all components. An organized reserve was included, and the college-based Reserve Officers' Training Corps (ROTC) continued to provide reserve officers. The US Military Academy remained the primary source of Regular Army officers. The nine Regular divisions were to be maintained at full strength, ready to deploy overseas. The Guard and Reserve divisions would be filled with volunteers or draftees and would be prepared to join the Regulars in a reasonably short period of time. The law increased the size and clout of the Militia Bureau in the War Department. The General Staff was significantly expanded at the same time, and the army school system was retained, reflecting the superb wartime performance of Staff College–trained officers.

Peacetime Doctrine and Training Philosophy

Devising a structure for the army was only one of the challenges facing the nation in 1919. The army also needed to develop doctrine for future training and operations. The wartime debate concerning infantry tactical doctrine was settled by Pershing's insistence that open warfare was the proper way to train and use American infantry. Following the war, an analysis was conducted by the AEF of the wartime performance of the infantry. This assessment reaffirmed open warfare tactical doctrine.

While in Germany, many of the 1st Division's officers helped study the war. These activities were an extension of the after-action review process conducted by Summerall and the AEF during the war. These efforts led to a revision of the *Army Service Regulations*, to the creation of a coherent staff manual,[47] and eventually to the improvement in tactical training done in the infantry and artillery schools in the 1920s and 1930s. In the short run, the army studied the design of the infantry division, concluding that the large square division of the European war was fundamentally sound but that personnel policies and attitudes toward the infantry were flawed.

Pershing established a board of officers in early 1919 to consider "the lessons to be gained from the experiences of the recent war" and to determine how "they affect the tactics and organization of Infantry." Known as the Lewis Board, because it was headed by Major General E. M. Lewis, the committee of five officers sent questionnaires to the officers still in Europe. With input from these queries, the board developed recommendations to guide future tactical organization in the army. Some of the men whom the board asked for personal input were George C. Marshall, Malin Craig, Frank McCoy, Fox Connor, Adna Chaffee, and Theodore Roosevelt Jr. Many of these officers, and especially Marshall, played a crucial role in infantry training and doctrine in the 1930s.[48]

The Lewis Board determined that the most important tactical lesson of the war was that "decisive results can only be accomplished by the offensive." The offensive power of an army is determined by the quality of its infantry, and "war is decided by man rather than armament." The infantryman must rely on his rifle, and "the training of our infantry should by all means be in open warfare and designed to foster the offensive spirit." The board concluded that the machine gun was the greatest obstacle to a successful offensive and that means needed to be developed "for putting hostile machine guns out of action." Close cooperation between the artillery and the infantry was part of the solution to the problem of how to overcome enemy machine guns. The attachment of mortars, tanks, and aircraft to the infantry was also identified as an important way to overcome strong defenses.[49]

The Lewis Board recommended that the 250-man infantry company be retained and that each battalion should consist of four infantry companies, commanded by a lieutenant colonel. The board concluded that the square division of two infantry brigades, each with two infantry regiments of three battalions, provided the sustained manpower and heavy firepower needed for offensive operations. The division was to contain an artillery brigade of three regiments and additional machine-gun and engineer battalions to support the infantry.[50] Many of the support units and two of the artillery regiments were to continue to use horse-drawn transport, and the board recommended that the motorized machine-gun battalion of the wartime division be eliminated. Such motorized units were to be assigned to divisions as needed.[51]

Many officers, including Pershing, favored a reduction in the division to three regiments, each with three battalions of three infantry companies and one machine-gun company. These officers believed that the smaller "triangular" division would be easier to maneuver and support. The army conducted additional studies of division size and structure in 1919 and 1920, the result of which was a compromise. The division remained "square," with four infantry regiments in two brigades. The division was reduced to just under 20,000 officers and men by removing the 155mm howitzer regiment from the artillery brigade, eliminating the separate machine-gun battalions, and reducing the infantry regiments by 700 men each.[52] Until 1939, this square division remained the structure of American infantry divisions. The 1st Division consisted of the 16th, 18th, 26th, and 28th Infantry Regiments and two infantry brigade headquarters. The artillery brigade was retained, although the 5th Artillery was reassigned, leaving the 6th and 7th Artillery Regiments in the division.

Although the Lewis Board missed the importance of the mechanization of future warfare, it provided sound advice about infantrymen and the infantry that was ignored by the nation and the army during the remaining wars of the twentieth century. These recommendations dealt with the nature of the individual infantryman, the replacement system, and the leadership needed in the tactical environment faced by infantry units.

Since infantry was critical to successful offensive operations, it was essential that the infantry soldiers of the future be of as high a quality as any other soldiers in the army. This conclusion was based upon the consensus of the Lewis Board that the US Army of 1918 had not produced fighting formations that could have matched the German army of 1914:

> Even if it had been possible at the beginning of the war to put against the German Army of 1914, our army of October 1918, division for division, there is a grave probability that faulty discipline, the untrained leadership and the lowering of average intelligence in our infantry to so favor other branches, would have resulted in disaster. . . . [T]hese conditions resulted from a very faulty policy with respect to infantry.[53]

The fundamental error that prevented American infantry from reaching "the standards required by modern war" was the mistaken belief that "infantry could be quickly trained and its officers and noncommissioned officers could be quickly made from average material." As a result, too many of the best-qualified soldiers were assigned to specialty branches, leaving the infantry units with the "leftovers of the draft."[54] Company commanders ran out of the kind of men who make good NCOs, especially since open warfare requires infantry leaders of intelligence, physical stamina, and personal courage. The board pointed out that when a division lost as many as 7,000 men in combat in two weeks there were insufficient qualified survivors to train replacements and to restore the infantry units to full combat efficiency.

The Lewis Board called for elevating the status of infantry soldiers to equal that of any other branch and recommended that the infantry not be called upon to provide many of its best men to fill specialty jobs. "The American People, Congress, and the Army itself, must be made to accept as a matter of course such improvements in the infantry service as will place that service highest in the estimation of the people and of the Army, and as will give it the personnel and training which the safety of the country demands."[55] Sadly, this advice was not followed in World War II, Korea, or Vietnam.[56]

The 1st Division Circus

While Congress debated the organizational future of the army and the army officer corps studied the lessons of the recent war, the division assembled at Camp Taylor, Kentucky. In many ways, Summerall and his officers faced challenges similar to those faced by McGlachlin during the occupation of Germany. There was no immediate military threat to whip up enthusiasm for rigorous training. There were few entertainments and positive distractions to keep the soldiers occupied in their camp in middle America. The army also faced a chronic shortage of funds for training and maintenance.

The division had entertained itself in Germany with a circus. This tradition was resumed in Kentucky. By the spring of 1920, plans were well along for an elaborate circus that Summerall planned to use to entertain the men and as an advertising format for recruitment. By early July, Lieutenant Colonel Harcourt Hervey had organized the circus and was conducting rehearsals before it set out for Chicago, Indianapolis, and Louisville. The circus included four elephants, five lions, fourteen monkeys, a buffalo, and numerous trained dogs. Performing were 220 soldiers, supported by another 130 men. The Midway had space for fifteen concession booths, a roulette room, and a "freak show." Thirty-seven clowns, a twenty-four–man monkey team, and a Wild West show performed under the big top. The finale was a "battle of the tanks," with ten army tanks taking part in a mock battle.[57]

The circus cost about $6,000 to operate from the middle of July until early August. Portable bleachers accommodated 6,000 fans, and admission was one dollar for adults and fifty cents for children. The performers and support soldiers shared 15 percent of the profit. There is no indication in the records whether the circus made money, but it certainly kept many soldiers busy and provided positive publicity for the division and the army.

Summerall also raised $20,000 as the division's share of the costs of a 1st Division monument in Washington, DC. The monument, near the Old Executive Office Building and the White House, was finished and dedicated in 1924. Today it is a moving and appropriate memorial to the men and

women of the 1st Infantry Division who have given their lives in combat in
our nation's wars since 1917.

Shortly after the circus returned from its tour, in August 1920, the War
Department ordered the division to move to Camp Dix, New Jersey. This
move was part of the realignment of the army to fit the organizational
and stationing plan prescribed by the National Defense Act of 1920. The
1st Division completed the move, using rail and motor transportation, by
mid-October.[58]

The Dispersion of the 1st Division: 1920–1939

The National Defense Act of 1920 authorized 293,000 officers and enlisted
men for the Regular Army. The army's goal was to maintain nine Regular
infantry divisions in federal service, spread across the nation in nine corps
areas. Maintaining an army whose authorized strength was nearly three
times as large as the prewar force proved a difficult task. Congress provided
too little money to maintain the authorized troop levels. The $21-per-month
pay was too low to attract well-qualified enlistees, especially in the boom-
ing economy of the 1920s, when even unskilled laborers could earn that
much in a week.[59] A soldier's routine was at best not exciting and at worst
marked by drudgery. By 1921, the budget was too small to allow realistic
training, research for new weapons, and proper maintenance of the material
on hand. The Republican administrations of the 1920s refused to request
the large sums of money needed to build sufficient permanent billets for a
larger standing force. The army, in other words, was anything but a growth
industry for a young man to join.

Desertion was a major concern of the army during the 1920s and early
1930s. In 1920, the annual desertion rate stood at 6.9 per thousand soldiers.
In the 1st Division, the rate varied from 4.7 to 9.1 per thousand.[60] Summerall believed at the time that "the fundamental cause of desertion is instability of character, a thing that is, I think, beyond the power of the military
to remove." A 1920 study by the General Staff concluded that desertion
rates varied in an inverse relationship with morale. "The causes which pro-
duce lack of contentment with the service undoubtedly increase desertion
and prevent reenlistment."[61] While the army could not control factors outside the army, like high civilian pay, it could affect length of enlistment and
conditions of service. Conditions of service affected morale the most. The
quality of barracks, food, pass and furlough privileges, and recreation facilities affected morale directly. Most of these factors could be influenced by
unit commanders. "The commander who looked after his soldiers' health,

welfare, and living and working conditions could appreciably hold down losses."[62]

Desertion plagued the 1st Division just as it did the rest of the army. For example, only 38 percent of the men leaving the division's units at Fort Hamilton in the years 1926 through 1929 completed their enlistment. More than 22 percent of the soldiers leaving the service from Fort Hamilton in this period deserted. Another 20 percent of the annual losses bought out their enlistment. Logically, the Great Depression provided an increased economic incentive for men not to desert. Nonetheless, nearly 20 percent of the men leaving the army units at Fort Hamilton in the period 1931 to 1934 deserted. About 8 percent of the total strength of the 1st Division units at Fort Hamilton deserted annually, and another 8 percent purchased their discharge.[63] Army policy allowing men to purchase the remainder of their enlistment contract was beyond the control of unit commanders. Desertion proved equally hard to prevent, although the army increased rations and tried to improve living conditions.

The army did not solve its peacetime desertion problems. However, it maintained its troop strength because of the decline in the authorized manpower levels. The 1st Division remained consistently under its authorized strength of 10,380 soldiers and well below its 19,385 wartime level. (See Table 4.1 to put the strength of the division into perspective.) The other Regular Army divisions faced similar problems, forcing the army to inactivate many battalions and regiments and eventually to retain only the 1st, 2nd, and 3rd Infantry Divisions with active division and brigade headquarters.

In the early 1920s, the 4th through the 9th Divisions were skeletonized, each with a cadre strength of about 2,500 officers and men. By 1928, attempts to maintain the 7th through the 9th Divisions were abandoned, allowing the army to fill the 1st through the 6th Divisions to an average of about 6,250 men. In 1934, the chief of staff, Douglas MacArthur, reconstituted the nine Regular Army infantry divisions, although he was unable to provide more than 3,000 men to the 5th through the 9th Divisions.[64]

The adjustments to peace included major realignments of army bases. As appropriations declined, the army found it impossible to maintain the large number of posts envisioned by the National Defense Act. Many posts closed.[65] The 1st Division's move to Camp Dix in 1921 allowed the division to remain together for training and administration. Camp Dix also was large enough to provide training grounds and ranges for the Guard and Reserve units in the Northeast, and the active army was expected to help with their training. However, the 1st Division soon was ordered to relocate to Camp

Table 4.1. Regular Army and 1st Division Strength, 1919 to 1939*

Year	Authorized	Active Army Total	1st Division
1920	293,000	200,355	6,673
1921	162,000	227,799	8,671
1922	137,000	146,507	6,514
1923	137,000	131,254	—
1924	137,000	140,943	—
1925	137,000	135,254	7,237
1926	137,000	133,443	6,691
1927	130,749	133,268	7,272
1928	130,749	134,505	7,507
1929	130,749	138,263	7,363
1930	130,749	138,452	8,532
1931	130,749	139,626	8,264
1932	130,749	134,024	7,739
1933	130,749	135,684	8,354
1934	130,749	137,584	7,473
1935	130,749	138,569	7,874
1936	177,000	166,724	8,178
1937	177,000	178,733	8,792
1938	177,000	184,126	—
1939	225,000	188,565	9,712

* NA, RG165, CSA Statistical Reports, Boxes 4, 6, 14, for the years 1920–1939. Most strength figures are for 30 June of the appropriate year.

Meade, Maryland. This move probably was prompted by the poor condition of facilities at Dix, as a 1924 inspector general's report indicated:[66]

> The buildings are all of the temporary war time cantonment type of construction and are practically all in very poor physical condition. The underpinning of floors is rotting out, the floors in many instances sagging badly, roofs are leaking, plumbing in general is in miserable condition, resulting in considerable waste of water, door and window sash and frames have been wantonly damaged in many buildings, and the electrical fixtures have, in many instances, been torn out by marauders.[67]

The difficulties encountered by the division and the army in trying to carry out this move illustrate the poor financial condition of the army. A conference was held at Camp Meade on 22 December 1921 to determine whether or not Camp Meade possessed suitable barracks and housing for the soldiers and families of the division. The division needed 346 sets of family quarters for married officers and enlisted men and 107 sets of bachelor officer quarters. Camp Meade had available only 186 quarters for married and 63 sets for bachelor officers—62 of these quarters were occupied by Camp Meade staff. An additional 185 married officers' quarters and 150 sets of married noncommissioned officers' quarters were needed. The camp quartermaster estimated that it would cost $130,000 to provide the additional married quarters and another $83,000 to repair troop barracks.[68] There was no money in the budget for these projects.

The proposal to move the division to Meade was dropped in early 1922. At the same time, the army decided to disperse the Regular divisions to regimental posts throughout the United States. This allowed the army to house its soldiers in the permanent barracks and forts of the prewar army, many of which were in better condition than the temporary camps built to house the wartime forces. If the army's authorized strength had remained at the initial level of 293,000 men, and if Congress had provided adequate funding, the army would have preferred to maintain its active divisions in large bases like Taylor or Dix, facilitating regiment-, brigade-, and division-level training.

As authorized troop levels fell, the army chose to reduce the peacetime strength of its infantry regiments, rather than to eliminate regiments. The chief of infantry believed that retention of regiments with about one-third of their wartime strength allowed the army to retain a reasonable nucleus for emergencies. The dispersion of regiments across the country also allowed the army to maintain training relationships with Reserve officers at low cost and to maintain contacts with communities and political elites. Most regiments were reduced to two battalions of about 400 men each, while the third battalion was reduced to a small cadre. This structure allowed more colonels and lieutenant colonels to command than would have been possible if the army had eliminated regiments and maintained active-duty regiments at around 3,000 men each.[69] But no division was capable of performing its wartime mission in the period from 1920 to 1939 due to reduced strengths and inadequate training.

The 1st Division dispersed to small forts in New York and New Jersey in 1922. The 1st Brigade's headquarters and the 16th Infantry were stationed at Forts Wadsworth and Jay, New York, and the 18th Infantry was housed in Forts Slocum, Schuyler, and Hamilton, New York.[70] The 2nd Brigade's headquarters was in Madison Barracks, New York, and its 26th Infantry Regiment moved to Plattsburg Barracks, New York. The 28th Infantry Regiment resided in Fort Niagara, New York. These post were large enough to accommodate regimental strengths of between 700 and 1,000 men.[71] Division headquarters remained at Fort Hamilton during the 1920s and 1930s, with the 1st Military Police Company and several other headquarters and support elements stationed at Camp Dix, New Jersey.[72] For the most part, the units of the division remained in these scattered posts until 1939. With no money for division-level training, it was impossible to prepare the division for war.

Training was difficult for units larger than a platoon. None of the New York City–area forts had rifle ranges adequate for long-range fire. A scaled-down training facility, called the 1,000-inch range, was used for machine-gun and rifle training in the small posts, but units had to travel to Stony Point, New York, or Camp Dix, New Jersey, for rifle practice and qualification. The infantry regiments found marksmanship training hindered by their need to guard facilities and to provide soldiers for recruiting duty. There was a serious shortage of officers in many units, and the infantry found it difficult to maintain an 80 percent "qualified" rifle marksmanship standard. For example, in 1924, only two companies of the 16th Infantry Regiment qualified 80 percent of their soldiers. The regimental commander reported that this poor performance was due to lack of interest on the part of some of the men, the poor condition of the rifles, and a shortage of officers.[73]

There were few opportunities for battalion-level maneuvers except at Camp Dix, and there is no evidence that such training was conducted from 1922 to 1938. The daily schedule of all units of the division was dull and repetitive. A typical monthly diary entry for 1st Brigade, from October 1922, noted that the "organizations of the Brigade performed the usual garrison duties in their respective posts during the month."[74] The routine varied seasonally. In the summer, the division supported Reserve officer training, allowing the troops to conduct rifle and machine-gun marksmanship training. In garrison, the duty day typically ended by noon, with the afternoon devoted to fatigue details and maintenance of equipment and buildings. Officers were expected to use the afternoons for professional study and physical conditioning.

As late as February 1939, the 1st Division had great difficulty in providing its troops with facilities in which to conduct antiaircraft practice in the New York area.[75] It was virtually impossible in the 1920s and 1930s to train the infantry with tanks, and only at Camp Dix did the division have a chance to conduct exercises with the infantry and artillery working together.

Officer Development and the Army Promotion System

The army chiefs of staff in the 1920s and 1930s believed that World War I was not the last time the army would be called on to fight a modern and heavily equipped land power. Palmer's and Pershing's testimony to the Senate in 1919–1920 emphasized that the nation would have to fight another day in Europe or Asia and that it was necessary to establish a military structure that allowed the nation to prepare for such a contingency. Although Congress failed to provide the funds to maintain more than half of the Regular Army envisioned in the National Defense Act of 1920, it did provide for 12,000 Regular officers and 80,000 Reserve officers.[76] To prepare these officers for war, the army remained committed to its school system, even as its appropriations were aggressively cut by Congress.

The ROTC provided a steady stream of educated men to serve as junior reserve officers. By 1928, ROTC units were operating on 325 college campuses, with 6,000 lieutenants receiving their commissions annually. These men would provide the vast majority of the army's company- and field-grade officers in any major war. The 1st Division contributed to the training of these officers during the annual summer camps held at Camp Dix, providing technical instructors and demonstration units. This commitment to the development of army leaders was a crucial investment for future mobilizations.[77]

In the early 1920s, the army consolidated its officer promotion system and established a single promotion list for most officers. This list replaced the system in which promotions had been made by the separate branches from lists each branch maintained. By using seniority as the primary criteria for promotion, it prevented the more talented officers, like George Marshall, from advancing faster than some of their obviously less talented contemporaries. But the single system provided uniform standards for promotion across all branches.[78]

Promotion remained slow throughout the interwar period. In 1922, Congress reduced the Regular Army officer corps by over 1,000, to roughly 12,000 officers. By 1925, it was clear that there was a "hump" in the officer corps created by the extraordinarily large number of officers brought into the army from 1917 to 1920. The groups of officers from these few years constituted 6,014 of the 10,003 officers below the rank of colonel in 1925.[79] It would take twenty-three years for all of these men to make major with normal attrition of about 4 percent annually. Since promotion was strictly by seniority, officers who entered the service after 1920 could expect to spend twenty-two years as lieutenants and captains in a standard career of forty years. The army and Congress studied the matter intensely but found no easy solution.

Officer efficiency reports were considered as measurement tools to cull the ranks, but no authority was sought or given to the army to involuntarily retire officers with substandard performance records. Part of the problem may have been that the officer performance evaluation system that was created in 1918 quickly became inflated. In 1921, 730 officers were rated unsatisfactory or inferior. In 1922, this number decreased to 381, and from 1923 to

1941, no more than 3 of the more than 11,000 officers rated received a rating of inferior, and fewer than 100 officers were considered unsatisfactory. The number of officers rated as superior or above average increased from 3,746 in 1921 to 9,941 in 1936. In 1936, 18 of 11,609 officers were rated as unsatisfactory.[80]

Promotion was slow, pay low, and training uninspiring in the army and the 1st Division in the 1920s. Things got worse with the onset of the Great Depression. In 1930, Congress forced officers to take an unpaid furlough equal to 8.5 percent of pay, and in 1934 Congress cut the pay of all federal employees by 15 percent. Many post commanders allowed married soldiers to establish vegetable gardens on unused plots of land, and mess halls were authorized to sell meals at cost to married enlisted soldiers and their families.[81]

The army had a strict policy that enlisted soldiers in the lowest three grades could not be married. In the 1st Division, this policy was consistently ignored. At Fort Hamilton, where the division headquarters and the 18th Infantry resided, between 10 and 12 percent of the total enlisted population in the first three grades were married in 1933 and 1934. Some officers felt that married junior enlisted men could not be good soldiers because they were forced to seek additional employment to feed their families. The inspector general concluded that "there are, however, exceptions to the foregoing, particularly in the case of married men who are furnished quarters on the reservation. These men are usually above average in efficiency." The division retained a number of these married junior soldiers, in open violation of the army policy against the enlistment of married men.[82] This issue was not resolved until 1938, when the deputy army chief of staff, George Marshall, recommended to the chief of staff that the army continue to refuse to enlist men with dependents, but that "marriage will not affect re-enlistment of those in the first three grades."[83] This pragmatic policy was adopted.

The steady decrease in appropriations in the early 1930s made it difficult for the army to maintain its many small posts. The inspector general found the post hospital at Fort Hamilton "barely adequate" in his 1933 visit:

> The ward in the permanent building was filled. The temporary building is not desirable as a ward in cold weather. . . . The personnel is not adequate for the additional ward. This hospital takes care of the personnel of the New York Port of Embarkation and casuals arriving on the transports. . . . With the limited space in the building it is practically impossible to make examinations of women and children.[84]

Six years earlier the inspector general report had noted similar problems, and little had been done to remedy the defects in the intervening six years. Throughout the army, facilities steadily deteriorated, in spite of efforts made by local commanders to repair buildings using troop labor.[85]

Army Service in the Great Depression

The Great Depression generally made life more difficult for the army. Most departments of the federal government suffered significant budget cuts from 1929 to 1934. Until 1935, little money was made available to the War Department to fund weapons research. Congress even came close to reducing the active-duty army officer corps from 12,000 to 10,000 officers, a move that was prevented by Senate action. The chiefs of staff from 1930 to 1939, Douglas MacArthur (1930–1935) and Malin Craig (1935–1939), warned Congress and the administrations that the army was unable to protect adequately the nation's interests overseas or to defend the continental United States. Until 1935, these warnings fell on deaf ears as the federal government attempted to ameliorate the economic effects of the Depression. In 1935, Congress authorized an increase of the army's active enlisted strength to 165,000. President Franklin D. Roosevelt, however, allowed the War Department to spend only enough money to bring the army to 147,000 enlisted men. Only in 1938, with the threats of war growing around the world, did Roosevelt agree with Congress to fund the full 165,000 soldiers.[86]

The procurement of modern motor vehicles, tanks, and weapons was equally delayed, although MacArthur had ordered the army to begin motorization in 1931. The process of replacing mules and horses was slow but steady. By 1938, the 5th Artillery's 155mm howitzers were pulled by new Indiana trucks, and the unit was able to carry all of its soldiers in motor vehicles. In 1938, the army was given $17 million for procurement, allowing it to set in motion the production of the M1 Garand rifle and a series of light tanks. As a result, that summer the 1st Tank Company was able to road march its new M2A2 tanks to Camp Dix for training exercises in support of the 424th Infantry.[87] Procurement of modern equipment, nevertheless, remained slow.

The shortage of funds created a strange penny-pinching mentality in the army. For example, in 1935, the 1st Division and II Corps commanding generals were required to approve personally a decision to spend $4 extra for each of two sets of Firestone "mud-snow" tires for the 26th Infantry's trucks.[88] Such a situation was far from unique.

One of the more fortunate developments from the army's viewpoint in the

1930s was the establishment of the Civilian Conservation Corps (CCC). The CCC provided work for over 275,000 young American males by 1934. The army spread the 1,330 CCC companies across the rural areas of the nation. Colonel George Marshall, then commander of the 8th Infantry Regiment in South Carolina, for example, supervised the development of nineteen camps. The 1st Division was heavily involved in the CCC mission in New York. In October 1933, 20 of the 23 officers and 132 of the 402 enlisted men of the 18th Infantry Regiment were working with the CCC.[89]

The CCC mission significantly hindered unit training, but it did have a number of positive effects. It allowed the army to provide some exposure to discipline to hundreds of thousands of young men, thus creating a reserve of sorts for the army in an emergency. Thousands of Reserve officers were called to duty to run the camps, and many of them remained on active service through 1945. After the creation of the CCC, with its need for officer leadership, there were no serious congressional attempts to cut the size of the Regular Army's officer corps.[90] The CCC mission also allowed the army to interact with Americans in a positive manner. Young men learned to respect the army and its officers, providing a valuable counter to the antimilitary feelings widely prevalent in America. This was in stark contrast to the unfavorable impression the army had made in the early 1930s when it was used by the federal government to disperse bonus marchers in Washington, DC. And it was a much better mission for the army of a free country than were the riot-control and antistrike missions that the army was ordered to prepare for in the early years of the Depression.[91]

Throughout the interwar period, the army maintained nine Regular Army and eighteen National Guard divisions, even though they were understrength or skeletonized. As early as April 1922, the chief of infantry, Major General C. S. Farnsworth, had identified the reasons why the army was wise to stick to the policy of maintaining active duty divisions and as many infantry regiments as possible:

> The efficiency of a military organization depends very largely upon its morale, which in turn depends upon its history, traditions and prestige. These, together with other qualities, give it a soul which should not be destroyed without serious consideration, and which cannot be re-created on short notice. . . . At least one complete and assembled division should form an immediately available and mobile force. This division should serve as a practical school of command and administration through which infantry officers may be passed for visualization and practice with larger units.[92]

The skeletonized divisions thus were available to provide the framework for a rapid expansion of the army. Because of them, the army was better prepared for mobilization in 1940–1941 than it had been in 1917. When mobilization commenced in 1940, the 1st Division's cadre was ready to absorb and train the 10,000 new soldiers needed to bring it to full strength. In this process, the traditions that had been maintained in the division were an essential part of the creation of what was to be one of the greatest combat teams of World War II.

5

Mobilization for War
The Expansion and Training of the
Big Red One, 1939 to November 1942

AT 0753 HOURS ON 7 DECEMBER 1941, Japanese warplanes struck the US Pacific Fleet in Pearl Harbor. Within two hours, the attackers had destroyed or damaged 18 major warships and over 180 airplanes, killing 2,403 Americans.[1] Seven days later, in a strategic miscalculation nearly as great as the German decision to implement unrestricted submarine warfare in 1917, Adolf Hitler declared war on the United States. All that was left for Franklin Delano Roosevelt and Congress to do was to recognize that a state of war existed between the United States and Germany and Japan.

The United States was better prepared for war than at the onset of any previous major conflict in its history. In December 1941, the US Army had 1.6 million men under arms, with thirty-six divisions, including three armored divisions, on active service.[2] The US Navy, whose preparations for a war against Japan had begun in 1934, was strong enough to absorb the losses suffered at Pearl Harbor, stop the Japanese fleet in the Battle of the Coral Sea in April 1942, and decisively defeat the Japanese navy in the Battle of Midway in June 1942. The US Army Air Forces, made virtually independent in the mid-1930s, had developed the aircraft types that by 1943 would enable American air forces to hammer Germany with long-range bombing. Because the air force and navy required two to three years to build a major warship or field an aircraft, the potency of the US Navy and US Army Air Forces early in the war (1942–1943) bears witness to the fact that the United States was not disarmed when the war began.[3]

The 1st Infantry Division on the Eve of the European War

When Hitler's armies smashed the Polish army, in September 1939, the 1st Infantry Division's 8,000 soldiers remained scattered in battalion-size posts across New York and northern New Jersey. The Springfield '03 rifle remained the principal infantry weapon and the 75mm cannon the standard artillery piece. The division was organized as a square division of two brigades, with an authorized war strength of over 19,000 men in four infantry and three artillery regiments. The army was just preparing to begin production of the M1 Garand semiautomatic rifle and the 105mm howitzer to arm its infantry and artillery. However, the division and the army would not receive these superb weapons until 1940–1941. Douglas MacArthur had ordered the replacement of horses by motor vehicles in the early 1930s, and the two-and-one-half-ton truck would soon arrive in the divisions.[4]

Most of the training conducted by the division in the 1930s was carried out by platoons, companies, and battalions on its scattered posts. Ceremonial duties also took up a lot of time. Soldiers of the division provided honor guards for the World's Fair in New York, for the British royal family's visit, and for presidential events in the Hudson Valley.[5]

Training opportunities began to improve in 1935 when the army received money to conduct army-level command-post exercises and field maneuvers. The 1st Division took part in the First Army maneuver at Camp Pine (now Fort Drum), New York, in August. The division worked with the National Guard's 26th, 27th, and 43rd Divisions and elements of six Reserve divisions in exercises by over 36,000 troops designed "to test the ability of the First Army to concentrate simultaneously[,] . . . prepare for field service, train all echelons in logistics, and provide field training for all components of the First Army."[6] These exercises were the first of their kind involving Guard and Regular divisions since World War I:

> The First Army maneuver in 1935 was one of a number of training exercises that culminated in the Carolina Maneuvers of late 1941. The maneuvers were invaluable tools for training, doctrinal development, and assessment of equipment and senior officers. For example, Colonel George Marshall concluded from his experiences as Commandant of the Infantry School and his work with the 33rd Division in Illinois that significant changes needed to be made in staff procedures and the issuance of field orders and missions.[7]

Six years later, Marshall got a chance to tackle such problems for the entire army. Large-scale field exercises gave him the opportunity to identify problems that stood in the way of creating the kind of officer corps needed to win the next war.

The Triangular Division

On 1 September 1939, George C. Marshall became the chief of staff of the US Army. One of his first decisions was to reorganize the infantry divisions of the Regular Army into a "triangular" structure. The division was to consist of three infantry regiments, supported by two regiments of field artillery.

As a consequence of these changes, the 28th Infantry Regiment, the artillery brigade headquarters, and both infantry brigade headquarters disappeared from the 1st Infantry Division. The army had conducted limited tests of the triangular structure in 1937, but little came of the results. In late 1939, the 1st Infantry Division was reorganized, along with several other Regular divisions. In March and April 1940, IV Corps conducted maneuvers to test the new structure at Fort Benning, Georgia, with the 1st, 5th, and 6th Infantry Divisions.[8] In May, the 1st Infantry Division submitted after-action reports assessing the performance of the division in its new configuration. The division commander, Brigadier General Karl Truesdell, believed that the new structure enhanced the maneuverability of the division. However, a number of serious deficiencies were noted.[9]

The artillery units lacked a coordinating headquarters capable of massing artillery fires. Truesdell recommended that a divisional artillery headquarters be established to ensure the coordination of artillery fires and the proper supervision of ammunition supply. The 5th Artillery Regiment's and the division's reports urged that a single artillery organization replace the two artillery regiments and that the 75mm guns be replaced by 105mm howitzers. The reports further recommended that additional 155mm batteries be assigned to the medium artillery battalions.[10]

Truesdell further determined that an assistant division commander was needed to serve as second in command to provide continuous operational capability in a unit expected to operate twenty-four hours a day. The assistant division commander and the division chief of artillery, Truesdell suggested, should be brigadier generals. The two brigadier generals already in the division serving as the infantry and artillery section chiefs should be converted to the new positions. Finally, the division's report recommended that an armored car troop and an aerial observation squadron be added for reconnaissance purposes, and that light tanks, antitank guns, another truck company, an additional medical company, and extra signal capability be provided as units of, or regular reinforcements to, the triangular division.[11] The army adopted many of the modifications recommended by the 1st Infantry Division.

Although the size of an army infantry division fluctuated during the 1940s, the army determined the basic structure and size through the experiences and conclusions gathered during the large maneuvers of 1940–1941. The strength of the infantry division in June 1941 was set at 15,245 soldiers. During the war, this strength was reduced to 13,412 men in 1943 and raised to 14,253 soldiers by 1944.

The three infantry regiments each had between 3,340 and 3,068 men authorized. The number of vehicles of all kinds grew from 1,834 in 1941 to 2,114 in 1945, as more trucks and armored half-tracks were added to give the division greater mobility. Three light artillery battalions armed with 105mm howitzers and one medium battalion with 155mm howitzers provided the division with a total of 48 artillery tubes in 1941 and 66 artillery pieces from 1943 on. A unit of light aircraft provided the artillery with a reconnaissance capability, and an armored reconnaissance troop was added to the division. The army also decided that tank and antitank battalions would be attached to the infantry divisions as needed for specific missions rather than permanently assigned.[12]

Army Training and Peacetime Maneuvers: 1940–1941

The 1st Infantry Division's part in the IV Corps maneuvers in Georgia reflected the rapid changes that the army underwent from September 1939 to September 1940. On 6 November 1939, the 6,300 soldiers of the division left their posts in the Northeast for training at Fort Benning. When they arrived at the Harmony Church cantonment, they occupied a site hastily carved out of the Georgia pinewoods. The soldiers of the 1st Division finished the camp by building mess halls and headquarters and erecting pyramidal tents to live in. General Truesdell noted that "winter in a pyramidal tent is no picnic, not even in Georgia, and the winter of 1939–1940 was one of the coldest. Harps Pond froze over solidly."[13] For the next seven months, the division would grow and train.

Although the division's strength did not exceed 8,000 men in June 1940, the division's officers steadily improved its capabilities for war. Truesdell oversaw the development of standard operating procedures (SOP) that shaped the way the division would fight. One of the more important provisions of the tactical SOP was the organization of regimental combat teams. These three teams brought together the infantry regiments with units of engineers, signal troops, and medical personnel in teams that habitually worked together. Each of the three combat teams routinely had the same artillery battalion in direct support, although the division commander, through his artillery commander, retained the ability to mass the fires of all artillery units as needed. Armor and reconnaissance units could easily join the combat teams, as they were to do throughout World War II.[14]

Following the triangular division tests, the Big Red One moved to Louisiana to participate in maneuvers. These exercises were the largest military training operations conducted in the United States to that date. They were also the first operational exercises of the army's tactical corps headquarters, made possible by the expansion of the Regular Army to 227,000 men in September 1939. The maneuvers allowed commanders to identify shortcomings inherent in new organizations. They demonstrated the lack of modern equipment of all kinds, as the nation was just gearing up for possible war.[15] The triangular structure passed its tests and was adopted for all of the Regular Army divisions in 1940. The National Guard divisions were not reorganized as triangular divisions until 1942.

While the army tested its new organizations, Hitler's forces smashed the French army and drove the British from Northwest Europe. France surrendered and Britain stood alone. These events convinced the Roosevelt administration and Congress to dramatically increase American military resources. Between June and September 1940, Congress increased the active army to 375,000 men, instituted the first peacetime conscription in American history, and appropriated nearly $3 billion for the mobilization of military resources. The Regular Army no longer had the "leisure" to fill, arm, and train the nine Regular infantry divisions fully before it dealt with 600,000 draftees. Consequently, Marshall recommended that the National Guard's eighteen infantry divisions be called up to provide the units in which the conscripts would train for their one year of active service. A congressional resolution on 27 August authorized the order to call the Guard to active duty, and Roosevelt signed the order on 16 September 1940.[16]

Following the Louisiana exercise of May 1940, the 1st Infantry Division returned to New York, where the men hoped for time off. This was not to be. In August, the regiments were brought together at Camp Pine, New York, to take part in maneuvers with the 26th Infantry Division. When these exercises ended in late August, the division returned briefly to its posts for what would be its last stay in New York. There, the division's immediate task was to absorb 5,500 conscripts. These men increased the division to 13,645 soldiers by 31 December. At the same time, many officers were reassigned to Guard units and training centers to prepare for the expansion of the army. By July 1941, 56,700 Reserve officers had joined the active army, providing 75–90 percent of the lieutenants and captains in the Regular Army divisions at that time.[17]

The US Army faced a daunting task in late 1940 and early 1941. It had to mobilize and fill nine Regular and eighteen National Guard infantry divisions. It had to create three armored divisions, field new weapons from rifles to tanks, and receive and train 600,000 draftees. The chief of staff, George Marshall, created the General Headquarters to direct the training of the new soldiers and units. Brigadier General Lesley McNair served as chief of staff of GHQ, and Marshall served as its commanding general. In theory, the GHQ was envisioned to be the equivalent of the AEF of World War I once the army was called on to deploy overseas. Ultimately, GHQ never deployed, since the army sent forces to multiple theaters of operations around the globe. In 1942, the War Plans Division of the General Staff assumed the operational and planning functions of the army, giving Marshall the staff he needed to conduct global strategy and operations. The GHQ, renamed the Army Ground Forces in 1942, retained the mission to train the army. It performed near miracles in its task of training the eighty-nine divisions that eventually made up the US Army in World War II.[18]

The Big Red One was more fortunate than many units because it was one of the first divisions to deploy overseas in 1942 and, therefore, was not as heavily levied for officers and men to provide cadre for other units. The division used the GHQ-directed training program, which called for thirteen weeks of individual basic training followed by another thirteen weeks of combined unit training for companies, battalions, and regiments. Once these phases were complete, the program called for several months of training for the division as part of a corps, culminating in large army maneuvers.[19]

With the collapse of France in May 1940, the army realized that if the United States got involved in a European war the army would have to fight its way onto the European continent. Consequently, the War and Navy Departments created an army-navy force to develop and test joint amphibious doctrine. To prepare the 1st Division for its role as the army component of this joint organization, the army directed Truesdell to provide two infantry battalions for amphibious training. In early December 1940, the 3rd Battalions of the 16th and 18th Infantry Regiments moved to Edgewood Arsenal, Maryland, to begin the new mission, while the remainder of the division moved to Fort Devens, Massachusetts.

The United States lacked an amphibious warfare doctrine in 1940. There also was little of the special equipment needed for assault landings on defended beaches. Over the next two years, the Big Red One played a prominent role in the development of amphibious doctrine and equipment. The 3rd Battalion, 16th Infantry, conducted the first amphibious training on Chesapeake Bay, near its cantonment at Edgewood Arsenal. The navy provided wooden lifeboats similar to those used on ocean liners. Each carried fifty soldiers and was propelled by eight sets of oars. The battalion commander, Lieutenant Colonel Ray Cavanee, pushed his soldiers hard, earning a reputation as "one of the meanest officers" with whom many of the old-timers ever served.[20]

After their initial training in Maryland, the division's two amphibious training battalions deployed to the Caribbean to take part in mock assaults against Puerto Rico. These operations marginally improved the techniques and equipment used in the Chesapeake. The navy provided rope ladders for the soldiers to climb down into the assault boats. Motor launches carried the assault troops to the beach. The soldiers still had to disembark over the sides of the boats. Once ashore, the troops tended to mill about rather than quickly organize as platoons and companies and fight their way inland.

Realizing that "a well-trained company with artillery support would have prevented a successful landing," Lieutenant Colonel George Hays, the Task Force G3, identified three major shortcomings that could be fixed through training and doctrine. "First, the landings needed to be conducted over a wider front to prevent stacking of units as waves of troops came in. Second, the troops must be trained to rush ashore and seize inland positions. . . . Third, initiative and personal leadership must be fostered in small-unit leaders."[21]

The amphibious training battalions rejoined the division at Fort Devens in the middle of a bitterly cold winter. They brought invaluable experience to share as the division rotated its infantry battalions through amphibious training at Buzzard's Bay, Massachusetts. By June 1941, the 1st Infantry Division was part of the 1st Joint Amphibious Force, along with the 1st Marine Division. On the West Coast, the 3rd Infantry Division was also involved in amphibious training on Puget Sound.[22] In July and August, the Big Red One took part in amphibious operations near Camp Lejeune, North Carolina. During assaults along the Carolina coast, the 26th and 16th Regimental combat teams landed simultaneously, using the new Higgins boats with the bow ramp. The troops moved inland rapidly, securing the beachhead. This exercise demonstrated how far doctrine and practice had come in less than a year. Nonetheless, GHQ was not satisfied with many aspects of joint operations and the training of the navy and army units for amphibious assaults.[23]

From the division's perspective, the amphibious training conducted during the summer of 1941 was invaluable. Stanhope Mason, who was soon to be the G3, remembered that "this experience not only made the 1st Infantry Division the only U.S. Army division with amphibious training, but it provided a means of staff know-how which was also unique in the army."[24]

Carolina Maneuvers: November 1941

Following joint training in North Carolina, the division returned to Fort Devens and continued individual and small-unit training.[25] Since it was designated as part of the Joint Amphibious Force, the division initially was not slated to take part in the army maneuvers in Louisiana or North Carolina. The navy, which was responsible for the joint task force, was unwilling to allow the division to be committed to large force-on-force exercises at a time when the joint force might be called on for overseas duty. Nonetheless, Major General Donald Cubbison, who had assumed command of the division on 13 January 1941, lobbied hard to have the division involved. Cubbison noted that the division was capable of rapidly redeploying to a Carolina port if needed and that the Carolina maneuvers would be invaluable training. McNair agreed, and the Big Red One was assigned to the First Army for the Carolina maneuvers.[26]

The 1st Division moved from Fort Devens to Samarcand, North Carolina, in October.[27] The division was part of VI Corps, commanded by Major General Truesdell. For the next six weeks, the division trained for the war games. Lieutenant General McNair designed the Carolina maneuvers to pit the First Army against the IV Corps and the I Armored Corps. The First Army was to cross the Pee Dee River in southwestern North Carolina and drive to Monroe to forestall a Red force invasion. Major General Oscar Griswold's force was to attack east across the Catawba River to prevent Blue forces from crossing that barrier in the other direction.[28]

Griswold, following an audacious plan, launched his two armored and one motorized divisions in a dash to the Pee Dee to disrupt the Blue force's crossing sites. Initially, Red's mechanized forces contained the crossings of Blue's I and II Corps, allowing Red's infantry divisions to move east and engage First Army's infantry. On the northern flank, however, the 26th Infantry Division crossed the Pee Dee and moved steadily west against the 4th Infantry Division. First Army exploited this success by committing the 1st Infantry Division the next morning against the 4th Infantry Division. The advance of the 1st and 26th Infantry Divisions on 17 November pushed the 4th Division back and then turned it south, bending Red's lines into the shape of a seven.

The Blue force then established secure bridgeheads and moved troops across the Pee Dee by the evening. Truesdell recognized the danger to his left flank. In response, he ordered the armored divisions to attack the 1st and 26th Infantry Divisions. Poor communications and wide dispersal of units again prevented the armored forces from concentrating sufficient power to overcome VI Corps' infantry units.

The armored divisions failed to drive the 1st and 26th Infantry Divisions back on 18 November, and by evening, Griswold's forces had been driven back. The next morning Griswold launched the 1st Armored Division around the flanks of VI Corps, hoping to encircle the 1st and 26th Infantry Divisions. The Big Red One stood firm, and the bulk of the 1st Armored Division was encircled and destroyed by strong First Army forces. During the next two days, First Army steadily ground down the Red forces. With little more to be gained from the maneuvers, McNair called a halt on 21 November.[29] After four days' rest, the 1st Infantry Division took part as a motorized unit in the second phase of the Carolina maneuvers, when the division again performed well.

The Louisiana and North Carolina maneuvers were the graduation exercises of the newly mobilized Army of the United States. The maneuvers gave General Marshall a means to assess senior leaders. Of the forty-two senior commanders in the maneuvers, thirty-one were not up to the demands of modern warfare. None of those men commanded a combat unit in World War II. Eleven senior commanders received significant commands overseas. Younger officers, such as Dwight D. Eisenhower, Terry Allen, William Simpson, and Omar Bradley, performed well and later commanded American forces in combat.[30]

Home to Fort Devens and Final Stateside Training

The 1st Infantry Division profited from its maneuver experiences. The soldiers felt victorious. Although later experience would demonstrate how much the Big Red One still had to learn, the soldiers' belief that they were ready for combat was an important ingredient in their later survival as a division in North Africa. With this sense of success and competence, the troops loaded onto trucks for the long drive to Fort Devens, where they expected to spend the winter. By 6 December 1941, the entire division was at home station.[31]

On Sunday, 7 December, the soldiers of the Big Red One learned of the Japanese attack. That evening, General Cubbison assured the War Department that the division was ready to travel to the West Coast to defend the nation from attack. Although not sent to California, the division was not destined to stay at Fort Devens. On 14 February 1942, the division was on the road to Camp Blanding, Florida, where it was to conduct jungle training.[32] Seventeen passenger trains carried the infantry, and the artillery battalions, engineers, and support units drove to Florida in their trucks and jeeps. The engineers' half-tracks, earth auger, and most of the division's jeeps were shipped to Blanding on 129 railroad flatcars. The rail trip took thirty-four hours; the road-march units made the journey in five days.[33]

Camp Blanding, near Jacksonville, was a mobilization site for National Guard divisions. When the 1st arrived, the 36th Infantry Division was using the post. While there was some friction between soldiers of the two divisions in the clubs, there was enough room on the base to allow both divisions to conduct rifle training and limited artillery practice. The assistant division commanders, Brigadier Generals Theodore Roosevelt Jr. and Terry De La Mesa Allen, respectively, did a good job of keeping the rivalry of the units under control.[34]

The move to Blanding was the division's first step toward combat in 1942. Many officers' and enlisted soldiers' wives followed their husbands to Florida, determined to spend as much time as possible with their spouses before they shipped overseas. These women found housing in short supply and expensive in the surrounding communities. "Reports from Camp Blanding indicate that the situation as to renting quarters in the nearby civilian communities is generally unfavorable."[35] These women saw little of their husbands, but what time they did share with them was precious. For many, this was their last opportunity to be with those they loved.

By early 1942, the division's permanent units had been assigned. The 16th, 18th, and 26th Infantry Regiments made up the cutting edge of the division, each with three infantry battalions. The 5th, 7th, 32nd, and 33rd Artillery Battalions provided fire support, with the 5th Artillery Battalion equipped with 155mm howitzers and the other units armed with 105mm howitzers. The 1st Recon (Reconnaissance) Troop, the 1st Engineer Combat Battalion, and the 1st Signal Company provided combat support services, while the 1st Medical and the 1st Quartermaster Battalions provided combat service support. The 601st Tank Destroyer (TD) Battalion joined the Big Red One at Blanding, beginning an association that would last through the North African campaign.

While the division trained in Florida, British and American leaders developed the strategy that ultimately defeated Germany, Italy, and Japan. As early as August 1941, President Roosevelt and Prime Minister Winston Churchill had agreed that if the United States entered the war the two allies would pursue a "Germany First" strategy. Because Germany's resources were far greater than Japan's, and because Germany was situated in the middle of the most economically developed continent in the world, outside of North America, the American and British staffs concluded that Germany was the most dangerous foe. Further, they decided that they should do all they could to keep Russia in the war. Priority to Europe offered the best chance of encouraging and aiding the Russians. Roosevelt and Marshall also understood that the United States needed to do all it could to prevent the defeat of Great Britain, and this was best done by a Germany First strategy.[36] To execute this strategy, the two allies agreed eventually to send American and British armies into Northwest Europe. For this amphibious operation, code-named Bolero, the United States would mass air and ground forces in Britain.[37]

With the Bolero plan in place, the US Army began to identify the thirty divisions that it hoped to have in Britain ready for an invasion of France in 1943. The 1st Infantry Division, as one of only eight combat-ready divisions in early 1942, was high on the list of units to be sent. On 18 May, the division moved from Camp Blanding to Fort Benning, Georgia, to take part in maneuvers with the 36th Infantry and the 2nd Armored Divisions.[38] Major

General Cubbison was assigned to command the artillery replacement training center at Fort Bragg, North Carolina, and Terry Allen assumed command of the Big Red One. Allen was promoted to major general in June. Brigadier General Roosevelt continued to serve as the assistant division commander, and Colonel Norman Cota served as the division's chief of staff.[39]

George Marshall's selection of Terry Allen to command the Big Red One initiated a close relationship between the soldiers of the Fighting First and the charismatic and iconoclastic Allen. A cavalryman, Terry de la Mesa Allen had seen some of the toughest fighting of World War I as an infantry battalion commander in the St. Mihiel and Meuse Argonne campaigns. Marshall had enough faith in Allen's qualities as a combat leader to have him promoted directly from lieutenant colonel to brigadier general. This made Allen one of the youngest generals in the US Army.[40]

Teddy Roosevelt was as feisty and charismatic as Allen and a proven combat leader. The son of President Theodore Roosevelt, Brigadier General Roosevelt had fought bravely and successfully as an infantry company, battalion, and regimental commander in the Big Red One in World War I. He had been wounded twice and had demanded to return to his unit after barely recovering from his wounds. Like Allen, he had George Marshall's total confidence.

With its new command team, the 1st Infantry Division briefly settled in to the Harmony Church cantonment on Fort Benning, Georgia, after a long road march from Florida. During the next four weeks, the division practiced offensive operations. Training was as realistic as possible, with emphasis placed on air-ground liaison and close artillery support. Although the artillery performed well, "the troop margin of safety was too realistically close and one soldier was killed by a short round."[41] After these maneuvers, the War Department ordered the division to move to Indiantown Gap, Pennsylvania, to make final preparations for embarkation for Britain.

The Deployment to Britain for Training

Most of the division traveled to Britain on the Cunard luxury liner, the *Queen Mary*. An advanced detachment consisting of the 2nd Battalion, 16th Infantry, and small parties from other units sailed on 1 July on two British transports, the HMT *Maloja* and the HMT *Duchess of Bedford*. The quartering parties arrived in Liverpool on 13 July. From there they moved to Tidworth Barracks, England, to prepare for the division's arrival. Tidworth was a permanent barracks used previously by British cavalry units. Situated near the Salisbury Plain training grounds, it provided reasonably good facilities to house and train the division. The *Queen Mary* sailed from New York on 2 August, arriving in Glasgow, Scotland, on 8 August. The great liner sailed without escort, relying on her speed to evade U-boats. Only when she neared Ireland was she joined by destroyers and cruisers, which provided antiaircraft protection.

During the voyage to Scotland, Terry Allen provided the troops with some extremely useful advice about Britain and how allies should act toward their hosts:

> You will find the English people polite, friendly and helpful. . . . We are proud to have as allies these people who stood single-handed against the enemy in 1940 . . . and who have held out alone for two years since then. The measures of our mutual success is going to depend a lot on the measure of our coopera-tion. So with this in mind, avoid doing things which might lead to needless ill-feeling. . . . Don't compare their country in a disparaging way with ours. Don't mock or sneer at manners, dress or prejudices just because they happen to be different from ours.[42]

Allen was wise to remind his soldiers that "we are good, but let's not sound off about it. These people have been in the fight for three years. We have not seen action yet. Until we have, any big talk about how good we are or what we are going to do would sound pretty second-rate." The message closed by observing that "one inconsiderate foreigner abroad can do his country more harm than can be undone by a whole flock of goodwill ambassadors."[43]

The soldiers disembarked on 8 August and traveled to Tidworth Barracks. By 10 August, the division had closed in to that station. Some of the soldiers immediately felt comfortable in England. As Lieutenant Joe Dawson wrote, "The loveliness of this country has been written in every form of literature and I honestly confess that everything said thus far has been an understate-ment. Thus far I have experienced a most happy time and the people of England are indeed most gracious."[44] Terry Allen anticipated that he would have as much as another year to prepare the division for the invasion of Western Europe.

As it turned out, Allen and his officers did not have much time to ready the troops for combat. As the Big Red One crossed the Atlantic, Allied plan-ning changed. Crises in the Soviet Union and North Africa threatened the survival of Russia and the British position in Egypt. In Russia, the German summer offensive seemed capable of destroying the Russians' will and abil-ity to continue the war. In North Africa, Field Marshal Erwin Rommel's *Afrika Korps* drove the British out of Libya and threatened Egypt. While the British rallied near El Alamein, Churchill convinced Roosevelt that the best way to keep Russia and Britain in the war was to commit American ground forces to North Africa in 1942.[45] On 23 July 1942, Roosevelt ordered Marshall to prepare for offensive operations in the Mediterranean region.[46]

Planning for Operation Torch commenced immediately. Roosevelt and Churchill appointed Major General Dwight D. Eisenhower as the Allied commander for the invasion. On 13 August 1942, as the 1st Infantry Division settled in to Tidworth Barracks, the combined chiefs of staff of Britain and the United States approved the directive to Eisenhower to invade North Africa and, in conjunction with the British forces, to drive the Axis Powers from North Africa. The first phase of this operation would be a British offensive at El Alamein, commencing on 23 October. This would be followed by Allied landings in French Morocco and Algeria. Once the Allies had secured Morocco and Algeria, they were to drive into Tunisia, while General Bernard Montgomery's British Eighth Army drove west across Libya.[47]

Torch

The Allied planners prepared the invasion of North Africa in London. Eisenhower's staff was composed of British and American officers, with the combat-experienced British providing the senior commanders. There would be three simultaneous amphibious assaults. The Western Task Force, from the United States, was to strike French Morocco near Casablanca to secure the Strait of Gibraltar and to neutralize units of the French navy in Morocco. The Central Task Force was to land near Oran, Algeria, to seize that port, secure the lines of communications west and east, and then join the British First Army in the drive to Tunis. Central Task Force was commanded by British Commodore Thomas Troubridge at sea and Major General Lloyd Fredendall, commanding general of US II Corps, on land. The 1st Infantry Division, with Combat Command B (CCB), 1st Armored Division, attached, was to make the main assaults.[48]

The great unknown of Operation Torch was whether or not the 120,000 French troops in North Africa would fight hard or quickly surrender and join the Allies. The planners believed that the French would probably fight the British since the British had attacked the French navy in 1940 to prevent its vessels from being available to the Germans. They hoped the French would allow American troops to land unopposed.[49]

While the planners worked through the issues related to the first combined Allied operation, the assault units conducted amphibious training. The 1st Infantry Division rotated its regimental combat teams through the Combined Operations Training Center near Rosneath, Scotland, in September. Brigadier Generals Teddy Roosevelt and Clift Andrus supervised this training while Allen prepared the division plan in London.

In mid-October, the division boarded ships for the journey to Algeria. On the night of 17 October 1942, the convoy sailed from the Firth of Clyde to Loch Linnhe, where a final dress-rehearsal exercise known as Mosstrooper took place. Brigadier General Clift Andrus, the division artillery commander, critiqued the exercise before the task force returned to its anchorage in the Clyde estuary.[50]

Central Task Force's plans were finished in late September. General Allen and his staff completed their tactical plan, published as division Field Order One, on 10 October. During the planning, Stanhope Mason, the division G3, identified a major problem in combined Allied amphibious operations. There were differences in terminology for the various beaches between the British and the Americans and between the American army and navy. Mason learned that the British had "a definite method of marking which has much to commend it." He noted that the beach on which the division was to land east of Oran, which had been designated as "Z," had three major parts:

> The British Navy designates these, looking shoreward from the sea from left to right, [as] red, white, and green. This corresponds to the ships' [night running] lights, that is, red for port, white for center or stern, and green for starboard. . . . Under this system of marking, the right battalion of the 18th Infantry lands on Z, Green, West, and so on across. The same system is being employed for the Y Beach landings. . . . If this system of designating beaches is agreeable to the services involved there would be less chance for error and confusion over terminology, and I recommend that we agree on its use.[51]

The British method of designating assault beaches was adopted for Torch and for later amphibious operations.

On 26 October, the Central Task Force ships carrying the Big Red One departed from Scotland. For eleven days, Admiral Troubridge led his convoy southwest into the Atlantic and then east through the Strait of Gibraltar, entering the Mediterranean on 6 November. The following evening, the task force anchored off the beaches west and east of Oran.[52]

Central Task Force planned to capture Oran by enveloping the city (see Map 8). Major General Fredendall's II Corps was in charge of the operations. The 1st Infantry Division's combat teams were to land west and east of Oran early on 8 November. The two forces would then advance on Oran in a pincer movement along the coastal roads. Most of CCB, 1st Armored Division, was to land east of Arzew after the 1st Infantry Division had secured the beach and adjacent roads. CCB was to sweep inland to Ste. Barbe-du-Tielat to cut off enemy reinforcements and to secure an airfield near Ste. Barbe. Then CCB was to drive north to join the assault into the city.

Simultaneously, a task force of the 1st Armored Regiment was to land nearly 30 miles west of Oran at Mersa Bou Zedjar, sweep inland to Lourmel, and join CCB in the vicinity of Valmy. Two ships were to land 400 soldiers of the US 6th Armored Infantry Regiment in Oran's harbor to seize the port facilities before the French could destroy them.[53]

Combat Team (CT) 26, composed primarily of the 26th Infantry Regiment and the 33rd Field Artillery Battalion, was to land 20 kilometers west of Oran, on Y Beach, near Les Andalouses. CT26 was to secure the western flank of the operation and drive east to capture the high ground west of Oran known as Djebel Murdjadjo. The 26th Infantry was to support the final drive into the city from the west. The assistant division commander, Teddy Roosevelt, would accompany Colonel Alexander Stark's Blue Spaders.[54]

Major General Allen was to command the eastern landings of the division at Z Beach, 16 miles east of Oran, on the broad open beach east of the coastal village of Arzew. The 1st Ranger Battalion, led by Lieutenant Colonel William Darby, was to land on the western flank of the division to seize French coastal artillery batteries. Colonel Frank Greer's CT18 was to make the assault on the western side of Z Beach (on Z Green), while Colonel Henry Cheadle's CT16 landed on the left flank of the division (on Z White and Red). CT18 was to seize Arzew and drive toward the eastern outskirts of Oran. CT16 was to secure the Arzew beachhead for the landing of the tanks of CCB, 1st Armored Division, and move west through Fleurus, protecting the left flank of the division as it moved toward Oran.[55]

The 1st Infantry Division in Operation Torch: The Seizure of Oran

The Germans and Italians spotted the hundreds of Allied ships in the western Mediterranean, but they decided that the convoys were headed east to reinforce Montgomery's army in Egypt. Consequently, the Axis Powers concentrated their submarines, surface warships, and aircraft in positions to intercept the Allied flotillas in the strait between Sicily and North Africa. As a result, the Allied Central and Eastern Task Forces sailed unmolested throughout 7 November. Shortly after dark, the convoys changed course to the west and, at approximately 2330 hours, dropped anchor 5 miles offshore and commenced the assault.[56]

The French Oran Division numbered about 9,100 infantrymen scattered in small village garrisons and in Oran. Another 4,000 soldiers manned twelve batteries of coastal artillery along the coast from Les Andalouses to Arzew. The French had forty tanks and armored cars and three squadrons of horse cavalry in the area as well. The II Corps intelligence summary of

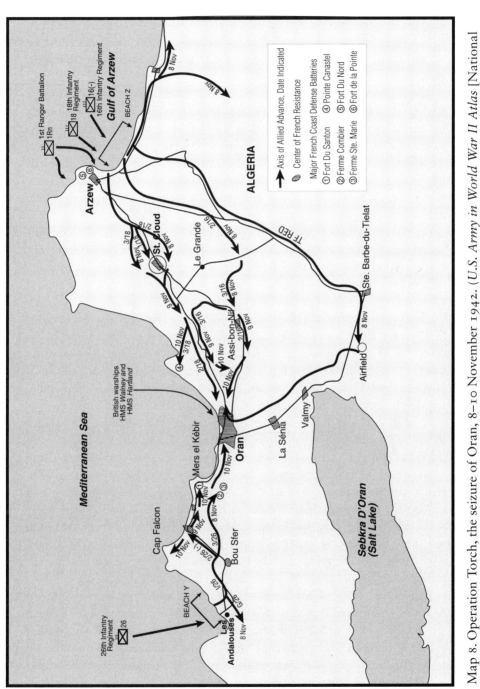

Map 8. Operation Torch, the seizure of Oran, 8–10 November 1942. (*U.S. Army in World War II Atlas* [National Historical Society, 1995])

20 September 1942 noted that the Oran garrison commander, General Paul Hippolyte, was anti-Vichy, but the overall French commander in Algeria, General M. L. Koetz, was anti-British.[57] Allen told the division to be prepared for stiff resistance but also to watch for any French troops trying to surrender and to facilitate their efforts.[58]

At X Beach, a force organized around a battalion of the 1st Armored Division and the 591st Engineer Boat Regiment landed unopposed (Map 8). By 0900, the tanks were ashore and a company from the 13th Armored Regiment was on its way inland to Lourmel. Meeting only minor resistance, the task force cleared Lourmel, established a blocking position southwest of that town, and pushed its main elements east to Misserrhin. Finding Misserrhin occupied by hostile French troops, the task force bivouacked for the night.[59]

On Y Beach, CT26 loaded its assault boats just before midnight on 7 November. While the British cruiser *Aurora* engaged a French convoy that blundered into the area, the heavily loaded infantrymen climbed down the nets into the bouncing boats below the five troopships. The first wave started the 6-mile run to shore at about 2345. It took well over an hour to reach the beach, which fortunately was not defended. The 3rd Battalion landed first, on the eastern side of Y Beach, followed by the 2nd Battalion in the center. The most troubling mishap for the first wave was the discovery that there was a sandbar paralleling the shore that prevented the assault craft from reaching shore. Inside the sandbar, the water was 4–5 feet deep, and a number of jeeps and guns foundered and had to be recovered later.[60]

Once it was clear that Y Beach was undefended, the second wave of landing craft approached the beach and the transports moved to within 2,000 meters of shore. By 0500, 2,670 men and 33 vehicles had landed, including Battery B, 33rd Field Artillery.[61] The artillery battery, specially armed with light 75mm howitzers, was attached to 3rd Battalion, 26th Infantry, and advanced to firing positions 2 miles east of Bou Sfer. By 1100, Batteries A and C had landed. The artillerymen served as infantry to protect the beach area until their 105mm howitzers came ashore late in the afternoon. Before daylight on 9 November, all of the battalion's howitzers were ashore and in position to support CT26.[62]

As planned, the 3rd Battalion, 26th Infantry, assembled east of Les Andalouses and moved inland to secure Bou Sfer. The capture of Bou Sfer, on the northern slopes of Djebel Murdjadjo, was the first step of the combat team's advance to Oran. Leaving Company L in Bou Sfer, John Bowen's 3rd Battalion continued east to Ferme Combier. There, at about 0730, the battalion "was pinned down by vicious fire" from the crest of Djebel Murdjadjo.

Unable to move without heavy casualties, and lacking artillery and armor support, Bowen ordered his men to dig in.[63]

While the 3/26th moved east, the 2nd Battalion pushed Company G and the battalion's antitank platoon west to El Ancor to establish a blocking position to protect the western flank of the combat team. The rest of the battalion advanced east to Ain el Turk and Cape Falcon, the location of a French artillery battery. Shortly after Company G had established a position near El Ancor, three French light tanks attacked. Within minutes, the Americans destroyed the tanks, leaving three hulks burning on the road. To the east, however, 2nd Battalion was unable to reach the French artillery batteries on Cape Falcon and Djebel Santon, north of Djebel Murdjadjo, before their fire forced some of the transports to weigh anchor and move farther offshore. The French forts placed effective artillery fire on the 2nd Battalion, forcing it to dig in for the night about 2,000 yards to the west of Ain el Turk.[64]

As the two assault battalions advanced, the 1st Battalion, 26th Infantry, landed and established reserve positions near Les Andalouses. During the night of 8 November, Lieutenant Colonel Verdi Barnes's 33rd Field Artillery Battalion hammered the French batteries to the north and east. By nightfall, the situation was stable. Casualties had been light, and a stream of French prisoners indicated that the defenders' hearts were not in the struggle. On the beach, logistical units established supply dumps and pushed food, water, and munitions forward.[65]

Brigadier General Roosevelt arrived at Colonel Stark's command post at Bou Sfer during the afternoon of 8 November, injecting energy into CT26's operations. French resistance in front of Bowen's 3rd Battalion was the biggest challenge facing the combat team. Roosevelt sent Company C, 1st Engineers, forward to reinforce Bowen. The engineers, mounted in M3 half-tracks, negotiated the long, twisting road from Bou Sfer to Bowen's positions and from there used their .50-caliber machine guns to neutralize the French positions around the Ferme Ste. Marie. The 26th Regiment's Cannon Company also reinforced the 3rd Battalion, providing fire from its 105mm cannons against French bunkers. For the remainder of 9 November, Bowen's men slowly worked their way toward the crest of Djebel Murdjadjo supported by the engineers and artillery fire.[66]

While the 3rd Battalion fought its way up Djebel Murdjadjo, the 2nd Battalion advanced through sniper fire into the village of Ain el Turk. The village was secured by 1600, 9 November, allowing the battalion to advance along the coast to Bouisseville. To the north of Ain el Turk, a French artillery unit fought to the last in the face of an assault by Company F. Fewer than a quarter of the French artillerymen survived the engagement. By afternoon, 2nd Battalion had reached Bouisseville, where it held up for the night.[67]

On 9 November, faced with strong resistance on Murdjadjo, Colonel Stark committed Major Robert Tucker's 1st Battalion on the right of Bowen's 3rd Battalion. Tucker's men moved through Bou Sfer and seized Hill 510, on the crest of Murdjadjo. This move allowed the 33rd Artillery to establish an observation post overlooking the plains west of Oran. By evening, the three battalions of CT26 were in a line facing Oran, with the 33rd Artillery prepared to support an assault into the city.[68]

Operations on Beach Z

The Torch plan called for two-thirds of the 1st Infantry Division to land 20 miles to the east of Oran near the small port of Arzew. The naval force of thirty-four transports and twenty escorting warships anchored 5 miles off the Gulf of Arzew at about 2345, 7 November. The 1st Ranger Battalion was attached to the division for the assault. The rangers landed on the western flank of Z Beach to capture French forts and artillery batteries north of Arzew. Two ranger companies landed directly in Arzew Harbor, where they captured the surprised garrison. Meeting some resistance, three ranger companies landed on the headlands north of Arzew and overcame the defenders of the French batteries there by 0400. After daybreak, French sniper and mortar fire from the west of Arzew caused minor difficulties to the rangers and navy personnel who had landed to operate the port. Nonetheless, by 0630 the area had been secured.[69]

CT18, with the 32nd Field Artillery, landed on the western side of the 3-mile-long beach east of Arzew beginning about 0120, 8 November. Colonel Frank Greer's 3rd and 1st Battalions landed side-by-side. The 3rd Battalion moved northwest to the edge of Arzew, where it met some resistance. At about 0400, the battalion seized a barracks, capturing sixty-two French soldiers. The battalion overcame more serious resistance in the port with fire from its 60mm mortars, capturing 13 seaplanes and 200 prisoners before moving west of town. The 1st Battalion, 18th Infantry, met no resistance when it landed, allowing Major Richard Parker to reorganize his battalion and push inland toward St. Cloud.[70]

The first check imposed by the French on the 18th Infantry's advance happened west of Renan, where Parker's men ran into French armored cars. Men of Company C destroyed four cars with rifle fire and antitank grenades. A fifth armored car advanced about 400 yards toward the battalion before it was destroyed. After this fight, Company C reached the edge of St. Cloud and launched a hasty attack to seize the town center. The leading infantrymen were met by rifle, machine-gun, and artillery fire and recoiled to avoid heavy losses.[71]

While the 1/18th was advancing inland, Major Ben Sternberg's 2nd Battalion landed, followed shortly by the 32nd Field Artillery Battalion. By 0840, the first two howitzers of the 32nd came ashore with the antitank and cannon companies of the regiment. The cannon company and artillery moved inland to support Parker's 1st Battalion near St. Cloud. The 2/18th reorganized and then pushed inland through Renan, to positions on the southeastern side of St. Cloud. By 1530, these reinforcements and the 1st Battalion launched a coordinated attack against St. Cloud.

The French defenders met these moves with heavy fire, preventing the American infantry from getting a toehold in the village. St. Cloud was a tough nut to crack. The town's stone buildings made perfect defensive positions. The vineyards surrounding the town gave the defenders clear fields of fire, since the vines were newly planted and fairly short. The town was defended by the 16th Tunisian Infantry Regiment and a battalion of Foreign Legion infantry. These units were supported by fourteen 75mm guns, numerous machine guns and mortars, and four 37mm antitank guns.[72] The French were in no mood to surrender, and once the initial American attack had been repulsed and blood shed, both sides were up for a fight. Colonel Greer now committed most of CT18 to the capture of St. Cloud, since that village blocked the most direct route to Oran.

After the second attack was repulsed, Greer brought his 3rd Battalion to positions to the north of St. Cloud. French artillery fire slowed the advance of the 3rd Battalion. Nonetheless, by dark, CT18 was arrayed with its infantry battalions in a semicircle around St. Cloud. At 2100, Terry Allen told Greer to seize St. Cloud with an assault to be launched at 0700, 9 November.[73]

The remainder of the combat power of the division was CT16. CT16 landed its 1st and 3rd Battalions unopposed, beginning about 0100, 8 November. Colonel Henry Cheadle's regiment was to seize and protect the eastern side of the beach for the subsequent landing of CCB, 1st Armored Division. The 3/16th landed on the right, next to CT18. Initially, there was some confusion because the assault boats came in too far west. This was overcome as the battalion reorganized and moved to make contact with CT18. By 0730, the battalion had occupied the high ground east of Fleurus. For the remainder of 8 November, Lieutenant Colonel Frederick Gibb's 3rd Battalion moved west under intermittent fire. By 2200, the troops had occupied Fleurus without serious resistance and advanced west another mile.[74]

Major William Cunningham's 1st Battalion, 16th Infantry, landed on target to the east of 3rd Battalion. The 1st Battalion quickly set out eastward

along the coastal road to La Macta. The infantrymen surprised French garrisons along the coast, taking many prisoners without suffering any casualties.
Between La Macta and En Nekala, 5 miles inland, the battalion established
positions to protect the left flank of the division and to cover the landing of CCB on Z Beach. The French garrison in La Macta put up a stiff
fight, forcing the battalion to make an assault supported by Battery A, 7th
Field Artillery. La Macta fell at 1330, and En Nekala was occupied without
resistance.[75]

The personnel of the 7th Field Artillery Battalion came ashore after daylight on 8 November. At 1224, 8 November, Battery A fired its first rounds
in support of the 16th Infantry at La Macta. Once in that village, the battery
moved to firing positions south of town and registered fires on the La Macta
Bridge. The next morning, when a battalion of French infantry counterattacked from the south, the gunners opened direct fire against French machine gunners and infantrymen. Six artillerymen were wounded before the
French retreated.[76]

First Infantry Division's success on 8 November allowed CCB, 1st Armored Division, to land unopposed. Light tanks and armored cars were
brought ashore by shallow-draft oil tankers that the British had modified to
make the prototypes of the vessel known as the Landing Ship, Tank (LST).
The British had cut the bows off these "Lake Maracaibo" tankers and fitted
a ramp to the vessel to allow vehicles to load and unload through the bow.[77]
Lacking the larger LSTs in 1942, the Sherman tanks were unloaded at the
dock in Arzew Harbor, delaying their availability for battle until after that
port was captured.

Ashore by 0820, a task force of light tanks and infantrymen drove 25
miles south. By 1115, the armored column had secured the crossroads at Ste.
Barbe-du-Tielat and reached the French Tafaraoui Airfield. At 1215, the task
force captured the airfield. As the tankers finished this job, a French ammunition train approached on the nearby railway. The task force captured the
train and prepared to send a column north to seize La Senia Airfield. Tafaraoui Airfield received its first Allied planes at about 1630. Although French
resistance prevented CCB from capturing La Senia, CCB's task forces cut the
main rail and road routes into Oran on D-day. The wider pincer movement
around the city had gone as planned. On 9 November, the armored forces
were ready to join the 1st Infantry Division in its closer encirclement of the
port.[78]

During most of 9 November, Terry Allen focused his attention on the
division's missions to protect II Corps' eastern flank and to drive as swiftly
as possible into Oran. Communications with Roosevelt and CT26 were

sporadic, but Allen knew that they were making progress up Djebel Murdj-adjo.[79] Things did not go as well east of Oran.

The attack by Colonel Greer's CT18 against St. Cloud, at 0700, 9 November, was repulsed by heavy French fire. Only a few platoons made it to the outskirts of the town before Greer ordered a retreat. Greer called for reinforcements and planned for another attack with all of his battalions at 1400. Allen initially decided to support Greer's attack with a battalion from CT16 and all available artillery. However, at 1355, Allen entered Greer's CP and ordered the barrage and attack cancelled. Instead, Allen ordered Greer to leave his 1st Battalion, reinforced with Company K, to contain the French in St. Cloud while the remainder of CT18 and most of CT16 bypassed St. Cloud and drove toward Oran. This was perhaps Allen's best decision of the operation. He refocused the division's main effort on its primary mission, and he spared the civilian population of St. Cloud the losses that additional fighting in the town would have caused.[80]

During the afternoon and evening of 9 November, Allen, Brigadier General Lunsford Oliver of CCB, and Colonel Claude Ferenbaugh, the II Corps operations officer, developed the plan for the final assault on Oran. The attack was to begin at 0715 the next day. Five infantry battalions were to move along the roads from St. Cloud and Arzew into the eastern section of the city. CCB, 1st Armored Division, was to launch task forces into the southern side of Oran, bypassing French resistance in Valmy and La Senia. CT26 was to attack the western side of Oran from Djebel Murdjadjo. Allen's order to the division for this operation was a masterpiece of brevity. In fewer than a hundred words, the order directed the combat team commanders to follow the routes and scheme of maneuver indicated on an attached map overlay. Allen made his intent clear in his order: "Nothing in Hell must delay or stop this [attack]."[81]

Allen could direct a complicated maneuver with a short order because training over the past year had prepared his leaders to do so using SOPs. Allen and Roosevelt also had instilled in the division's commanders a clear understanding of Allen's intent and philosophy in tactical situations. George Marshall sent a copy of this field order to President Roosevelt as an example of how far the army had progressed from the multipaged orders that had so irked Marshall during the 1930s war games and the long orders of World War I.[82]

During the night of 9–10 November, US Colonel d'Alary D. Fechet delivered the attack orders to Colonels Greer (CT18) and Cheadle (CT16). Gibb's 3rd Battalion had been moving steadily northwest during the night of 9 November when it received instructions to retrace its route south from

the Arcole–St. Cloud Road and join the 2nd Battalion on the road into
Oran from Fleurus. Somehow Gibb's tired infantrymen successfully made
this move by 0600, falling in behind the 2nd Battalion on the designated
road.

The 2nd Battalion, 16th Infantry, also had continued its advance west at
about 1700, 9 November. It encountered French resistance about 2 miles
west of Assi Bou Nif, which it quickly overcame. Receiving the order to continue into Oran, Cheadle ordered the 2nd Battalion to resume its advance
at about 0200 so as to reach the division's designated line of departure by
0715. At around 0730, 10 November, the 3/16th started to move into Oran.
As the infantry advanced, the cannon company suppressed French artillery
and machine guns to the west of the Ferme St. Jean Baptiste. Otherwise, the
advance was unopposed. With the 3rd Battalion following as a reserve, the
infantry of 2nd Battalion entered Oran by 1030.[83]

Meanwhile, east of the city, the 3rd Battalion, 18th Infantry, captured
French artillery batteries on the coast near Pointe Canastel, while the 2nd
Battalion headed toward Arcole, on the road to Oran. The 2nd Battalion
overran Arcole at about 1030. About 200 French soldiers surrendered, indicating that French morale was cracking. At around 1100, the 32nd Artillery,
reinforced by a battery of the 5th Artillery, hammered the French artillery
at Pointe Canastel and La Briqueterie, facilitating the capture by the 3rd
Battalion, 18th Infantry, of those coastal positions. Greer's 2nd Battalion
reached the outskirts of Oran at about 1000 and awaited orders to enter the
city.[84]

Teddy Roosevelt and Colonel Stark had not received much information
from Allen during the first two days of the battle. Finally, late on 9 November, Allen was able to have a message dropped by a British Spitfire telling
Roosevelt to "shoot the works on F[ield].O[rder]. No. 1 at once."[85] By that
evening, the 1st Battalion, 26th Infantry, had consolidated positions on top
of Djebel Murdjadjo, and the 3rd Battalion was preparing to advance down
the mountain on the road into Oran. The 2nd Battalion, 26th Infantry, had
cleared the French out of Ain et Turk but had not taken the batteries of Fort
du Stanton. Late on the morning of 10 November, the 3rd Battalion's attack
toward Oran was cancelled by General Fredendall, who had received word
that Oran was on the verge of surrender.[86]

The capture of Oran was accomplished by armored task forces of CCB
acting in accordance with the corps plan. As the infantrymen of CT16 entered the outskirts of Oran, at about 1100, they noticed a tank coming out
of Oran, toward their positions. Before they opened fired, they identified the
white star on the front. The tank was from the 1st Battalion, 1st Armored

Regiment, and had been sent to notify the 1st Infantry Division that the French had agreed to a cease-fire to commence at 1215.[87]

Immediately upon the implementation of the cease-fire, and before the final terms were completed, Allen ordered his combat team commanders to secure the critical installations in Oran. CT18 secured the dock and the coastal defense installations; CT16 sent two battalions into the center of Oran to protect government buildings, water-supply facilities, and electrical installations. These actions were taken as part of the preinvasion plan in which high priority was given to the need to protect the infrastructure of Oran so as to facilitate future operations. CT26 used its 3rd Battalion to secure the western side of the city and its 2nd Battalion to seize La Senia Airfield.[88]

The final armistice was signed at 1230, 10 November. The French were left in command of the city with the responsibility to provide civilian and military police. American forces took control of and guarded all critical installations. Central Task Force headquarters moved into the Grand Hotel the next morning. As things quieted down, the Big Red One withdrew its troops to assembly areas outside the city.[89]

Assessment of the Division's Role at Oran

General Allen was pleased with the conduct of his troops: they successfully conducted a night amphibious invasion, secured the beachhead, and conducted converging attacks on a large city. The regimental combat team concept combining infantry, artillery, and engineers in a single organization proved its worth. Allen noted, however, that additional armored support and reconnaissance assets were needed in the combat teams and the division. The division's ability to operate on two widely separated fronts and to maneuver day and night vindicated the triangular divisional structure.

Allen further noted that there had been too few troopships and landing craft available for the operation, making it impossible to keep the combat teams and their subordinate battalion landing teams intact in the initial landings. The difficulties in landing heavy artillery and transportation equipment hindered operations. Inadequate communications equipment made command and control difficult.

Losses had been remarkably light, due in part to the surprise achieved by the night landings. The 1st Medical Battalion treated 314 wounded soldiers. There are no records available for the number of men treated and returned to duty by the medical companies that were attached to the combat teams. Combat Teams 16 and 18 reported a total of 65 men killed in action and

196 men wounded. The artillery battalions suffered a total of seven battle casualties, only one of whom was killed. No record of losses seems to exist for CT26 beyond the report that 96 wounded were treated by the 2nd Clearing Platoon, Company D.[90] Nonetheless, the 1st Infantry Division had been baptized again in combat, a quarter-century after its first actions on the French countryside.

6

Tunisia
The Division Comes of Age

THE 1ST INFANTRY DIVISION PERFORMED WELL in Operation Torch, vindicating its training and demonstrating the high quality of its leaders. Fighting the Vichy French, however, was not the same as fighting the German Wehrmacht. For the next four months, the Big Red One was denied the chance to fight as a united division against the Axis forces. Instead, its units were committed piecemeal in Tunisia. Although Generals Allen and Roosevelt were two of the few proven American commanders in North Africa, their talents were wasted until disaster overtook the American forces at Kasserine, in February 1943.

The Allies' First Drive to Tunis: November–December 1942

The Torch landings were the first step in securing French North Africa before the Germans and Italians could move significant combat power to Tunisia. The plan called for a rapid advance east from Algiers to secure the Tunisian ports of Bizerte and Tunis. General Kenneth Anderson's Eastern Task Force, soon to be renamed the British First Army, was to push east while American units secured Morocco and Algeria.

The Eastern Task Force began its drive to capture Tunis on 10 November by sending a British brigade by sea to Bougie, 100 miles east of Algiers. The 6th Battalion, Royal West Kent Regiment, landed in the Gulf of Bougie the next morning. There was little French opposition. By 12 November, the British had secured Bougie and the airfield farther east at Djidjelli. The same day, another British naval force landed a Commando battalion unopposed in the port of Bone, 125 miles from Bizerte.[1]

The Germans reacted forcefully to these landings. Luftwaffe units occupied the airfields around Bizerte and Tunis without resistance and then attacked the anchorage at Bougie on 11 and 12 November. The British lost three transports and an antiaircraft ship. These German successes were the first of many over the next three months as their possession of the all-weather airfields in Tunisia allowed German aircraft to support Axis ground operations. The inability of the Allied air forces to secure bases closer to the action was a crucial factor in German tactical success.[2]

Anderson also sent forces overland to Tunisia, hoping to get to Tunis before the Axis could build up a strong presence. A task force from the 78th British Infantry Division moved from Bone, Algeria, on 14 November, to the port of Tabarka, Tunisia (Map 9). This advance was accompanied by airborne drops of British and American paratroopers who captured the airfield at Youks-les-Bains, near Tebessa, 120 miles inland. By 16 November, the British had secured Tabarka and were poised to move farther east. Over the next two days, a British brigade occupied Djebel Abiod as the 78th Division moved east. It was hoped that Eastern Task Force units would be well established in northern Tunisia and ready to seize Bizerte within a week.[3]

The Torch landings forced the French to make difficult decisions. Hitler summoned Vichy representatives to Germany and demanded that the French resist the Allied invasions. The French in Algeria and Morocco opposed the landings with varying degrees of vigor, but their capitulations on 10 and 11 November caused the Germans to hasten forces to Tunisia to disarm the French troops. On 9 November, the Vichy government notified the Germans that they could use the Tunisian airfields. By that evening, German aircraft and ground personnel started to arrive. German paratroopers landed at the same time to protect the airfields. Over the next three weeks, the Germans and Italians poured 15,000 troops and 581 tons of supplies into Tunisia by air. At the same time, they sent ground forces to Tunisia by sea. On 12 November, Italian transports entered the Bizerte Harbor carrying 340 men, 17 tanks, 4 guns, 55 trucks, 40 tons of ammunition, and 101 tons of fuel.[4]

On 11 November, the Germans occupied Vichy France. Fortunately for the Allies, the French scuttled their main fleet in Toulon. Once the independence of Vichy ended, several of the French commanders in Tunisia shifted their allegiance to the Free French Forces. The French garrisons in Bizerte and Tunis were not so lucky, due to their commanders' indecision. The Germans disarmed the French troops in Tunisia, gaining complete control of the area.[5]

From the soldiers' perspectives, it was good to have the French as allies again. Members of the 1st Infantry Division did their "utmost to reestablish the intimate contact of the past with these friends of ours and since their resistance to us was of necessity we hold no animosity for them." Americans fortunate to cultivate relationships with Frenchmen learned that "their lot has been one of almost unspeakable sorrow." The entrance of the United States into the war made that struggle one of "the whole world rising in answer to the challenge of freedom."[6]

Meanwhile, Anderson's troops continued their advance toward Bizerte. Anderson, however, found it difficult to supply his forward forces, and the weakness of Allied airpower allowed the Luftwaffe to attack Allied lines of communications at will. On the other side, Hitler determined that it was essential for the Axis forces to hold North Africa. Therefore, he committed increasing amounts of men and equipment to the Tunisian theater and selected Field Marshal Albert Kesselring to serve as the commander for Axis efforts in the Mediterranean. Kesselring quickly took hold of the situation in northern Tunisia and created a coherent front in the path of the Allied advance.

In a series of sharp engagements in northern Tunisia, from 18 to 23 November, the Germans stopped the British advance. Further movement toward his objectives would require Anderson to bring up additional combat units to defeat the enemy forces in the good defensive terrain of mountainous northern Tunisia.[7] Consequently, Eisenhower sent CCB, 1st US Armored Division, to join the British advance and ordered II Corps to provide artillery units to reinforce the British and French. The first units of the Big Red One to see action against the Germans did so, therefore, as part of a conglomerate Allied force, rather than as part of a unified division.

The Scattering of the Division to Tunisia

On 19 November, the 5th Field Artillery Battalion was ordered to move east the next morning. Allen was not pleased to send his units piecemeal into Tunisia, but he sent the 5th Artillery off with the division band playing "When the Caissons Go Rolling Along" as the batteries trooped past the division color guard.[8]

Lieutenant Colonel Robert Tyson's 5th Artillery Battalion drove from Oran to Arba in four days and reported to the British 78th Division. On 24 November, the artillerymen continued east to Souk Ahras, where they joined the 11th Brigade. The battalion's mission was to support the British drive along the Medjerda River Valley through Medjez el Bab, Tebourba, and Djedeida. If the 11th Brigade could capture Djedeida, it would rupture the German defenses. The 11th Brigade was one of three columns Anderson set in motion to capture the critical crossroads of Mateur and Djedeida. Units of CCB, 1st US Armored Division, also were parceled out to support these British efforts.[9]

On 27 November, the British ordered Colonel Tyson to move the 5th Artillery to positions northeast of Tebourba. The battalion reconnaissance party reached Tebourba only to find that the Germans occupied the town. The battalion halted while British infantry drove the Germans east. The next day, 11th Brigade ordered the 5th Artillery to reconnoiter a site north of Djedeida, 7 miles beyond Tebourba. The reconnaissance party arrived at Tebourba during a German air attack and discovered that Axis ground forces were between them and Djedeida. Nonetheless, Tyson received orders to move his battalion to positions northeast of Djedeida that night.

At about 2100, Tyson set out for Djedeida with his S3 (operations officer) and battery commanders to find suitable firing positions. The battalion was to follow in two hours. Just as the battalion was preparing to move, a British officer from 11th Brigade arrived with orders canceling the movement. A battalion liaison officer left immediately to notify Colonel Tyson of the change. He never contacted Tyson and his party. Instead, at 0430, 29 November, several members of Tyson's reconnaissance team returned to the battalion bivouac and reported that they had run into heavy enemy fire west of Djedeida. Tyson, his S3, and three battery commanders failed to get away and were presumably killed or captured.[10]

The battalion executive officer, Major L. G. Robinson, reorganized the battalion for combat before receiving orders to move to positions east of Tebourba and to fire in support of the 11th Brigade. On 30 November, the 5th Artillery commenced firing. Over the next twenty-four hours, the battalion supported British efforts to repel an Axis counterattack. On 1 December, the artillerymen fired at targets to the north, east, and south of their positions. "There was intermittent bombing, dive-bombing, and mortaring of our positions during the entire day." Batteries A and B received counterbattery fire but could not change positions due to the need to continue firing. By evening, the Germans had closed in on Tebourba as the 5th Artillery fired over a 1,000 rounds, leaving just fifty rounds total with the guns.[11] The battalion's after-action report summarized the action:

> With no resupply in prospect, the Bn Cmdr [battalion commander] requested authority to withdraw to more secure positions. Our infantry, 2 Co.'s of the Surreys, 11th Brigade, were holding a bridgehead at El Bathan, 1 mi W of Tebourba. . . . It was reported that during the day the road Medjez-Tebourba had been cut off by another enemy armored force which had bypassed our troops at Djedeida and Tebourba. . . . No orders had been received from the CRA [Commander, Royal Artillery] for 48 hours. . . . The Bn Cmdr decided to withdraw to SW of Tebourba.[12]

The battalion drove through Tebourba just before it fell to the Germans and then rolled along the road to Medjez el Bab to positions west of town. The battalion's S4 (logistics officer) reported that there would be no ammunition resupply for at least five days, and the 11th Brigade ordered the artillerymen to be prepared to fight as infantrymen. On 3 December, Battery A was given all available ammunition and attached to the 175th Armored Field Artillery Battalion. The mission of the 175th Artillery was to serve as an antitank screen east of Medjez to protect the town and a nearby airfield.

The 5th Artillery's antitank platoon bolstered roadblocks west of Mateur. On 8 December, the rest of the 5th Artillery moved west as part of an Allied withdrawal to a defensive line between Bedja and Medjez el Bab.[13]

The saga of the 5th Artillery was part of a larger battle in which the enemy had stopped the Allied advance toward Djedeida and Mateur and then counterattacked to expand their Tunisian bridgehead. In this effort, Kesselring's forces deployed elements of the *10th Panzer Division* reinforced by some of the new Tiger tanks. German lines of supply were less than 50 miles long, while Anderson's supply lines stretched 200 miles to Algiers. Additionally, the Luftwaffe's air superiority over the battlefield enabled it to provide close air support to Axis ground forces.[14] Reluctantly, Eisenhower accepted Anderson's advice to suspend the offensive until the logistical situation could be remedied and the Allied air forces could provide air support.

The 1st Infantry Division also was called on to send four infantry battalions to Tunisia to fight under British or French command. The first to go was the 3rd Battalion, 26th Infantry. On 20 November, Company I, 3rd Battalion, 26th Infantry, boarded C-47 transport planes at the Tafaraoui Airfield for the one-hour flight to Bleda, Algeria, 185 miles inland.[15]

The next morning, Company I, 26th Infantry, flew another 375 miles east to Youks-les-Bains, where the men boarded trucks for the 65-mile trip to Feriana, Tunisia. After a few hours' rest, the company traveled to Gafsa, where it arrived on 22 November. Company I was the lead unit of Lieutenant Colonel John Bowen's 3rd Battalion, whose mission was to secure the town and a nearby airfield. When the infantrymen got to Gafsa, they encountered German paratroopers. After a short engagement, four Germans surrendered, and Company I dug in. Another small German unit attempted to move into Gafsa later that day, but Company I forced it to withdraw.[16]

The Allied seizure of Gafsa opened a new front. Located in central Tunisia, Gafsa was on the road running west to east toward the port city of Gabes. If the Allies could seize Gabes, they would cut off Axis forces in northern Tunisia from Field Marshal Erwin Rommel's army in Libya. Conversely, by holding Gafsa, the Allies blocked Axis forces from moving northwest through Feriana and on to Tebessa, Algeria. Such a move by the enemy would threaten the Allied position in northern Tunisia.

By 30 November the 3rd Battalion, 26th Infantry, had arrived in central Tunisia as part of a task force with the 503rd Airborne Infantry Regiment. Bowen's 1,000 soldiers made up the majority of the American force. The 701st TD Battalion, an engineer detachment, a company of paratroopers, and miscellaneous French forces augmented the 3rd Battalion.[17] Most of the enemy in the area were Italians who had been rushed in from Libya to prevent the Allies from cutting Tunisia in half on the Gafsa-Gabes line.

On 1 December, Companies I and M of the 26th Infantry, accompanied by Company B, 701st TD Battalion, and a French infantry company, moved northeast toward Faid, about 75 miles away. Intelligence reports indicated that about 200 Germans and Italians were entrenched on the high ground overlooking Faid Pass, on the road to the Tunisian coast. On 2 December, Bowen launched an attack against the Axis positions. After some progress, heavy machine-gun and artillery fire stopped the infantrymen short of their objective. The next morning, the Allied force was attacked by German dive-bombers, the first of many such attacks.

On 3 December, a French infantry battalion and a battery of 75mm guns arrived. After a barrage from the French guns and American 81mm mortars, French and American infantry attacked the pass. The French circled to the east of the Axis positions while Company I moved in from the north. By 1700, the pass was in Allied hands and 125 enemy troops had surrendered. The 26th Infantry lost five men killed and fourteen wounded. For the next week, the task force maintained outposts in Faid and nearby Sidi bau Zid. The only threat to these positions and Gafsa came from German air attacks. On 11 December, Bowen's battalion moved to Feriana to defend that base and the airfield at Youks-les-Bains. Outposts were maintained in Gafsa and on the roads east to Faid and Maknassy.[18]

The two remaining battalions of the 26th Infantry moved into Tunisia in December to operate under French command. In mid-January, the 1st and 2nd Battalions moved to Sbeitla, about 50 miles northeast of Feriana. The 26th Infantry Regiment was dispersed to defend the roads across central Tunisia because of growing concern that the Axis forces might launch an offensive in the area to envelop the British army in northern Tunisia from the southeast and cut it off from its supply bases in Algeria.

The war for most of the 26th Infantry Regiment from December 1942 to early February 1943 was characterized by raids and counterraids and long periods of guard duty. On several occasions, Italian raiders got the best of the American outposts around Gafsa. On 16 January, for example, English-speaking Italians penetrated the defenses of Company I and killed or wounded eleven men. The Italians got away with four prisoners. By then, the Allied force around Feriana and Gafsa had grown to over 2,300 men, including the 3rd Battalion, 26th Infantry. Allied outposts and patrols operated as far east as El Guettar. Unfortunately, the Allies' logistical situation did not allow them to launch a drive toward Gabes.

The problems inherent in the intermingling of battalion-size units from three different nations without having worked out the logistical and command difficulties were evident in Allied operations in Tunisia in 1942 and early 1943. American and British radios could not operate on the same frequencies. The British logistical system could not provide the ammunition needed by American units. British commanders forgot their American units at critical times. French forces were inadequately armed, and there was little real cooperation between them and the British.

The 18th Combat Team Joins the Battle

When Eisenhower suspended the offensive in early December, he did so with the understanding that the British, French, and American forces would resume the push east before the end of the year. The command structure in Tunisia remained confusing, to say the least. French troops reported to a French general, Americans remained under the command of Fredendall and Eisenhower, and British troops received their orders from Anderson. Anderson was to coordinate the actions of the Allied contingents, but only through the three separate national ground commanders.

Individual battalions and companies received insufficient logistical and staff support. It was this situation that seriously irritated Terry Allen. His pointed comments to Eisenhower's and Fredendall's staffs created an impression that Allen was not a team player. Worse, Fredendall had not yet established a forward command post that could support the American units moving east.

On 7 December, CT18 received orders to march overland from Oran to Algiers. The next morning, the 18th Infantry moved east, accompanied by the 32nd Field Artillery Battalion. The team reached L'Arbe, 20 miles south of Algiers, on 9 December. During the next six days the combat team prepared for action.[19] By 18 December, CT18 was at Ghardimaora, Tunisia, awaiting further instructions from British 5 Corps. They did not have to wait long. The British commander ordered Colonel Greer to move CT18 east to the vicinity of Medjez el Bab to take part in 78th Division's drive toward Tunis.[20]

The Allies' offensive was to begin on the evening of 24 December. Anderson concentrated his offensive power along the Medjerda River. To make a drive northeast from Medjez el Bab toward Tebourba possible, the 78th British Division had to capture a ridge on the north side of the Medjerda known as Djebel el Ahmera. This mountain, which dominated the highway and railroad along the river, was nicknamed Longstop Hill by the British. The 2nd Battalion, Coldstream Guards, was to capture Longstop on the night of 22 December, making it possible for British and American units to drive northeast along the Medjerda the next day. CT18 was to send its 1st Battalion to relieve the Coldstream Guards and then to hold Longstop. The 3rd Battalion, Coldstream Guards, was to seize the village of Grich el Oued on the south side of the river at the same time.[21]

Djebel el Ahmera (Longstop Hill) was a complex of mountains running from the southwest to the northeast along the northern side of the Medjerda River Valley. The highest of the five points on Longstop was defended by a company of the German *754th Infantry Regiment*. One company of the *754th* also held the small railway station of Halte d'el Heri in the Medjerda Valley. This station controlled the gap between the mountain and the river. Company A of the Coldstream Guards was to seize it on the night of 22 December and then hand it over to Company A, 1st Battalion, 18th Infantry.

The Coldstream Guards captured Point 290 on Longstop Hill and Halte d'el Heri after the defenders ran out of ammunition and retreated. Lieutenant Colonel Robert York's 1st Battalion, 18th Infantry, moved forward as planned but failed to find its British guides due to the miserable visibility of the rainy night. It was early morning before York found the British battalion commander. However, before they could coordinate the relief of the British troops, the commander of the 1st Guards Brigade ordered the Coldstream Guards to withdraw. In this confused situation, the British did not realize that they had cleared only the first three of the five points of Longstop and that the point known as Djebel el Rhar, just east of Point 290, was high enough at 243 meters to allow the Germans to place effective fire on the higher point.[22]

Company B, 18th Infantry, was the first unit to discover that German troops occupied Hill 243 and the lower slopes of Hill 290. Consequently, the GIs began a slugging match with the Germans to clear the final two humps of Longstop. While this action was going on, Company A and half of the regimental antitank platoon approached Halte d'el Heri from the west. There they ran into an ambush and lost all but one officer and thirteen men. The Germans retained control of the railroad station in the Medjerda Valley.

Realizing that the loss of Longstop would open the direct route to Tunis, Kesselring ordered the *69th Panzergrenadier* and the *7th Panzer Regiments* to counterattack. The *Panzergrenadiers* assaulted Longstop early in the afternoon, enveloping York's B and C companies from the northwest. By 1500, the Germans had driven York's men off Hill 290. Within an hour, 1st Battalion, 18th Infantry, struck back. The Germans, however, stopped the attack, forcing York's men to dig in on the southwest of the dominant crest.

Colonel Greer, commander of CT18, convinced the 1st Guards Brigade to reinforce York's hard-pressed command. During the night of 23–24 December, the Coldstream's 2nd Battalion returned to Longstop. The British battalion commander passed one company through Company B, 18th Infantry, to drive the Germans off the dominant ground. At 1700, 24 December, the British attacked, supported by fire provided by the 32nd Field Artillery Battalion and British artillery. By dusk, the Coldstream again had driven the

Germans off Hill 290. Only then did the British realize what they earlier had failed to appreciate: Hill 243 to the northeast was critical to holding Longstop.[23]

During the night, York moved his two uncommitted infantry companies into positions alongside the British, expecting a German counterattack. His situation was less than bright. "Communication and control was most difficult. Wire lines were cut and broken and the SCR 536 radio became wet and failed to function due to the heavy rain which fell throughout the battle."[24] Even more troubling, the forward observers from the 32nd Artillery left their positions on Hill 290 to shelter for the night in the village of Chassart Teffaha, causing a two-hour delay in the artillery support the next morning.[25]

The Germans struck back with attacks by the *69th Panzergrenadier Regiment* from the east and tanks of the *7th Panzer Regiment* along the north side of Longstop. During the battle, the British company on Hill 290 withdrew without notifying York, leaving 1st Battalion's 81mm mortar platoon exposed. York shifted a French infantry company that had just arrived into position to defend the battalion's left flank, but this unit withdrew when German tanks approached. Faced with fire from three sides, York ordered his men to retreat to positions near Chassart Teffaha. By noon, the remnants of York's command were in defensive positions near that village. At 1400, two companies of the Grenadier Guards relieved the 18th Infantry, allowing the exhausted soldiers to fall back to Medjez el Bab. On 26 December, York and his men reached a regimental assembly area at Teboursouk.[26]

The debacle on Longstop was the last Allied attempt to seize Tunis before the Germans could consolidate their bridgehead. York's battalion lost 356 men killed, wounded, or missing. Lacking replacements, Colonel Greer was forced to levy men from his other battalions to refill the depleted ranks of the 1st Battalion. The Coldstream Guards lost 178 men. German losses were heavy, but far fewer than the attackers had lost. Eisenhower agreed to suspend offensive operations for the next month while reinforcements, supplies, and airfields were pushed forward. For Terry Allen, the decimation of the 18th Infantry Regiment was totally frustrating, especially since the regiment remained detached from the division.[27]

The 1st Division Moves East

The 1st Infantry Division finally received orders on 14 January 1943 to deploy all of its units still near Oran, to Guelma, Algeria. Once at Guelma, the division was to constitute the reserve for the Allied Forces Headquarters (AFHQ). No attempt was made to reunite the scattered units of the division already in Tunisia. CT16 moved by rail and road early on 17 January, followed by the rest of the division. It took nearly a week to get the division in place.

As the division moved to Guelma, the German *Fifth Panzer Army* launched attacks to drive the Allies out of the passes of the mountain range in central Tunisia known as the Eastern Dorsal. The German army commander, General Juergen von Armin, knew that it was essential to prevent the Allies from advancing through those passes toward the Tunisian coast. From 18 to 25 January, German kampfgruppen attacked the inadequately armed French XIX Corps.[28]

Kampfgruppe Weber launched the northern attack along the Kabir River on 18 January, with a subsidiary thrust west against the southern flank of the British 5 Corps. This latter attack secured the high ground west of a reservoir that provided most of the water for Tunis. Weber's main effort to the southwest through Pont-du-Fahs and toward Rebaa Oulad Yaha was a more serious move. By the evening of 18 January, the Germans were near Sidi Said. From there, they could continue southwest toward Siliana or south through Hir Moussa and into the Ousseltia Valley. The lightly armed French troops in the Kabir Valley retreated, creating a crisis for Eisenhower. If the Germans drove west, they threatened Anderson's troops in northern Tunisia. If they continued south, they could destroy the French XIX Corps and secure the Eastern Dorsal.[29]

Eisenhower received frantic calls from General Alphonse Juin asking for reinforcements to stop the Germans and to help extricate isolated French units. On 19 January, Eisenhower ordered Anderson to send British troops to Rebaa Oulad Yaha to maintain contact with the French and block further enemy advances. He also directed Fredendall to send CCB, 1st Armored Division, to join the French. CCB reached Kesra, 15 miles west of Ousseltia, the next morning. There the French commander ordered the armor unit to attack north along the Ousseltia Valley to drive *Kampfgruppe Weber* back.[30]

The piecemeal commitment of the Big Red One continued when II Corps ordered Terry Allen to send CT26, consisting of Colonel Alexander Stark's 26th Infantry Regiment (less the 3rd Battalion in Gafsa) and the 33rd Field Artillery Battalion, to Sbeitla on the evening of 19 January. After an all-night journey by truck, "through some of the narrowest and most difficult roads in Tunisia, [with] steep upgrades and inclines, hairpin turns, and dirt roads," CT26 reached Sbeitla. After another night move, the team reached a bivouac site near Ousseltia.[31]

On 21 January, Fredendall ordered Allen to send Colonel d'Alary Fechet's CT16 and the 7th Field Artillery to Maktar, Tunisia. Fechet was to occupy a sector of the new Allied front after CCB had secured positions in the north end of the Ousseltia Valley. Meanwhile, the British 36th Brigade responded to French pleas for help. Moving through Rebaa Oulad Yaha on 21 January, the 5th Battalion (the Buffs) established blocking positions in the Kabir Valley near Sidi Said. By then, the main German effort had turned south toward Ousseltia.

As the British dug in, CCB attacked northward in the Ousseltia Valley. By the end of the day, the armor had pushed the enemy forces back far enough to allow isolated French units to escape. The Germans, however, dug in west of Kairouan Pass, 5 miles east of Ousseltia. Early the next morning, the French ordered CCB to drive north to link up with the British 36th Brigade near Hir Moussa. The 1st Battalion, 13th Armor, attacked to the northeast at about 1430 hours, 22 January, but German resistance stopped the advance well short of its objective.[32]

In response to this action, II Corps ordered CT26 committed to the Ousseltia area. At the same time, Fredendall ordered the 2nd Battalion, 16th Infantry, and the 7th Field Artillery to the Rabaa Oulad Yaha area to reinforce the British 36th Brigade.[33]

CT26 moved from Sbeitla to an assembly area near Ousseltia on 23 January. Upon arrival, the combat team received orders to attack Kairouan Pass, supported by the 7th and 33rd Artillery Battalions. The 2nd Battalion attacked at 0900, 25 January, advancing for three hours before encountering Italian troops. By that time, Lieutenant Colonel Clarence Beck's men had reached the top of Djebel Ribana, on the south side of the pass. At about noon, German 88mm guns opened fire from concealed positions. The 2nd Battalion dug in and called for counterbattery fire from the 33rd Artillery. Verdi Barnes's artillery crews delivered accurate fire on the German positions, silencing the 88s.

At 1600, 2nd Battalion, 26th Infantry, resumed its attack to clear the reverse slope of the djebel. The 33rd and 7th Artillery Battalions protected the infantrymen with a rolling barrage. "Resistance was so ineffective that the positions on Djebel Rihana were occupied and some sixty prisoners taken." Finding Italian morale low, Colonel Stark launched a night assault to seize Djebel Labirech on the northern side of the pass.[34]

Lieutenant Colonel Gerald Kelleher's 1st Battalion, 26th Infantry, moved out at 0200, 26 January, toward its objectives. The infantrymen moved along the eastern slopes of the djebel, hitting the Italians' southeastern flank. "Bayonets were fixed as the men charged up the hills. The attack had been a complete surprise. Men sleeping at their posts were quickly overrun, and organized resistance put up by small bands of men was quickly ended by using automatic rifles."[35] Kelleher's men captured ninety prisoners, ten machine guns, and considerable stores of food and water while suffering few casualties. CT26 dug in, while the 33rd Field Artillery planned fires on the eastern slopes of the two captured djebels. A section of the 601st TD Battalion covered the road to the east against an armor attack. By mid-afternoon, Axis artillery had registered fire on the American positions. Attempts to reach them with artillery counterbattery fire failed due to the extreme ranges involved, and calls for airpower went unanswered. All that Stark could do was move his command post and the firing positions of the 33rd Artillery closer to the pass.

The enemy did not counterattack the 26th Infantry, although American observers noticed movement to the east. To provide his command with early warning, Stark sent Company F forward on the morning of 27 January to occupy the near slope of Djebel Halfa. Stark also sent Company E to protect Company F's flank. German and Italian troops reacted with machine-gun fire from the higher slopes. Artillery from both sides joined the fray during the day. When German infantry moved to outflank his positions, Stark ordered Companies E and F to withdraw. A platoon of Company F provided a rear guard, but in the process was cut to pieces, losing fifty-two men.

While German infantry of the *756th Infantry* maneuvered to the front, the Luftwaffe bombed the combat team's command post and artillery positions. The antiaircraft fire of the 443rd (Antiaircraft) Artillery (AA) failed to down any enemy planes, but it did deter low-level bombing. Late that afternoon, CCB ordered Stark to withdraw all of CT26 except for 2nd Battalion, 26th Infantry, to an assembly area near Sbeitla. This move was accomplished with no enemy interference.[36]

While CT26 was serving with CCB, CT16 received orders from II Corps to move to the northern end of Ousseltia Valley. On 27 January, 2nd Battalion, 16th Infantry, was attached to a British brigade near Sidi Said. The next day, the British commander ordered Lieutenant Colonel Joe Crawford to position one of his companies on Hill 727, also known as Conical Hill. This hill provided an excellent observation post in the path of Axis forces trying to push southwest toward Rebaa Oulad Yaha or south into Ousseltia Valley. On 31 January, elements of the German *334th Infantry Division* attacked. Company G, 16th Infantry, successfully defended itself on Conical Hill, as did the British troops on its flanks. The cost was high—Company G suffered over 100 casualties and was reduced to about 40 effectives before it rejoined the battalion. Crawford's battalion remained with the British until it rejoined the 1st Infantry Division on 3 February.[37]

Finally, on 29 January, Terry Allen received orders to move the remainder of the division to Ousseltia Valley to serve with the French XIX Corps. There Allen assumed command of Allied units and CT16 along the 30 miles of front from Pichon in the south to the northern end of the valley. The division G3, Frederick Gibb, established the command post 3 miles south-west of Ousseltia. Colonel Fechet moved the 1st and 3rd Battalions, 16th Infantry, into defensive positions and assumed control of the 2nd Battalion, 26th Infantry, in its positions on the western side of Kairouan Pass. The 1st Division had six French infantry battalions and two Tabors of Goums, native Moroccan mountain troops, to defend the southern half of the valley. Brigadier General Teddy Roosevelt Jr. commanded the southern sector while Colonel Fechet controlled the northern. The 1st Engineer Battalion provided a mobile reserve along with Company C, 601st TD Battalion, and Company A, 70th Tank Battalion.[38]

The enemy did not attack the Big Red One's sector in Ousseltia Valley, and "activity in this sector was largely restricted to continual active patrolling and to artillery fire."[39] A minor attack by two German companies caught the 60th Goum, Tabor Number 1, by surprise at Si bou Abda on 2 February. The Goumiers lost about 122 men killed and wounded. This was a surprise, since the irregular infantry were renowned for their ability to attack Axis troops when and where least expected. Roosevelt, who spoke fluent French, did an outstanding job organizing his conglomerate command, according to Terry Allen's report to General George Marshall. Roosevelt also made special efforts to provide modern arms and equipment to the French.[40]

The scattered units of the Big Red One now began to reunite. The 5th Field Artillery Battalion was returned to Allen on 4 February. CT18 reverted to division control as well. But confusion in Allied command relationships continued. For example, on 2 February, Allen sent a memo to the commander of the British 90th Artillery Battery explaining the confusion surrounding the deployment of the artillery unit: "Various orders were received regarding your status. At noon yesterday, this headquarters was informed by our corps commander (19th Corps, French) that your battery was attached to this division. . . . We later heard that your status had been changed last night, and that you now reverted to control of 19th Corps. . . . We will inform you as soon as we have any further definite information."[41] On 4 February, the 1st Infantry Division was ordered by both the US II Corps and the French XIX Corps to deploy the 1st Recon Troop to different missions. The division was under the command of the French XIX Corps, although US II Corps was responsible for its logistical and administrative support. As Allen wrote to Fredendall, "It is confusing to receive conflicting directives regarding the disposition of units assigned to the Division. However, I assume that the need for this Reconnaissance Troop to the south is a dire emergency. . . . Therefore, I have directed the 1st Reconnaissance Troop to report to Colonel Stark . . . and have reported my action in this case to General

Koeltz."[42] Ultimately, the 1st Recon Troop remained with the division as part of XIX Corps.

Coordination of the movement of Allied units within the XIX Corps area remained inadequate, due in part to the lack of sufficient communications equipment by the French. On several occasions, "CCB, in executing Corps orders for reconnaissance and other missions, . . . narrowly avoided fatal results due to the lack of coordination between units concerned." Stanhope Mason, the 1st Division's new chief of staff, recommended to XIX Corps that all movement of units in the division's sector be ordered through the division headquarters.[43]

During February, the division needed a significant number of replacements. Having found that many of the new soldiers were poorly trained in critical field skills, Terry Allen established a training camp at Guelma, Algeria, to acclimate the new men and teach them basic combat skills. Allen also recommended that the camp be used by both the 1st and 34th Infantry Divisions and that a British offer for American soldiers to use British training facilities should be accepted.

General Allen recognized the shortcomings of the replacements because he understood the condition of the infantry units firsthand. As his temporary aide, Lieutenant Joe Dawson, wrote in a letter on 15 February,

> When we visited the front lines we went to every unit on the whole sector and the General personally spoke to nearly every man up there. We also visited the observation posts that were often well forward of the front lines themselves. There is nothing that is more inspiring than to have a general walking along the front lines when the bullets are flying, talking with the men and looking around with the same air one would assume walking down Austin Avenue.[44]

Another major concern of Allen's was the inadequate air support he received while in the Ousseltia area. In letters to General Carl Spaatz, General Louis-Marie Koeltz, and Jonathan Anderson, Allen enumerated the twenty-five requests made by the 1st Infantry Division for aerial support or reconnaissance from 29 January to 13 February. Only nine of the requests were granted: none of the air missions damaged the enemy.[45] This unsatisfactory situation was partially a result of the continuing shortage of all-weather air bases, but it was also caused by the lack of adequate ground-air control procedures and practices.

The Luftwaffe, in contrast, flew from bases just east of Kairouan Pass. As a result, Allen reported that "daylight movement of combat vehicles in the Valley brought almost immediate strafing. Two German planes, particularly, nick-named 'Ike and Mike' by the soldiers were very annoying in their strafing and diving tactics. Even a lone jeep was a fair target for 'Ike and Mike.'"[46]

During the second week of February, Allen considered launching an attack to secure Kairouan Pass. However, it became clear that French XIX Corps would have to be pulled back to maintain contact with Allied units that had been pushed back by the enemy farther south. Consequently, Allen concluded that it would be a waste of lives to seize ground that would be soon abandoned. This was a wise decision, since XIX Corps ordered the division to withdraw to the high ground on the western side of the valley on 15 February.[47]

The Battles of Kasserine Pass

As part of the Axis efforts in January to control the passes through the Eastern Dorsal, strong elements of the *21st Panzer Division* moved to seize Faid Pass east of Sbeitla. The German division attacked two battalions of French infantry in the pass on the night of 29–30 January. The French stubbornly held on to positions in the village of Sidi bau Zid and in Faid Pass, hoping that American reinforcements would come to their aid. Combat Command A (CCA), 1st Armored Division, received the mission to relieve the French. However, the combat command failed to push its armor to Faid Pass in time to dislodge the attackers. A small task force did reach Sidi bau Zid, but stopped when it observed Germans to the south. At about 1430, CCA halted for the night, leaving the French to their own slim resources.[48]

When the Germans struck Faid Pass, CT26 (minus its 2nd and 3rd Battalions) had just moved to Sbeitla to serve as part of II Corps reserve. At 0030, 30 January, Colonel Stark received orders to move CT26 to Djebel Lessouda, 7 miles west of Faid Pass where CT26 was attached to CCA. The combat team reached the Lessouda area that evening and prepared to attack the next morning. The plan called for the team's single infantry battalion to advance across the open ground between Djebel Lessouda and Faid, while a battalion of armor attacked on the right, south of the Sbeitla-Faid Road. Amazingly, considering the enemy's dominating positions, the two available infantry companies of 1st Battalion, 26th Infantry, captured several low hills west of Faid Pass. But the tank battalion bogged down in soggy ground and lost nine tanks to German antitank fire.[49]

The 33rd Field Artillery tried to suppress the antitank guns, but CCA could not make progress. At 1320, CCA ordered Lieutenant Colonel Gerald Kelleher to withdraw his infantry to Lessouda. Kelleher extricated his companies in the early hours of darkness. Throughout the battle, CCA failed to concentrate its forces or coordinate the attacks of separate battalions. The best chance to recapture Faid Pass had been lost. As the official history concluded, "Prompt decisive action could well have saved Faid Pass and altered the grim course of the Tunisian campaign in the coming weeks."[50]

Fredendall ordered CCA to make another attempt to seize Faid Pass. The new plan called for the 1/26th to attack from positions east of Lessouda to seize Djebel Ain Rebaou, on the south side of Faid Pass. The 1st Battalion, 6th Armored Infantry, was to attack simultaneously from Sidi bau Zid. The 33rd Field Artillery opened a preparation barrage at 1130, 1 February, followed half an hour later by the advance of Kelleher's infantrymen. The 1/6th Infantry failed to attack on time, leaving Kelleher's men on their own. The Germans held their fire until they were at the base of the djebel. Then they unleashed a hail of artillery, tank, and machine-gun fire. Kelleher's men were slammed to the ground, as were the soldiers of the 1/6th Infantry, who finally had moved forward. The two battalions retreated 4 miles west to Sidi bau Zid, where they remained for the next five days. CT26 lost 120 men in its attempts to recapture Faid Pass. On 8 February, CT168, of the 34th Infantry Division, relieved CT26, allowing the latter to return to Sbeitla to refit.[51] Eisenhower's failure to force Anderson and Fredendall to employ battalions and regiments as part of coherent divisions again had proven costly.

Fredendall's failure to recapture Faid Pass and the abortive operations of Combat Command C (CCC), 1st Armored Division, at Sened and Maknassy farther south, convinced the Germans that they could secure all passes through the Eastern Dorsal and might even push forces across the high Tunisian Plain between the Eastern and Western Dorsals. The loss of Faid Pass forced II Corps to assume a defensive stance. Worse, Fredendall scattered the combat commands of the 1st Armored Division from Gafsa to Sbeitla. To reinforce his long front, Fredendall also arranged to have CT18 move from the British First Army to the vicinity of Rebaa Oulad Yaha, while Stark's CT26 (-) shifted to Feriana, northwest of Gafsa. The initiative lay with the enemy.

On 13 February, Eisenhower, Anderson, and Fredendall agreed to hold an outpost line between the Western and Eastern Dorsals with positions at Gafsa, Sidi bau Zid, and Pichon (Map 9). This line would protect the airfield at Thelepte and the approaches to the passes through the Western Dorsal. The concern was to protect the right flank of Anderson's British First Army as it prepared for a spring offensive. These dispositions also protected II Corps' supply installations around Tebessa.[52]

As the Allies moved units, von Arnim launched an attack with the *10th* and *21st Panzer Divisions* to capture Sidi bau Zid and Djebel Lessouda. CCA, 1st Armored Division, and CT168 held Djebel Lessouda, Sidi bau Zid, and Djebel Ksaira when the Germans attacked on 14 February. The

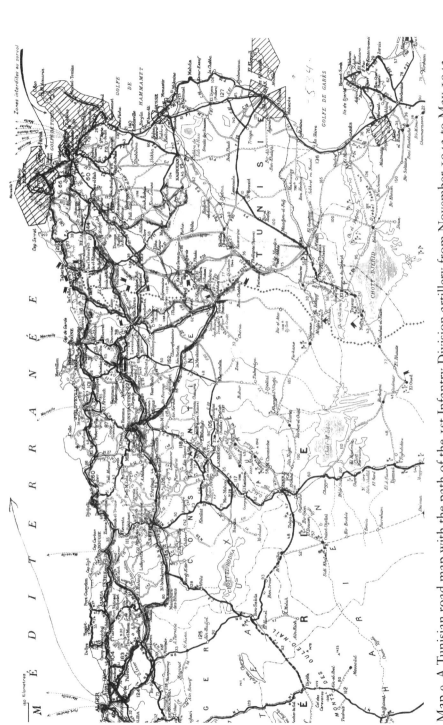

Map 9. A Tunisian road map with the path of the 1st Infantry Division artillery from November 1942 to May 1943 marked by the commander, Brigadier General Clif Andrus. (McCormick Research Center Collections)

Germans pinned down the 168th Infantry with frontal assaults while armored forces maneuvered around the flanks of the American positions. By afternoon, CT168 and much of CCA were surrounded. German air attacks also destroyed the 17th Field Artillery Battalion. Those elements of CCA that still could move retreated west to Sbeitla, leaving the infantrymen of CT168 on Djebels Lessouda and Ksaira, south of Faid Pass.[53]

Allied intelligence failed to identify the *10th Panzer Division* in the attack, which made Anderson unwilling to release British forces to aid the beleaguered Americans. Making things worse, Fredendall was not far enough forward to get a sense of what was happening, and Major General Orlando Ward, commanding general of the 1st Armored Division, was not in charge of his division's scattered combat commands, thanks to the piecemeal way Fredendall had committed them.

Meanwhile, with CCA's headquarters in Sidi bau Zid about to be surrounded, the command moved west to Sbeitla. This move sparked panic among some artillery units, beginning a mad dash by American units toward Sbeitla. According to the commander of the 168th Infantry, CCA's commander "fled so fast he even left his codebook."[54] The only thing between the Germans and Sbeitla was Lieutenant Colonel William Kern's 1st Battalion, 6th Armored Infantry. Brigadier General Raymond McQuilin ordered Kern to establish a blocking position at a crossroads on the road to Faid. This position became known as Kern's Crossroads.[55]

Major General Ward now was given charge of the battle and prepared to launch CCC in a counterattack to relieve the stranded troops on Djebels Lessouda and Ksaira. This attack got under way at 1240, 15 February. Moving cross-country, the force was led by three columns of tanks with antitank units on the flanks and mounted infantrymen following. East of Kern's Crossroads, the columns had to cross three wadis—deep, dry streambeds. At the first wadi, an attack by German Stuka dive-bombers failed to slow the columns. At the second wadi, the Luftwaffe again attacked, but the Americans continued east, overrunning several German antitank positions. At the third wadi, German artillery opened fire, forcing the tank crews to button up. As the tank columns emerged from the wadi, the *5th* and *7th Panzer Regiments* sprang an armor ambush. Caught by surprise by German tank fire, nearly every American tank was destroyed. As this debacle unfolded, American infantry and artillery units retreated to Kern's Crossroads. The American tank battalion lost 313 men and 50 tanks, bringing 1st Armored Division's losses to 98 tanks, 1,200 men, 57 half-tracks, and 29 artillery pieces in two days.[56]

The units surrounded on Djebels Lessouda and Ksaira were doomed. Ward ordered the men on Lessouda to break out that night, empowering Major Robert Moore to lead his 1/168th Infantry to safety. Eventually, Moore and

432 of his 904 soldiers made it to Sbeitla. Colonel Thomas Drake's CT168 on Djebel Ksaira started west too late. Dawn found those who could walk scattered across the open ground west of Sidi bau Zid. German infantry and armor rounded up most of Drake's command. Only one officer and several hundred hungry GIs staggered back to American lines. The 168th Infantry Regiment lost about 2,200 men, most as prisoners.[57] The Germans had maimed CCA and CCC and were encouraged to continue their offensive.

Earlier, on 13 February, II Corps had ordered Colonel Stark to send the 1st Battalion, 26th Infantry, and one battery of the 33rd Field Artillery to Kasserine Pass, 25 miles west of Sbeitla. CT26 had been in the Feriana region recovering from its actions around Faid Pass. The combat team was in the process of training 125 replacements for the 1st Battalion. It also had been given the mission to defend the pass to the west of Feriana. The 1st Battalion, 168th Infantry, was attached to CT26. Stark remained with his headquarters in Feriana while Gerald Kelleher's 1st Battalion, 26th Infantry, moved to Kasserine.[58]

Kelleher's infantrymen reached Kasserine Pass on 14 February and joined the 19th Engineer Regiment in a line that ran across the main road from Sbeitla to Tebessa. To the north of the pass, Djebel Semmama rose to 1,356 meters, and to the south, Djebel Chambi stood guard at 1,544 meters. These mountains dominated the pass and the valley to the northwest (the Bahiret Foussana). To the southeast of the pass, the village of Kasserine stood on the road east to Sbeitla. A wadi carved by the Hatab River bisected the pass and was the boundary between the 26th Infantry and the engineers (Map 10).

Kelleher's men held the north side of the pass, with all companies positioned in the pass and with one platoon from Company A on the southern slope of Djebel Semmama. The 19th Engineers deployed three companies on the south side of the pass, with one platoon on the edge of Djebel Chambi and one company in reserve. The engineer regiment was a construction unit equipped with dump trucks and grading equipment. The engineers were armed with rifles and light machine guns and had yet to see combat. A platoon of tank destroyers and a company of light tanks backed up the two battalions. Efforts to cover the front with mines were begun too late, in the early hours of 19 February. Most of the mines were strewn on the rocky ground since the infantrymen lacked the tools to bury them.[59] It was unclear which American commander was in charge of the defense.

After the German victories west of Faid Pass, on 15 and 16 February, and the defeat of the 1st Armored Division by Rommel's armor at Sbeitla on 17 February, Fredendall ordered II Corps to withdraw to the passes in the Western Dorsal at Bou Chebka, Kasserine, and Thala to prevent further enemy advances. The French XIX Corps established positions at Kesra and at Sbiba, where CT18 was attached to the 34th Infantry Division to defend

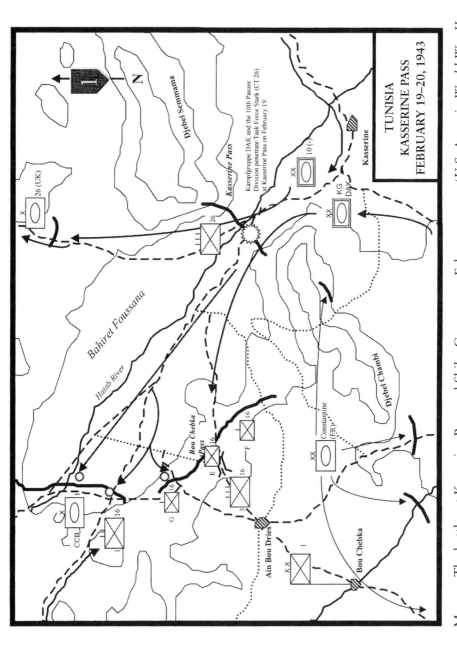

Map 10. The battles at Kasserine Pass and Sbiba Gap, 19–20 February 1943. (*U.S. Army in World War II Atlas* [National Historical Society, 1995])

the pass.[60] On 18 February, believing that Axis forces were planning a major move against Kasserine Pass and Tebessa, Fredendall ordered Stark to leave the 1/168th Infantry and the 175th Field Artillery west of Feriana and move the remaining elements of CT26 east of Tebessa. Bowen's 3rd Battalion, 26th Infantry, remained near El Mar el Abiod, 20 miles west of Feriana, to guard the approach through the Western Dorsal to Tebessa. As German pressure increased, Fredendall ordered Stark to assume command of the two battalions in Kasserine Pass.[61]

On 18 February, the 33rd Field Artillery deployed to support the tenuous line across the pass. A French battery with 75mm guns was attached to the 33rd. Efforts to register the artillery were made difficult by German artillery fire. When Colonel Stark reached Kasserine Pass at 0300, 19 February, he determined that the defenders had failed to put sufficient force on the dominant terrain of Djebels Semmama and Chambi. The engineer battalion's positions were especially poor. "Machine guns were badly sited, foxholes were too shallow, and barbed wire remained mostly on the spools. Nearly every man had entrenched on the floor of the pass, rather than the adjacent heights."[62] Little could be done before the Axis forces attacked that morning.

The battle for Kasserine Pass commenced in the early dawn of 19 February, as German and Italian infantry infiltrated on to the djebels overlooking the pass and Axis tanks attempted to drive through the center of the American defenses. Accurate fire by the flat trajectory French 75s and the plunging fire of the 33rd Artillery's howitzers drove the enemy armor away. But the Axis artillery observers on the dominant terrain enabled their artillery to bring accurate fire on Stark's command post and front lines. At about 1035, thirty-five to forty German trucks began unloading infantrymen in front of the American positions. These troops moved on to Djebel Semmama, where a desperate stand was made by elements of Company A to prevent the Germans from seizing the southern slope of the mountain.[63]

Stark called for reinforcements and dispatched the regimental scout platoon toward the northern djebel. He also sent the engineer reserve company to the northern flank, although the engineers, given their lack of combat training and experience, could do little to stop the Germans. II Corps responded to Stark's calls for help by sending three companies of the 3rd Battalion, 39th Infantry, forward. These units did not arrive until the afternoon. Stark immediately committed the companies piecemeal to bolster his lines. Company I, 39th Infantry, arrived first and occupied positions in the center of the pass. Stark sent Company L to the north to reinforce Company A, 26th Infantry, on Djebel Semmama, and he split up Company K to reinforce Companies B and C, 26th Infantry, in the pass. These moves were completed just before the Germans launched a determined attack at 1530.[64]

By then, the enemy had secured Djebel Semmama and had infantry on Djebel Chambi in the south. Artillery fire cut the telephone lines connecting the front lines to the command post and to the 33rd Artillery. As a result, Stark had no idea what was happening in the pass 3 miles east of his command post, and the artillery had to fire blind against suspected enemy positions. As dark fell, the companies on the front line were surrounded and a German attack was under way on the northern flank. The 33rd Artillery and its attached French battery pulled back 1,000 yards and continued to fire at preregistered targets.[65]

During the night, stragglers from the 1st Battalion, 26th Infantry, and the 39th Infantry drifted past the regimental command post. Stark ordered the companies on the valley floor to withdraw to the high ground on the flanks, but enemy troops were in firm possession of the djebels, and the American companies disintegrated. By dawn, 20 February, the only remaining American units were the tank platoons of Company I, 13th Armor, and the antitank company of the 805th TD Battalion. Stark planned to use these elements to retake Djebel Semmama. This attack never got under way, since the tanks and tank destroyers got into a close-range fight with German tanks in the center of the pass.

In response to Stark's calls for help, a small British task force attempted to drive down the road from Thala to Djebel Semmama, but "the Germans on the high ground were too strongly entrenched and the British forces succeeded only in gaining the lower slopes at the cost of losing all of their tanks." The after-action account by the 33rd Artillery describes the battle:

> The action on the 20th which had continued all the night . . . was much the same as the previous day with heavy shelling of the front and infantry infiltrating our lines. The engineers on the right had fallen back and our battery OP's were lost. . . . A liaison officer was sent to the left sector to work with the reinforcing infantry which was going in on that flank. Fires were prepared by the 33rd FA Bn [Field Artillery Battalion] and the French battery to support this action. . . . They were never called for. About 1230 hours the report came in from the artillery liaison officer that the CP [command post] of the 19th Engineers was being over-run and that tanks had broken through on the left. This left the artillery unprotected [from] foot troops which at this time were observed coming down the mountains to the rear. Permission was requested and granted for the artillery to go out of position.[66]

The artillery attempted to cover the retreat of the infantrymen and engineers to the west, but German infantry advancing on both sides of the Hatab River threatened to cut off the firing batteries. The French artillerymen were forced to destroy their guns before American trucks could retrieve them. As the artillery displaced west, a tank battle was observed in the center of the pass between Company I, 13th Armored Regiment, and the heavier tanks of *Kampfgruppe DAK*. With the road north to Thala already cut and the enemy close to crossing the road to Tebessa, the 33rd Artillery gave up the fight and retreated to positions 20 miles west of Kasserine Pass.[67]

By 2030 hours, 20 February, the command post of the 1st Battalion, 26th Infantry, was surrounded, and the battalion S3 had been killed as he attempted to rally his men. Kelleher was captured but, in the confusion, escaped after posing as a medical officer. With the German artillery observation posts able to call for accurate fire on the defenders and the frontline units shattered, there was little choice but for Stark to order a retreat. As the 26th Regiment's history concluded, "The only troops not surrounded or actively engaged were the remnants of Co. I, 13th Armor, the remainder of the 805 TD, and a new 894 TD Bn which had arrived on the scene this afternoon. What was left of Co. A, 26th Infantry, and Co. L, 39th Infantry was left on the high ground to the left; What was left of the 19th Engineers and the 1st Battalion, 26th Infantry, was still on the high ground to the right."[68]

The 1st Battalion, 26th Infantry, lost eight officers and 235 enlisted men in the battle at Kasserine Pass. Kelleher and most of his company commanders survived, providing a leadership cadre around which to rebuild the unit. Fortunately, Rommel turned his armor north toward Thala, rather than west against CCB and CT26.[69]

The American defeats in the battles from Faid to Kasserine Pass were a direct result of the poor leadership exercised by Fredendall. His use of elements of various divisions intermingled in ad hoc formations confused the troops, made communications a constant challenge, and failed to exploit the command and control capabilities of the headquarters and staffs of the 1st and 34th Infantry and the 1st Armored Divisions. Until the battles around Kasserine, Eisenhower condoned Fredendall's conduct of operations and failed to make him use divisions as the basic tactical organization. One of the few positive things that came out of the debacles of February was a change in the commander of II Corps and the reunification of the units of the Big Red One.

The First Division at Bou Chebka

While CT26 was operating at Feriana, the 1st Division, with CT16, withdrew to the western side of the Ousseltia Valley. On 19 February, as Rommel's armor attacked at Kasserine, Allen was ordered to move the division to Ain Bou Dries, 15 miles west of Kasserine Pass, to block Bou Chebka

Pass. Teddy Roosevelt Jr. remained in the Ousseltia Valley to command the 2nd Battalion, 26th Infantry, and three French infantry battalions holding the line. CT18 was part of the 34th Infantry Division's line to the south of Task Force Roosevelt, helping that division defend Sbiba. CT16 set out on 19 February, and the remainder of the division moved the next night. The division's command post was in operation 5 miles north of Bou Chebka late on 20 February 1943.[70]

Allen also assumed command of the French Constantine Division, whose units were deployed to block the roads running northwest from Feriana to Ain Bou Dries. The 2nd Battalion, 16th Infantry, established defensive positions in Bou Chebka Pass. The 3rd Battalion established positions behind the pass. The 1st Battalion dug in to the north, on the right flank of CCB on Djebel el Hamra, to help the 1st Armored Division prevent an enemy advance from Kasserine Pass along the road to Tebessa.[71]

The most serious German attack toward Tebessa was made by *Kampfgruppe DAK* on 21 February. Concentrated fires of four artillery battalions, including the 33rd Artillery, stopped this attack cold. Rommel's attack north to Thala from Kasserine that morning also was stopped, but only after the British suffered heavy losses.

Early on 22 February, Rommel launched another attack with Panzergrenadiers against the 2nd Battalion, 16th Infantry, in Bou Chebka Pass. Taking advantage of the mist and fog, the grenadiers forced Company G to retreat, leaving five howitzers of the 33rd Field Artillery in German hands. However, when the fog cleared, the Germans were exposed to the massed fires of the 7th and 33rd Artillery Battalions and the direct fire of 2/16th Infantry. This defense was orchestrated by Generals Clift Andrus and Terry Allen. In an attempt to sidestep the 1st Infantry Division's positions to the north, Rommel ordered another attack at 1100 by the *8th Panzer Regiment* and the Italian *Bersaglieri Regiment* against the 1st Battalion, 16th Infantry, and CCB on Djebel el Hamra. The 1st Battalion and the 13th Armored Regiment stopped this attack before it got close, again relying on heavy artillery concentrations.

With the German grenadiers pinned down and Rommel's armor committed to the north, Allen ordered the 16th Infantry to retake Hill 812. The 3rd Battalion led the attack, supported closely by Joe Crawford's 2nd Battalion. The 7th and 33rd Artillery Battalions joined the fray with heavy supporting fires. The Panzergrenadiers were driven off the hill, and the captured guns of the 33rd Artillery were recovered.[72] This well-coordinated division attack on 22 February was in stark contrast to the frittering away of battalions that had been so common in the II Corps attacks around Faid Pass. Allen noted in his report to George Marshall: "As the lines of our infantry reached their positions, the Germans broke and ran. Some 400 surrendered to a group of 13th Armored Regiment tanks on reaching the valley [floor]. Our attack was followed by a counter-attack by Combat Command B of the 1st Armored Division from the northeast side of the valley."[73]

The fighting was intense, and men unintentionally emerged as heroes. In one platoon's assault, led by a lieutenant,

> all went well till a mortar shell landed almost on top of him blowing his leg off. Then it seemed all hell broke loose and the rest of the platoon was forced to fall back. Amid heavy fire this soldier suddenly turned around and started back toward the Lt. One could see him reach him. . . . The soldier dropped his rifle and as calmly as if he were in the garden of some quiet secluded spot far from any danger, he carefully picked up the Lt and started walking very slowly and carefully to our lines. . . . He brought him on back to the lines and gently laid him down in a protected spot. We went over to him and asked him why he had done it? He said, "Seems like he needed a little help so I thought I best fetch him back." The Lt was rushed to the aid station thence to a hospital where he will be OK though missing a leg.[74]

Such actions blunted the last German attempts to break the American lines. On 25 February, 1st Armored Division, with CT16 attached, pushed east toward Kasserine Pass. The Germans, however, had withdrawn, leaving a battlefield strewn with mines and booby traps. By mid-morning, American and British troops converged on Kasserine Pass. The entire Western Dorsal was in Allied hands.[75] Eisenhower was given another chance to straighten out the snarled command relationships of the forces in Tunisia.

On 19 February, the Allies established the 18th Army Group to coordinate the operations of the British First Army, the French XIX Corps, and the US II Corps. Sir Harold R. L. G. Alexander assumed command of these forces and of Bernard Montgomery's British Eighth Army, which had just reached the Axis defensive positions known as the Mareth Line in southern Tunisia.[76] As the enemy shifted divisions to southern Tunisia to face the Eighth Army, the 1st Infantry Division assembled near Bou Chebka. Terry Allen summarized the experiences of the division accurately in March:

> Marked success attended the efforts of the Division when it was possible to operate under Division control and take advantage of the teamwork and morale so thoroughly instilled during training periods. Losses have been suffered, which are part of the cost of belonging to the "Fighting First," but in no case was there any disorganization, and the Boche was made to pay in kind. Casualties in the officer personnel have been particularly heavy and indicated the active leadership of the junior officers.[77]

The Axis February offensives in Tunisia inflicted considerable casualties on the Allies. The Germans claimed that they captured over 4,000 prisoners and destroyed hundreds of Allied tanks, trucks, and artillery pieces.[78] The inexperienced Allied leaders made many mistakes. They committed units piecemeal, badly tangling logistical and command lines of communication, and failed to use the command and control assets of the three American divisions in Tunisia. Eisenhower finally realized his mistakes of selecting and retaining Fredendall in command. With George Marshall's approval, he replaced Fredendall with George Patton on 6 March 1943.

Realizing that his forces could not break through the Allied defenses west and north of Kasserine Pass and at Sbiba, Rommel ordered his units to withdraw from the Western Dorsal and to establish a line that ran northeast from Gafsa through Sbeitla and on to Pichon. Behind this line, the Axis forces established their main defenses along a line from El Guettar through Faid to Fondouk. Rommel's forces had to hold this line if they were to prevent the American forces in southern Tunisia from driving through the passes to the Gulf of Gabes. Such a move would cut off the German-Italian army in the Mareth Line from the *Fifth Panzer Army* and the Axis supply bases around Tunis and Bizerte. Recognizing this situation, General Alexander gave Patton's II Corps the mission to drive through the Eastern Dorsal to Gabes, on the Tunisian coast.

The Big Red One Reunites

Once it became clear that Rommel had withdrawn from Kasserine Pass, the Allies pushed cautiously east to the Axis line. But the next order of business for the 18th Army Group was to reorganize the forces to establish national and division integrity. As part of this effort, in early March, Major General Terry Allen assembled his scattered units near Marsott, north of Tebessa. Most units of the division spent the first two weeks of March resting and training. Allen continued the divisional school that he had established in February to train replacements.

The school concentrated on discipline, physical conditioning, and marksmanship. Allen insisted that "discipline must be exemplified by the *prompt* execution of orders, by military bearing and the proper wearing of the uniform, by careful attention to saluting discipline and by general demeanor of all individuals." The well-known insistence by Patton for strict adherence to uniform regulations played a part in Allen's instructions concerning discipline and demeanor. But Allen emphasized to all commanders that combat training "must be stressed to acquire the battle wisdom necessary to inflict maximum losses upon the enemy, with the minimum losses to our-selves."[79]

The division also worked to get back those division veterans who had been evacuated to rear-area hospitals due to illness or wounds, and who had recovered. As the *History of the 26th Infantry in the Present Struggle* notes,

> The enlisted men who fell sick or were wounded were often shunted from place to place, and sometimes never did get back to their own outfit. When some of our boys went AWOL from a convalescent hospital, and reported to the colonel that they had done so only because they had a general feeling that they weren't going to be sent back to their own outfit, then Colonel Stark and his staff de-cided that arrangements should be made with the hospitals and depots to return the valuable soldiers; . . . What hastened that decision was receiving from the replacement depots more than once contingents of air force, quartermaster and medical men as infantry replacements. It imposed an additional strain of train-ing these men in a combat zone.[80]

The value of the reunification for the division's morale and efficiency cannot be overstated. For the first time since November 1942, the three infantry battalions of the 26th Infantry Regiment were together. Specialty units such as the regimental cannon company could operate as a unit to support the infantry. The artillery battalions of each combat team could work as part of Clift Andrus's Division Artillery, allowing the division to efficiently mass the fires of all four battalions. The 1st Medical Battalion could finally sup-port the division in the manner in which it was organized. The division commander and staff could control operations with the assets necessary to fight and win. After its reunification in Tunisia, the Big Red One never lost a battle.

George Patton's selection as II Corps commander pleased Terry Allen. Allen and Patton had known one another in the prewar army. They were selected for promotion to brigadier general on the same list. In a letter to his wife, Mary Frances, Allen reported that "Patton is our new corps com-mander and is doing awfully well. It seems like old times to see some of the old cavalry faces."[81] However, in spite of this previous friendship, Patton had a job to do, and he ruffled a lot of feathers. Eisenhower's instructions to Patton gave him the mission to rehabilitate II Corps and its divisions. Patton had to reequip his armor with over 200 replacement tanks, restore the con-fidence in those units that had been badly battered, and plan a major attack in 18th Army Group's offensive. All this had to be done in two weeks.[82]

In his efforts to instill a fighting spirit across his corps, Patton did some maladroit things. In the case of the 1st Infantry Division, Patton's decision to urinate in Terry Allen's slit trench near the command post in March engendered a fair amount of resentment. Patton's most reliable biographer, Martin Blumenson, points out that Patton meant no disrespect to Allen personally. Instead, he was trying to show disdain for a defensive attitude that he believed permeated II Corps. The immature gesture backfired. Patton also insisted that soldiers shave daily and wear neckties when not in the line and helmets with straps attached at all times. Many of the soldiers of the 1st Infantry Division, after nearly a year of the casual leadership styles of Terry Allen and Teddy Roosevelt, resented such rules, which they perceived as "chicken-shit." Blumenson concludes, in Patton's defense, that "he had to be ruthless, for he had only eleven days to shake his troops out of slovenly habits and into a state of alertness. At the same time, he expedited the arrival of new equipment, clothing, and mail."[83]

The Big Red One was the only division in II Corps not in need of rehabilitation of the type that Patton was instituting. Allen's emphasis on training and discipline before Patton arrived prove that the two generals held similar beliefs about getting soldiers ready to fight. Although Eisenhower and Patton entertained doubts about the tactical abilities of Major General Orlando Ward, commanding general of the 1st Armored Division, they had complete confidence in Allen's and Roosevelt's combat leadership. Patton selected the Fighting First to carry out the first stage of the American attack in March because of his faith in the division.

While the division regrouped around Marsott, the enemy attacked in northern Tunisia to weaken the British First Army. Von Arnim's columns pushed the British back on 26 and 27 February, but Anderson parried the German thrusts with reserves. By 3 March, the Germans had been stopped. *Fifth Panzer Army* lost 22 tanks and over 1,000 men while destroying just 16 British tanks. Another 49 German tanks were disabled, leaving just 6 operational tanks in the German formations in northern Tunisia by 1 March.[84]

Because General Anderson needed to shift the 1st British Parachute Brigade from its positions near Bou Arada to meet the German offensive, General Alexander called on II Corps to provide an infantry regiment to hold the line near Bou Arada. On 3 March, II Corps alerted the 1st Infantry Division to commit CT26 for defensive operations in support of the British. This assignment came the same day that Colonel George Taylor assumed command of the 26th Infantry from Colonel Stark. By 2130, 3 March, CT26 and the 33rd Field Artillery Battalion were on the road northward. Taylor and his new command became acquainted while holding a section of the British lines until 10 March. During the nights of 8–9 and 9–10 March, French units replaced CT26, allowing Taylor's men to return to 1st Infantry

Division control. The combat team had suffered few casualties and used the time in the line to integrate hundreds of replacements it had received to fill the gaps created by losses at Faid and Kasserine Passes.[85]

The Allied armies were now ready to begin to drive the Axis forces from Tunisia. The struggle would be difficult, and, in the process, the American army would further develop the expertise needed to defeat the Wehrmacht.

7

Offensive Operations
Gafsa to Victory in Africa

PATTON'S ASSUMPTION OF COMMAND BROUGHT badly needed focus and energy to American operations. His orders were clear and his intent to close with and destroy the enemy was evident. Patton believed in American soldiers and in the 1st Infantry Division. In subsequent operations, there would be no dribbling out of units, and ground taken would be held. Patton understood that a big part of his mission was to redeem the reputations of the American fighting man and of the US Army's officer corps. To do this, Patton relied on the combat capabilities of the Big Red One. For the first time since the capture of Oran, Terry Allen had control of the entire division. With his leadership, the 1st Infantry Division would demonstrate the endurance, flexibility, and combat power of an infantry division structure when it was employed as a coherent force.

Offensive Operations of the Big Red One:
17 March–7 April 1943

As CT26 rolled back to Marsott, Patton ordered the division to seize Gafsa on 17 March. By 16 March, the 1st Infantry Division had shifted southeast, nearer to Bou Chebka. During final preparations for the Gafsa attack, the division continued to train replacements. For example, on 10 March, the 26th Infantry Regiment sent five combat veteran officers and eleven enlisted men to the training camp near Marsott to instruct newly arrived soldiers. Special emphasis in this training was placed on the laying, detection, and removal of mines and booby traps. As the operations officer of CT26 noted, mines and booby traps posed a mortal threat at all times:

> We are now to finish this Tunisian campaign. . . . Each of you shall have his part in this operation—we need YOU. And to do our best to keep YOU with us, we want you to know about mines and booby traps. In this operation we shall be up against all the trickery the Nazi can contrive against us—in short, dirty pool. The two things that you must continually be on guard against are mines and booby traps. . . . Don't be a curiosity hunter on the battlefield—or even off it. Leave all enemy equipment alone.[1]

172

As the infantry and engineers honed their combat skills, the Division Artillery refined techniques to mass artillery fires and ensured that forward observers were ready to accompany the infantry. During this final preparation, Allen also placed emphasis on training for night offensive operations.[2]

The 1st Infantry Division's attack against Gafsa was part of II Corps' Operation Wop. The operation was a supporting attack to draw enemy reserves away from the offensive by Montgomery's Eighth Army against the *First Italian Army*. Patton's plan called for the Big Red One to seize Gafsa while the 1st Armored Division protected its northern flank. General Alexander, lacking confidence in American commanders and troops, limited Patton's freedom of operation. Therefore, the attack was designed to halt once Gafsa was captured.[3]

The division's plan to take Gafsa was straightforward. The three combat teams would attack early on the morning of 17 March after moving 50 miles by truck from Bou Chebka to Gafsa. The assault positions were cleared of mines and secured in advance by the 1st Engineer Battalion. CT18 was to strike from the northeast, CT16 would advance from the northwest, and the 3rd Battalion, 26th Infantry, was to move in from the west. The 1st Ranger Battalion was attached to the division to move east of Gafsa to scout the road toward El Guettar. The infantry assault was to be preceded by an air attack and artillery barrage.[4]

The combat teams reached their attack positions by 0315, 17 March. II Corps delayed the attack until 1000, due to poor visibility, which delayed planned air strikes. At ten, the division commenced its envelopment of Gafsa. While CT18 and the 601st TD Battalion cut off the place from the east, the 3rd Battalion, 16th Infantry, advanced toward Gafsa from the northwest. At 1220, Company I, accompanied by Teddy Roosevelt Jr., entered the battered town. The Italian garrison had escaped, leaving mines and booby traps.[5]

The Battle of El Guettar

The division lost contact with the enemy as it rolled into Gafsa. That was unacceptable to General Allen, who ordered the 1st Ranger Battalion to continue toward El Guettar, 11 miles east. Allen told the battalion commander, Bill Darby, that "it is vitally necessary to resume close contact with the enemy."[6] He also positioned CT18 so that it could advance. By late afternoon, 18 March, the rangers had seized El Guettar without opposition. The division then shifted artillery and logistical units to Gafsa for further offensive operations.[7]

The weather was miserable. Rain fell steadily, delaying the attack on

Gafsa and turning the roads into quagmires and the wadis into streams. "Men were wet through to the bone, and sleep was impossible. The onrushing water tore at lines and disrupted communications. Linesmen and crews were out all through the night, tracing breaks, laying new wire, keeping communications intact among the battalions of the regiment, the Division, and the Corps groups."[8] Everyone dealt with knee-deep mud and slippery roads, making repositioning a time-consuming and exhausting process. As the combat teams got into place to defend Gafsa, new orders arrived from II Corps.

While the 1st Infantry Division was seizing Gafsa, Montgomery's Eighth Army attacked the *First Italian Army* in the Mareth Line. Montgomery launched the British 30 Corps head-on against the entrenched Italians and Germans. The attackers made several minor penetrations, but the Germans drove them back out. By 20 March, it was apparent to Alexander that the Eighth Army was not going to romp through the enemy's defenses. Consequently, Alexander gave Patton approval to exploit his success at Gafsa by pushing toward El Guettar, hoping to draw Axis reserves from the south.[9]

Late on 20 March, Patton instructed Allen to plan "an attack along the axis Gafsa-Gabes. . . . You may be called upon to put it into effect tomorrow."[10] The 1st Infantry Division was to advance from El Guettar toward Gabes while the 1st Armored Division was to drive to Maknassy Pass, northeast of El Guettar, threatening the communications of the *First Italian Army*. General Alexander still restrained Patton from driving across the Eastern Dorsal toward Gabes and Sfax.[11]

The 1st Armored Division reached Station de Sened on 20 March. Major General Ward, however, moved his division cautiously toward Maknassy, not reaching there until the next afternoon. Once he arrived, Ward halted his armor rather than pushing the remaining 5 miles into the pass on the road to Sfax. This pause allowed the Germans to switch forces to Maknassy Pass, preventing a breakthrough to the plains of southern Tunisia. Patton was not pleased. Meanwhile, the 1st Infantry Division consolidated its hold on El Guettar and sent patrols toward the hills to the east.

For the first time in the campaign, American troops were fighting as divisions controlled by an American corps headquarters. While two veteran divisions led the advance, the less experienced 9th and 34th Infantry Divisions remained in reserve. Patton's grip on the reins was firm and his orders clear.

Nonetheless, the Eastern Dorsal remained a formidable barrier for II Corps to cross. As Stanhope Mason remembered:

> We had to advance from hilltop to hilltop along an east-west ridge which had numerous gullies running along sides of the hills at right angles to the ridge.

These formed natural defensive positions. There was no concealed approach in those barren, rocky hills. Tactical options were so restricted by the terrain there were basically only two ways to get the job done. One was to make a frontal attack. That would be the quickest way to do it, but the cost in casualties resulting from such WW I trench warfare tactics was wholly unacceptable to Gen. Allen. The second and habitually used method was a combination of night attack, artillery concentration, and maneuver.[12]

Terry Allen had trained the division for night operations, which were slow. Patton was constantly pushing him to speed up the advance. This pressure was "felt throughout the Division, but Gen. Allen was able to absorb most of it without the profligate expenditure of lives."[13]

The main road from El Guettar to Gabes was Highway 15 (Map 11). This asphalt road ran southeast across a low ridge that was an extension of Djebel el Ank, about 4 miles east of El Guettar. Highway 15 then continued across open ground and climbed into a saddle between Djebels Kheroua and Mcheltat. To control Highway 15, the 1st Infantry Division had to secure the ridges that ran in an arc about 7 miles east of El Guettar. The secondary road that ran east from town was called Gumtree Road, because of the type of trees that grew along it. Gumtree Road crossed Djebel el Ank in a low pass between Hill 623 on its south and Hill 890, on Djebel Orbata, on its north.

Allen planned a night attack to seize the hills through which the two roads ran. On the north flank of the division, CT26 and Darby's 1st Ranger Battalion were to secure Djebel el Ank and the pass between Hills 623 and 890. In the center, CT18 was to seize Hill 336 on Highway 15 and continue east to secure Djebels Kheroua and Mcheltat. CT16 was division reserve, with one battalion and the 7th Field Artillery protecting Gafsa and one battalion ready to move forward on trucks from El Guettar to a defensive line along the ridge at Hill 336 that overlooked Wadi el Keddab. Once the initial objectives were taken, CT26 was to take Bou Hamron, 2 miles east of el Ank Pass, and CT18 was to overrun Djebel Berda south of Highway 15. The Big Red One could then open the route to Gabes.

Darby's rangers opened the operation at 2200 hours, 20 March, with a night march over Djebel Orbata to Hill 890. The next morning, Darby reported that his men were ready to attack the Italian camp in the pass and that the 3rd Battalion, 26th Infantry, was in position to join the assault.[14]

The rangers launched a bayonet attack that caught the Italians completely unprepared. Many Italians surrendered, as Lieutenant Colonel John Corley's 3rd Battalion, 26th Infantry, joined the fray. By 0755, Corley reported that his men were advancing through el Ank Pass with "not much opposition."

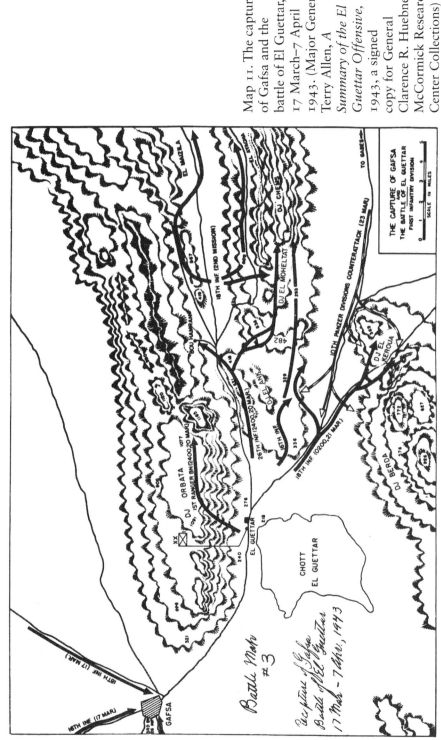

Map 11. The capture of Gafsa and the battle of El Guettar, 17 March–7 April 1943. (Major General Terry Allen, *A Summary of the El Guettar Offensive*, 1943, a signed copy for General Clarence R. Huebner, McCormick Research Center Collections)

At the same time the 1st Battalion, 26th Infantry, moved east along the south side of the pass, giving the Italians no place to run in that direction. Darby's men continued along the high ground to the north of Gumtree Road, protecting CT26's flank. All units called for artillery fire against fleeing Italians. Before the end of the day, the 33rd Field Artillery had fired fourteen fire missions.[15] Due to these successes, Colonel Taylor brought his command post into the pass and moved his 2nd Battalion forward to secure the high ground north of the road. Djebel el Ank was in American hands by midday. As the infantry drove the enemy from the pass, the 1st Engineers removed the mines that infested Gumtree Road, opening it to truck and ambulance traffic.[16]

To the south, the 18th Infantry advanced in the early hours of 21 March along Highway 15. At 0530, patrols reached the southwest ridge of Djebel el Ank, near Hill 336, and reported that the area was clear. The 2nd and 3rd Battalions continued moving until they ran into Italian positions northeast of Wadi el Keddab. As Greer's men crossed the open terrain east of Hill 336 they were hit by enemy artillery fire. Calls for air support went unanswered, and the enemy guns were out of range of the division's artillery. Despite the lack of artillery support, CT18 continued forward.[17]

The Italians holding the ridges resisted with artillery and small-arms fire, but they did not make a determined stand. At 0752, Greer reported that his infantrymen were not facing stiff resistance and that "firing is getting further and further back. The enemy artillery is either knocked out or else it is moving back." By 0810, the 18th Infantry had taken its objectives, capturing a large number of prisoners. The Division G3, Frederick Gibb, ordered Greer to seize Djebel Mcheltat. As the infantry advanced, the 601st TD Battalion moved forward to provide protection from enemy armor. At 0901, the 601st reported that the "whole Italian army [was] in the bag."[18] This report was hyperbole, but the advance had gone well.

While the 3rd Battalion, 18th Infantry, advanced toward Djebel Mcheltat, the 2nd Battalion moved southeast toward Djebel Kheroua. When Greer reported enemy troops unloading from trucks 3 miles to the east, Gibb ordered the 3rd Battalion, 16th Infantry, to move by truck to positions astride the highway at Hill 336. There the battalion established a defensive line in case the enemy counterattacked. Since the 18th Infantry had outrun its artillery support, Andrus moved the 5th and 32nd Field Artillery Battalions forward. Terry Allen also ordered the cannon companies of the 16th and 26th Infantry Regiments each to send a platoon of self-propelled 75mm guns to CT18 to provide antitank protection for Greer's exposed infantrymen.

By 1630, CT18 had reached Hill 482 and Djebel Kheroua, and the 1st Battalion had swung into line between the 2nd and 3rd Battalions. Engineers worked to get 4,000 mines and three truckloads of barbed wire forward to the infantry positions. Stanhope Mason also asked II Corps to send the 899th TD Battalion forward to reinforce the 601st TD. One company of the 899th was identified as a reserve for the 601st, but II Corps would not allow it to move to El Guettar.

On the division's left, the 26th Infantry Regiment had moved to within a mile of Bou Hamron by 1620. At that time, Darby's rangers returned to El Guettar to prepare for another mission. It was slow going for the Blue Spaders, in large part because of minefields. In its after-action report, the 26th Infantry noted that "mines have now become of paramount importance in this campaign, in many cases causing far too much delay for advancing troops. The locating, marking, and removing of minefields must be a continual process."[19]

As the division advanced, the Luftwaffe attacked repeatedly. Fifteen Heinkel bombers hit Greer's men at 1450, and a short while later the 32nd Field Artillery lost two howitzers, an ammunition truck, and an artillery prime mover to a Stuka attack. Nonetheless, the division had reached most of its objectives, establishing a defensive arc running 5 miles east of El Guettar from Bou Hamron in the northeast to Djebels Mcheltat and Kheroua in the southeast.[20]

II Corps' offensive threatened to cut the Axis army group in half. In conjunction with a flanking movement by the Eighth Army west of the Mareth Line, it forced the enemy to take measures to protect the rear of the *First Italian Army*. In response, *Army Group Africa* ordered the *10th Panzer Division* to attack the 1st Infantry Division.[21]

As the *10th Panzer* moved into assembly areas 20 miles east of El Guettar, on 22 March, the 1st Infantry Division consolidated its positions (Map 11). The 3rd Battalion, 26th Infantry, occupied positions near Bou Hamron, while the 33rd Artillery moved into el Ank Pass. The 2nd Battalion faced southeast toward Hill 536, and Kelleher's 1st Battalion dug in on the eastern end of el Ank to protect the pass. The regiment saw little action during the day. Reconnaissance patrols advanced toward Sakkat and onto a piece of ground known as the Rass ed Dekhla. Taylor also made plans to seize Hill 536, which dominated Gumtree Road.[22]

Greer's infantrymen bore the brunt of the fighting on 22 March, as the 1st and 2nd Battalions, 18th Infantry, pushed south to capture Hill 772, the dominant terrain feature of Djebel Berda. This mission proved very difficult as Bob York's 1st Battalion ran into enemy machine guns and received punishing artillery fire from batteries out of range of Andrus's artillery. At 1820, Allen ordered Greer to have his 2nd Battalion join the attack, hoping to gain the crest of Berda before dark. Patton put strong pressure on Allen to push this assault, at one point revealing his frustration by saying, "Well Goddam it, get moving, and get there right away."[23]

Allen pushed Greer's attack because Djebel Berda dominated the open plains and Highway 15. The resistance Greer's men encountered forced Allen to conclude that the "enemy is stronger than [the] 18th [CT] thought it was."[24] As the day wore on, the division became concerned about enemy counterattacks. The engineers laid 4,800 mines in a belt from Hill 336 to the Chott el Guettar. Andrus repositioned his artillery to support a renewal of the attack, with the 5th and 32nd Field Artillery Battalions deployed east of Hill 336. From these exposed positions, the gunners could reach more of the enemy's artillery. Andrus also pressured II Corps to get air reconnaissance for 23 March so that he could locate the enemy artillery. II Corps eventually agreed and also released all of the 16th Infantry from its mission to defend Gafsa.[25]

The German Counterattack

At 0245, 23 March, the 26th Infantry commenced an attack to seize Hill 536 and establish contact with the exposed left flank of CT18. As this move got under way, the 601st TD Battalion informed the division command post that an enemy attack by at least ten tanks and two companies of infantry was under way along the Gabes Road. This was a concentrated effort by the *10th Panzer Division* to smash through the 1st Infantry Division and take El Guettar.

By dawn, seventy German tanks were advancing west along Highway 15. The tanks were accompanied by half-tracks carrying infantry. As the Germans reached the open ground between Djebels Kheroua and Mcheltat, more infantrymen arrived on trucks and dismounted. The phalanx continued, with the dismounted infantry moving with the tanks. When the Germans were 2 miles east of Hill 336, they divided their formation into three columns. One turned north, into the southern flank of the 3/18th Infantry, another continued along the Gabes Road toward Hill 336, and the third column moved west for about 2 miles and then turned north toward El Guettar. This last column cut behind the two battalions of the 18th Infantry on Djebel Berda.

The 601st TD Battalion fought tenaciously to stop the German armor along Highway 15, but the panzers caught two companies of the 601st by surprise. In the ensuing melee, those companies lost all of their antitank guns. By 0710, the remaining guns of the 601st had retreated through the 18th Infantry to join the artillery battalions east of Hill 336.

The right-hand German column pushed the infantrymen of the 3rd

Battalions of the 16th and 18th Infantry Regiments out of their foxholes on
the western side of Djebel Mcheltat. Using the folds of the terrain as cover,
the American soldiers fought a ferocious delaying action, forcing the Germans to dig them out of their positions in hand-to-hand fighting. The men
of Company K, 18th Infantry, threw more than 1,300 grenades as they clung
to their position for as long as possible. But the Germans fought through
the American infantry into the positions of the 5th and 32nd Artillery Battalions. The gunners of the 5th Artillery hammered the Germans:

> By 0930 hrs all wire communication in the [5th Artillery] Bn [battalion] had
> been knocked out and remained out despite repeated attempts to repair lines.
> Radio was becoming less effective. Our infantry withdrew to a line of ridges
> behind our gun positions from which our crews continued to fire missions by
> means of direct and indirect laying until threatened with being overrun by
> enemy infantry and tanks. At the last moment and just prior to arrival of rein-
> forcements, the personnel of the firing batteries withdrew on Bn order to the
> high ground behind the positions after destroying howitzers and other equip-
> ment which could not be withdrawn.[26]

A similar situation developed in the positions of the 32nd Artillery. Four
howitzers were operated as antitank guns, while the remaining eight hammered German infantry. Eventually, the gunners of the 5th and 32nd Field
Artillery Battalions were forced to destroy ten howitzers and retreat to the
division's final defensive line along the Wadi el Keddab. In the process, the
gunners destroyed a number of German tanks and broke the momentum
of the northern German column. The American artillerymen and infantry
held their positions long enough to allow Allen to move the 2nd Battalion,
16th Infantry, into defensive positions and to bring the lead company of the
899th TD Battalion into the fight. The remaining artillery and tank destroyers poured strong fire into the enemy, stopping the advance. By noon, the
northern German column was withdrawing to reorganize. As it did so, the
3rd Battalion, 26th Infantry, counterattacked south from Djebel el Ank to
relieve the pressure on the division's beleaguered center.[27]

As the battle unfolded, Allen called on all available resources. Patton
monitored the battle and his staff responded to Allen's requests. By 0730,
the 899th TD Battalion was rolling to El Guettar and a battalion of infantry
from the 9th Infantry Division was moving to Gafsa to relieve the 1st Battalion, 16th Infantry. Corps also pried loose air support from 18th Army
Group, although planes did not arrive until after 1000 hours. Before noon,
six new 155mm howitzers were sent to El Guettar from an ordnance depot

to replace the guns lost by the 5th Artillery, and all available artillery ammunition was being sent to the division.

The largest of the German columns had moved west, behind CT18, and then turned north toward El Guettar. As the forty to fifty German tanks in the column crossed the open ground southwest of Hill 336, the Division Artillery and the 601st TD Battalion hit them with every available weapon. Nearing the Chott El Guettar, the panzers ran into the 1st Engineers' minefield. Thirty German tanks were knocked out by artillery fires and another eight hit mines. Tanks that tried to maneuver around the mines became mired in the salt and sand flats of the Chott. At the same time, the infantrymen of the 18th Infantry on Djebel Berda plastered German infantrymen with mortar, rifle, and machine-gun fire. By 1100, the Germans were retreating in the south.[28]

Throughout the day the Luftwaffe attacked the division. The 105th Coastal Artillery Battalion (Antiaircraft) met the German planes with 40mm and .50-caliber fire, providing some relief. Most of the guns of Battery C and one platoon of Battery A were destroyed when the 5th and 32nd Field Artillery Battalions were overrun. Although they reported few confirmed hits, the antiaircraft gunners forced the enemy planes to fly erratic and inaccurate attack patterns. The Allied air forces provided little counter–air support.

At the height of the battle, a staff officer asked Allen if he wanted to move the division command post back from its exposed position. Allen replied, "I will like hell pull out, and I'll shoot the first bastard who does."[29] By 1200, the crisis had passed. Allen moved two battalions of CT26 south to reinforce the division's center. As the Germans retreated, the 3rd Battalions of the 16th and 18th Infantry Regiments counterattacked toward Djebel Mcheltat. This attack recaptured the gun lines of the 5th and 32nd Artillery Battalions, allowing the artillerymen to recover some of their equipment. To the south, Greer sent nineteen jeeps from his two battalions on Berda back to supply dumps in El Guettar. Thirteen of the jeeps survived the trip with badly needed small-arms and mortar ammunition.[30]

As the Germans withdrew, a company of the 899th TD followed aggressively. In the process, the inexperienced Americans ran into an ambush, losing four M10 tank destroyers. The Germans obviously remained dangerous as the division prepared to meet further attacks.

Resupply and reorganization were the critical tasks accomplished during the midday respite. Artillery ammunition stocks were low and could not be filled until after 1500. In a series of small attacks and moves in the afternoon, CT26 took over the front from Hill 482 north to Bou Hamron. At the same time, two battalions of the 16th Infantry helped CT18 reorganize the center, allowing Greer to keep his 1st and 2nd Battalions south of the highway on the slopes of Djebel Berda. The 1st Engineers manned the final defensive lines between the Chott El Guettar and Hill 336.

As the division readjusted the front, Patton notified Allen that the *10th Panzer Division* was going to renew its assault at 1600. By then, Allen was confident that the 1st Infantry Division could defeat whatever the enemy threw at it. When the Germans delayed their attack, Allen sent a message to the Germans asking why they were late. This message alerted the Germans that the Allies were deciphering their coded messages. The Germans changed their codes, denying the Allies information for the next week. In frustration with Allen's breach of security, Patton asked, "Terry, when are you going to learn to take this war seriously?"[31]

The German attack resumed at about 1645, when two battalions of the *7th Panzer Regiment* and two battalions of Panzergrenadiers appeared along Highway 15, between Djebels Kheroua and Mcheltat. The tanks remained out of range of the American tank destroyers while the German infantrymen moved on foot toward Hill 336. The attack was supported by artillery fire, and dive-bombers attacked Greer's infantrymen north of the road. The Luftwaffe failed, however, to suppress Andrus's artillery battalions. Division Artillery, reinforced by two corps artillery battalions, "crucified" the German infantry as they attempted to reach the division's antitank gun screen. Greer reported to Allen that the enemy were dropping like flies as his gunners used air bursts above their heads.[32] One eyewitness described the final German infantry assault of the day:

> Over two hundred Germans rose out of the ground before us on the very same ground that had been fought over by the tanks all morning long and in plain sight of all of us. How they got there is a mystery to me but sure enough there they were. Without the slightest hesitation they arose as one and started toward us, with their tanks behind them. . . . Then our artillery went to work on them with sky bursts that exploded shrapnel shells over their heads and literally cut them to pieces. It was murderous and deadly. . . . The whole thing was based on the fact that they expected us to run ourselves but as we chose to stand our ground and with the withering fire upon them the whole attack broke down.[33]

By 1830, the Germans were retreating. The division had survived the second crisis of the day.

The 1st Infantry Division, with the assistance of two artillery and two tank destroyer battalions, defeated the *10th Panzer Division*. Although heavy fighting continued until 7 April, the panzer division no longer had the punch it had used to such effect in Tunisia since December. The *10th*

Panzer Division lost at least forty tanks, or more than half its strength, and hundreds of infantrymen. American losses had been heavy, especially in the 18th Infantry, the 601st TD Battalion, and the 5th and 32nd Field Artillery Battalions. The Americans, however, replaced all equipment and most personnel losses, while the Axis units were unable to do so. The Division Artillery played a decisive role in the battle. The thirty-six howitzers of the three divisional 105mm battalions fired 4,319 rounds in one day, accounting for a majority of the enemy tanks destroyed.[34]

Victory in North Africa

Although the *10th Panzer Division* did not mount another assault toward El Guettar, the 1st Infantry Division remained alert. The *10th Panzer Division*, reinforced with elements of the *21st Panzer Division* and the Italian *Centauro Division*, remained in positions blocking Highway 15 and Gumtree Road. II Corps had succeeded in drawing significant German strength from in front of Montgomery. Alexander now instructed Patton to blow a hole through the Axis defenses and have the 1st Armored Division charge to the coast. Alexander directed that the 1st and 9th Infantry Divisions were to punch the hole, while the 34th Infantry Division was to launch another attack well to the north. Patton, deeply resentful of Alexander's dictation of the plan, prepared to comply.[35]

Since Major General Manton Eddy's 9th Infantry Division was to attack along the south side of Highway 15, the 1st Infantry Division reduced its front. Greer's battered CT18 was placed in reserve to refit. Taylor's 26th Infantry was on the left and Fechet's CT16 was on the right. The key pieces of terrain that II Corps needed to capture were Hills 369 and 772 south of the highway and Hills 482 and 574 to the north. With these in hand, Patton could unleash 1st Armored Division in a dash for Gabes.

The enemy was prepared for the corps attack. Units of the *10th Panzer Division* were interspersed with Italian soldiers of the *Centauro Division*. German infantrymen held the critical pieces of terrain. Although the enemy expected the main American effort north of Gumtree Road, they had sufficient forces on Djebels Mcheltat, Kheroua, and Berda to make Patton's offensive a costly enterprise.

The 1st Infantry Division was better prepared for the attack than the 9th Infantry Division. The veterans of the two regiments had been in the sector for a week. Patrols had located the enemy defenses, and the leaders of the Big Red One knew the ground. Coordination between the artillery and infantry was well practiced, and the commanders knew how to conduct offensive operations. The 16th Infantry crossed the line of departure at 0550,

28 March, with a strong advanced guard. At a large wadi southwest of Djebel Mcheltat, the leading infantrymen drew heavy machine-gun fire as flares illuminated the battlefield. Thirty Italian prisoners were captured, but resistance did not diminish.

The 2nd Battalion, 26th Infantry, took its initial objective (Hill 536) at 0635, and the 3rd Battalion, 26th Infantry, maneuvered south along Djebel Mcheltat to meet CT16. The 26th Infantry was advancing through compartmentalized terrain, allowing its men to bypass enemy machine guns and use artillery to destroy resistance. The CT16 was attacking across open ground covered by enemy observation and fire. As a result, the division's advance on the right ran into trouble. Roosevelt moved forward with CT16, providing Allen with first-hand information.

The 1st Battalion, 16th Infantry, had run into an obstacle covered by machine guns. Lieutenant Colonel Charles Denholm was wounded as he rallied his men. The battalion retreated to better cover, forcing Fechet to commit his 3rd Battalion to lead the advance and protect the 1st Battalion as it reorganized. Roosevelt reported that the 16th Infantry was "getting heavy artillery fire, CP [command post] being shelled continuously. The Ops not good. Observation bad." In this situation, Roosevelt recommended to Allen that "we immediately take up consideration of a flanking movement from the North by the 2nd Battalion of the 26th . . . striking in deep and following a line down to what we approximate the final objective."[36]

Roosevelt remained with the 16th Infantry, which was suffering heavy casualties. Efforts by the 26th Infantry to help clear Hill 482 continued. The terrain across Mcheltat, however, was too rough for half-tracks or tanks to traverse, making this an infantryman's fight. By 1235, the 3rd Battalion, 26th Infantry, was 2,000 yards from 3rd Battalion, 16th Infantry, and the 2nd Battalion, 26th Infantry, was still moving toward Hill 574. But the 16th Infantry was not able to advance. By 1350, 2nd Battalion, 26th Infantry, also had ceased to make progress. CT16 could not overcome the obstacles in its sector because of the heavy enemy fire, and CT26 was spread too thin to advance. At 1435, Allen decided to send the 18th Infantry's 2nd and 3rd Battalions to the battle. But it would take two hours to make this move. The Big Red One had been stopped, at least momentarily.[37]

As the division fought toward its objectives, the 9th Infantry Division launched its first night attack of the war in the early hours of 28 March. The lead battalion of the 47th Infantry became disoriented in the dark, mistaking Draa Saada el Hamra Ridge (Hill 290) for its objective of Djebel Kheroua (Hill 369). The 1st and 3rd Battalions captured most of el Hamra Ridge but could not seize its highest point. The 2nd Battalion, 47th Infantry, got lost as it moved to the south and remained out of contact for thirty-six hours. By the end of the day, the 9th Infantry Division was forced to regroup, having lost heavily to the entrenched enemy.[38]

The 16th Infantry Regiment also found it impossible to make progress on the north side of Highway 15. Because things had not improved by nightfall, Taylor committed Kelleher's 1st Battalion, 26th Infantry, in a drive along Djebel Mcheltat to help the 3rd Battalion fight through to CT16 and secure Hill 482.

Kelleher's attack commenced at 2000. By 0300, 29 March, the battalion had reached Hill 482, where it got involved in heavy fighting for possession of the heights. At dawn, Kelleher's men received fire from the west and from Hill 482. Company A was hit especially hard. The acting company commander remembered later: "This fire, in addition to sniping fire, proved very demoralizing to the troops." Attempts to have the artillery forward observer call for artillery support failed when German fire hit his radio operator and the radio. Fifty men of Company A retreated to a wadi where enemy artillery fire blasted them. The company lost 40 percent of its strength.[39] By the end of the day, the "battalion [had] suffered badly from heavy mortar fire and very accurate enemy sniping. It was not until near dark that we were able to get some of the high peaks."[40] The battalion, however, persisted in its fight to secure the hill. By the morning of 30 March, Company L had cleared the hills to the west. Communications to Division Artillery also were reestablished, allowing the 33rd Field Artillery to fire 3,000 rounds of 105mm fire in support.[41]

The costly battles by 1st Battalion, 26th Infantry, and the 16th Infantry ended successfully because the veteran leaders held their units together in the most difficult of circumstances. Their situation was no less severe than those experienced by the battalions of the 9th Infantry Division, but seasoned leaders and veteran troops produced very dissimilar results. The 1st Infantry Division continued to grind its way through the tough terrain north of Highway 15. As the famous war correspondent Ernie Pyle noticed, the troops "had made the psychological transition from their normal belief that taking human life was sinful, over to a new professional outlook where killing was a craft."[42]

At 0030, 29 March, the 16th Infantry launched another night attack against the southwest portion of Mcheltat. After a two-mile advance, the 2nd Battalion engaged the enemy's outpost line. By 0530, Fechet reported that his assault was making progress. At 0650 his lead battalion reached its objective west of Hill 482. The enemy retreated as the 16th Infantry advanced to meet CT26. By 0720, Fechet reported that the base of Hill 482 was secure and that the main threat was coming from south of Highway 15 in the 9th Infantry Division's sector.[43] In reality, Fechet's battalions were west of Hill 482, and it would take a day of heavy losses for the 1st and 3rd Battalions to clear the area.[44]

While the 16th and 26th Infantry Regiments fought for Hill 482, the 18th Infantry's attack progressed along Gumtree Road. Meeting light resistance, Greer's infantrymen reached Sakket. With the flank secured, the division turned its attention to Hill 574. But a push toward that point had to wait until the combat teams could be supplied and reorganized. The division dug in on the line from Hill 482 north to Djebel Hamadi and waited for further orders.

II Corps' attempt to open the road to Gabes with infantry attacks had failed. The 1st Infantry Division had made progress in the north, but the 9th Infantry Division failed to dislodge the Germans. The 34th Infantry Division also failed to make any progress at Fondouk el Aourareb. In this situation, Alexander ordered Patton to attempt another breakthrough with a thrust by the 1st Armored Division.[45] After a promising start, the attack broke down when the armor units encountered strong antitank defenses. Most of the ground gained by American infantrymen was retaken by the Germans.

On 1 and 2 April, the 1st and 9th Infantry Divisions made minor attacks and conducted patrols to prevent the enemy from launching a surprise counterthrust. Both divisions had suffered heavy casualties. The 9th Infantry Division lost over 1,300 killed, wounded, and missing. The Big Red One lost 126 killed, 1,016 wounded, and 159 missing, from 16 March to 6 April.[46] The men were exhausted after two weeks of sustained combat. Holding on became the order of the day.

Although there was some concern that the enemy was preparing an attack toward El Guettar on 3 April, the reality was that *First Italian Army* was retreating while the *10th* and *21st Panzer Divisions* were protecting its flank. By 4 April, all units reported that the Axis forces were preparing to withdraw. On 6 April, the Big Red One reached the final objectives of the original attack. The El Guettar campaign was over. When the 1st Infantry Division launched an attack at 0700, 7 April, it found the enemy gone.[47]

Once it was clear that the enemy had withdrawn, the division consolidated its positions and policed the battlefield. The 16th Infantry took charge of 2,000 Axis prisoners and moved them to prisoner pens near Tebessa. The 1st Engineers cleared minefields and repaired roads, and the 1st Quartermaster Battalion provided trucks to shuttle infantrymen back to Gafsa to bathe and pick up new boots and clothing.

Patton and Allen complimented the troops on their performance. In his 8 April letter to Allen, Patton summarized his assessment of the division's performance: "For twenty-two days of relentless battle, you have never faltered.

Over country whose rugged difficulty beggars description and against a vet-eran foe cunningly disposed, you have pressed on. Undeterred by cold, by lack of sleep, and by continuous losses, you have conquered. Your valorous exploits have brought undying fame to the soldiers of the United States."[48] After its successful actions, the division moved to Morsott, Algeria, 140 miles northwest of Gafsa, where it spent five days recuperating. During this brief lull, Terry Allen had the troops paint the division's insignia on the fronts of their helmets. The Red One was to be two-thirds the size of the shoulder patch. Officers were to paint their Red One in half-size, above their rank insignia. This recognition of unit pride and esprit was well deserved.[49] Nearly as important, "clear skies and a warm sun made the rest of the tired men a pleasant one. Bathing and washing of clothes were seen everywhere. Articles had been distributed by the ARC [American Red Cross] field repre-sentative. . . . The men began to lose that dazed look, and began sitting up and eagerly reading the bulletin board notices for entertainment."[50]

On 15 April, Colonel Taylor informed the 26th Infantry that it was to move north the next day to take over a section held by a British brigade. Taylor also notified the combat team that John Bowen was to take command of the 26th Infantry and that he was going to assume command of the 16th Infantry. During the next four days, the division followed the 26th Infantry north. With the rupturing of the Axis lines in southern Tunisia, the struggle for Africa had entered its final phase.

The Final Allied Offensive in Tunisia

The Allies failed to cut off the Axis forces in southern Tunisia from their bases at Bizerte and Tunis. Another operation was needed to destroy the enemy. The 18th Army Group's plan for the drive against the Axis bridge-head included an attack east to Bizerte by II Corps, in the northern corner of Tunisia. This placed the American divisions on the extreme left flank of the Allied forces, in the most rugged and compartmentalized terrain in Tunisia (Map 12). Major General Omar Bradley, who had taken command of II Corps when Patton returned to Algiers to plan the invasion of Sicily, was to work directly for General Alexander. South of II Corps, the British First Army was to drive northeast to seize Tunis while Montgomery's Eighth Army made a supporting attack. The French XIX Corps was placed in the line between the two British armies.[51]

II Corps was to attack toward Bizerte with two divisions abreast on a line from the Mediterranean coast to the corps' southern boundary, 7 miles northwest of Medjez el Bab. The 9th Division was on the corps' northern flank, and the Big Red One was on the south. Bradley intended to commit the 1st Armored Division through the 1st Infantry Division in a drive north along the Tine River after the infantry opened the road to Mateur.

Montgomery's Eighth Army initiated the offensive on the night of 19–20 April. At first, the British made progress against the Italians in the enemy's screen line. But the local German commander, Fritz Bayerlein, shifted reserves to the threatened area and made the British pay a high price in casualties and tanks for the capture of Djebel Garci. In the face of mounting losses, Montgomery suspended the attack.[52]

Before Anderson's First Army could commence its offensive, the Germans launched a spoiling attack west of Ksar Tyr. Although the Germans advanced 5 miles, they were stopped at the main British positions. The British then forced them back to their original line by the evening of 21 April. Anderson's offensive commenced the next morning, forcing von Arnim to commit the *10th Panzer Division* against the British 6th Armored Division. This opened a three-day armor melee that forced the British to suspend their offensive. Both sides lost heavily. In three days of vicious fighting, the Germans stopped the British southwest of Tebourba. The British lost ninety tanks, but the *Fifth Panzer Army*'s armored force was reduced to sixty-nine operational tanks and its fuel reserve was exhausted.[53]

The 1st Infantry Division's Last African Battle: Bedja-Mateur

The 1st Infantry Division held the southern portion of II Corps' front, between the Djoumine and Tine River Valleys, and was to make the main attack. The division deployed with the 26th Infantry on the left, the 16th in the center, and the 18th on the right. The 1st Recon Troop and the 81st Reconnaissance Battalion protected the division's northern flank along the Djoumine River and maintained contact with 9th Infantry Division. The 1st Battalion, 168th Infantry, from the 34th Infantry Division, reinforced the northern flank. The division's southern flank was protected by the attached 6th Armored Infantry Regiment. Andrus's artillery was reinforced by eleven battalions of artillery from the corps.[54]

The Germans in the area included three battalions of the Luftwaffe *Regiment Barenthin* and two battalions of the *755th Regiment* of the *334th Infantry Division*. The Germans had organized defensive zones around each of the major hills in the sector, making it necessary for the division to strike them simultaneously.[55]

The division attacked on Good Friday, 23 April. John Corley's 3rd Battalion, 26th Infantry, made a noisy demonstration toward Hill 499 to draw

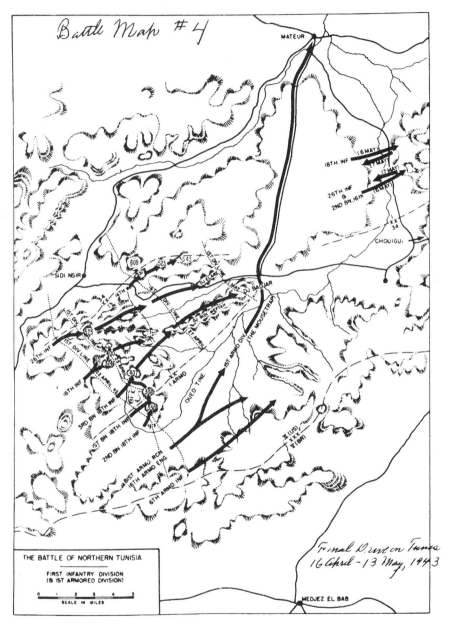

Map 12. The battle of Northern Tunisia, 16 April–13 May 1943. North
of Medjez el Bab is Longstop Hill, where the 18th Infantry fought in
December 1942. (Major General Terry Allen, *A Summary of the Final
Drive on Tunis,* 1943, a signed copy for General Huebner, McCormick
Research Center Collections)

German attention away from the regiment's main thrust by the 2nd Battalion toward Hill 575 (Kef el Goraa). Knowing from earlier patrols that Hill 565 was not defended, Bowen had a company of Kelleher's 1st Battalion occupy 565 to support the assault on Kef el Goraa. Kelleher's men took Hill 565 with no resistance, but the 2nd Battalion ran into heavy enemy fire as it crossed the open ground south of Hill 575. During the attack, all the officers and the first sergeant of Company F were killed or wounded, leaving a staff sergeant named Searle in command. He reorganized the company, appointed new platoon leaders from among the sergeants and corporals, and continued the attack.

By 0830, 2nd Battalion's attack had stalled. Under intense enemy fire, Daniel was forced to withdraw his companies to a ridge 800 yards south. As the morning wore on, Kelleher's company on Hill 565 came under heavy fire as the Germans dug new positions on Kef el Goraa facing Hill 565.[56] The 5th, 33rd, and 68th Field Artillery Battalions hammered the defenses in unsuccessful efforts to suppress enemy fire. The 33rd Artillery alone fired 111 missions and 4,212 rounds from 23 to 26 April.[57] Nonetheless, CT26 was forced to dig in and reorganize for another attempt to take Hill 575. In the late afternoon, Allen ordered the 1st Battalion, 168th Infantry, to move into the positions held by the 26th Infantry's 3rd Battalion, freeing Bowen to reinforce the attack against Kef el Goraa. This move was not completed until the evening of 24 April.[58]

The 16th Infantry's attack in the division's center against Hill 400 did not meet opposition until it neared its objective at about 0745. At that point, Company K came under heavy fire. For the remainder of the day, the 3rd Battalion fought to clear the enemy from Hill 400 and to push on to Hill 394. In this effort, a series of hilltops had to be taken by the 2nd and 3rd Battalions. By dusk, the 3rd Battalion was still moving slowly toward Hill 394, and Taylor had sent Denholm's 1st Battalion toward Hill 469 to the east. The German resistance did not slacken, making it necessary to dig them out of every hole. The process was slow and costly. At 2145, Taylor reported to the division G3 that the "enemy [is] holding 394 in strength. [They] blasted L Company who tried to take it. 3d Bn moving fwd, situation getting under control and will have 394 by morning."[59]

During this slugging match against the *755th Regiment*, all of the officers in Company K were killed or wounded. "With this situation materially unchanged at 2300 hours, Colonel Taylor's order went out. . . . 'There will be a general attack all along the line at 0300. Take advantage of darkness. Watch the flank to the east.'"[60] By dawn, 24 April, CT16 held Hills 400 and 394. Taylor pushed his battalions forward, ensuring that his soldiers would not have to fight and die another day for the ground they had already taken.

CT18 also encountered fierce resistance. Ben Sternberg's 2nd Battalion reached Hill 350 at about 0445. With the aid of accurate artillery fire by the 32nd Field Artillery, Company G launched a bayonet charge against a position known as Windmill Farm. At the same time, Company E, led by Captain Carl Randall, attacked from the northeast, surprising and capturing thirty-five Germans. Within twenty minutes, Sternberg reported that his men had occupied their objectives. The Germans, however, counterattacked and drove Company G from Windmill Farm. At dawn, the enemy attacked Company E on Hill 350 before Randall's men could dig in. The assault drove Company E and other elements of the 2nd Battalion off the crest. Companies E and G suffered severe losses, but Greer ordered Sternberg to try again. At 1145, Company F, supported by tanks from the 1st Battalion, 13th Armor, launched another assault. During the attack, machine gunners fired 92,000 rounds and mortarmen fired 1,200 rounds. As Sternberg remembered, "The advancing infantry was subjected to intense mortar, artillery and machine-gun fire, but they never faltered. The support rendered by the tanks was excellent and the supporting fires of H Co., commanded by Capt. Robert E. Murphy, were superb." By 1320, Hill 350 was again in American hands. For its determined efforts, the 2nd Battalion, 18th Infantry, received one of the first Presidential Unit Citations awarded in World War II.[61]

On CT18's left flank, the 3rd Battalion fought its way toward Hill 407 against increasing resistance. By 0430, the battalion was pinned down by machine-gun fire. Company I maneuvered a platoon onto the crest just in time for it to be surrounded and captured by a German counterattack. Lieutenant Colonel C. P. Brown was forced by heavy losses to order a retreat into a draw just short of the base of the hill, where his battalion stayed for the remainder of the day. That evening, Lieutenant Colonel York maneuvered his 1st Battalion around the flank of 3rd Battalion to launch another attack at 0300, 24 April. By early morning, the 1st Battalion held Hill 407. During these attacks, the 2nd Battalion lost 43 killed, 161 wounded, and 20 missing, and the 3rd Battalion suffered 17 killed, 73 wounded, and 48 missing.[62]

In the center, CT16 spent the morning consolidating positions on Hills 400 and 394. The key to the center was Hill 469. By 1020, Denholm's 1st Battalion was working its way toward 469, and the priority target of Division Artillery became the German positions on that hill. At 1637 hours, Denholm's men were on Hill 469 cleaning out the last pockets of resistance. At the same time, the 6th Armored Infantry Regiment consolidated its hold on Hills 388 and 420.[63]

On the division's right, the 18th Infantry attacked at 0300, 24 April, to destroy the German positions on Hill 407. Following this, the regiment advanced east against light resistance for the next two days. On 26 April, Greer's lead battalion halted on Hill 341, known as Djebel Sidi Meftah, until the remainder of the division could reach the higher hills to the northwest.[64] With this success in the south, the division was ready to tackle the enemy's positions on Kef el Goraa.

The 26th Infantry launched its attack to take Hill 575 at 0300 on Easter Sunday, 25 April. The infantrymen followed a rolling barrage to the base of the mountain, at which point the artillery shifted to the top and reverse slopes. John Corley, who had recently been promoted to lieutenant colonel, led the attack with the 3rd Battalion. The regimental history recounts the attack:

> There was some scattered fire from the Germans as we neared the lines that had been staked out and measured so that blind firing could be effective. . . . Squads that advanced in touch with the flank squads found it easy to mop up the resisting points. In the darkness, the squads bunched closer together so that firing and grenades would not endanger the lives of our own men. . . . The first groups ran into the concrete emplacements. Some of these were mopped up with hand grenades; others had already been smashed by our artillery. Some were empty; the foe had retreated as soon as the troops had come into close range. Bayonets were fixed as the rest of the hill-mass was explored for remaining knots of resistance.[65]

By 0600, Corley's infantrymen had taken Kef el Goraa. The 26th Infantry had lost 17 killed, 111 wounded, and 1 missing since 23 April. The division now held a bulge in the German lines, with CT18 nearly to the road that runs from the Tine River to Mateur and the 26th and 16th Infantry Regiments in positions overlooking the road (Map 12). As a result, the Germans started to pull back to the last series of hills before Mateur.

In the midst of the successful assault against Hill 575, before dawn on 25 April, the 26th and 16th Infantry Regiments were hit by friendly artillery fire. The 1st Battalion, 26th Infantry, suffered two casualties. The 1st and 2nd Battalions, 16th Infantry, lost 40 wounded and 5 killed. This tragedy made Taylor's efforts to keep the 16th Infantry moving more difficult.[66]

On the morning of 25 April, Allen reorganized the division. He shifted CT26 east to the vicinity of Djebel Touta (Hill 444), allowing the 34th Infantry Division to take over the line along the Sidi Nsir Road. This move let the 34th Division get its infantry into the line for an attack to capture Hill 609, known as Djebel Tohent. The Germans had withdrawn to a defensive line anchored on Djebel Tohent and were inflicting damage on the 1st Infantry

Division to the south. Hill 609 had to be captured before the 1st Armored Division could drive to Mateur and Bizerte, less than 30 miles away.[67] The battle for control of Hill 609 was to rage for the next six days.

On 27 April, the 34th Infantry Division assaulted the hills between Sidi Nsir and Djebel Tohent. Hill 490 and a lower hill to the west had to be taken before the 34th Infantry Division could approach Hill 609. The infantrymen made limited progress in the face of heavy fire and failed to occupy Hill 490. At 1720, 27 April, the 1st Infantry Division learned that the 34th Infantry Division would try again the next day. During these operations, the Big Red One moved supplies forward and sent out reconnaissance patrols.[68]

It was now apparent that the attacks by the 34th Infantry Division against Hill 490 and then Djebel Tohent could succeed only if the Germans were driven from Hills 529 and 531. Consequently, on 27 April, Allen committed the 16th Infantry's 2nd Battalion to clear those hills on the boundary with the 34th Division and sent the 1st Battalion, 16th Infantry, east to take Hill 428. These missions were accomplished before daylight on 28 April. However, the new positions were exposed to enemy observation. By 0700, Taylor was reporting that his regiment was "having a sad time the way this thing is going. They [the 34th Division] did not move at the time given to me." Allen immediately contacted II Corps and reported that "those people haven't moved one inch and our people are completely stopped by fire from 609." In response, Allen received permission for the 1st Infantry Division's artillery to plaster Hill 609 in the 34th Infantry Division's sector with high explosives and smoke rounds.[69]

While CT16 attempted to secure Hills 529 and 531, CT26 advanced northeast from Djebel Touta to Djebels Berakine and el Anz, and CT18 moved east toward Djebel Badjar. Once el Anz and Badjar were in American hands, the 1st Armored Division could move up the Tine Valley. Hill 609 remained the key to success. By 0900, enemy artillery fire had pinned down the 2nd Battalion, 16th Infantry, on Hill 531 and Denholm's 1st Battalion had halted on Hill 476. To the east, the 26th Infantry was unable to clear Djebel el Anz because of artillery fire from eight locations, including Hill 609. The Germans were defending every hill in the area with a determination derived from the knowledge that this was their last set of defensible positions south of Mateur.[70]

On 29 April, the 34th Infantry Division attempted to envelop Djebel Tohent with infantry supported by tanks. However, German artillery and machine-gun fire decimated the attackers short of their objectives. Thus, the 16th and 26th Infantry Regiments continued to take a pounding in their exposed positions. It was clear to Allen that his division would have to lend a hand in the encirclement of Hill 609. By seizing Hill 558, 4,000 yards east-northeast of Hill 609, Allen reasoned that the Germans would be forced to withdraw from Djebel Tohent.[71]

Allen ordered CT16 to seize Hills 523 and 545. Colonel Taylor assigned the mission of taking Hill 523 to Denholm's 1st Battalion, while the 3rd Battalion was to clear the eastern slopes of Hill 531. Denholm's battalion moved north during the night of 29–30 April. By 0215 hours, the battalion had reached the base of Hill 523; here Denholm's men fixed bayonets and attacked. By 0445 they had cleared the crest, where the infantry set up parapets in an all-around defense. When Denholm attempted, however, to move a company northeast to Hill 545, which overlooked his positions on 523, he learned that a deep fault separated the two hills and that his men could not get to 545. This was to prove disastrous for 1st Battalion.[72]

Once Denholm's command reached the top of Hill 523, Allen called for a company of tanks to reinforce it. Unfortunately, it would take several hours for the tanks to arrive. In the meantime, the enemy counterattacked, enveloping Denholm's battalion. Artillery fire and enemy infantry cut the wire communications to the hilltop, making it impossible to provide artillery support to the battalion. By 1045, the situation was desperate. After several hours of trying to push support forward, the division G3 learned that the Germans had overrun Denholm's positions and that American prisoners had been spotted on Hill 545. It was later learned that Denholm and about 150 of his men had been captured. The remaining men of his battalion were killed, wounded, or dispersed.[73]

Later, on 30 April, Taylor launched a counterattack with Joe Crawford's 2nd Battalion supported by Sherman tanks. Crawford's infantrymen reached the top of Hill 523 and repulsed a German attack at around 1520. From then until dark, Division Artillery fired every available weapon against the enemy attempting to attack Crawford's men. Nonetheless, by 2100, Taylor reported that Crawford was "not going to be able to hold either hill. 2nd Bn is being pushed vigorously. Enemy around 523 again in strength. L and D cos. have been driven off hill. Artillery fire will probably not be effective after dark."[74]

The division did all it could to help the 2nd Battalion, 16th Infantry. Bowen sent the 26th Infantry's 2nd Battalion to relieve the 3rd Battalion, 16th Infantry, thus making it available to support Crawford. Two companies of the 1st Engineers joined CT16 to serve as infantry, and Division Artillery responded to every call for fire. Nonetheless, it was clear that the enemy again had Hills 523 and 545. The division could not advance until the 34th Division took Djebel Tohent. The 26th Infantry Regiment defeated seven enemy counterattacks at Djebel el Anz in this period, and CT18 remained committed on the eastern end of the long division front. The division was out of reserves and had suffered over 2,000 casualties since the beginning of the offensive.[75] As a result, General Bradley ordered Allen to make no further movement until the 34th Infantry Division secured Hill 609.[76]

Just when the situation seemed darkest, the 34th Infantry Division cleared the hills around Djebel Tohent. The fighting all along the Tunisian front had taken its toll on the enemy's ability to resist. The breaking point came on 1 May, when American attacks shattered the last coherent Axis defenses and destroyed the last enemy reserves. The steady advance of the 9th Infantry Division to the north forced the Germans to begin a general withdrawal. The 1st Armored Division was ready to drive to Mateur. Facing this unrelenting pressure, *Fifth Panzer Army* ordered a withdrawal toward Bizerte and Tunis on the evening of 1 May.[77]

As the Germans retreated, the 1st Infantry Division pushed forward across its front. By the evening of 2 May, CT16 had patrols on Hills 523 and 545. At the same time, the 34th Infantry Division assumed responsibility for the northern sector of the 1st Infantry Division.[78] Over the next two days, the Big Red One pulled the battered 16th Infantry Regiment out of the line and moved the 26th and 18th to positions overlooking the Tine River south of Mateur.

On the morning of 3 May, the 1st Armored Division drove north. CT18 facilitated this by pushing patrols east. By mid-morning, it was clear that there was an opportunity to push forward from the positions of CT26 as well. By 0920, Greer had troops across the Mateur Road, and Allen ordered the two combat teams to ignore hills to the flanks of their advance.[79] That afternoon, elements of the 1st Armored Division occupied Mateur. Over the next three days, the *Fifth Panzer Army* fell apart.

The 1st Infantry Division made one final attack in North Africa, on 6 May. This action was a costly failure, and there was later some debate between Bradley and Terry Allen as to whether or not Bradley had authorized the attack. The division's records indicate, however, that II Corps was fully aware of the attack before it was launched. The division's chief of staff, Stanhope Mason, also confirms in his memoirs that Bradley was aware of the operation and that the corps commander took no action to cancel the attack.[80]

While II Corps was advancing toward Bizerte, the 1st Infantry Division held a defensive line facing east along the Tine River, south of Mateur. Wishing to expedite the destruction of the Axis forces and to facilitate an advance by the 34th Infantry Division to the south, Allen planned to attack with two regiments abreast across the Tine. The objectives for the assault were a series of hills from which the Germans had been firing at the division.

At 0300, CT18 and CT26 began the assault. By 0420, CT18 reported that its 1st Battalion was on Hill 121 and its 3rd Battalion was on the forward slope of Hill 232. Then things went wrong. "At daylight direct 88mm artillery fire and machine gun fire forced [Company A] to side slip to a defiladed position south of 232 where it remained throughout the day. Company C moved to 202 where it was pinned down by heavy machine gun and artillery fire."[81] Bowen's 26th Infantry was even less fortunate. By 0500, its 3rd Battalion was being plastered by artillery and machine-gun fire, and the 2nd Battalion had run into a minefield. It was clear that the "enemy [was] not pulling [out]."[82]

CT26 on the right advanced into a well-organized German defense and by 0600 was fighting to hold on to its gains. When Allen ordered a company of tanks to cross the river and aid CT26, it found that there were no fords across the Tine. A bridge put in earlier broke after four tanks crossed, and those tanks found the ground too soft to allow further maneuver. As this transpired, Greer reported to the G3 that the soldiers of the 18th Infantry were in a fight for their lives:

> I need help. 3rd Bn has gotten lost, one company is in the wadi east of 232. We were driven off the hill. 1st Bn is in [the] wadi on 232 and may be cut off if we don't get help. Resistance is strong and we are getting hell. 2nd Bn is making progress toward the hill but there is something forming in back of the hill. We have arty on it. I can't get the tanks across the ford the engineers fixed up. I have got to have help.[83]

Allen ordered Greer to hang on, promising him that "we will straighten things out." Minutes later, CT18 reported that German machine guns had caught its 3rd Battalion in the open and inflicted heavy casualties: fewer than 100 men were still combat-effective. CT26 was in a similar situation, as artillery and mortar fire rained down on the exposed infantrymen. The 33rd Field Artillery alone fired 127 missions and 2,664 rounds in an unsuccessful attempt to destroy the German artillery and mortars.[84] As the division reported to II Corps, "The *Barenthins* are in front of us, evidently in strength and going to stand." And stand they did, capturing most of the survivors of Companies I and K, 18th Infantry, by 0800.[85]

By 1145, the G3 had decided that there was "not much hope of doing anything in [the] 18th sector." Therefore, he instructed Bowen to maneuver one of his battalions toward Greer's beleaguered companies, but only under the cover of darkness, which was still a long time off. CT16 remained in reserve with two battalions. Shortly after noon, the Germans counterattacked against the 3rd Battalion, 26th Infantry. Since Bowen's battalions were pinned down, it was impossible for them to aid Greer.[86]

Confusion reigned on the firing line and in the division headquarters. At 1320, Greer called the G3 again, asking, "What about some orders? We can't hold here. I am afraid I will be cut off. . . . If enemy counter-attacks 232 we are sunk." Allen, however, determined that the reserve (CT16) should be put in through the 26th Infantry's positions and maneuver north to aid Greer, and Gibb told Greer that "there will be no change until tomorrow." At the same time, Allen notified II Corps that the division was "definitely held up."[87]

As Greer feared, another German assault hit his 1st Battalion at 1755 hours. Artillery plastered his men, and enemy infantry were all around their positions. Greer believed that he needed to retreat before the Germans cut off the remnants of the regiment. Allen, however, refused permission for a retreat, fearing that such a move would uncover the left flank and rear of CT26. Nonetheless, Greer's men retreated, forcing Bowen to protect his regiment's left flank with whatever force he could scrape up. With his flank threatened, Bowen asked for orders. Allen responded by ordering the two regiments to "fight in place," even though Bowen reported that "I am exposed on ridge. Can be cut to pieces."[88]

By midnight, both combat teams had retreated west across the Tine River. Gibb reported to II Corps that "we got stuck out too far; all our rifle companies are down to the strength of a reinforced platoon. No contact. They will need a chance to get reorganized. We have been in too long."[89] For all intents and purposes the campaign was over. On 7 May, the chief of staff, Colonel Stanhope Mason, ordered the major subordinate units to prepare quartering parties to send to Oran.

Morale was not high in the headquarters as the infantrymen dug in on the west bank of the Tine. Rick Atkinson notes, in *An Army at Dawn*, that "Allen was chastened, and even loyalists doubted his judgement." To Bradley, the attack was "a foolish one undertaken without authorization."[90] Further, Bradley had come to believe that Allen was "the most difficult man with whom I have ever had to work . . . fiercely antagonistic to any echelon above that of division."[91]

On 7 May, the 9th Infantry Division entered the heavily damaged port of Bizerte and the 1st Armored Division reached the Tunisian coast. To the south, the British First Army captured Tunis. By 13 May, the Axis forces in Tunisia had collapsed. At least 275,000 enemy soldiers surrendered, including approximately 80,000 Germans.

Despite the setback on the Tine, Eisenhower held the 1st Infantry Division

in high esteem. On 16 April, he wrote to George Marshall, telling the chief
of staff that "both the First and the Ninth Divisions did a very workmanlike
job in the Gafsa area, with the First Division definitely showing the results of
its greater experience and consequent greater success." However, he erroneously believed that the division's "task was not as difficult as that facing the
Ninth Division."[92] In a letter written the same day to Bradley, Eisenhower
pointed out that "the 1st and 9th Divisions, particularly the former, have
established themselves reputations as sound fighting units, although it is
recognized by senior American and British officers that in certain aspects
their training is not all that it should be."[93] Near the end of the offensive in
the Beja-Mateur battle, Eisenhower again wrote to Marshall: "The British
liaison officer [at headquarters], who is an experienced veteran, stated cat-
egorically that the 1st U.S. Division is one of the finest tactical organizations
that he had ever seen."[94]

Eisenhower's admiration for the Big Red One did not, evidently, extend
to the leadership of Terry Allen. Eisenhower's letters to George Marshall in
April and May 1943 are full of praise for Patton, Bradley, Lucian Truscott,
Manton Eddy, Ernest Harmon, and others.[95] But he made no mention of the
leadership or fighting qualities of Allen or Teddy Roosevelt.

The 1st Division's Return to Oran

On 13 May, the Big Red One moved to Oran. The regiments were billeted in
small towns outside Oran, and the division headquarters was established in
Sidi Chami. Training for amphibious operations began almost immediately.
During this period of training in the hot North African spring, the soldiers
continued to wear wool uniforms rather than the more comfortable cotton
khaki clothing worn by the support and headquarters troops in Oran. This
and other restrictions imposed by Bradley and Patton did not sit well with
Generals Allen and Roosevelt or with the division's combat veterans.

During the following weeks, there developed an unhealthy relationship
between the combat troops and the support personnel in the Oran area.
Fights broke out between the division's veterans and the men who had supported them, and the military police had to intervene. The feeling developed
in II Corps headquarters that Allen and Roosevelt were condoning disre-
spectful attitudes by their men toward the officers and enlisted personnel in
the support units. Allen ordered Roosevelt to sort it out and court-martial
any soldiers guilty of improper conduct. But the situation, which became
known as the Oran Incident, reinforced Bradley's impression that Allen and
Roosevelt were weak disciplinarians. Bradley even claimed that this "incident (and others too numerous and trivial to mention) convinced me that

Terry Allen was not fit to command, and I was determined to remove him and Teddy from the division as soon as circumstances on Sicily permitted."[96]

Captain (later Lieutenant Colonel) Donald V. Helgeson's recollection of how the veterans of the Fighting First were treated during the weeks they spent living in tents near Oran illustrates the gulf of understanding that sometimes exists between senior leaders and the troops:

> I have never read anything describing the deplorable leadership and appalling treatment of those of us who returned to Oran (and Algiers) after the Tunisian campaign. The MBS [Medium Base Section] personnel, resplendent in their khaki uniforms and comfortably ensconced in their apartments and hotel rooms in the city, had declared every decent bar and night club off-limits to all but MBS personnel. We didn't even get clean uniforms (some still bloody from combat). We were shunned by all the permanent party who were living under better conditions than in the US. . . . We lived in crummy camps with medio-cre food, no entertainment or recreation, treated literally like stray dogs. . . . I blame Eisenhower, Patton, and all the rest who let this go on right under their noses. The 1st Division has been much maligned for their bad behavior in Oran and poor morale in Sicily. What can you expect? Not one word of gratitude or understanding from one senior officer for all the hardships and sacrifices we had endured![97]

There was one remarkably positive piece of news when the division got to Oran. Lieutenant Colonel Denholm and over 150 of his soldiers escaped shipment to POW camps in Italy and rejoined the division. The saga of Denholm and his men was dramatic. They were on an Italian ship in Tunis Harbor as the campaign ended. When the ship attempted to sail to Italy, on 6 May, it was repeatedly attacked by Allied aircraft. Its captain ran the vessel aground on the Tunisian coast after his crew abandoned ship. After hours of bombing, Denholm and the other prisoners got word of their plight to a French fisherman, who, in turn, alerted the Allied air forces about the human cargo trapped on the Italian steamer.[98]

Denholm and the other 16th Infantry veterans rejoined the division as it embarked on a rigorous schedule of training focused on amphibious operations. The US Army and the 1st Infantry Division again demonstrated a capacity to learn from combat experiences and to apply those lessons to deployed units and to the forces training in the United States.[99]

The infantry regiments analyzed the lessons learned in the Torch landings and practiced techniques to overcome earlier shortfalls. The men learned to use new amphibious warfare vessels such as the Landing Ship, Tank (LST), and the Landing Craft, Infantry (LCI). To do so, the infantry battalions rotated through assault courses on the beaches near Arzew. This training program was definitely needed—thousands of replacements had joined the division since the Torch landings. These men filled the gaps left in the division's ranks by the loss of over 3,900 casualties from 12 November 1942 to 13 May 1943. Of these losses, 634 were killed in action and 697 were missing. It was essential that the replacements be integrated into the combat teams and taught the intricacies of amphibious operations. The 1st Infantry Division accomplished these tasks in a remarkably short period of time. By the end of June, the entire division was aboard ships en route to Algiers to join an armada bound for Sicily.

The first American gun fired in France, 0605, 23 October 1917, by Battery C, 6th Field Artillery, commanded by First Lieutenant Idus R. McLendon. This 75mm gun was emplaced near Bathlemont-les-Bauzement, in the Ansauville sector. (US Army Photo SC5717, McCormick Research Center Collections)

The 16th Infantry in first-line trenches, Gypse Hill, near Einville, Meurthe-et-Moselle, France, 19 November 1917. (US Army Photo SC67139, McCormick Research Center Collections)

General John J. Pershing addressing officers of the 1st Division, Chaumont, France, 16 April 1918. Major General Bullard is seen in his wolf-fur coat. (US Army Photo SC10910, McCormick Research Center Collections)

The 26th Infantry training for Cantigny with French tanks at Breteuil, France, 11 May 1918. The 1st Division G-3 training officer, George C. Marshall, had the soldiers rehearse the battle in maneuvers on similar terrain. (US Army Photo SC12428, McCormick Research Center Collections)

Doughboys waiting for orders to take a machine-gun nest at Berzy-le-Sec, France, 21 July 1918. (US Army Photo SC16487, McCormick Research Center Collections)

A French-made Renault tank with a 37mm gun from Colonel George S. Patton's brigade, attached to the 1st Division, is assisted by the 1st Engineers, September 1918. (Donation of Mildred Friedrich Chapin, McCormick Research Center Collections. Chapin's uncle was Corporal William Friedrich of Company E, 1st Engineers, 1916–1919.)

Brigadier General Frank Parker (left) talking to Lieutenant Colonel Theodore Roosevelt Jr. of the 26th Infantry and Mrs. Eleanor B. Roosevelt, who was volunteering with the YMCA, in Romagne, Meuse, France, 13 November 1918. (US Army Photo SC35363, McCormick Research Center Collections)

The 1st Division circus parades past Cologne Cathedral, Rhenish Prussia, 4 August 1919. (US Army Photo SC162170, McCormick Research Center Collections)

The Victory Parade of the 1st Division, New York City, Fifth Avenue,
10 September 1919. (From the collection of Sergeant William M. Steamer, General
Summerall's chauffeur, US Army Photo SC63797, McCormick Research Center
Collections)

Horse-drawn 75mm guns of Battery D, 6th Field Artillery, on Pulaski Highway from
Fort Hoyle to Fort Meade, Maryland, for maneuvers in 1938. (Donation of Joseph
Furayter, McCormick Research Center Collections)

Troops climbing down a net from the USS *Kent* into Higgins boats, at Buzzards'
Bay, Massachusetts, 1941. (US Army Photo, McCormick Research Center
Collections)

General Lesley McNair, to the left behind mortar crew, and General George C.
Marshall, right, at 1st Infantry Division maneuvers on a mortar range, Camp
Blanding, Florida, 1 May 1942. (US Army Photo, McCormick Research Center
Collections)

Corporals of the 1st Ranger Battalion covering a French gun position captured at Arzew, Algeria, 8 November 1942. Many rocky positions had to be built up rather than dug in. (US Army Photo SC165327, McCormick Research Center Collections)

2nd Battalion, 16th Infantry, marching east through Kasserine Pass, Tunisia, 26 February 1943. Field Marshal Erwin Rommel decided to retreat after the 16th Infantry bloodied his Kampfgruppe, *Deutsches Afrika Corps*, at Bou Chebka. (US Army Photo SC167571, McCormick Research Center Collections)

Company D, 18th Infantry, in foxholes and slit trenches southeast of El Guettar, Tunisia, 23 March 1943. These positions overlook the Gafsa-Gabes highway. (US Army Photo SC171892, McCormick Research Center Collections)

Lieutenant Colonel Charles J. Denholm (left), 1st Battalion, 16th Infantry, after he was freed from an Italian prison ship in Tunis Harbor, with Colonel George A. Taylor, 16th Infantry, in Tunisia, 9 May 1943. Denholm was captured by German paratroopers at Hill 523, 30 April 1943. (US Army Photo SC171634, McCormick Research Center Collections)

Company A, 16th Infantry, advances from Nicosia toward the open ground around Troina, 28 July 1943. (US Army Photo SC185269, McCormick Research Center Collections)

Germans, while retreating to the northeast, dynamited this bridge between Mistretta and San Stefano, Sicily. Motorized equipment was delayed and the infantry proceeded on foot, 2 August 1943. (US Army Photo SC180230, McCormick Research Center Collections)

Major General Clarence Ralph Huebner (left) takes command of the 1st Infantry Division from Major General Terry de la Mesa Allen, 8 August 1943. (US Army Photo SC437660, McCormick Research Center Collections)

Troops in an LCVP approach Omaha Beach, France. Smoke is from naval gunfire supporting the landing, 6 June 1944. The tall man looking to the left has been identified as Ellsworth R. Clark of Headquarters Company, 1st Infantry Division. (General Stanhope B. Mason Collection, then colonel, chief of staff of the 1st Infantry Division, US Army Photo SC320901, McCormick Research Center Collections)

Assault troops with full equipment and landing craft, including LCT 583, jam Omaha Beach, 6 June 1944. Private First Class Harold Wordeman wears a helmet with the white bow of the engineers. (Photo taken by Captain Herman Wall, 165th Photographic Company, at Easy Red, around 1130. General Stanhope B. Mason Collection, US Army Photo SC189902, McCormick Research Center Collections)

Brigadier General Willard G. Wyman (left), assistant division commander, with two staff officers early in the Normandy campaign. Wyman led the 1st Infantry Division Advance Command Post in the assault on Omaha Beach. Arriving at 0830 hours, Wyman coordinated the assault with Brigadier General Norman D. Cota, directing CT116 and CT115, regiments attached for D-day. (US Army Photo, McCormick Research Center Collections)

A squad of the 18th Infantry riding an M4 Sherman tank of the 745th Tank Battalion into the liberated town of La Ferté-Macé, France, 14 August 1944. (US Army Photo, McCormick Research Center Collections)

Crowds meet Company D, 26th Infantry, in Liège, Belgium, 1944. Liberated Belgians greet Staff Sergeant Richard Tracy. (Donation of Bill Lee, Company D, McCormick Research Center Collections)

8

The Invasion of Sicily

WHILE THE 1ST INFANTRY DIVISION REPLENISHED its ranks and trained for amphibious operations, Allied forces prepared for the invasion of Sicily. Operation Husky, the code name given to the invasion of Sicily, was to be the first major Anglo-American offensive in Europe in World War II. The capture of Sicily would open the sea-lanes through the Mediterranean, thus saving an estimated 1.8 million tons of shipping per year, since ships no longer would have to take the long route from the Atlantic Ocean to the Pacific around Africa. Success in Sicily would further undermine Italian morale and willingness to continue the war, possibly leading to the early surrender of Italy. Such a result would force the Germans to divert divisions from France and Russia to Italy and the Balkans. Finally, an assault on Sicily would employ the large Allied forces still in North Africa.[1]

Command Relationships and the Plan

Sicily was chosen as the next Allied objective in part because American and British airpower could support operations there from Africa. Ten Italian and two German divisions defended Sicily in July 1943. Planners believed that the Allies could build up forces on the island faster than the Axis since all enemy reinforcements would have to cross the Strait of Messina from Italy. This route could be attacked by the Allied air forces and, if Messina itself could be seized quickly, the Axis divisions on the island might be cut off and captured.

Operation Husky was planned and executed under the direction of Allied Forces Headquarters, commanded by General Eisenhower. General Alexander's 15th Army Group commanded the American Seventh and the British Eighth Armies for the invasion. Lieutenant General George Patton led the Seventh Army. Bernard Montgomery remained commander of the Eighth Army. Alexander designated the Eighth Army to make the main attack on the southeastern Sicilian coast.

Patton specifically asked for the 1st Infantry Division to land in the center of the American sector. The 16th and 26th Infantry Regiments were to lead the assault, while the 18th Infantry was to serve as II Corps reserve. Two ranger battalions were attached to the division. CCB, 2nd Armored Division, was to land after the 1st Infantry Division had secured the beachhead.[2]

Why was the Big Red One called on again to carry out the critical mission of an amphibious assault? The short answer is that it was one of the best divisions available to conduct the dangerous and difficult task of landing on a hostile shore and establishing a lodgment. The longer answer is that Patton unequivocally told General Eisenhower that he had to have "those sons of bitches."

Operation Husky Begins: 10–12 July 1943

The American landings in southern Sicily were organized in two distinct areas. Naval Task Force 86 was to land the 3rd Infantry Division on Seventh Army's western flank, on both sides of the port of Licata (Map 13). CCA, 2nd Armored Division, was to come ashore as soon as possible to protect the 3rd Division from counterattacks by the German *15th Panzergrenadier Division*.

Omar Bradley's II Corps was to land along the Gulf of Gela. The 1st Infantry Division was to seize Gela and drive inland 12 miles to secure airfields between Gela and Niscemi. The 45th Infantry Division was to assault on the right side of the Gulf of Gela, seize Comiso, and link up with the British. Little planning had been done concerning what the Seventh Army was to do once ashore beyond protecting the flank of the British as they drove north.[3]

US Rear Admiral John L. Hall commanded Naval Task Force 81, which carried the Big Red One. Two light cruisers and thirteen destroyers protected the task force and were to support the initial landing with naval gunfire. The flotilla sailed from Tunis on 8 July. After passing Malta, the convoy turned north and approached Sicily, arriving in the Gulf of Gela late on the evening of 9 July. During most of the journey, the Mediterranean remained calm, but as the task force approached its destination, gale-force winds whipped the seas to a white froth. Eisenhower considered delaying the operation, but in the late afternoon of 9 July the winds abated. However, there was still enough force in the storm to roll the ships and landing craft violently. Just before midnight, the task force anchored 5 miles offshore from Gela. Operation Husky was about to begin.[4]

As the assault ships prepared to deploy, Lieutenant Joe Dawson wrote a last letter to his family:

> From the postmark you will note that this is being written just before we step into the great unknown of D Day and H Hour. What it brings forth I cannot hazard a good guess but whatever happens you can know that we shall do

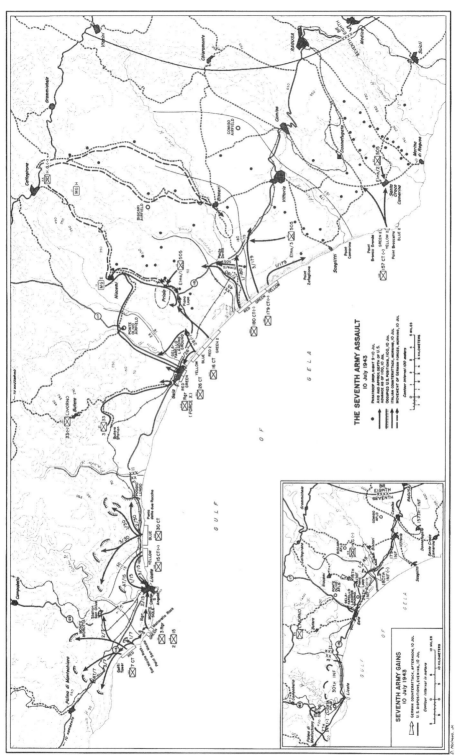

Map 13. The Seventh Army assault, 10 July 1943. (*U.S. Army World War II Atlas* [National Historical Society, 1995])

our best to live up to the heritage vested in us. I must admit that the business of fighting is beginning to become a bit wearisome now that we have been in actual combat for these many months and everyone of us are beginning to feel the pangs of homesickness and a fervent desire to get back home.[5]

The 1st Infantry Division commenced landing at 0245, 10 July. There was no preliminary naval gun bombardment, in the hope that the defenders would be caught off guard. There were no plans for air support since the air forces had refused to cooperate in the planning process. As far as the US Army Air Forces was concerned, it would manage the air campaign and determine what support was best for the ground troops.[6] Hence, there were no air-ground liaison teams with the infantry regiments.

Terry Allen had three regimental combat teams for the landings. CT16 was to land on the right and drive inland to link up with the 505th Parachute Infantry Regiment. CT26 was to land in the center and drive north to seize Ponte Olivo Airfield. Allen's third combat team was Force X, composed of the 1st and 4th Ranger Battalions, the 39th Engineer Battalion, and the 1st Battalion, 531st Engineer Shore Regiment. Commanded by Lieutenant Colonel William Darby, Force X was to seize Gela and protect the left of the division from counterattacks. The 505th Parachute Regiment, 82nd Airborne Division, was to be attached to the 1st Infantry Division once the amphibious troops linked up with the airborne.[7]

The Husky landings were lightly opposed. Lucian Truscott's troops easily secured the port of Licata. For the remainder of the day, the 3rd Infantry Division faced little opposition. The 45th Infantry Division also came ashore with little opposition, but the division's units were scattered widely by the rough seas and strong winds. The airborne operation failed totally. The inexperienced pilots of the 52nd Airlift Command scattered paratroopers across Sicily, missing the drop zones inland from the beaches at Gela. The failure to get the airborne regiment together on D-day was a major setback since the 505th Parachute Infantry Regiment was to have served as the 1st Infantry Division's reserve.

The landings of the Big Red One went smoothly in spite of sporadic op-position. The infantry came ashore as planned, although for men like Joe Dawson it was "a ticklish moment in one's life and can be likened to step-ping into the Great Unknown and only fate decides the issue for you, for the enemy was now fully alert and the air was filled with flying steel."[8] The battalions moved off the beaches as rapidly as possible in the soft sand and eliminated the Italian strongpoints in the area. By late morning, Darby's Force X had captured Gela, and the 1st Battalion, 26th Infantry, had made contact with the rangers. At about 1000, Darby's men directed naval gunfire to repulse an Italian counterattack, securing Gela.

The 26th Infantry landed with few losses and overran the Gela-Farello landing field. As the 1st Battalion moved west, the 2nd and 3rd Battalions pushed along Highway 117 to clear the hills north of Gela. During the afternoon, Bowen's men consolidated their positions and prepared to continue toward Ponte Olivo Airfield, 3 miles farther north. The 1st Battalion aided the rangers against an Italian tank attack in the afternoon and then dug in north of Gela.[9]

The 16th Infantry made it ashore with little difficulty. By 0930 hours, Charles Denholm's 1st Battalion, 16th Infantry, was near Piano Lupo and the intersection of Highway 115 and the road to Niscemi.[10] There the difficulties began, as Denholm found only a few paratroopers at the intersection, and they were being pursued by Italian tanks. Artillery observers ended the Italian armor threat with nineteen salvos of 5-inch gunfire from the destroyer *Jeffers*. With the Italians in retreat, the 1st Battalion, 16th Infantry, cleared the bunkers at the crossroads while Joe Crawford's 2nd Battalion dug in on the high ground west of Highway 115.[11]

The only Axis forces capable of launching counterattacks against the landings were the Italian *Livorno Division*, concentrated 30 miles north of Gela, and the German *Hermann Goering Panzer Division* at Caltagirone, 20 miles northeast. The tanks that attacked the rangers in Gela and CT16 on the Piano Lupo were 11-ton Renaults from the *Livorno Division*. While those Italians were being stopped, the commander of the *Hermann Goering Division*, General Paul Conrath, tried to launch an attack from Caltagirone to the beach areas of the 1st and 45th Infantry Divisions. This attack was delayed until mid-afternoon, giving the Americans time to dig in and to bring ashore artillery and antitank weapons.

The *Hermann Goering Division's* first attack struck 2nd Battalion, 16th Infantry, near Priolo at about 1400, 10 July. Crawford's infantrymen held their positions overlooking the Niscemi Road, where the German tanks could not get to them in their foxholes. But lacking heavy antitank weapons, the infantrymen were unable to stop the tanks from bypassing them. They did, however, force the accompanying German infantrymen to take cover. As the German tanks moved farther down the road, they encountered Denholm's battalion at the crossroads near Piano Lupo. Calls for naval gunfire by forward observers tipped the scales for the defenders, as the German panzers retreated to escape the hail of accurate 6-inch shells. A second German thrust later in the day also was stymied by naval gunfire, prompting the 16th Infantry to report to the division command post that the "tanks are withdrawing[;] it seems like we are too much for them."[12]

During the next twelve hours, the 1st Infantry Division worked feverishly to land its artillery battalions. Patton had allotted the division only ten Sherman tanks, and those got stuck in the soft sand when they landed. In the afternoon, Patton, in response to the failure of the airborne drop, ordered his floating reserve to land and to assemble behind the 1st Infantry Division. Colonel George Smith's CT18 came ashore during the night of 10–11 July. Encountering major difficulties with sandbars and plagued by the lack of proper landing craft, the 18th Infantry lost much of its heavy equipment in the high surf. Nonetheless, CT18 was ready for action on the beach shortly after daybreak.[13]

On the morning of 11 July, the 1st Infantry Division still lacked armor support. The regimental cannon companies and antitank guns were arriving, along with some howitzers of the artillery battalions. Making matters worse, German aircraft destroyed LST 313 along with most of the vehicles of the 33rd Field Artillery. Fortunately, the howitzers had been carried to shore aboard amphibious trucks designated DUKW. As day broke on 11 July, the six infantry battalions of CT16 and CT26 were digging in along the roads to Niscemi and Ponte Olivo Airfield. The 18th Infantry and a company from the 41st Armored Infantry Regiment had assembled behind the left flank of the 16th Infantry, and the 32nd Field Artillery Battalion was bringing its howitzers ashore. Unfortunately, German aircraft destroyed the ship carrying the 18th Infantry's jeeps and trucks. At that point, enemy forces counterattacked the beachhead.

The Battle for the Gela Beachhead: 11–12 July 1943

The Axis reaction to the Husky invasion was swift. The Italian *Sixth Army* had four Italian and two German divisions capable of offensive action in Sicily. During the night of 10–11 July, General Alfredo Guzzoni, commander of *Sixth Army*, ordered the *Livorno* and the *Hermann Goering Divisions* to drive the 1st Infantry Division into the sea. Once this was completed, the *Livorno* was to wheel west to attack the 3rd Infantry Division while the *15th Panzergrenadier Division* would strike Truscott's forces from the west. The *Hermann Goering Panzer Division* was to roll up the 45th Infantry Division and continue east to the British beaches. Although this was an ambitious plan, it posed a serious threat since no American armored units were operational in the Gela area.[14]

At about 0600, the *Livorno* and *Hermann Goering Panzer Divisions* attacked the 1st Division's front, from Gela to the Acate River. On the division's western flank, three columns of Italian tanks and infantry struck the rangers and the 1st Battalion, 26th Infantry, in Gela. Naval gunfire, augmented by the fire of captured Italian guns and a battery of the 7th Field Artillery, helped the rangers and infantrymen beat back the Italian infantry and destroy at least eight enemy tanks. For the remainder of the day, the 26th Infantry and Force X hung on to their positions.[15]

North of Gela, Lieutenant Colonel John Corley's 3rd Battalion, 26th Infantry, reached positions halfway to Ponte Olivo Airfield from Gela in a night advance before encountering elements of the *Hermann Goering Division*. Corley let the regiment headquarters know it was about to be hit by an armored thrust and requested artillery and antitank support. Corley's infantrymen dug in and prepared to ride out the storm. By 0800, German Mark IV tanks had struck the 3rd Battalion and then continued down the road toward the 2nd Battalion. When German infantry tried to follow the panzers, fire from Corley's foxholes prevented them from accompanying their armor.[16]

Under strong pressure, however, the 3rd Battalion withdrew south to positions between the 1st and 2nd Battalions. As they did so, Corley's men exacted a heavy toll from the Italian and German infantry. The heavy weapons platoons expended all available mortar and bazooka ammunition while covering the withdrawal of the companies to the new defensive line. As the 3rd Battalion fell in alongside the 2nd Battalion, the combat team's resistance steadied. The German tanks, now without infantry support, turned southeast into the center of the division's beachhead, between Gela and Piano Lupo.[17]

While Corley's men separated the German tanks and infantrymen north of Gela, Darby's rangers, supported by naval gunfire and the 33rd Field Artillery, plastered the Italian infantrymen and tanks that again were attempting to advance toward Gela. Using captured Italian 47mm guns, the rangers decimated the Italians. The official history notes: "The battering received during this attack on Gela finished the Livorno Division as an effective combat unit."[18] This was the last Axis threat to Gela.

The situation in the 16th Infantry's sector was equally threatening, as another Kampfgruppe of the *Hermann Goering Division* attacked south along the road from Niscemi. Joe Crawford's 2nd Battalion met this force north of Casa del Priolo. Without antitank guns or armor support, Crawford's men were forced back to their former positions west of the crossroads of the Niscemi Road and Highway 115. There the infantrymen dug deeper and called for fire support. Denholm's 1st Battalion also was forced back to positions near the crossroads, where it joined the 2nd Battalion. With strong support from the few guns of 7th Artillery that had arrived, the 16th Infantry repulsed the Germans with heavy losses on both sides.[19]

Stopped along Highway 115, German armor moved west of Piano Lupo and continued toward the center of the division over the open ground between Gela and Santa Spina.[20] When the two columns of German panzers converged, they were just 2,000 yards from the Mediterranean. At this point, the Germans thought that the 1st Infantry Division was re-embarking and that victory was in their grasp.[21]

Allen, seeing the danger posed by the German tanks, ordered the 18th Infantry to move to positions on the low dunes along Highway 115, facing north. He also ordered the 33rd Field Artillery to engage the panzers with direct fire. By 1000, the 18th Infantry could see forty German tanks advancing toward the sea. As Captain John B. Kemp, of the 3rd Battalion, 18th Infantry, remembered, many "riflemen of the regiment, rather than dig their holes deeper, rushed to the services of the firing platoons of the 18th and 26th Infantry [regimental] Cannon Companies and helped the firing batteries of the 33rd F. A. Battalion move [their howitzers] into new positions where direct fire was then put on the oncoming tanks." At that point, there was

> a beautiful exhibition of direct fire. The tanks penetrated and went into our rear areas, dangerously close to the beach. They were mostly on flat, barren ground, however, with no cover: and our guns were in good positions on a wooded hill east of Gela. By noon of July 11th, 14 enemy tanks had been knocked out. The 3rd Battalion suffered some casualties, but they were very light in proportion to the intensity of the attack.[22]

Joined by a newly landed battery of the 32nd Field Artillery, the 33rd Artillery and the cannon companies of the 16th and 26th Regiments destroyed half of the German tanks on the Gela Plain, ending the threat to the division's center. By early afternoon, the 1st and 2nd Battalions of the 16th Infantry had been reinforced by a company of Sherman tanks from the 2nd Armored Division.

Although the Axis forces had been driven back, the division's situation did not appear rosy at the end of the day. Casualties had been heavy and the beaches were congested with men and supplies. There was a possibility that the enemy would resume his assaults. Assessing the situation, Terry Allen decided that the Big Red One needed to seize the initiative. Therefore, he ordered the infantry regiments to make night attacks to seize the division's D-day objectives. These attacks, carried out in the early hours of 12 July, disrupted local German counterattacks that had been planned to cover their retreat the next day. Allen's decision to attack provided a boost to morale in the division. These attacks also initiated the 1st Infantry Division's advance across Sicily.

The Big Red One's defensive action at Gela ended Axis hopes of throwing the Allies back into the sea. The victory was due first and foremost to the infantrymen who held their positions when bypassed by enemy tanks and prevented Axis infantry from accompanying the tanks to the beach. The division's artillery, supported by naval gunfire, accounted for the majority of the forty-five German tanks destroyed on 11 July. These tank losses maimed the *Hermann Goering Panzer Division*.[23] Clift Andrus earned the Distinguished Service Cross for his orchestration of the division's supporting fires. The Allied air forces played little role in the victory. In fact, the Luftwaffe repeatedly attacked the troops ashore and sank a number of transports and warships offshore. Of the six requests made by Seventh Army for aerial missions on 10 July, none were filled, and on 11 July, the air force provided only one of five missions requested by the 1st Infantry Division.[24]

The battle for Gela ended on an extremely tragic note. Plans had been made to drop 2,000 paratroopers onto the Gela-Farello landing field on the evening of 10 July. Precautions were taken to alert Seventh Army units that 144 transport aircraft were to fly over the 45th and 1st Infantry Divisions from the east. At 2000, the 1st Division G3 ordered all units "not to fire on planes unless they commit a hostile act," and at 2100 hours the G3 section notified the division that a formation of C-47s would be overhead dropping American paratroopers at about 2000 or 2100. Unfortunately, the drop was postponed until the next night. During the intense fighting of 11 July, no messages were sent to the units reminding them that there would be a parachute drop that evening. In fact, the only mention of an airborne operation for that night in the G3 Log is an answer to a call from the 18th Infantry asking, "What's this I hear about parachutes?" In response, at 1900 hours, the G3 told the 18th Infantry to expect paratroopers to land in its vicinity that evening.[25]

At 2240, the first aircraft flew over and successfully dropped its paratroopers. When the second flight approached the release point near Biviere Pond the calm was rudely shattered by a lone machine gun.

> Within the space of minutes, it seemed as though every Allied antiaircraft gun in the beachhead and offshore was blasting planes out of the sky. . . . Control over Army and Navy antiaircraft gunners vanished. . . . Some paratroopers were killed in the planes before they had a chance to get out. Other paratroopers were hit in their chutes while descending. A few were even shot on the ground after they landed. It seems that each succeeding serial received heavier fire than those preceding it.[26]

Of the 144 C-47 aircraft in the operation, 23 never returned to Africa and another 37 were badly damaged; 60 pilots and 81 paratroopers were killed, and 132 were wounded.[27] There is no excuse, only explanations, for the disaster. During the two previous days, the Luftwaffe had regularly bombed the beachhead and ships, inflicting significant casualties. German bombers attacked less than an hour before the American planes arrived. The soldiers on the ground were tired and not properly alerted about the impending drop. Bradley was furious, and Eisenhower blamed Patton for the part that the Seventh Army played.[28]

The Advance Inland

According to the plan, the Eighth Army was to move rapidly north to Messina, forcing the enemy to withdraw from Sicily. Unfortunately, the Germans reacted swiftly, reinforcing the defenses facing the Eighth Army with the *1st Parachute Division*. Consequently, on 13 July, Montgomery, without notifying Alexander, decided to swing his forces farther west since they had failed to advance in their zone. This forced a major adjustment of the boundary between the US Seventh and British Eighth Armies.

No one notified Patton or II Corps. Montgomery's move usurped Highway 124. The 45th Infantry Division first learned of Montgomery's move late on 13 July when it encountered Canadian and British troops south of Vizzini. The confusion caused by the shift and the time it took to reorient Allied units gave the Axis forces time to withdraw from western Sicily and establish a defensive line protecting northeastern Sicily.[29]

The British failed to exploit the enemy's difficult situation on 12 July, but the 1st Infantry Division's night attack brought progress. On the division's left, the rangers successfully assaulted Italian positions on the hills between Gela and Butera, capturing most of an enemy infantry battalion. The 26th Infantry advanced north along Highway 117. Although encountering heavy enemy fire, the combat team overran Ponte Olivo Airfield by mid-morning.[30]

On the division's right, the 16th Infantry moved more slowly due to significant resistance from the rear guard of the *Hermann Goering Division*. During an intense firefight, Lieutenant Colonel Joe Crawford was badly wounded, but his 2nd Battalion, 16th Infantry, held its positions near Casa del Priolo, allowing Taylor to maneuver the 1st Battalion into positions facing northeast. Signs of fatigue became evident as Taylor reported that "we are open on our E[ast] flank, and after three nights of attack our boys are tired."[31] Nonetheless, Taylor's men continued to advance, and, by afternoon, Taylor felt that the road to Niscemi could be opened if he had a company of tanks.

In response to his and Taylor's concerns about the division's right flank, Allen moved the 1st Battalion, 18th Infantry, to positions facing east along the Acate River early on 12 July. This move was prudent. At 0900, the battalion repulsed German tanks that were attempting to move west.[32] This action was the last enemy offensive effort to interfere with II Corps' beachhead.

Having failed to drive the Big Red One into the sea, the Axis commanders agreed that their forces should retreat to a defensive enclave in the northeastern corner of Sicily. Their defenses were to run from Catania west to near Enna and then north to Sante Stefano. Once their units had withdrawn from western Sicily, they planned to withdraw again to a line from Catania to near Adrano, on the southwestern slopes of Mount Etna, and then curve to the northwest through Troina to the coast near San Fratello. The primary concern of the Germans was to delay the Allied offensive while ensuring that the German divisions in Sicily were not cut off.[33]

The 1st Infantry Division continued to move its regimental combat teams north during the next few days. On the division's left, Darby's rangers captured Butera and established contact with the 3rd Infantry Division. At that point, they became part of the II Corps reserve. The 26th Infantry moved steadily northwest, leapfrogging battalions on the road from Ponte Olivo Airfield to Mazzarino. During an advance of 10 miles on 13 July, Bowen's men met no resistance. After moving through the night, the 2nd Battalion occupied Mazzarino without a fight. Army civil affairs teams, organized to administer conquered territory, followed closely on the heels of the 26th Infantry.[34]

CT16 captured Niscemi on the morning of 13 July. However, with the order to stop short of Highway 124 so that the British could use that route, the 16th Infantry halted. CT18, which rejoined the division on the morning of 13 July, pushed northeast from Ponte Olivo Airfield against light resistance. On 14 July, both combat teams rested, since their route north was blocked by the new army boundary. That afternoon, Bradley ordered the 18th Infantry to send a patrol across the boundary to secure the junction of Highways 117 and 124. By the end of the day, the 16th Infantry was in contact with the Canadians on the division's right, and the 26th Infantry was in contact with the 3rd Infantry Division on the left, near Mazzarino.[35]

As CT26 pushed from Mazzarino toward Barrafranca on the night of 15–16 July, Allen shifted CT16 to positions north of Mazzarino, behind the 26th Infantry. Allen also moved CT18 by truck to Mazzarino. These moves took the greater part of a day. The heavy traffic in the division's rear, caused by the move west of the 45th Infantry Division, complicated the tactical moves and made resupply, engineer, and medical activities more difficult.[36]

In spite of the challenges of moving artillery, supplies, and infantry, CT26 resumed its advance toward Barrafranca at 0100, 16 July. Kelleher's 1st Battalion led on the winding road toward the town, hoping to occupy the hills west of Barrafranca without opposition. The *15th Panzergrenadier Division*, however, had other plans. Before dawn, enemy fire ripped into Kelleher's companies, forcing the men to dig in. As the 2nd Battalion tried to maneuver around the left of the 1st Battalion, it was hit by German artillery fire, which drove the infantry to seek cover. Bowen quickly threw the 3rd Battalion into the fight on the east side of the road to Barrafranca, expanding his front. But the enemy fire was so heavy that by 0600 the regiment was pinned down.[37]

The battle for Barrafranca lasted for most of the day. For the Germans, it was essential to halt the 1st Infantry Division in order to give Axis units in western Sicily time to move east. Consequently, the Germans committed tanks in repeated counterattacks to keep the 26th Infantry from seizing the town and the road junction just to the north. During the morning, Bowen's situation looked desperate. At 1002, he reported that sixteen tanks had broken through his lines and that "tanks [are] running all over us. Situation confused."[38] Allen called for armor support and encouraged Andrus to get artillery support to the beleaguered infantrymen. II Corps also attached the 70th Tank Battalion to the Big Red One and ordered the 2nd Armored Division to send a company of Sherman tanks to Allen as well. Andrus moved three artillery battalions into positions to support Bowen, while Allen ordered Taylor to move a battalion of the 16th Infantry forward to reinforce CT26.[39]

These actions paid off. During the morning, the 26th Infantry repulsed two enemy armored thrusts with well-directed artillery fire. The regimental history records the action:

> At 0840 hours, the enemy tanks attacked the 3rd Battalion, sweeping past the town barriers and hitting the extended companies' lines. Company I and Company L, out in front, had more favorable ground from which to fight back, and the other companies fell back until they too found cover suitable for setting up mortars and machine guns against enemy armor. The reluctance with which the companies fell back and the persistence with which they returned to the attack must have proven quite a thorn in the side of the German armored units.[40]

At the same time, the 1st and 2nd Battalions held their positions west of Barrafranca. By mid-afternoon, the 3rd Battalion, 16th Infantry, had maneuvered into position on the left of Bowen's team, and tanks had arrived to provide a base of fire against the enemy tanks. During the fight, at least eight German tanks were destroyed. Having established superior firepower and with four battalions of artillery support and a company of light tanks accompanying them, Bowen's infantrymen resumed their advance. By 1700, the 26th Infantry had secured the dominant terrain around the town, and the tanks of the 70th Tank Battalion entered Barrafranca. The Germans retreated. CT26 consolidated positions north of town and buttoned up for the night.[41] During the early hours of 17 July, CT16 passed through Barrafranca and occupied Pietraperzia. The 1st Recon Troop and elements of the 16th Infantry continued north as well, establishing blocking positions on Highway 122 before dark. This move cut off a major route of escape for the enemy to the west.[42]

Allied Plans Adjust

While the 16th and 26th Infantry combat teams pushed northwest, the 45th Infantry Division shifted to the west of the 1st Infantry Division. After passing through Mazzarino, late on 16 July, the 157th Infantry attacked Pietraperzia. Finding the town occupied by the 16th Infantry, the 45th Division continued to move toward Caltanissetta, which it occupied by 1600. Three hours later, Santa Caterina fell, giving the 45th Infantry Division possession of Highway 121. To the east, the Canadians advanced, especially after the Germans gave up the fight for Barrafranca. It seemed that Patton's Seventh Army was on the verge of cutting Sicily in two.[43]

A change in Allied plans now gave II Corps the mission of driving north from Caltanissetta through Petralia and on to the sea at Cefalu (Map 14). The 45th Infantry Division was to advance on the corps' left through Santa Caterina and then northwest to Cerda. The 1st Infantry Division was to move north from Pietraperzia, through Villarosa, Alimena, and Petralia.[44]

Taylor's CT16 was to seize the high ground east of Caltanissetta at 0100, 18 July, as the first step in the advance. The 26th Infantry was to remain in its assembly area while all available trucks in the division moved CT18 to Villarosa, once that town was secured by Taylor's troops. The 16th Infantry jumped off from positions north of Pietraperzia as planned. Within forty-five minutes, the infantrymen had crossed the Salso River and were calling for the 1st Engineers to repair the bridge on the road to Caltanissetta. CT16 captured a few Germans as the enemy retreated. The II Corps now had relatively clear sailing to the north. At 0115, the 45th Infantry Division reported that it had taken Caltanissetta, while CT16 occupied its objective with two battalions and pushed reconnaissance units toward Enna. The only resistance to these moves came from artillery and mortar fire directed at the division's right flank.[45]

The British 30 Corps, however, failed to keep up with the division. Consequently, the *15th Panzergrenadier Division* was able to threaten 1st Infantry Division's eastern flank. By the afternoon of 18 July, 1st Recon Troop and tanks of the 70th Tank Battalion had encountered German tanks on the road east of Caltanissetta, and German artillery fire made it too risky for Allen to move CT18 forward until after dark. Consequently, Taylor pushed patrols

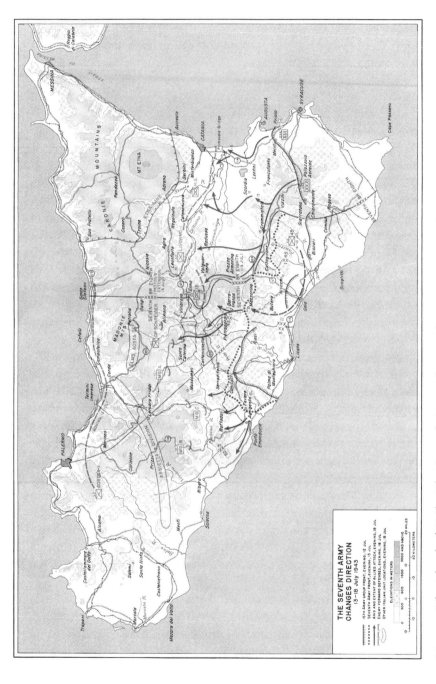

Map 14. The island of Sicily. The Seventh Army changes direction, 13–18 July 1943. (*U.S. Army World War II Atlas* [National Historical Society, 1995])

east to locate the enemy artillery and rescheduled the move of CT18 until after dark.[46]

Based on new instructions from II Corps, Allen ordered Taylor's CT16 to move east along Highway 122 to attack Enna. CT18 was to secure Villarosa. The biggest problem faced by CT18 was traffic congestion. By 1615, Smith's leading battalion was on the high ground west of Villarosa, where it made contact with the enemy. Smith ordered the 1st and 3rd Battalions to dismount from their trucks and seize the high ground around the town. "The 1st Battalion made good progress, but the 3rd Battalion was unable to advance because of heavy mortar, machine gun, and artillery fire." While Smith prepared a night attack, the German rear guard in Villarosa withdrew, allowing the 18th Infantry to secure the town the next morning.[47]

While CT18 was opening the route north, the 16th Infantry moved toward Enna. During 19 July, patrols met no major resistance until they were hit by artillery fire near the junction of Highways 122 and 117. In response, Taylor deployed the 1st and 3rd Battalions in a cross-country maneuver to seize the high ground southeast of Enna. As the GIs advanced, the Germans evacuated Enna, allowing the 16th Infantry to reach the outskirts of the town during the night of 19–20 July. Tanks of the 70th Tank Battalion, along with the 3rd Battalion, 16th Infantry, occupied Enna the next morning. While the 2nd Battalion regained contact with the retreating Germans, the regiment's Intelligence and Reconnaissance Platoon made contact with the 26th Infantry near Villarosa.[48] Once CT18 had secured Villarosa, Allen moved CT26 through Caltanissetta, to Villarosa, where Bowen's rested troops prepared to pass through the 18th Infantry and continue the advance toward Alimena.

The 1st Infantry Division's progress north on 18–20 July unhinged the Axis defenses in Enna, forcing the Germans to fall back to their final defensive line. On 19 July, Bradley swung the 45th Infantry Division to the northwest toward Villafrati, leaving the Big Red One to move toward Alimena and Petralia.

On 20 July, General Alexander again changed the scheme of maneuver for 15th Army Group. Eighth Army was to continue hammering at the German defenses north of Catania and to push 30 Corps toward Agira and Adrano. Seventh Army was to advance toward Messina.

The 1st Infantry Division's part in the new plan was to seize Petralia and then swing east along Highway 120 to Nicosia. The 45th Infantry Division was to advance along the coast road. During the early hours of 21 July, the 26th Infantry moved out in a column of battalions. Lieutenant Colonel Derrill Daniel's 2nd Battalion led the advance over the mountains from Villarosa to Alimena, followed by the 3rd Battalion. During the night, the battalions leapfrogged one another as the leading battalion secured the mountaintops along the route. By dawn, Daniel's men were in a position to attack Alimena. Although enemy tanks were observed north of Alimena, 2nd Battalion's troops entered the town without serious opposition. To that point, the greatest hindrance to the advance had been the miserable condition of the road and the need for the engineers to repair two bridges. The engineers used dynamite to blast a bypass around a dry streambed so that tanks could catch up with the infantry.[49]

Although Alimena fell without a fight, enemy on the heights north of town continued to fire on the approaches from the south. To clear up this situation, Bowen sent Daniel's battalion to seize the high ground. The regimental history summarized the resulting action:

> Meanwhile in town, the civilians and remaining enemy soldiers had gotten the wrong impression as to our intentions. Though the town was now in our hands, the snipers began firing at our troops and on the tanks. The tanks ignored the fire for a while in the hope that the civilians would see that we did not mean to blow them off the map. But when the sniping fire continued, then the tanks began moving down the streets, methodically cleaning out nest after nest.[50]

It took the greater part of the day for the 26th Infantry to clear out the snipers in Alimena. This situation forced Allen to postpone the movement of CT18 and was serious enough that he spent the afternoon in Bowen's command post. Roughly 250 Italian soldiers surrendered during the fighting. That evening, Allen notified his G3 that "I think they are about through here for tonight."[51] During the night, patrols cautiously moved north to the hills overlooking the village of Bompietro, on the road to Petralia.

Shortly after dawn, on 22 July, the 1st and 3rd Battalions, 26th Infantry, supported by light tanks, attacked Bompietro. The tanks, however, failed to coordinate their move with the infantry. As the tanks reached the edge of town, they received intense enemy mortar and artillery fire and fell back to the positions of the 1st Battalion, 26th Infantry. "Amid a storm of curses and maledictions from the dug-in infantry," the tanks "attracted heavy artillery the way sugar gathers bees." The tankers withdrew farther south as the 3rd Battalion moved forward to help. As a result, both infantry battalions were pinned down by enemy fire. Things got worse. At about 0930, an American air mission hit the 26th Infantry, inflicting significant casualties.[52] The aviators and II Corps blamed the 26th Infantry for failing to mark its positions with yellow smoke. Bowen replied, "That does not excuse them for bombing behind the front lines."[53]

More productively, Bowen and Brigadier General Clift Andrus prepared an infantry and armor assault, supported by artillery fire, to seize the town. This attack succeeded. John Corley's 3rd Battalion rolled into Bompietro and began the laborious process of digging out snipers, while the 1st Battalion cleared the hills around the town. CT26 captured 800 Italian prisoners.[54] Exhausted by three days of intense combat, the men of the 26th Infantry dug in around Bompietro as the 18th Infantry moved through to continue the drive to Petralia.

While the 1st Infantry Division was assaulting Alimena and Bompietro, the 45th Infantry Division reached the north coast of Sicily and the 2nd Armored Division reached Palermo. On 23 July, Palermo surrendered. In ten days, Truscott's provisional corps captured 53,000 prisoners, 189 artillery pieces, and over 400 vehicles. After mopping up scattered resistance, the 82nd Airborne and the 2nd Armored Divisions assumed occupation duties and the 3rd Infantry Division prepared to relieve the 45th Infantry Division.

With the provisional corps pinched out of the line, the only American troops in contact with the enemy were in the 1st and 45th Infantry Divisions. The British Eighth Army did not have similar success as it and II Corps bore the brunt of fighting the Germans. With western Sicily secure, Patton reinforced Bradley's drive east, hoping to reach Messina before Montgomery's Eighth Army.

The Drive East

The zone of operations for II Corps was divided into two corridors by the Madonie Mountains. Only two north-south roads connected the corridors (Map 14). The 1st Infantry Division was to advance east along Highway 120, through Gangi, Sperlinga, Nicosia, and Troina. This route passed along the southern slopes of the Madonie Mountains. "The road was narrow and crooked, with steep grades and sharp turns." Mountains along the highway provided the enemy with ideal defensive positions. An advance east required the attacker to secure these heights, as well as the low ground between them.[55]

CT18 passed through the 26th Infantry and moved north from Bompietro to Petralia on 23 July. By mid-afternoon, the 18th Infantry had two battalions on the hills around Petralia, and it occupied the town without resistance. At this point, Bradley ordered the 1st Infantry Division to swing east. The 18th Infantry reached Gangi the next morning. By the evening of 24 July, patrols of the 18th Infantry made contact with elements of the 45th Infantry Division to the north. Over the next twenty-four hours, CT18 moved to Gangi and prepared for an advance to Nicosia, while CT16 remained in reserve in Enna. To the west and south of Gangi the 1st Engineers repaired bridges and cleared mines along the roads, allowing the division's artillery battalions to move forward to support the infantry battalions.[56]

By this point in the campaign, some members of the division had developed a fatalistic attitude to warfare:

> The ever presence of death and horror brings a callousness to human suffering for one becomes so wrapped up in self preservation that it is impossible to sustain moral fortitude when one's own life is so constantly exposed. Nevertheless one experiences compassion even tho the times are difficult to allow one to feel anything but cold hatred towards those who deny peace and human freedom, especially when it becomes intimate to one's own self and to those whom association through perilous times have brought into close friendship. It is exemplified by the growing feeling of urgency to get this dirty job over as quickly as possible before one loses the delicate balance that makes the difference between civilization and barbarism.[57]

The division had to keep attacking. Allen's scheme of maneuver was to have CT26 move east along Highway 120 toward Sperlinga, while the 18th Infantry either passed through the 26th or reinforced Bowen's troops if they met heavy resistance. Division Artillery controlled eleven battalions of artillery, and the 70th and 753rd Tank Battalions were attached to the division for the operation.

During the night of 23–24 July, the 26th Infantry shuttled its 1st and 2nd Battalions by truck from Petralia to a ridge east of Gangi. The 3rd Battalion moved to an assembly area nearer Gangi and prepared to follow. On the morning of 24 July, Major Walter Grant's 1st Battalion, 26th Infantry, moved east on the north side of the highway toward its initial objective, Hill 825. Daniel's 2nd Battalion set out on the south toward Hill 937. The advance over the rugged terrain was slow, and it was mid-afternoon before the battalions neared their objectives. As Daniel's infantrymen approached Hill 937, they were pinned down by enemy fire. In response, Bowen ordered Grant to swing Company B south to positions from which its mortars could support the 2nd Battalion. At the same time, Allen called for artillery to plaster Hills 825 and 937.[58]

Both battalions reached their objectives in the early evening. Grant found Hill 825 to be a barren slab of rock impossible to dig in on. He also had to occupy Hills 844 and 908 nearby, since they dominated 825. To the south, Daniel put one company on Hill 937, while the remainder of his battalion consolidated lower heights. At the same time, Allen alerted CT18 to prepare to move through the 26th Infantry and drive toward Sperlinga. Before this could happen, early on 25 July, the Germans counterattacked. On the south, Company G was thrown off Hill 937. To the north, Grant reinforced his positions on Hill 825, repulsing German patrols in the process.[59]

Faced with more opposition than expected, Terry Allen brought all three infantry combat teams into the battle and used flanking maneuvers to pry the enemy from the dominant terrain. Bowen initiated the maneuver by sending Corley's 3rd Battalion south, behind the 2nd Battalion, to capture Hill 962. At the same time, on the evening of 25 July, Smith's 18th Infantry moved from Gangi to the north, outflanking the Germans on Hill 825. CT18's mission was to head east toward Highway 117, north of Nicosia. If successful, this move could unhinge the German defenses in Sperlinga and Nicosia. To support these maneuvers, II Corps returned CT16 to the division and attached the 4th Tabor of Goums to Allen's command. Because the Goumiers were native Morrocan troops whose specialty was moving across mountainous terrain, Allen put them on the northern flank to assist the 18th Infantry's advance toward Mount Sambughetti.[60]

CT16 arrived in Gangi on 25 July. The next afternoon, its infantry battalions moved south, around the 26th Infantry. The Germans reacted to these maneuvers. The commander of the *15th Panzergrenadier Division*, General Eberhard Rodt, reinforced *Group Fullriede*, widening the battle and preventing the battle group from being encircled. During the next several days, in a series of violent attacks and counterattacks, the Big Red One and the Germans fought to control the key terrain along Highway 120. Hills 825, 927, and 962 changed hands at least twice on 26 July. Even with artillery superiority, Andrus's gunners could not silence the enemy artillery. Many infantrymen concluded that "the hills rise here and as usual we force our way ever upward. Someday I hope we shall be able to fight downhill for a change."[61]

Allen's use of maneuver paid off. CT18, accompanied by the Moroccan Goumiers, fought its way to the top of Mount Sambughetti on 27 July. In a sharp fight for the 4,500-foot crest, the combat team captured 200 Italian soldiers. This success allowed Smith's men to move to Highway 117, threatening the Germans in Nicosia from the north. It also enabled forward observers to adjust artillery fire on the enemy south of the peak.[62] Meanwhile, CT16 and CT26 hammered away at the enemy along Highway 120, while Allen ordered Smith to prepare to send a battalion south to encircle Nicosia. By the evening of 27 July, each of the nine rifle companies of the 26th Infantry held a mountaintop along the highway and the 16th Infantry was moving farther south of the highway, toward Nicosia. These moves threatened to trap the enemy in Sperlinga.[63]

In response, General Rodt withdrew *Group Fullriede* from west of Nicosia during the night of 27–28 July. When two battalions of the 16th Infantry attacked Sperlinga at dawn, 28 July, they found the place empty. At 1000, Company I, 16th Infantry, led the drive into Nicosia. The town was defended by an Italian garrison that had not gotten word of the German withdrawal. For about an hour, the 3rd Battalion, 16th Infantry, fought house-to-house against snipers and machine gunners before forcing 700 Italian soldiers to surrender. While this fight was under way, reconnaissance patrols pushed 2 miles northwest toward Cerami, where they encountered machine-gun fire from caves along the highway. Attacks by the 1st and 2nd Battalions the next day cleared the caves, allowing CT16 to occupy the high ground west of the Cerami River and south of Highway 120.[64]

North of Nicosia, the 18th Infantry and the Goumiers cleared the hills along Highway 117. During these operations, American P-51 Mustang fighters strafed the 16th and 18th Infantry Regiments. These incidents, on 29 July, sparked a heated exchange between the division and corps staffs. II Corps concluded that the bomb line had been drawn too close to the forward units. The corps G3 also directed the 1st Infantry Division to push CT18 north to help the 45th Infantry Division clear its sector of Highway 117. The division's G3, Frederick Gibb, replied that "incidently [*sic*], we've got one or two Germans in front of us." The order stood, however, as Bradley had already told Allen to send the battalion north.[65]

On the morning of 30 July, the 1st Battalion, 18th Infantry, entered Mistretta, just north of the boundary with the 45th Infantry Division. The battalion met little resistance, and its greatest difficulty was moving supplies from Gangi to the frontline companies. Since there was no road open, any food, ammunition, and water had to be carried forward on the backs of mules and men, while the wounded had to be moved back on stretchers.[66]

The 1st Division's drive to Nicosia coincided with the 45th Infantry Division's advance to Santa Stefano and the 1st Canadian Division's to Agira (Map 14). Most Italian units crumbled when attacked, and the Germans were withdrawing to the Etna Line. However, the officers and men of the 1st and 45th Infantry Divisions were exhausted, and both units had suffered heavy casualties. Therefore, Patton ordered the 3rd Infantry Division to relieve the 45th Infantry Division. Patton also summoned the 9th Division from Africa to replace the Big Red One. However, most of the 9th Infantry Division would not be able to relieve the 1st Infantry Division before 4 August. In the meantime, Bradley told Allen to keep the pressure on the Germans by capturing Cerami and Troina. Bradley attached the 39th Infantry Regiment and the four battalions of the 9th Division Artillery to the 1st Infantry Division for this mission.[67]

On to Troina

On 30 July, Bradley's intelligence officers had convinced him that the Germans had no intention of defending Troina. Seventh Army intelligence believed that the Germans had developed a strong defensive line running from Adrano north along the eastern side of the Simeto River, and then across the Caronie Mountains to San Fratello. Therefore, it was believed at higher headquarters that the Germans would withdraw from Troina once the 1st Infantry Division applied pressure. In reality, the German Etna Line ran west from Adrano through Troina and north to San Fratello. This line was held by the *29th Panzergrenadier* and the *15th Panzergrenadier Divisions*. The 3rd Infantry Division faced the *29th Panzergrenadier Division* in the northern sector. The 1st Infantry Division would be attacking the *15th Panzergrenadier Division*. To make matters worse, Troina was surrounded by ridges that dominated the terrain between Cerami and Troina. Colonel Stanhope Mason described Troina in his memoir: "Troina sat atop a conical hill, the highest in the vicinity, approached by a hairpin road. The entrenched German defenders, protected by stone buildings, had an open field of fire and an excellent observation point. The valleys below were devoid of natural cover. But Troina sat astride the main roads to Messina and had to be taken."[68]

On 30 July, the 1st Infantry Division's infantry moved into assembly areas where the soldiers could sleep, eat a warm meal, and replace worn-out equipment. During the day, patrols pushed east toward Cerami. On 31 July, the Goumiers moved into Capizzi unopposed. CT39 advanced through the 16th and 18th Regiments and occupied Cerami without resistance by 0900. The intelligence reports seemed correct. When pressed, the enemy would withdraw.[69]

Although Allen had alerted Bowen for a move of CT26 through the 39th Infantry once Cerami was secured, he now decided to continue the advance toward Troina with CT39's battalions only. To support CT39, General Andrus moved eleven artillery battalions to positions near Cerami. At the same time, II Corps withdrew the 70th and 753rd Tank Battalions to give the tankers badly needed rest.[70]

When CT39's soldiers advanced toward Troina on 31 July, they were hit by artillery and mortar fire and encountered German machine-gun positions along the high ground 2 miles east of Cerami. Artillery support was poorly coordinated and too few artillery battalions could reach the enemy. Allen ordered Andrus to sort out the problems, but poor roads and inadequate communications made this hard to do. After losing "a few casualties and [capturing] seventy-five prisoners," CT39 dug in for the night. Nonetheless, it still seemed feasible for the 39th Infantry to capture Troina without

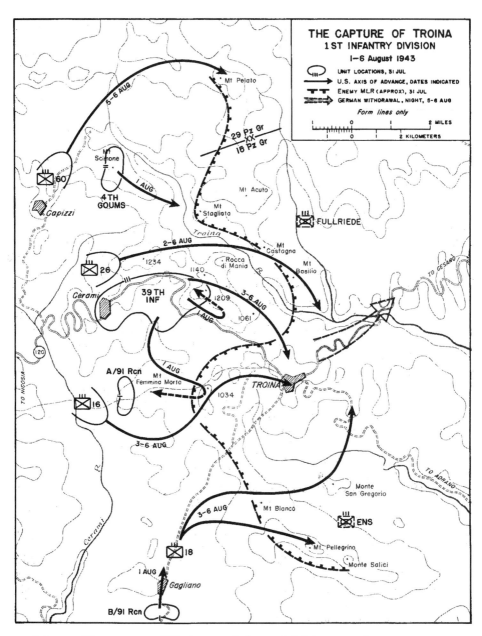

Map 15. The capture of Troina, 1st Infantry Division, 1–6 August 1943.
(Lieutenant Colonel Albert N. Garland and Howard McGaw Smyth, *Sicily
and the Surrender of Italy* [Chief of Military History, Department of the
Army, 1965])

reinforcements, so Allen again decided not to commit the 26th Infantry. Allen ordered CT39 to attack Troina again the next morning, 1 August.[71]

The 39th Infantry's routes of advance were to the southeast, along Highway 120. On the left, the 3rd Battalion moved about a mile before German fire plastered the exposed infantrymen. The regiment pulled back to Hill 1209; to the south the 2nd Battalion dug in. These moves were fortuitous. Around noon, the 2nd Battalion, with help from Andrus's artillery, repulsed a counterattack. The 1st Battalion, 39th Infantry, also was stopped in its advance on the right, toward Hill 1034.

All further moves toward Troina by the 39th Infantry, on 1 August, were stopped by enemy fire. At dusk, several counterattacks struck the 1st Battalion, 39th Infantry, driving its companies back, leaving them "badly disorganized." German infantrymen from *Group Ens* dug in on Hill 1034 while the 1st Battalion retreated a mile west. One of the few pieces of good news was that the attached 91st Reconnaissance Battalion had occupied Gagliano, threatening the left flank of the Germans in Troina. General Allen now realized that it would take a lot more force for the division to capture Troina.[72]

On the evening of 1 August, Allen decided to deploy Bowen's CT26 on the left of CT39 and use both regiments to drive the Germans from the hills north and west of Troina. Once the 26th Infantry captured Mount Basilio, Allen believed forward observers would be able to adjust fire on the German artillery positions along Highway 120, northeast of Troina, allowing Andrus's artillery to silence the enemy guns. Bowen's capture of Mount Basilio also would threaten the Germans' escape. The plan called for the 4th Tabor of Goums to move from Mount Scimone to Mount Stagliata to protect the left flank of the 26th Infantry.[73]

At 0500, 2 August, Derrill Daniel led the 2nd Battalion, 26th Infantry, across its line of departure. The 1st Battalion followed, about a mile behind, while the 3rd Battalion remained in reserve. To the north, the Goumiers encountered heavy fire as they tried to cross the Troina River. That was as far as they got that day. On the right of the Blue Spaders, the 39th Infantry could not advance due to heavy enemy fire. During the morning, it became apparent to Allen that CT39 was exhausted. The best it could do was to hold its positions.[74]

At 1030, Allen informed Bradley that the division was preparing another envelopment attack for 3 August. "We are planning another Nicosia and do it ourselves. 26th and 16th will both make end runs and pull the guards [German flanks] back. Appointment to have an early breakfast." In response, Bradley observed that "apparently there is a lot in there." Allen agreed, noting, "It's been built up, they need that main road. This [next attack] will mean we will be able to turn over to the 9th Division a tight sector. If it is all right with you we will do this." Bradley answered, "OK."[75] Meanwhile, the 26th Infantry doggedly pushed east, securing Rocca di Mania before digging in for the evening.

The division's plan for 3 August called for an attack by three combat teams and the Goumiers. In the north, the 26th Infantry and the North Africans were to capture Mounts Castagna and Basilio and interdict Highway 120 to Cesaro. The 39th Infantry was to maintain pressure in the center. George Taylor's 16th Infantry, reinforced by the 2nd Battalion, 18th Infantry, was to attack in the south to capture Hill 1034, a mile southwest of Troina, while the other two battalions of the 18th Infantry advanced northeast along the road from Gagliano to Troina. This pincer movement was designed to encircle the *15th Panzergrenadier Division* or force Rodt to order a retreat.

The attack commenced at 0300, 3 August. In the north, the 26th Infantry moved steadily forward, capturing Mount Basilio. Resistance then stiffened, as bypassed enemy snipers and machine guns forced the regiment to spend the morning clearing the hills west and north of Mount Basilio. The 39th Infantry also advanced in the night, establishing two battalions on Mount San Silvestro by mid-morning. By then, German artillery had found the range of the two regiments, bringing to bear a heavy rain of shells. A new type of German mine also made life miserable for the American troops. Encased in a wooden box, it proved very difficult to find before it blew off someone's legs. To ease the pressure from the German artillery, Allen called for air strikes against the enemy positions. These had some success, although one group of fighters attacked the Goumiers, forcing them to retreat. During the afternoon, *Group Fullriede* counterattacked the two battalions of CT26 on Mount Basilio. Although the 26th Infantry repulsed the Germans in hand-to-hand combat, it was clear that the regiment could not advance with its flanks exposed. The northern pincer of the division's assault had failed to cut the highway from Troina to Cesaro.[76]

On the division's southern flank, the 2nd and 3rd Battalions, 16th Infantry, moved forward during the night. By daybreak, it seemed that the lead companies of Major Charles Horner's 3rd Battalion would be able to secure Hill 1025, less than a mile from Troina. *Group Ens* responded vigorously to this threat. By 0625, Companies K and L reported that they were on the hill, but the Germans brought to bear tremendous firepower, decimating the exposed infantrymen. Although John Mathews's 2nd Battalion maneuvered to the right, on the road into Troina, it was unable to lessen the pressure on the 3rd Battalion.[77]

Fearing that the Germans would launch a counterattack against the 16th Infantry, Allen ordered Taylor to swing his 1st Battalion around the right flank of his 2nd Battalion, hoping that the new direction of attack would ease the pressure on the 3rd Battalion. Allen also ordered the 2nd Battalion, 18th Infantry, to move east about 4,000 yards to outflank the Germans south of Troina. For the remainder of the day, the battle seesawed back and forth.[78]

American casualties had been heavy, with companies in the 16th and 26th Infantry Regiments down to 30 or 40 men, out of a normal strength of around 180. A few replacements arrived, but the regiments kept most of these new men to the rear. German losses also had been heavy. The *15th Panzergrenadier Division* lost at least 1,600 men in the first two days of August. During the night of 3–4 August, the German *XIV Panzer Corps* committed its last reserves to Troina. The steady pressure exerted by the Big Red One was helping the Allied operations to the north and east. But as long as Rodt held Troina, the Etna Line could be defended.[79]

The fourth of August brought more costly fighting. The regiments jumped off at 0300. In the north, the Goumiers failed to move forward in the face of heavy artillery fire. This exposed the left flank of the 1st Battalion, 26th Infantry, as it moved to secure Mount Stagliata and the low ground between Rocca di Mania and Mount Basilio. The Germans retained positions on Mount Acuto from which they directed fire to the south. By 0930, Walter Grant's men were pinned down. It was all Bowen's regiment could do to hold its previous gains. To the south, the 39th Infantry was unable to advance due to counterattacks during the night that drove its 2nd Battalion off Hill 1140. This situation exposed any advance by CT26 to Germans on Hills 1209 and 1061. The Germans' right flank was not going to be turned.[80]

On the division's right, the 16th Infantry renewed its push to secure Hill 1034 and to advance along the Gagliano Road into Troina. Colonel Taylor reported to Allen that the "whole ridge seems to be well defended and covered as noted yesterday, for I and L Companies have both been receiving small arms and mortar fire from the vicinity of Hill 1034." Although Taylor tried to maneuver the 1st Battalion around the German positions, heavy enemy fire made movement by his men nearly impossible. The 3rd Battalion was stopped, although the 1st Battalion made some progress.[81] When the 1st Battalion reported that its companies were moving to secure several hills to the east of 1034, Allen ordered Taylor and Driscoll to keep their units as concentrated as possible in case the Germans counterattacked. This was timely advice. At 1045, *Group Ens* launched a strong armor-infantry assault against the 3rd Battalion, 16th Infantry.[82]

This counterattack against CT16 (nicknamed the Rangers) was one of several during the day that came close to driving the Rangers off Hill 1034. Horner's men hung on, helped by the fire of six artillery battalions. For several hours, enemy patrols attempted to encircle Company I, but artillery fire stymied those efforts. But there was to be no further American advance in the area until a way was found to suppress the German artillery.[83]

CT18 (nicknamed the Vanguards) made the most progress on 4 August. By midday, Smith's 1st and 2nd Battalions had crossed the Gagliano Road and were approaching the slopes of Mount Pelegrino. German resistance and the rugged terrain slowed the Vanguards' advance. Resupply could only be accomplished by mule trains, and all casualties had to be carried out by manpower. Troina was not going to be flanked easily from the south.[84]

It was painfully clear that the 1st Infantry Division could not drive the Germans out of Troina without additional help. Allen requested air attacks against the *15th Panzergrenadier Division*, and finally II Corps made the division its priority for air support. A plan was developed for a coordinated air-artillery attack against the German positions. A total of 72 P-51 fighters would strike in two waves, at 1700 and 1715, 4 August. Andrus's artillery force would fire from 1645 to 1700, 1710 to 1715, and 1725 to 1730. Then the four infantry regiments would launch a general push toward their objectives.[85]

The artillery-air bombardment took place as planned. The infantry moved out as the last aircraft departed. For several hours, the battalions moved forward, and reports indicated a decrease in enemy fire. The 26th Infantry even reported that "the enemy is completely unnerved." CT16 took Hill 1034, and the 18th Infantry reached the upper slopes of Pelegrino. As the evening wore on, resistance increased and the American advance halted as the exhausted troops dealt with Germans to their rear and flanks. Nonetheless, the concentrated use of artillery and air attacks, closely followed by a coordinated infantry advance, had shown great promise. Allen requested another joint air-artillery operation to support an assault the next morning. Bradley disapproved the request, giving air priority for 5 August to the 3rd Infantry Division.[86]

The German Resistance Cracks

The 1st Infantry Division's operations against Troina were part of a larger Allied push against the Germans holding the Etna Line. The Eighth Army continued to attack the *1st Parachute* and *Hermann Goering Divisions*, while the 3rd Infantry Division advanced against the *29th Panzergrenadier Division* along the north coast. The Big Red One was hammering at the pivot of the Etna Line and the *15th Panzergrenadier Division*. By 5 August, the 1st Infantry Division's attacks caused General Rodt to ask permission to withdraw his division 6 kilometers. This request was denied, but British advances to the east made it clear that the time was near when the Axis forces would have to withdraw from Sicily. In the meantime, Rodt concentrated his remaining reserves against CT26 and CT39, since these units threatened the *15th Panzergrenadier Division*'s escape route north of Troina.[87]

On 4 August, the 9th Infantry Division established assembly areas near Nicosia. Hoping to get into the fight as soon as possible, the 9th Infantry Division commander, Manton Eddy, proposed to Bradley that he send the 60th Infantry Regiment into the line north of CT26. By moving from Capizzi to Mount Pelato, the 60th Infantry would relieve pressure on the 26th Infantry and threaten the northern flank of the *15th Panzergrenadier Division*. Bradley approved this plan. On 5 August, the 60th Infantry and the 4th Tabor of Goums set out from Capizzi. At the same time, the 1st Infantry Division launched yet another attempt to capture Troina.[88]

Allen's plan of action on 5 August differed little from previous operations. CT26 and CT39 were to put pressure on *Group Fullriede*. Taylor's CT16 was to consolidate its hold on Hill 1034 and move as close to Troina as possible. The 18th Infantry was to secure Mounts Pelegrino and Salici and drive across the Adrano Road east of Troina.

The 26th and 39th Infantry Regiments had suffered too many casualties, especially among noncommissioned officers, to make much headway on the morning of 5 August. Enemy fire hammered the exposed troops, causing additional losses and a retreat by the 2nd Battalion, 39th Infantry. Two battalions of the 26th Infantry were cut off by German infiltrators, forcing the air-drop of ammunition, food, and water. There was even concern that counterattacks in the coming night might drive the exhausted troops from their positions.[89]

The 16th Infantry was in no better shape. The 3rd Battalion held Hill 1034 with companies reduced to platoon size. The men were exhausted, and *Group Ens* showed no sign of giving up the high ground west of Troina. On the right, Smith's 18th Infantry fought its way to the peaks of Pelegrino and Salici before being stopped by German infantrymen supported by artillery and mortar fire. At 0920, Lieutenant Colonel Frederick Gibb notified II Corps that "everything [is] held up generally along last line given yesterday."[90]

As Allen was discussing the action with his staff, the Germans decided that the time had come to withdraw from Sicily. The first stage was to pull the *29th* and *15th Panzergrenadier Divisions* back to new positions. This move commenced in the Troina sector during the evening of 5 August. The next morning, when the exhausted soldiers of the 1st Infantry Division resumed their probes toward Troina, they met only scattered resistance. By 0855, the men of the 16th Infantry had cleared the battered town. The division command post received similar reports from the other infantry regiments.[91]

The battle for Troina was over. At the same time, Eddy's 9th Infantry Division resumed control of its 39th Infantry and Division Artillery and prepared to move through the 1st Infantry Division to continue the advance toward Cesaro and Messina.

A New Commander

On 5 August, as he planned the final push on Troina, Terry Allen received a letter from II Corps headquarters notifying him that he and Teddy Roosevelt Jr. were to surrender command of the division to Major General Clarence Huebner and Colonel Willard Wyman. Stunned, the exhausted Allen ordered his chief of staff to prepare orders for Huebner's assumption of command.[92] The next evening, Huebner took command of the division in which he had held every rank except general during his career. The loss of Allen was painful. In Huebner, the Big Red One gained another great commander.

For many members of the division, the relief of Terry Allen and Teddy Roosevelt made the sense of letdown felt after Troina more pronounced. Why was a successful command team removed after the Big Red One had accomplished every mission assigned to it in Africa and Sicily? The short answer is that Allen and Roosevelt were exhausted after two campaigns and the stress that accompanied the preparation for two amphibious invasions. Both leaders had been in the front lines day and night. They lived up to Marshall's and Patton's expectations, and their division exhibited few of the weaknesses shown by other divisions in their first battles. But the steady personal toll of battle sapped the generals' strength. Therefore, they were relieved of command so that they could get much-needed rest and so that the 1st Infantry Division could get fresh leadership.

Allen returned to the United States, where Marshall assigned him to command the 104th Infantry Division. In the fall of 1944, Terry Allen and the Timberwolves arrived in northern Europe and did a magnificent job for the rest of the war. Teddy Roosevelt remained in Europe, where he eventually served as assistant division commander of the 4th Infantry Division.

Joe Dawson summed up the change of command about as well as anyone, on 6 August 1943:

> Terry [Allen] left tonight and with him went a record unequaled by any general officer in the divisions of the U.S. Army. We've been through a lot and we all feel keenly his going though it is to a higher post of duty. I should like to be with him. Our new C.O. is a grand soldier of the old school from all accounts but I'll reserve judgment till I see him in action. Terry leaves with the end of this bitter battle today and I somehow feel that this one was the toughest we have yet had.

It is a mark of great credit to him that we have always delivered in the pinches and have lived up to our creed: No Mission too difficult, no sacrifice too great![93]

The Fighting First would have plenty of opportunity to evaluate Clarence Huebner in training and battle.

The Costs and Importance of Operation Husky and the 1st Division's Contributions

The 1st Infantry Division's capture of Troina ended the Sicily campaign for most of the division. The 9th Infantry Division passed through the Big Red One, captured Cesaro on 8 August, and pursued the retreating Germans. After a brief rest, the 18th Infantry Regimental Combat Team joined the 9th Infantry Division for the push to Messina. Although the regiment did not catch up with the Germans, its soldiers had to deal with mines and booby traps that exacted a steady toll of casualties. On 16 August, patrols from the 18th Infantry met elements of the 3rd Infantry Division on the coastal road west of Messina. The 3rd Infantry Division entered Messina during the night of 16–17 August, just as the last German troops escaped by ferry to the Italian mainland.[94]

Operation Husky had accomplished most of its objectives. The Big Red One was instrumental in the success of the invasion. Its stand at Gela, its drive through the mountains of central Sicily, and its role in cracking the German defensive line at Troina vindicated Patton's and Bradley's decisions to use the division and its commander, Terry Allen, in the most critical parts of Operation Husky. After its hard-won successes, the division took no further part in the war in the Mediterranean region. It was slated to move to England, to prepare for Operation Overlord, the cross-Channel invasion of France.

9

Operation Overlord

THE 1ST INFANTRY DIVISION ENDED ITS MISSION IN SICILY when the 18th Infantry Regimental Combat Team withdrew from active operations and rejoined the division. The soldiers were grateful to be out of the line and anticipated a period of rest. When they had time to think about their future there were no expectations that they would be going home. Instead, the training programs initiated by Major General Clarence Huebner made it clear to the troops that further combat awaited them. The next challenge for the Big Red One was to prepare for its third amphibious assault against a hostile shore.

Allied Strategic Decisions: May–August 1943

The most important Allied strategic decision of World War II was made in December 1941 when Roosevelt and Churchill agreed that the highest priority of the coalition was the defeat of Germany. This remained the central tenet in Allied planning for the rest of the war.[1]

After the conquest of Sicily, the Americans insisted that operations in Italy be carried out only by the forces in the Mediterranean region and that seven veteran divisions be sent from the Mediterranean to England to build the nucleus of the force for the cross-Channel invasion. After a series of conferences in 1943, Roosevelt and Churchill reaffirmed that priority for troops and shipping should be given to the invasion of France, tentatively slated for May 1944. These decisions determined the fate of the Big Red One for the rest of the war.[2]

The 1st Infantry Division and Major General Clarence Huebner

At the end of the Sicily campaign, the 1st Infantry Division needed time to recuperate from over thirty days of continuous combat. Captain Joe Dawson, the new commander of Company G, 2nd Battalion, 16th Infantry, observed on 22 August:

> Deep in the heart of the regiment I am lost as to the "big" picture as my time is
> well occupied with details on the functioning of this company of mine. We are

now just beginning to relax [two weeks after leaving combat] from the nerve strain of battle and the result is I must have plenty for my men to do in order to prevent unrestrained "relaxing." We are now in the throes of bathing, delousing, and clothes washing and house keeping, but the men are doing swell.[3]

During the following three months the division initiated a rigorous training program. Huebner tightened discipline. Colonel Stanhope Mason, the division's chief of staff, experienced this when, on 7 August, his jeep was flagged down by a military policeman who warned him that the general and his aide were carrying a pocket full of traffic tickets and were personally handing them out all over the sector. The official speed limit was 20 mph, and Mason, whose jeep had been traveling at 35 mph, slowed his driver down.[4]

The 1st Infantry Division had been through a great deal. Fortunately, the division was full of competent leaders who understood the challenges and were just as interested as their commanding general in rejuvenating the command and preparing it for combat. For example, Colonel John Bowen, in a letter to Huebner, described several of the challenges facing the 26th Infantry Regiment on 10 August 1943:

In general, individual and unit morale is excellent. This can be attributed to the esprit de corps of this regiment [26th Infantry], the long unbroken string of victories in which the regiment has participated, and the knowledge that this regiment has participated in every 1st Division action and has taken every assigned objective without exception. . . . On the other hand, the command is recovering from a state of exhaustion induced by the long and virtually constant combat. Many of the old-timers are depressed to find so few of their old comrades still with them. To many, the thought of continued combat without respite is disturbing.[5]

The surgeon of the 26th Infantry, Major J. W. Henderson, echoed this sentiment in his assessment of the health of his regiment:

The mental attitude of the command, as I have observed it, is in general poor. The soldier appears discouraged and his discouragement is based not on the defeat of any unit in battle, but on the constant removal of original members of the unit as a result of casualties. There is no thought of defeat of the Regiment or Division, but there is a strong feeling that it is only a question of time until the individual soldier, himself, is killed or wounded. If some assurance could be given the soldier in this regiment that there would be some rest for him and that he would not take part in every battle of this war, as many now feel they will, it might result in an improvement of general attitude.[6]

The key to the future health of the division lay in restoring and maintaining the soldiers' self-confidence, morale, and discipline. These three attributes were interrelated. As Colonel George Taylor observed, good morale comes from

> a willing spirit; it is inside a man and will come out when put to the test. . . . If you want morale, raise your standards high and sell them; point to pride in unit; train for a purpose; carefully gauge the capabilities of your men so as not to overtax them; work them hard but never fail to reward them; always be just and fair; never let them fail and you will have morale.[7]

The division remained in Sicily until late October. In the meantime, the division moved 150 miles southwest to assembly areas near Licata. There the troops established camps with showers, squad tents, dining halls, and recreational facilities. Efforts were made to provide the soldiers with competitive sports, trips to historic sites, and opportunities to swim in the Mediterranean. Nonetheless, a lot of time was available for men to be bored, feel homesick, or indulge in self-pity.

Huebner's training program stressed soldier skills such as rifle marksmanship, map reading, and first aid. The program included physical conditioning, close order drill, and long road marches. Platoons, companies, and battalions practiced communications procedures and tactical fire and maneuver. Officers participated in command post exercises to hone their decision-making skills.[8] New soldiers benefited along with the veterans. By engaging the troops' energy in a full schedule of training, Huebner lessened boredom and strengthened the troops' self-confidence and pride.

Efforts also were made to ensure that the soldiers received awards for their accomplishments and courage during the recent fighting. Huebner, Andrus, and Wyman participated in awards ceremonies throughout the division. Commanders talked to the troops about their significant contributions to the victory in Sicily. These efforts, and the chance for the men to sleep, eat, and bathe, helped to restore morale.[9]

The Big Red One faced a serious health problem once the fighting ended on Sicily. Malaria was widespread and took its toll on exhausted men who were ill-equipped with the protective gear and preventive medicines. In August 1943, the 1st Medical Battalion admitted 2,538 patients for disease, compared to 560 for injuries and wounds. In September, it admitted 2,436 men for disease and 149 for injuries. Most of the disease cases were caused by malaria or yellow jaundice, which was caused by the atabrine the men took to combat malaria. Commanders provided the men with protective netting, atabrine pills, exercise, and a proper diet to prevent the ravages of malaria. These efforts paid off, as the number of patients admitted for disease in October decreased to 1,049.[10] Cooler weather helped, although the troops were more than ready to leave Sicily when they received movement orders in late October.

The Division Returns to England

In September, Seventh Army notified Huebner that the 1st Infantry Division was to return to England to train for the cross-Channel invasion.[11] The staff coordinated transportation and prepared movement orders for the division. The troops embarked on four British transports in Augusta, from 18 to 21 October.[12] Sailing on 23 October, the ships stopped briefly in Algiers before moving through the Strait of Gibraltar. After an uneventful trip around Ireland, the convoy arrived in Liverpool, England, on 5 November. During the voyage, commanders provided training to keep troops occupied most of the day. Schedules included calisthenics, rifle exercises, map reading, Browning automatic rifle (BAR) training, and first aid. Schools also were conducted for officers and noncommissioned officers.[13]

When the troops disembarked in Liverpool, they boarded trains for the journey to their billets near the city of Dorchester, in southern England. The companies and batteries were distributed in villages throughout the county with all of the men given quarters in barracks, houses, or public buildings. For the first time since October 1942, the troops were no longer living in tents or out in the open. For the next seven months, Dorset was the home of the Fighting First.[14]

The division was reasonably well housed during the winter of 1943–1944. This situation helped maintain morale while the troops trained rigorously. Lieutenant Jean Peltier, of Battery A, 33rd Artillery, described his billets and his unit's facilities in Dorset:

> Piddlehinton, despite its name, was a very nice camp. There was no mud as all the streets and parking areas were hard surfaced. The buildings were new. There was plenty of space for everyone. There was a large gymnasium and auditorium. There was a [British-run recreation club] run by a very efficient Mrs. Little and a group of volunteer girls who wore uniforms. The canteen supplied doughnuts, tea, coffee, "canned" music, beer, etc. There were billiard tables and a ping pong table in the other rooms. To us, this was next door to heaven.[15]

Training for Overlord: November 1943–May 1944

Once the troops were settled, training resumed. During November and December, emphasis was placed on marksmanship and squad- and platoon-level exercises. The soldiers practiced extensively with M1 rifles, machine guns, bazookas, grenades, M1 carbines, and pistols. Weapons squads practiced with 60mm and 81mm mortars and 37mm and 57mm antitank guns. Each infantry platoon conducted one night exercise per week in addition to daytime tactical training. The cannon and antitank platoons of the infantry regiments underwent an intensive training cycle that culminated in a four-day, live-fire problem.[16]

At the same time, units received their full complement of equipment, and the infantry regiments reorganized under special tables of organization with a 15 percent overstrength in personnel. The 37mm antitank guns were replaced by more powerful 57mm guns. The cannon companies replaced their 75mm self-propelled guns with towed 105mm howitzers. With new equipment and adequate training areas, the Big Red One was ready to step up the tempo of its preparations for its third amphibious assault of the war.[17]

The division also identified lessons learned in Sicily. Colonel George Taylor wrote a paper analyzing the psychological aspects of infantry leadership in combat. This paper was disseminated throughout the army. General Andrus continued to improve the ability of artillery units to rapidly mass fires against a single target. The key to this capability was radio and wire communications. Artillery units found that if they maintained two forward observer radio nets in each artillery battalion, using the 608 series radio as the Fire Direction Center's base radio, they could talk with forward observers up to 12 miles away. They also maintained the capability to connect the infantry battalions with telephone wire.[18]

In January 1944, the division began a second phase of training. The troops continued to practice individual soldier skills while the infantry and engineer platoons learned how to assault fortified positions and to fight in towns. Conditioning marches were lengthened to as long as 50 miles. In February, the program gained momentum. Mock invasion maneuvers were held in Weymouth Harbor along with English Home Guard units, honing defensive combat techniques.[19] The infantry regiments conducted command post exercises that included the units that made up the combat teams (artillery, engineer, medical), and two of the division's regiments took part in training exercises at the Assault Training Center at Woolacombe, England.[20]

Most of the soldiers who took part in the D-day assault of Overlord underwent some training at the Woolacombe center. The 16th and 18th Infantry Regiments conducted beachhead operations in February. The center emphasized demolition techniques, mine-clearing, and infantry assault tactics. While the 26th Infantry Regiment did not train at Woolacombe, the 115th and 116th Infantry Regiments of the 29th Infantry Division, which were to be attached to the Big Red One during the invasion, went through the center at least once each.[21]

In March, full-scale rehearsals of amphibious landings were conducted on the Slapton Sands beaches near Strete, Devon. Operation Fox, on 11 March, allowed CT16 and CT116 to work together under division control. "This operation was supposed to be a full-scale rehearsal for the landing on Omaha Beach, but there were three major exceptions. First, nobody was shooting at them as they landed; second, the men performed no demolitions or live-firing; and, oddly, for this exercise the 116th Infantry went in on the left of the 16th Infantry."[22] No tanks took part in the assault, but engineers practiced the removal of beach obstacles and mines.[23]

The Overlord Plan

In December 1943, Churchill and Roosevelt selected General Eisenhower to serve as the Allied commander for Operation Overlord.[24] Eisenhower, who had matured significantly as a senior commander during Torch and Husky, was the right man for the immensely difficult job of harnessing the British and American armed forces for the invasion. As President Roosevelt told his son, Eisenhower "is the best politician among the military men. He is a natural leader who can convince other men to follow him."[25]

When Eisenhower arrived in London in January 1944, he inherited an Overlord plan. The planners, after careful study, had determined that the invasion should be made along the Normandy coast near Caen. The goal was to get ashore and seize a lodgment area that included Normandy and Brittany. Once the lodgment was secure, the Allies planned to build up overwhelming forces on the continent with which to launch an offensive against the Germans. The tactical details of the plan were left to the men chosen to command the operation.[26]

Lieutenant General Omar Bradley was selected to command the American 1st (later 12th) Army Group and the US First Army.[27] In his role as ground forces commander, General Bernard Montgomery developed the tactical plan for the invasion. The assaults were to be carried out by five infantry and three airborne divisions. The British Second Army was to land on beaches from Arromanches to the Orne River with three infantry divisions, while the 6th Airborne Division was to land by parachute and glider along the Orne River to secure the crossings below Caen. The D-day objectives of Second Army were Caen and Bayeux.

The US First Army was to conduct amphibious assaults with two infantry divisions on beaches west of the British. The 4th Infantry Division, as part of VII Corps, was to land on Utah Beach on the east coast of the Cotentin Peninsula. The 1st Infantry Division was to spearhead the assault of V Corps on Omaha Beach, 15 miles east of Utah Beach. The 82nd and 101st Airborne

Divisions were to land in drop zones inland from Utah Beach, between the Douve River and the sea, to secure crossings over the Douve near Carentan. Once the Allied beachheads were connected, the First Army was to send VII Corps north to capture Cherbourg while the British drove south and east from Caen to secure the open ground needed to build airfields.[28]

The 1st Infantry Division, designated Force O, was to seize the Omaha beachhead and drive south to secure the terrain between the Aure and the Drome Rivers. The division was to make contact with the British 30 Corps to the east. The 29th Infantry Division was to land behind the 1st Infantry Division, with the mission of driving south and southwest to link up with VII Corps. The 1st Division was reinforced with the 115th and 116th Infantry Regiments and the 741st, 743rd, and 745th Tank Battalions. Following the initial assault, the 26th Infantry Regiment was to come ashore with the 29th Infantry Division. Once the beachhead was secure, the two regiments of the 29th were to return to their parent organization and the 26th Infantry was to rejoin the Big Red One.[29]

The tactical plans for the 1st Infantry Division's part in Overlord were given to the regiments in late February. From then on, training focused on the D-day missions. The plan called for an amphibious assault led by the 16th and 116th Combat Teams against a beach, code-named Omaha, between the villages of Colleville-sur-Mer and Vierville-sur-Mer. Omaha Beach was about 5 miles wide. Bluffs barely inland from the high tide point overlooked the beach. On the eastern half of the beach, a shingle, or low ridge, of round stones up to 10 yards wide and backed by sand dunes stood between the bluffs and the water. On the western side of the beach, a retaining wall and road separated the shingle and water from the bluffs. Five draws provided potential vehicle access routes from the beach to the high ground to the south (Map 16).[30]

The beach was infested with steel barriers and abatis, with mines often attached. German concrete pillboxes, connected by trenches, lined the bluffs. Strong positions blocked the draws and minefields and barbed-wire barriers choked the five avenues through the bluffs.[31] Allied intelligence identified the German *716th Infantry Division* as the force manning the defenses on Omaha Beach and the British beaches to the east. This division was a "static" unit with no transport and little offensive capability. A similar division, the *709th*, defended the eastern Cotentin coast, with a regiment on Utah Beach. The *91st Infantry Division* and the *6th Parachute Regiment* were the only offensive-capable German units thought to be in the area. The *91st Division* was spread across the southern Cotentin Peninsula to guard against an airborne attack. First Army failed to warn the assault units that the *352nd Infantry Division* had moved into positions defending

Omaha Beach in late March. Thus, instead of facing a single regiment of a static division, the 1st Infantry Division was to meet a fully capable infantry division.[32]

The infantry companies were reorganized into three assault platoons each. These platoons had two sections of about thirty-five men, a number that fit the troop-carrying capacity of the smallest landing craft. The assault sections included two rifle teams, a wire-cutting team, a bazooka team, a 60mm mortar team, and a demolition team. The men were to carry only essential supplies and demolitions, such as the bangalore torpedo, which was a long series of pole sections full of explosives that fit together and could be slid under wire barriers and ignited to blow a gap. The special assault platoons trained as units beginning in February.[33]

Engineer demolition teams were to land with the leading infantry companies. While the infantrymen dealt with the enemy on the bluffs, the demolition teams were to blow gaps in the beach obstacles so that the following waves of boats could safely land. The line companies of the 1st Engineer Combat Battalion were attached to the regimental combat teams, providing them with the capability to clear barbed wire and mines.[34]

Efforts were made to provide tank support for the infantry from the onset of the operation. The 741st and the 743rd Tank Battalions each provided thirty-two specially equipped duplex drive (DD) tanks for the first wave. These tanks were to be launched from landing craft tanks (LCTs) 5,000 yards from shore for the swim to the beach. The armor battalions' remaining tanks were to land from LCTs. Sherman tanks of the 745th Tank Battalion were to begin arriving with the second assault wave on LCTs. The tanks were to provide support to the assault platoons against fortified positions and to help defeat any German counterattacks.[35]

During the spring, the men "worked as they had never worked before. . . . It was tough, grueling work—work that tasked minds and muscles almost as they would be tasked in the real thing that was to follow."[36] Joe Dawson, wrote to his family on 1 May:

> I am singularly optimistic about the whole thing and I know that it will be a great show because I've got a group of men that are as good as they come in anybody's army. Yes I would say they are a coach's dream. We're ready this time, so I can assure you success! . . . There will doubtless be *many* who will suffer death as a result of the next big conflict, but the final achievement will indeed be worth the price. Just know that and pray for its speedy fruition.[37]

By early May, Force O was ready for its dress rehearsal. This operation, code-named Fabius I, was carried out at Slapton Sands from 4 to 7 May. In spite of rough seas and rain, the exercise went as planned. The 16th Infantry landed on the left and the 116th landed on the right, as they were to do on D-day. The combat teams swiftly moved inland to consolidate a "beachhead maintenance line." Unfortunately, the personnel who operated the landing craft in the rehearsal were not the same men who operated the boats on D-day.[38] During a similar rehearsal for Force U and the 4th Infantry Division, known as Operation Tiger, German torpedo boats attacked the convoy carrying the assault troops. The Germans sank three LSTs, drowning as many as 700 Americans.[39]

Operation Fabius was the last rehearsal for the units bound for Omaha Beach. For the remainder of May, the division water proofed vehicles, cleaned up the camps around Dorchester, and stored personal gear and equipment not needed in the coming battle. On 17 May, the troops moved into the marshaling camps near the port of embarkation.[40] By the end of the month, the division was task-organized.

Operation Overlord: D-day

At echelons of command well above the 1st Infantry Division, Generals Eisenhower and Montgomery made the critical decisions concerning the invasion. Eisenhower selected 5 June as the primary date for D-day. The three airborne divisions were to begin their drops shortly after midnight. The time at which the amphibious landings were to start, known as H-hour, was set for three hours before high tide and as close to dawn as possible on each of the invasion beaches. For Omaha and Utah Beaches, H-hour was 0630. This timing allowed roughly thirty minutes of daylight for the navy's bombardment before the troops landed and enough light for the landing craft commanders to identify navigational features on the shore. It also allowed three hours for the engineers to open barriers through the obstacles before high tide covered them. The British assault to the east was to commence at 0725 due to differences in tides.[41]

During the last week of May, the combat teams loaded their equipment aboard their share of the more than 5,000 ships and craft that were to carry the invasion force to Normandy. From 1 to 4 June, the soldiers embarked at Weymouth, Portland, and other nearby ports, and the convoys for Omaha assembled in Weymouth Harbor. On 3 June, forecasts of horrible weather for 5 June forced Eisenhower to postpone the invasion for at least a day. After twenty-four nerve-wracking hours of waiting by the supreme commander, meteorologists predicted that conditions would be adequate for the operation on 6 June. Making one of the most important Allied decisions of the war, Eisenhower ordered the invasion to begin on 6 June 1944.[42]

During the next forty-eight hours, the invasion fleet left port, formed convoys, and forged its way to Normandy. Squadrons of minesweepers cleared gaps through minefields in the English Channel. Overhead, thousands of planes protected the convoys and continued to bomb the coastal defenses and the French rail system. In the early hours of 6 June, the American and British task forces reached their transport areas off the Normandy coast. At 0130, the invasion commenced when the airborne divisions jumped into drop zones on the flanks of the invasion.

The transport area for Force O was about 23,000 yards (12 miles) north of Omaha Beach. Once there, the assault units transferred to landing craft for the long run to the beach. The weather was rainy, with waves as high as 6 feet and a wind of 15–25 knots. It was a long trip to shore for the 16th and 116th Regiments. As one battalion commander observed, "After having been battered about on the unusually rough sea for more than two hours, and having been drenched by cold spray from the outset, a great majority of the soldiers in the assault waves were overcome by seasickness. Men who had been chilled by their wetting, cramped by immobility in the small and fully loaded craft, were not in the best condition for strenuous action on landing."[43]

While the assault boats moved south through heavy seas, 329 heavy bombers dropped 13,000 bombs on the coast. However, due to the heavy clouds, the bombers used instruments to find the target area and unloaded their ordnance several seconds late to avoid hitting friendly troops. Most of the bombs hit south of the defenses, inflicting little damage on the enemy.[44]

The German *Seventh Army* reacted to the airborne drops by putting its forces on full alert. As reports of the invasion filtered to higher headquarters and to Hitler's staff in Bavaria, the byzantine organization of the German command structure in France worked in the Allies' favor. The *Seventh Army* controlled few reserves, and Rommel's headquarters could only commit one armored and one mobile infantry division (the *21st Panzer* and *91st Infantry Divisions*) to action without Hitler's permission. Hitler controlled the majority of the armored divisions in France, and his staff was unwilling to wake the Führer in the morning as news of the invasion reached Germany. Consequently, the closest armored reserve, the *I SS Panzer Corps* with the *12th SS Panzer* and the *Panzer Lehr Divisions*, was not ordered to move toward Caen until late in the afternoon of D-day. These two panzer divisions did not get into the battle until 8 June.[45]

At 0535, German artillery behind Omaha Beach opened fire against the approaching landing craft. Within minutes, Allied warships responded with counterbattery fire. The volume of naval fire on the beach area was less than planned due to poor visibility. Few German positions were silenced. The infantry, engineers, and tankers would have to crack the defenses. The initial naval gunfire, however, detonated many German mines on the beaches, facilitating engineer operations later in the morning.[46] The Luftwaffe proved impotent in the face of overwhelming Allied air superiority.

The first assault wave hit Omaha Beach at approximately 0630. Eight infantry companies were to land in eight zones across the beach, closely followed by engineers (Map 16). DD tanks were to land before the infantry, having swum in from their off-load points 4 miles out to sea. On the western flank, four assault companies of the 116th Infantry were assigned beach sections named Dog Green, Dog White, Dog Red, and Easy Green. Their missions were to seize the draws on the western half of the beach and to protect the engineers as they destroyed the obstacles. Unfortunately, only Company A, 1/116th, hit its designated beach. The three remaining companies of CT116 (E, F, and G) were carried east and scattered by the strong winds and the fast easterly current. Most of F and G landed about 1,000 meters east of Company A. Company E came ashore farthest east, intermingling with the 16th Infantry.[47]

Company A, 116th Infantry, was left to face the concentrated fire of the German positions near the draw leading to Vierville-sur-Mer. When the Higgins boats dropped their ramps, the enemy unleashed a hail of fire at the exposed infantrymen. German fire hit two-thirds of the men in Company A in the first twenty minutes. Those who survived were pinned down at the base of the seawall. Over 90 percent of the company were casualties. As Steven Ambrose describes it, "In the lead Company A boat, LCA 1015, Capt. Taylor Fellers and every one of his men were killed before the ramp went down. It just vaporized."[48] Nonetheless,

> its sacrifice was not in vain. The men had brought in rifles, BARs [Browning automatic rifles], grenades, TNT charges, machine guns, mortars and mortar rounds, flamethrowers, rations, and other equipment. This was now strewn across the sand at Dog Green. The weapons and equipment would make a life-or-death difference to the following waves of infantry, coming in at higher tide and having to abandon everything to make their way to shore.[49]

Company C, 2nd Ranger Battalion, landed as planned to the west of Company A. The rangers met a wall of fire that killed or wounded half of the men before they got to dry land. For the next few hours the survivors hung on for their lives at the base of the bluffs.

East of Company A, eight DD tanks made it ashore because the skippers of the LCTs carrying the tanks took them all the way to shore. Once the tanks landed, however, German guns destroyed most of them. Company F and elements of G, 116th Infantry, came ashore opposite the heavily fortified

Les Moulins Draw. "For the men of F and G Companies, the 200 meters or more journey from the Higgins boats to the shingle was the longest and most hazardous trip they had ever experienced, or ever would."[50] One-quarter of the men of Company F were hit, including most of the officers. A nucleus of Company F reached the relative safety of the shingle, where the men waited for the next wave.[51]

The experience of the 16th Infantry, on the eastern half of Omaha, was similar to that of the 116th. Heavy seas, underwater obstacles, and intense enemy fire destroyed many craft and caused high casualties before the assault companies reached shore.[52] Boats were blown east, scattering the sections. Companies L and I drifted well to the east, and it took them an hour to get back to the beachhead. Most of the DD tanks supporting CT16 foundered in the high waves. Those few that reached shore became targets for German artillery fire. Casualties were high, but, through good fortune, four boat sections of Companies E and F, 16th Infantry, landed in a soft spot, between the Saint-Laurent and Colleville-sur-Mer Draws. There, for some unknown reason, the Germans had not manned all of the positions on the bluff. The Americans below lost only two men as they made their way to the shingle.[53]

The remainder of Companies E and F landed in front of the pillboxes guarding the Colleville Draw. Nearly half of the men of Company E were hit by enemy fire. Many wounded men drowned, and the survivors crawled to the shingle without most of their equipment. According to the 16th Infantry's after-action report, the survivors were "pinned down on the beach by extremely heavy fire from concrete fortifications, machine-gun emplacements, and sniper nests, which remained intact through severe naval and air bombardment. Casualties were extremely high."[54]

At around 0700, another eight tanks from the 741st Tank Battalion landed from LCTs. Within minutes, most were knocked out by German guns. Engineers landed with the infantry as planned. However, with little cover from tanks or friendly infantry, the engineers were able to clear only four lanes through the barriers for the following landing craft. Of the engineers, 40 percent were hit by enemy fire. The brigade commander, the S2 (intelligence officer), and the S3 (operations officer) of the 5th Special Engineer Brigade died trying to accomplish their mission.[55] Fifteen engineers earned the Distinguished Service Cross for their bravery on the beach. However, with only four lanes cleared, boats that attempted to beach did so with the high risk of hitting obstacles or mines.[56]

While the first wave struggled to survive, the landing craft of the second wave reached Omaha. These vessels carried the remainder of the four initial assault battalions of the 16th and 116th Infantry, two battalions of combat engineers, naval shore fire control teams, and the advance elements of

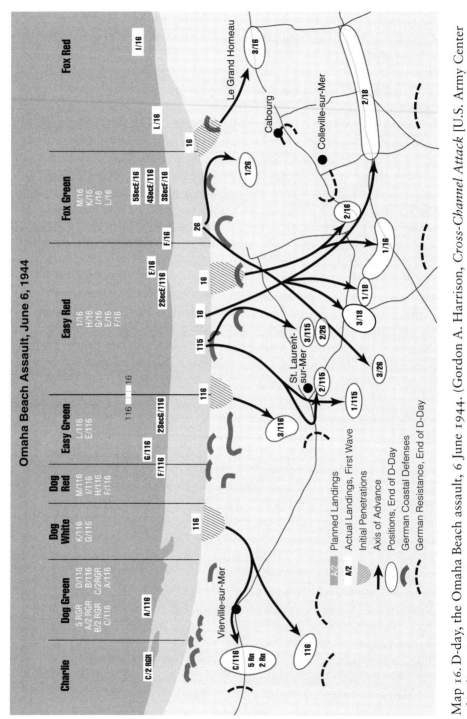

Map 16. D-day, the Omaha Beach assault, 6 June 1944. (Gordon A. Harrison, *Cross-Channel Attack* [U.S. Army Center of Military History, 1993])

the artillery and medical units. On the western half of the 116th Infantry's sector, elements of the 1st Battalion, 116th Infantry, landed close to where Company A had been destroyed. The battalion command group landed at the base of the cliffs on the far western side of the beach and was pinned down for the rest of the day. Most of the heavy weapons of the 1st Battalion were lost in the rising tide. Only Company C, 116th Infantry, which landed between the Vierville and Les Moulins Draws, made it ashore as a cohesive unit without heavy losses. The 5th Ranger Battalion followed Company C into the relatively safe area, but two companies of the 2nd Ranger Battalion landed in front of the Vierville Draw and lost nearly half of their men.[57]

In the zone of the 2nd Battalion, 116th Infantry, the heavy weapons company and 2nd Battalion headquarters landed in front of Les Moulins Draw, suffering the same fate as Company F. The battalion commander, Major Sidney Bingham, rallied several sections of Company F and unsuccessfully attacked the defenses. Meantime, the 3rd Battalion landed east of Les Moulins. While the units were intermingled, most of the men made it across the beach in one piece.

At about 0730, Brigadier General Norman Cota, assistant division commander of the 29th Infantry Division—and the senior officer of that unit working for Major General Clarence Huebner—landed with Company K, along with Colonel Charles Canham, commander of the 116th Infantry Regiment. By then, the 116th had two intact forces ashore. With the leadership of Canham, Cota, and numerous NCOs and junior officers, Company C, between the Vierville and Les Moulins Draws, and the 3rd Battalion, east of Les Moulins, began to turn the tide of the battle.[58]

Cota and Canham concluded that the plan to attack the fortifications in the Vierville and Les Moulins Draws had been overcome by events. Instead, the troops at the seawall and the shingle needed to blow the barbed-wire obstacles in their path, cross to the base of the bluffs, climb the bluffs between the draws, and attack the enemy strongpoints from the flanks. Cota led soldiers across the beach, over the seawall, through the minefields, and up to the bluffs. There he established a command post and pushed small groups of men up the bluffs. Canham, "with his right arm in a sling and a .45 Colt in his left hand . . . was yelling and screaming for the officers to get the men off the beach." Soldiers began to move forward in small groups. These groups made it to the top and began the process of clearing out the defenses. Behind them, the engineers began to clear the obstacles.[59]

On the 16th Infantry's side of the beach, similar confusion and intermingling of units occurred as the remainder of the combat team arrived. In the process, the 16th Infantry's executive officer was killed, along with thirty-five men, when their boat took a direct hit. Colonel George Taylor, who landed at 0800 with the remainder of the command group, made it to the cover of the shingle by crawling through the surf and across the fire-swept beach. The remaining two companies of 2nd Battalion (G and H) and most of 1st Battalion landed in front of the Colleville Draw at approximately 0730. As Captain Joe Dawson, commander of Company G, remembered, "This caused severe intermingling and confusion on the already crowded beach. Reorganization was accomplished under continued heavy fire. Much equipment was lost and casualties mounted."[60]

Dawson made it ashore with his communications sergeant and company clerk at about 0730: "As they jumped, a shell hit the boat and destroyed it, killing thirty men, including the naval officer who was to control fire support from the warships." Dawson had expected to find a path cleared up the bluffs by Company F. What he found was "nothing but men and bodies lying on the shore." Realizing that "there was nothing I could do on the beach except die," Dawson gathered survivors and began the process of blowing the obstacle on the shingle and moving across the dunes and swampy ground between there and the base of the bluffs.[61] As Dawson related to his family,

> All the weapons of war seemed to be concentrated on that naked, exposed bit of sand and the miracle of it all was the fact that I still cannot tell just how I crossed it or how my men managed—*but we did!* Though many fell as we moved through this storm of steel, they didn't falter an instant, but came on without stopping. . . . My company pressed on, . . . and only pausing a few seconds to get their breath stormed the heights commanding the beach and with this successful assault we were able to secure the beach for the other units to come ashore.[62]

In the center of the 16th Regiment's sector, Sergeant Philip Streczyk of Company F blew one of the first breaches in the enemy wire along the shingle with a bangalore torpedo, opening the way toward the bluffs.[63] Lieutenant John Spaulding, of Company E, exploited Streczyk's opening by leading the remnants of Company E across the swamp and dunes along a path found by Streczyk. While these men crossed the open ground, a section of Company G provided covering fire. In this area of Omaha, few enemy soldiers manned the defenses overlooking the beach. Once at the bluff, Spaulding led his men along a faint trail through the heavily mined bushes to the top. Halfway up, they encountered a machine gun. After Sergeant Fred Bisco's bazooka failed to knock out the machine gun, Spaulding decided to rush the position. Spaulding later recalled: "As we rushed it the lone German operating the gun threw up his hands and yelled, 'Kamerad.' We needed prisoners for interrogating so I ordered the men not to shoot."[64]

Once on top of the bluff, Spaulding's force attacked west toward the German defenses around the Saint-Laurent Draw. Using grenades, bazookas, and bayonets, the men cleared out four concrete shelters, two pillboxes, and five machine-gun nests. By the time this was accomplished, only 83 men of Company E remained unhurt, out of an original strength of 183 men.[65] This action cleared one of the exits from the beach and reduced the amount of fire being directed at the men landing below. Dawson's Company G, operating a short way east, gained the crest and moved south toward Colleville. After clearing the pillboxes overlooking the draw, Spaulding and his men "started down the communications trenches [between German bunkers]. The trenches led to the cliff over the beach. We were now behind the Germans so we routed four out of a hole and got thirteen in the trenches."[66] Recognizing the success of the 16th Infantry, the assistant division commander, Brigadier General Willard Wyman, radioed General Huebner asking him to "reinforce 2nd Battalion, 16th Infantry, at once."[67]

Meanwhile, on the eastern edge of Omaha, Company L, 16th Infantry, had landed forty-five minutes late (at 0715) and out of sector. When the men reached shore, they sheltered beneath the bluffs abutting the beach. Of the 187 men in the company, 123 made it to the bluffs. Over the next few hours, Company L and stragglers from other units fought their way south. Supported by tanks and naval gunfire, they assaulted enemy positions in the draw northeast of Colleville. By 0900, they had subdued them with surprisingly small losses. Later in the morning, the force, now best described as 3rd Battalion, 16th Infantry, repulsed a counterattack by elements of the *352nd Infantry Division*. In this action, Lieutenant Jimmie W. Monteith was killed while leading his men and consistently exposing himself to enemy fire, earning the Medal of Honor posthumously. This small victory secured the left flank of Omaha Beach.[68]

While scattered groups moved off the beach and up the bluffs, Colonels Taylor and Canham and Brigadier Generals Wyman and Cota attempted to bring order out of chaos and get the soldiers to move off the beach. Taylor succinctly summarized the options for the troops along the beach when he told groups of men that "there are only two kinds of people on this beach: the dead and those about to die. So let's get the hell out of here! . . . If we're going to die, let's die up there."[69]

Critical Point

By 0900, 6 June, it seemed to those in the command ship USS *Ancon* that the assault on Omaha had failed. The air force and the navy had not suppressed the defenses. There were far more enemy troops defending the area than expected. The DD tanks had failed to get to shore in sufficient numbers to suppress the German bunkers. The first two waves of infantry and engineers had landed too far east, and the units were badly intermingled. The obstacles on the beach had not been cleared, and landing craft were blown out of the water as they approached the shore. Smoke obscured the area, and there seemed to be no units larger than platoons operating under control of officers. In this situation, the commander of the 7th Naval Beach Battalion halted further landings until the congestion on the beach could be cleared.[70]

The commander of V Corps, Major General Leonard Gerow, briefly considered halting further landings and sending the remaining regiments of Force O across the British beaches to the east or Utah Beach to the west. This option was possible because on those beach areas the Allies had been remarkably successful.

As Gerow contemplated his options, the situation on Omaha Beach underwent a major transformation. West of Omaha Beach, the 2nd Ranger Battalion, commanded by Lieutenant Colonel James Rudder, captured the German fortifications on Pointe du Hoc, removing a major threat to the invasion fleet from the 155mm guns thought to be there. On the western half of Omaha, elements of 5th Ranger Battalion and 1st Battalion, 116th Infantry, found a soft spot in the defenses between the Vierville and Les Moulins Draws and moved on to the bluffs. The 3rd Battalion, 116th Infantry, breached the German defenses west of the Saint-Laurent Draw and advanced toward Saint-Laurent-sur-Mer. These moves and those by the 16th Infantry to the east were facilitated by the heroic action of American and British destroyers, which sailed as close to the beach as possible to deliver accurate fire from their 5-inch guns against enemy positions. Although few naval gun fire control parties were in operation, the destroyers observed the sources of enemy fire and then targeted those locations. This method of engagement silenced dozens of German machine guns and artillery pieces.[71]

To the east, the 1st and 2nd Battalions, 16th Infantry, moved into the western part of Colleville-sur-Mer by 1100. These two battalions cleared enemy machine-gun nests from the fields around Colleville and fought to drive a determined enemy from positions in the village. By dark, they had established defensive positions on the Vierville–Saint-Laurent Road. Meanwhile, on the eastern end of Omaha Beach, the 3rd Battalion, 16th Infantry, cleared Exit F1 of enemy troops and fought its way to Le Grand Hameu, where it dug in to secure the eastern flank of the division and V Corps.[72]

At 1000, Gerow ordered the 115th and 18th Regimental Combat Teams to begin landing. By this time, many landing craft coxswains had decided to ram their vessels through the barriers rather than wait for engineers to clear them. At 1030, LCT 30 and LCI 544 (Landing Craft, Infantry) steamed at full speed through the obstacles, firing their 20mm and .50-caliber guns at the defenses. Under this covering fire, and that of two destroyers firing from barely 1,000 meters offshore, the 37th and 146th Engineer Battalions landed with bulldozers and began to clear gaps through the dunes on either side of the Saint-Laurent Draw. To the east of the draw, the 16th Infantry neutralized the enemy on the bluff, while to the west the 3rd Battalion, 116th Infantry, cleared the pillboxes overlooking the draw.[73]

The 115th and 18th Infantry Regiments landed together in front of the Saint-Laurent Draw. Although the 115th was farther east than planned and the troops were badly intermingled, most of the men got ashore unscathed. By about 1100 hours, there were sufficient troops ashore to begin the push inland while clearing the last pockets of resistance on the bluffs. The 115th Infantry moved up the Saint-Laurent Draw and drove the Germans out of Saint-Laurent-sur-Mer. This action secured the exit of Draw E1, allowing engineers to clear lanes through the dunes and the enemy barriers. By mid-afternoon, American vehicles were using the road up the draw. The 115th Infantry ended the day in positions south of Saint-Laurent, while the 3rd Battalion, 116th Infantry, dug in 500 yards to the northwest of Saint-Laurent.[74]

Once ashore, the 2nd Battalion, 18th Infantry, assumed the mission of the 2nd Battalion, 16th Infantry, to secure the high ground south of Colleville-sur-Mer. The men of the 2nd Battalion, 18th Infantry, crossed the beach while receiving heavy machine-gun and mortar fire from their flanks. According to the regiment's after-action report, "With disregard for this heavy enemy opposition the battalion pushed across the beach covered with uncleared minefields and up over the steep beach embankment to close with the enemy. Before this intense onslaught of our troops the enemy were forced to withdraw resulting in the capture of this vital ground. By 1223 hours the leading elements of this battalion were in Colleville-sur-Mer."[75] The 1st Battalion, 18th Infantry, followed the 2nd Battalion up the bluff to positions on the right of the 16th Infantry near Colleville. The 3rd Battalion, 18th Infantry, suffered heavy casualties while landing and then moved into an unmarked minefield where it lost more men. In this action, Private Carlton W. Barrett, of the 18th Infantry, spent much of the day pulling wounded comrades out of the surf in front of the Saint-Laurent Draw, earning the Medal of Honor. By 1530, the 3rd Battalion was digging in 1,500 meters south of the beach.[76]

Even before the momentum along the bluffs shifted in favor of the American infantrymen, the artillery of the Big Red One began to come ashore. The 7th Field Artillery Battalion's forward observers landed with the first two waves of the 16th Infantry. Twenty artillerymen were killed, wounded, or missing, and most of their communications gear was lost. Later, when the infantry climbed the bluff, the forward observers joined their assigned companies, although only a few had operational radios. The 7th Artillery command group landed near the Colleville Draw at 0827 and came under German machine-gun fire. "The CP group made their way off the beach and reorganized in an abandoned enemy emplacement. Advance was almost impossible in face of fire from commanding enemy strong points."[77]

The 7th Artillery Battalion's command post could not be established until Captain Robert Woodward, the battalion communications officer, led an attack against machine-gun nests in the area. Woodward and his men killed seven and captured twenty-six Germans, opening the way for the command group to set up the command post "about 300 yards off the beach atop the fortification now abandoned."[78]

The 7th Artillery's howitzers were off-loaded from their transport into DUKWs at about 0430. From then until 1300, the ungainly amphibious trucks circled offshore waiting for the beach master to allow them to land. At 1300, the first DUKW landed the first howitzer. Of the twelve howitzers in the battalion, six were lost when their DUKWs were swamped. The remaining six guns landed in three separate places, and it took the battalion three hours to get them into position. Battery C fired its first rounds against German machine-gun nests at 1615. The 7th Artillery's after-action report concluded that "this is believed to be the first artillery mission fired by Force Omaha in France."[79]

The 1st Infantry Division included a number of attached artillery battalions for D-day. Three of these attempted to land their howitzers during the late morning and afternoon of 6 June. The 111th Field Artillery Battalion lost eleven of its 105mm howitzers when the DUKWs carrying them foundered in the heavy seas or were hit by enemy fire. The 58th Armored Field Artillery lost three of its self-propelled 105mm howitzers when the LCT they were riding hit a mine and blew up. The 62nd Armored Field Artillery landed only two of its guns. The surviving guns of these battalions joined the 7th Field Artillery before dark.[80]

Once the 18th Infantry Regiment was ashore, the 32nd Field Artillery Battalion began its ride to the beach. The first elements of the battalion arrived at Easy Red Beach at 1030. The howitzers and vehicles came in during the afternoon, after the naval beach parties and engineers had cleared paths through the barriers. By 2030, ten of the 32nd Artillery's howitzers were in position 200 yards north of Colleville-sur-Mer. Twenty-eight artillerymen of the 32nd were killed or wounded and twenty-five vehicles were lost during the day, but the battalion was ready to support the infantry along the Beachhead Maintenance Line.[81]

The 33rd and 5th Field Artillery Battalions did not land until 7 June, D+1, due to beach congestion. Both battalions made it ashore with just three men wounded. The 105mm howitzers of the 33rd and the 155mm howitzers of the 5th Artillery were in firing positions by 2030, 7 June. Their safe arrival indicates how quickly the infantry combat teams had recovered from the initial losses on the beach and secured the beachhead.[82] Nonetheless, in spite of heroic efforts, the field artillery failed to play its hoped-for role in supporting the infantry on D-day. Fortunately, the superb fire support provided by the destroyers, amounting to thousands of 5-inch rounds in close support, contributed immensely to the outcome of the battle.[83]

The Beachhead Secured

The decisions to land CT18 and CT115 marked the turning point of D-day. Brigadier General Wyman, the senior officer of the 1st Infantry Division on Omaha Beach for most of 6 June, played a key part in these decisions. He provided effective coordination of the four infantry combat teams landed thus far. On his orders, the infantrymen of the 18th Infantry pushed toward the first ridge paralleling the coast to the south, the Beachhead Maintenance Line, clearing out German machine-gun nests and artillery positions as they advanced.[84] It was not an easy mission, as the "Germans had most of the gates and breaks in the hedges zeroed in with rifle and machine guns." With Company E in the lead, 1st Battalion fought its way south with the 3rd Battalion advancing to its right. By 2400, the 18th Regiment had crossed the Vierville-Colleville Road and had dug in. During the night, the Germans tried unsuccessfully to penetrate the regiment's positions. These positions on the Beachhead Maintenance Line provided protection from possible German counterattacks for the follow-on forces.[85]

Late in the morning of 6 June, General Gerow ordered the 26th Infantry Regiment to land. This decision was prompted in large part because the 16th Infantry had taken such a pounding on D-day that it was no longer capable of offensive action. The 26th Infantry landed on the eastern portion of Omaha Beach near the Colleville-sur-Mer Draw in mid-afternoon. By then, most German resistance in the area had been overcome by the 16th Infantry, allowing the 26th to come ashore with few losses. Lieutenant Colonel Frank Murdoch's 1st Battalion, with tanks from the 745th Tank Battalion, moved to the high ground north of the village of Coburg, about 500 meters inland, to establish positions protecting the left flank of the division. Derrill Daniel's 2nd Battalion and John Corley's 3rd Battalion moved about a mile south of the beach to fill a gap in the front between the 115th and the 18th Infantry Regiments and prepared to resume the advance toward Formigny the next morning.[86]

By the end of 6 June, the Big Red One held a much smaller beachhead

than envisioned in the plan. The main position was a narrow sector between Saint-Laurent and Colleville-sur-Mer, held by the 16th, 18th, 26th,
and 115th Infantry Combat Teams. The 2nd and 5th Ranger Battalions and
the 116th Infantry held another enclave a mile to the west, at Vierville, with
a tenuous supply line back to the beach east of the Vierville Draw. All units
were short of vehicles, artillery support, and supplies. Most of the tanks of
the 741st and 743rd Tank Battalions had been lost, and only a few of the
tanks of the 745th Tank Battalion were ashore. Compared to the plan or to
the progress on the other D-day beaches, this was a disappointing result for
the sacrifice of the soldiers of the 116th and 16th Infantry Regiments who
had borne the brunt of the enemy defensive fire and suffered the most from
the adverse weather, strong currents, and high waves.[87]

The human cost of D-day, especially on Omaha Beach, was high, although
it is impossible to provide an exact figure of the 1st Infantry Division's or
V Corps' losses. The V Corps personnel officer listed losses as 2,374 men
killed, wounded, or missing on 6 June. Of these, the 1st Division lost 1,190
soldiers, and the 29th Division lost 743 men. Corps units lost the remaining
441.[88] The 16th Infantry Regiment's Daily Casualty Report for the period
from 0630, 6 June, to 1200, 7 June, lists a total of 1,044 casualties. Of
this number, 363 men were listed as missing and presumed to be stragglers.
Later Casualty Reports indicate that 341 of those stragglers returned to duty
with the regiment by 25 June, leaving the regiment's net loss at 681 men
killed, wounded, or missing for the first thirty-five hours of the Normandy
campaign.[89]

The after-action reports of the artillery battalions listed their losses for 6
and 7 June as fifty-three men killed, wounded, or missing. The 16th Infantry Regiment's Daily Casualty Report list the losses of the 7th Field Artillery Battalion as thirty-eight killed, wounded, or missing in that period.
The records of the V Corps G1 list the 1st Infantry Division losses for the
period 6 to 10 June as 144 killed, 1,310 wounded, and 356 missing.[90] It is
abundantly clear that losses were heavy, especially in the 16th and 116th Infantry Regiments. The 16th Infantry lost roughly 18 percent of its assigned
strength, and at noon, 7 June, the regiment was short 1,044 men. Similar
losses occurred in the 116th Infantry.

The 1st Medical Battalion performed magnificently on D-day. Each regimental combat team had a Collecting Company attached to it from the
medical battalion, and each infantry battalion had a medical section of
about fifteen men, including the battalion surgeon. The 1st Medical Battalion established a clearing station on Omaha Beach at 1730. The Clearing Company lost fifty-one men killed, wounded, or missing in June 1944,
the majority of them on 6 June. The after-action report of the 1st Medical

Battalion does not list the number of men treated for wounds on 6 June. The company treated 233 wounded on 7 June and a total of 950 wounded by the end of the month. The company treated an additional 1,171 men during this period for various diseases and 182 for injuries.[91]

Medical personnel contributed immeasurably to the success of the invasion while facing the same dangers experienced by the combat troops. Company A, 1st Medical Battalion, was the Collecting Company attached to the 16th Infantry. The company's litter teams attempted to reach shore twice during the morning before the landing craft they were aboard was set on fire by enemy shells. After rescuing sailors and soldiers from burning holds and treating the wounded, the tired men got onto another landing craft and returned to the beach at 1700. They joined a team of medics led by Major Charles Tegtmeyer, the medical officer of the 16th Infantry, in efforts to save as many wounded men as possible. These medical personnel worked closely with the medical detachments of the naval beach battalions and the 60th and 61st Medical Battalions. The wounded who survived D-day owe their lives to these medical personnel.[92]

Much had not gone according to plan. Only 100 tons of supplies, of a planned 2,400 tons, had been landed. Ammunition shortages were widespread. The beachhead was scarcely a mile deep, and German artillery could still hit the beaches. German machine-gun nests and snipers continued to hold out, and many obstacles remained along the beach. The 16th and the 116th Infantry Regiments had suffered heavy losses during the assault, and it would be a full month before the 16th Infantry Regiment would resume offensive operations.[93]

The Beachhead Expands: 7–9 June 1944

The success of the British to the east of Omaha on 6 June convinced the Germans that the landings north of Caen were the main Allied effort.[94] Consequently, the German *Seventh Army* committed its armored reinforcements in a counterattack against the British. The *352nd Infantry Division* was left to contain the Omaha beachhead, while the *91st Infantry Division* and the *6th Parachute Regiment* tried to counterattack VII Corps on the Cotentin Peninsula. Although V Corps continued to expect a counterattack during the next week, the Germans focused their efforts against the British.[95]

As to the Omaha beachhead, Huebner planned to continue the attack on the morning of 7 June with the five infantry regiments already ashore. During the night of 6–7 June, most of the 745th Tank Battalion landed and sent tanks to join the 16th, 18th, and 26th Regimental Combat Teams, while the 743rd Tank Battalion supported the 115th and 116th Regimental Combat

Teams. A steady buildup of artillery continued, providing elements of seven artillery battalions to support the advance.

The 1st Infantry Division needed to accomplish two missions on 7 June. It had to advance far enough inland to put the beaches out of German artillery range, and it needed to link up with the British to the east at Port-en-Bessin and with VII Corps to the west at Isigny (Map 17).[96]

Huebner assigned the lightest missions for 7 June to the 16th Infantry Regiment. The 1st and 2nd Battalions cleared Germans out of the area between the beach and Colleville-sur-Mer. Company G, 2nd Battalion, secured Colleville, capturing fifty-four Germans. The 3rd Battalion, with tanks of Company B, 745th Tank Battalion, advanced along the coast road to Huppain, overlooking Port-en-Bessin. The infantrymen and tanks met little resistance, securing the town by 1700. There the 3rd Battalion waited to link up with the 47th Royal Marine Commando.[97] The 1st Battalion, 26th Infantry, moved south to Russy and then east toward Mount Cauvin, an important vantage point overlooking the Aure River. The battalion commander described the action: "As darkness was falling, we attacked into Etreham, and onto Mount Cauvin. By daylight, we had established a defense line forward of Etreham and on the south slopes of Mt. Cauvin. The next morning (8 June) Company C met a party of British commandos, so the Allies were linked up."[98] In the division's center, Huebner attached the 3rd Battalion, 26th Infantry, to CT18 for the main effort to push to the original D-day objective line on the high ground from Trévières to Blay. Five tanks from the 741st Tank Battalion supported the 1st Battalion, 18th Infantry, and twenty tanks from the 745th Tank Battalion worked with the other two battalions of the 18th Infantry Regiment. By noon, the 1st and 2nd Battalions were across the Bayeux-Isigny Highway, where they ambushed German bicyclists.

At 1400, the 1st Battalion, 18th Infantry, secured Engranville, while the 3rd Battalion, 18th Infantry, pushed through Surrain, crossed the Aure on an intact bridge, and seized Mandeville. On the combat team's right flank, however, the 3rd Battalion, 26th Infantry, ran into German machine-gun positions in the hedgerows north of Formigny and was stopped for the rest of the day. Formigny was not captured until the next morning. On the eastern flank of CT18, the 2nd Battalion, 18th Infantry, crossed the Aure River and captured the village of Mosles, on the road to Bayeux. Elements of the German *916th Infantry Regiment* held on to Trévières and manned a thin line south of Mandeville and Mosles, but there was no well-organized German defense in the area.[99]

On the division's right flank, the 115th Infantry cleared Germans out of the area of Les Moulins and attacked to the southwest toward Vacqueville. The 2nd and 3rd Battalions, 116th Infantry, spent the day destroying the

German positions in and around Vierville, while the 1st Battalion, 116th Infantry, and the 5th Rangers drove toward Pointe du Hoc, where Colonel Rudder's 2nd Ranger Battalion was under attack. German resistance remained strong on the western flank of Omaha throughout the day. The 115th Infantry made only a limited advance, and the column of rangers and the 1st Battalion, 116th Infantry, did not reach Rudder's men until the next day. Meanwhile, the 175th Infantry Regimental Combat Team, 29th Infantry Division, came ashore and prepared to advance toward Isigny the next day. As the day waned, Major General Charles Gerhardt assumed command of the 29th Infantry Division's units at 1700.[100]

By the end of 7 June, only scattered enemy resistance continued north of the Aure River. The 1st and 29th Infantry Divisions were firmly established in the bridgehead, and the 2nd Infantry Division had begun to land. Armor and artillery units were flowing ashore while the engineers improved the exits from the beach and the roads immediately inland. The heaviest fighting on 7 June took place in the British sector, where units of the *I SS Panzer Corps* faced the British. On the Cotentin Peninsula, the 82nd and 101st Airborne Divisions established contact with the 4th Infantry Division in spite of fierce German resistance around Ste. Mère-Église and north of Carentan. As Allied airpower impeded the movement of German reinforcements, the 90th Infantry Division began to arrive. The Allies were winning the race to build up superiority in Normandy.

Huebner's priorities for the 1st Infantry Division on 8 June were to secure the remainder of the D-day objectives and improve contact with the British along the Drome River. CT18 was to seize Formigny and the high ground east of Mandeville. The 16th Infantry Regiment became the division reserve. Huebner ordered Colonel John Seitz to concentrate the 26th Infantry on the eastern flank, near Mosles, for an advance east through Ste. Anne to link up with the British 50th Division. This move offered a chance to isolate the German *726th Infantry Regiment* and the *918th Infantry Battalion* in a pocket between the British and American forces south of Port-en-Bessin.

The 1st Battalion, 18th Infantry, seized Formigny with the attack by Company B, clearing the enemy from between the 29th and 1st Infantry Divisions. This released the 3rd Battalion, 26th Infantry, for a midday move to Mosles. The rest of CT18 pushed toward the low ground south of Mandeville, but the strong German resistance in Trévières made it dangerous to push too far south. Consequently, the major offensive effort of the division on 8 June took place between Mosles and Ste. Anne.[101]

Late on 7 June, Huebner released the 2nd Battalion, 26th Infantry, to the control of CT26. The 2nd Battalion moved during the night to Mosles, where it took over the positions of 2nd Battalion, 18th Infantry, at dawn and waited for the rest of the 26th Infantry to arrive. The 3rd Battalion did not reach Mosles until after noon, and the 1st Battalion, 26th Infantry, met enemy resistance in its attack from Etreham to the south, across the Aure. Finally, at 1800, the 3rd Battalion, accompanied by tanks of the 745th Tank Battalion, advanced east. Infantrymen moved along both sides of Highway N13 with the tanks driving in the center. As the tank-infantry team moved, the tanks sprayed likely ambush positions with machine-gun fire. Led by Company I, John Corley's battalion reached Ste. Anne at 0100 and established positions facing east and south. A patrol led by Technical Sergeant T. Dobol moved farther east to Vaucelles, hoping to meet the advancing British. Instead, Dobol met the advance guard of a German counterattack.[102]

The converging attacks by the British 56th Brigade from Bayeux toward Sully and the 26th Infantry Regiment from Mosles threatened to cut off elements of the *352nd Infantry Division* and the *30th Mobile Brigade* in a corridor running south from Port-en-Bessin to Vaucelles. To avert this encirclement, General Dietrich Kraiss, commander of the *352nd*, ordered the German units in the area to retreat after dark, on 8 June. The line of withdrawal was through Vaucelles and Ste. Anne. Shortly after the 3rd Battalion, 26th Infantry, had established hasty fighting positions, German infantry, and possibly some light tanks, attacked. They struck from the north as well as the east, surprising Company L. A confusing melee ensued. John Corley repositioned his tanks to the threatened sector; Huebner sent additional armor; and the 33rd Artillery provided artillery support. The 3rd battalion held on to Ste. Anne, although casualties in Company L had been heavy and it was impossible to move toward Vaucelles until the battalion reorganized. However, the British were unable to hold their positions in Vaucelles, and most of the Germans in the corridor escaped through a gap along the Drome River.[103]

The counterattack at Ste. Anne was the last German offensive action near Omaha Beach. The battle shifted to the area known as the Bocage, characterized by small farm fields encircled by hedgerows of earth, brush, and trees that made it extremely difficult to coordinate tank-infantry teams and artillery. On 9 June, the 2nd Infantry Division entered the V Corps front between the 29th and the 1st Infantry Divisions (see Map 17). At the same time, General Gerow ordered the three divisions to attack south.

The Drive to Caumont-l'Éventé: 9–13 June 1944

The 1st Division's next objective was Caumont-l'Éventé, a town on a high ridge along the Bayeux–St. Lô highway. Gerow attached the 743rd and 745th Tank Battalions, the 635th TD Battalion, the 102nd Cavalry

Reconnaissance Squadron (M), and several V Corps artillery battalions to the division. Huebner planned to advance with CT18 on the right flank and CT26 on the left. The 745th Tank Battalion supported CT26, and the 743rd joined CT18.

Huebner kept the 16th Infantry Regiment in reserve, allowing Colonel Taylor time to integrate replacements. The 16th Infantry received just 7 replacements by 13 June, although 140 of the men listed as missing also rejoined their companies by then. From 13 to 15 June, 736 new soldiers were assigned. By 24 June, 1,202 replacements, 44 men from hospitalization, and 341 stragglers had joined the regiment, bringing its strength to 3,840 men. This was 181 more men than the unit had assigned on 5 June. By the end of the month, the 16th Infantry was ready for commitment to the heaviest combat duties.[104]

The division attacked south during the afternoon of 9 June. On the right, CT18 made progress against German rearguard positions. By late evening, the 1st and 3rd Battalions had broken through the defenses and had reached the railroad line that runs from Bayeux to Carentan (Map 17). To the east, CT26 moved against diminishing resistance, seizing the village of Agy at 2000 hours. During this period, the 32nd Field Artillery fired 13 missions and 356 rounds against suspected enemy positions, while the 33rd Field Artillery fired 7 missions and 285 rounds. Although the division had plenty of artillery support, there were few targets to use it on, indicating the German front had been broken.[105]

The attack continued on 10 June, as the 3rd Battalion, 18th Infantry, reached Vaubadon and the 1st Battalion occupied La Commune. Near the village of Vaubadon, a line of resistance was encountered as the 18th Infantry crossed the fields north of town. However, the bravery of men like Staff Sergeant Arthur F. DeFranzo overcame the German machine-gun nests in the area, allowing the 1st Battalion to occupy Vaubadon. In this action, Sergeant DeFranzo "courageously moved out in the open to the aid of a wounded scout" when his unit was ambushed. Wounded himself, but refusing aid, as his Medal of Honor award citation noted,

> DeFranzo reentered the open field and led the advance upon the enemy. There were always two machine guns bringing unrelenting fire upon him, but Staff Sergeant DeFranzo kept going forward, firing into the enemy and one by one the enemy emplacements became silent. While advancing he was again wounded, but continued on until he was within 100 yards of the enemy position and even as he fell he kept firing his rifle and waving his men forward. . . . In this action Staff Sergeant DeFranzo lost his life, but by bearing the brunt of the enemy fire in leading the attack, he prevented a delay in the assault which would have been

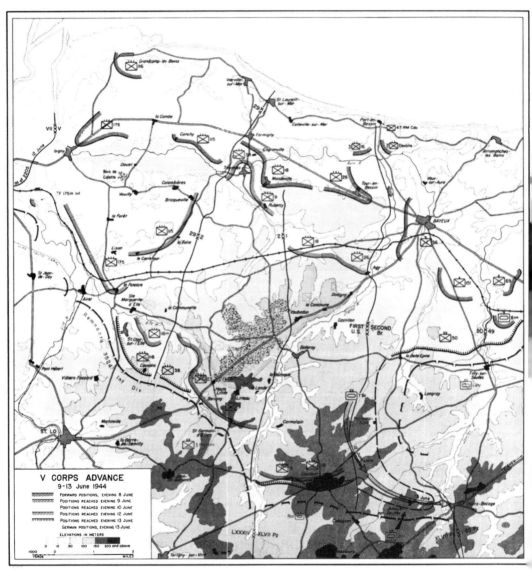

Map 17. V Corps advance, 9–13 June 1944. (Gordon A. Harrison, *Cross-Channel Attack* [U.S. Army Center of Military History, 1993])

of considerable benefit to the foe, and he made possible his company's advance with a minimum of casualties.[106]

By denying the Germans time to establish defenses in depth in the hedgerows of the Bocage, men such as DeFranzo made it possible for the division to advance. This and similar small-unit actions made it look deceptively easy for the Big Red One to push south to Caumont from 9 to 13 June.[107]

From Vaubadon, the 18th Infantry sent patrols south to Balleroy and Castillon, which they found undefended. The 26th Infantry did not advance as far as CT18 on 10 June, since the British to the east were lagging. Seitz's regiment swung its line counterclockwise to the south, with Agy as the pivot, keeping pace with CT18 to its west and the British to the east. On 11 June, the 2nd Battalion, 18th Infantry, cleared the Bois de Baugy in the center of the division's sector, while the 3rd Battalion, 18th Infantry, occupied Balleroy. The 1st Battalion, 26th Infantry, occupied La Butte, east of Balleroy, by 2200 hours, 11 June.[108] These advances were over short distances—the division used most of the day to rest the troops and to move artillery and supplies forward, close to the line of advance.

Even though only minor resistance by small German units was encountered on 10 and 11 June, Huebner maintained a cautious advance due to concern for the division's flanks. In fact, the division was driving into a wide gap in the German defenses, causing great concern to enemy commanders. Only the reconnaissance battalion of the *17th SS Panzergrenadier Division* filled the gap to the south between the German *LXXXIV Corps* near St. Lô and the *I SS Panzer Corps* west of Caen.[109] The decisions by Huebner and Gerow not to aggressively drive the division into the gap in the German defenses caused the Allies to miss a major opportunity to unhinge the German defenses in the British sector.

The division's final push to Caumont commenced on 12 June, when the 18th and 26th Combat Teams each deployed two infantry battalions on line. The 102nd Cavalry Squadron screened the eastern flank of the division and sent reconnaissance troops ahead of the advancing infantrymen. Tanks accompanied the infantry, and the division's artillery battalions steadily displaced forward to support the advance. On the left, the 26th Infantry met some resistance in Ste. Honorine de Ducy but quickly overcame the enemy. Action was so light that the 33rd Field Artillery fired just thirty-nine rounds on 11 and 12 June. As dusk approached, the 1st and 2nd Battalions reached Caumont and the ridge to its east. Caumont was occupied by the Germans, so the combat team dug in and prepared for a coordinated attack the next morning.[110]

The 18th Infantry jumped off according to schedule at 0630 hours, 12 June, meeting little opposition. The 1st and 2nd Battalions moved from phase line to phase line until they occupied their objectives and dug in. The regimental command post set up operations in Sallen, about 3 miles north of Caumont.[111] The 32nd Field Artillery Battalion, with the 62nd Armored Field Artillery attached, supported the advance. The 32nd Artillery fired only four missions and a total of twenty-seven rounds on 12 June.[112]

Early on 13 June, the 2nd Battalion, 26th Infantry, seized Caumont-l'Évente, while the 1st Battalion cleared the ridge east of town. The 1st Engineer Battalion spent the remainder of the day clearing the streets while the 26th Infantry established defensive positions in the village and along the ridge to the east. The 18th Infantry dug in on a line running from Caumont to the village of La Vacquerie. For the remainder of June, the 18th and 26th Regiments maintained their defensive positions while the 16th Infantry remained in reserve.[113]

The V Corps drive south by the 29th, the 2nd, and the 1st Infantry Divisions pushed the Germans out of the Forêt de Cerisy and gave the Omaha beachhead breathing room. By mid-June, the Allies and the Germans feverishly worked to reinforce their forces in Normandy.

The Results

The Big Red One successfully led V Corps across Omaha Beach and onto the overlooking high ground on D-day. The subsequent advances over the next three days by the 1st and 29th Infantry Divisions connected the American forces on the Cotentin Peninsula with the British forces to the east. The resistance on the beaches and bluffs overlooking Omaha was far greater than expected, and the effects of Allied air and naval bombardment were less than hoped. However, the 1st Infantry Division and other V Corps units overcame German resistance and seized the critical ground to secure the beachhead and land the follow-on forces safely, ensuring the success of Operation Overlord.

10

Crusade in Europe
The Drive to Germany

ONCE THE 1ST INFANTRY DIVISION HAD SECURED Caumont-l'Évente, on 13 June, the division halted its advance because the British to the east had been stopped by the Germans' determined defenses, and the 2nd Infantry Division to the west had been stopped short of St. Lô in the Bocage. For the next four weeks, the 18th and 26th Infantry Regiments, reinforced by the 745th Tank and the 635th Tank Destroyer Battalions, remained in defensive positions waiting for the neighboring forces to catch up.

First Army's priorities in June remained the capture of Cherbourg and the accumulation of the forces and supplies needed to continue the offensive. From 10 to 30 June, VII Corps fought its way across the Cotentin Peninsula and pushed north to capture Cherbourg. The three other corps of First Army (VIII, XIX, and V) tried to push south to positions along the high ground from Lessay to St. Lô. First Army achieved little in its June attacks, even after VII Corps entered the front.

The Allies operated in two types of terrain in Normandy. The British fought in the generally open farmland around Caen. The Americans had to fight their way first across swamps north of Lessay and then through the region known as the Bocage. The Bocage is an area compartmentalized by a series of ridges running from the southwest to the northeast. Small fields and orchards surrounded by hedgerows are the predominant agricultural pattern. The hedgerows consist of a mound of dirt topped by a thick hedge, making it impossible to see more than 100 yards. Thus, every field was a ready-made defensive position that was extremely difficult to attack with armor or infantry.[1]

The Caumont Interlude

Although nearly a million Allied soldiers had landed by the end of June, the lodgment in Normandy remained remarkably shallow. Consequently, Bradley launched a series of attacks in July to push the Germans south and gain a suitable line of departure, from Lessay to St. Lô, for an offensive toward Avranches and Brittany.[2]

While the rest of First Army carried out these attacks, the 1st Infantry Division remained in defensive positions near Caumont. Although the Germans did not attack these defenses, they patrolled the front actively and shelled the American positions routinely.

From the perspective of the soldiers in the foxholes, it was not so routine. As Lieutenant William Dillon remembered, "My platoon always had a front line hedge row—always!"[3] As early as 15 June, the Germans "launched strong attacks which worked up to the main line of resistance" before they were stopped cold, "with 100 percent casualties to the attacking squads."[4] Thomas McCann, of the 18th Infantry, pointed out that "from the beaches to August fighting in the area was handicapped by the hedgerows. You would go on patrol and while you were on one side of the hedge the enemy was on the other side going in an opposite direction. We had observation posts on houses, churches, on the edge of clearings, any place where we could see into the enemy lines."[5] The division's casualties were not heavy, but there was a steady strain on the troops and morale sagged as it became clear that it was going to take a long time to get to Berlin.

The 18th Infantry's after-action report noted that "this stable situation was put to use in the much needed training in all types of patrols. With combat and ambush patrols constant contact with the enemy was maintained. . . . The troops were kept on a constant alert to cope with any surprise attempt by the enemy to pierce our lines." The four weeks in a static position afforded the infantry regiments time to assimilate replacements and to train their soldiers in how to operate as part of tank-infantry teams in the Bocage. For the first time, infantrymen and tanks were taught how to function as an integrated unit. "All in all, the situation afforded an excellent training period."[6]

The 26th Infantry reported similar experiences. By early July, "it had become SOP for the 2nd Battalion positions near and in Caumont to receive a daily mortar and artillery pounding by the enemy. . . . The 1st Battalion [east of Caumont] was also very heavily shelled." Caumont's civilian population was evacuated due to the shelling, although the inhabitants were given passes to return to their homes periodically. By mid-July, the lovely town had been leveled. The regiment also sent patrols "to scout out the enemy terrain and to lay mine fields."[7]

Not all of the patrols turned out favorably, as Lieutenant Dillon of the 16th Infantry remembered: "At noon on the 6th (July) I went back for dinner and Capt. Kenckle said to stay after I ate so they could zero me in on a patrol I would take out that night. . . . Capt. Kenckle said I could take up to 10 men and any weapons I wanted. . . . We took Thompson sub-machine guns, carbines, a bazooka, and whatever the men wanted and left about midnight."[8] Dillon's patrol encountered Germans and Lieutenant Dillon was wounded and captured. After a brief stint in a German aid station, he escaped and joined French partisans. On 3 August, he was liberated, along with eighty-nine American airmen, by Patton's Third Army.

Casualties in the division during its stay around Caumont were relatively light due to the well-protected positions of the infantry and the lack of major attacks by either side. From 7 to 13 June, the 1st Medical Battalion's Clearing Company treated an average of seventy-eight wounded soldiers per day. From 14 June to 15 July, the company treated fewer than twenty per day. The loss of medical personnel dropped dramatically from forty-five medic casualties in June to one in July. Although additional wounded were treated by the three Collecting Companies, which operated with the combat teams, the casualty figures of the Clearing Company reflect the overall trends.[9] Most of the casualties were infantrymen. The artillery battalions lost ninety-six men killed, wounded, or missing in June and twenty-nine in the first two weeks of July.

The weather during June and most of July in Normandy was miserable. Storms lashed the coast, making logistical operations difficult. By 26 June, Captain Joe Dawson was heading his letters to his family with the words "Cold and Wet—Normandy":

> Now today I've spent in mere routine dreariness that marks so many days of warfare. It is cold and raining and most uncomfortable with the shelling of the "heinies" adding torment to discomfort. But there's nothing to do but huddle a bit closer in the ground and believe me my hole is plenty deep. I somehow get a little comfort, however, and if the wet, damp, cold would lift, I'm sure my leg would lose its stiffness.[10]

Low clouds and limited visibility also made it difficult for the air force to provide air support or to interdict enemy reinforcements and supplies. On several occasions, the British cancelled attacks when the bombers could not see to drop their bombs, and, as late as 24 July, Bradley had to postpone major operations until the weather cleared.

While the division was holding the line around Caumont, Generals Huebner, Gerow, Bradley, and Eisenhower presented awards honoring the courage of the soldiers during the invasion. Gerow also ordered a number of units to nominate fifteen soldiers each for the award of the Distinguished Service Cross for their actions in June.[11] Men selected for the award included Norman Cota, Willard Wyman, George Taylor, Joe Dawson, John Spaulding, Raymond Strojny, Philip Streczyk, and Walter Ehlers. Ehlers later was awarded the Medal of Honor. When Eisenhower visited the 16th Infantry

Regiment, he remarked, "You are one of the finest regiments in our Army. I shall always consider the 16th my Praetorian Guard."[12]

After his visit to Normandy in early June, Eisenhower assessed the quality of the American divisions in Normandy in a letter to George Marshall: "On the showing to date I would rate the 1st and 9th Divisions as tops; the 4th, 29th, 2nd, and 79th as good, and the others largely untested."[13]

The division's defensive operations at Caumont saved it from the heavy losses experienced by most of First Army's divisions that took part in attacks to secure suitable positions for future operations. Nonetheless, the division's soldiers lived in constant danger. As Lieutenant John Walker, of the 16th Infantry, noted in his memoir, "It is impossible for anyone not having experienced it to understand how utterly exhausted, both mentally and physically, a soldier becomes. The bad uncooked, greasy canned food; the wet uncomfortable hole in the ground that serves as a bed at night and a home during the day . . . the hopeless future that offers him nothing but a continuation of his present, tired, aching state and more attacks."[14]

The division had to deal with a number of battle fatigue casualties, caused by the constant stress and strain of the front lines. Frank Murdoch, commander of 1st Battalion, 26th Infantry, noted years later that even the bravest men eventually reached a point where they would break. Veterans of North Africa and Sicily got to this point in France or Germany unless they were killed or wounded first. Murdoch pointed out that the infantry commanders recognized this phenomenon and rotated soldiers periodically to jobs in the rear where they could recuperate.[15]

The procedure for such casualties was to evacuate them to an Exhaustion Center near the 41st Evacuation Hospital. The center attempted to restore combat fatigue patients to fighting fitness and return them to their units. However, medical officers found that most of the cases from the 1st Infantry Division in June were unqualified for further combat, even after treatment, and were capable only of limited service duties. The decision as to whether or not a soldier was fit for combat was a medical one. If a unit returned a soldier to the hospital whom it believed was no longer psychologically fit, a report was made by the unit surgeon through medical channels to the army surgeon. Action was then taken to reclassify the soldier.[16]

The Big Red One suffered a steady stream of casualties in its Caumont positions. For the period 11 June to 8 July, the division lost 117 men killed, 1,994 wounded, and 86 missing in action.[17] Many of the wounded recovered, and Major General Huebner worked to have these men returned to their units. On 1 July, the V Corps G1 decided that "wounded in action cases will, if at all possible, be returned to their former units."[18] A few days later, Major General Gerow notified Huebner that First Army "has issued instructions to all of the Replacement Battalions servicing the various corps to return immediately to units from which they came, all personnel evacuated either in the U.K. or from the continent."[19]

This policy made sense until First Army realized that it caused major imbalances in the strength of infantry divisions. When a division suffered losses it presented a requisition to the personnel system for replacements. When the 16th Infantry Regiment lost over 1,000 men in early June, the division requisitioned replacements. By 26 June, the 16th Infantry had received 1,206 replacements and was 273 men stronger than it had been before the invasion.[20]

During this period, the 1st Infantry Division received 2,260 replacements, and 343 wounded soldiers had rejoined the division. However, since the division was no longer authorized the augmented strength of 16,805 men that it had for Overlord, it was overstrength on 8 July by about 2,300 soldiers (15,601 on hand, with an authorized strength of 13,986).[21] Since roughly 1,700 members of the division were wounded from 6 to 26 June, the division could become even further overstrength as men returned from the hospitals.

By August, V Corps policy was that personnel "who have been evacuated to medical installations outside this command . . . will be returned to their former organizations only in the event that such organizations are below authorized strength and have a vacancy in the appropriate grade." Commanders were encouraged to consider deferring requisitions and promotions so that former members of their organizations could be returned upon completion of their convalescence.[22]

First Army Attacks: 1–14 July 1944

In early July, First Army launched attacks to secure the high ground along the highway from Lessay to St. Lô. VIII Corps struck first on 3 July. After four days of fighting in the swampy terrain north of that town, the corps had suffered heavy losses and taken little ground.[23] On 4 July, VII Corps attacked from south of Carentan toward Périers. Four days of tough fighting and heavy losses bought less than 2 kilometers of ground.[24] The Germans met these attacks from well-integrated defensive positions, and with sharp counterattacks.

On 7 July, XIX Corps widened the attack to the east when its 30th Infantry Division assaulted across the Vire River and seized the high ground around St.-Jean-de-Daye. The next morning, Bradley sent the 3rd Armored Division across the river to exploit the crossing and break the German line. Unfortunately, the 3rd Armored Division and the 30th Infantry Division got snarled up in the tight bridgehead, while heavy rains turned the area into a quagmire. The offensive faltered, and the *Panzer Lehr Division* counterattacked to close the breach. The results in the hedgerows south of the Vire were again heavy losses and little terrain taken.[25]

Bradley attempted to broaden the offensive to the east of the Vire by launching part of V Corps toward St. Lô. After a costly battle, St. Lô finally was taken on 19 July. However, First Army failed to break through the German defenses. Eisenhower, in a letter to General George Marshall, assessed the reasons for this failure:

> The first of these, as always, is the fighting quality of the German soldier. The second is the nature of the country. Our whole attack has to fight its way out of very narrow bottlenecks flanked by marshes and against an enemy who has a double hedgerow and an intervening ditch almost every fifty yards as ready-made strong points. The third cause is the weather. Our air has been unable to operate at maximum efficiency and on top of this the rain and mud were so bad during my visit that I was reminded of Tunisian wintertime. Even with clear weather it is extraordinarily difficult to point out a target that is an appropriate one for either air or artillery.[26]

First Army lost 40,000 men killed and wounded in these attacks, of whom roughly three-quarters were infantrymen, in exchange for the rubble of St. Lô and limited gains.[27] Another method was needed to break through the German defenses.

Cobra

This attrition strategy weakened the German forces and prevented them from accumulating reserves for a counteroffensive. Enemy losses in Normandy exceeded 102,000 soldiers by 17 July, and their personnel system could only replace about 12 percent of those men. Due to the Allies' attacks across a wide front, German divisions arriving in Normandy were committed piecemeal. German artillery was unable to match the quantity or quality of Allied artillery, and the enemy lost more than 445 tanks, assault guns, and antitank guns by mid-July. While the Allies could replace lost material, the Germans could not. As one German officer concluded, "Although our troop morale is good, we cannot meet the enemy materiel with courage alone."[28]

The Allies considered several alternatives to break the stalemate. Amphibious assaults along the western coast and airborne landings behind the enemy lines were ruled out for a variety of reasons. First Army implemented tactical fixes, such as better tank–infantry–artillery teams, and technical solutions, such as tank-mounted plows to cut through the hedgerows, that helped move the assaults forward. Nonetheless, the GIs never achieved a breach that the Germans could not close.[29]

Then, on 11 July, General Bradley envisioned a tactical approach to break the stalemate—an attack that was to combine massive aerial bombing along a narrow front with a powerful thrust by armored and infantry divisions. Such an operation, it was hoped, would shatter the defenses so that the exploitation forces could pour through the gap in a torrent so powerful that German reserves could not stanch it.[30] Eisenhower approved Bradley's concept. At about the same time, General Montgomery decided to attempt a similar approach to smash through the German defenses east of Caen. Since there were not enough aircraft available to attempt the two attacks simultaneously, Eisenhower allowed Montgomery to launch his operation first.

Operation Goodwood commenced on 18 July, when 2,100 Allied aircraft dropped 8,000 tons of bombs on a 2-kilometer front near Caen. Three armored divisions then advanced 3 miles against the stunned defenders. By noon, however, the British tanks had outrun their artillery and infantry support just as they encountered another belt of German antitank guns. The defenses proved too strong as the Germans committed their remaining mobile reserves. The British lost 5,537 men and 500 tanks in exchange for 34 square miles of ground.

As Montgomery planned Goodwood, Bradley prepared Operation Cobra. The area selected for the breakthrough was west of St. Lô, between the villages of Montreuil and Hebecrevon. The box for the bombardment and penetration was 7 kilometers wide and 2.5 kilometers deep. The plan called for 2,896 bombers and fighter-bombers to drop 5,000 tons of bombs in the box in a short period of time. Two infantry divisions were to attack immediately following the aerial bombardment, thus catching the enemy off guard. Once the infantry divisions had penetrated the forward defenses, they were to turn to the flanks, allowing one motorized infantry and two armored divisions to charge through the gap. Once through the gap, most of the exploitation force was to wheel toward the Norman coast southwest of Coutances, isolating the Germans in front of VIII Corps.[31]

Bradley selected Major General Joe Collins and VII Corps to control the offensive. Bradley's plan called for the 9th and 30th Infantry Divisions to make the initial penetrations. The 1st Infantry, with the 2nd and 3rd Armored Divisions, was to exploit the breakthrough. Collins decided to have the exploitation force drive toward Coutances, instead of passing south of that city, and to have it stop short of Coutances to allow VIII Corps to advance.[32]

The 1st Infantry Division's Preparations for Cobra

The 1st Infantry Division turned over its sector to the 5th Infantry Division on 13 July and moved to an assembly area near Colombières.[33] By 15 July, the soldiers of the Big Red One had their first chance since early June to enjoy hot showers, warm food, and clean uniforms. For five days, they replaced worn-out equipment, slept in tents, and enjoyed band concerts. Huebner presented awards to soldiers, including thirty Silver Stars to members of the 7th Field Artillery Battalion.[34]

Colonel George Taylor was promoted to brigadier general and assigned to the 4th Division. Lieutenant Colonel Frederick Gibb was reassigned from his position as division G3 to command the 16th Infantry Regiment. Colonels George Smith and John Seitz remained in command of the 18th and 26th Infantry Regiments, respectively, and Brigadier General Clift Andrus continued as the Division Artillery commander. Major Elisha Peckham was promoted to lieutenant colonel and remained in command of the 3rd Battalion, 18th Infantry. The other veteran battalion commanders remained with their units, giving the division a battle-hardened leadership cadre.[35]

While in the Colombières area, Colonel Seitz and the staff of the 26th Infantry Regiment had the sad duty of attending the funeral of Brigadier General Teddy Roosevelt Jr., who had died of a heart attack on 12 July while serving as the assistant division commander of the 4th Infantry Division.[36] Major General Raymond Barton submitted a recommendation for the Medal of Honor for Roosevelt to First Army. Eisenhower and Bradley believed that the appropriate award was the Distinguished Service Cross, but they forwarded the original recommendation to Marshall. Marshall made sure that Roosevelt got the Medal of Honor.[37]

The rest period near Colombières was short-lived. On 19 July, the division moved to St. Jean-de-Daye, 5 kilometers north of the line of departure. By the next evening, the division's combat teams, including the 745th Tank, and the 634th and 635th TD Battalions, were in their final assembly areas.[38]

The VII Corps plan called for CCB, 3rd Armored Division, to join the 1st Infantry Division. Huebner attached its 1st Battalion, 33rd Armored Regiment, to CT18. Each of the infantry combat teams had a company of tanks from the 745th Tank Battalion and at least one company of antitank guns. First Army assigned truck companies to the division to enable it to carry all of its soldiers in motor vehicles. The mission of the 1st Infantry and the 2nd and 3rd Armored Divisions was to follow the assault divisions through the bombardment box to exploit the breakthrough (Map 18).[39]

Operation Cobra

Bradley planned for Operation Cobra to commence on 21 July. Miserably wet weather, however, forced a three-day delay. On 24 July, the sky seemed to be clearing enough for the bombers to see their targets, and the order was given to launch the aerial bombardment. But the return of bad weather forced another delay. Some of the bombers did not get word to abort their mission, and a number of bombs fell short. These bombs hit positions of the 30th Infantry Division, killing 25 men and wounding 131. Since Collins had withdrawn the three divisions along the line of departure 300 yards to prevent friendly bombs from hitting them, those divisions had to retake their former positions. This forced a costly battle as the 9th, 4th, and 30th Infantry Divisions fought to within 100 yards of the Périers–St. Lô Road by dusk. The air attack and ground action on 24 July alerted the Germans to the pending offensive, making it imperative for Bradley to begin the operation quickly.

On 25 July, 1,500 heavy bombers dropped 3,300 tons of bombs on the target, and 380 medium bombers followed with 650 tons. Finally, 550 fighter-bombers dropped 200 tons of bombs and napalm on the German positions. Unfortunately, some bombs fell short, killing 111 American soldiers and wounding 490. Among the dead was Lieutenant General Lesley McNair, commanding general of Army Ground Forces, who had come to observe the offensive. Bitter recriminations followed. Eisenhower swore he would never again use heavy bombers in a tactical support mission.[40] In spite of the disorganization caused in the assault divisions, Collins ordered the ground attack to begin.

The effects of the bombardment on the Germans were devastating. The bombing on 24 July disrupted the communications of *Panzer Lehr*. When a major ground attack did not follow, *Panzer Lehr*'s commander concluded that an offensive was not in the offing. The heavy pounding the next day took him by surprise and smashed his forward defenses. The bombs overturned tanks, buried machine guns and antitank guns, and stunned soldiers: "It was hell. . . . The planes kept coming like a conveyor belt, and the bomb carpets came down, now ahead, now on the right, now on the left. . . . The fields were burning and smoldering. The bomb carpets unrolled in great rectangles. . . . My front lines looked like a landscape on the moon and at least seventy percent of my personnel were out of action."[41]

At least a thousand Germans died in the aerial attack, and only a dozen tanks and assault guns remained operational to face the onslaught of seven American divisions.[42]

VII Corps' attack did not kick off as planned. Only one regiment in the 9th Infantry Division and one battalion in the 30th Infantry Division moved forward at H-hour. Many of the assault units were stunned by the bombing. High casualties disrupted two regiments, while all assault companies of the 4th Infantry Division were delayed as they evacuated casualties from the bombing. Only the swift action by the 9th Infantry Division to replace the shattered 3rd Battalion, 47th Infantry, with the 1st Battalion, 39th Infantry, enabled the drive to gather momentum. By noon, the 30th Infantry Division was moving into the breach.[43]

Enemy strongpoints slowed the advance south of the Périers Road. By mid-afternoon, the leading troops had moved only 2 kilometers, forcing Collins to make one of the most important decisions of his life. With all three assault divisions reporting slow progress, Collins had to decide whether or not to commit the exploitation forces.

Sensing that the enemy defenses were porous, Collins launched the exploitation forces. By 1735 hours, the 1st Infantry Division, with CCB, 3rd Armored, was moving south along the Marigny Road and the 2nd Armored Division had started down the St. Gilles Road. By midnight, the 30th Infantry Division had taken Hebecrevon and cleared most resistance from the road north of St. Gilles, opening the way for the 2nd Armored. On the west, the 9th Infantry Division pushed to within 3 kilometers of Marigny, clearing the road for the 1st Infantry Division. In the center, the 4th Infantry Division captured La Chapelle-en-Juger, 2 kilometers south of the Périers Road.[44]

Because the roads south were not open when Collins issued the order to move on 25 July, the 1st Infantry Division reorganized its columns to put infantry and armor in front in place of the attached 4th Mechanized Cavalry. CCB, 3rd Armored Division, led the advance down the Marigny Road in the early hours of 26 July, while CT18 moved south on the east side of the road. CT16 followed the 18th Infantry and CT26 remained in reserve. While the 1st Infantry Division moved out, the 9th, 4th, and 30th Infantry Divisions continued to eliminate scattered resistance, facilitating the advance of CT18 and the 1st Division Artillery. By mid-afternoon, *Panzer Lehr* had ceased to be combat-effective.[45]

The 1st Battalion, 18th Infantry, led the advance toward Marigny, its first objective near a road junction on the Coutances–St. Lô Road. At 1410 hours, the battalion reached La Chapelle-en-Juger, having bypassed small pockets of enemy. As the 1st Battalion neared Marigny, it encountered strong resistance.

A and B Companies were literally drenched all of the way with shell-fire; every other hedgerow contained a stubborn pocket of resistance that had to be liqui-

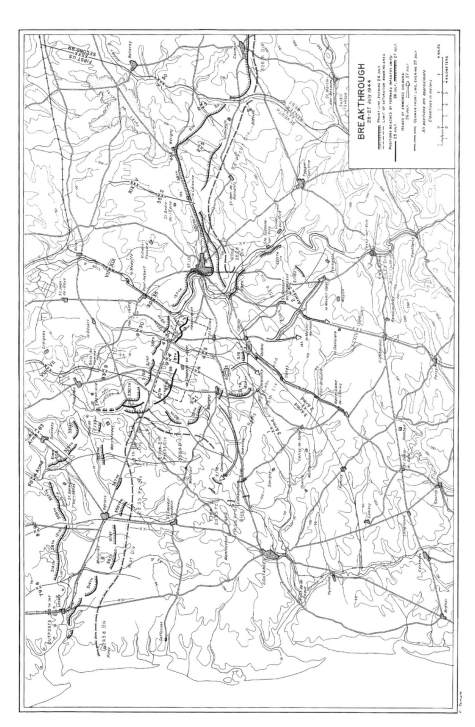

Map 18. The breakthrough, 25–27 July 1944. (Martin Blumenson, *Breakout and Pursuit* [U.S. Army Center of Military History, 1993])

dated before the advance could continue. B Company killed a dozen Germans [and] captured three dozen others. The battalion couldn't make use of the supporting tanks because of the terrain. In addition to the fact that it was naturally rugged, the ground had been completely torn up by the aerial bombardment of the previous day.[46]

The 3rd Battalion maneuvered west of town and then south to seize Hill 100, while the 1st Battalion tried to maneuver around the east side. The 3rd Battalion, however, could not bypass Marigny because of fire from the town, and a reconnaissance at this point showed that a deliberate tank-infantry attack was needed to eliminate the enemy. During the night of 26–27 July, however, the Germans pulled most of their troops out of Marigny, allowing CT18 to eliminate their rear guard in a bitter fight the next morning. When the 3rd Battalion attempted to push south to the Coutances Road, it met a hail of machine-gun, mortar, and artillery fire. The attack stalled and the battalion dug in for the rest of the day. The 18th Infantry's actions at Marigny made it possible for CCB, attached to 3rd Armored Division, and CT16 to swing west, even though the road junction south of town was not in American hands. Once CT18 had control of Marigny and Hill 100, Huebner ordered Smith to send his 2nd Battalion west to Comprond to reinforce CCB.[47]

Due to the resistance in Marigny, CCB maneuvered cross-country during the night to reach the road to Coutances. On 27 July, the combat command rolled west until it encountered elements of the *2nd SS Panzer* and the *17th SS Panzergrenadier Divisions* 4 kilometers from Coutances. Huebner also ordered CT16 to accompany CCB to the west to protect its flanks. The 16th Infantry, with two companies of the 745th Tank Battalion and two antitank companies attached, left its trucks north of Marigny on the morning of 27 July and moved southwest with its infantrymen mounted on tanks. The combat team met little resistance until it neared Marigny, where Company I was attacked by about 100 Germans and several tanks. A daylong battle developed as the Germans tried to push east and Lieutenant Colonel Charles Horner's men fought to open the way west. Shortly after dusk, Horner's tanks and infantry crushed the German force and continued west. Colonel Gibb moved his 1st and 2nd Battalions forward behind the 3rd Battalion. By midnight, CT16 was 5 kilometers west of Marigny and had caught up with CCB.[48]

While the armor and infantry advanced, on 26 July, the Division Artillery moved its guns forward. During the day, the artillery fired just eight missions, most against tanks. By late afternoon, the 32nd Field Artillery had occupied positions near La Chapelle-en-Juger, and the 7th had set up near Montreuil, where its howitzers could reach targets south and west of Marigny. The 7th Artillery fired one mission on 26 July while losing nine men wounded by enemy artillery fire. The 5th and 33rd Artillery Battalions reached positions among the bomb craters near La Chapelle-en-Juger during the early hours of 27 July.[49]

The 26th Infantry Combat Team was the last to move south. On 28 July, "shortly after it had moved through Marigny, the column ran into heavy road traffic and had to move at a snail's pace from there to its destination. The motorized column moved to within 300 yards of its final position, de-trucked, and pushed forward. The 3rd Battalion on the right, and the 1st Battalion on the left, met scattered resistance, losing one tank and capturing five prisoners."[50] The 3rd Battalion made contact with the 16th Infantry at about 1830 hours, while the 1st Battalion coordinated with the 3rd Armored Division to the southeast.[51]

By the evening of 27 July, it was clear that the German defenses had been shattered. Enemy attempts to close the breach failed, while VII Corps destroyed the last reserves of the German *Seventh Army* in the process. The German army commander, General Paul Hausser, had barely established a north-south defensive line east of Coutances to prevent the 1st Infantry Division from cutting off the Germans retreating to the south. The destruction of *Panzer Lehr* opened a gap that only wishful thinking could fill. As the enemy scrambled to establish a front, the 1st Infantry and the 2nd and 3rd Armored Divisions began a move south that doomed the enemy positions in western Normandy.[52]

Breakout: 28 July–31 July 1944

Collins began the breakout phase of Cobra on 27 July, when he ordered the 3rd Armored Division to drive through the center of the Cobra Gap toward Carantilly and Cerisy-la-Salle (see Map 18). CCA, 3rd Armored Division, including the 2nd Battalion, 26th Infantry, pushed through La Chapelle-en-Juger and reached Carantilly that evening. The next morning, the drive continued against decreasing resistance. On the evening of 28 July, CCA was abreast of CT26, between Savigny and Cerisy-la-Salle. The 2nd Armored Division also pushed south through the debris of the German *LXXXIV Corps*, and by the evening of 27 July its CCB reached Notre-Dame-de-Cenilly. The next day, 2nd Armored Division established blocking positions farther west to prevent the enemy from escaping along the roads from Coutances. Over the next two days, the armored division smashed numerous attempts by

German units to escape. By 30 July, 2nd Armored Division had killed an estimated 1,500 enemy soldiers and had captured 4,000, while losing fewer than 400 of its own men.[53]

While Huebner reoriented the 1st Infantry Division southward, on 29 July, Collins returned 3rd Armored Division's CCB to Major General Leroy Watson's command and ordered him to lead his division south to maintain momentum. After a day of reorganization and movement on the crowded roads behind the 2nd Armored Division, the 3rd Armored Division launched its attack on 30 July. On the division's east flank, CCB entered Hambye around noon, where it paused while engineers repaired a bridge. Infantrymen of CT26 made this possible by fording the stream and driving German machine gunners from the far bank. There, the 3rd Battalion, 26th Infantry, established a bridgehead and repulsed a counterattack.[54]

Late that afternoon, CCB resumed its drive to Villedieu-les-Poêles, but increasing resistance caused it to halt at dusk. CCA made less progress along narrow and unpaved secondary roads. When it reached Gavray it found that the Germans had destroyed the bridges across the Sienne River, forcing CCA to halt. It took several hours to organize artillery and infantry for an attack across the river. When the advance commenced in mid-afternoon, the infantrymen moved so cautiously that an armored battalion commander, Lieutenant Colonel Leander Doan, dismounted from his tank to lead the assault. Only scattered fire met the infantrymen of CCA, and the crossing was secured. Most of a day had been lost as the 3rd Armored Division settled down for the night.[55]

Collins was so disgusted with 3rd Armored Division's lack of initiative that he decided to move the 1st Infantry Division into the lead. He attached 3rd Armored's CCA to Huebner's command and CCB to the 4th Infantry Division. CT26 rejoined the 1st Infantry Division, and Collins told Huebner that "you can go as fast as you like." The 1st Infantry Division assumed the axis of advance of CCA for its drive south to Brecey.[56]

Reacting quickly, Huebner shifted CT18 to Gavray to follow the armored force moving toward Brecey. By the afternoon of 31 July, the division was rolling, and the rear command post notified the forward command post that "we are feeding a continuous column" of units south.[57] The western column reached L'Épine that evening, where it slammed into a column of retreating Germans. American tankers destroyed a number of enemy vehicles and scattered the rest. CCA then dug in astride the Villedieu-Avranches highway at L'Épine for the night. As it did so, CT18 continued to move south toward L'Épine.[58]

Task Force Doan, composed of tanks and infantrymen, commanded by

Lieutenant Colonel Doan, led the advance along the division's eastern axis, followed by CT26. Doan bypassed Villedieu and continued south toward Brecey. Using air support to clear suspected ambush sites, Doan's column reached Brecey before dark. There, Doan's men surprised a group of Germans, which they quickly rounded up. Since the bridge over the Sée River south of town was damaged, Doan had his infantry prepare a hasty ford by placing rocks in the river bottom. Infantrymen crossed the stream, followed by tanks and half-tracks. This audacious move allowed the task force to push another 3 miles before halting for the night.[59]

While the Big Red One's task forces were crossing the Villedieu-Avranches Road (29–31 July), the 4th and 6th Armored Divisions drove through scattered German units and captured bridges over the Sée and Sélune Rivers, near Avranches. These divisions became part of Lieutenant General Patton's Third Army on 31 July. With the capture of these crossings and Avranches, the German defenses were unhinged from the Normandy coast. The Allied armies now had an opportunity to drive around the Germans' southern flank and head east to the Seine.[60]

As the enemy defenses disintegrated, the 1st Infantry Division suffered few casualties. The 1st Medical Battalion treated 231 wounded on 27 and 28 July, but only 16 during the next three days. On 1 August, the battalion treated 239 wounded; it treated 212 from 2 to 7 August. During the remainder of August the unit admitted 7 wounded men per day.[61]

Pursuit: August 1944

On 31 July, Huebner ordered his combat teams to catch up with the retreating enemy. CT26 followed Doan's task force to secure Hill 242, south of Brecey. CT18 continued moving behind the 26th Infantry as the division's frontage narrowed. Due to congested roads, the 26th Infantry was not able to reach Brecey until the morning of 1 August, where the combat team captured 250 Germans. The division sent the following report to VII Corps on the night of 31 July: "We have been fighting all afternoon between our objective and the railroad down to [coordinates] T-355267; infantry and antitank guns and scattered resistance forced them [the leading task force] to deploy. The column stretches on the road miles behind and blocks the infantry column following."[62]

On 2 August, the division continued toward Juvigny. Task forces of tanks and infantry led the combat teams on the roads with close air support above. The enemy deployed mines and occasional roadblocks to slow the division, forcing the tank- and truck-mounted infantrymen to dismount frequently to eliminate resistance. As infantrymen cleared the routes, armored task forces bypassed roadblocks. In this fashion, the division moved from Les Cresnays to Mortain, which the 18th Infantry occupied on 3 August. For the next four days, the 18th Infantry remained in Mortain while the remainder of the division occupied positions near Juvigny. On 4 August, the 18th Infantry repulsed a German attack east of Mortain, inflicting heavy losses on the enemy.[63]

On 5 August, Huebner received word that the 9th and 30th Infantry Divisions would relieve the 1st Infantry Division in the Mortain area on the night of 6–7 August, allowing the division to advance toward the Mayenne River.

CT26 set out on the afternoon of 6 August, accompanied by an armored task force. By midnight, the infantry battalions were deployed along the Mayenne River, from Mayenne 15 kilometers south to Montigeroux. CT16 occupied Mayenne. Smith's 18th Infantry moved to Ambriéres, where it established positions to protect the division's left flank. The division remained in the Mayenne area for the next seven days. As the 18th Infantry after-action report noted, "Within this period readjustments were made within the regiment and maintenance of motors, weapons and equipment took place in preparation for a further drive into France."[64]

On 13 August, the division swung to the northeast to seize La Ferté-Macé. CT26 attacked on the right of the road from Mayenne to La Ferté-Macé, while CT18 led on the left. Gibb's CT16 followed. Although the leading task forces encountered some resistance, the advance was steady. The 32nd Artillery Battalion shifted its guns three times during the day but fired no missions. By evening, the division had covered half of the 50 kilometers from Mayenne to La Ferté-Macé. On 14 August, the advance resumed, and by the end of the day the leading task forces were just south of La Ferté-Macé.[65]

On 15 August, the 18th Infantry occupied La Sauvagère, 6 kilometers northwest of La Ferté-Macé, and the 26th Infantry seized La Ferté-Macé. The 16th Infantry dug in west of La Sauvagère to block enemy escape routes.[66] The next morning the division consolidated positions on the flank of a huge pocket of Germans in central Normandy. As the enemy retreated, the division found itself no longer in the front lines. For eight days, the Big Red One remained in place as a battle raged between Falaise and Argentan, where the Allies attempted to encircle the Germans. La Ferté-Macé became a rest center for the troops, with movie facilities and Red Cross canteens. This respite came to an end on 24 August when the division shuttled its units 170 miles east to join VII Corps near Corbeil, on the Seine River.[67]

On 27 August, the 1st Infantry Division crossed the Seine on pontoon bridges. On 28 August, the 26th Infantry advanced to Meaux, where it captured an intact bridge over the Marne River. After the division crossed the Marne, on 28–29 August, it turned northeast toward Soissons. By that evening, the 33rd Field Artillery Battalion was in positions near the American World War I monument at Château-Thierry, and the lead elements of CT26 were in Villers-Cotterets.[68] During its advance, the division met little resistance and casualties were light.[69]

The Drive to the Siegfried Line: September 1944

During August, the Allied armies destroyed the coherence of the German forces in Normandy so thoroughly that it was impossible for the enemy to establish another defensive line in France. Although the Allies missed an opportunity to cut off at least twenty enemy divisions in the Falaise Pocket, German losses, from 6 June to mid-September, totaled 500,000 men, including 200,000 men isolated in coastal fortresses. The British and American armies captured roughly 50,000 Germans in Normandy during August.[70] Nothing stood between Germany and the Allied forces except thousands of destroyed bridges.

During the advance there often were insufficient truck units available to carry the infantry forward. Consequently, infantrymen frequently moved on foot, covering as many as 25 miles per day. The weather remained warm with infrequent rain, allowing the Allied air forces to provide air support to the spearheads. But it also forced the marching infantrymen to eat the dust of passing vehicles. Troop morale remained high in spite of the dust, heat, and long foot marches as it became clear to the men that there was a chance the war in Europe might be over by Christmas.[71]

After clearing out pockets of Germans around Soissons, the 1st Infantry Division resumed its advance, with CT18 reaching Laon on 31 August. The 3rd Armored Division captured a bridge over the Aisne River at Soissons, and the 103rd Antiaircraft Artillery Battalion was detached from the 1st Infantry Division to protect it. On 1 September, CT26 moved 85 miles northeast from Soissons to Vervins, France, and then the next day another 27 miles to Avesnes, Belgium, where it caught up with the enemy.[72] To the west of VII Corps and the 1st Infantry Division, as many as 50,000 Germans were retreating toward Mons, hoping to get to Germany. On 2 September, the 3rd Armored Division drove a long finger into Belgium, with its tip east of Mons, cutting the enemy escape route. CT18 followed the armored thrust, reaching Bavay, Belgium, just north of the French-Belgian border, on 3 September. The same day, CT16 entered Guise, to the west of Vervins and southwest of Mons.[73]

As the soldiers of the division entered Belgium, the Belgian people welcomed them enthusiastically, although sometimes too quickly. The after-action report of the 26th Infantry describes such a scene on 2 September:

> The town of Avesnes gave an unprecedentedly warm welcome to the troops of the combat team. At one crossroads leading out of town, a group of civilians out to welcome one of the tanks attached to the team was taken under fire by an enemy SP 88, and nine civilians [were] killed. The Civil Affairs Officer moved into town, and finding that both the mayor and Sub-Prefect had left town since they had collaborated with the enemy occupying forces, an election was held and a new mayor elected by the town council. The new administration began clearing out the debris littering the highways and streets, and posted new proclamations.[74]

On 2 September, Huebner learned that thousands of Germans were fleeing from the area between Mons and the Belgian border. In response, Huebner ordered CT18 to clear the enemy out of the Bois de la Lanière, along the highway from Bavay to Charleroi. At the same time, the 2nd Battalion, 16th Infantry, moved into the woods to cut the road, while the 1st Battalion, 26th Infantry, reinforced roadblocks on the southwestern side of Mons.

Early on 3 September, the 1st Battalion, 26th Infantry, reached the intersection of the Bavay-Binche Road with the Maubeuge-Mons Road and encountered thousands of Germans. A free-for-all firefight developed. For the remainder of the day, the 1st Battalion defended the road junction and captured many Germans. During the same period, the 2nd Battalion, 16th Infantry, reached the crossroads on the Bavay-Binche Road in the Bois de la Lanière, where it encountered thousands more. For the next two days, firefights broke out between the disorganized Germans and American blocking positions. In nearly every case, the Big Red One's soldiers overwhelmed the enemy, forcing thousands to surrender in what became known as the Mons Pocket.[75]

The 18th Infantry also engaged Germans in and around Bavay on 3 and 4 September. In two days of heavy fighting, the 1st and 3rd Battalions killed hundreds of Germans and captured 1,100 prisoners. The regimental history describes the chaotic scenes:

> In Bavay a German antiaircraft unit was entrenched with orders to hold the town at all costs. Our advance guard deployed and attacked swiftly, with heavy fighting ensuing throughout the day. The 1st Battalion sustained a number of casualties, including four officers. The enemy, however, suffered very heavily, over 150 were killed and wounded and 400 men taken prisoner. Late in the day

an enemy column sought to enter the town from the woods to the southwest. Again the Germans were dealt a swift and deadly blow, this time to the tune of losing seven killed, fifty prisoners, and six trucks and wagons destroyed.[76]

The 3rd Battalion, 26th Infantry, captured another 1,100, while the 2nd Battalion, 16th Infantry, bagged still more. American casualties were light. For example, Company E, 2nd Battalion, 16th Infantry, lost two men while capturing 1,500 Germans. The 3rd Armored Division also contributed around Mons, bringing total German losses to over 25,000 prisoners.[77] On 4 September, the 1st Infantry Division mopped up around Mons while the 3rd Armored Division drove toward Dinant, on the Meuse River, where unexpectedly strong resistance had halted the 9th Infantry Division.[78]

On 6 September, Huebner ordered Combat Teams 18 and 26 to advance toward the German border. CT26, moving on the division's left flank, reached Eghezée, Belgium, by early afternoon, 7 September. The 18th Regimental Combat Team kept pace on the right, traveling "through a massive wreckage of German vehicles, wagons, and guns of all caliber that had been caught on the road by our air force. The advance was unopposed and the Regiment received a rousing reception from thousands of civilians who lined the streets of Charleroi, where it bivouacked for the night."[79]

The Gamble at the Westwall: September 1944

As Eisenhower's armies approached the German frontier, fifty-four full-strength Allied divisions faced sixty-three badly understrength enemy divisions. Allied tank superiority was approximately twenty-to-one, and the British and American air forces completely outnumbered the Luftwaffe.[80] American intelligence estimates were rosy, predicting that the Germans would be unable to make a stand until they had retreated behind the Rhine River. At the worst, Allied intelligence officers thought that the enemy would only be able to fight a delaying action in the fortifications known by the Allies as the Siegfried Line and by the Germans as the *Westwall*.[81]

During the pursuit, the Allied armies moved much faster than planned. In less than a hundred days after D-day, the First Army had reached the German frontier, a place that planners had anticipated reaching 230 days later. Consequently, Allied logisticians had insufficient time to establish the supply depots, pipelines, and railways needed to sustain Eisenhower's armies. By early September, the iron hand of logistics had intervened. All available trucks were diverted to hauling supplies forward from depots over 200 miles to the rear. The troops did without fresh food and clean clothes, however, and there was still a shortage of fuel and ammunition. By the time the First

Army reached the German frontier, it had less than five-days' supply of artillery ammunition, and only a third of the tanks of the armored divisions were operational.[82]

Nonetheless, Eisenhower, Montgomery, and Bradley agreed that the best course of action was to continue the pursuit, hoping to prevent the Germans from manning their frontier defenses before the Allied troops swept through. As part of First Army's main effort, the Big Red One continued east with VII Corps.

The 1st Infantry Division Hits the Westwall

After its victory in the Mons Pocket, the 1st Infantry Division crossed the Meuse north of Liège and approached the German frontier between Henri Chapelle, Belgium, and Aachen, Germany. On 11 September, CT18 and CT16 encountered sporadic enemy artillery fire and roadblocks. As the division approached the frontier, resistance increased, causing Huebner to order the combat teams to stop and prepare a more concentrated approach for the next morning (Map 19).

The time to gamble had come. The VII Corps commander, Joe Collins, requested permission from Lieutenant General Courtney Hodges to launch his three divisions against the Siegfried Line, hoping to find enemy positions empty or their defenders so demoralized that his columns could break through quickly. Hodges approved Collins's request. Collins ordered the 1st Infantry Division to carry out a "reconnaissance in force to the Siegfried Line, [and] develop the enemy situation, prepared to exploit any weak points in the line."[83] The 3rd Armored Division was to advance on Huebner's right to penetrate the Siegfried Line as well. The 47th Regimental Combat Team of the 9th Infantry Division was to advance on the right of the armored division to protect that flank from German counterattacks.

VII Corps was going to attempt to rupture the *Westwall* between Aachen and the large forest 10 kilometers to the east. The German defenses in this area had two distinct parts: a forward line of dragon's teeth and pillboxes along the German border, and a second set of fortifications 7 kilometers inside Germany. The city of Aachen was a major obstacle as well, and Collins intended to bypass it. If VII Corps could drive through the corridor east of Aachen and breach the defenses between Verlautenheide and Mausbach, it would have relatively open terrain to the Rhine River (Map 19).

The VII Corps reconnaissance commenced the morning of 12 September. In the 1st Infantry Division's zone, the 1st Battalion, 16th Infantry, led on the right, from Herve, Belgium, striking bunkers in the Aachen municipal forest. On its left, the 3rd Battalion, 18th Infantry, moved into the forest

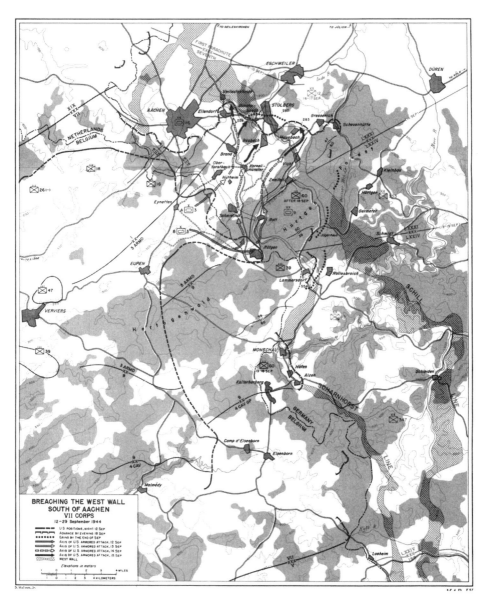

Map 19. Breaching the *Westwall* south of Aachen, VII Corps, 12–29
September 1944. This map includes Gressenich in the Hürtgen Forest.
(Charles B. McDonald, *The Siegfried Line Campaign* [Chief of Military
History, Department of the Army, 1963])

from Aubel, Belgium. Both battalions ran into strong resistance. By noon, the regimental commanders had to reinforce their lead battalions. For the remainder of the day, the 18th Infantry fought a nasty battle that barely pushed the enemy back to its bunker line. On the right, "the 16th Combat Team moved rapidly, and by nightfall, the 1st Battalion of the 16th Combat Team had entered the Scharnhorst Line, capturing many pillboxes, either inadequately manned or in some cases unmanned. The 3rd Battalion, 16th Combat Team attacked to the right of the 1st Battalion and at nightfall had been unable to make any noticeable penetration in the line proper."[84] The Germans reacted to 1st Battalion's success with a counterattack, which, although beaten back, indicated that Aachen could not be seized by a coup de main.

At the same time, the 3rd Armored Division sent two combat commands into the approaches of the Stolberg Corridor, the relatively open area between the hills east of Aachen and the Hürtgen Forest, about 10 kilometers from the city. On CCB's right, Task Force Lovelady (under Lieutenant Colonel William Lovelady), advanced through Roetgen before encountering dragon's teeth, mines, and a crater along the road to Rott. Uncertain as to what lay ahead, it laagered and prepared for a deliberate attack the next morning. Task Force Smith, the left prong of CCB, was stopped short of Schmidthof, in front of the *Westwall*. CCA, on the left flank of 3rd Armored Division, encountered enemy antitank guns 1,000 yards short of the Siegfried Line, northeast of Eynatten. After losing three tanks, CCA stopped for the night. Because of the German reaction, Collins ordered the 1st Infantry Division to establish positions around the south and east of Aachen to protect the flank of the 3rd Armored Division and to begin the encirclement of the city. Collins directed the 3rd Armored Division to attack in the Stolberg Corridor through the two tiers of German defenses and seize Eschweiler, north of Stolberg. The 47th Infantry was to protect the 3rd Armored's right flank by securing Zweifall and Vicht, on the edge of the Hürtgen Forest.[85] In preparation for this attack, 1st Battalion, 26th Infantry, was shifted to CCA, where it assembled in a forest east of Eynatten for its part in the assault against the defenses south of Oberforstbach.[86] These deployments initiated VII Corps' deliberate attack to break through the Siegfried Line.

Soldiers of Company M, the heavy weapons company of the 3rd Battalion, 18th Infantry, take cover in the dragon's teeth of the Siegfried Line to avoid the mortar fire near Stolberg, Germany, 22 September 1944. (US Army Photo SC194637, McCormick Research Center Collections)

A machine-gun crew of the 26th Infantry uses a pile of wreckage for cover while firing on an enemy position in Aachen, Germany, 15 October 1944. (US Army Photo SC195461, McCormick Research Center Collections)

The 3rd Battalion, 18th Infantry, advances on a road in the Stats Forest outside of Langerwehe in the Hürtgen Forest campaign, Germany, 5 December 1944. (US Army Photo SC248227, McCormick Research Center Collections)

A US tank destroyer, left, and a German Mark IV tank (with spaced armor around the turret) at Dom Bütgenbach, December 1944. (US Army Photo SC198278, McCormick Research Center Collections)

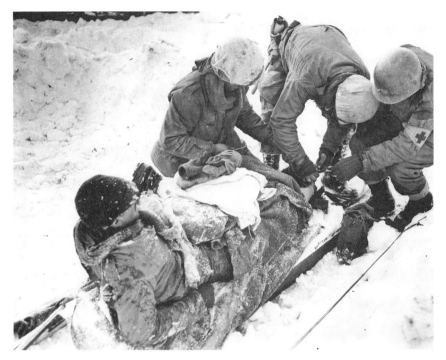

A soldier of the 26th Infantry with leg wounds from a mine is given medical attention on a sled, Büllingen, Belgium, 29 January 1945. Many soldiers also suffered from frostbite due to the freezing cold and deep snow. (US Army Photo SC199652, McCormick Research Center Collections)

This snapshot, labeled "Negro 4th Platoon," of Company K, 26th Infantry, was taken by Henry M. Pokorski near Ukerath, Germany, 25 March 1945. African American rifle platoons joined the 1st Division in the Rhineland campaign. (Donation of Henry M. Pokorski, McCormick Research Center Collections)

Sergeant Ron Myers leads the way into Riefensback, in the Harz Mountains campaign, Germany, 14 April 1945. (US Army Photo SC206362, McCormick Research Center Collections)

Soldiers of the 26th Infantry board boxcars at Kelheim, Germany, 1946. These World War II veterans boarded a Victory ship at the port of Le Havre, France, to return home to Camp Kilmer, New Jersey. (Private First Class Dwight Lund album, McCormick Research Center Collections)

Private First Class Pichierre, 18th Infantry, guards the door to Rudolf Hess's cell at the Nuremberg city jail to prevent a suicide attempt, 24 November 1945. (US Army Photo SC220076, McCormick Research Center Collections)

Sergeant Thomas Tacco issues orders to a squad of the 16th Infantry. The 1st Infantry Division was completely integrated by the fall of 1950. (US Army Photo, McCormick Research Center Collections)

Company C, 1st Battle Group, 16th Infantry, with the 16th Infantry Band and villagers, parades to the hamlet of Otzweiler for an Easter egg hunt in 1960. (US Army Photo, 1958–1963, McCormick Research Center Collections)

1st Battalion, 18th Infantry, 2nd Brigade, landing with the 1st Infantry Division colors in Vietnam, 12 July 1965. (US Army Photo, McCormick Research Center Collections)

A soldier of the 2nd Battalion, 16th Infantry, motions a Vietnamese woman to keep her children's heads down during a firefight with the Vietcong, 16 January 1966. (US Army Photo SC626305, McCormick Research Center Collections)

Second Lieutenant Robert J. Hibbs, Company B, 2nd Battalion, 28th Infantry, holding a Vietcong flag. Lieutenant Hibbs was posthumously awarded the Medal of Honor for action on 6 March 1966. (Donation of William Hibbs, McCormick Research Center Collections)

Major General William E. DePuy with Sergeant Vaughn Lewis, squad leader, 1st Platoon, Company B, 2nd Battalion, 28th Infantry, at a war game, the commanding general's new tactic, on 26 January 1967. (US Army Photo, McCormick Research Center Collections)

The 1st Battalion, 26th Infantry, in an airmobile assault from "Huey" helicopters at a landing zone in classically Vietnamese terrain consisting of coarse wild grass and sparse jungle like that at Ap Gu. This photo of the Blue Spaders was taken in 1969. (US Army Photo, McCormick Research Center Collections)

Soldiers of Company C, 2nd Battalion, 28th Infantry, on a tank of the 2nd Battalion, 34th Armor, rout a Vietcong base camp south of Phu Loi on 5 April 1967. (US Army Photo, McCormick Research Center Collections)

Engineers with bulldozers and infantry in armored personnel carriers cooperated in Operation Paul Bunyan, summer 1967. (US Army Photo, McCormick Research Center Collections)

The aero rifle platoon of the 1st Squadron, 4th Cavalry, 1968. From the collection of Cliff Richeson, the platoon radio telephone operator, who is seen to the lower right. Lieutenant Sam Copela was the platoon leader. (Donation of Cliff Richeson, McCormick Research Center Collections)

Company A, 2nd Battalion (M), 2nd Infantry, patrolling along the Song Be River, northeast of Lai Khe, on 18 August 1968. Each platoon had four M113 armored personnel carriers, or "tracks." (US Army Photo, McCormick Research Center Collections)

Self-propelled guns of the 8th Battalion, 6th Artillery, such as these, were with Lieutenant Colonel Charles C. Rogers's 1st Battalion, 5th Artillery, at Fire Support Base Rita on "Fright Night," 31 October–1 November 1968. (US Army Photo, McCormick Research Center Collections)

The colors of 1st Infantry Division arrived from Vietnam at Forbes Air Force Base, Topeka, Kansas, on 8 April 1970, on their way to the division's home post at Fort Riley, Kansas. (US Army Photo, McCormick Research Center Collections)

Abrams tanks with mine plows cleared the way for the 1st Infantry Division (M), 24 February 1991. Armored combat engineer earthmovers had torn gaps in the berm. This snapshot was taken by Major Steven Goligowski, S-3, Division Support Command, on 26 February 1991. (Donation of Major Steven Goligowski, McCormick Research Center Collections)

"Welcome to Iraq, courtesy the Big Red One," 26 February 1991. This snapshot was taken by Allen C. Smith of the 16th Infantry. (Donation of Allen C. Smith, McCormick Research Center Collections)

I I

The Battles of the German Frontier

VII CORPS' ATTEMPT TO CRASH THROUGH THE *Westwall* before the enemy could man the fortifications failed, necessitating a deliberate attack to penetrate the German defenses. Corps commander Joe Collins hoped that the penetration of the Siegfried Line east of Aachen would cause the Germans to evacuate the city, sparing the corps from a house-to-house fight. Therefore, he ordered the 1st Infantry Division to seize the hills south and east of Aachen to protect 3rd Armored Division's flank as it attacked east through the Stolberg Corridor. His decisions set in motion a series of battles around and for Aachen.

The Breaching of the Siegfried Line: 13–19 September 1944

CT16 and CT18 renewed their attacks south of Aachen on 13 September.[1] The 18th Infantry fought its way steadily through the bunker line in the Aachen Forest. The 3rd Battalion ended the day facing Aachen from the southwest, with its left-hand units at the junction of the borders of Belgium, Holland, and Germany (see Map 19). To the regiment's right, the 1st Battalion broke through the pillbox line and seized Brandenberg Hill, 3 kilometers south of Aachen. From there, the 18th Infantry could observe enemy activity in the city and protect the left flank of the division. For the remainder of the month, CT18 held these positions and maintained contact with XIX Corps to the west.[2]

Meanwhile, the 16th Infantry pushed north through the Scharnhorst Line defenses and toward the hills east of Aachen to protect the left flank of VII Corps' main attack. The 3rd Battalion, 26th Infantry, supported CT16's mission by replacing the 3rd Battalion, 16th Infantry, in the fight to control the southern part of the Aachen Forest, allowing Gibb to move Lieutenant Colonel Charles Horner's battalion north to join the rest of CT16 in a drive toward Brand.[3]

The 26th Infantry, minus its 1st Battalion, assumed CT16's task in the Aachen Forest, using bangalore torpedoes, bazookas, and tank guns to subdue the bunkers. For the remainder of September, the 26th Infantry consolidated its positions and probed the defenses on the southern edge of Aachen.[4]

The 3rd Armored Division attacked toward Stolberg on 13 September. Task Force Lovelady blasted a hole through the *Westwall* north of Roetgen and pushed on to Rott, where it ran into a Germa Münsterbusch n Panther tank and several antitank guns. Losing four tanks and a half-track before destroying the German tank and guns, Lieutenant Colonel William Lovelady decided to stop for the night just north of Rott. The other task force of CCB stalled in front of Schmidthof.

CCA, on the left, had better luck after a rough start. Task Force Doan pushed its infantry across the dragon's teeth (concrete antitank barriers) and into the bunker line south of Oberforstbach before machine-gun fire pinned down the infantrymen. Tanks could not follow since German fire prevented the 23rd Engineers from blowing gaps in the obstacles. Just as things were getting desperate for Doan's men, someone found a path through the dragon's teeth a few hundred yards to the south. German farmers had created this road by filling in the teeth with dirt so that they could move their equipment to their fields beyond. After checking for mines, tanks pushed through the gap and moved to support Doan's infantry. CCA exploited this situation by sending the 1st Battalion, 26th Infantry, and two platoons of tanks to reinforce Task Force Doan in a drive to Nütheim, a village that dominated the area on the German side of the Scharnhorst Line (see Map 19).[5]

Major Francis Adams led the 1st Battalion, 26th Infantry, from the Eynatten Woods into the dragon's teeth in a column of companies, intending to advance 1,500 meters to the northeast and attack Nütheim from the flank while Task Force Doan attacked from the southwest. When Company A reached the teeth near twilight it was plastered by mortar and machine-gun fire. In spite of losing three platoon leaders, the company moved through the defenses and headed toward a burning barn west of Nütheim. Using the burning barn as a beacon, Companies B and C followed Company A through the obstacles and moved north. By dark, Company A had reached a road near Kroitzheide. After cutting German telephone lines along the road, the company retraced its steps to the ridge a kilometer north of Nütheim where it rejoined Major Adams and the remainder of the battalion.

As Adams assembled his battalion west of Nütheim, Doan's tanks fought their way through the remaining bunkers of the Scharnhorst Line and joined the 1st Battalion, 26th Infantry, at about 2200. Once together, Doan and Adams decided to wait until morning to make a coordinated tank-infantry assault against Nütheim. The next morning, Company B, 26th Infantry, supported by tanks, cleared Nütheim, while Company C captured pillboxes southwest of the village. In these actions, the infantrymen poured rifle fire into the bunker's openings until a tank could get close enough to fire a cannon round through the embrasure. This tactic worked well. The 26th

Infantry also used self-propelled 155mm guns to fire a concrete-penetrating round into pillboxes. Although the rounds did not penetrate the bunker wall, they often caused concussions, which could force the defenders to surrender. By the end of 14 September, CCA and the 1st Battalion, 26th Infantry, had ruptured the Scharnhorst Line, allowing engineers to open more lanes through the fortifications.[6]

On 14 September, CCA advanced through Brand to the southern edge of Eilendorf, where it encountered the Schill Line. With its left flank protected by the 16th Infantry, the armored task force destroyed enemy assault and antitank guns it encountered along the way. CCB also made steady progress, as its left-hand task force moved from Schmidthof to Kornelimünster, and Task Force Lovelady pushed on from Rott, crossed the Vicht River, and reached the Vicht again south of Mausbach by nightfall (Map 19). There, Lovelady's infantrymen from the 36th Armored Infantry Regiment waded the river and captured a group of 88mm guns. German resistance was ineffective, largely because the *LXXXI Corps* was forced to commit its reinforcements piecemeal against the three spearheads of American armor and infantry.[7]

The next morning, CCA brought up more units to the Schill Line and waited for the 16th Infantry to consolidate positions around Eilendorf and then aid in an attack against German fortifications in Münsterbusch. By noon, CT16 had cleared Eilendorf and its 2nd Battalion was pushing toward Münsterbusch.[8] CCB continued its drive as Lovelady's men overran Mausbach, and Task Force Mills reached Büsbach, in the division's center. Task Force Lovelady thus had succeeded in breaching the Schill Line at Mausbach. All that the 3rd Armored Division needed to do was to capture Büsbach, Stolberg, and two hills east of Stolberg for a gap to be opened wide enough for VII Corps to drive toward the Rhine.[9]

The Germans, however, were determined to drive VII Corps out of the Schill Line and retain Aachen. In what has been called the "German miracle in the west," Germany was able to find the manpower and the matériel to refit a number of divisions decimated at the fronts during the past four months. On 16 September, the leading regiment of the *12th Infantry Division*, which had been reconstituted in central Germany, began to arrive by rail in Düren, 20 kilometers east of Stolberg. This division was full-strength, with three infantry regiments, four battalions of artillery, and 14,800 men. In order to stop the 3rd Armored Division, the German corps commander ordered the regiments to move immediately upon arrival into the lines between Aachen and the Hürtgen Forest. On 16 September, the *27th Fusilier Regiment* detrained and moved to Verlautenheide, from where it was to attack Eilendorf the next day. On 17 September, the other two regiments of the *12th Infantry Division* arrived and moved west to halt CCB near Mausbach.[10]

On 16 September, Collins ordered the 3rd Armored Division to widen the breach in the Schill Line. CCA, reinforced by the 1st Battalion, 26th Infantry, attacked enemy positions in Büsbach to close a gap between it and CCB to the east. Using a self-propelled 155mm howitzer, Company B, 26th Infantry, fought its way through Büsbach to the edge of Münsterbusch while Company A fought its way around the east side of Büsbach, capturing three large pillboxes in Brockenberg. As the infantrymen fought house-to-house, German artillery and small-arms fire intensified. Many men, like Major Armand Levasseur, the S3 of the 1st Battalion, 26th Infantry, "realized that the picnic, wine, and flowers campaign of France and Belgium was at an end. Now at last, the German was fighting on native soil, so resistance was expected to stiffen."[11]

As the Blue Spaders cleared Büsbach, CT16 joined CCA's attack against the hill between Eilendorf and Münsterbusch known as the Geisberg. After fierce fighting and the loss of at least six tanks, the 16th Infantry consolidated positions on the hill as elements of the 3rd Armored pushed a mile past the line of bunkers. From there, the tankers encountered stiff resistance and stopped well short of Stolberg. Even though CCA's drive had stalled, the seizure of the Geisberg strengthened the 1st Infantry Division's positions around Aachen and broke the contact between the *116th Panzer* and *9th Panzer Divisions*.[12]

The Germans counterattacked on 17 September. German infantry charged across open ground with bayonets fixed and were met by heavy fire from the 16th Infantry and the 32nd Field Artillery Battalion. After receiving over thirty fire missions and 708 rounds from the 32nd Artillery, few Germans made it to the foxholes of the 16th Infantry, and those who did were cut down by machine-gun and rifle fire. The *27th Fusiliers* tried once more in the afternoon to drive the 1st and 2nd Battalions out of their positions around Eilendorf, with similar results. By the end of the day, the *Fusiliers* had sustained hundreds of casualties, while the hardest-hit battalion of the 16th Infantry had lost two men killed and twenty-one wounded. The enemy attempted several more times during the month to dislodge CT16, with no success.[13]

At midday, 17 September, CCB attempted to capture the dominant ground north of Mausbach known as the Weisenberg. They ran head on into the *89th Infantry Regiment* and a battalion of the *48th Grenadier Regiment*. The Germans drove back CCB a kilometer toward Mausbach, forcing the 3rd Armored Division to reinforce CCB with the 1st Battalion, 26th Infantry. Over the next four days, CCB and the *12th Division* fought for possession of the Weisenberg. In the end, the 1st Battalion, 26th Infantry, captured the hill with an infantry assault at dawn, on 20 September. In the process, the 1st Battalion's strength fell to about 40 percent, and the tank battalions of the 3rd Armored Division were reduced to fewer than twenty tanks each. The Germans had succeeded in plugging the hole in the Schill Line. Stout enemy resistance and Allied shortages of supplies and replacements ended the VII Corps offensive in the Stolberg Corridor.[14]

The Battle for Aachen: Closing the Ring, 1–10 October 1944

With the drive in the Stolberg Corridor stopped, First Army was forced to capture Aachen the old-fashioned way, house by house. The first step toward the seizure of the city was to have the XIX and VII Corps encircle it (Map 20).

The Big Red One had already gone a long way toward doing that by driving the Germans out of the fortifications to the southwest, south, southeast, and east of Aachen. To complete the encirclement, the division needed to capture Verlautenheide and two hills northeast of Aachen known as Crucifix Hill and the Ravelsberg. XIX Corps' 30th Infantry Division was to penetrate the Siegfried Line 15 kilometers north of Aachen and drive southeast to close the ring around the city at Würselen. Once the ring was closed, CT26 was to seize Aachen from the German *246th Infantry Division*. The encirclement and capture of Aachen was First Army's priority mission. It was scheduled to begin on 1 October, when the 30th Infantry Division was to cross the Wurm River and assault the German pillboxes near Rimburg, Germany. The 1st Infantry Division was to begin its attacks on 8 October.[15]

Huebner faced this difficult mission with too many places to defend and too few combat units. In order to free CT18 for its assault against Verlautenheide, Huebner asked Collins to provide units to take over the 18th Infantry's positions southwest of Aachen. Collins assigned the 1106th Engineer Combat Group with two battalions of combat engineers to relieve the 18th Infantry by 2 October. During the relief, the 32nd Field Artillery Battalion provided artillery support to the engineers. On 1 October, the 32nd quietly remembered its reorganization day when, four years earlier, it had been renumbered from 2nd Battalion, 7th Field Artillery. The battalion's after-action report notes that "all men were from this battalion and the officers were chosen from the [7th] regiment. Through this four years the battalion has fought separately from the division and with it. Out of the original complement of officers there remains only four of the original officers, with two more appointed from the ranks."[16]

Once its 1st and 2nd Battalions were relieved from its southern sector,

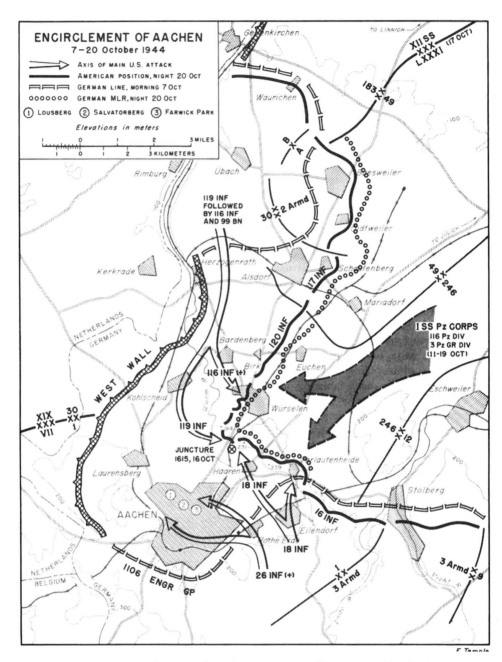

ENCIRCLEMENT OF AACHEN
7–20 October 1944

AXIS OF MAIN U.S. ATTACK

AMERICAN POSITION, NIGHT 20 OCT

GERMAN LINE, MORNING 7 OCT

GERMAN MLR, NIGHT 20 OCT

① LOUSBERG ② SALVATORBERG ③ FARWICK PARK

Elevations in meters

3 MILES

3 KILOMETERS

TO LINNICH

Gelsenkirchen

XII SS
XXX (17 OCT)
LXXXI

183 X 49

Waurichen

100

Ubach

Besweiler

119 INF
FOLLOWED
BY 116 INF
AND 99 BN

30 X 2 Armd

Rimburg

100

dtweiler

TO JULICH

Kerkrade

Herzogenrath

117 INF

Schopfenberg

49 X 246

Alsdorf

Mariadorf

NETHERLANDS
GERMANY

120 INF

WEST WALL

Bardenberg

Birk

Euchen

I SS Pz CORPS
116 Pz DIV
3 Pz GR DIV
(11–19 OCT)

Eschweiler

116 INF (+)

Wurselen

Kohlscheid

200

XIX 30
XXX XX
VII   1

119 INF

200

246 X 12

JUNCTURE
1615, 16 OCT

Haaren

rlautenheide

200

Laurensberg

18 INF

Stolberg

AACHEN
① ② ③

16 INF

18 INF
Dothe Ex

Eilendorf

200

3 Armd X 8

NETHERLANDS
BELGIUM

1106 ENGR GP

GERMANY

200

26 INF (+)

XX
3 Armd

Tucht R.

300

F. Temple

Map 20. The encirclement of Aachen, 7–20 October 1944. (Charles B. McDonald, *The Siegfried Line Campaign* [Chief of Military History, Department of the Army, 1963])

the 18th Infantry moved to an assembly area near Eilendorf, where its 3rd Battalion held the front lines between CT26 to the south and CT16 to the east. There the soldiers bathed, changed uniforms, ate hot meals, and slept. The infantrymen took refresher training on how to assault bunkers using bangalore torpedoes, bazookas, flamethrowers, and satchel charges. A battery of self-propelled 155mm howitzers, a company of Sherman tanks, and a company of M10 tank destroyers prepared to support the attack as well. There was time for the leaders to study maps of their objectives. As one contemporary account noted, "Our terrain study was precise and detailed— every bit of enemy activity was noted and recorded—every pillbox closely watched—every likely approach studied—every last discernible fold in the ground tucked away in our memories for future reference."[17]

By 7 October, CT18 was ready. Artillery forward observers and air controllers joined the companies to provide fire. One survivor remembered: "Extensive plans were made, every known or suspected enemy position plotted, artillery concentrations placed where we might need them, and all possible supporting weapons enlisted in our aid."[18]

As the 18th Infantry got ready to attack, CT26 prepared for its drive into the city. The 1st Battalion, 26th Infantry, returned to the regiment on 22 September so badly depleted that General Huebner placed it in a reserve position to allow the battalion to rest and to absorb hundreds of replacements. The 26th Infantry established a rest center where soldiers could bathe, eat warm meals, and sleep. Remarkably, the 26th Regiment's after-action report notes that "mail has been exceptionally good, considering the long supply lines, and the fact that the Division Rear was some 250 miles back in Meaux, France."[19]

As the offensive neared, CT26 sent patrols into the outskirts of Aachen to locate enemy positions. These patrols identified the *246th Infantry Division* and confirmed that the *116th Panzer Division* had withdrawn. They also determined that roughly 15,000 civilians of the city's original population of 165,000 had refused to obey evacuation orders and that the garrison was receiving a steady stream of supplies through the gap to the north of Eilendorf. By 3 October, patrols of 2nd Battalion, 26th Infantry, reached the railway line along the southern side of Aachen, and the battalion secured the eastern suburb of Rothe Erde. The battalion account notes: "Excellent observation posts enabled constant surveillance of a large portion of the city of Aachen, making it possible to zero in mortars and artillery batteries and also providing opportunity for reconnaissance for future operations."[20] The Germans reacted strongly to the American patrols, often initiating firefights in the area along the outskirts of the city. On several occasions, the Blue Spaders used captured German mortars to hammer enemy positions. As the regiment kept up the pressure on the defenders, the commanders planned the assault they were to lead once CT18 closed the routes into the city between Verlautenheide and the Ravelsberg.[21]

The Germans recognized the threat to Aachen and attempted to drive the 16th Infantry from its positions between Eilendorf and Stolberg. On 3 October, the 3rd Battalion, 16th Infantry, repulsed a counterattack by the *27th Fusilier Regiment* supported by eight assault guns and an artillery barrage. Counterfire by the Division Artillery aided the 16th Infantry, but Huebner took the threat seriously enough to order CT26 to have reinforcements ready to move into CT16's positions and to ask Collins to prepare a task force of tanks and infantry to join the fight if necessary. By the end of the day, the 16th Infantry had repulsed the *27th Fusiliers* without commitment of the reserves. Nonetheless, it was clear that the attack against Verlautenheide could start only when the 30th Infantry Division was close enough to the linkup point to support the 18th Infantry.

On 2 October, the XIX Corps offensive near Rimburg kicked off. Overcoming serious resistance along the forward defenses and repulsing several counterattacks, the 30th Infantry Division, reinforced by the 2nd Armored Division, made sufficient progress to allow Huebner to order CT18 to attack on the morning of 8 October (Map 20).[22] Fortunately, most German reserves had been sent to resist the XIX Corps attack.[23]

The 2nd Battalion, 18th Infantry, attacked Verlautenheide at 0400, 8 October. After a fierce struggle and house-to-house fighting, the battalion secured the village while receiving intense enemy mortar and artillery fire. The 1st Battalion launched its attack through Verlautenheide at 0900 to seize the bunkers on Crucifix Hill. Captain Bobby Brown's Company C, 18th Infantry, had the mission of securing Crucifix. Although German artillery fire took a heavy toll of Brown's men as they moved from Eilendorf to Crucifix Hill, the attack did not falter. Approaching the hill from the east, Brown's men hit the pillboxes from the rear, where there were significantly fewer firing ports. Captain Brown set the example, as an eyewitness reported. "Utilizing all that vital terrain study we had, [Brown] moved to the [pill]box with a pole charge. Shortly after the blast a few remaining survivors, those who had been in the box rather than outside of it, gave up. Number one had fallen."[24]

For the remainder of the day, Company C's infantrymen fought from pillbox to pillbox, finally clearing the hill and the ridge to the south by 1630. As this fight raged, the 3rd Battalion launched its drive to clear the ridge between Haaren and Crucifix Hill. Within two hours, the battalion had seized the ridge and established positions facing Aachen. CT18's attack carved a thin salient into the German positions and brought the division within 1,500 meters of its final objective for the linkup with the 30th Infantry Division. On 9 October, Companies B and I, 18th Infantry, seized the Ravelsberg. The attack, according to the regimental after-action report, "operated so smoothly that within a few hours the objective was taken without a fight. . . . Though handicapped by darkness, pillbox after pillbox was by-passed and the objective was reached."[25]

The main supply route into Aachen was cut. For the next two weeks, the Germans repeatedly attacked the 18th and 16th Infantry Regiments in attempts to reopen communications with the *246th Division* in Aachen. Fortunately, the Germans committed their reserves piecemeal against the well dug-in 16th Infantry on the eastern side of the 1st Infantry Division's salient between Verlautenheide and Eilendorf, rather than at the more exposed positions on Crucifix Hill and the Ravelsberg.

By 5 October, the German commander in the west, Field Marshal Gerd von Rundstedt, decided to commit the *3rd Panzergrenadier* and the *116th Panzer Divisions* to the battle to drive XIX Corps back through the Siegfried Line. These divisions then could push 1st Infantry Division off the hills northeast of the city. Rundstedt stipulated that these reserves were to be employed together under the command of the *I SS Panzer Corps*, and only after all of their units had arrived. Due to Allied bombing of the German rail system, these divisions still had not arrived by 8 October. By then, the 1st Infantry Division's successes forced the *Seventh Army* commander to commit the regiments of the *3rd Panzergrenadier Division* as they arrived. On the evening of 14 October, the *29th Panzergrenadier Regiment* and a dozen Tiger tanks of the *506th Panzer Battalion* attacked the 16th Infantry Regiment between Verlautenheide and Eilendorf.[26]

The Assault and Capture of Aachen: 11–21 October 1944

On 10 October, with CT18 in possession of its objectives and XIX Corps moving toward Würselen, Huebner sent two officers into Aachen to deliver an ultimatum to the German commander. If the garrison did not surrender within twenty-four hours, aerial bombardment and artillery fire would level the city and the division would destroy all remaining resistance. The German commander, Colonel Gerhardt Wilck, refused to surrender. At noon, 11 October, Colonel Seitz's CT26 commenced the assault.[27]

Seitz had the 2nd and 3rd Battalion, 26th Infantry, for the battle, while the 1st Battalion remained in reserve. Division Artillery controlled the fires of twelve artillery battalions to support the infantry, and each infantry platoon had a tank or tank destroyer attached for direct fire support. On 11

October, fighter-bombers opened the attack by dropping 62 tons of bombs on Aachen. Artillery battalions fired another 169 tons of high explosives. The next day, the air force dropped another 199 tons of bombs while the artillery fired over 5,000 shells. At the least, the preliminary bombardment adversely affected the defenders' morale and disrupted their communications.

By the morning of 13 October, the ground assault was under way, with Derrill Daniel's 2nd Battalion advancing on the 26th Infantry's left and John Corley's 3rd Battalion operating on the right (north). Corley's mission was to clear the factory area between Aachen and Haaren and then secure the hills on the northern edge of the city known collectively as the Lousberg (which included Salvatorberg and Farwick Park). Corley made steady progress, clearing the factory area and reaching the base of the Lousberg that evening. As the 3rd Battalion advanced, it used a 155mm self-propelled gun to blow holes in the apartment buildings in its path. Once a hole was blown, infantrymen entered the building and used hand grenades, flame-throwers, and bayonets to root enemy soldiers out of the cellars and attics. The next day, Company I, 26th Infantry, reached the observatory on top of the Lousberg and Company K entered Farwick Park. For the next two days, the 3rd Battalion battled elements of the *404th Infantry Regiment* and an SS infantry battalion for possession of the Kurhaus and the Palast Hotel. The Germans counterattacked repeatedly, trying to throw Corley's men back, but with the use of a 155mm self-propelled gun and all other available fire, the 3rd Battalion secured Farwick Park and moved on toward the observatory on the overlooking hill. By the evening of 16 October, Corley's men had secured the Lousberg.[28]

Meanwhile, Daniel's 2nd Battalion advanced into the heart of the city, fighting for every building. Daniel's tank-infantry teams moved steadily forward using a grid system of checkpoints to ensure that platoons did not get ahead of the friendly units to their flanks. This prevented the Germans from attacking Daniel's men from the rear. The sewer system proved to be a special problem as the enemy used it to infiltrate behind the advancing infantrymen and strike from the rear. Daniel's men solved that problem by covering every manhole cover with rubble. On 16 October, Huebner ordered the two battalions to hold in place while the rest of the division repulsed German counterattacks against the 16th and 18th Infantry Regiments. The Germans also tried to push Company L, 26th Infantry, off Observatory Hill (part of the Lousberg), but it held firm and then counterattacked.[29] By 17 October, the German attacks along the division's eastern flank had been defeated and the 30th Infantry Division had closed the ring around Aachen. No more German reinforcements or supplies could enter the city.[30]

As the fighting raged in Aachen, the *3rd Panzergrenadier Division* again attempted to capture the ridge held by the 16th Infantry between Eilendorf and Verlautenheide. During the early hours of 15 October, German infantry infiltrated into a gap between Company G, 16th Infantry, and Company G, 18th Infantry. This move was parried and the enemy was thrown back. At about noon, a battalion of the *29th Panzer Regiment*, with Tiger tanks, attacked Companies I and G, 16th Infantry. To their south, a battalion of the *8th Panzergrenadier Regiment* moved forward along the railway line. Anticipating these moves, the 7th Field Artillery coordinated the fire of six artillery battalions to plaster the open ground to the east of the 16th Infantry's positions. As Sergeant Don Wilson, of nearby Company F, remembered, "We knew they were coming. . . . Their artillery barrage . . . [continued] for an hour or more. It was later reported that over 3,000 rounds fell in our area. . . . When the barrage lifted, we could hear them singing rousing marching songs as they came through the woods."[31]

The panzer division commander observed the American artillery falling on his attacking infantry and concluded: "It was obvious that an advance through this fire was impossible." Nonetheless, the Tiger tanks made it through the barrage and commenced to fire into Company G's foxholes.[32] Some Panzergrenadiers also made it through the protective barrage and joined the Tigers in the fighting positions of the 16th Infantry. Colonel Gibb reacted by calling for air strikes and continuous artillery fire, and by moving four self-propelled tank destroyers forward. Colonel Smith brought his reserve company to the interregimental boundary, and General Huebner alerted the 1st Battalion, 26th Infantry, for possible action.

None of the reserves had to be committed. At 1430, the US 492nd Fighter Squadron attacked the German armor and infantry with 500-pound bombs and .50-caliber machine guns. General Collins, who was visiting the division, was so impressed by the P-47 Thunderbolts' action that "he sought the number of the squadron in order to commend the pilots."[33] Artillery battalions continued to throw tons of explosives at the attackers while the men of 2nd Battalion grimly met the enemy with grenades, rifles, and bayonets. Joseph Pilck, a platoon sergeant in Company G, 16th Infantry, remembered:

The next day the Germans attacked us. We stopped them—but they kept attacking us and attacking us, again and again. . . . The Germans kept trying to knock us off that hill, also known as "Dawson Ridge." . . . The last three days that I was there, the enemy broke through, took part of the ridge, and dug in. That was Oct. 16, 1944. My job was to knock them out, which I did with what few men I had left (approximately 17 men). They [Company G] kept me covered while I knocked out three machine guns and one rifleman. Just before that, about 4 o'clock, I was hit in the right shoulder with a piece of shrapnel. It didn't hit any bones, so the medic patched me up. . . . They finally hit me in the right knee and broke my leg. By this time it started to get dark—and I was put out of commission for good.[34]

Sergeant Pilck received the Distinguished Service Cross for his actions on Dawson's Ridge. At around 1500, the last of the enemy retreated, leaving hundreds of dead on the field. The 16th Infantry restored its lines, replenished its ammunition, and awaited the next attack.[35]

The *3rd Panzergrenadier Division* launched another attack that night against Company G. German tanks and infantry overran a squad position and captured an antitank gun. Dawson's men tried to drive them out, assisted by a tank destroyer, but the enemy fire was too heavy for the men to make progress. With his positions overrun, Dawson called for artillery fire on his own foxhole line.[36] The artillery fire prevented the enemy from digging the rest of the company out of its holes. At dawn, the battered German grenadiers withdrew from Company G's front while making another attack against Company I. The 2nd Battalion S3 visited Companies G and I in the late morning and reported the situation to the battalion CP:

> I just returned from G and I Companies. Things are a little rough—in fact very rough. Here is the story. In front of I Company Jerries are in the woods at 894446, then go down a little trail to a junction, then go southwest to the next trail junction down to 895444, Jerries lined up there. The pillbox lost by I Company is occupied by eight officers and their bodyguards, according to a P[risoner of] W[ar]. . . . Dawson (G Company) doesn't know if he can hold another attack through there. The men are worn out.[37]

But these assaults were the last gasps for the Panzergrenadiers. On 16 October, Companies G and I recaptured their positions, leaving the ridge in the hands of the Big Red One.[38] Throughout the defense of Dawson's Ridge, the Division Artillery played a crucial role. The 7th Field Artillery Battalion fired 6,347 rounds of 105mm, while the 5th Artillery fired over 1,200 rounds of 155mm. This was at a time when the 12th Army Group was experiencing a severe shortage of 105mm and 155mm artillery ammunition.[39]

The Germans also attempted to drive the 18th Infantry from Crucifix Hill. The 1st Battalion, however, repulsed every enemy attempt to dislodge them. As the official history points out, "The regimental commander, Colonel Smith, [even] succeeded in freeing two rifle companies to seize a fourth objective on 10 October. This was Haaren, a suburb of Aachen controlling the highway to Jülich between Crucifix and Ravels[berg] Hill.[40] For his actions in the seizure and defense of Crucifix Hill, Captain Bobby Brown received the Medal of Honor.[41]

On 16 October, the 30th Infantry Division secured Würselen, closing the ring around Aachen.[42] The 26th Infantry continued methodically to clear a path across Aachen. Due to the division's shortage of infantry units in the face of enemy counterattacks, General Collins attached a tank-infantry task force from the 3rd Armored Division to the 1st Infantry Division to help clear and retain the Lousberg. The 2nd Battalion, 110th Infantry, also joined the 26th Infantry on 19 October, when it went into the line on the left of Daniel's 2nd Battalion. These reinforcements allowed Daniel and Corley to concentrate their remaining infantry for the final push against the city.[43] By 21 October, Colonel Wilck saw the handwriting on the wall as Corley's men approached his command bunker on Lousbergstrasse with a 155mm gun. After several attempts to surrender, Wilck sent two American prisoners, Sergeant Ewart Padgett and Private James Haswell, outside with white flags. A few hours later, Wilck surrendered the ancient capital of the Holy Roman Empire to Brigadier General George Taylor, the new assistant division commander of the 1st Infantry Division.[44]

The Germans suffered heavy losses attempting to hold Aachen. The 30th Infantry Division captured 6,000 prisoners in its drive, while the 1st Infantry Division captured another 5,600. The *3rd Panzergrenadier* and *116th Panzer Divisions* suffered heavy losses in their counterattacks against the 1st Infantry Division. Although Aachen had little military utility beyond its location on the line of communications into Germany, it stood symbolically for Hitler's Thousand-Year Reich. No German could mistake the significance of the city's fall.[45]

The Costs of Breaching the Siegfried Line

The battle for Aachen took a toll on the Big Red One. In October 1944, the 1st Medical Battalion admitted more wounded men to its Clearing Station than in any previous month, including June 1944. In addition to the 995 wounded that were treated, the Clearing Station admitted 1,392 men for illnesses of various kinds.[46] Due to supply shortages, many members of the division had not received overcoats, rubber boots, or field jackets. As the weather worsened, the number of men admitted to the Clearing Station in November for various illnesses jumped to 2,146. Just as alarming, the number of neuropsychiatric casualties rose from an average of 133 men per month, from June through September, to 279 men in October.[47] A disproportionate percentage of these casualties were infantrymen.

The effects of continuous operations on the soldiers were evident. The division had been in contact with the enemy since 25 July, with only short periods of respite. The soldiers were exhausted, and casualties due to accidents rose alarmingly from 219 in September to 394 in October. Combat losses had been heavy since the beginning of the assault on the Siegfried Line, and most of the infantrymen and engineers of the division had remained in the front lines for weeks at a time. The arrival of cold and rainy weather further contributed to the troops' misery as they faced determined resistance to every advance. No wonder men like Joe Dawson could make the following observations in a letter home on 28 October: "My nerves are somewhat shattered as a result of such constant pressure these past bitter months, yet my faith remains unshaken and God has always answered my prayers for strength. You who have seen life for many years know wherein I say that these bitter tragic months of terrible war leave one morally as well as physically exhausted."[48]

Shortly after writing this letter, Dawson was wounded a second time and evacuated to the United States to recover. Unfortunately, the rest of the division could not be pulled out of the line to recuperate for any appreciable length of time due to a shortage of infantry divisions in the European Theater. In fact, Collins soon called on the Big Red One to lead the main offensive effort again.

First Army's November Offensive: 16 November–4 December 1944

First Army's capture of Aachen and its penetration into the *Westwall* were two of the few pieces of good news for the Allies by the end of October. In September, Montgomery's 21st Army Group had failed to fight its way across the Meuse and the Rhine Rivers in Operation Market Garden. In October it failed to drive the Germans out of the Scheldt estuary (the sea approach to Antwerp), forcing Eisenhower to loan Montgomery the 104th Infantry and the 7th Armored Divisions for that purpose. Severe logistical problems precluded an all-out Allied offensive in October, allowing the German army to recover. Eisenhower was aware that the opportunity to exploit the victories of the summer was slipping away, but it was not until November that the necessary supplies and forces could be assembled for another major offensive.[49]

In early November, the 104th Infantry Division joined VII Corps and occupied the front held by the 1st Infantry Division east of Aachen. This gave VII Corps three infantry divisions and one armored division for the offensive, allowing Collins to move the 1st Infantry Division to a narrow sector near Mausbach, where the division was to make the main effort. Collins attached the 47th Infantry Regiment to the Big Red One for the initial assault. The corps' mission was to attack to the northeast to seize crossings over the Roer River near Düren, with 104th Infantry Division on the left, 1st Infantry Division in the center, and 4th Infantry Division on the right. An aerial bombardment, known as Operation Queen, was to precede the ground attacks.[50]

The weather remained cold and rainy during most of November. The men of the 26th Infantry made themselves as comfortable as possible in the damp woods around Schevenhütte by building log huts and wooden walkways. The soldiers of the 18th Infantry, in the forest south of Stolberg, experienced equally miserable weather as the rain and wet snow fell continuously. Roads became a morass of mud, and foxholes filled with water. The 16th Infantry rotated a battalion at a time to a rest camp in Brand, where the men got four days out of the line. Each regiment also sent some soldiers back to the division rest camp in Herve, Belgium, where they could sleep in a bed, enjoy a USO show, and visit the Red Cross canteens. All three infantry regiments received replacements and did their best to orient the new men and prepare them for combat in the Hürtgen Forest. But with less than a week before the start of the offensive, the units accomplished little training.

The Hürtgen Forest was the hardest route for an army to follow from Aachen to the Roer or Rhine Rivers. Dense stands of fir trees covered the numerous ridges and steep valleys of the region. The few good roads in the area ran from Monschau in the southeast to Düren in the northwest, providing the Germans with good all-weather supply routes. The First Army was conducting an attack from the west to the east, and few good roads ran from the Stolberg Corridor into or across the Hürtgen Forest. The soggy ground and dense woods of the area made it very difficult for tanks to support the infantry. German infantry had reinforced the naturally defensible terrain by building log-covered bunkers and strewing the area with minefields and barbed wire. The few villages in the area were on the high ground along the roads between Monschau and Düren, giving the enemy additional defensive works.

On 16 November, the weather cleared sufficiently for the aircraft of Operation Queen to see the target area. Fog at airfields in England and France, however, prevented many bombers from getting into the air. As a result, fewer bombs were dropped than planned during the hour-long bombardment before the ground forces attacked. There were very few friendly casualties on the ground due to the depth of the safety zone, but few enemy positions were hit either. The major appreciable effect of the bombing was to diminish enemy artillery fire on the first day of the offensive.[51]

The 16th Infantry attacked Hamich from a line of departure just west of Schevenhütte. The 1st Battalion led with Companies A and C, followed by Company B and a platoon of tanks. The infantry quickly ran into the *48th Infantry Regiment*, of the *12th Division*, in log-reinforced bunkers. Calling on the 7th Field Artillery for support, the infantrymen pushed about a kilometer through the forest, reaching the northern edge overlooking Hamich at about 1500. As they dug in, they were hit by a counterattack. Supported by four battalions of artillery, the 1st Battalion held its positions, as Company B moved up to reinforce the line. With all three companies on hand, Lieutenant Colonel Driscoll tried a late-afternoon assault to seize Hamich. As the infantrymen emerged from the woods, German artillery fire hammered them, inflicting heavy losses. The men withdrew to their foxholes to wait for armor support. The tanks, however, could not make it through to Hamich along the narrow, muddy forest roads, forcing Driscoll to call a halt for the remainder of the day.[52]

While Driscoll's men were moving north, the 3rd Battalion, 16th Infantry, moved around the 1st Battalion's left to get to Hill 232. Due to their movement and the 1st Battalion's progress, the Germans in Gressenich found themselves flanked and withdrew during the night. On the morning of 17 November, the 47th Infantry occupied Gressenich, opening the road to Hamich. That afternoon, tanks and tank destroyers joined Driscoll's battalion in another attempt to take Hamich. The attack failed, in large part because of the heavy losses that the 1st Battalion already had suffered. As a result, Colonel Gibb ordered Charles Horner's 3rd Battalion to take Hamich.

At daybreak (about 0800 hours), 18 November, Horner's men attacked Hamich. After eight hours of house-to-house fighting, the 3rd Battalion secured the village. Just before dusk, Horner's men repulsed a counterattack led by five tanks, with the timely intervention by a squadron of American P-47 fighters. Meanwhile, Gibb ordered Walter Grant's 2nd Battalion to swing left behind the 3rd Battalion, pass through the forest west of Hamich, and attack Hill 232. At 1400, with support from fifteen battalions of artillery, the 2nd Battalion's infantrymen drove a battalion of the enemy off the ridge and dug in.[53]

Every advance or maneuver made by the 16th Infantry during the first three days of the drive was met by German artillery fire and counterattacks. During one of these counterattacks against Company C, near Hamich, Sergeant Jake Lindsey helped his platoon leader, Lieutenant James Wood, repulse an attack by tanks and infantry. Driving the tanks away with rifle grenades, Lindsey helped stop six infantry assaults on the platoon's position. Finally, after being wounded and running out of ammunition, Lindsey jumped out of his foxhole and attacked a squad of Germans with his bayonet. He is credited with killing three, capturing three, and driving two others off. By the end of the engagement, over one hundred Germans lay dead in front of the platoon. Woods was captured, but Lindsey survived to become the hundredth infantryman to earn the Medal of Honor in World War II.[54]

On 18 November, Huebner committed the 3rd Battalion, 18th Infantry, to reinforce the 16th Infantry. Companies I and K joined the 16th Infantry's drive to capture Wenau and Heistern the next day. "The attack was very slow and costly. The battalion was advancing through the heavily wooded area south of Wenau and German artillery inflicted many casualties upon our infantry." Nonetheless, by nightfall on 19 November, the 3rd Battalion, 18th Infantry, reached the edge of Wenau and hunkered down for the night.[55] The next morning the battalion occupied Wenau and then moved west to attack Heistern. By dusk, the 3rd Battalion had entered Heistern and cleared the southern half of it in house-to-house fighting.

While CT16 and CT18 fought to secure Hamich Ridge and Wenau, the 26th Infantry struggled to push north through the forest east of the Schevenhütte-Langerwehe Road. According to the regiment's after-action report, "intense mortar and artillery fire hitting the trees was inflicting casualties upon the advancing companies. The enemy was well dug-in and defended the clearings, fire-breaks, and trails in the woods with mortar and machine-gun fire. Progress was extremely slow, for the thick woods meant that the areas the battalion moved through had to be thoroughly cleared."[56] As the day wore on, engineers improved the trails so that tanks could join the infantry. At the same time, the 1st Battalion committed one company to close a gap opening between the 2nd Battalion and the 8th Infantry Regiment of the 4th Division to the east. During this move, Germans opened fire on the 1st Battalion from positions that had been bypassed by the lead companies. After a frustrating day, Colonel Seitz ordered the battalions to dig in for the night.[57]

The next morning, the 2nd Battalion, 26th Infantry, resumed its attack. Immediately, Daniel's men ran into mines and barbed wire, forcing Seitz to commit Company A to work through a ravine on the left of 2nd Battalion to bypass the defenses. Company A made little progress as enemy machine guns ripped into the exposed infantrymen. At dusk, Seitz again had the battalions button up for the night. On 18 November, tanks and tank destroyers finally reached the 2nd Battalion using roads built by the 1st Engineer Battalion. While the armor took the German bunkers under fire, Companies B and C tried to maneuver to the enemy's flank. Both companies made little progress before the regiment quit for the night.[58]

On 19 November, as casualties mounted, Seitz brought the 3rd Battalion through the 2nd Battalion's positions and launched another attack against the German bunkers. Led by a tank equipped with a bulldozer blade, the 3rd Battalion pushed through the woods to Hill 272 and a trail junction west of the village of Laufenberg. As the 3rd Battalion advanced, Company G repulsed a counterattack on the regiment's right and the 1st Battalion pushed to the northwest toward the Schevenhütte-Langerwehe Road. By 1600, the 1st and 3rd Battalions reached their day's objectives and again were ordered to dig in for the night.[59]

The final period of the 1st Infantry Division's operations in the Hürtgen Forest commenced on 21 November. On the left, two battalions of the 18th Infantry passed through the 16th Infantry and attacked Langerwehe. After seven days of brutal fighting, CT18 reached its objective. The regiment cleared Langerwehe and dug in. To the west, the 104th Infantry Division pushed forward, securing positions northwest of Langerwehe.[60] The 18th Infantry held Langerwehe and the village of Luchem until relieved by the 9th Division on 4 December.[61]

While the 16th and 18th Infantry Regiments secured the objectives on the left flank, the 26th Infantry continued its efforts to reach Jüngersdorf and Merode. On 21 November, the 1st Battalion passed through the 3rd Battalion to attack to the northeast. After two days of hard fighting and heavy losses, the regiment could measure its progress only in hundreds of yards. From 24 to 26 November, the 26th Infantry stayed in place and eliminated bypassed enemy positions. On 27 November, Corley's 3rd Battalion resumed the drive to Jüngersdorf. Corley's men moved relatively rapidly, in large part because the 18th Infantry's seizure of Langerwehe threatened the enemy in Jüngersdorf with encirclement. At 1530, they entered Jüngersdorf. For the remainder of the day the 3rd Battalion, supported by tanks, cleared the enemy out of the village. The next morning, the battalion repulsed a counterattack.[62]

On 29 November, the 2nd Battalion, 26th Infantry, passed through the 1st Battalion and moved toward Merode. Taking advantage of artillery support, Companies E and F crossed the open ground east of the forest and reached the houses on the western edge of Merode at about noon. Sidney Miller, a lieutenant in Company F, described the advance toward Merode in a memoir he prepared in the 1980s:

> At the appointed time to advance on the morning of the 29th, the squad leaders started their men out with an eye toward possible snipers, advancing over the crest of the rise of ground preceding the down slope [to Merode]. . . . The second and third platoons were on my right and E Company to the right of them with two tanks. We hadn't proceeded too far before encountering small arms

fire and with the initial advance down went the two new lieutenants along with a number of others who had been advancing standing up. . . . One of our aid men had taken off his bag and was about to apply gauze and tape to a downed man when the snipers shot him. There were so many evidently wounded or dead that Tom [Sheffield, his platoon sergeant] went over to pick up the aid bag and as I approached him, his head snapped side ways and when he turned and looked at me I could see he had been shot through the mouth and it looked like half his jaw or teeth were gone. . . . I gave him two shots of morphine and motioned him to go back over the hill. . . . The din was terrific as we were under heavy mortar and artillery fire. . . . As it got dark we buttoned up for the night.[63]

Two tanks accompanied the companies but were quickly knocked out. The companies requested additional armor support, but before any action could be taken a battalion of the *5th Parachute Regiment* counterattacked. A short time later, the companies reported that heavy fighting was in progress and that artillery fire from Schlich was hammering them. The last messages from Company F reported that enemy paratroopers, supported by tanks, were thrusting against its positions. The isolated infantrymen faced annihilation or capture.

The next morning, Lieutenant Miller surrendered his platoon. As Miller remembered, "They lined us up outside of the building with our hands on our heads and I thought for sure they were going to mow us down and I think they would have had not the prisoner intervened on our behalf as I had treated him fairly [when I captured him the day before]."[64] J. C. Hill, another member of Company F, remembered the prisoners' journey to Germany: "We were marched for days through village after village, being pointed out as prisoners of the elite 1st U.S. Infantry Division—to boost morale."[65]

The regimental headquarters heard nothing further from Companies E and F.[66] The 33rd Field Artillery Battalion did its best to provide counter-battery fire, but it was impossible to locate the German artillery without forward observers.[67] Without a reserve there was little that could be done quickly enough to help Daniel's forward companies. Tanks tried to get to Merode along the forest trail, but they were blocked by two tanks disabled in the initial advance. The regimental after-action report describes the results of efforts to aid the beleaguered infantrymen:

A combat patrol sent out to contact the two companies was turned back by heavy enemy mortar, machine gun, and small arms fire, and by tank fire. Attempts to pull bogged down tanks, which were blocking the way for other

vehicles, out of the road leading to the town were futile, since the trails were
under heavy artillery fire. Artillery fire was laid on the far end of the town at
1105 hours. The day passed with no news from the companies. At 1845 hours,
a prisoner gave some idea of what had happened. German infantry and tanks
had cut the companies off after they had entered the town, closing in on them
from the woods above and below the town. In the evening, the 1st Battalion,
18th Infantry, relieved the 3rd Battalion [26th Infantry]. Plans were drawn for
using the 3rd Battalion to drive on Merode and relieve whatever elements of the
two companies were still holding out.[68]

In the end, it was futile to throw more men into the fight for Merode, especially since armor and effective artillery support could not be guaranteed for
the effort. According to the division history, prisoners "taken later reported
that the remnants of Companies E and F, 2nd Battalion, 26th Infantry had
been captured when their ammunition was gone, December 1, 1944."[69]

On 2 December, General Collins notified Huebner that the division had
done all that could be expected and that the 9th Infantry Division would
take over the 1st Division's sector. By 7 December, the 18th and 26th Infantry Regiments and most of the artillery battalions were in assembly areas in
southeastern Belgium to recover from their ordeal in the Hürtgen. The 16th
Infantry remained in the line until 11 December, when two of its battalions
moved to a rest area. The 2nd Battalion stayed in defensive positions until
13 December.[70] At Aubel, the men moved into tents, had access to warm
showers and hot meals, and were given a chance to sleep without being
shelled. A few lucky men got passes to Paris.[71] The soldiers of the 18th
Infantry were billeted in homes in and around Plombiers. The regimental
after-action report noted: "It was a tired, bedraggled, but glorious group
of men who returned from the violent, explosive front facing Duren to the
quiet, peaceful ground over which the regiment had advanced three months
before."[72] It seemed that the division could look forward to an extended
period of rest.

The 1st Infantry Division suffered enormous casualties for its conquest
of 11 square miles of German soil. The 1st Medical Battalion treated 6,163
casualties in its Clearing Station in November and another 493 in the first
six days of December. The division lost 507 men killed in action and 345
men missing.[73]

The losses in November and the first week of December included at least
653 neuropsychiatric casualties (combat fatigue). An unknown number of
men received treatment for combat fatigue or exhaustion in battalion aid
stations as well. The sharp rise in such casualties reflected the cumulative
strain of battle on the soldiers. The medical system did all it could to treat

neuropsychiatric patients. The primary means of treatment was for the division's medical units to provide the affected soldiers with warm food, rest, and quiet as soon as possible, and as close to their units as possible, for about twenty-four hours. With this treatment, many of these men returned to their platoons within several days. If, however, there were too many other casualties in the system, as there were in the 1st Infantry Division in November 1944, the unit aid stations and the Collecting Companies evacuated more combat fatigue casualties to the rear. The farther a man went to the rear for treatment, the more likely it was that he would be permanently affected, and the less likely it was that he would be able to return to his unit.[74] The rate of such casualties treated in the division's Clearing Company peaked in November.

Rest and Recuperation: 6–16 December 1944

The division had lost many veteran and trained personnel, although it was remarkably close to full strength when it came out of the line (with the exception of 2nd Battalion, 26th Infantry).[75] Replacements had arrived throughout the battle, but the infantry battalions had not had time to acclimate and train the new men. This was especially unfortunate, since many replacements sent to Europe were not trained infantrymen. This situation occurred because the army had underestimated the rate of loss of infantrymen and because the personnel system failed to meet even the inadequate estimates of needed replacements. Consequently, many men who joined the division lacked infantry skills. The best that can be said is that the division's infantry strength was replenished.[76]

On 11 December, Major General Clarence Huebner became the deputy commander of V Corps. Brigadier General Clift Andrus became the commanding general of the 1st Infantry Division. Huebner later assumed command of V Corps.

The Battle of the Bulge Begins

Fate or luck would not allow the Big Red One to enjoy its well-earned period of recuperation. On 16 December, the Germans launched a counteroffensive against First Army. In what the Germans called *Wacht am Rhein*, three German armies struck the thinly manned defenses of VIII Corps from Losheim to just north of Luxembourg City and the southern half of V Corps, between Monschau and Losheim. Allied intelligence had anticipated a German counterattack but thought that it would take place on the Roer Plain east of Aachen. The magnitude and the location of the enemy's thrust surprised nearly every intelligence officer and commander from Eisenhower's head-quarters in Paris to VIII Corps headquarters in Bastogne. Eisenhower im-mediately read the situation correctly, while Bradley was slow to see it as a major counteroffensive.[77]

The German attack against the critical north shoulder of the Bulge struck V Corps' 99th Infantry Division at dawn, east and northeast of Büllingen, Belgium, and at Monschau, Germany (Map 21). Although the 99th had only been in the line for a month, its infantrymen were protected in log and earth bunkers and its leaders had acclimated themselves to combat. The Germans made little headway initially, as the Americans met their assault with heavy fire. At midday, the *12th SS Panzer Division* committed tanks to get things moving. By dusk, several of the battalions of the 99th Infantry were fighting for their lives in the forests. Fortunately for V Corps, the veteran 2nd Infan-try Division was just a few kilometers west, where it had been conducting an attack against the Siegfried Line. The division halted its offensive and pre-pared to occupy positions behind the 99th Infantry Division. Over the next two days, the 2nd Infantry Division established a defensive front, anchored on the Belgian villages of Krinkelt and Rocherath, through which the 99th Infantry skillfully withdrew. By 18 December, the 2nd and the 99th Infantry Divisions had prevented the Germans from opening the two northern routes to the northeast and were digging in on Elsenborn Ridge.[78]

As the Germans attacked, General Eisenhower concluded that *Wacht am Rhein* was a major offensive and ordered 12th Army Group to move divi-sions from Ninth Army and VII Corps south to reinforce V Corps, and to have Third Army shift forces north to bolster VIII Corps.[79] As a result, on 16 December the 26th Infantry, accompanied by the 33rd Field Artillery Battalion and Company C, 745th Tank Battalion, was ordered to move to Camp Elsenborn, 25 miles south of Verviers.

The 3rd Battalion, 26th Infantry, set out for Elsenborn at 0400, 17 De-cember. Moving without lights, the trucks reached the camp at 0700. Since Colonel Seitz was on leave, Lieutenant Colonels Van Sutherland and Frank Murdoch directed the regiment's deployment. When they reported to the Elsenborn command post of the 99th Infantry Division, they received or-ders to occupy positions south and east of Bütgenbach, 7 kilometers south of Elsenborn. By 1400 hours, the 3rd Battalion had reached Bütgenbach, where it was joined by Daniel's 2nd Battalion. Sutherland determined that the key terrain was southeast of town, at a crossroads known as Dom Büt-genbach. This position blocked the roads to Bütgenbach from Büllingen to the east and from Moderscheid to the south.[80]

On 18 December, the 2nd and 3rd Battalions established a foxhole line in an arc around the crossroads. Daniel's companies dug in at the intersection,

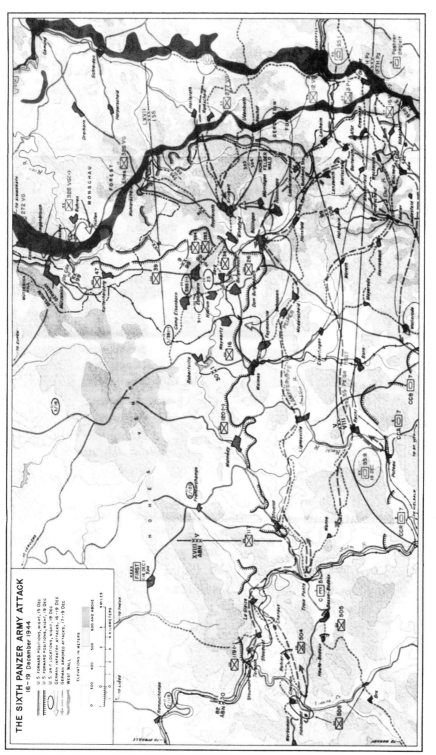

Map 21. The *Sixth Panzer Army* attack, 16–19 December 1944. The 1st Infantry Division held the northern shoulder of the Bulge at Bürgenbach. (Hugh M. Cole, *The Ardennes: Battle of the Bulge* [Chief of Military History, Department of the Army, 1965])

while Corley's men dug in to the east and northeast to anchor the regiment's left flank on Bütgenbach Lake. Company K dug in between Bütgenbach and Dom Bütgenbach, northwest of 2nd Battalion, to protect Daniel's right flank.[81] The 2nd Battalion, 26th Infantry, thus established its positions astride the road that the German plan had designated as Panzer Route C. This road ran from the frontier at Losheim, Germany, through Büllingen and Bütgenbach, and on to Liège, Belgium. It was essential to the attackers' success that their forces open this route so that the *1st SS Panzer Corps* could reach the Meuse River crossings.

By the time the 26th Infantry arrived in Bütgenbach, the 2nd and 99th Infantry Divisions had already upset the enemy's timetable. During the night of 18–19 December, the battered regiments of the 99th finished withdrawing through the 2nd and moved to Elsenborn. To their southwest, CT26 held Dom Bütgenbach, astride Panzer Route C. Unable to break through at Elsenborn, the *Sixth Panzer Army* ordered the *12th SS Panzer* and the *3rd Parachute Divisions* to swing south and open the route through Bütgenbach.[82]

On 16 December, First Army ordered the remainder of the 1st Infantry Division to be prepared to move on six hours' notice. The next afternoon, the 18th Infantry moved to Eupen to operate against German paratroopers believed to have landed, in a region known as the Hohe Venn. Over the next two days, the 3rd Battalion sent companies on sweeps along the roads from Eupen to Malmédy. Only a few German paratroopers were encountered. On 19 December, the 3rd Armored Division assumed responsibility for Eupen's security and CT18 rejoined the division. By the evening of 20 December, the 1st and 3rd Battalions, 18th Infantry, were laagered near Sourbrodt, and the 2nd Battalion had reinforced the 26th Infantry.[83]

Combat Team 16 moved south on 18 December to Robertville and established defensive positions. Patrols confirmed that Germans were moving west along the road from Moderscheid to Malmédy. The 1st Infantry Division's mission was to prevent the Germans from turning north. To carry out this mission, Andrus ordered Smith to move his combat team into a line from Waimes to Weywertz. On 20 December, Walter Grant's 2nd Battalion moved south and drove the Germans out of Waimes and established contact with the 30th Infantry Division. The 3rd Battalion, 16th Infantry, occupied positions south of Weywertz and linked up with the 26th Infantry. The 1st Battalion remained in reserve in Robertville.[84]

The Battle of Bütgenbach:
18–24 December 1944

The 26th Infantry was in the path of the main German effort of the Battle of the Bulge on 18 December (see Map 21). Fortunately, the 2nd and 3rd

Battalions had time to dig deep fighting positions and to reinforce them with overhead cover of logs and earth before the *12th SS Panzer* and the *3rd Parachute Divisions* attacked. When the regiment arrived, Lieutenant Colonels Murdoch, Daniel, and Corley noted that fog was making visibility poor during the early daylight hours. Consequently, they placed the regiment's 57mm antitank guns in the forward foxhole line, enabling the guns to support the infantry during limited visibility situations. The fire from the small antitank guns also would identify targets for the 3-inch guns of tank destroyers that were 300 yards behind the front lines. This decision was immensely important, because it made the best use of the 57mm guns and gave the infantrymen close-in antitank support.

There was little activity in front of CT26 on 18 December. Patrols from Company K observed enemy armor in Büllingen, and the 33rd Artillery fired 1,700 rounds at suspected targets. The real show started at 0225 hours, 19 December, when German infantrymen and tanks attacked Company E just south of the intersection. As Company E opened up with every available weapon, Daniel called for artillery fire on pre-plotted locations. In less than an hour, three German tanks were knocked out and the attacking infantry scattered. Daniel reported during the action: "Much happening out there. We are killing a lot of Germans."[85]

By this time, Brigadier General Andrus had established the division command post in Sourbrodt. Colonel Seitz also had returned from leave to resume command of CT26. At around 1000 hours, Company A moved a kilometer south of Bütgenbach, where it and Company B linked up to reinforce the western flank of 2nd Battalion. Shortly after that German infantry, supported by two tanks, struck Company E from the south along the Moderscheid Road. One of the tanks was destroyed by a 57mm antitank gun before the gun was disabled by a Panzerfaust rocket. Daniel again called for artillery support, and the exposed enemy found themselves smothered by fire. The Germans retreated. For the rest of the day, German artillery and mortar fire plastered CT26. The day ended when American mortar fire repulsed enemy patrols probing Company K's positions northwest of the battalion's command post.[86]

By 19 December, V Corps had established an impressive artillery concentration around Elsenborn to support the 2nd, 99th, and 1st Infantry Divisions. This allowed the corps to provide massive artillery concentrations to any section of its line. At the height of the battles south of Bütgenbach, as many as 10,000 rounds were fired in one mission to support the 26th Infantry. The 33rd Field Artillery Battalion alone fired 2,642 rounds on 19 December. The thin line of infantrymen could not have survived the German assaults without such massive artillery support.

Even with artillery support, the 26th Infantry faced a daunting challenge.

On 20 December, the *12th SS Panzer Division* threw a battalion of Panzer-grenadiers supported by twenty tanks against Daniel's lines. At 0330, they attacked Companies E and F, hoping to break their hold on the intersection and open the road to Bütgenbach. The attack was supported by mortar and artillery fire that drove Daniel's men into their foxholes. A number of tanks reached the lines between Companies E and F and continued toward Büt-genbach. It looked as if the Germans were going to break through. The in-fantrymen, however, remained in their foxholes, pouring fire into the ranks of German infantry who tried to follow the tanks. At the same time, Daniel called on the 33rd Artillery to bring all available fire onto 2nd Battalion's positions while tanks and tank destroyers behind the foxhole line engaged the German tanks that had gotten through. As additional German armor ap-proached the American foxholes, the crews of the 57mm antitank guns held their fire until their targets were within point-blank range. This increased the chance that a hit would disable the tanks, but it exposed the gun crews to German fire.

Losses were heavy on both sides, and the situation called for unbelievable bravery. For example, Corporal Henry F. Warner,

> serving as a 57mm antitank gunner with the Second Battalion . . . was a major factor in stopping enemy tanks during heavy attacks. . . . In the first attack, launched in the early morning of the 20th, enemy tanks succeeded in penetrat-ing parts of the line. Corporal Warner, disregarding the concentrated cannon and machine gun fire from two tanks bearing down on him, and ignoring the imminent danger of being overrun by the infantry moving under tank cover, destroyed the first tank and scored a direct and deadly hit upon the second. A third tank approached to within five yards of his position while he was attempt-ing to clear a jammed breach block. Jumping from his gun pit, he engaged in a pistol duel with the tank commander standing in the turret, killing him and forcing the tank to withdraw.

Warner survived the encounter but on the following day was killed while destroying another tank in a point-blank duel. He received the Medal of Honor posthumously.[87]

On 21 December, Daniel committed his reserve platoon to support Com-pany E, as enemy tanks stalked his command post. Seitz sent Company C forward to Daniel, allowing him to reinforce Company F and reconstitute a two-platoon reserve. After antitank guns knocked out two of the five enemy tanks around 2nd Battalion's command post, the Germans withdrew and a brief quiet settled over the battlefield. Seitz took advantage of this lull to send mines and three more antitank guns to Dom Bütgenbach and to request engineers to help lay the mines. Before this help could arrive, the Germans launched three more attacks. These efforts were defeated due, in large part, to the artillery's effective fire. In the afternoon, another Panzergrenadier battalion supported by six tanks made the final try of the day to break Daniel's lines. The pattern of the earlier attempts was repeated: the Blue Spaders refused to retreat, and every available weapon threw metal at the enemy. By nightfall, the Germans gave up for the day.[88]

On the morning of 21 December, the *3rd Parachute Division* struck the 2nd Battalion, 26th Infantry, in Company G's sector. The regiment's after-action report described the fighting that followed:

Six German tanks were destroyed by the artillery fire which fell close to the forward positions, and the flames of these lit the area of fighting. Enemy tanks succeeded in penetrating the lines this time through G Company's position. When antitank fire was placed upon these, the German tanks took refuge behind some buildings near the battalion CP, and fired upon the rocket-gun teams that tried to get within range. In an effort to drive the enemy tanks out, mortar fire was called down upon the battalion positions. When these tanks left the shelter of the buildings, the antitank crews fired upon them. It was slow work. . . . By 1600 hours, all enemy tanks . . . had been destroyed. Meanwhile, the infantry again held their positions and endured wave after wave of attacks by enemy infantry who persisted in moving through our terrific artillery barrage and came to close grips with our infantry. Our infantry fought the hostile tanks and infantry with hand grenades, rocket guns, BARs, and rifle grenades. Machine guns were in almost constant operation, and the crews of tanks, tank destroyers and antitank guns remained at their posts until they had either destroyed the enemy or had been destroyed.[89]

By the afternoon of 21 December, Daniel was forced by his losses to consider shortening his lines. Colonel Seitz, however, promised Daniel that replacements were on their way, and General Andrus sent the 2nd Battalion, 18th Infantry, to reinforce the 26th Infantry. These moves allowed Seitz to shorten the front of the 1st Battalion south of Bütgenbach and to reinforce Daniel with a platoon from 3rd Battalion. The next morning, 376 replacements joined the 26th Infantry, with most of them going to the 2nd Battalion. On 23 and 24 December, another 326 men joined the 26th Infantry, bringing the regiment to over 2,950 officers and men. The 613th TD Battalion also joined the division on 22 December, providing additional antiarmor protection with its self-propelled 90mm guns.[90]

While the 26th Infantry was fighting for its life, the 16th Infantry improved its positions near Waimes. On 20 December, German paratroopers made a half-hearted effort to dislodge the 2nd Battalion. With help from the 7th Field Artillery, Walter Grant's infantrymen repulsed the attack and continued to fortify their positions. The 1st Battalion occupied backup positions north of Waimes, around the village of Bruyères. The 3rd Battalion also repulsed enemy probes south of Weywertz, thus protecting the western flank of the 26th Infantry. For the remainder of the month, the 16th Infantry sowed mines and maintained contact with the enemy through active patrolling.[91]

On 22 December, Andrus ordered Smith to send the 1st Battalion, 18th Infantry, to Bütgenbach to help the 26th Infantry repulse Germans who had fought their way into the village through the 1st Battalion, 26th Infantry. Before Lieutenant Colonel Henry Learnard's men got to Bütgenbach, the 26th Infantry drove the enemy off with heavy losses on both sides. During the night of 22–23 December, the 1st Battalion, 18th Infantry, replaced the 1st Battalion, 26th Infantry, on the lines south of Bütgenbach, allowing Frank Murdoch's battalion to move closer to the 2nd Battalion, 26th Infantry. At the same time, the 2nd Battalion, 18th Infantry, occupied the line southwest of the town, and Colonel Smith assumed control of the center of the division's front with his 2nd Battalion in reserve near Nidrum.[92] From then until the end of the month, the Big Red One held the north shoulder of the Bulge.

The Battle of the Bulge: 23 December 1944–15 January 1945

It was apparent that the Germans had failed to break V Corps' defenses. Backed by powerful artillery resources, the 1st Infantry Division helped to destroy the offensive capability of at least five German divisions. By holding the ground south from Monschau to Dom Bütgenbach, and from Dom Bütgenbach west to Malmédy, V Corps prevented the *Sixth Army* from turning north and from supplying the lead Kampfgruppe of the *1st SS Panzer Division* in La Gleize, to the west. As a result, the Germans shifted their main effort to the *Fifth Army*. By 27 December, Collins's VII Corps had met and destroyed the German armored units that made it farthest west, near Ceney, Belgium, and Patton's 4th Armored Division had relieved the encircled 101st Airborne in Bastogne. Any threat that the enemy would reach the Meuse River, let alone Antwerp, was at an end.

The shift in the German main effort was noticed by the 1st Infantry Division on 23 December, when artillery forward observers saw armored vehicles moving east from Büllingen. These vehicles were part of the *12th SS Panzer Division* trying to move west along roads farther south. The remainder of the day was quiet for the 26th Infantry, until, as its after-action report notes, "towards evening, two enemy tanks to the front of I Company were taken under our tank and mortar fire, and one of the enemy tanks was destroyed. The enemy crew abandoned the second tank which was hit and set afire. 2nd Battalion patrols established that 30 tanks had been knocked out in their area alone." For the remainder of December, the 2nd Battalion remained around Dom Bütgenbach, while the 1st and 3rd Battalions, 26th Infantry, secured its flanks.[93]

The after-action report of the 18th Infantry sums up the situation:

> The tactical plan of employment of the 1st Division called for our holding the newly organized line for an indefinite period of time. Immediate steps were taken to prepare as strong [a] defensive position as possible. For several nights running, engineers, riflemen, antitank men, and pioneers toiled ceaselessly to sow minefields, erect road blocks, prepare dummy-gun positions, and string barbed wire. At the same time our reconnaissance patrols were very active, carrying the fight to the enemy's lines. These actions were small but bitter. In reality, the Bütgenbach sector . . . became a deadly training ground for our high percentage of new men.[94]

On 23 December, the temperature dropped below zero, the wind blew fiercely, and snow covered the Ardennes with a white blanket. While the clearing of the skies was welcome during the day, allowing Allied airpower to plaster the German columns to the south, the nights were bitter, as one of the coldest winters of the century settled on the region. To ease the misery of the soldiers, engineer units constructed squad and platoon shelters with timber cut in the nearby woods and installed stoves to warm the men. As New Year's Eve approached, Colonel George Smith considered the future with the following thoughts: "What the new year would bring only time would tell; however, if spirit and determination were any criteria, our regiment was ready to do even greater deeds in contributing to the foe's downfall in 1945."[95]

The Battle of the Bulge ended when VII and XII Corps counterattacked the northwestern and southwestern tips of the German penetration. While the enemy was pushed east, First Army and V Corps prepared to resume the push to the Rhine. For the 1st Infantry Division, December had been a harrowing month, with high casualties and nearly miraculous results at Dom Bütgenbach. And yet, when the next Allied offensive opened in January 1945, the Big Red One would play a major role.

12

The Last Offensive against Germany
January to May 1945

THE BATTLE OF THE BULGE WAS THE COSTLIEST American battle of World War II. It was also a strategic victory for the Allies and a disaster for the Germans. The Germans used most of their reserves and over half of their available armored vehicles, artillery, and aircraft in the offensive. Hitler gambled his last stakes on a victory in the west. He lost, permanently weakening the Wehrmacht on all fronts. In a real sense, the Nazi animal had come out of its lair to fight, enabling its enemies to destroy much of its remaining strength.

By the end of December, the Germans had depleted the resources they needed to stave off an anticipated Russian winter offensive. The German divisions in the west were so badly battered that they would be unable to halt the Western Allies when they resumed their advance toward the Rhine River.[1] Eisenhower and his generals prepared to resume offensive action in the Bulge as early as 27 December and to begin a major drive toward the east in early January 1945. Eisenhower's overall strategy remained unchanged. The Allied armies were to push the Germans back to the Rhine all along the front in preparation for the final drive into Germany. Once sufficient forces were arrayed along the Rhine, the Allies planned to cross the river, encircle and destroy the German armies in the Ruhr and Saar industrial areas, and then push east to meet the Russians on the Elbe River. Eisenhower had three army groups, nine armies, twenty corps, and seventy-three full-strength divisions to carry out this strategy against von Rundstedt's eighty badly depleted and poorly supported divisions.[2]

The last offensive of Eisenhower's armies began with the reduction of the bulge in the American lines (see Map 22). During the initial phase of the Allied offensive, V Corps remained in position on the northern shoulder of the Bulge as the VII and XVIII Airborne Corps pushed the enemy back. The Allied attacks took place in horrific weather. The temperature dropped well below freezing and remained there. Snow fell nearly every day. Advancing infantrymen waded through waist-deep snow, and drifts higher than a Sherman tank blocked the roads. Behind the front, the roads were covered with ice, and it was common for tanks, trucks, and artillery pieces to slide off. German resistance was generally light, except in the villages that dotted the Ardennes. Both sides recognized the importance of these as strongpoints and as places where soldiers periodically could get out of the cold. Generally, the Americans advanced slowly during the day, clearing the roads as they moved and fighting for the villages as they came upon them. At night, the Germans withdrew, sowing the roads and fields behind them with mines. Most American casualties during January 1945 were caused by frostbite, trench foot, and wounds inflicted by mines.[3]

The 1st Infantry Division Offensive: 14 January–5 February 1945

During the first two weeks of January 1945, the 1st Infantry Division remained in defensive positions. The 26th Infantry held the ridge between Büllingen and Dom Bütgenbach in an arc around the crossroads just east of Dom Bütgenbach. The 18th Infantry Regiment held a south-facing line from Bütgenbach to Oberweywertz, and the 16th Infantry defended positions from there to Waimes.

The 26th Infantry's after-action report noted that "the snow had piled into such high drifts that a tank dozer was in use to push aside paths to the company [command posts]."[4] Trench foot and frostbite casualties outnumbered combat casualties, as the 1st Medical Battalion treated 516 disease cases and 117 wounded soldiers in the first two weeks of January.[5] Most companies rotated men with symptoms of cold-weather injuries to their field kitchens, where those soldiers could dry their feet, change their socks, and get a warm meal. For the several thousand replacements who joined the division in this period, such as Raymond Gantter, living in a foxhole in such cold weather was the worst memory of the war. Gantter describes some of the challenges in his autobiography, *Roll Me Over: An Infantryman's World War II*:

> It was a beautiful and grim Christmas Eve. Shorty and I spelled each other on guard throughout the bitter cold night. The cold I could endure, but an additional misery landed on me in the middle of the night. I got the GIs! That's always a tragedy, of course—although in normal life, with the luxury of a civilized bathroom at hand, it would seem only an embarrassing annoyance—but this time the tragedy was of major proportions. You see, our dugout was on a crest of a hill, smack in the middle of an open field and with never a bush or tree to provide cover. It's not modesty that bothers us, you understand: it's snipers. . . . A half-naked man crouching on a hilltop is a defenseless creature.[6]

On 14 January, Huebner called on the 1st Infantry Division to spearhead the V Corps drive. The only silver lining was that the enemy was often surprised by the division's attacks because they considered the weather too bad for offensive action.

The division's initial mission was to open the route to St. Vith by seizing the village of Ondenval and by clearing the road through the hills south of that village (see Map 22). The 23rd Infantry Regiment joined the Big Red One for the offensive. To protect CT23's flank, the 1st Infantry Division needed to secure the woods on the Bütgenbacher Heck. Brigadier General Clift Andrus planned to have CT23 attack on the right to clear the Ondenval Gap, while the 16th and 18th Infantry Regiments captured the village of Schoppen and the Bütgenbacher Heck, respectively.[7]

The offensive commenced on 15 January, as 3rd Battalion, 18th Infantry, moved slowly through the deep snow toward the Bütgenbacher Heck. To the west, the 3rd Battalion, 16th Infantry, accompanied by a company of tanks from the 745th Tank Battalion, seized the high ground northeast of Faymonville while the 1st Battalion, 16th Infantry, fought its way into that village against fierce resistance. Edmund Driscoll's 1st Battalion fought from house to house for the rest of the day, losing several tanks to Panzerfausts in the process. By that evening, the battalion had lost seventy men and still had not secured the entire village. Lieutenant Colonel Charles Horner's 3rd Battalion also lost about seventy casualties as it fought its way to a line running east from Faymonville. After a brief rest that night, Driscoll's men cleared the rest of the village the next morning, allowing the 2nd Battalion, 16th Infantry, to move toward Schoppen.

To the west of CT16, the 23rd Infantry Regiment captured Ondenval in a dawn attack but then ran into strong resistance in the Ondenval Gap. To support this effort, General Andrus sent a battalion by truck from its reserve position to the village of Ligneuville to join CT23. Lieutenant Colonel Learnard's 1st Battalion, 18th Infantry, reached Ligneuville in the afternoon of 17 January. There the soldiers detrucked and prepared to attack to the east, over a 1,200-foot-high mountain known as the Wolfsbusch, into the flank and rear of the German defenses.[8]

Learnard's men waded through waist-deep snow to reach the top of the Wolfsbusch at midnight. There they rested for a few hours as Learnard and the company commanders planned an assault down into the enemy's positions. Early on 18 January, the battalion moved out in the face of a blizzard. As they moved through the forest, using compasses to stay on course, they encountered and captured a German patrol. When they reached the German positions, they took the enemy by surprise. The haul of prisoners included the battalion commander and staff of the *2nd Battalion,*

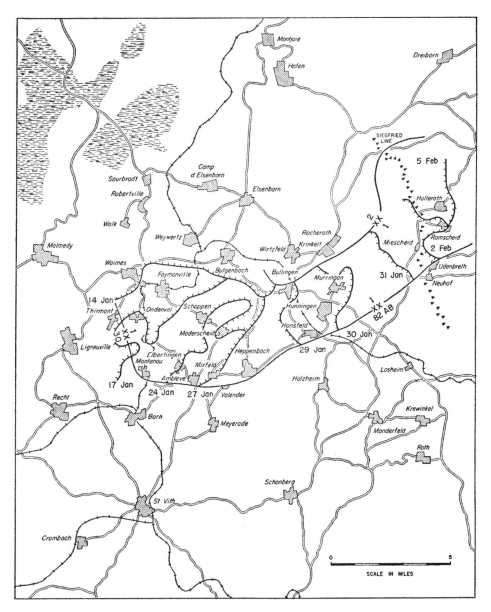

Map 22. The Ardennes campaign from Waimes, Belgium, 14 January 1945, to Hollerath, Germany, 5 February 1945. (H. R. Knickerbocker et al., *Danger Forward* [Society of the 1st Division, 1947])

8th Parachute Regiment. Learnard's men also captured three 88mm guns, a battery of 105mm howitzers, and a number of half-tracks and trucks.[9]

The 18th Infantry next turned south on 19 January in a two-pronged assault against Montenau. Captain Richard Lindo's Company C, 18th Infantry, attacked from the north while Company A moved through the woods and struck Montenau from the west. Task Force Lindo and Company A overwhelmed the German garrison, which had not expected anyone to attack in such weather.[10] These assaults opened the Ondenval Gap for the 7th Armored Division's move to St. Vith.

On 19 January, CT16 continued its drive to secure Schoppen. Charles Horner's 3rd Battalion "set out in the worst weather encountered by the 16th Infantry during all its campaigning in World War II," according to the regimental history. "Snow was knee-deep on the level and drifted to two to three times that depth where the wind could get at it." Although the soldiers were exhausted by plowing through the snow, the Germans in Schoppen were surprised and their outposts quickly eliminated. By noon, Horner's men had secured the village and Company K had pushed another 500 meters south. At the same time, the 1st Battalion, 16th Infantry, captured the high ground overlooking Eibertingen, thus maintaining contact with CT23 to the west.[11]

The division's attacks from 15 to 19 January accomplished their purposes and enabled V Corps to send the 7th Armored Division to St. Vith, further threatening the German forces to the west with encirclement. This forced the enemy's *Fifth Army* to continue its retreat. For the next four days, the division consolidated its positions as the 18th Infantry captured Moderscheid. The 3rd Battalion, 18th Infantry, lost 259 men in these actions, including 85 soldiers killed. Cold-weather injuries remained prevalent.[12]

The 26th Infantry pushed patrols and then companies east and south. It met little resistance and found many abandoned positions. By mid-January, it was clear that the German retreat from the area of the Bulge was well under way. On 24 January, the 1st Battalion, 26th Infantry, assaulted German positions around the Morscheck crossroads, on the road from Moderscheid to Büllingen. Captain Don Lister's Company C led the attack, described in Rocco Moretto's memoir, *Memorable Experience:*

> At 0300 we started out in what was to be the coldest weather that I'd experienced in my whole lifetime. It was so cold that the snowsuits were frozen stiff and crackled as you moved. . . . The snowsuits blended in perfectly with the snow as they moved down the road, and no opposition was met till the 1st Platoon swung to the east. At that point they were met with fire from two machine guns and about a squad of riflemen. We very quickly gained fire superiority,

killing four of the enemy and six were taken prisoner. . . . Additional Germans were caught in their dugouts [and] surrendered without firing a shot.[13]

This action made it possible to swing the division's line to face in a more easterly direction.

In response to the continued German withdrawal and the success of the V Corps attacks, First Army accelerated the offensive. To bring the most force to bear, Hodges adjusted the boundaries of the XVIII Airborne and V Corps, shifting the 1st Infantry Division into the airborne corps so that it could join the 82nd Airborne Division in an attack to the Siegfried Line. This attack was to commence on 28 January, allowing time for the two divisions to reorient their logistics, artillery, and infantry.[14]

The weather continued to be miserably cold, with snow falling nearly every day. It took several days to turn the 1st Infantry Division to the east and narrow its front. On the evening of 27 January, the 26th and 18th Combat Teams were in place. CT26, on the left (north), was to drive through Büllingen and Mürringen and move northeast through the Rocherrath Forest to Hollerath, Germany. CT18, on the right, planned to move east and northeast through Hepscheid, Honsfeld, and Hünningen before crossing the Rocherrath Forest to seize Ramscheid and Udenbreth, Germany. The 16th Infantry was the division's reserve. The German *89th Volksgrenadier Division*, with two badly depleted regiments, manned the defenses in the villages along the way and the bunkers of the *Westwall* between Hollerath and Udenbreth.[15]

The offensive commenced at 0400, 28 January. On the right, the 18th Infantry's 1st and 2nd Battalions took Hepscheid and Heppenbach by 1000 hours with few losses. In Heppenbach, the 2nd Battalion captured 125 prisoners while Company A rolled through Hepscheid on tanks to secure the bridge east of town. Both battalions pushed another 500 meters to the forested high ground overlooking Honsfeld. This success allowed the 32nd Field Artillery to move to firing positions near Moderscheid.[16]

Colonel John Seitz's CT26 enjoyed equal success. At 0200, the 3rd Battalion attacked Büllingen, with Company K on the south side of the road and Company L on the road with tanks from the 745th Tank Battalion. As the regimental after-action review noted, "When L Company ran into stubborn machine gun fire, I Company swung to the left of the pinned down company and cleared the enemy from the western outskirts of the town. By 0930 hours the town was cleared and the enemy pushed out of their positions. . . . Again, the tank dozers cleared a path for the tanks and tank destroyers to get into the town."[17] Just before midnight, Seitz sent the 2nd Battalion east to clear the woods between Büllingen and Mürringen. The next morning, the 1st Battalion joined Daniel's 2nd Battalion in an attack into Mürringen. "Resistance was spotty, and the main obstacles in the path of the battalions were the deep snow, the blown bridges at the edge of town, and the minefields before and in town." Mürringen was secured by 1000 hours, 29 January, allowing the 5th and 33rd Field Artillery Battalions to displace to firing positions in and around Büllingen.[18]

To the south the 18th Infantry resumed its attacks at 0115 hours, 30 January, against Honsfeld. Infantrymen rode into the village mounted on tanks and half-tracks. Resistance collapsed as the tanks sprayed the defenders with cannon fire and machine guns. By 0700, sixty-nine Germans had surrendered, allowing the 3rd Battalion to continue toward Hünningen.

While CT18 cleared Hünningen, on 31 January, the 2nd Battalion, 26th Infantry, made a night attack to eliminate enemy resistance between the two regiments. Once that mission was completed, the 1st Battalion, 26th Infantry, passed through the 2nd Battalion, entered the Rocherrath Forest, and moved toward the Siegfried Line. To the north, the 2nd Infantry Division overcame strong resistance in Wirtzfeld and captured Krinkelt and Rocherrath, while to the south the 82nd Airborne captured Lanzerath. These advances protected the 1st Infantry Division's flanks and allowed the Big Red One to plan a final push across the German border. By the evening of 31 January, the divisions of V and XVIII Corps had reached the fortifications of the Siegfried Line.[19]

As the 18th Infantry reached the German border, reconnaissance elements noticed German civilians digging snow out of the pillboxes of the Siegfried Line. Word of this passed quickly to XVIII Corps Artillery, which ordered 240mm and 8-inch fires placed on the pillboxes. The 26th Infantry met enemy tanks as its infantrymen approached the border, but the tank destroyers of the 634th TD Battalion drove them off. By dusk, the two leading combat teams of the division were in positions along the border and were working to bring food, armored vehicles, and ammunition up to the front. To the northwest, there was a 500-meter gap between the 1st and 2nd Infantry Divisions that the 2nd was moving to fill, while to the south the 82nd Airborne was in contact with the 18th Infantry. XVIII and V Corps prepared to penetrate the *Westwall*.[20]

At 0300, 1 February, the 1st Battalion, 26th Infantry, attacked enemy positions a mile west of Hollerath, Germany. Companies A and C got to within a quarter of a mile of Hollerath before German fire forced them to ground. The battalion commander, Major J. K. Rippert, ordered Company B to maneuver to the north to outflank the enemy, but it was halted by intense enemy fire. Finally, Rippert pulled the battalion back to the woods to the west and dug in. For the next thirty-six hours, Colonel Seitz arranged for a deliberate attack to be supported by heavy artillery, flamethrowers, and engineers with demolition charges.[21]

During 2 February, the 18th and 26th Combat Teams cleared the woods behind them of snipers and wandering patrols of Germans and brought forward tanks, flamethrowers, and bangalore torpedoes to use against pill-boxes. At the same time, the 32nd and 33rd Field Artillery Battalions moved to within range of the front lines and prepared to support an assault.[22]

On 3 February, the Big Red One launched an attack against the Siegfried Line between Hollerath and Ramscheid. To the south, the 3rd Battalion, 18th Infantry, spearheaded the advance of CT18. The leading companies ran into wire entanglements, mines, booby traps, and entrenched enemy on the high ground west of Ramscheid. As the regimental after-action report noted, "The enemy had the advantage of positions, firing his automatic weapons from reinforced bunkers and concrete pillboxes. Meanwhile, the 2nd Bat-talion had left the woods and was advancing across a clearing towards the pillboxes that surround the town." Infantry assault teams destroyed nine pillboxes, allowing the 2nd Battalion to reach its objective. The 3rd Battal-ion advanced to the north of the town and attacked it from the northeast. Surrounded and pounded by heavy fire, the Germans in Ramscheid surren-dered or died.[23]

The 26th Infantry captured Hollerath at 1230 hours. The 3rd Battalion, backed by the direct fire of self-propelled 155mm and 8-inch guns, blasted through the pillboxes and secured the high ground west of Hollerath. By 1430, the pillbox line was broken. The 1st Battalion attacked at the same time and found abandoned pillboxes, possibly reflecting the psychological effects of the heavy guns used in a direct-fire mode against bunkers. By dusk, the regiment had established positions at the crossroads east of Hollerath.[24]

The offensive of January 1945 was carried out successfully in some of the worst winter weather of the century in Western Europe. The 1st Infantry Division suffered more casualties in the January offensive than it had in its defensive fighting in December 1944. The 1st Medical Battalion's Clearing Station treated 2,114 sick and wounded soldiers in December and 2,758 in January. Many of these men returned to duty. There was a 20 percent increase in the number of men treated for disease in January, reflecting the cold-weather injuries suffered as the infantrymen waded through the deep snow and lived for days in open foxholes. The number of neuropsychiatric patients fell from 188 in December to 92 in January, while the number of injuries rose from 300 to 616.[25]

These statistics do not reflect the misery and suffering involved in the fighting. For example, men wounded during the advance were sometimes covered by snow, making it difficult to find them before they froze to death. Allen Towne, a medic serving with the 18th Infantry, described what happened in one case:

> We received [in Hünningen on 6 February] two infantrymen in the aid station who had been out in a ditch, wounded, and had been covered with snow for at least 24 hours. They were both in deep shock and, after much difficulty, we finally got the plasma needles into their veins (the veins were sunken and very small). They responded to the plasma, and we could see the color coming back into their gray faces as the plasma bottles drained. . . . This time, both men lived.[26]

There is no way of knowing how many wounded men died due to exposure and shock before they could be treated. It is truly remarkable that in such a situation the division's soldiers continued to attack. Their sacrifice helped eliminate the Bulge and initiate the final offensive against Germany, but the costs were high. First Army lost 39,672 casualties in its January operations.

The Drive to the Rhine River: February–March 1945

By the evening of 3 February, the 1st Infantry Division had punched a hole through the Siegfried Line and established defensive positions facing east. First Army then ordered the 99th Infantry Division to replace the Big Red One. Over the next five days, the division disengaged and moved north to join the 8th Infantry Division along the Roer River near Kleinau, Germany.

A week later, the 1st Infantry Division was in its new sector waiting for the floodwaters of the Roer to subside sufficiently so that the combat teams could assault across the river and drive to the west bank of the Rhine. During the move north, the troops spent a few days in rest areas to shower, change clothes, clean weapons, and maintain their vehicles.[27] The weather changed significantly in early February, as the cold snow gave way to cold rains. Trench foot remained a major problem, and movement along the narrow roads of the Hürtgen Forest remained difficult due to deep mud.[28]

While waiting for the Roer to recede, Combat Teams 16 and 26 prepared for an assault crossing between Udingen and Kreuzau, Germany. The 299th Engineer Battalion joined the division to assist the 1st Engineer Battalion with the operation. The plan called for the engineers to ferry a battalion of infantry from each combat team across the river in small M2 assault boats. Once the infantry secured the far banks, the engineers were to build treadway bridges for the armor and artillery to cross.[29] To the north, the 8th

Infantry Division was to cross at the same time. The 18th Infantry Regiment remained in an assembly area near Vicht, 15 kilometers west of the Roer. There, on 25 February, Colonel George Smith relinquished command of the regiment to Lieutenant Colonel John Williamson and became assistant division commander of the 104th Infantry Division, then commanded by Major General Terry Allen. Shortly thereafter, Smith was killed in action.[30]

By 22 February, the Roer had receded sufficiently to allow the Ninth Army to begin Operation Grenade, an assault crossing by two corps. VII Corps attacked to protect the right flank of Ninth Army. During the night of 22–23 February, six infantry divisions crossed the Roer using assault boats, infantry bridges, and powered landing craft. The swift current proved to be a major obstacle, making it difficult for the engineers to ferry the infantrymen across or get the foot and vehicle bridges built. Fortunately, the Germans failed to counterattack while the bridgeheads were vulnerable. By the evening of 23 February, all six American divisions were across, allowing them to expand their bridgeheads the next day.[31]

Bradley and Hodges capitalized on the success of the Ninth Army and VII Corps by sending III Corps across the river beginning on 25 February. However, instead of assaulting across as planned, the 1st Division sent its first troops over the Roer on the already-secured bridges of the 8th Infantry Division.[32]

The 2nd Battalion, 16th Infantry, crossed at 0830, 25 February, and moved south along the east bank to Niederau. By noon, the 3rd Battalion had reached Niederau as well. Tanks and tank destroyers accompanied the infantry while the 5th and 7th Field Artillery Battalions provided covering fire. At 1500, two infantry battalions seized Kreuzau. CT16 moved farther southeast toward Drove while the 3rd Battalion, 26th Infantry, crossed the river. As the 16th Infantry progressed south, the 1st Engineers put in bridges near Kreuzau for the 1st Battalion, 16th Infantry, and the rest of the 26th Infantry. By dark, all of CT16 was across.[33]

The next day, the remainder of the 26th Infantry crossed the river and pushed south to clear the eastern bank all the way to the Mausauel Hill, near the division's southern boundary. CT26 protected the southern flank as the other two combat teams pushed east. The 18th Infantry crossed the Roer on 26 February. The regimental combat teams encountered light resistance as they pushed to the Neffel River. By 27 February, all of the 1st Infantry Division's artillery battalions were in positions between the Roer and Neffel Rivers, and a bridgehead on the Neffel had been secured by the 18th Infantry near Dorweiller.[34]

On 1 March, the 9th Armored Division advanced on the southern flank of the 1st Infantry Division as part of a widening drive to the Rhine. By the first week of March, it was clear to most German generals that they could not stop the Allied drive short of the Rhine, but Hitler refused to allow them to conduct an orderly withdrawal. Continued bad flying weather was one of the few things that prevented Allied aircraft from turning the German's piecemeal retreat into general chaos.[35] Across the Western Front, Eisenhower's armies all were involved in the offensive to the Rhine. The major question was: Which army would be able to capture a bridge intact over the river?

By the morning of 1 March, the 1st Infantry Division was deployed along the Neffel River. Although the advance had gone well, the Germans defended nearly every village in the path of the division, and many of these fights were costly. For example, the 18th Infantry's after-action report describes the action in the town of Pingsheim, near the Neffel River, on 28 February:

> C Company . . . assaulted Pingsheim. Here the company encountered stiff enemy resistance. C Company was pinned down in open flat terrain outside the town after having a meeting engagement with an enemy company. Slowly driving the enemy before them, suffering severe losses which deprived the unit of many of its leaders, the company encountered the main defenses of the town. When C Company finally managed to enter the town, B Company was sent to aid in the final assault. This company attacked the town from the east and forced the garrison of two officers and 126 men to surrender.[36]

The division continued toward the Rhine between Cologne and Bonn for the next five days. The 18th and 26th Combat Teams forced crossings of the Neffel and pushed to the Erft Canal, which they reached by 4 March. A task force of tanks and infantry from the 18th Infantry and the 745th Tank Battalion protected the division's left flank as it advanced, while the 26th Infantry protected the right flank (Map 23). On 4 March, the 18th Cavalry Reconnaissance Squadron took over CT18's left-flank mission, allowing the 18th to rest its troops for two days in an assembly area near Norvenich.[37]

On 6 March, the 1st Infantry Division turned southeast to seize Bonn and the crossings of the Ahr River. Andrus ordered the 16th and 18th Combat Teams to capture Bonn while CT26 protected the division's left flank. On 7 March, the division advanced to within 4 kilometers of Bonn and prepared for the final assault on the city.

The enemy situation in Bonn was unclear. The Rhine bridge was still intact, and numerous German units and refugees were using it to escape to the east side of the river. There were reports that remnants of the *1st SS Panzer Division* were in the area, and the regimental commanders of the 16th and 18th Infantry Regiments, Colonel Gibb and Lieutenant Colonel Williamson,

Map 23. The reduction of the Ruhr Pocket and advance to the Elbe and Mulde Rivers, 5–18 April 1945. The 1st Infantry Division locations from Belgium and the Rhineland to Czechoslovakia included Namur, Liège, Aachen, Düren, Bonn, Remagen, Siegen, Lippstadt, Paderborn, the Harz Mountains, Halle, Plauen, Hof, and Karlsbad. This map also includes the Cold War locations of Aschaffenburg, Würzburg, Schweinfurt, and Bamberg. (US Military Academy map)

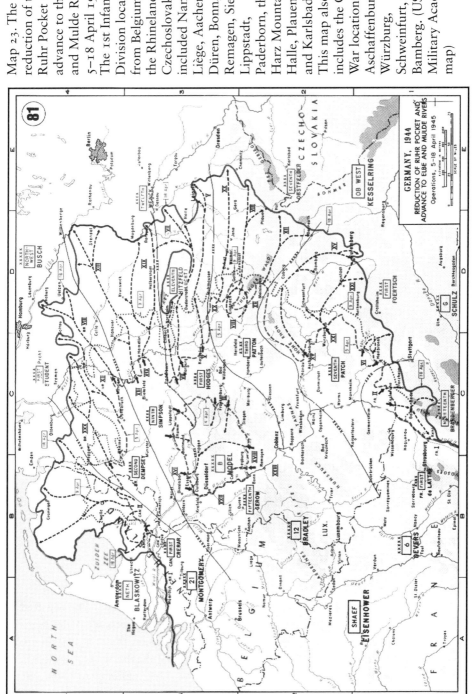

anticipated that the roads into the place would be defended by the usual array of machine-gun nests, minefields, and antiaircraft units with 20mm and 88mm guns used in a direct-fire mode.

Gibb's CT16 attacked at 0400, 8 March, without artillery preparatory fires, hoping to surprise the enemy. The 1st and 3rd Battalions, 16th Infantry, moved in two columns down two main roads into Bonn. The 3rd Battalion made it to the city's center and the bank of the Rhine before stirring up much resistance, securing its objectives by dawn. The 1st Battalion had a little less luck, but by noon it also was at its objectives in the heart of the city. A contemporary account of the 16th Infantry's advance noted: "So successful was the night attack that American soldiers mingled freely with German soldiers who never knew what was going on. One German asked what panzer division was moving down the road. In many instances, sentries were disarmed before they knew what was happening."[38] For the next twenty-four hours, the two battalions held positions in Bonn, and the 2nd Battalion, 16th Infantry, moved forward to protect their lines of communications.

To the south, CT18 had to fight through a series of small villages to reach Bonn. The 1st Battalion, 18th Infantry, accompanied by tanks and self-propelled tank destroyers, moved forward at first light and by 0930 had cleared Duisdorf. Williamson next maneuvered the 2nd Battalion, 18th Infantry, around 1st Battalion to secure Endernich. After securing the villages of Odehoven and Gielsdorf, the 18th Infantry made contact with the 16th in the suburb of Alfter. The next morning, Williamson committed the 3rd Battalion for the final drive into Bonn.[39]

By noon, the 1st Infantry Division had secured Bonn. Unfortunately, the Germans blew up the bridge over the Rhine. Andrus gave the 18th Infantry responsibility for control of the city, with 1st Recon Troop attached for the mission. The 1st Engineer Battalion spent the next few days clearing rubble and mines from the roads and streets. CT26 and the 18th Cavalry Group secured the left bank of the Rhine north of Bonn. For the next five days, the division remained in place.[40]

The Integration of African Americans into the 1st Division

As the division fought to the Rhine, it received thousands of replacements. In March 1945, 81 officers and 2,779 enlisted soldiers joined the Big Red One. This was not unusual—the division had received replacements regularly throughout the war. However, on 10 March 1945, the first of three infantry platoons of African American soldiers joined the division, integrating, for the first time, white combat units. Each infantry regiment received one platoon of blacks who had volunteered for frontline service as infantrymen.

The US armed forces essentially remained racially segregated during World War II, with 800,000 blacks serving mostly in service and combat service units. Also, by late 1944, a number of segregated African American combat units, including the 92nd Division in Italy and the 761st Tank Battalion in Third Army, had served in combat. Although black units with white and black officers had served for years, truly integrated units did not exist.[41]

A severe shortage of infantry replacements in the European Theater, however, developed in the fall of 1944. The losses suffered in the Battle of the Bulge exacerbated this shortage of infantrymen, and Eisenhower's counteroffensive promised to continue the high loss of infantrymen. The army, however, could not train enough white soldiers to fill the need for infantrymen in 1944–1945. Therefore, during the fall of 1944, Eisenhower ordered General J. C. H. Lee, commanding general of the Communications Zone (COMZ) of the European Theater, to select white soldiers from service units in the COMZ for retraining as infantry replacements. Lee did so, but even with an aggressive culling process of able-bodied men, too few white replacements were found to fill the shortage of infantrymen. In December, Lee proposed to Eisenhower that black soldiers then serving in the COMZ should be offered a chance to volunteer to serve as combat soldiers in all-white divisions. Eisenhower approved this proposal.

The response by African Americans was heartening. By February, 4,562 African American soldiers had volunteered, including many noncommissioned officers willing to accept a reduction in rank for the privilege of serving as infantrymen. These men were organized into platoons and sent to the 16th Retraining Depot at Compiègne, France, for a course in weapons training. The platoon leaders and sergeants were white combat veterans from those divisions willing to accept the service of black infantrymen.

According to their depot commander, the black volunteers "approached their work with a will." Once trained, the new infantrymen were made available in platoons. The first thirty-seven platoons were ready for assignment by 1 March 1945. On 10 March, twenty-five platoons joined First Army divisions, including the Big Red One.[42]

The first platoon to arrive in the division was assigned to Company K, 26th Infantry. Lieutenant Frank Leggett and Staff Sergeant Boheen served as platoon leader and platoon sergeant. The leaders selected to lead the African American platoons were, according to General Albert H. Smith, "the most experienced young infantry leaders available." The 16th and 18th Infantry Regiments received their platoons of black soldiers on 12 March, when they joined those regiments' B Companies. The replacements received their division shoulder patches immediately.[43] For the next three days, the black soldiers underwent the same refresher training given to all of the division's infantrymen in assembly areas near Bonn.

The new platoons accompanied their regiments into the Remagen Bridgehead and took part in First Army's offensive from 17 to 24 March. They did well in combat. In its first action, the soldiers of the Fourth Platoon, Company B, 18th Infantry, inflicted "great casualties on the enemy, capturing many prisoners and had only one casualty themselves." In their next action, the platoon was involved in a very heavy firefight. Although a number of black soldiers and their platoon leader were wounded, the platoon held its positions until ordered to retreat with the rest of the company.[44]

The story was the same in the division's other regiments. On 3 April, the Fourth Platoon, Company K, 26th Infantry, overwhelmed an enemy 20mm gun crew, killing four and capturing two Germans. This platoon continued to fight well to the end of the war, with conspicuous success at Krugsreuth, in the Harz Mountains, on 29 April, where it cleared the town and captured ten Germans.[45] Unfortunately, at least some members of the African American platoons experienced racist prejudice in the division. For example, when Bruce M. Wright and the other members of a black platoon joined the 26th Infantry, one white captain said, "I never thought I'd live to see the day when a nigger would wear the Big Red One."[46] Wright earned two Purple Hearts in the war, including one as a medic on Omaha Beach, on 6 June 1944, and the other when wounded in Germany, where he also earned the Bronze Star. After the war, he graduated from New York Law School and eventually became a justice on the New York State Supreme Court.[47]

Some of the soldiers, at least, were pleased to have the replacements, and many leaders and soldiers welcomed them as full members of the division. The 18th Infantry's history concluded that African Americans' "action in the battles that followed was comparable to that of the other platoons of the regiment . . . and a source of deep pride to its members."[48]

The Crossing of the Rhine and the Ruhr Pocket

As First Army approached the Rhine in March, Bradley instructed Hodges to clear the river's left bank to a junction with Patton's Third Army and then hold the line of the Rhine until the 21st Army Group launched its carefully planned assault over the river to the north.[49]

As First Army approached the Rhine, the Germans blew the bridges. Then, through a series of mishaps and misfortunes on the part of the Germans, and through the initiative of a number of American soldiers, the leading armored task force of 9th Armored Division captured the Ludendorff railroad bridge at Remagen intact, on 7 March. When III Corps headquarters was informed that Brigadier General William Hoge's combat command was sending its lead company, commanded by Lieutenant Karl Timmerman, across the span, the reaction was immediate. III Corps notified First Army, and First Army began to shift every available engineering resource to support the establishment of a bridgehead over the Rhine. Lieutenant Timmerman got across the bridge in spite of the Germans' exploding of preplaced demolitions. Amazingly, the bridge was thrown straight up with the blast, but settled back onto its supports, allowing Timmerman to be the first Allied soldier across the Rhine and for his company, from the 27th Armored Infantry Battalion, to secure the abutments on the far shore.[50]

During the next twenty-four hours, 8,000 American troops crossed the bridge, and every available antiaircraft unit was sent to the area to protect the crossing. Lacking reserves, the Germans failed to eliminate the expanding bridgehead and, by 11 March, were barely holding a defensive line 5 kilometers east of the river using a hodgepodge of units, including remnants of *Panzer Lehr Division* (300 men, 15 tanks), *9th Panzer Division* (600 men, 15 tanks), and *106th Panzer Brigade* (5 tanks). The *11th Panzer Division*, with 4,000 men and 25 tanks, was promised to the commander, General Fritz Bayerlein, but it became stranded for several days near Düsseldorf due to lack of fuel (Map 23).[51]

On 15 and 16 March, the 1st Infantry Division was shifted to VII Corps and crossed the Rhine. Although the Ludendorff Bridge collapsed shortly thereafter, the engineers had sufficient pontoon bridges and ferries in operation to continue the buildup east of the river. On 13 March, Eisenhower decided to have First Army serve as the southern pincer of a massive encirclement of the Ruhr industrial area in support of Montgomery's 21st Army Group's offensive north of the Ruhr. Hodges moved his most aggressive corps commander, Joe Collins, across the Rhine to lead the attack.[52]

The 1st Infantry Division's mission was to occupy positions on the right of the 78th Infantry Division and then attack to expand the bridgehead eastward. CT18 and CT26 moved across the Rhine on 15 March and occupied positions formerly held by the 78th. The 16th Infantry and the division's artillery followed during the next two days, establishing assembly areas and firing positions near the towns of Honnef and Rheinbreitach.[53]

On 17 March, Combat Teams 18 and 26 attacked the high ground near Orscheid and Grafenhoven. The main resistance to the advance was the difficult terrain and German artillery. Heavy concentrations of counterbattery fire suppressed the enemy artillery, allowing the infantry battalions to maneuver against the villages and hilltops critical to the advance. By the next morning, both infantry regiments had secured their objectives. During the next two days, VII Corps continued to push the 78th, 1st, and 104th

Infantry Divisions forward in a series of attacks that advanced the lines about a kilometer a day.

In the face of this offensive, the Germans stripped armor from other parts of their front and prepared a counterattack.[54] However, in the face of the continuing American attacks, the enemy found it necessary to commit his armor piecemeal. When the Germans launched counterattacks on 23 and 24 March, they lacked sufficient power to require more than the commitment of local reserves by the 1st Infantry Division to stop them. In fact, in the face of these German attacks, all three of VII Corps' divisions continued to gain ground.[55]

The 78th Infantry Division reached the Sieg River on 21 March, and Hodges and Collins agreed that the time was ripe to launch the 3rd Armored Division through a line of departure held by CT18. The plan called for the 3rd Armored to crash through the thin German defenses and move rapidly east toward Marburg. The 78th Division was to protect the left flank from the Rhine to the Cologne-Frankfurt autobahn, and the 1st and 104th Infantry Divisions were to move behind the 3rd Armored Division, with the 1st Division on the left (north).[56]

The 1st Infantry Division organized for this drive with its normal three combat teams. Each team was built around an infantry regiment, with a company of tanks and another of self-propelled tank destroyers from the 745th Tank and the 634th TD Battalions attached. The three 105mm howitzer battalions continued to support their habitual regimental teams, the 7th Artillery with the 16th Infantry, the 32nd with the 18th, and the 33rd with the 26th Infantry. A platoon of engineers from the 1st Engineers served with each team, and the remainder of the engineer and the medical battalions joined the 1st Recon, the 1st Signal, and the 1st Quartermaster Companies as Division Troops. The Division Artillery controlled the 5th Field Artillery Battalion with its 155mm howitzers, as well as two attached battalions of medium artillery (the 193rd and the 957th Artillery Battalions).[57]

The Ruhr Pocket: 25 March–17 April 1945

The offensive to encircle the Ruhr region began on 25 March (see Map 23). The 3rd Armored Division smashed through the porous German lines and rolled 12 miles east on the first day. The 16th and 18th Infantry Regiments facilitated this advance by securing the line of departure and by pushing northeast along the Sieg River. Although the Germans were heavily overmatched, the fighting remained often intense at the small-unit level. For example, CT18 repulsed a dozen counterattacks on 24 and 25 March. The history of the 18th Infantry Regiment considers this battle, near the village of Ukerath, "the last of its kind in the war." Nonetheless, after repulsing two counterattacks, the 18th Infantry, reinforced by the 3rd Battalion, 26th Infantry, captured Ukerath and secured the line of departure.[58]

To the left of the 18th Infantry, CT16 pushed to the Sieg River and then moved east, leapfrogging battalions as it moved. The regiment's history notes:

> The fighting was beginning to be some of the heaviest the 16th had had since Hamich. . . . The fighting for a few minutes was at extremely close range. A platoon leader killed a German, with his Tommy gun, so near him that the dying man fell on top of the lieutenant who was crouched in a ditch. . . . Close teamwork between the First and the Third Battalions saved the Third from a severe counterattack. B [Company, 1st Battalion,] adjusted heavy [artillery] fire on the enemy, breaking the formations before they could start an attack.[59]

The Division Artillery played a critical role in this push. The 7th Field Artillery Battalion fired an average of 1,500 rounds per day of 105mm to support CT16, from 22 to 26 March. The 5th Field Artillery fired nearly 3,000 rounds in the same period.[60] The artillery broke up most enemy counterattacks before they could get to the American positions, and the tanks and tank destroyers with each team added a final punch to the rifle and machine-gun fire of the infantrymen.

Most German resistance in front of First Army collapsed on 26 March, allowing a race to begin to encircle the Ruhr before *Army Group B* could escape. To the north, the Ninth Army crossed the Rhine and crashed eastward against an increasingly disorganized enemy (see Map 23). As the 3rd Armored Division continued its drive, General Andrus deftly leapfrogged the 1st Infantry Division's combat teams along the Sieg River to prevent the enemy from striking south into the flank. Behind the division, the 4th Armored Cavalry Group entered the line, freeing troops of the 1st Infantry Division for further movement. By 28 March, the 3rd Armored Division had crossed the Lahn River at Marburg, over 90 kilometers from the line of departure. On 30 March, CT18 entered Siegen as the VII Corps hooked to the north toward Paderborn.[61] The next day, Ninth Army and First Army closed the Ruhr Pocket near Lippstadt.

During the first week of April, the division moved to the eastern end of the Ruhr Pocket to prevent the escape of the enemy. By 4 April, the division was relieved of this role and rejoined VII Corps for the drive across Germany to the Elbe River. On 15 April, Field Marshal Walter Model ordered all boys and old men in *Army Group B* to drop their weapons and head for home. Fighting in the Ruhr Pocket ended on 18 April, as over 317,000 Germans surrendered. The Ninth and First Armies lost roughly 1,500 men killed and 8,000 wounded in this triumph.[62]

The Final Push

After the Ruhr Pocket closed, the 1st Infantry Division moved to the Weser River to establish a bridgehead for the 3rd Armored Division. All units were motorized or mechanized by this time, making the 65-mile move east fairly easy. During this move, Lieutenant Colonel Frank Murdoch assumed command of the 26th Infantry as Colonel Seitz moved to the 69th Infantry Division.[63]

During the afternoon of 8 April, Combat Teams 16 and 18 crossed the Weser in assault boats. The 16th Infantry secured Furstenberg and the high ground nearby, encountering light resistance. The 3rd Battalion, 18th Infantry, crossed near Lauenforde without meeting any resistance. Engineers established bridges, allowing the armor and artillery to cross the next morning. The 3rd Armored Division then passed through and drove east alongside the 104th Infantry Division, following a route south of the Harz Mountains through Nordhausen and Sangerhausen toward Halle. The 1st Infantry Division received the mission of clearing enemy forces out of the Harz Mountains.[64]

As the VII Corps crossed the Weser, on 8 April, Hitler ordered the *Eleventh Army* to hold a line along the Leine River, between Göttingen and Northeim, while the *Twelfth Army* moved into the Harz Mountains from where it was to counterattack against the First Army. These grandiose goals were unattainable. On 9 April, the 3rd Armored Division crossed the Leine near Northeim, followed closely by the 1st Division. On 10 April, the Big Red One began the task of clearing the Harz Mountains.

CT26 moved through the mountains on the northern flank, while CT16 was in the center and CT18 moved along the southern part of the sector. The terrain was heavily forested with many villages. Movement was confined to the sparse road network, with crossroads and villages as the daily objectives of the battalion task forces. The Germans built numerous roadblocks of trees and boulders, but most were not defended. Periodically, the combat teams ran into entrenched German infantrymen supported by tanks, forcing the lead company to deploy tanks and tank destroyers to cover its infantrymen as they cleared out the German positions. Once a roadblock area was secured, engineers removed the barrier and mines, allowing the column to advance. For the next two weeks, the division fought its way through the Harz Mountains, finishing its mission on 25 April. The combat teams captured thousands of prisoners, in the process destroying the *Twelfth Army*.[65]

Since most resistance was overcome by the infantry and armor teams, the artillery battalions fired few missions each day, especially after the division crossed the Weser and Leine Rivers. Casualties in the artillery battalions were very light, with a total of two men killed and nine wounded in the 5th, 7th, and 32nd Field Artillery Battalions in April.[66] The engineers, in contrast, worked nearly around the clock clearing roadblocks and mines and maintaining roads.

On 30 April, after five days of rest in assembly areas in Thuringia, the division moved 150 miles south to join V Corps along the Czechoslovakian border. The combat teams deployed along a line from near Hof (CT26), to Selb (CT16), to Cheb (CT18). During the first five days of May, the combat teams restricted their activities to patrolling and to capturing thousands of Germans fleeing to the west. On 5 May, the division attacked toward Karlsbad, Czechoslovakia. For two days, the infantry-tank teams moved forward against light opposition, until receiving orders to cease hostilities at 0815 hours, 7 May 1945. This order was accompanied by the wonderful news that the German forces had surrendered, effective 8 May.

The Big Red One had played an important role in the "Last Offensive." After holding the northern shoulder of the Bulge in December, the division counterattacked to drive the enemy back to its starting line. At the end of January, the division carved a hole through the Siegfried Line and took part in the offensive across the Roer. In March, the division pushed to the Rhine, captured Bonn, and entered the Remagen bridgehead, to play an important part in the breakout achieved by First Army. From then until the end of the war the Fighting First helped close the Ruhr Pocket, seized crossings over the Weser, and drove through the Harz Mountains. During these operations, the division captured tens of thousands of prisoners and cleared hundreds of towns and villages of remnants of the Wehrmacht.

Summing Up

The 1st Infantry Division had been overseas since the summer of 1942 and had served in 443 days of combat. During that time, it took part in three amphibious assaults and earned battle streamers for its flag in recognition of its role in the campaigns in Algeria–French Morocco, Tunisia, Sicily, Normandy, northern France, Ardennes-Alsace, Rhineland, and Central Europe. The division's losses totaled 21,023 men, with 4,325 dead, 1,241 missing, and 15,457 wounded. Roughly 9,600 of the wounded returned to duty. The initial strength of the division of 14,851 was maintained during the war by 28,892 replacements.[67]

The 1st Infantry Division had superb senior leadership throughout the war. Terry de la Mesa Allen and Theodore Roosevelt Jr. prepared the division for its operations in North Africa and Sicily and led it through the Battles of El Guettar and Gela. Clarence Huebner and Willard Wyman trained the Big Red One for its date with destiny on D-day and led it from the breakout at Cobra to the capture of Aachen. Finally, Clift Andrus and George Taylor guided the division through the Battle of the Bulge and the "Last Offensive" across Germany.

These officers were first-rate leaders. But it was the regimental, battalion, company, and platoon leaders who ensured that the division accomplished its missions. Throughout the war, these officers and noncommissioned officers trained the soldiers, maneuvered the companies and platoons against the enemy, and captured or held the ground needed for victory. From Arzew to Troina, from Normandy to the Harz Mountains, these leaders accomplished the most difficult of combat tasks.

The heart of every military unit, however, is its enlisted soldiers. The men of the Big Red One performed magnificently throughout the war. They pioneered amphibious warfare for the US Army; they carried out three assault landings; they faced down the *Hermann Goering Panzer Division* at Gela; they led the way ashore on Omaha Beach; and they pushed through the Hürtgen Forest. In the process, 16 soldiers earned the Medal of Honor (nine posthumously), 161 received the Distinguished Service Cross, and over 21,000 earned the Purple Heart.[68] But these statistics do not indicate the full scope of the soldiers' courage and fortitude. The way in which the men of the division stoically endured the miserable conditions of a Tunisian winter, of a Normandy summer, and of a Hürtgen autumn is beyond belief. The soldiers' steadiness under fire as German tanks attacked the infantry at El Guettar, Gela, Aachen, and Bütgenbach was incredible. These actions testify to the courage and commitment of the 43,743 soldiers who made up the Big Red One in World War II.

13

The Occupation of Germany
and the Cold War

ON THE MORNING OF 7 MAY 1945, the 1st Infantry Division received a message: "The Supreme German High Command has signed surrender terms of all land, sea, and air forces to take effect at 0001, 9 May 1945. No more offensive action will be taken."[1] When the 26th Infantry requested permission to move a battalion into the next town to its front, the division operations officer refused permission and informed the regiment that "the CG does not want to jeopardize the life of another soldier."[2]

With the end of hostilities in Europe, most Americans anticipated that the troops would be coming home soon. Few Americans envisioned the commitment that was to be made by the United States to protect the security of Western Europe. And yet, in 1945, the US Army was a critical component of American European policy. Within the next few years, it became evident to the Harry Truman administration that the United States needed to deter Soviet aggression in Europe. The only way to do that was to commit armed forces to Europe to bolster the political morale and military capabilities of regional allies. The US Army was to remain the heart of the American commitment in Europe as the Cold War developed in the late 1940s and early 1950s. Central to the army in postwar Europe for the next eleven years was the Big Red One.

Operation Eclipse: Disarming the Enemy

When the war in Europe ended, the 1st Infantry Division helped execute Operation Eclipse. Operation Eclipse was the plan to disarm the Wehrmacht, enforce the terms of a German surrender, establish law and order in occupied territories, and redistribute the Allied forces into the occupation zones agreed to at the Yalta Conference. The operation included the tasks of caring for and repatriating displaced persons and former prisoners of war and the apprehension of war criminals.[3]

By 9 May, the 1st Infantry Division had created reception areas on the roads into the division's sector from the east and a concentration area on the western side of its front lines where POWs, displaced persons, and former Allied POWs could be sorted out. The infantry regiments maintained

355

a continuous front to prevent unauthorized people from moving into Germany and operated reception stations to control the flow of people. No one anticipated the magnitude of the operation, and there was little guidance about who to let through and who to turn back to Czechoslovakia.[4]

The magnitude of the migration under way in Europe in 1945 was staggering. Over seven million German soldiers surrendered to the Western Allies in April and May. Another two million were captured by the Russians. The British and American armies had to deal with at least 6 million non-Germans who had performed forced labor in Germany, most of whom wanted to go home. More than two million former Allied POWs were scattered across the former Reich, and several million ethnic Germans were fleeing from the Soviet advance in the east. Finally, hundreds of thousands of former concentration camp inmates needed immediate medical care and food.[5] The 1st Infantry Division found itself dealing with most of these categories of people.

The 26th Infantry Regiment's reception center quickly filled with POWs. As the regimental after-action report notes, "All day long [on 9 May] and far into the night they streamed into the reception center at Schonbach using every means of locomotion known to man—by foot, horse drawn carts, bicycles, motorcycles, automobiles and even by plane. Within the next few days over 25,000 dirty, bedraggled Germans found their way up the hill into the reception center."[6] At the reception station, the regiment disarmed the enemy, sprayed them with DDT to deter typhus, and then sent them on to the concentration area where they were to be sorted. The 18th Infantry reported that it processed 18,000 POWs in its center, while the 16th Infantry received 27,000 prisoners, including 300 women, on 9 May alone.[7]

During the next week, the division aided thousands of wounded German soldiers who had been evacuated from Prague to protect them from the Red Army. The 1st Medical Battalion provided as much help as it could, but the division had inadequate capabilities to care for so many wounded. Women and children accompanied the German army as well, and no one knew what the policy was toward them. Finally, after a flurry of messages, V Corps ordered the division to keep the women and children in the reception stations until a special camp was established for them.[8]

Meanwhile, Eisenhower's headquarters dealt with the issues of what to do with displaced persons, fleeing civilians, and POWs. Those Germans east of the boundaries of the American and British zones of occupation were disarmed by the Red Army. Germans fleeing from eastern Germany were turned away by the British and Americans and told to return to the Soviet zone. Foreign workers in Germany were repatriated. POWs captured before the surrender were disarmed and screened to identify SS troops, General

Staff officers, and suspected war criminals. POWs not in those categories were released to go home as soon as possible. Members of the SS, General Staff officers, and suspected war criminals were kept in custody for further interrogations. After the surrender of the Wehrmacht, those German soldiers not already POWs were disarmed and treated as disarmed enemy troops. By labeling them disarmed enemy troops, rather than POWs, the Allies did not have to feed them. If they had been classified as POWs, they would have been entitled by the Geneva Conventions to the same rations received by Allied soldiers. This would have posed a severe logistics problem for the Allied armies.[9]

On 11 May, the 1st Infantry Division established a 5-mile-wide buffer zone between American and Soviet forces. No more Germans were allowed to pass through American lines. This posed a humanitarian problem to the men of the Big Red One. There were thousands of civilians in the neutral zone in front of the division, along with an estimated 50,000 German soldiers. Many of these people expressed, as the Division G3 reported to V Corps, "their panic over the approaching Russians."[10] In addition, thousands of wounded German soldiers remained in hospitals between Cheb and Karlsbad, and it was feared that the Russians would not treat these men in accordance with the Geneva Conventions. On 12 May, however, V Corps repeated its order to the division that "you will process what POWs you have behind our lines but you will take no more." It was necessary for the corps to send another message to the division, shortly thereafter, reiterating that "under no conditions are displaced civilians or enemy to come through our lines."[11]

During May and June, the Allies processed and released most of the German soldiers held in western Germany. The first to go home were farmers, coal miners, and transport workers to get the German economy in operation before winter. On 18 May, POWs over fifty years of age were released except for the excluded categories, and in late June the Allies discharged all German POWs except for the special category personnel. Those Germans held by the Western Allies whose homes were in the Soviet zone were kept until an agreement was reached with the Soviet authorities for their return.[12]

The Allies kept over 100,000 suspected SS personnel and war criminals in custody for at least another year. Prosecutors reviewed their records and interviewed witnesses to determine who would stand trial as major criminals and who would be released to German courts for judgment as minor criminals. Ultimately an International Military Tribunal tried sixty-three leading war criminals in Nuremberg, and German courts dealt with thousands of lesser criminals.[13] Allied prosecutors opened 3,887 case files for suspected major war criminals. They tried 1,672 of these people in Allied military courts: 878 were convicted of mass atrocities and 538 were found guilty of lesser offenses.[14]

The occupation governments hoped that the displaced person burden would disappear as people returned to their homes. Unfortunately, the rise of Communist tyranny in Eastern Europe drove a stream of refugees across the occupation zones' borders. This flow of humanity was joined by hundreds of thousands of Jews who had survived the death camps and sought refuge in the United States or Palestine. Refugees of German ethnicity became the responsibility of the German people. Jews and other foreign nationals remained the responsibility of the Allied authorities. As late as 1950, 101,631 displaced persons were in camps and another 71,000 lived in the German community. These uprooted people posed a major threat to law and order in western Germany.[15]

The 1st Infantry Division remained along the Czech-German border until early June. The Division Artillery processed at least 70,000 German POWs and 15,000 former Allied POWs. Unknown numbers of civilians passed through the division's sector as well. Most of the division's part in Eclipse was completed by 20 May. From then until 5 June, General Andrus kept the troops occupied with limited tactical training, awards ceremonies, and athletics. The 1st Battalion, 18th Infantry, received the Distinguished Unit Citation for its actions in Normandy. The 3rd Battalion, 18th Infantry, received the same award for its defense of Crucifix Hill in October. Staff Sergeant Max Thompson received the Medal of Honor for his action near Haaren, Germany, in October 1944.[16]

All in all, as Colonel John Williamson concluded in the 18th Infantry's after-action report, "May 1945 was a glorious month . . . for it saw the 18th Infantry reach its final objective and accomplish its mission in the War of Europe and stand among so few Regiments who, from the campaigns in Africa, fought and fulfilled their role in bringing the greatest military force known to time to its knees in complete and final victory."[17]

Demobilization

The most important thing that happened to the Big Red One in late May 1945 was the departure of the first contingent of men from the division to the United States to be demobilized.[18] When the war ended, the army had a system to award demobilization points to soldiers according to the length of their time in the service (1 point per month), time overseas (1 point per month), number of children under eighteen (12 points each up to 36), and awards they had received (5 points each). Soldiers with 85 or more points, as of 12 May 1945, were to be sent home first. Men with fewer than 85 points were eligible to remain in Germany with the occupation forces or to be shipped to the Pacific Theater to fight the Japanese.[19]

Eisenhower hoped that his command would have a month to organize the redeployment of divisions to the Pacific and the United States. However, on 8 May, the War Department announced that the process would begin on 12 May, with at least 17,500 men to return home for discharge in May and another 35,000 in June. Marshall made this announcement early because of the pressures from the public and Congress to get the boys home. As Marshall told Eisenhower, "I fear that the weight of public opinion in the U.S. will be such that unless the task is handled properly we may be forced to take measures that will interfere with redeployment and result in a prolongation of the Japanese war."[20]

Between 5 and 8 June, the 1st Infantry Division was relieved of its responsibilities along the border and deployed to occupation duties in Bavaria. Men with 85 points and higher were pulled out of the division and sent to a large assembly area near Châlons-sur-Marne, France, and assigned to divisions headed to the United States. Nearly 90,000 men redeployed from Europe to the United States in May, greatly exceeding the target of 17,500. Supreme Headquarters Allied Expeditionary Force (SHAEF) allowed those soldiers to carry war trophies home, with the exception of explosives and nonmilitary articles removed from enemy dead. War trophies included German weapons, and the 5,000 men of one of the first units shipped home (the 28th Infantry Division) carried 20,000 souvenir weapons back to the United States.[21]

There were over three million American troops in the European Theater in May 1945. In May and June, 402,459 soldiers departed, with 23,479 going directly to the Pacific and another 187,220 heading to the Pacific through the United States. Over 191,000 men shipped out for the United States to be discharged. In July, 391,910 soldiers left Europe, with 72,238 going to the Pacific and 227,141 destined there after a stay in the United States. The remaining 91,679 soldiers went home to be discharged. In this process, two army group headquarters, six corps headquarters, and thirteen divisions left Europe by the end of July.[22] The 1st Infantry Division became part of the occupation force that was to remain in Germany.[23]

The division felt the impact of demobilization immediately. A large percentage of its veterans left in the first three months after the victory in Europe. Men with lower points joined the division from units that had been selected to redeploy. It was not until October that the 1st Infantry Division received a few replacements from the United States who had been drafted before the war ended. As a result, the cohesion and the combat readiness of the Big Red One steadily declined. The division, however, had little time to train the new men, making it hard to integrate them into its units.

By the end of the summer, the division was fully employed as occupation troops. The infantry regiments and Division Artillery were assigned areas of responsibility scattered from Aschaffenburg to Nuremberg (Map 24). For example, the 5th Artillery Battalion was quartered in Ansbach, where it operated a POW center. In September, the 5th Artillery moved to Ober-dachstetten to join the 1st Engineer Combat Battalion and the 701st Ordnance Company for occupation duties in *Landkreise* (administrative district) Ansbach. On 15 November 1945, the 5th Artillery moved to Aschaffen-burg and assumed control of the *Landkreise* of Alzenau and Aschaffenburg, where it operated four displaced persons camps. The battalion's after-action report notes: "Throughout the period [of October through December], redeployment of personnel continued, attended by a serious shortage of both officers and enlisted personnel which was not relieved until the last week of the period."[24]

Throughout the fall, the strength of the US Army in Europe declined. By 1 January 1946, over 2.5 million troops had departed, leaving 622,789 American soldiers in Europe.[25] By then, the 1st Infantry Division was dispersed as part of an occupation force that initially was expected to be about 400,000 men.[26] During the next six months, the War Department reduced the occupation force to roughly 200,000 men. The US forces in Germany were to consist of three infantry divisions and a mobile police force.[27] The changes in occupation troop levels made it difficult for commanders to plan for the training, housing, and support of these forces.

The Early Occupation of Germany: 1945–1946

The US Army had been preparing for the occupation of Germany since 1940. In an attempt to profit from the army's experiences as an occupation force in Germany from 1918 to 1923, the army judge advocate general, Major General Allen Gullim, prepared Field Manual 27–5, *Military Government* (1940), to guide the planning for the occupation of future enemy nations. In 1942, an army school of government opened at the University of Virginia to train military occupation administrators. By the fall of 1942, the army was involved in the governance of North Africa, and army civil affairs teams accompanied Patton's army and the 1st Infantry Division into Sicily. Although the army underestimated the difficulties of its occupation tasks in Germany, it at least had trained several thousand civil affairs officers to direct military government.[28]

Map 24. The occupation zone of the 1st Infantry Division in Germany and Austria, 1947. Grafenwöhr would be a training area throughout the Cold War. (H. R. Knickerbocker et al., *Danger Forward* [Society of the 1st Division, 1947])

When the Allies overran the Rhineland, the Fifteenth Army assumed control of the occupation, using civil affairs teams to control and feed the German population.[29] Once the war ended, all German government ceased, the German military was disbanded, and the German police forces were disarmed. Operation Eclipse was intended to prevent disorder and to facilitate the establishment of the military occupation of Germany. The 1st Infantry Division found itself scattered across a large region supporting the civil affairs teams of the military government.[30]

The 18th Infantry Regiment established its headquarters in Scheinfeld, with its 2nd Battalion around Würzburg and its 1st Battalion detached for service in Nuremberg. The 18th Infantry operated three POW camps and provided the general security for the countryside. The regiment's after-action report explains: "The primary mission of occupation was again carried out. Road blocks, road patrols and security checks were maintained. 'Double Check,' a coordinated security check and search operation in two phases, was carried out within the entire Regimental area. Illegal possession of US property and lack of proper identification were the primary things of importance uncovered. Work projects for winterizing all troop billets, PW Camps and Displaced Persons Camps were receiving full attention."[31]

The 16th Infantry occupied *Landkreis* Bamberg. The regiment secured ammunition dumps in Bamberg and Breitengüssbach. It ran POW compounds in Bamberg, Adelsdorf, and Neuhaus and a displaced persons camp in Bamberg. The troops carried out an extensive program of clearing enemy ammunition, weapons, and wrecked vehicles from their areas of responsibility. The regiment's after-action report notes: "In no cases was it necessary to employ troops to subdue armed resistance, riots, or insurrections by the civilian population."[32]

The 26th Infantry Regiment occupied Nuremberg. The regiment protected the court of justice established by the Allies to try the most notorious of the war criminals. At the end of December, the regimental history reported the regiment's accomplishments:

The intensive campaign to provide the Nurnberg Area with sufficient fire wood has been completed. Repairing the buildings and maintaining security for the installations and personnel of the Office of Chief of Council [of the war crime trials] continues. The rubble clearance program continues in the operation of about fifteen kilometers of narrow gauge railroad. As all first and second priority roads have been cleared, it is intended that rubble clearance be given over gradually to civilian agencies.[33]

As winter approached, the division distributed food and fuel to displaced persons and POW camps. The troops supervised German prisoners in road repair work and assisted the military government in enforcing curfews and occupation regulations. The division also was responsible for the management of Jewish displaced persons.[34] Personnel shortages, turbulence, occupation duties, and dispersion made command and control and tactical training difficult.[35]

Relations of the occupation troops with the German population evolved during the occupation. From September 1944 to May 1945, SHAEF maintained a strict "nonfraternization" policy between the troops and the enemy population. All social contact was forbidden. American soldiers were to talk to Germans only while on duty and to restrict all contact to official business.[36]

After 8 May 1945, the army found it difficult to maintain a nonfraternization policy. News reports that implied that American soldiers were coddling the enemy population, even women and children, brought complaints from American politicians and the Truman administration. The army intensified efforts to convince the soldiers that all Germans were war criminals and that it was a security risk to have social contacts with them. But it was impossible to enforce the strict separation policy. Many GIs found it difficult to view the malnourished German children as enemies. The troops also discovered that Germans were willing to cooperate in the violation of the orders against fraternization. By July, Eisenhower had delegated the shaping of policy about social contacts to his subordinate commanders.[37]

The best evidence of the disobedience of the nonfraternization policy was the rise in the venereal disease rate from 50 cases per 1,000 soldiers in May to 190 cases per 1,000 in August, and then to 250 cases per 1,000 men in December 1945.[38] Hundreds of enlisted men and officers, including six generals, were punished for fraternization. Attempts to enforce nonfraternization had put the army "in a position that was both ludicrous and potentially dangerous. No amount of pious exhortation could, once the fighting had ended, convince the soldiers that they were not the chief and possibly intended victims. . . . Fittingly, non-fraternization did not end, it disintegrated." The tendency of many commanders to look the other way when their soldiers violated the policy harmed discipline as rules were selectively obeyed. On 1 October, the Allies ended the policy.[39]

During the first six months, the 1st Infantry Division had few difficulties with the German population beyond fraternization. Security in most areas was good, with the exception of occasional attempts by displaced persons or renegade Germans to steal food, fuel, and clothing, all of which were in critically short supply. Most of the disturbances faced by the occupation troops in the first year, including looting, thefts, and burglary, were caused by the 600,000 displaced persons still in the American zone.[40]

By October, the level of violent crimes and depredations committed by displaced persons had increased sufficiently that the American Control Council decided to issue firearms to the German police. The 26th Infantry's after-action report notes that "acts of lawlessness on the part of the DP's [displaced persons] were investigated by this section [the military government detachment in Nuremberg] because they constituted a security threat." As winter approached, the 26th Infantry assumed a greater role in the administration of the displaced persons camps in its area and worked closely with the United Nations Relief Agency in solving problems caused by displaced persons.[41] The problems associated with displaced persons and malnutrition were difficult to work out until the German economy began to recover.

During the winter of 1945–1946, the redeployment of troops to the United States continued. In early January, however, an announcement in *Stars and Stripes*, the US military newspaper, that the number of men to be returned each month to the United States was to be dramatically decreased sparked demonstrations by soldiers in Frankfurt, London, and Paris. The demonstrations were peaceful, and General Joseph McNarney, commanding general of the US forces, allowed the soldiers to hold meetings and discuss their grievances with commanders. The soldiers got their point across. On 15 January 1946, the War Department announced that redeployment and demobilization would continue at a higher rate than first announced. As a result, the troop strength of the European command and the occupation forces continued to fall.[42] There is no evidence as to whether or not men of the Big Red One took part in the demonstrations, but the continued rapid transfer of troops exacerbated the division's severe personnel shortages.

During the first six months of 1946, 3,998 soldiers left the 26th Infantry, while only 2,462 men joined the regiment. As the unit noted, "The adverse effect on general military efficiency of this, a seventy percent turnover in personnel, does not need detailed discussion."[43] The 5th Field Artillery Battalion reported that its strength was down to 30 percent in April, and by June the artillery battalion had just 15 percent of its officers and 65 percent of its authorized enlisted strength. "Until the last few days of this period, redeployment outweighed replacements until the unit was barely skeletal."[44] By late summer, the 18th Regiment's after-action report observed:

> The evils born out of redeployment and rapid turn over of personnel continued without appreciable change. Too many of the soldiers of the occupation force were not a credit to the United States. Insofar as it pertains to the preparation of the Germans to receive democracy, the average soldier was ineffective, being, as he was unprepared to assume or carry out his assigned responsibilities. Soldier-civilian incidents were numerous.[45]

Personnel shortages continued into the spring of 1946. The 26th Infantry lost 1,444 officers and enlisted men during the first quarter of 1946 and it received 782 replacements. Since the 26th was responsible for supporting the war crimes tribunal, it received priority for replacements; the other regiments experienced steady losses until the army caught up to the need for new soldiers in the summer. It was August before the 18th Infantry finally received 2,292 replacements from the 14th Infantry, which was disbanded. This infusion of men, and a decrease of occupation duties during the summer, allowed the 18th Infantry to concentrate its battalions in three bases around Bamberg.[46]

Replacements began to arrive in Germany in appreciable numbers in early 1946. Most of these men were inadequately trained, having undergone just thirteen weeks of training. All of the units of the 1st Infantry Division created training programs for replacements, further diverting strength from occupation duties. By June 1946, the superb combat division that had sliced across Germany was gone. As the 26th Infantry regiment reported, "The lack of an efficient training program coupled with the departure, through redeployment, of trained men and the receipt of grossly untrained replacements has rendered the Regiment ineffective as a fighting unit."[47]

Discipline and Disorder

American soldiers were a major factor in an increased crime rate in Germany in 1946. Until the redeployment was completed, thousands of veterans with too much time on their hands remained in Germany. There were numerous complaints, many substantiated, by Germans about rapes, murders, and thefts carried out by Americans. The crime committed most often by American troops was black market activity, especially before 1948. GIs were forbidden to sell or barter goods to Germans. The demand for goods, however, was so great that it was tempting for some soldiers to steal food, clothing, and cigarettes from supply depots and military exchanges to sell on the black market.[48]

In one case, in September 1946, soldiers in Amberg robbed the post exchange of watches and cameras, which they intended to sell. In this case, US agents and the German police raided the suspects' apartments and recovered most of the stolen goods. Three soldiers were apprehended and punished.[49] After the 18th Infantry moved to Frankfurt, in December 1946, it encountered increased black-market activities, as the regimental after-action report indicates:

> After the arrival of the Regiment in Frankfurt, Germany, it was noted that black market rings operated by both Allied and German professional crooks seemed to flourish on a large, well organized scale. Positive indications of the above came to light by the method used in stealing which occurred in the Regimental Area. Objects stolen included personal possessions of miscellaneous categories, food stuffs, and equipment. In numerous cases vehicles were found stripped of

essential parts. As part of a study of this matter it was concluded that most of
these stolen articles reached black market operators either by way of American
soldiers or German employees of the 18th Infantry, or both.[50]

The army made strenuous efforts to curtail such activities. However, the
German economy was nearly at a standstill in 1945–1946, and the German
people were receiving fewer than 1,200 calories each per day. People sought
food, clothes, and fuel from the occupation troops. Germans paid exorbi-
tant prices in German and occupation currency or offered household goods,
jewels, military memorabilia, and sex for goods. An illicit market flourished,
and many American soldiers reaped the rewards. When caught, they were
punished for black-market activities, but only the revival of the economy and
a sound German currency in 1948 reduced the scope of the black market.

During the planning for the occupation of Germany, Allied leaders had
worried that a Nazi resistance movement might develop. Occupation units
were required to report any such activity in their quarterly reports. The Big
Red One provided at least half of the occupation force in the American zone
after the autumn of 1945, and its regimental and battalion quarterly reports
indicate that there was no such resistance from 1945 to 1948.

The Arrival of American Families

From the beginning of planning for the occupation of Germany, the army
intended, as a long-term morale measure, to allow married soldiers to bring
their families to Germany.[51] In the autumn of 1945, the US command ordered the theater engineer and surgeon to plan for the establishment of bases
for families and medical facilities to serve them. In January 1946, the War
Department approved the sites selected for family housing, and the first
families arrived in Bremerhaven in late April. Although it would take years
to construct adequate facilities, Congress approved funds for the construction of housing in May. By the summer of 1946, post exchanges, movie
theaters, medical clinics, and quarters were ready for servicemen's families in
some locations. In October, American schools opened. The arrival of families coincided with a decrease in the venereal disease and crime rates and
fostered a long-term positive relationship of American military families with
the German people.[52]

A number of American soldiers had long had wives and sweethearts with
them in Europe. There were no rules against fraternization with the British
population, and nature had taken its course. Some officers, like Frank Murdoch, a battalion commander in the 26th Infantry, met their future wives
early in the war. Frank was engaged to marry when he deployed to North

Africa in 1942. When he returned to England from Sicily in 1943, his fiancée was waiting for him. In April 1944, Murdoch requested permission to marry. The division's chief of staff told him he needed to wait an additional thirty days, due to an army policy requiring a "cooling off" period. Murdoch appealed the decision to Major General Huebner, knowing how imminent the invasion was. Huebner pointed out to Murdoch that if the date on his request was postdated by thirty days, then Huebner could approve it and Frank and his fiancée could marry right away. The Murdochs married on 7 April 1944 and celebrated their sixtieth anniversary in 2004.[53]

The Murdochs were not unique. By June 1946, the army had provided transportation to the United States for 34,125 wives and 11,160 children of American servicemen. From the autumn of 1945 on, the army recognized that soldiers would fall in love with Germans. With the end of prohibitions on fraternization, many GIs found Germans receptive to romantic advances. Many relationships ended without marriage but with children. Many were solemnized by German or American religious authorities, and the United States military recognized these unions. The size of the American family presence in Germany increased accordingly.[54]

Combat Readiness and Training

By the end of 1946, the 1st Infantry Division and the police force known as the Constabulary were the only American combat formations in Germany. Both were understrength, and no tactical training had been conducted in the past year. Living conditions were often substandard. For example, when the 18th Infantry Regiment moved from Amberg to Frankfurt in October, there were serious morale problems directly related to working and living conditions:

> The men of the Regiment . . . were required to assume a strenuous guard routine from a billet area entirely unsuited to [the] requirements of US troops. Housing was of the apartment type with inadequate or non-existing heating and plumbing facilities. Likewise, dayrooms were small, poorly equipped and largely without purpose. Club facilities were extremely poor in comparison with others of the Frankfurt area. No planned social program was in effect to provide men with "off duty" recreation of a desirable character. On the other hand, guard commitments often necessitated, for an individual, successive tours of several days' duration. . . . The resultant poor morale was evidenced by extremely high venereal disease and courts-martial rates.[55]

The 18th Infantry Regiment consolidated support functions and worked to improve its troop billets. The Service Company removed forty truckloads of debris from its billets and motor pool. But, as the regimental report concluded, the Engineer Utility Section of Frankfurt, "slow and unreliable, estimated eighteen months as the time required to provide basic facilities. Consequently, the men and officers of this regiment were required to live throughout October, November, and December in these squalid surroundings."[56]

Many infantry replacements who joined the 18th Infantry in 1946 were of the lowest mental category of recruits (Category V), and 10 percent of them were judged "undesirable and recommended for separation from the service." The regiment asked permission to attach Polish guard units to the regiment and to reduce the guard requirements.[57] The personnel situation in the 18th Infantry was representative of that in the US Army worldwide.[58]

The military readiness and capability of the army forces in Germany reached their lowest point in 1947. By then, the United States had recognized that the Soviet Union posed a serious threat to Western Europe. Consequently, the Truman administration took a number of steps to face the challenges of the Cold War against Communism. The reorganization of the American command in Europe was part of this process; major changes in the occupation policies and the missions of American forces in Germany were another. The 1st Infantry Division and the Constabulary ceased to be an army of occupation and became the major defenders of German freedom. The Big Red One shifted its attention from the enforcement of occupation rules to preparation for potential combat.

The 26th Infantry Regiment was the first unit to benefit from the changes in the political environment in Europe. On 2 April 1947, having completed its missions with the International Military Tribunal in Nuremberg, the regiment moved to an army training area near Grafenwöhr, Bavaria, to construct and operate a training center. The regiment built or refurbished rifle and machine-gun ranges, a bayonet course, and a parade ground. The soldiers also constructed a tent camp capable of accommodating 1,200 soldiers. Company B, 1st Engineers, and the 535th Heavy Signal Construction Company repaired roads and water lines and provided electrical service to billets and training areas. Recreation facilities were built, including volleyball and horseshoe courts, a Service Club, and a library. The US Army had begun a long-term commitment to the Grafenwöhr Training Area.[59]

The 1st Infantry Division commander, Major General Frank W. Milburn, opened the training center on 5 May 1947. The 26th Infantry conducted squad-level training for four infantry companies and two artillery batteries during the next four weeks, ending this first cycle of training on 31 May. The second cycle began on 16 June, and five more infantry companies and three artillery batteries underwent training.

The units that went through the training at Grafenwöhr were at about 50 percent strength. The 5th Field Artillery Battalion, for example, had only 14 officers and 243 enlisted men on 30 June 1947, or roughly half of its authorized strength. In October, the 18th Infantry Regiment had 1,961 officers and men in the two battalions scattered around Frankfurt, and its 1st Battalion remained on detached duty in Bremerhaven. Nonetheless, training at Grafenwöhr was a major tonic to unit morale and efficiency.[60] Although little platoon-level training took place, the instruction was a step forward. The Big Red One had begun the arduous process of re-creating a combat-ready division.[61]

In July 1947, the 26th Infantry was filled to its authorized strength (a total of about 3,000 men) and all of the regiment moved to Grafenwöhr. The regiment was the core of the US European Command (EUCOM) reaction force. Again known as the 26th Regimental Combat Team, it was to prepare for potential combat operations anywhere in Germany and was expected to be able to deploy to any point in the occupation zone within twenty-four hours. The 5th and 33rd Field Artillery Battalions provided artillery support. The regiment also was "to develop the most highly trained, best appearing, and most efficient organization in the U.S. Army."[62]

Brigadier General Fay Prickett commanded the training center and oversaw the training of the 26th Infantry Combat Team. The 5th Constabulary Regiment, stationed in Augsburg, was designated as the second regimental combat team of the EUCOM contingency force to provide a reserve "to move promptly to control any uprising or general disturbance before it resulted in destruction of life or property."[63]

Since there was no danger of an uprising by either the German population or any remaining hardcore Nazis, EUCOM took steps to reorganize the Constabulary. Its authorized strength dropped from 33,000 men to 18,000 during the summer of 1947. In September, one-third of the Constabulary squadrons were inactivated, and the 5th Constabulary Regiment was consolidated as part of the EUCOM reserve. EUCOM also forecast that all Constabulary units would be deactivated over the next three years as the German government assumed responsibility for the internal security of the American occupation zone. Lieutenant General Huebner, EUCOM chief of staff, pointed out to the newly organized Department of Defense: "The question of which tactical units were to remain in the European Command had not been settled, but informal discussion had favored an infantry division."[64]

This reorganization took place as the nation recognized the Communist threat and the need to increase and revitalize American armed forces. Congress authorized, in 1948, renewal of the Selective Service Act to provide the men needed for the expanding armed services. Congress also reaffirmed the importance of the National Guard and the Army Reserve to national defense. By 1950, twenty-seven National Guard divisions and twenty regimental combat teams had been organized, and an Air National Guard had been created to increase the wartime potential of the US Air Force.[65]

During the first four years after World War II, the Truman administration relied upon nuclear weapons as the primary deterrent against a Soviet attack in Europe. Army forces were seen as subsidiary to the air force and navy, whose units would deliver the nuclear weapons in the event of a war. Ground forces in Germany were to deter opportunistic attempts by the Russians to extend their sphere westward. They basically served as a trigger to an American nuclear response. The Berlin Blockade of 1948 seemed to validate the reliance on air forces as the deterrent to Russian aggression. In this environment, the 1st Infantry Division remained the only American ground combat unit in Europe by 1948 and the only one of the army's ten active divisions authorized to be at full strength.[66]

The Berlin crisis led to the reorganization of the 16th Infantry Regiment, which had ceased to operate as a coherent unit in late 1946.[67] In April 1948, the officer and NCO cadres from the 18th and 26th Infantry Regiments formed a new regiment, with most of its enlisted soldiers coming from service units in Germany. The new unit was redesignated the 16th Infantry Regiment on 7 July and officially rejoined the 1st Infantry Division. The 3rd Battalion, 16th Infantry, remained in Berlin. The 1st and 2nd Battalions and regimental headquarters took part in EUCOM maneuvers in September with the rest of the Big Red One before moving to Grafenwöhr for training in October. By the end of 1948, the 16th Infantry (minus the 3rd Battalion) had established winter quarters in casernes (military barracks) near Nuremberg, where the regiment adopted its nickname, "The Rangers."[68]

The Regular Army was inadequate for its Cold War missions in 1947–1948. The army's and air force's combined strength in June 1947 was 1,070,000. The army had roughly 220,000 soldiers stationed overseas, with 118,916 officers and enlisted personnel in Europe.[69] The 1st Infantry Division and the rest of the army were equipped with weapons remaining from World War II. This situation reflected, in part, that the US government was still uncertain of the role of ground forces in the nuclear war environment.[70]

The Racial Integration of the Army and the Reorganization of EUCOM

The 1948 Selective Service Act was one of several steps taken to find the manpower needed by the services to face the Soviet threat. President Truman also ordered the integration of African Americans into formerly all-white units, and Congress created the Women's Army Corps, giving women the opportunity to serve in the Regular Army for the first time on a professional basis. These moves initiated a long process of integration of women and people of color into the armed forces. Racial integration had an immediate impact on the 1st Infantry Division.[71]

The 1st Infantry Division had played an important part in the use of African American infantry platoons in 1945. Three platoons had performed magnificently in the division.[72] Following the war, African Americans mainly served in all-black units.[73] As the need for more occupation troops became acute in 1947, EUCOM created additional African American infantry units. In the summer of 1947, the Big Red One oversaw the training of the 370th and 371st Infantry Guard Battalions at Grafenwöhr. Organized with African American personnel from inactivated support units, these battalions were to guard installations.[74] Because many of these black soldiers had low test scores and lacked education beyond the fifth grade, Lieutenant General Clarence Huebner ordered the 1st Infantry Division to establish a training and education program at Grafenwöhr. This program was very successful. The 370th and 371st Infantry Battalions performed impressively, as all indicators of discipline and efficiency demonstrated. EUCOM continued the program at new facilities on Kitzingen Air Base, where black replacements were sent for remedial training and education as necessary. By June 1950, 200 instructors provided education to over 2,900 soldiers at a time, and, according to a 1950 European Command estimate, "the command's education program was producing some of the finest trained black troops in the Army."[75]

In early 1948, the secretary of defense characterized the army's policy concerning the service of black Americans as an attempt to extend to all soldiers equality of opportunity, "without renouncing segregation." This policy reflected national practices and prejudices, and the army remained segregated. President Truman, however, took a major step toward racial equality with Executive Order 9981, on 26 July 1948. This order created the President's Committee on Equality of Treatment and Opportunity in the Armed Forces to study policies concerning the employment of people of color in the services. This committee concluded that all positions in the military should be opened to all Americans. Further, race or color should no longer be a factor in selection for promotion or schooling, and the assignment of personnel should be based on the needs of the services and individual ability. Finally, the committee recommended that African Americans should no longer be restricted to service in segregated units and that quotas on blacks in the service should be abolished.[76]

President Truman accepted these recommendations, with a significant amount of skepticism by the leadership of the armed services, including army commanders in Germany.[77] In the next year, the European Command implemented Truman's executive order cautiously.

African American soldiers were assigned to the 1st Infantry Division in an all-black unit on a permanent basis for the first time in 1949. By 30 June 1950, the division's strength included 14 African American officers and 893 enlisted men. It is difficult to know how these men were received or treated by their fellow soldiers. Nonetheless, although EUCOM maintained segregated battalions into the 1950s, Truman's integration policy moved the army forward on its long journey to full racial integration.[78]

The Cold War and the Resurgence of Army Readiness: 1948–1953

The year 1948 also brought momentous changes to the international situation and to the organization of American forces in Europe. Communists seized power in China and Czechoslovakia, and the Soviet Union imposed a blockade of all land and water routes into Berlin. Increased Russian intransigence in occupied Germany stemmed in part from the success of American efforts to revitalize the German economy and establish democratic government in West Germany. The European Recovery Program, named the Marshall Plan in honor of George Marshall, who conceived its main ideas, was enacted by Congress in early 1948. This measure promised financial aid to European governments and proved to be one of the shrewdest and most successful foreign aid measures in history. As a result, the economies of Western Europe began a remarkable resurgence, directly contributing to the American postwar economic boom.

The Western Powers in Germany agreed to unify their occupation zones and to allow the German *Länder* (states) to form the Federal Republic of Germany (i.e., West Germany). Soviet threats over Berlin drove the Allies closer together. As a result, ten European nations joined the United States and Canada in the North Atlantic Treaty Organization (NATO), promising mutual defense in the case of attack.[79]

The US Army maintained roughly 90,000 soldiers in Germany in 1948. The recognition by the US government and Congress that Communist forces posed a threat to American security and interests brought about significant changes in American defense policy. Efforts were initiated to bring the ten army divisions on active duty to full strength and to provide the resources to make them combat ready. On 29 September 1948, EUCOM headquarters ordered the 1st Infantry Division to reorganize under a new table of organization and to devote its efforts to the tasks of becoming combat ready.[80]

The reorganized division was considerably larger than its World War II equivalent. Its total strength was 18,751 men. The three infantry regiments (16th, 18th, and 26th) were assigned 3,773 soldiers each, including heavy mortar companies to replace the regimental cannon companies and heavy tank companies to replace the antitank companies. The 63rd Heavy Tank and the 48th Antiaircraft Artillery Automatic Weapons Battalions joined the division, while the four artillery battalions (5th, 7th, 32nd, and 33rd) constituted the 3,668-man-strong Division Artillery. The 1st Engineer and 1st Medical Battalions joined the 1st Military Police, 1st Quartermaster, 1st Signal, and 1st Reconnaissance Companies as the division troops. EUCOM also attached transportation, ordnance, and quartermaster units to the division to provide support and mobility. The 122nd (Negro) Transportation Battalion, with its six segregated truck companies, was included with these attachments.[81]

In August, EUCOM held its first large tactical exercise, giving the 1st Infantry Division a chance to work with a British regiment. Exercise Normal was a graduation exercise for the division, allowing it for the first time in three years to maneuver its regiments. Defects in communications and maintenance were identified, and additional training resources were provided to the 16th Infantry Regiment and the signal and ordnance companies. In 1949, the frequency of field training exercises increased. EUCOM Exercise Snowdrop (17–23 January 1949) revealed weaknesses in command and control procedures and unit mobility. As a result, the tempo of the division's tactical training increased. Exercise Showers (18–24 April 1949) was "the first serious postwar test of the tactical and logistical functioning of the U.S. Army units of the European Command." Seventy thousand troops took part, including air and naval units. The level of proficiency of all participants was significantly higher than it had been in previous exercises.[82]

EUCOM completed its exercise program for 1949 with Exercise Harvest in September. Over 110,000 soldiers, including nearly every soldier in the US Army, Europe (USAREUR) took part. Harvest included greater participation by air force and naval units and allowed EUCOM to showcase its combat capabilities to foreign observers. The exercise included French troops, and umpires allowed the 1st Infantry Division to conduct free-play force-on-force maneuvers. Observers noted that morale was especially high and that the division demonstrated improved mobility and tactical capability.[83]

At the battalion level, the reorganization of the division and the focus on tactical training improved morale and combat capabilities. Soldiers and officers spent a great deal of time in the field and at the Grafenwöhr training area, where they fired their individual and crew-served weapons. Replacements continued to join the division, making it important to continue training at all levels. For example, the 5th Field Artillery Battalion received 371 enlisted replacements in the fall of 1948, increasing it to full strength for the first time in three years. The battalion conducted training in its local garrison during the winter of 1948–1949 to integrate the new soldiers. Following this training, the battalion conducted live-fire practice at Grafenwöhr. At the same time, the division's training office prepared programs of instruction for use by all divisional units to bring new soldiers up to required standards.[84]

This increased training significantly improved morale and discipline. The rates of venereal disease and reports of absence without leave decreased steadily in 1949. Although incidents related to alcohol abuse remained high, efforts to provide adequate billets and recreational facilities to all units provided more off-duty relaxation and entertainment for the mostly all-male soldier population.[85]

The Korean War Buildup: 1950–1952

By the spring of 1950, USAREUR was an operational headquarters within EUCOM. The deputy commanding general of EUCOM served as the chief of staff of that organization and as the commanding general of USAREUR. The mission of USAREUR was focused on the training, operation, and support of its two major combat formations, the 1st Infantry Division and the Constabulary. These tactical organizations remained the only American ground forces in EUCOM in early 1950.[86]

The 1st Infantry Division spent a great part of 1950 at the Grafenwöhr training area. The opportunity to concentrate the division at one location allowed the staff to handle the maneuver battalions and enabled the service units to support the combat organizations away from their fixed garrison locations. An inspection report concluded that such training increased the combat readiness of the division even though the training area was too small to allow maneuver training by units larger than a battalion.[87]

In June 1950, the international situation changed dramatically with the North Korean Communist invasion of South Korea and the United Nations intervention. The US Joint Chiefs of Staff feared that the Soviet Union might take advantage of the American commitment of forces to Korea to attack West Germany. These fears increased when the Soviets began to arm East German army units and increased their own military presence in East Germany. Consequently, the United States decided to assign more land and air forces to Western Europe. The US Seventh Army was activated to oversee the buildup and operations of the ground forces.

In October 1950, USAREUR ordered the 1st Infantry Division to activate the 6th Infantry Regiment at Grafenwöhr using cadre from the Big Red One. The 6th Infantry was then assigned to the Berlin Military Post, where it absorbed the 3rd Battalion, 16th Infantry, which was designated the 3rd Battalion, 6th Infantry. By the end of 1950, the 6th Infantry had become the Berlin garrison. The 16th Infantry provided cadre for the reactivation of its 3rd Battalion, which joined the 1st Infantry Division in West Germany.[88]

The 1st Infantry Division also provided 1,320 officers and men to form the 4th Infantry Division in November. An African American infantry battalion in the 4th was formed around a cadre of black soldiers from the Big Red One as well. As the trained soldiers formed new units, a steady influx of newly drafted men filled the ranks, forcing the 1st Infantry Division to focus its training efforts during the winter of 1950–1951 on basic soldier skills and small-unit operations.[89]

A major influx of additional ground forces to Germany took place during 1951. In January, there were 86,000 American army troops in Germany. By the end of the year, Seventh Army controlled two corps and five army divisions with 234,000 soldiers. Another 21,000 air force and navy personnel served in EUCOM. The first of the four additional divisions to arrive was the 4th Infantry Division from Fort Benning, Georgia, in May. In June, the 2nd Armored Division arrived. These divisions were joined that autumn by the 28th and 43rd Infantry Divisions, both newly activated National Guard divisions.[90] The V and VII Corps headquarters deployed to Germany to provide tactical control over the five divisions.

The increase of army troop strength placed a tremendous strain on training areas and support structures. In response, EUCOM acquired additional training areas, housing areas, and motor pools from the German government. It took time to build or remodel barracks and to construct schools and housing for family members. Recreation facilities and programs for unmarried soldiers received special attention, and, by the end of 1951, great strides had been made to provide additional movie theaters, post exchanges, clubs, and athletic facilities. These efforts paid off, as indicators of discipline and morale, such as venereal disease, absence without leave, crime, and courts-martial rates increased only modestly in 1951 and declined in 1952.[91]

With a Soviet attack a possibility, the EUCOM leadership discussed whether servicemen's families should be allowed in Germany. While recognizing the dangers involved, General Manton Eddy, the commanding general of USAREUR, recommended to the EUCOM commander that the army continue to allow families to accompany servicemen for the following reasons:

For ten years the armed forces have been in varying degrees of emergency. A large number of our officers and enlisted personnel have been separated from their wives and children much of that time. We cannot revert to the Spartan life of field soldiers with every international crisis and still retain our integrity and morality as an Army. In the changed world of today, we should accustom ourselves to the atmosphere of tension that surrounds us and seek as normal an existence as possible. This includes *the right* to have our dependents with or near us if this is at all reasonable. Whether an individual will accept the risks and inconveniences of this should, in general, be up to him.[92]

General Thomas T. Handy, EUCOM commanding general, concurred and recommended to the army chief of staff that dependents should be allowed to remain in the command unless war appeared imminent. He based his decision on the "moral, morale, and stabilizing influence of dependents in the command" and on the "psychological effect that returning dependents would have on the Germans and other Western Europeans, who, he thought, would leap to the conclusion that we were abandoning them to the Russians."[93]

Adding to the challenges of acclimating and training 122,000 new personnel during 1952, the army in Europe initiated a policy of full racial integration. Roughly 14 percent of the force in Europe was African American. The aptitude scores and educational levels of black replacements rose in 1952, although they still reflected the baneful effects of racial segregation in the United States.[94] Previously, black replacements had been assigned to segregated units, with the exception of those with certain technical skills. This changed in 1952 as African American replacements were assigned first to combat units, such as the 1st Infantry Division, and then to the combat support and service support units. Black soldiers integrated the formerly white infantry and artillery battalions of the Big Red One with little difficulty. The goal remained to have the percentage of African American soldiers in all types of units reflect the overall percentage of blacks in the total army. EUCOM insisted that no unit was to consist solely of African Americans "and that the program should be carried out with no publicity."[95]

By the end of the year, most combat units and 40 percent of the service units in Germany had been racially integrated. Difficulties arose, as men were transferred from their units and friends, and morale suffered in some cases. Nonetheless, surveys indicated that "most unit commanders felt that morale remained at an unexpectedly high level despite the difficulties caused by integration."[96] It took another year and a half before all USAREUR units were integrated.[97] Racial integration improved overall manpower utilization and the efficiency of formerly segregated units. The results of Army Training Tests, Annual General Inspections, and Command Maintenance Inspections "showed generally that integration had raised the level of performance of former all-Negro units and had improved their capability to perform their mission. Moreover, integration had not decreased the combat effectiveness of former all-white units."[98]

The deterrence of Soviet aggression in Europe and the restoration of South Korean independence changed the nature of the struggle to contain Communism. With the death of Joseph Stalin, tensions between the West and the Soviet Union eased, allowing the United States to reduce troop strength overseas. The quality of life for the soldiers of the Big Red One in Germany improved steadily from 1952 to 1954. A program of housing and barracks construction eased the shortage of family housing and provided adequate quarters for single soldiers. Relations with the German population continued to improve, especially after West Germany became a sovereign nation and entered NATO. The 1st Infantry Division remained part of Seventh Army, with division headquarters in Würzburg and the regimental combat teams stationed in Schweinfurt (16th), Aschaffenburg (18th), and Bamberg (26th). The division's mission remained "to assist in providing for the security of Western Germany and preventing armed aggression by Soviet-bloc countries."[99]

The Big Red One's Return Home

A constant problem experienced by army forces in Europe from 1946 to 1955 was personnel turmoil caused by the assignment of soldiers to Europe for tours of duty of two to four years. This turmoil forced the 1st Infantry Division to spend a great deal of time training new personnel. In 1954, the army experimented with the assignment of platoons instead of individual replacements to the 1st and 9th Infantry Divisions. This system allowed the platoons to train in the United States and move to Europe "combat-ready." Although it did not eliminate the need to integrate the platoons into companies and battalions, it did increase the cohesion of the incoming platoons. In October 1954, the Department of the Army issued regulations for the rotation of entire divisions between the United States and Europe. The 1st Infantry Division was selected as the first division in Europe to "gyroscope" back to the United States, in exchange for the 10th Infantry Division stationed at Fort Riley, Kansas.[100]

The intent of the program was to increase stability, cohesion, and the combat capability of divisions by keeping the personnel together for three years, during which time they would train as a division in the United States and then deploy overseas for thirty-three months. When its overseas service was complete, the division would return to the United States and those soldiers who did not remain in the service would be replaced by new soldiers.

As far as possible, the Gyroscope program intended to have the families of married personnel accompany them. Career soldiers would spend up to seven years in the same division, and men who enlisted for three years would hopefully spend all of their service time in the same unit.[101]

Homecoming: 1955

The 1st Infantry Division arrived in New York Harbor aboard the navy ship *Upshur* on 23 July 1955, where it received the most impressive reception given any military unit since the end of World War II. It deserved this welcome. From 1945 to 1955, the Big Red One had remained on the forward edge of the free world prepared to repel Soviet aggression. Its soldiers developed positive relations with the German people and reinforced their willingness to commit their future to democracy, NATO, and a close alliance with the United States.

After its triumphant return to New York, the 1st Infantry Division was stationed at Fort Riley, Kansas. In 1958, the army reorganized its divisions into what were known as Pentomic divisions. The purpose of the Pentomic organization was to enable army units to fight on the nuclear battlefield that the Eisenhower administration's "New Look" had assumed would be the future of land warfare. The idea was to give the division five independent battle groups. The battle groups were tactically self-sufficient and able to operate widely separated from each other. They were to remain dispersed when the enemy's use of nuclear weapons was imminent, thus presenting a smaller target for nuclear weapons. The underlying premise was that large conventional forces were no longer necessary.[102]

The 1st Infantry Division was the first division to convert to the Pentomic structure, in 1957. The infantry regiments were reorganized into five battle groups. Each battle group had four infantry companies assigned (later increased to five). The Division Artillery headquarters was inactivated, and only two artillery battalions supported the division. The 7th Field Artillery consisted of five batteries of 105mm howitzers, and the 1st Battalion, 5th Field Artillery, was equipped with Honest John rockets and 155mm howitzers. The division strength decreased from about 17,500 to 13,700 soldiers. The 1st Medium Tank Battalion, 69th Armor, and the 1st Armored Cavalry Squadron, 4th Cavalry, provided armor support. The 9th Transport Battalion, equipped with armored personnel carriers, provided a pool of tactical vehicles to move the infantry on the nuclear battlefield.

A much smaller division staff was included in a "provisional" brigade command and staff group. The 1st Engineer, 1st Medical, 701st Ordnance, and the 121st Signal Battalions were joined by the 1st Quartermaster,

1st Aviation, and the 1st Administrative Services Companies to support the battle groups. The army believed that the Pentomic division would be more flexible and less vulnerable on the nuclear battlefield of future warfare.[103]

Many veteran combat leaders questioned the rationale of the reorganization. General Willard Wyman, Continental Army Command commanding general in 1956, believed that the design was flawed because it was an attempt to replace infantrymen with "push-button weapons" such as the Honest John and Davy Crockett nuclear-equipped rockets. Wyman felt the Pentomic division was a move away from having an army organized to carry out a number of important combat missions: "Until the day when a submarine can take a hill and a B-52 occupy a city, I predict the Army division will continue to be the decisive instrument of military force in the arsenal of democracy."[104]

The Pentomic divisions initially were to rotate between the United States and overseas. However, the Gyroscope concept was too expensive to continue at the division level. It required an army of twenty-four active divisions, at a time when the Eisenhower administration was looking for ways to cut the size and costs of conventional land forces. The divisions that moved to Germany faced significant degradation in combat readiness when they arrived overseas in new operational and social environments. Discipline problems increased significantly, in part because it was hard to find enough senior noncommissioned officers to man the divisions going overseas, leaving units with inexperienced NCOs. Finally, the army found it necessary to continue to assign individual replacements to the divisions that gyroscoped to Europe to keep them at authorized strength. The division-level rotation system was abandoned in 1958.[105]

Beginning in late 1958, battle groups from divisions in the United States rotated with battle groups in overseas divisions. This new approach broke the historic affiliation of the infantry regiments of the 1st Infantry Division as the battle groups of the 16th, 18th, 26th, and 2nd Infantry Regiments left the division and were replaced at Fort Riley by battle groups of the 8th Infantry Division from Germany. The Society of the First Division was outraged, believing that "the Pentagon planners have apparently overlooked the most important factor . . . the man." The *Bridgehead Sentinel* quoted Henry Baldwin, the military correspondent of the *New York Times*, who wrote, "The Army's present difficulties may further increase when the Army's gyroscope operation . . . shifts fully from divisions as the unit rotation to battle groups. This plan will break up tactical units that have trained together and have a common battle tradition—like the famous 1st Division—and will disperse some of the component parts to other parent units with a consequent impairment of unit pride and morale."[106] By early 1959, four of the division's battle groups had no historic connection with the Big Red One.

The army also increased the artillery component of the Pentomic divisions by adding four artillery battalions to the original two. A 105mm howitzer–equipped battalion supported each battle group, and the other two battalions served the division with 8-inch and 155mm howitzers and Honest John rockets. The army also changed the primary mission of the 1st Infantry Division from that of a combat-ready deployable force to a training division.

From 1958 to 1961, the 1st Infantry Division conducted basic and advanced recruit training at Fort Riley with a reduced cadre of 6,100 officers and soldiers. These troops trained about 5,000 recruits at any one time in eight-week-long basic courses and sixteen-week advanced infantry courses. The division also supported reserve units' summer training and the summer camp of Reserve Officer Training programs. The division worked to maintain esprit and a sense of affiliation in its cadre and trainees, but it was a difficult challenge given the nature of a training unit.[107]

By the early 1960s, it was evident that the conceptual basis for the Pentomic division was flawed. President Eisenhower had believed that the advent of nuclear weapons made large ground forces obsolete and that large army formations would present a lucrative target. He also reasoned that the American nuclear arsenal, largely wielded by the air force, provided an effective deterrent to war because the Communists would be unwilling to risk being attacked by nuclear weapons for minor or major territorial gains. If a war broke out, it would be ended rapidly by the use of atomic weapons, and the army would be needed only to occupy the defeated nation and control the remaining population after the nuclear exchange. Consequently, the Eisenhower administration starved the army of funds during the late 1950s while it lavished resources on the navy and air force.[108]

Communist aggression in Southeast Asia in the 1950s disproved the theory that the Soviets or the Chinese Communists would not risk nuclear war by deploying conventional forces. The Soviet Union also developed significant nuclear forces of its own, counterbalancing US nuclear weapons and making "mutual assured destruction" an effective deterrent to American use of atomic weapons to stop aggression.

Army training exercises and tests also revealed a number of problems with the Pentomic design. There were too many subordinate organizations for the division commander to control. There were too few infantrymen in the battle groups to conduct sustained operations. The lack of intermediate headquarters forced the division commander to deal directly with as many as sixteen subordinate units, including the five battle groups and engineer, artillery, medical, and maintenance organizations. The battle groups did not prove well suited to conventional (non-nuclear) operations. Finally, commanders found it difficult to organize the Pentomic units for special missions without weakening the division's combat power. By 1959, the Pentomic organizational premises were under attack from within and without the army.[109]

The election of John F. Kennedy as president in 1960 ended the Pentomic era. Kennedy believed, along with many army officers, that the most likely future wars would require conventional ground forces to operate against a growing Communist threat. Kennedy ordered the army to reorganize its divisions for conventional warfare and to increase its special operations forces.

While the Kennedy administration was settling in, the Big Red One ended its mission as a training command and was designated part of the deployable strategic reserve. The division was brought up to wartime strength. The artillery battalions deployed to Fort Sill, Oklahoma, for intensive live-fire training. The two armored battalions spent four months at Fort Irwin, where they could fire their 76mm and 90mm tank guns and maneuver over the wide expanses of that California post. And the infantry battalions spent several weeks training in the Pike National Forest in Colorado. The division also accomplished another first when its entire 1st Battle Group, 12th Infantry, deployed by air force jet transports to Germany for a training exercise. This was the first such aerial movement of US troops.[110]

In mid-1964, the Big Red One became a division with three brigade headquarters, eight infantry and two armor battalions, a Division Artillery headquarters, and four artillery battalions. This structure was known as the Reorganization Objectives Army Division (ROAD) and continued to be the division design for the remainder of the twentieth century. The traditionally affiliated infantry regiments returned to the 1st Infantry Division, which was now mechanized, but the regimental headquarters were not reactivated. Battalions were attached to the brigades rather than assigned as situation and mission required.

The organizational experimentation of the 1950s created a great deal of turmoil. Historic unit relationships were broken, and an impersonal approach to personnel assignments weakened bonds between soldiers and their divisions. The return to a triangular structure enabled the Big Red One to begin to restore the sense of esprit and loyalty that had been a characteristic of the division from 1917 to 1958. The span of control of the division commander was reduced again to about seven major subordinate commands. But as the division made progress in these areas, the US government decided to commit major ground units to South Vietnam.

14

The Vietnam War and the Big Red One
Deployment and First Battles

THE US ARMY'S OFFICIAL HISTORY describes the entry of the 1st Infantry Division and other large American tactical organizations into the Vietnam War in the following manner:

> In early 1965 a Communist insurgency seemed close to toppling the South Vietnamese government. Refusing to accept the loss of its Asian ally, the United States committed combat units to the field of battle. In the spring and summer the first Army brigades arrived, establishing bridgeheads, and began to conduct operations. During the second half of 1965 divisions deployed, and in November and December the Army fought its first big battles.[1]

Why a Land War in Vietnam?

French and South Vietnamese efforts to prevent Communist advances in South Vietnam had failed consistently since 1950. (Map 25.) By 1964, American advisers with the Army of Vietnam (ARVN) were engaged in operations against Communist forces. Nonetheless, the ARVN continued to lose control of major portions of the country to the Vietcong, the derisive term applied to Communist guerrillas by the South Vietnamese government. In early 1965, an American air offensive was launched against North Vietnam in retaliation for Vietcong assaults against an American air base at Pleiku. These air attacks did nothing to affect the deterioration of ARVN forces or to lessen the will of the Communists to defeat the South Vietnamese government. In fact, on 8 February, Vietcong units killed twenty-three American advisers in an attack at Qui Nhon.[2]

The arrival of American Marines in Da Nang did not cow the enemy. On 30 March, a car bomb destroyed the US embassy in Saigon, killing twenty Vietnamese and two Americans. On 1 April, President Lyndon Johnson authorized General William Westmoreland, commanding general of the United States Military Assistance Command, Vietnam (MACV), to commit American ground troops to offensive operations.[3] By the end of March, the army chief of staff had concluded: "Time is running out swiftly in Vietnam, and temporizing or expedient measures will not suffice."[4] The army alerted combat units for deployment, as the Joint Chiefs of Staff urged the Johnson administration to meet Westmoreland's request for forty-four additional combat battalions.

As a result, the Marine contingents around Da Nang were increased and three army brigades were alerted for deployment. The first army combat brigade to arrive in Vietnam was the 173rd Airborne, which deployed to protect Bien Hoa Air Base in early May (Map 26). The 173rd established its base camp northeast of the airfield, facing War Zone D, a region in which the Vietcong operated. By mid-May, the paratroopers were patrolling in the jungle near their base and, on 15 May 1965, the 2nd Battalion, 503rd Airborne Infantry Regiment, conducted the first helicopter assault landing of the American war in Vietnam.[5]

The Big Red One Deployment to Vietnam

On 5 June, Westmoreland noted that the increase in American combat units would bring the total US force in South Vietnam to 175,000 soldiers. In his view, the reinforcements would provide "a substantial and hard hitting offensive capability on the ground to convince the V.C. [Vietcong] that they cannot win."[6] The additional battalions would go a long way toward providing the 500,000 soldiers that the army estimated would be needed in Vietnam for at least five years. The Joint Chiefs of Staff, however, were unwilling to ask for this many troops openly, and the Johnson administration was doing all it could to dampen domestic political opposition to a war in Asia, including "equating opposition to his [Johnson's Vietnam] policy with abandonment of American soldiers on the front line."[7]

Once the president had approved Westmoreland's request for additional troops, the army selected the 101st Airborne, the 1st Cavalry, and the 1st Infantry Divisions to provide a brigade each for deployment.[8] On 14 April 1965, the army ordered Major General Jonathan Seaman, commanding general of the 1st Infantry Division, to prepare a brigade for deployment within the next thirty days. Seaman selected the 2nd Brigade, which then was the division's rapid deployment force. A week later, Seaman traveled to the Pentagon, where he learned that the situation in Vietnam was deteriorating and that the leading brigade had to be ready to ship to Vietnam by 30 June. In mid-May, Seaman received confirmation that the 2nd Brigade would join the 173rd Airborne Brigade in Vietnam.[9]

Seaman attempted to make the 2nd Brigade "the best possible brigade out of my own resources," and, consequently, "I really tore that division apart," as substandard officers and noncommissioned officers were replaced with the best available men from the division's other two brigades. He also

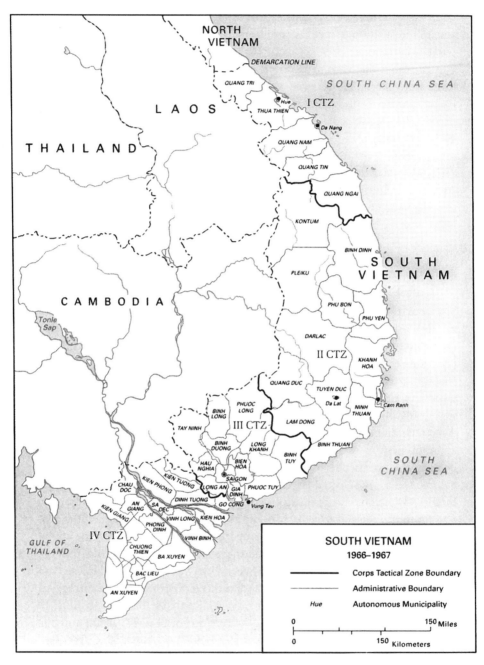

NORTH
VIETNAM

DEMARCATION LINE

QUANG TRI

SOUTH CHINA SEA

LAOS

Hue
THUA THIEN   I CTZ

Da Nang

THAILAND

QUANG NAM

QUANG TIN

QUANG NGAI

KONTUM

BINH DINH

SOUTH
VIETNAM

PLEIKU

CAMBODIA

Tonle
Sap

PHU BON

PHU YEN

DARLAC

II CTZ

KHANH
HOA

QUANG DUC

TUYEN DUC

Da Lat

NINH
THUAN   Cam Ranh

BINH
LONG

PHUOC
LONG

LAM DONG

TAY NINH

III CTZ

BINH
DUONG

LONG
KHANH

BINH THUAN

BINH
TUY

HAU
NGHIA

BIEN
HOA

KIEN TUONG

SAIGON

SOUTH
CHINA
SEA

CHAU
DOC

KIEN PHONG

LONG AN

GIA
DINH

PHUOC TUY

AN
GIANG

SA
DEC

DINH TUONG

GO CONG

Vung Tau

KIEN GIANG

VINH LONG

KIEN HOA

GULF OF
THAILAND

PHONG
DINH

IV CTZ

VINH BINH

CHUONG
THIEN

BA XUYEN

BAC LIEU

AN XUYEN

SOUTH VIETNAM
1966–1967

— Corps Tactical Zone Boundary
.... Administrative Boundary
Hue   Autonomous Municipality

0   150 Miles

0   150 Kilometers

Map 25. The Republic of South Vietnam, 1965–1966. (John M. Carland,
Stemming the Tide, May 1965 to October 1966 [U.S. Army Center of
Military History, 2000])

stripped the 1st and 3rd Brigades of any equipment needed to provide the 2nd Brigade its full authorization of equipment.[10] Thus the 2nd Brigade moved out to port with the best available leaders and material, but the process undoubtedly made it harder for the rest of the division to prepare for its anticipated deployment to Vietnam.

The 2nd Brigade, commanded by Colonel James Simmons, included the 2nd Battalion, 16th Infantry, the 1st and 2nd Battalions, 18th Infantry, the 1st Battalion, 7th Artillery, and Battery C, 8th Battalion, 6th Artillery. Company-size units rounded out the brigade combat team. The soldiers and their equipment traveled by rail from Fort Riley to Oakland Army Terminal in California, where they were loaded onto ships. Passing under the Golden Gate Bridge on 25 June, the soldiers heard officially that they were headed to Vietnam to defend American port facilities then under construction at Qui Nhon, in north-central Vietnam.[11]

Before the brigade reached Vietnam, its destination changed, due to the increased Communist threat to Saigon. The 2nd Battalion, 16th Infantry, and the 2nd Battalion, 18th Infantry, were to move to Bien Hoa with most of the brigade. The 1st Battalion, 18th Infantry, and one battery of artillery were to proceed to Cam Ranh Bay, where the navy was building a port.[12]

After dropping the 1st Battalion, 18th Infantry, off at Cam Ranh Bay, the *General W. H. Gordon* sailed to Vung Tau, where, on 14 July, the rest of the 2nd Brigade disembarked. Over the next three days, the troops moved by truck and transport planes to a base camp site southwest of Bien Hoa Airfield (Map 26). There the brigade was assigned to the operational control of the 173rd Airborne Brigade. Its first mission was to construct a fortified camp on one of the approaches to Bien Hoa to provide a safe base for the brigade and to protect the airfield from Communist attacks.[13]

The men worked fast to clear the jungle and brush from the area and to build bunkers with solid overhead cover for protection from enemy mortar and artillery fire. On the night of 18–19 July, the Vietcong made their first attack against the 1st Infantry Division, inflicting the first casualties. The brigade completed its fortifications and encampment by the end of the month, in spite of heavy rains and nightly enemy sniper fire.[14]

The 2nd Brigade arrived in Vietnam with its infantrymen still equipped with the M14 rifle, instead of the lighter M16 rifle. The M14 rifle was replaced during the next year. The 8th Battalion, 6th Field Artillery, brought a battery of 8-inch howitzers, giving it a range advantage of 2,200 meters over its two 155mm-equipped batteries. The infantry battalions left their armored personnel carriers (APCs) in the United States and became dismounted infantry units. General Seaman had to argue determinedly to equip

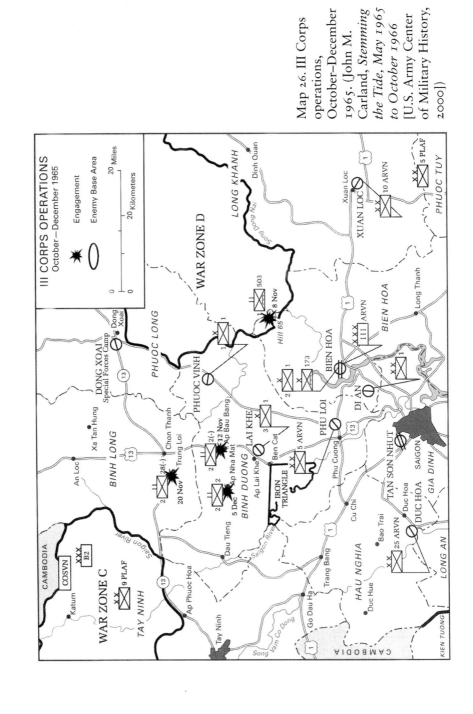

Map 26. III Corps operations, October–December 1965. (John M. Carland, *Stemming the Tide, May 1965 to October 1966* [U.S. Army Center of Military History, 2000])

the cavalry squadron with armored vehicles and the artillery with its 8-inch howitzers.[15]

On 22 July, the commander of the 2nd Battalion, 16th Infantry, Lieutenant Colonel Lloyd Burke, became the division's first senior officer wounded when his helicopter was shot down. Burke was evacuated to the United States, the first such evacuee of many. On 8 September, the 2nd Battalion, 16th Infantry, carried out the brigade's first battalion-size operation near Bien Hoa. On this action and on the battalion's next foray 15 kilometers north of Bien Hoa, the troops made no contact with the enemy. Finally, on 23 September, Colonel Simmons maneuvered two battalions against Vietcong positions located in the earlier sweep. During a four-day fight, the 2nd Battalion, 16th Infantry, and the 2nd Battalion, 18th Infantry, attacked Vietcong in dug-in positions, which they overran.[16]

As the 2nd Brigade commenced operations, the rest of the 1st Infantry Division prepared to move to Vietnam. Seaman sent 140 soldiers to Hawaii to train in the 25th Infantry Division's jungle warfare course. These men returned to Fort Riley and became instructors for the Intensified Combat Training Program in the division. Stressing day and night patrolling, navigation, weapons training, and communications procedures, the course enabled the division to integrate the new soldiers who had replaced the men pulled from the 1st and 3rd Brigades to fill the 2nd Brigade.[17]

Because General Westmoreland wanted only dismounted infantry and no tank battalions, the 1st and 2nd Battalions, 2nd Infantry, from the 5th Infantry Division replaced the 1st Division's two tank battalions, and the 1st Battalion, 26th Infantry, and the 1st Battalion, 28th Infantry, turned in their M113 APCs. These four infantry battalions, plus the 1st Battalion, 16th Infantry, and the 2nd Battalion, 28th Infantry, completed the nine infantry battalions, counting the three already deployed, of the Big Red One in Vietnam.[18]

The troopers of 1st Squadron, 4th Cavalry, replaced their M114 reconnaissance vehicles with the M113 APCs, a vehicle that General Don Starry characterized as "the best land vehicle developed by the United States. . . . It could absorb hits and continue operating." A steel gun shield was provided for the APC's .50-caliber machine gun, and two M60 7.62mm machine guns were added, making it the Armored Cavalry Vehicle (ACAV). The ACAV gave the 1/4th Cavalry tremendous firepower.[19]

The division was short 250 officers and 3,000 enlisted men in July, and Seaman overcame these shortages by stripping soldiers from units not scheduled for deployment. The historical report of the 1st Battalion, 26th Infantry, noted:

As the departure date approached, personnel turbulence increased. The battalion experienced a turnover exceeding one third of the number of personnel authorized during the final 45-day period prior to departure. The late receipt of the movement order (some people were required to depart 9 days after the movement order was received) created an extreme hardship on many personnel. Relocation of dependents and settling of personal affairs assumed a role of importance.[20]

During August and September 1965, advance parties selected sites for the division's base camps in Vietnam. Meanwhile, the troops and equipment moved to the West Coast, where they had embarked on ships for the voyage to Vietnam. The ships reached Vung Tau and Saigon Harbors in October. From those ports, the soldiers and equipment moved to their base camps (Map 26). The division headquarters and the support battalions were located at Di An; the 1st Brigade moved to Phuoc Vinh, farther north; the 3rd Brigade established its base at Lai Khe; the Division Artillery established its headquarters near Phu Loi; and the 2nd Brigade remained at Bien Hoa, 10 kilometers northeast of Di An. These locations were astride the main avenues of approach to Saigon from the Vietcong-infested War Zones C and D and the Iron Triangle. The move of the 1st Infantry Division to its bases was completed without incident or injury. At the end of what was known as Operation Big Red, the 2nd Brigade reverted to division control, reuniting the division.[21]

The first task for the newly arrived units was to establish fortified base camps. Carl Bradfield, of the 1st Battalion, 26th Infantry, remembered his first day's activity with the Blue Spaders:

> Everybody was busy hacking down elephant grass, which can grow as high as twelve feet and is so dense, one cannot see two feet in any direction. . . . There was only one tool used to clear as much grass away as possible before nightfall—the machete. . . . Men chopped, hacked and sliced the tall grass down . . . as the machetes worked hard and fast, the high grass and the jungle undergrowth began to form a clearing. . . . Nevertheless, work had to stop because "Charlie" (VCs [the Vietcong]) would be visiting us in the dark. . . . Occasionally, on those first hot sticky nights, a burst of rifle or machine gun fire came in our direction. We were a whole brigade of greenhorns, so it wasn't clear who was shooting at us.[22]

The men of the division were not greenhorns for long. General Westmoreland laid out a strategy that would pit America's finest units against a hardened enemy.

Westmoreland's Strategy: 1965

Secretary of Defense Robert McNamara asked General Westmoreland in July 1965 how he planned to use the additional forces he was receiving. Westmoreland's response was to develop a three-phase strategy in which the US units would serve as the vanguard of anti-Communist forces to expand South Vietnamese control over the areas of the country contested by the Communists and then destroy the enemy in its lairs.

Saigon and the logistics installations around the capital were essential to the success of Westmoreland's strategy. The security of the capital was also critical to the survival of the South Vietnamese government. If Westmoreland's plan was to succeed, American units had to take the fight to the enemy and drive it away from the major cities in their areas of operations. General Seaman was charged by Westmoreland to begin the first of three envisioned phases:

> Seaman's formations [1st Infantry Division and 173rd Airborne Brigade] would operate in a fan-shaped area opening northward from Saigon over a distance of some fifty-five kilometers. The land surface favored combat and varied from grasslands to rolling forested hills, few over seventy meters high. The road network thinned out rapidly to the north, but Highway 13—III Corps' main north-south artery—ran through and beyond the security zone. . . . Because it coursed between the two well-entrenched enemy strongholds to the north, War Zones C and D, securing it was one of Seaman's top priorities [see Map 26].[23]

The Communists facing the 1st Infantry Division totaled 16,000 regular soldiers of the *B2 Front*. This organization included five regiments of about 3,000 men each, organized in two divisions—the *5th* and *9th People's Liberation Army Front (PLAF) Divisions*. The *B2 Front* could count on the support of about 14,000 local Communist guerrillas. These soldiers provided logistical support, intelligence, and reinforcements whenever given an opportunity.[24]

The 1st and 3rd Brigades of the 1st Infantry Division generally faced War Zones C and D and the *9th PLAF*, while the 2nd Brigade and the 173rd Airborne Brigade faced the *5th PLAF* and protected ARVN's III Corps headquarters at Bien Hoa and the division's headquarters at Di An. Three ARVN divisions were also in the III Corps region to help defend Saigon.[25]

The Battle of Ap Bau Bang

The first major battle fought by the Big Red One took place in early November 1965 as the division was clearing Vietcong forces away from Highway 13, north of Lai Khe. The 173rd Airborne Brigade joined the fight by sending its three infantry battalions into the western edge of War Zone D. On the morning of 8 November, the 1st Battalion, 503rd Infantry, was ambushed by a battalion of the *271st PLAF Regiment*. The troops repulsed Vietcong attempts to overrun their positions and forced the Communists to withdraw. Although the paratroopers defeated the enemy, the Vietcong had initiated and terminated the action on their terms, a pattern that was to be disturbingly familiar throughout the Vietnam War.[26]

On 4 November, the 3rd Brigade, 1st Infantry Division, received the mission to clear Highway 13 from Lai Khe to Bau Long Pond. This operation was dubbed Bushmaster I. Lieutenant Colonel George Shuffer's 2nd Battalion, 2nd Infantry, set out on 10 November to secure the highway. Shuffer divided the 13-kilometer-long stretch of road into three zones, assigning one to each of his three rifle companies. Troop A, 1/4th Cavalry, and Battery C, 2nd Battalion, 33rd Artillery, supported the infantry. The rifle companies swept their sectors along the road during the day and pulled into fortified night defensive perimeters (NDPs) in the evening. The ARVN 7th Regiment passed through the area of responsibility of the 2nd Battalion, 2nd Infantry, without incident on 10 and 11 November, while American civil affairs teams handed out food and clothing to the villagers of Ben Dong So and Bau Bang.[27]

While Shuffer was putting his units into their NDPs on 11 November, the commander of the *9th PLAF Division* decided to attack Shuffer's command post near Bau Bang. Five Vietcong battalions moved into positions around Shuffer's NDP during the night of 11–12 November, planning to attack just after the Americans began to move out of their laager the next morning. By dawn, the Communists had set up mortars, recoilless rifles, and machine guns in Bau Bang and had laid telephone wire to the assault units.

The Vietcong attacked at about 0605, as the men of Company A and Troop A started to move out. While the Communists' mortars and machine guns laid down a barrage from the north of the American perimeter, a battalion of enemy infantry moved undetected to within 40 meters of 3rd Platoon, Troop A, 1/4th Cavalry, on the southwest corner of the American NDP. The cavalrymen met the enemy with fire from their 7.62mm and .50-caliber machine guns and then mounted their ACAVs and charged. This counterattack drove the Vietcong back in disarray, allowing Shuffer to get his other units into defensive positions.[28]

In spite of this repulse, the *9th PLAF Division* continued its attempts to overrun Shuffer's task force.

The Viet Cong had little more success in the two attacks that followed. In the first, as they crept close to the American position through high brushes and then dashed toward the concertina wire, they met fire from troopers in stationary armored personnel carriers and from infantrymen in foxholes and retreated. In the second, a number of them rushed the American line from the southeast across Highway 13, but Shuffer's men were again ready and beat them back.[29]

At around 0700 hours, the Vietcong launched a fourth attack against Shuffer's NDP from the southern edge of Bau Bang. Supported by mortar, recoilless rifle, and machine-gun fire from the village, the attackers reached the American perimeter. A suicide squad got through the wire and threw satchel charges into a howitzer position, killing two and wounding four crewmen. The gunners of Battery C, 2nd Battalion, 33rd Artillery, responded by lowering their 105mm tubes to fire level with the ground and smashed the attackers with fifty-five rounds of high-explosive shells. Fighter-bombers joined in at the same time, dropping napalm, cluster bombs, and fragmentation "iron bombs." This curtain of metal drove the surviving Communists back to Bau Bang.[30]

The Vietcong launched a final assault at 0900 to cover the withdrawal of their surviving soldiers. By then, American artillery, mortars, and aircraft had leveled Bau Bang. As Companies B and C, 2nd Battalion, 2nd Infantry, arrived, the last of the attackers fled, carrying their wounded. While the Vietcong had initiated and terminated the action, the *9th PLAF Division* suffered a major setback in its failure to destroy the isolated American task force. The *9th PLAF Division* lost at least 146 men killed and left weapons and equipment on the battlefield. They killed 20 and wounded 103 American soldiers.[31]

During the following week, the 3rd Brigade continued Operation Bushmaster I along Highway 13, from Lai Khe to the Michelin Plantation. On 14 November, the 2nd Battalion, 28th Infantry, and the 2nd Battalion, 33rd Field Artillery, moved by truck from Lai Khe to Chon Thonh, on the southwestern edge of the Michelin Plantation, to establish blocking positions. The 1st Battalion, 16th Infantry, and the 2nd Battalion, 28th Infantry, deployed southeast of the plantation by helicopter and worked their way through the jungle toward the 2/28th Infantry. After six days of slogging through the bush, the infantrymen found little of note and were ordered to return to Lai Khe.

The 2nd Battalion, 28th Infantry, again planned to move overland along Route 239 to Lai Khe. However, as the column set out, Route 239 turned into a muddy morass as monsoon rains drenched the area. The rifle companies and the accompanying artillery batteries bogged down, moving at about 100 meters per hour. When the column approached the hamlet of Trung Loi, 8 kilometers west of Highway 13, the lead company encountered Vietcong on both sides of the road. A firefight ensued.

When the Vietcong's *272nd Regiment* brought recoilless rifles and mortars into the fight, American helicopter gunships arrived, plastering the brush on the south side of the road. The gunships drove a number of the enemy on to the road where infantrymen killed some of them. By 1900, American and South Vietnamese fighter-bombers joined the fray, dropping napalm and cluster bombs along the north side of the road. Vietcong resistance dissolved as the Communists withdrew. By 2000, the column resumed its march eastward to Highway 13. During the next two days, the column moved without incident to Lai Khe, ending Operation Bushmaster I. The Communists killed 6 and wounded 38 American soldiers, while losing an estimated 40 to 140 men killed. Although the Big Red One again held the field at the end of the day, the Vietcong had decided where the fight was to take place and when it would start and end.[32]

The Battle of Nha Mat: December 1965

Shortly after the 3rd Brigade returned to Lai Khe, the Vietcong overwhelmed the ARVN 7th Regiment in the Michelin Plantation. General Seaman immediately instructed Colonel William Brodbeck to move one artillery and two infantry battalions to Dau Tieng to protect the 7th Regiment while it regrouped. The 3rd Brigade units reached Dau Tieng Airfield the next day. On 30 November, acting on intelligence that Vietcong units were in the southeastern corner of the plantation, Seaman ordered 3rd Brigade to destroy the enemy. Seaman reinforced Brodbeck with a third infantry battalion, enabling him to maneuver two infantry battalions while the third protected the brigade's forward camp.[33]

On 1 December, the 3rd Brigade initiated Operation Bushmaster II by moving two battalions by helicopter into the Michelin Plantation at Landing Zone (LZ) Dallas. For three days, the 2/2nd and 1/16th Infantry Battalions searched for the enemy while the 2/16th Infantry secured the 2/33rd Artillery and the brigade command post on LZ Dallas. On 5 December, Lieutenant Colonel Shuffer's 2nd Battalion, 2nd Infantry, encountered a bunker complex held by the *272nd PLAF Regiment*. As Company A tried to maneuver around the enemy's flank, Company B was attacked and driven across a road. Realizing that he was in the midst of a large enemy force, Shuffer established a defensive perimeter, with Company A on the west, C along the south, and B on the east. Shuffer's command group filled in the gap along the north. For the next four hours, the "Ramrods" held this perimeter as the *272nd* tried to overrun them.[34]

Brodbeck gave Shuffer priority for all available fire support, including artillery, helicopter gun teams, and air force fighter-bombers. Shuffer employed this firepower in a manner similar to that used during the fight near Trung Loi. He assigned the area on the north side of his laager to the helicopter gunships, that on the east to the fighter-bombers, and the ground south and west to the artillery. As the gunships, artillery, and fighter-bombers hammered the Vietcong, the enemy attempted to move closer to the American positions to protect themselves from the supporting fires. Shuffer's infantrymen, however, maintained a high volume of small-arms and mortar fire, preventing the Communists from getting close enough to do so.

Meanwhile, as Company B held off the attacks from the east, Companies A and C pushed southwest into the bunker complex. As the infantrymen advanced, they followed a rolling artillery barrage. Eventually, the enemy lost heart and retreated. The withdrawal turned to a rout under the hail of American fire, allowing Shuffer's men to secure the bunker complex. In the process, the Communists abandoned their dead, the heavy weapons, and a great deal of equipment. Although the Ramrods did not pursue the enemy, they counted 301 Vietcong bodies on the field, while losing 39 dead and 119 wounded themselves.[35]

Brodbeck terminated Operation Bloodhound (Bushmaster II) on 9 December. The 2nd Battalion, 2nd Infantry, and Battery A, 2nd Battalion, 33rd Artillery, earned Valorous Unit Awards for their actions on 5 December.[36]

The War Expands: 1966

The Communists' ability to suffer heavy losses in 1965 while increasing their forces in South Vietnam posed a major dilemma for Westmoreland and for the Johnson administration. Lieutenant General Stanley Larsen, the commander of I Field Force (an ad-hoc command unique to this situation), bluntly wrote to Westmoreland: "We are not engaging the Vietcong with sufficient frequency or effectiveness to win the war in Vietnam."[37] In response, the MACV commander directed his commanders to intensify operations and to develop "imaginative, aggressive tactics" to force the Communists to fight on US terms. Nonetheless, Westmoreland believed that his divisions had stemmed the Communist tide of victory, giving the South Vietnamese army an opportunity to regroup while American units initiated phase two of his strategy to take the battle deep into enemy-held areas.[38]

For the 1st Infantry Division, 1966 opened with too few troops in its area of operations to carry out the expanded mission. In addition to its three brigades, the division had attached to it the 173rd Airborne Brigade. With just thirteen maneuver battalions, the division could not hope to defend the major cities in III Corps and still launch major operations into War Zones C and D and the Iron Triangle. Westmoreland recognized that III Corps' area was the critical region of South Vietnam and directed his first major reinforcements to the Saigon area in early 1966.

The 25th Infantry Division began arriving in Vietnam in January. Its 3rd Brigade moved to the Central Highlands, but the division headquarters and its 1st and 2nd Brigades joined the Big Red One in III Corps, with their main base in Cu Chi (see Map 26). To control the two divisions in the area, Westmoreland created II Field Force. At the same time, Lieutenant General Larsen's headquarters in the II Corps area was redesignated I Field Force. By the end of April, 36,000 American and 39,000 ARVN troops were in the III Corps area ready to initiate Westmoreland's strategy.[39] At the same time, the Communist forces in the region increased to over 60,000 men.[40]

The 1st Infantry Division had two major tasks: it had to take the battle to the enemy's strongholds, and it had to secure the Cu Chi area for the safe arrival of the 25th Infantry Division. On 7 January, the 3rd Brigade attacked the Vietcong in the Ho Bo Woods, 10 kilometers southwest of Lai Khe. For five days the air force hammered enemy camps with B-52 bomber strikes in support of infantry sweeps of the woods. Although the brigade found over 10 tons of rice and numerous caches of supplies, the enemy avoided contact. On 12 January, the brigade returned to Lai Khe. Six men of the division were killed and forty-five were wounded, most by booby traps and mines.[41]

After a brief rest in Lai Khe, the 3rd Brigade deployed for Operation Buckskin to clear Hau Nghia Province of the enemy. The brigade established a forward base at Trung Lap from where its infantry battalions and a troop of 1/4th Cavalry swept the flat open terrain. These sweeps revealed no Vietcong units, although the brigade found base camps used by the enemy to store supplies and hide troops. On 24 January, Brodbeck moved the brigade to Cu Chi, where his men found a trench and tunnel system that ran throughout the area. Brodbeck's soldiers explored and destroyed as many tunnels as possible before turning the area over to the 2nd Brigade, 25th Infantry Division, on 30 January.[42] In the words of the official history, "the tunnels of Cu Chi would torment the 25th Division for years to come."[43]

In February the 1st Infantry Division launched its largest operation of the war thus far. Operation Mastiff targeted the *9th PLAF Division*, in the Boi Loi Woods and the area southwest of the Michelin Plantation in Tay Ninh and Hau Nghia Provinces. On 21 February, Seaman deployed 2nd Brigade from Dau Tieng to the northern and western sides of the area of operations, while 3rd Brigade and the Quarterhorse (1/4th Cavalry) moved into positions on the southern and southeastern side of the zone. The two forces then advanced toward one another. Although the troops found enemy camps and arms caches, they encountered only platoon- or company-size Vietcong units. The following fight, reported in the Mastiff after-action report, was typical of the actions encountered:

> The 1st Bn, 18th Inf (-) conducted a heliborne assault into LZ Betty [on 21 February] utilizing two lifts beginning 0954. The battalion closed on Betty [at] 1026 and commenced sweeping east with the recon platoon blocking on the east. Light contact was made by C Company resulting in 1 VC KIA. Mines, booby traps, and small arms fire were encountered in the vicinity of XT507376 resulting in 1 U.S. KIA, and 7 U.S. WIA. The battalion closed on Position Steel and established blocking positions for the night.[44]

After six days of searching, Seaman terminated Operation Mastiff—14 soldiers of the division had been killed and 94 were wounded. The division reported 61 enemy bodies on the field. During the operation, the division captured 198 tons of rice, 22 base camps, and numerous medical supplies and documents.[45] Again, however, the Communists avoided the big battles that would have allowed the Americans to mass firepower against the Vietcong main force battalions.[46]

In the midst of Operation Mastiff, the 1st Engineer Battalion was called upon to construct an all-weather road connecting Route 13 near Ben Cat to Route 16, south of Phouc Vinh. The 1st Brigade was to protect the engineers. The engineers deployed on 7 February and for six weeks labored to construct the road. Using tank dozers, cranes, scoop loaders, and rollers, the engineers cleared the route of mines, quarried laterite gravel from three quarries in the area, and built the road. The Vietcong made three attempts to delay construction, none of which inflicted any major damage on the 1st Engineer Battalion. On 3 March, Troop C, 1/4th Cavalry, escorted a column of engineer vehicles back to Di An, signaling a successful conclusion of the engineer's portion of Operation Rolling Stone. The 1st Engineer Battalion lost three men killed and twenty-nive wounded while constructing 18 kilometers of all-weather road.[47]

The Battle of Tan Binh: 24 February 1966

1st Brigade was very active as it protected the engineers along the road east of Ben Cat. Colonel Edgar Glotzbach assigned one infantry battalion to protect the work crews while his other two infantry battalions searched for the enemy. Periodically the battalions would rotate missions. During these operations, the Vietcong struck the brigade base camp near Tan Binh, evidently thinking they could overrun the command post.

The *9th PLAF Division* massed 1,800 soldiers around the 1st Brigade's base camp on the night of 23–24 February for a dawn attack. However, an American listening post spotted the enemy moving in the dark and opened fire. This alerted the soldiers of the 1st Battalion, 26th Infantry, Company B, 1/28th Infantry, and Troop B, 1/4th Cavalry, who manned their foxholes and armored vehicles around the perimeter. Between 0130 and 0300 hours, the Communists laid down a barrage of small-arms, mortar, and recoilless rifle fire against the American positions but refrained from attacking. At first light, the two batteries of 105mm howitzers of the 1st Battalion, 5th Artillery, in the base camp lowered their tubes and fired 166 rounds of high explosives directly into enemy positions.

Groups of Vietcong were seen moving close to the perimeter, giving the defenders clear targets. Finally, at 0530, Vietcong infantry made an uncoordinated attack against the American positions. The Blue Spaders and the Quarterhorse repulsed this assault, inflicting heavy casualties on the enemy. By 0645, the battle was over as the enemy retreated, leaving at least 142 dead and numerous weapons on the field.[48]

During Operation Rolling Stone, civil affairs and psychological operations teams distributed propaganda leaflets and safe conduct passes in the villages along the road. American soldiers also helped villagers rebuild damaged houses while medical teams treated hundreds of civilians for minor medical problems. As a result of the security provided by the 1st Brigade, two South Vietnamese district chiefs visited their districts for the first time in years. Sadly, after Operation Rolling Stone ended, the South Vietnamese armed forces were unable to secure the area, allowing the Vietcong to reestablish control over the population.[49]

The Battle of Lo Ke: March 1966

Following Operation Mastiff, the 3rd Brigade tried new methods to lure the enemy into battle. Based on intelligence that the *9th PLAF Division* was operating north of Lai Khe, Lieutenant Colonel Kyle Bowie's 2nd Battalion, 28th Infantry (the Black Lions), deployed to the Lo Ke Rubber Plantation, on 3 March. This move initiated Operation Boston/Cocoa Beach. Bowie's men moved on foot to the area just west of Bau Bang and established a fortified base camp. Expecting a fight, Bowie had extra ammunition and supplies flown in to his battalion. On 4 March, two of Bowen's companies made sweeps around his camp. One of the companies found a trench system to the north. That night, the Black Lions established listening posts outside the defensive perimeter and waited.

The night of 4–5 March passed without incident. The next morning, as the outposts prepared to come in, the patrol on the northern side heard noises. The patrol's leader, Second Lieutenant Robert J. Hibbs, observed through his Starlight scope—a device that used ambient light to illuminate targets in the dark—a column moving along a nearby trail. Hibbs watched this group of women and children carry supplies to a rendezvous near the northwest corner of the plantation with a Vietcong infantry company. The enemy company continued south toward Hibbs's position after picking up supplies. As they did so, Hibbs positioned his claymore mines to cover the route the enemy was advancing along and notified Colonel Kyle of the situation.

When the enemy entered the claymores' kill zone, Hibbs detonated the mines, showering the Vietcong with steel flechetes. At the same time, Hibbs's men threw grenades at the enemy and began to withdraw on their lieutenant's command. During the withdrawal toward the battalion NDP, Hibbs and his platoon sergeant stopped to help a wounded comrade. As they did so, two Vietcong machine-gun crews opened fire, badly wounding the two leaders. Hibbs ordered his patrol to continue toward the NDP with the wounded while he turned toward the enemy machine guns with his M16 rifle and pistol. Hibbs's attempt to destroy the guns diverted the enemy's attention from his men, but Hibbs was hit again and fell. Before he died, he smashed his Starlight scope, preventing the enemy from using it. For this action, Robert Hibbs received the Medal of Honor posthumously, the first soldier of the Big Red One to earn the medal since 1945.[50]

The Vietcong then attacked the northern side of Kyle's perimeter. The Black Lions met this assault with mortar and small-arms fire, driving the enemy back into the woods. This attack was followed by another from the northeast and a third from the east. Kyle called for air strikes as his men laid down a heavy sheet of fire to prevent the Vietcong from getting close to their foxholes. Air force fighter-bombers dropped 500-pound bombs on the attackers. After several more attempts to penetrate the perimeter, the Communists retreated.

Although Brodbeck committed the 2nd Battalion, 2nd Infantry, to the chase the next morning and had the area thoroughly searched over the next two days, the enemy got away. By the time the operation ended, on 8 March, the Vietcong had lost an estimated 199 men killed. The 1st Infantry Division lost 15 men, 6 of whom died when their helicopter crashed on 5 March.[51]

The Spring of 1966: Situation in the II Field Force Area of Operations

In spite of American efforts, Communist strength in the II Field Force area (also known as III Corps) increased significantly in early 1966. The

Communist Central Office for South Vietnam (*COSVN*) continued to function somewhere along the Vietnam-Cambodian border, near or in War Zone C. From there, General Nguyen Chi Thanh directed the efforts of three Communist divisions. These three divisions were reinforced by five battalions of artillery of various calibers and the elite North Vietnamese *70th Guard Regiment*. The latter infantry unit protected Thanh's *COSVN* headquarters.[52]

General Westmoreland believed that Thanh intended to launch a major offensive against Saigon during the rainy season in May or June. To forestall this offensive, General Seaman, the new II Field Force commander, ordered Major General William DePuy, the new division commander, to launch the Big Red One in a preemptive strike against Thanh's forces.

William DePuy had served as MACV operations officer. As such, he had studied and analyzed operations in Vietnam and had developed ideas about how operations should be conducted against the Communists. DePuy believed that the division needed to find "the enemy with the fewest possible men, and . . . [then] destroy him with the maximum amount of firepower."[53] DePuy believed that artillery shells were cheaper than men's lives and that the purpose of the infantry was to advance artillery forward observers to positions from which they could direct fire against the enemy. Every operation conducted by the division while DePuy was commander was organized so that the infantry units maneuvered within the range of American artillery.[54] DePuy was criticized by some on Seaman's staff for abandoning the tactical concept of having infantrymen physically "close with and destroy the enemy" rather than doing the job with firepower.[55]

DePuy had a profound impact on the 1st Infantry Division. He took a deep interest in the techniques of combat operations. For example, he developed a foxhole with firing ports facing to the left and right fronts, rather than facing directly toward the enemy. Each of these "DePuy foxholes" protected similar positions to their right and left, interlocking observation and fire but denying the enemy an opening to fire at directly. These positions were covered with logs and sandbags to protect the soldiers from enemy mortars and artillery. DePuy "as he walked among positions in the jungle, lectured officers and NCO's on how to construct proper defenses."[56] The DePuy foxholes and the concept of interlocking fires became standard in much of the army.[57]

DePuy insisted that the division's units train whenever possible. This was critical because the army had set soldiers' Vietnam tours at one year, rather than the duration of the war. There would be roughly a 10 percent turnover of personnel every month. Each brigade established a jungle warfare training school for new men, and periodically DePuy gave battalions time out of action to hone tactical skills.

DePuy's approach to operating the division was to maneuver battalions against the enemy and to use helicopters to make the Big Red One an air-mobile division in all but name. DePuy later commented:

> It was my idea to go after the Main Forces wherever they could be found and to go after them with as many battalions as I could get into the fight—what was later called "pile-on." . . . To do this required a very agile and fast moving division, a division which was, in fact, airmobile. My efforts were to create just such a division. I took it as my main mission to defeat all the Vietcong Main Forces north of Saigon in the III Corps zone. . . . So as soon as I got there, I moved the division around a lot.[58]

Operation Abilene: 30 March–15 April 1966

DePuy's first large-scale offensive action came at the end of March in Operation Abilene. Abilene was a search and destroy operation in Long Khanh and Phuoc Tuy Provinces, east of Saigon. The goal was to strike the *5th* and *94th PLAF Regiments* thought by MACV intelligence to be in the area. The division's zone of operations was between Highways 1 and 15, with the brigades beginning their search for the Vietcong in Phuoc Tuy Province (see Map 27). On 30 March, the attached Royal Australian Regiment and a tank platoon from the 1/4th Cavalry secured the site for the division's forward command post and logistics base. The 2nd and 3rd Brigades commenced inserting their infantry battalions into landing zones the same day. Once on the ground, the infantry made methodical sweeps of the jungle where the Vietcong regiments were suspected to be. For the next ten days the division had only minor contacts with the enemy.[59]

DePuy had the infantry battalions shift their search areas repeatedly in order to catch the enemy off guard. Each day, the infantry made contact with only small enemy units, making it impossible to take advantage of the available firepower. Numerous caches of supplies were found, including 1,241 tons of rice, 51 tons of salt, and 5,000 gallons of kerosene. Although the division destroyed 54 base camps, a small-arms factory, and a printing press, none of these material losses permanently degraded Vietcong capability.[60]

American medical units treated 1,500 villagers for minor ailments, and civil affairs teams helped rebuild homes and villages and distributed 25 tons of food. But as before, the South Vietnamese had insufficient forces available to secure the area permanently.[61]

The only major combat action of Abilene took place on 11 April, when the 2nd Battalion, 16th Infantry, found the base camp of the *D800 Battalion*, forcing the Vietcong to fight. The action commenced when Company C

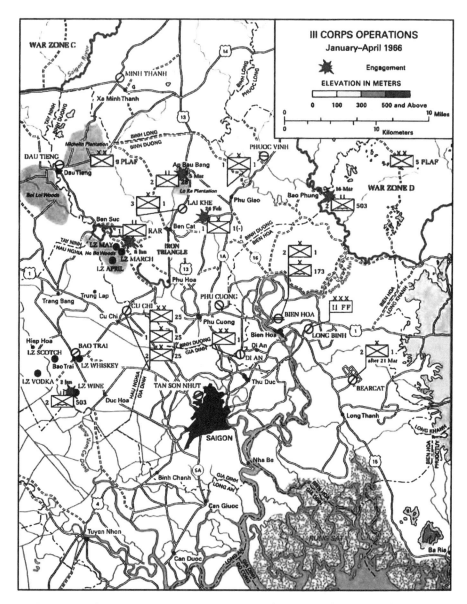

Map 27. III Corps operations, January–April 1966. (John M. Carland, *Stemming the Tide, May 1965 to October 1966* [U.S. Army Center of Military History, 2000])

engaged a platoon of VC at YS 535855. The engagement resulted in five VC KIA (B[ody] C[ount]), two US KIA and 12 US WIA. The VC attempted to break contact at 1525 and moved to the northwest. C Company pursued, maintaining contact and at 1525 halted to evacuate casualties. Although unknown at this time, the position selected was approximately 100 to 200 meters from a battalion base camp. Dense jungle growth restricted visibility to 15 meters and prevented the company from finding the VC installations.[62]

At 1735 hours, the Vietcong opened a heavy barrage against Company C from all directions of the landing zone. This fusillade was followed by three separate attacks by Communist infantry against the hastily dug positions of the Americans. The men of Company C held their ground, repulsing each assault with support from the 1st Battalion, 7th Artillery, and from helicopters dropping flares during the night. The next morning, Company A, 2/16th, and Company B, 2/18th Infantry, cut their way through the jungle to join Company C. By then, the Vietcong had retreated, leaving forty-one bodies on the field.[63] On 15 April, General DePuy ended Operation Abilene and moved the troops back to their base camps.

Operation Abilene established only temporary American control over the villages of Phuoc Tuy and Long Khanh. When the division returned to base, the area returned to enemy control. The 1st Infantry Division found the bodies of 92 enemy in the area. The Big Red One captured 36 small arms and 2 mortars. In the process of inflicting these losses on the Vietcong, the division lost 48 men killed and 135 wounded.[64]

In DePuy's final analysis,

> Operation Abilene demonstrated conclusively that the 1st Infantry Division can move—and move rapidly—by airmobile operations. In a period of 16 days, the major land area of Phuoc Tuy Province was covered with sufficient thoroughness to provide assurance that the *5th* and *94th Vietcong Regiments* were not present in strength. . . . A number of lessons were learned. . . . However, the Vietcong have suffered a tremendous loss of prestige in Phuoc Tuy Province by failing to oppose U.S. Forces.[65]

Nonetheless, the enemy avoided contact with American forces when they felt it was to their advantage to do so.

Operation Birmingham

II Field Force next ordered DePuy to carry out a similar strike in Tay Ninh Province, where Communist facilities were believed to be in War Zone C.

The Vietnam-Cambodian border ran along the western and northern sides of Tay Ninh, giving *COSVN* units access to sanctuary in neutral Cambodia. Allied intelligence estimated that there were numerous hospitals, rest camps, and supply dumps in War Zone C, especially along the border. It was believed by MACV that there were probably only two Vietcong battalions in the zone. Other Communist units transited the area and used its facilities on a periodic basis.[66]

DePuy deployed the 1st and 3rd Brigades into Tay Ninh Province on 23 April. A forward division command post was established near Tay Ninh Airport, while the 1/4th Cavalry and the artillery battalions moved overland to Dau Tieng. The next morning, the division took advantage of good flying weather to fly four infantry battalions to landing zones in War Zone C. Over the next six days, the two brigades conducted battalion-size search and destroy missions. The division found large caches of food and a Vietcong training center, complete with electric generators and five large classrooms.[67]

Although DePuy maneuvered all available battalions through War Zone C, no major contact was made until 30 April, when Lieutenant Colonel Richard Prillaman's 1st Battalion, 2nd Infantry, received small-arms fire from the Cambodian side of the Rach Cai Bac River. Prillaman's soldiers returned fire and called in artillery and air strikes. As Prillaman's men maintained a heavy volume of fire against the enemy, Company A, 2/16th Infantry, maneuvered to the flank of another Vietcong position to the north of the two battalions. The 1/2nd Infantry, then, in the words of the division's after-action report, "closed with the VC forces (estimated at a battalion on the east bank) and killed 42 VC plus another 75 (probable)." Communist losses included 54 men killed on the eastern side of the river and another 100 probably killed on the western bank. The action ended when the Vietcong retreated deeper into Cambodia.[68]

Operation Birmingham continued with minor contacts until terminated on 16 May. During the operation, 118 enemy bodies and 130 weapons were found and another 307 enemy were thought to have been killed. The 1st Infantry Division destroyed 3 hospitals, 66 base camps, 4 munitions factories, and 6 fuel dumps. The Vietcong lost 2,103 tons of rice, 323 tons of salt, and 35 tons of wheat. During Birmingham, 62 soldiers of the Big Red One died and another 324 suffered wounds; 21 American helicopters received damage, as did 8 armored vehicles.[69]

General DePuy believed that "Operation Birmingham was another highly successful operation in which the division again demonstrated its ability and willingness to move rapidly to a distant area of operations for the conduct of extended jungle operations while retaining high morale and fighting effectiveness. This operation was the first deep penetration of War Zone C since 1961."[70]

The Enemy Offensive that Might Have Been

During Birmingham, MACV received intelligence that *COSVN* was planning a major offensive during the monsoon season. Defectors told interrogators that the *9th PLAF Division* was moving two regiments from War Zone D to C, to attack Loc Ninh before 10 May 1966.[71]

Although the enemy did not attack before 10 May, ARVN units encountered the *271st* and *273rd PLAF Regiments* in the hills west of An Loc. A Vietcong soldier's diary found in early May outlined plans for four regiments to attack Loc Ninh. DePuy decided to launch another preemptive operation to forestall the Communists.[72] Brodbeck's 3rd Brigade carried out the search and destroy operation from 19 to 26 May. Although the three infantry battalions searched aggressively for the enemy, they made no major contacts. After a number of air assaults and sweeps through the jungle, the troops captured one clip for a pistol, a shaped charge explosive, and some papers. The only good news was that no American soldiers were killed or wounded. By 26 May, all units were back in their bases.[73]

There also were numerous battalion-level operations in the spring and summer of 1966. One unusual one was Operation Lexington III, carried out by the 1st Battalion, 18th Infantry (the Vanguards), from 21 May to 9 June in the Rung Sat Special Zone along the Saigon River. The battalion used helicopters and navy assault craft to move as the soldiers attempted to prevent the Vietcong from interdicting shipping. The Vanguards carried out numerous sweeps of the river and hit the enemy with seven ambushes. At least 29 Vietcong were killed and 30 weapons were captured before the battalion returned to base.

The major problems the 1st Battalion, 18th Infantry, encountered were malarial swamps, immersion foot, and heavy rains. The men could operate in such a wet environment for only forty-eight hours before they needed several days to dry out and treat sores and infections. During the operation, the battalion's mortars accidentally shelled the village of Dong Ha. Seven Vietnamese civilians were killed and thirty wounded. The battalion surgeon and medical personnel rushed to the village to care for the wounded. Many were evacuated by helicopter to American hospitals. The division G5 (civil affairs officer) arranged for compensation for the families of the victims, and the Vanguards delivered food and building materials to Dong Ha.[74]

In the midst of such operations, commanders found that replacements

were not adequately trained. For example, the Vanguards' after-action report concluded: "New arrivals have a tendency to fire prior to identifying
the enemy or insuring that moving objects are not friendly troops. Green
troops must be indoctrinated to let the enemy close, with the idea of a first
round kill." Further training was necessary for radio operators on how to
set up the taller 292 antennas for the radios carried by the platoons and
companies.[75] Such problems were endemic, as Lieutenant Colonel Paul Gorman found when he assumed command of the 1st Battalion, 26th Infantry, in June and learned that parts of the 292 antenna were used for other
purposes, such as pointers in staff briefings.[76] Training replacements was a
major challenge for the division as it received nearly 6,000 replacements in
the first half of 1966 alone.[77]

Operation El Paso II/III: 2 June–3 September 1966

Although the division had not encountered the enemy in its sweeps around
Loc Ninh in May, MACV intelligence continued to report that General
Thanh was planning a major push in Binh Long Province. Initially, 3rd
Brigade moved north to help the ARVN 5th Infantry Division defend Loc
Ninh, on 2 June. The first major contact came on 8 June, when Troop A,
1st Squadron, 4th Cavalry, engaged two Vietcong battalions near Ap Tau O.
The Communists initiated the action by detonating a mine against the lead
tank of Captain Ralph Sturgis's column.

Over the next six hours the enemy attacked the column as the men of the
Quarterhorse engaged them with canister, small-arms, and machine-gun fire.
The fighting was often at close quarters:

> Captain Copes [in charge of Troop A's maintenance elements] saw Sgt Norris
> in need of help so he tried to get him into his M113. While doing this a VC
> threw a 75mm shell packed with explosives into the M113. The bomb landed
> in Captain Copes' lap. He quickly grabbed the bomb with his left hand and at
> the same time grasped his M-16 rifle with his right hand. He heaved the bomb
> package up and out of the track, and upon quickly turning his head, he saw the
> VC that threw it. He instantly aimed the M-16 and killed the VC and ducked
> back inside the M113 just before the bomb exploded outside the track's rear.[78]

The Communists had waited days for a chance to ambush an American
convoy. They engaged the column from "fortified revetments [made by] using 55 gallon diesel drums and sandbags for walls. The drums were filled
with dirt for greater strength." Several tanks and a number of APCs were

damaged by recoilless rifle fire, but the Vietcong had the worst of the engagement as air strikes and artillery pounded their positions.[79]

The enemy was in full retreat by 1800 hours, having lost at least ninety-three men killed, including a battalion commander. The Vietcong's failure to coordinate the assaults of their two battalions gave General DePuy time to bring American firepower to bear. The fact that they had chosen to attack an armored force also was their misfortune. As DePuy commented, the enemy had "swallowed some bad bait."[80] Reinforcements from the 2nd Battalion, 28th Infantry, arrived as the enemy withdrew. The Quarterhorse collected thirty small arms and one 57mm recoilless rifle on the battlefield and confirmed the attackers were from the *272nd Regiment*. This intelligence caused DePuy to deploy the 1st Brigade to Binh Long and to establish a command post near An Loc. Operation El Paso II thus became a two-brigade operation.[81]

During the next three weeks, the division encountered small groups of enemy. In most cases, the Vietcong broke contact after losing a few men. The 2nd Battalion, 28th Infantry, inflicted the most damage on the Communists in this period when, on 11 June, the *707th Battalion* of the *273rd PLAF Regiment* made a stand in a bunker complex north of Loc Ninh. Fighting continued all day as Lieutenant Colonel Kyle Bowie committed his entire battalion against the Communists. Under the cover of intense artillery fire, the Vietcong defense collapsed. The *707th* lost 98 dead before it could escape from the battle. Bowie's victory was not cheap, as his recon platoon was outflanked by a counterattack and lost 19 men killed. Total American losses were 33 dead and 33 wounded.[82]

DePuy continued to send forces throughout Binh Long Province to pursue the enemy. However, no contact was made with major Vietcong units until the 1st Squadron, 4th Cavalry, began to conduct "Roadrunner" operations along Highway 13, from An Loc south to Phu Loi. These operations were designed to lure the enemy out to ambush the armor columns, thus allowing the division to pile on with troops and firepower.

During one of these efforts, Lieutenant Colonel Leonard Lewane's 1/4th Cavalry and Lieutenant Colonel Herbert McChrystal's 2nd Battalion, 18th Infantry, secured the division's forward base at Quan Loi. The armored cavalry squadron patrolled the area while the infantry battalion protected the base and reinforced the Quarterhorse when necessary. On 30 June, the cavalrymen moved north toward Loc Ninh, looking for the enemy. Shortly after 0930 hours, the armored column encountered Vietcong on the western side of Highway 13, just beyond a rice paddy. In the first thirty minutes of contact, recoilless rifles knocked out four of Troop B's M48 tanks. Lieutenant

James Flores, the troop commander, reported the action to Colonel Lewane, who was overhead in a helicopter, and requested fire support.[83]

Lewane diverted fighter-bombers to Flores's position where their bombs helped screen the withdrawal of Troop B to a rally point north of a bridge site. The Vietcong maintained contact and poured a heavy volume of fire into the rally point where Troop B was reorganizing. As the engagement developed, Captain Stephen Slattery, Troop C commander, moved his platoons toward Troop B's location to help evacuate the wounded and to suppress the enemy fire. As Troop C moved,

> several of the infantry riding on the personnel carriers were hit as mortar rounds started falling into the area. Capt. Slattery ordered the platoons to deploy and push out the perimeter, primarily to the north. The 3d Platoon was operating northwest of the crossroads, 1st Platoon to the east, and 2d Platoon west and southwest. . . . Checkpoint 1 was becoming very jammed with C Troop maneuvering and vehicles returning with B Troop wounded.[84]

At this point, Lewane ordered Troop C to join Troop B. As the troop moved north 2nd Platoon was hit by enemy fire. A wounded tank commander and loader were evacuated from their vehicle and the column continued. As they went, the cavalrymen threw hand grenades at the enemy, who were able to get close to the vehicles because of the thick brush. Finally Troop C reached Troop B. Lewane ordered Slattery to deploy his platoons in a semicircle to screen the withdrawal of Troop B. As the troopers maneuvered, the division concentrated artillery fire north and east of the action and directed air strikes to the west. On the request of Captain Slattery, cluster bombs of the fighter-bombers were moved in as close as possible to the perimeter. Under the protection of Troop C and the fighter-bombers, Lieutenant Flores withdrew his troop south to Checkpoint One, where he regrouped his command.[85]

Shortly after Flores got to the checkpoint, Company A, 2/18th Infantry, arrived by helicopter. The infantrymen boarded the armored vehicles of 3rd Platoon, Troop C, and moved north to reinforce Slattery. After dropping the infantrymen off, 3rd Platoon moved east to push the Vietcong away from a potential landing zone. The cavalrymen, however, ran into a Communist bunker, where the platoon leader, Lieutenant Charles D. Cole, was wounded along with several of his men. The platoon withdrew to the main perimeter under covering fire from 1st Platoon. At about the same time, Company B, 2/18th Infantry, arrived by helicopter and reinforced the cavalrymen. The infantry companies, now under the command of Lieutenant Colonel McChrystal, maneuvered against the Vietcong positions. Enemy fire then began to slacken as they retreated.[86]

Over the next three days, General DePuy deployed the 1st Battalion, 2nd Infantry, and the 1st Battalion, 28th Infantry, in pursuit. The South Vietnamese also committed regional forces to help block escape routes. On 2 July, the 2nd Battalion, 18th Infantry, was hit by mortar fire and a dawn assault. This attack was met with artillery and small-arms fire and 61 fighter-bomber sorties. The action ended around 0900, as the enemy retreated. Enemy losses in the Battle of Srok Dong were 270 killed (body count) and an estimated 300 men probably killed. The Americans captured 40 small arms and 23 crew-served weapons. American losses were 19 killed and 94 wounded; 11 armored vehicles were damaged, and a personnel carrier and a helicopter were destroyed.[87]

Based on the success of the armored cavalry squadron in luring the enemy into an action, General DePuy ordered Colonel Sid Berry to plan another Roadrunner operation. The mission was "to position forces and conduct reconnaissance in force to lure VC forces to ambush/attack the column, enabling the 1st Brigade to destroy VC forces by offensive action."[88]

Operation Olympia/El Paso commenced on 9 July, as Troops B and C, 1/4th Cavalry, and Company B, 1/2nd Infantry, moved southwest from Highway 13 toward Minh Thanh along Route 245. To tempt the Vietcong to attack, information was leaked that the column, known as Task Force Dragoon, was escorting bulldozers and trucks and that the armored elements were weak. Intelligence officers estimated that a battalion of the *272nd Regiment* was in the area, and Berry's staff identified the most probable locations where the Vietcong would strike and planned artillery fire and air strikes accordingly.[89]

At 0700, Task Force Dragoon, commanded by Lewane, set out from An Loc and turned southwest onto Route 245. Thick brush along the roadway restricted movement to the road, where tanks were interspersed with the APCs and a mechanized flamethrower vehicle of each cavalry troop. The infantrymen rode on the tracks of Troops B and C. After moving 2 kilometers south of the road junction, the column reached open terrain and spread its formation. As they moved, the tanks sprayed suspected ambush sites with machine-gun fire. No enemy activity was observed, however, as the task force secured and crossed a bridge along the route. At that point, Lewane ordered the column to increase speed.

The column continued without incident until 1110 hours, when Lieutenant Jack Lyons, of 1st Platoon, Troop C, reported Vietcong crossing the road ahead. More enemy followed as Troop C's tanks began to fire. All hell then broke loose, as mortar and recoilless fire hit the column. After a short delay, Lewane determined that the ambush force was north of the road, allowing him to direct preplanned artillery fire into this area. The Vietcong were in foxholes along the north edge of the road and evidently had not occupied those positions until the task force was in the ambush kill zone.[90]

As soon as the Vietcong attacked, Task Force Dragoon created a goose egg position along the road. This allowed Berry to coordinate the fire of helicopter gunships, fighter-bombers, and artillery against the enemy. Berry also started Major John Bard's 1st Battalion, 18th Infantry, toward the battle. As Bard's men moved overland, the 1/28th Infantry prepared to move by helicopter to a landing zone northeast of the fight, while the 1st Battalion, 16th Infantry, and the 2nd Battalion, 2nd Infantry, were alerted for movement to positions north of the Vietcong force. These moves were designed to trap the enemy.[91]

The 1st Brigade enveloped the enemy over the next few hours. Task Force Dragoon remained in blocking positions along Route 245 as the 1/28th Infantry made contact on its right with a large Vietcong force. The 1/18th Infantry drove northeast with its right flank on the road and its left-hand elements 500 meters into the jungle, while the Ramrods and Rangers attempted to cut off the enemy's escape. Contact was made throughout the afternoon with small groups of fleeing Vietcong, but the undergrowth prevented the closure of the ring and many got away. As darkness fell, the 1st Brigade held positions roughly surrounding the initial Vietcong locations, and air strikes continued through the night. But the battle was over. Attempts to catch the remnants of the *272nd PLAF Regiment* failed.[92]

Operation Olympia achieved significant results. The 1st Brigade found 239 enemy bodies and 54 weapons on the field and captured 8 Vietcong. Perhaps another 304 Communists were killed in the jungle as they retreated. While 25 Americans died and another 113 were wounded in the Battle of Minh Thanh Road, the *272nd* was no longer capable of offensive action.[93]

By mid-July, the 1st and 3rd Brigades had engaged and defeated two regiments of the *9th PLAF Division*, foiling their hopes of taking part in an offensive. The Vietcong abandoned their camps in Binh Long Province. During the operation, which terminated at the end of September, the 1st Infantry Division found a total of 825 dead enemy and estimated that it probably killed another 1,249. The division destroyed hundreds of camps and supply bases and captured tons of food and other supplies. In the process, 125 Americans died and another 424 were wounded. DePuy concluded: "Operation El Paso inflicted a severe defeat on the *9th Vietcong [PLAF] Division*, completely frustrating the monsoon offensive in the northern III Corps area, and represented an important learning process throughout the 1st Infantry Division."[94]

Operation Amarillo and the Phu Loi Fight

As El Paso came to an end, DePuy sent Sid Berry's 1st Brigade into action along Routes 1A and 16, between Di An and Phuoc Vinh. The brigade was to support the 1st Engineer Battalion as it worked on the roads and to protect supply convoys. During one of these operations north of Tan Binh, on 24–25 August, a nighttime patrol from Company C, 1st Battalion, 2nd Infantry, found itself in the bunker complex occupied by the Vietcong *Phu Loi Battalion* (Map 28). The fifteen men of the patrol took cover in a bunker, radioed for help, and commenced to fight for their lives. In response, Major Richard Clark, acting battalion commander of 1/2nd Infantry, ordered the rest of Company C to move toward the action, accompanied by 2nd Platoon, Troop C, 1/4 Cavalry.[95] Captain William Mullen's men found movement difficult and encountered heavy fire. As the firing increased, Berry ordered Clark to send the remainder of 1/2nd Infantry toward the sound of the guns. Berry also asked DePuy for helicopters to lift the 1st Battalion, 16th Infantry, to a landing zone west of the *Phu Loi Battalion* to prevent its escape.

By 1100 hours, DePuy had learned that Company C, 1/2nd Infantry, had suffered "many casualties," leading DePuy to make this action the division's priority fight.[96] By then, Lieutenant Colonel Paul Gorman had moved his 1st Battalion, 26th Infantry, toward the fight from the south, and the 1st Battalion, 16th Infantry, had landed to the west and was pushing toward the battle. To cut off an escape route through the village of Bong Trang, Gorman moved Company B west, with the infantrymen riding on the tracks of Troop A, 1/4th Cavalry. At the same time, his Company C moved north to help Company C, 1/2nd. The Blue Spaders reached the Ramrods at about 1600.[97]

During the afternoon, DePuy notified Colonel Berry that the 2nd Battalion, 28th Infantry, was going to arrive by air. By then, things were not going well on the battlefield as Company B, 1/2nd Infantry, met withering fire in its attempts to reached Mullen's Company C. In three futile assaults, Company B lost dozens of men without breaking through. Only the arrival of the APCs and tanks of Troop C, 1/4th Cavalry, eased the pressure on Clark's besieged units. According to the official history, when Captain Steve Slattery's troopers reached the clearing, they "entered a scene of disarray. Wounded and dead littered the battleground, and some of the men had become separated from their superiors and were no longer firing their weapons."[98] Berry's attempt to surround and overwhelm an enemy force clearly was not working out well.

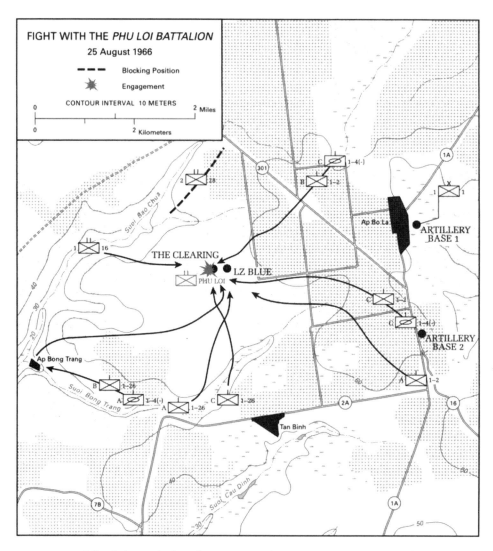

Map 28. The fight with the *Phu Loi Battalion*, 25 August 1966. (John
M. Carland, *Stemming the Tide, May 1965 to October 1966* [U.S. Army
Center of Military History, 2000])

At about 1625 hours, the 1/16th Infantry reached the Vietcong base camp
and joined the fight. The *Phu Loi Battalion* met the arriving Americans
with heavy fire from bunkers around the clearing and along the trails in
the area (Map 28). The action was confused as the 1st Battalion, 2nd Infantry, moved in from the east and the Blue Spaders moved from the south.
By 1700, it appeared that the heaviest fighting involved the intermingled

soldiers of Company C, 1/2nd Infantry, Company C, 1/26th Infantry, and Troop C, 1/4th Cavalry. At least fifty men from these units were wounded and two were killed.[99]

Many of the American units on the ground were so disorganized that Colonel Berry was forced to land and personally take command of the ground action, at about 1430. Major Clark was killed as he and Berry were discussing the situation, and the 3rd Brigade's executive officer assumed command of the 1/2nd Infantry. Berry, a veteran of the early fighting in the Korean War, told Gorman later that it was "the worst battle scene I had ever witnessed." From the south, Gorman's Blue Spaders (Companies A and B) swung north at Bong Trang and advanced through the brush to the clearing. The arrival of Gorman's force with a platoon of armored cavalry swung the tide toward the 1st Brigade. Berry put Gorman in command of the intermingled battalions, and the American units established NDPs.[100]

As the *Phu Loi Battalion* withdrew, snipers remained active, nearly killing Gorman and Berry when they met on top of a tank in the clearing. Berry resumed his role as brigade commander and attempted to encircle the enemy, whom he hoped were caught between the 1/2nd and the 1/26th Infantry. Most of the *Phu Loi* escaped during the night. Early the next morning, fighter-bombers dropped napalm in the confined space between the American battalions. After one canister hit near Gorman's command group, Gorman asked Berry to continue bringing the ordnance in close. However, after another canister fell too close and killed and wounded several men, Berry ended the air strikes.[101] When they attacked, the American infantry found that the enemy was gone. They also found the bodies of six members of the patrol that had initiated the action. The remaining nine survived, having stayed in their bunker through the battle.[102]

During the remainder of 26 August, 1st Brigade soldiers searched the area and cleaned up the debris from the previous day's fight. The initial reports indicated that the brigade had 30 men killed and 183 wounded. The 1st Brigade found 53 enemy bodies and captured 6 more Vietcong alive. The 1st Brigade after-action report listed friendly losses for the nine days as 41 killed, 34 of them on 25–26 August.[103]

Colonel Berry concluded that "this battle presented on a grand scale the tactical difficulty often previously encountered at company level in the jungle: The tendency to bring up units on line for frontal attack instead of enveloping the enemy position by wide maneuver."[104] Inexperienced leadership and the difficulties of jungle warfare explained some of the tactical problems noted. By the summer of 1966, the 1st Infantry Division had been in Vietnam for nearly a year. Most of the brigade, battalion, and company commanders, nearly all of the NCOs, and most of the soldiers who originally moved with the division from Fort Riley had rotated back to the United States. Lessons learned in the fall of 1965 had to be relearned. This process became even harder when the army restricted command tours to six months.

The Autumn of 1966: Frustration

At the end of operations, the men of the 1st Infantry Division returned to their bases knowing that they had kept open the lines of communications into Saigon. They also weakened the enemy's ability to maintain forces close to the capital. But the large-scale operations failed to provide security for the population outside of those places where American and allied forces were stationed. Such missions also put a continual strain on American soldiers, as mines, malaria, ambushes, and the damp environment took their toll.

Having inflicted major losses on the enemy in Roadrunner operations, DePuy hoped to repeat success by conducting a division maneuver that would tempt the Communists to commit large units against American convoys or seemingly isolated battalions. On 9 October, DePuy deployed the 1st and 3rd Brigades with seven battalions of infantry, the Quarterhorse, and the 2nd Battalion, 34th Armor, for Operation Tulsa.

Tulsa was a giant Roadrunner-type operation along Highway 13, between Phu Cuong and An Loc (see Map 27). During the first phase, the 1st Brigade moved to Quan Loi, east of An Loc, and deployed its battalions from An Loc. The 3rd Brigade operated from Lai Khe, with its units in action north along Highway 13. DePuy controlled the operation from a command post in Lai Khe. The two brigades swept the area looking for ambush sites while clearing the highway of mines and booby traps. The infantry and armor also protected engineers as they repaired the bridges and culverts along the route. From 9 to 11 October, the division met no resistance and prepared Highway 13 for the passage of supply convoys from Phu Cuong to An Loc.[105]

During the next five days, the first supply convoys since early August moved to An Loc. Civilian traffic also was restored. During this period, infantry and armor checked the road for mines every morning and looked for evidence of ambushes. The Communists chose not to contest the division's control of the highway, having learned from the earlier pounding they took when they challenged American armor and firepower in that area.[106]

DePuy ended Operation Tulsa on the evening of 16 October, having proven that when the US Army deployed a full division along a 60-kilometer stretch of highway it could ensure the safe passage of civilian and military traffic. But he had failed to find and fix the enemy's main force units.

The division initiated Operation Shenandoah in the same area of operations on 17 October. Shenandoah was a reconnaissance in force designed to lure the enemy into battle. The 1st and 3rd Brigades conducted search and destroy missions to find the regiments of the *9th PLAF Division* in the jungle areas west of Highway 13 and along the road between An Loc and the village of Minh Thanh.

On 28 October, four 1st Brigade battalions encountered a battalion of the *272nd PLAF Regiment* near Minh Thanh Plantation. The action began when Colonel Berry deployed two infantry battalions and Troop A, 1/4th Cavalry, to where intelligence indicated the enemy were operating. Company B, 1st Battalion, 26th Infantry, made the first contact when men of the 3rd Platoon "heard voices on the trail, and alerted the platoon. All together, its soldiers faced left and opened fire, neatly ambushing an enemy column of about 50 well armed men coming down the trail."[107] The Communists retreated, only to run into the company's 2nd Platoon, which had deployed across the trail. Reeling from a second deadly volley, the Vietcong ran back into 3rd Platoon, losing more men.

As the action developed, Lieutenant Colonel Gorman swung Company C, 1/26th Infantry, into a blocking position north of his Company B. Although the enemy did not run in that direction, fighter-bombers arrived and plastered the retreating Vietcong. As the aircraft departed, an artillery aerial forward observer brought the 155mm howitzers of Battery B, 1st Battalion, 5th Artillery, to bear against a fleeing column of enemy. Company B followed the barrage to the south, preventing the Communists from establishing a stable firing line.[108]

As the Blue Spaders developed the contact, Colonel Berry moved his other three infantry battalions into positions to the west, south, and east of the contact, completing a "box-type ambush," with the Vietcong in the center and Gorman's men to the north. The four American battalions established NDPs around the box, but there were gaps in the jungle between each of the battalions. Berry used all available artillery to close those gaps by firing throughout the night, hoping to hit anyone trying to escape. The suspected Vietcong locations were also plastered by artillery and air strikes.[109]

The next morning, the 1/26th Infantry moved into the box from the north and the 1/28th Infantry advanced from the east. The sweep revealed two base camps and seventy-four dead Vietcong. Although 1st Brigade searched the area for the rest of the day, no contact was made. After three more days of fruitless search and destroy missions, DePuy ended the operation on 2 November.[110]

DePuy's frustration with the Vietcong's success in avoiding the major engagements he sought in Operation Shenandoah was short-lived. Within two days, the Big Red One was alerted to move in mass to defeat an offensive launched by the *9th PLAF Division*.

Operation Battle Creek/Attleboro

By October 1966, the Communists had decided to launch large-scale operations to isolate and destroy American or South Vietnamese units while expanding their control of the South Vietnamese countryside. In the III Corps area of operations, Senior Colonel Hoang Cam, commander of the *9th PLAF Division*, received orders to "destroy a 'vital' element of the enemy, support the local movement, oppose enemy pacification and expansion efforts, break the oppressive government control, widen friendly liberated areas, and provide security and protection for storage facilities and base areas of Dung Minh Chau [War Zone C]."[111]

Colonel Cam planned to begin his offensive by attacking the newly arrived 196th Light Infantry Brigade in Tay Ninh Province (see Map 27). The 196th struck first when it deployed its battalions to the jungle northwest of Dau Tieng. In a complicated tactical plan, Brigadier General Edward de Saussure moved his units into the jungle in a search and destroy operation. In the words of the official history, "the operation went badly from the start. With no linkup plan, little appreciation of the enemy and terrain, and command and control difficult, the two blocking and four attacking forces quickly became separated from one another, lost in the jungle. Shortly before noon an enemy force of unknown size attacked the western blocking company in tall elephant grass, killing the company commander and inflicting heavy casualties."[112] For the remainder of the day, de Saussure and his battalion commanders worked to reorganize the troops on the ground and relieve the company under assault. In the process, four more companies suffered heavy losses. By nightfall, the 196th had formed two NDPs.

The meeting engagement between the 196th and the *101st PAVN [People's Army of Vietnam] Regiment* caused Colonel Cam to adjust his plans, as the *9th PLAF* concentrated to destroy the 1st and 2nd Battalions of the 27th Infantry. The *271st* and *272nd PAVN Regiments* attacked the next morning against Tay Ninh West and the American base at Suoi Da. They inflicted significant damage at both places and diverted de Saussure from the fighting involving the 27th Infantry and the *101st PAVN Regiment*.[113] Cam moved his headquarters to within a kilometer of that battle and brought up reinforcements.

On the morning of 4 November, the American units near the Ba Hao River began to move out of their NDPs in search of the enemy. After going a short distance, they stumbled into the *101st PAVN* in a bunker complex, initiating a battle in which the North Vietnamese had most of the tactical advantages. American casualties were heavy, as the enemy launched human-wave assaults in attempts to overwhelm the 1st Battalion, 27th Infantry. De Saussure tried to move additional forces to the fight, but as a portion of the 4th Battalion, 31st Infantry, arrived by helicopter, it was pinned down by Communist fire. By the end of the day, two American battalions remained in contact. As this situation developed, Seaman alerted General DePuy and the 1st Infantry Division for action. That evening, DePuy was ordered to take over the 196th Brigade and commit his division against the *9th PLAF*.[114] DePuy quickly moved his command post to Dau Tieng and ordered three infantry battalions to move to the area north of Dau Tieng on 5 November. Operation Battle Creek, later renamed Attleboro, lasted for the next three weeks.

On 5 November, the *101st PAVN* again tried to overrun the two isolated American battalions. These attacks were repulsed with the aid of air and artillery strikes, and enemy casualties rose to nearly 200 killed. By the end of the day, the 1/27th Infantry had been reinforced by the 2/27th Infantry, ending the crisis. Over the next two days, the battered battalions disengaged.

The 1st Infantry Division's 2nd and 3rd Brigades arrived during the next three days, allowing DePuy to search for the *9th PLAF*. The first task was to return to the battlefield northwest of Dau Tieng to recover American bodies and to assess the damage inflicted on the *101st PAVN*. The 1st and 2nd Battalions, 28th Infantry, found 17 American bodies and 70 enemy corpses. On 8 November, the 1/28th Infantry, was attacked by two enemy battalions as it prepared to leave its NDP. After three assaults, the Communists gave up. The battalion lost 21 men killed and 42 wounded; 305 enemy bodies littered the field, and the 1/28th picked up 58 weapons.[115] On 9 November, the 1st Brigade joined the operation.[116]

Cam's plan to destroy a significant American force had been foiled by the Big Red One's rapid reaction to the 196th Brigade's debacle. On 26 November, Operation Attleboro ended with the redeployment of the 2nd Brigade to Bien Hoa. The 1st Infantry Division lost 45 men killed and 195 wounded, while killing at least 845 enemy. In the process, the division captured 8 prisoners, 108 weapons, tons of ammunition and mines, and 1,131 tons of rice.[117]

Results

The 1st Infantry Division accomplished a great deal during its first year and a half in Vietnam. It prevented the Communists from destroying the Army of Vietnam forces in the III Corps region. It established battlefield dominance over enemy main force units. DePuy and his brigade and battalion commanders developed techniques to coordinate air strikes, helicopter gun-ships, and artillery in support of infantry and armor. The division's soldiers demonstrated time and again their ability to stand toe to toe with the enemy in battle and to come out winners. The division inflicted heavy losses on the Vietcong, forcing them by the late summer to avoid major contact with American units. The division also defended the logistics infrastructure in the Saigon area.

15

The Year of Decision?
The 1st Infantry Division in Vietnam, 1967

By Christmas 1966, US forces had been in-country for longer than a year and had defeated North Vietnamese attempts to destroy the South Vietnamese government. How the war could be ended in a way acceptable to the United States and its allies, however, remained unclear. General William Westmoreland believed that MACV would have sufficient combat power in the coming year to sustain offensive operations throughout the country. Offensives by American and allied forces would inflict heavy casualties on the enemy, moving Westmoreland's attrition strategy closer to its goal of making the war so costly for North Vietnam that it would end its invasion of South Vietnam.[1]

The fighting in 1966 indicated that American and allied forces had hurt the enemy significantly. MACV believed that Communist losses were about 7,000 dead per month. American casualties through October totaled roughly 5,700 dead and 26,800 wounded. By the end of 1966, there were over 351,000 American troops in the country, but Communist strength also increased to roughly 283,000 soldiers. Allied intelligence estimated that another 202,000 Communist troops would arrive in South Vietnam in the coming year, as American strength increased to 480,000 men.[2]

The most pressing challenge facing American commanders was to force the enemy to fight battles that would end in high Communist casualties and minimal allied losses. Major General DePuy had concluded that the best way to kill the enemy at a rate that would exceed his reinforcements was to find Communist units with the smallest possible force and to use American firepower to pulverize them.[3] With this in mind, DePuy developed operations, such as Roadrunner, to tempt the Communists to leave their hidden base camps to attack seemingly exposed and weak American units, as they had in the Battle of Minh Thanh Road. In order to give infantry units more firepower, mobility, and protection, the army "remechanized" a number of infantry battalions, including the 2nd Battalion, 2nd Infantry.

Operation Cedar Falls

In the autumn of 1966, Westmoreland planned a major push into War Zone C, where he hoped to find and destroy the *9th PLAF Division* (see Map 26). However, Westmoreland's intelligence officer recommended that an offensive be launched first against the Communist base area known as the Iron Triangle, northwest of Saigon. MACV had concluded that this region was the logistics and headquarters base for the Vietcong *Military Region (MR) 4*. Westmoreland was receptive to his G2's suggestion and sent him to discuss it with Lieutenant General Jonathan Seaman, the II Field Force commander. Seaman, whose 1st and 25th Infantry Divisions would conduct the offensive, agreed that it made sense to eliminate the closer threat before invading War Zone C.[4]

The operation against the Iron Triangle was named Cedar Falls. The Iron Triangle was bounded on the west by the Saigon River, on the east by the Thi Tinh River, and on the north by the jungles of the Thanh Dien Forest (Map 29). Local force companies and perhaps five or six understrength Vietcong battalions were based in the area, along with the logistical facilities of MR 4. The *272nd PLAF Regiment* also frequented the area, but air strikes had driven it north toward War Zone C.[5]

Cedar Falls was a hammer and anvil operation by the 1st and 25th Infantry Divisions, reinforced by the 196th Light Infantry and the 173rd Airborne Infantry Brigades and two squadrons of the 11th Armored Cavalry Regiment (ACR). The 25th Infantry Division, with the 196th Light Infantry Brigade and its own 2nd Brigade, formed the anvil by occupying defensive positions along the western side. The Big Red One, with its 2nd and 3rd Brigades, the 197th Airborne Brigade, and the 11th ACR, acted as the hammer, striking toward the Saigon River from positions along the Thi Tinh River and in the Thanh Dien Forest. The hammer units were to push the enemy toward the 25th Infantry Division.[6]

The village of Ben Suc, in the northwestern corner of the triangle, was a major Vietcong medical facility. The early seizure of this village was deemed essential. The 1st Battalion, 26th Infantry, commanded by Lieutenant Colonel Alexander Haig, was to initiate Cedar Falls with the quick capture of Ben Suc. Once the village was secure, South Vietnamese troops were to screen and then evacuate the population to a camp. Three nearby villages also were to be cleared and their populations relocated. Once the villagers had been removed, the villages, tunnels, base camps, and jungles in the area were to be destroyed.[7]

The insertion of Haig's battalion went off like clockwork on 8 January. At precisely 0800, 60 helicopters of the 1st Aviation Battalion flew into the

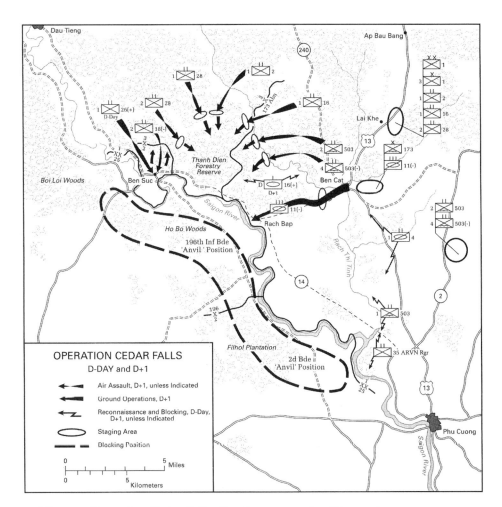

Map 29. Operation Cedar Falls, 8–9 January 1967. (George L. MacGarrigle, *Taking the Offensive, October 1966 to October 1967* [U.S. Army Center of Military History, 2000])

fields around Ben Suc and landed 420 Blue Spaders. Follow-on helicopter lifts brought in another infantry company to finish the seal around Ben Suc as well as teams of interpreters to screen the population. As the initial helicopters came in at treetop level, interpreters with loudspeakers instructed the villagers to remain in their homes. Most of the villagers complied, although forty Vietcong were killed as they tried to escape. The only US casualties occurred when a platoon stumbled into a minefield and lost four men.

Over the next few days, three ARVN infantry battalions sorted out the population and moved the people and their possessions to relocation camps.

By 12 January, 5,987 people, 247 water buffalo, 225 cattle, 158 oxcarts, and 60 tons of rice had been moved by truck, helicopter, and boat. Most of these people had served the Vietcong in varying capacities. Eventually, they were resettled in a new village to the south. After the villagers were clear, the 1st Engineer Battalion destroyed the intricate three-level-deep tunnel system under Ben Suc. Searches of the tunnels revealed 7,500 Vietcong uniforms, 800,000 vials of penicillin, and tons of rice.[8]

While the Blue Spaders cleared Ben Suc, five more battalions flew into landing zones in the Thanh Dien Forest, creating a seal to the north. Simultaneously, Task Force Deane, consisting of the 173rd Airborne Brigade and two squadrons of the 11th ACR, moved into line along the eastern leg of the triangle and began to push west. By 9 January, the triangle was sealed. The only major event occurred when the 25th Infantry Division engaged a Vietcong battalion in the Filhol Plantation, near the southeastern corner of the triangle. This enemy force fled in the afternoon after taking a pounding by artillery and air strikes.

From 8 to 18 January, American troops searched the triangle. Only light and occasional enemy contact took place as the infantry moved through the Thanh Dien Forest and Task Force Deane advanced west from the Thi Tinh. The Americans killed over 750 Vietcong and captured another 280. An additional 512 Communists surrendered to the *Chieu Hoi* (Open Arms) program, designed to allow Vietcong to switch their allegiance to the Saigon government. The large number of weapons captured was unprecedented, as the hammer forces seized 23 crew-served weapons and 590 individual firearms. The advancing units found 3,700 tons of rice and a half-million pages of Communist documents in the tunnels and bunkers in the area. American losses totaled 72 killed and 337 wounded.[9]

Operation Cedar Falls included innovative combat engineer operations reminiscent of the Bocage or Aachen battles of World War II. Lieutenant Colonel Joseph Kiernan, commander of the 1st Engineer Battalion, concluded:

> Starting with the construction of the D. S. Bailey Bridge at Ben Cat on 21 Dec 66, and ending with the demolition of the tunnel complexes on 26 Jan 67, Operation Cedar Falls was without exception the most significant combat engineering operation of the war to date. New concepts of jungle warfare using dozers to open heretofore inviolable VC strongholds; the emergence of a new "Secret Weapon," the dozer-infantry teams; and combined acetylene and HE (high explosive) tunnel demolitions; all have proven unique, successful, and of tremendous value to future operations.[10]

Kiernan's engineers were joined by the 168th Engineer Battalion, which was in charge of all available bulldozers from the 79th Engineer Group. The two engineer battalions used regular bulldozers, tank dozers, and Rome plows to clear swaths through the jungle and along the major roads. The Rome plows were dozers with a special blade developed by the Rome Caterpillar Company of Rome, Georgia. This blade was more curved than the regular blade and had a sharply honed lower edge that formed a point and could slice through trees up to 3 feet in diameter. Bars on top of the blade prevented trees from falling onto the tractor. Infantrymen in armored personnel carriers protected the engineers from snipers. These dozer-infantry teams cleared over 2,700 acres of jungle, carved a new road to Ben Suc, and opened landing zones in the forests.[11]

Cedar Falls was a success by nearly every measurement. The enemy's ability to support operations near Saigon was degraded. The Iron Triangle, cleared of its population, became a "specified strike zone" in which any activity was considered hostile and could be engaged free of restrictions. Many Communists were killed and even more surrendered.

II Field Force now was free to move against War Zone C without a major Vietcong stronghold to its rear. DePuy wrote: "Although I do not expect the war to end quickly, I believe this has been a decisive turning-point in the III Corps area; a tremendous boost to the morale of the Vietnamese Government and Army; and a blow from which the VC in this area may never recover."[12]

Operations Tucson and Junction City

As Cedar Falls began, II Field Force finished plans for Operation Junction City. Two preliminary operations were intended to position the 1st and 25th Infantry Divisions on the fringes of War Zone C without arousing Communist suspicions. The 25th Infantry Division initiated these maneuvers on 2 February with Operation Gadsden, a search and destroy operation along the Cambodian border by the 196th Light Infantry Brigade and the 3rd Brigade, 4th Infantry Division. The two brigades cleared the area without major engagements and built bases and landing zones from which they could operate during Junction City.[13]

During the second preparatory operation, known as Tucson, the 1st Infantry Division interdicted enemy communications between the two war zones and established firebases and landing zones in the area. The Northern Rice Route, as it was called, ran through the Long Nguyen Secret Zone and the Michelin Plantation from War Zone C to War Zone D. Intelligence indicated that the *272nd PLAF Regiment* frequented the area.[14] General John Hay, the new division commander, employed the 1st and 3rd Brigades for the operation.

On 14 February 1967, the 3rd Squadron, 5th Cavalry, attached to the Big Red One, and two infantry battalions deployed to blocking positions between the village of Bau Long on Highway 13 and the Michelin Plantation. From these positions, the tanks and ACAVs of the 3rd Squadron, 5th Cavalry, the infantrymen of the 1st Battalion, 16th Infantry, and the 2nd Battalion, 28th Infantry, served as the anvil onto which Hay hoped the 3rd Brigade's hammer would smash the enemy. At the same time, the Quarterhorse and the 2nd Battalion, 2nd Infantry (M), moved down two axes from Minh Thanh Plantation to push the enemy to the 1st Brigade. The 1st Battalion, 2nd Infantry, and the 2nd Battalion, 18th Infantry, conducted search and destroy operations between the two mechanized units to prevent the Vietcong from escaping.[15]

Good weather facilitated airmobile operations and the armor sweeps. Although only a few Vietcong were engaged, the division uncovered supply dumps, base camps, and bunker complexes, all of which were destroyed. Casualties were light, with three Americans killed and sixty-five wounded. The enemy lost thirteen killed and five men captured. The operation further reduced the Communists' ability to support sizable forces in the Saigon area, pushed the Vietcong back into War Zone C, and allowed the 1st Infantry Division to position forces on the edge of War Zone C.[16]

Operation Junction City commenced on 22 February 1967. It was the largest American operation of the war thus far. At various times, the 1st Infantry Division was reinforced by the 173rd Airborne Brigade, the 1st Brigade, 9th Infantry Division, most of the 11th Armored Cavalry Regiment, and several small ARVN units. The 25th Infantry Division took part in the operation with its 2nd Brigade, the 3rd Brigade, 4th Infantry Division, and the 196th Light Infantry Brigade. The immediate purpose was to find and destroy *COSVN* and the *9th PLAF Division*.[17]

The concept of Junction City was to create a giant inverted horseshoe around the area of operations with five brigades and then to have two brigades attack north to destroy enemy forces in the horseshoe. On 22 February, the 196th Light Infantry Brigade and the 3rd Brigade, 4th Infantry Division, established blocking positions on the western side of the horseshoe. The six infantry battalions involved moved by helicopter and overland from base camps they had established during Operation Gadsden without opposition.[18]

The same day, the 1st Infantry Division moved three brigades into positions along the northern and eastern sides of the horseshoe. Three infantry battalions air-assaulted into landing zones along the north of the horseshoe to interdict routes into Cambodia. They met only sporadic small-arms fire. The 2nd Battalion, 503rd Airborne Infantry, parachuted into a secure drop

zone on the northeastern corner of the horseshoe, while the other two battalions of the 173rd Brigade moved into position by helicopter. The units
suffered only minor injuries as they landed, having achieved complete surprise.[19] The 2nd Battalion, 2nd Infantry (M), and the 1st Squadron, 4th
Cavalry, moved their armored vehicles into positions on the eastern side of
the horseshoe, reinforced by the 2nd Battalion, 28th Infantry. Farther south,
the 1st Battalion, 16th Infantry, deployed along Route 4 to secure the lines
of communications.[20]

To complete the southern portion of the ring, the 11th Armored Cavalry
Regiment and the 2nd Brigade, 25th Infantry Division, moved into positions
along Route 247, with the cavalry on the east and the 2nd Brigade on the
west. By nightfall, 35,000 American soldiers were around what was hoped
to be the location of the most important Communist headquarters in South
Vietnam.

On 23 February, the 11th Armored Cavalry and the 2nd Brigade, 25th
Infantry Division, drove into the horseshoe. For five days, they moved north
searching for the enemy. The rugged terrain and thick brush was the only
resistance they encountered. By the evening of 27 February, the first phase
of Junction City was complete. It was, in the words of the official history,
"the largest non-battle of the war." Somehow *COSVN* slipped through the
encircling forces and reached Cambodia. The *9th PLAF* avoided major contact with the attackers. Known Communist losses were 54 killed, while 28
Americans died.[21]

The Big Red One's first major contact of Junction City occurred on 28
February, when Company B, 1/16th Infantry, ran into a battalion of the
101st PAVN Regiment 15 kilometers north of a Special Forces camp at
Suoi Da. The North Vietnamese battalion was moving west toward Route 4
when it encountered Company B near the Prek Klok River. The 3rd Platoon
was leading through the heavy jungle with the 2nd and 1st Platoons following. Captain Donald Ulm's company was using cloverleaf-pattern patrols to
search its route of advance when the 3rd Platoon received small-arms fire
from the east. Captain Ulm concluded that he faced a large force, since there
were at least three machine guns employed against his men. He called for
artillery support from a battery of the 2nd Battalion, 33rd Artillery.[22]

For the next four hours, Company B fought for its life against the larger
Communist force. Neither side was dug in. Both maneuvered units to the
flanks in attempts to encircle their enemy. Captain Ulm remained calm during the confused fighting, directing artillery fire and air strikes against the
enemy. During the action, Company B formed a perimeter and marked its
positions with smoke grenades to enable forward air controllers to adjust
air strikes and helicopter gunships onto the enemy. In the end, American

firepower prevailed. Company B maintained its cohesion and repulsed re-peated assaults by the *101st PAVN*. After losing at least 167 men killed, the Communists retreated, just as Company B, 2nd Battalion, 28th Infantry, arrived to reinforce Ulm's company. American losses totaled 25 men killed and 27 wounded.[23]

Following what has been called the Battle of Prek Klok I, on 28 Febru-ary, Operation Junction City settled back into a tedious routine of search and destroy missions. On 1 March, General Hay redirected the efforts of the division to an area east of Route 4, hoping the Big Red One would encounter the *101st PAVN Regiment* again. On 4 March, the 1st Brigade, 9th Infantry Division, joined the operation, allowing General Hay to rotate battalions back to their base camps periodically for rest, a warm meal, and fresh socks.[24]

During the next ten days, the division searched for the enemy with little success. Then, on 10 March, Communist mortars opened a barrage against the Prek Klok fire support base. As the last mortar rounds fell, two battal-ions of the *272nd PLAF Regiment* assaulted the perimeter held by the 2nd Battalion, 2nd Infantry (M). For seven hours, the Vietcong tried to overrun the mechanized battalion's APCs in their positions around the base. Each assault was met by small-arms and machine-gun fire. The commander of the Ramrods, Lieutenant Colonel Edward Collins, coordinated artillery fire and air strikes as well. None of the enemy reached the perimeter. By 0500 the next morning, the Vietcong had retreated, leaving 196 men dead on the field. Three Americans died and 38 were wounded. As in previous battles, the division used a linear boundary, like Route 4, as the fire coordination line for air and artillery support, making it possible to use all available fire support throughout the battle.[25]

The Communists again remained elusive, until 20 March, when the *273rd PLAF Regiment* struck Fire Support Base 14, which was protected by Troop A, 3rd Squadron, 5th Cavalry. The Vietcong attacked shortly after midnight from the southwest, west, southeast, and northeast of the perim-eter. As the division's after-action report notes, "Immediate fire support was provided in the form of artillery fires, air strikes delivering bombs, CBU [cluster bombs], and napalm, gunships, and 'dragon ships.' This fire support continued throughout the battle."[26] In spite of the fire support, the Vietcong continued to assail the perimeter, forcing Captain Raoul Alcala, Troop A commander, to request reinforcements. In response, Lieutenant Colonel Sid-ney Haszard, the squadron commander, sent two armored cavalry platoons to the firebase. These platoons arrived in the middle of another Vietcong assault and drove through heavy fire to reinforce Troop A.[27]

When news of the attack reached Lieutenant Colonel Paul Gorman, the

1st Infantry Division operations officer, he called on every resource to support Alcala. Artillery swung into action; air force fighter-bombers arrived in a seemingly endless stream; and Troop C, 1st Squadron, 4th Cavalry, was alerted for action. Brigadier General James Hollingsworth, the assistant division commander, flew to the battle to orchestrate the fire support from his helicopter for the rest of the night. At around 0220, Captain Alcala ordered his five platoons to counterattack. This action surprised the enemy, allowing Alcala's men to recover their damaged tracks and wounded men who had escaped from burning personnel carriers.[28]

The Vietcong regrouped and launched another effort to overrun the firebase at around 0300. Lieutenant Colonel Haszard had decided by then to join Alcala's command and assist in the direction of battle. In the words of the after-action report,

> At the same time [as the enemy attacked], the squadron commander, LTC Haszard, in a M-113 and followed by another M-113, moved up Highway 13 and drove into the heaviest part of the Vietcong attack, where a seal of US artillery fire had been placed. As the squadron commander's track came within sight of the perimeter, his vehicle was struck by either an artillery or a recoilless rifle round. The round knocked out his engine and killed his right gunner. Two minutes earlier LTC Haszard had been acting as the right gunner.[29]

General Hollingsworth watched from his helicopter in the light of flares and tank searchlights and later described what he saw: "Haszard performed a very gallant act under fire when he dismounted his vehicle and proceeded to move the escort vehicle into position to tow his damaged vehicle into the perimeter. . . . I was particularly interested in his getting inside the perimeter so that in case the troop commander's communications were knocked out, I would still have communications with the forces on the ground."[30] Haszard hooked up his track to another and had it towed into Alcala's perimeter while warding off Vietcong attackers.

For the next four hours, air strikes pounded the enemy while the cavalrymen fired a steady stream of machine-gun fire and canister rounds at Vietcong trying to pull away their dead. Helicopters from the 1st Aviation Battalion also landed to drop off ammunition and evacuate twenty-six severely wounded troopers.

The *273rd* made its last assault at around 0500, just as F-100 Super Sabre fighter-bombers dropped cluster bombs and napalm. The F-100s were so low that one was hit by ground fire and crashed, killing the pilot. But the bombs and napalm ended the fight as the Vietcong broke and ran, leaving 227 men dead. Three Americans died and sixty-three were wounded. Again, massive firepower and the firm resolve of American soldiers soundly defeated the Communists.[31] The Communists avoided contact for the next ten days, until they saw an opportunity to destroy a seemingly isolated American infantry battalion near a small village known as Ap Gu.

The Battle of Ap Gu

By late March, the new II Field Force commander, Lieutenant General Bruce Palmer, was about to end Junction City when intelligence indicated that the *271st PLAF Regiment* was moving across War Zone C toward Katum. Palmer ordered the operation to enter a second phase on 18 March, hoping to intercept the Vietcong regiment. Consequently, the Big Red One continued to cast a wide search and destroy net. On 24 March, General Hay ordered the 2nd Brigade to establish bases approximately 6 kilometers south of the Cambodian border. The brigade headquarters set up operations at Fire Support Base Charlie near Sroc Con Trang and prepared to deploy its battalions.[32]

During the afternoon of 30 March, the 1st Battalion, 26th Infantry, conducted an airmobile assault into LZ George, named after Captain George Joulwan, the battalion's S3 (operations officer). After clearing the landing zone of mines and booby traps, the battalion established an NDP. The soldiers dug foxholes and covered them with wood and sandbags to protect themselves from mortar fire. The "Dobol positions," as the battalion called their DePuy foxholes, had their firing ports cut to face the sides rather than toward the front. Each position therefore protected its neighbors. Lieutenant Colonel Alexander Haig, the battalion commander, ensured that his soldiers continued to improve their positions. The battalion was supported by artillery batteries at Fire Support Bases Charlie and Thrust.[33]

Meanwhile, the *9th PLAF Division* had ordered the *271st Regiment* to meet the *70th Guard Regiment* near LZ George and launch an assault against the 1st Battalion, 26th Infantry. On 31 March, just after Haig had sent Captain Brian Cundiff's Company C into the jungle to search east of the landing zone, the enemy approached. The *70th Guards* moved into the woods northwest of LZ George and the *271st* approached through the jungle to the east. Shortly before 1300, the battalion reconnaissance platoon found signs on the trees in the woods to the northwest warning Americans not to enter. When the platoon moved into the woods, it was met by a hail of small-arms fire. Reconnaissance had found the *70th Guards*. In the process, the point man was killed and the platoon was pinned down.[34]

Lieutenant Richard Hill quickly reported his situation to the battalion. Haig called for artillery support and air strikes and ordered Company C to retrace its steps to the NDP. Meanwhile, Captain Hansen started his platoons toward the action and Captain Rudy Egersdorfer ordered Company A to start back toward the landing zone from the south, each captain acting on his own initiative. As Company C moved west, it encountered an occupied bunker and took several casualties, slowing its return to the NDP. By then, Company B was in contact with the *70th Guards*. By 1415, the situation was serious enough for Hay to order the 1st Battalion, 16th Infantry, to prepare to reinforce the Blue Spaders. By 1553 hours the first helicopter lift of the Rangers was en route to LZ George.[35]

Meanwhile, Haig lifted off in a helicopter to coordinate fire support. What he saw was not good. The reconnaissance platoon and Company B were engaged with a clearly superior Communist force. Lieutenant Hill had been killed, and both units had suffered casualties. Haig ordered Egersdorfer to have Company A set up a line through which Company B and the reconnaissance platoon could withdraw. As he was issuing these instructions, Haig's helicopter was hit by enemy fire and crashed. Haig and the pilot evacuated safely from the ship, and George Joulwan took off in another chopper to coordinate the action while the battalion commander joined the companies on the ground.[36]

After skillful maneuver, Egersdorfer's men established a firing line forward of Company B to cover that company's and the reconnaissance platoon's move to the NDP with their wounded. As the Blue Spaders withdrew, the first lift of the 1st Battalion, 16th Infantry, landed in LZ George.

By 1800, the Rangers were on the field and the Blue Spaders were in their NDP. The Blue Spaders lost seven men killed and forty-two wounded during the day. As night approached, the 1st Battalion, 16th Infantry, established an NDP west of LZ George.[37]

Realizing that there were at least three Vietcong battalions in the area, the Blue Spaders and Rangers prepared for an enemy attack. The division G3, Paul Gorman, informed Haig that signal intelligence indicated that "tomorrow morning all hell [is] going to break lose . . . be prepared."[38] While Gorman arranged fire support, Haig visited every bunker in his NDP, encouraging the men to improve their positions. Listening posts were established outside the perimeter, and efforts were made to feed the soldiers a hot meal.

During the night, listening posts heard enemy movement. Around 0520, the first mortar rounds crashed into the battalions' perimeters. A barrage also hit 2nd Brigade headquarters at Fire Support Base Charlie, keeping the brigade headquarters there busy as the *271st* attempted to overrun LZ George. Fortunately, the enemy did not attack Fire Support Base Thrust and its three batteries to the southeast of LZ George.

When Haig heard the first incoming mortar round land, he ordered his battalion to full alert. At the same time, the listening posts in front of Company C fired their claymores at nearby Vietcong and retreated to the perimeter. The main assault of the *271st Regiment* struck the bunker line at the northeast corner of the NDP as enemy infantry followed close on the heels of the men from the listening posts. The Communists employed rocket-propelled grenades (RPGs), claymores, and machine guns to support the attack. Although Charlie Company hit the attackers with every weapon available, Vietcong broke into the perimeter and overran several bunkers before being stopped near the company's command bunker. In an exchange of grenades and small-arms fire, First Sergeant Al Cooper killed several Vietcong at close range with his M16 before being hit by grenade fragments. Cooper vividly remembered the action years later:

> A platoon sergeant came back with his arm practically blown off: I took him to B Company's positions. A man gave me a cup of coffee—best cup of coffee in my life. Captain [Brian Cundiff] told me to get on a Medevac helicopter and get out of there. A round had gone through his canteen. Water ran down his leg: He thought he had been hit. The person who said he was not scared was insane.[39]

The *271st PLAF Regiment* launched five assaults during the next two hours. Most of the assaults hit Companies B and C, allowing Haig to use his reconnaissance platoon to reinforce Company C's counterattack to drive the Communists back out of the perimeter. The battalion's efforts were bolstered by helicopter fire teams, which used their machine guns, rockets, and miniguns on the wood line to the northeast. Artillery fire and fighter-bombers also hit enemy troops to the east and northwest, further isolating the critical piece of the battle.

The last Communist attempt to break the perimeter came at 0700, just as fighter-bombers dropped napalm and cluster bombs 30 meters from the American positions. Hundreds of Vietcong were in the killing zone. The survivors were strafed by F-4 Phantoms "equipped with miniguns, which fire so rapidly that they sound like an enormously loud chainsaw biting into a tree trunk."[40] Vietcong who survived turned and ran to the northeast. The Battle of Ap Gu was over, and the *9th PLAF Division's* efforts to destroy a major American unit had failed.[41]

As the Communists retreated, Hollingsworth ordered the 1st Battalion, 2nd Infantry, and the 1st Battalion, 16th Infantry, to pursue the enemy. The Vietcong, however, fled so rapidly that no major contact was made by either advancing battalion. Haig's soldiers evacuated 102 American wounded and the bodies of 17 dead comrades. During the next day and a half, the Blue

Spaders buried 491 enemy dead in and around their perimeter and the positions of the 1st Battalion, 16th Infantry. Later sweeps of the area brought the number of enemy bodies found to 609. In addition, 5 Vietcong and 50 weapons were captured.[42]

Operation Junction City continued for another two weeks. The *9th PLAF Division* was so badly mauled that it withdrew to Cambodia to refit. The Big Red One had been able to operate with near impunity throughout War Zone C, in spite of a concerted effort by *COSVN* and the *9th PLAF Division* to inflict a major defeat on an American unit.[43] *COSVN* claimed that its forces killed 13,500 Americans. The actual figure was 282.

Pacification Efforts

American successes in 1966 created a period in which the South Vietnamese could carry out "Revolutionary Development" programs to end Vietcong control in the countryside and increase support for their government. The 1st Infantry Division participated in these efforts. However, to minimize the impact of pacification efforts on combat battalions, the division created the Revolutionary Development Task Force (RDTF) to carry out pacification and development programs. These programs where designed to encourage enemy soldiers to desert the Communist cause and to convince the rural population that its best hopes for peace and security lay with the Saigon government.

The RDTF was led by a lieutenant colonel and included a "modest compliment of communicators, intelligence specialists, drivers, and other mission essential personnel." The RDTF totaled fifteen officers and thirty-two enlisted soldiers equipped with small arms, jeeps, and radios. A few of the task force members spoke Vietnamese, but most possessed "no particular qualifications for their task."[44]

The RDTF was designed to free tactical unit commanders from the responsibilities of planning and coordinating revolutionary development missions. The tactical unit commanders were called into an operation just before execution, and the RDTF commander provided them with the details of the plan to be carried out. A typical mission was the pacification efforts undertaken at the village of Tan Binh, in Binh Duong Province, on 26 December 1966.

The pacification of Tan Binh called for a seal and search operation. Two infantry battalions and an armored cavalry troop surrounded the village. Once the village was sealed off, South Vietnamese police, intelligence specialists, and reconnaissance troops entered and searched for Vietcong operatives and supporters. Communist defectors from Tan Binh provided intelligence that was used to focus the search for any known enemy. During the two-day seal and search of Tan Binh, all males ages 15 to 45 were rounded up and sent to an interrogation camp for questioning. The women and children remained in the village. Anyone fleeing the area was treated as an armed Vietcong and killed by the soldiers of the 1st Brigade.[45]

Since Tan Binh was a known Communist base, the population was not treated to the carnival atmosphere used in villages with a neutral population. American combat troops remained outside the village and maintained "an attitude of professional detachment and efficiency." The RDTF entered the village with the South Vietnamese who were in charge of the operation. Colonel Paul Gorman concluded that "in our experience these operations have done much to build respect among American soldiers for their Vietnamese comrades in arms—more than any other operation we conduct."[46]

During the next year, the 1st Infantry Division carried out a number of missions as part of II Field Force's "Lam Son 67" operations. Often one brigade would be committed to pacification efforts while the other two maintained pressure against enemy main force units. The brigades rotated missions and did not have long-term responsibility for a region or group of villages. Heavy personnel turnover, due to the one-year tour length, removed experienced soldiers and replaced them with hastily trained recruits, making it difficult to maintain the professional and detached demeanor necessary for successful pacification. Worse, once a village or district was pacified, the South Vietnamese government withdrew its forces for duties elsewhere. In most cases, when the ARVN units left, the Communists reasserted control of the area. Pacification could have achieved its purposes only if there had been sufficient South Vietnamese forces available to protect the pacified areas permanently.

In 1967, Communist troop strength in South Vietnam increased, causing President Johnson to increase American forces in the country to 525,000. The North Vietnamese met these increases by accelerating the flow of replacements to the south, so that by mid-1967 half of the soldiers in Vietcong units were North Vietnamese Regulars.

As the war escalated, the 1st Infantry Division maintained a routine that included stints in the jungle searching for the enemy, periods of dreary guard duty at the base camps, and short periods of intense combat. James Shelton, who joined the division as a major in July 1967, describes his memories of the division in his book, *The Beast Was Out There*: "When I arrived in the 1st Division in July 1967, I could clearly sense an attitude of resentment toward General Hay on the part of those who had served under General DePuy. This resentment was not necessarily a result of anything

Hay had done poorly. Most old timers simply felt that DePuy could not be replaced."[47]

Shelton identified serious problems with the American personnel policies in the war that were having a major impact on the division's tactical capabilities.

> General Hay was faced with a turnover rate of perhaps 80 percent in the soldiers in the combat units of the division. Since the division had arrived in Vietnam in July 1965, there had been a wholesale turnover of combat personnel in July 1966, and again in July 1967. . . . A one-year tour of duty had been established for all U.S. personnel in Vietnam, causing the turnover phenomenon, and very few men would volunteer to extend.[48]

The Big Red One no longer enjoyed the advantage that a large cadre of veteran soldiers and leaders had contributed to and inculcated during previous wars. Along with this loss of institutional memory, the soldiers' work remained hard and dangerous, particularly in infantry battalions. As Shelton remembers, "For men assigned to combat units, sleep normally came from exhaustion; and many nights were as exhausting as the days. The oppressive heat and the boredom of army food did not help. . . . Many men were so tired that they didn't bother to eat." Such hardships, along with the ever-present danger of combat and the threat of malaria, made the year in Vietnam a long one for all members of the division.[49] Nonetheless, the war continued.

Operation Manhattan: 23 April–11 May 1967

Despite increased emphasis on pacification in 1967, the 1st Infantry Division continued to conduct large operations. Operation Manhattan was one of these. While the 2nd Brigade conducted pacification missions around Di An, the 3rd Brigade and two squadrons of the 11th Armored Cavalry Regiment swept the area from the northwestern portion of the Iron Triangle to the Michelin Plantation and from the Saigon River east to Highway 13.[50]

Operation Manhattan produced no big battles, but the maneuvering units found numerous arms and supply caches, including the largest capture of enemy weapons by Americans in Vietnam, by the 2nd Battalion, 18th Infantry. The Vanguards captured 347 rifles and over 300,000 rounds of ammunition in a deserted base camp. By the end of the operation, on 11 May, the 1st Infantry Division and 11th ACR claimed to have killed 123 Vietcong and captured 21 prisoners of war. Over 300 Vietnamese civilians were evacuated from the area and resettled elsewhere. The engineers cleared large swaths of jungle along the roads in the area, facilitating future operations. American losses were 15 soldiers killed and 133 wounded.[51]

While Operation Manhattan was under way, the *COSVN* commander planned to bombard Bien Hoa Air Base with 122mm rockets. The planned attack by the *84A PAVN Artillery Regiment* coincided, accidentally, with Hay's commitment of most of the 1st Infantry Division and the 11th ACR to Operation Manhattan. Hay also had sent 1st Brigade north to An Loc to thwart a Vietcong attack predicted to begin some time after 30 March. These troop movements uncovered the infiltration routes from Cambodia to the southwestern edge of War Zone D, allowing the enemy to move the rockets to within their 11-kilometer range of Bien Hoa.[52]

Thanh's preparations did not go unnoticed. American Special Forces encountered elements of the *84A PAVN Artillery* and reported seeing unusual loads being carried by the enemy. Air force security police captured an infiltrator near Bien Hoa on 8 May and learned that his mission was to identify aircraft parking locations on the air base. On 10 May, an air controller spotted elements of the *273rd PLAF Regiment* moving south toward Bien Hoa and called in air strikes to disperse the enemy force. A Special Forces team was sent to the area and found fifty-three enemy bodies and captured three men from the *273rd Regiment*. These prisoners confirmed that many North Vietnamese had joined their regiment and that an attack would take place before Ho Chi Minh's birthday on 19 May. One prisoner reported that his unit was escorting artillerymen carrying four "DKZ," the Communist designation for the Soviet 122mm rocket system. This report was forwarded to the 1st Infantry Division G2 late on the evening of 11 May, too late for analysts to put the information together concerning the Communist plan. That evening, the *84A PAVN* and the *273rd PLAF Regiment* fired 53 rockets and 150 mortar and recoilless rifle rounds into Bien Hoa Air Base, destroying 49 aircraft. The 173rd Airborne Brigade was responsible for the base's security but had taken no extra defensive precautions, even after one of its patrols reported a Vietcong probe the evening before.[53]

Operations Dallas and Billings

The attack on Bien Hoa indicated that the enemy had replenished their ranks and intended to carry out major operations during the monsoon season. The II Field Force commander ordered Hay to continue pacification efforts with one brigade and to use two brigades to put pressure on the Communists in War Zone D and the nearby Long Nguyen Secret Zone.

Operation Manhattan, therefore, was followed in quick succession by Operations Dallas and Billings. In Operation Dallas, the 1st Infantry Division and the 11th ACR searched for enemy forces and installations in areas on both sides of Route 16. The Vietcong, however, refused to fight, allowing the division and the cavalry regiment to move freely through the woods and jungles but denying them the battles so favorable to American firepower. From 17 to 25 May, the 1st and 2nd Brigades killed nineteen Vietcong, while losing four men killed and eighty-one wounded. General Hay claimed that the operation helped reduce the Communists' ability to fire 122mm rockets at Bien Hoa and Saigon.[54]

Operation Billings, from 12 to 26 June, was a major effort to inflict damage on the *9th PLAF Division* "in an area extending east from the Song Be River to Route 1A and north from Phuoc Vinh to Highway 13 lateral."[55] On 14 June, the 1st Battalion, 16th Infantry, encountered the *271st PLAF Regiment*. In an intense fight, the Rangers killed sixty-two enemy.[56]

On 17 June, the 1st Battalion, 16th Infantry, and 2nd Battalion, 28th Infantry, converged at LZ X-Ray. As the units met, a patrol reported enemy approaching from the northwest. The American battalions formed a defensive perimeter and prepared for a fight. At about 1245 hours, Company B, 2nd Battalion, 28th Infantry, received fire and, at 1325, an infantry assault hit the perimeter. The *271st PLAF Regiment* attacked for over an hour and, at one point, penetrated the defenses before being thrown out by counterattacks. Fighter-bombers, attack helicopters, and artillery hammered the Vietcong throughout the battle, inflicting heavy casualties. By 1500 hours, the enemy was in retreat. Hay, fearing another attack, sent Lieutenant Colonel Richard Cavazos's 1st Battalion, 18th Infantry, to LZ X-Ray at about 1900. Hay placed Cavazos in command in the landing zone since he was the most combat-experienced battalion commander in the area.[57] But the battle was over.

The two battalions of the *271st Regiment* involved in the fight lost an estimated 274 men killed and one captured. The 3rd Brigade lost 35 men killed and 150 wounded.[58] The Communists retreated north, rather than toward War Zone D. Hay had anticipated that the *271st* would move east, and the B-52 strikes and artillery bombardments to interdict the enemy fell on empty jungle. For the next nine days, the Big Red One tried unsuccessfully to engage large enemy units. However, the enemy's attempt to destroy the American forces on LZ X-Ray was his last effort to inflict heavy losses on the 1st Infantry Division.[59]

The division lost 57 men killed and 197 wounded during Operation Billings; it claimed to have killed 347 Communist soldiers. The division captured 1 prisoner, 2 weapons, 238 rounds of ammunition of all types, and 5 grenades and destroyed over 200 bunkers and huts. Major General Hay concluded that "Operation Billings was the most successful operation conducted by the 1st Infantry Division since Operation Junction City."[60] Not everyone agreed with this assessment, as Shelton notes:

> Although Billings was called a success, U.S. casualties were 47 killed and 197 wounded. Enemy killed were reported as 347. Regardless of the reported number of enemy killed, which was always suspect, the American death toll was the division's largest for a single operation . . . up to that time. The men who participated in Operation Billings, most of whom were veterans of the war, did not consider it a victory.[61]

The fundamental problem was that search and destroy missions carried out by companies or battalions were more dangerous than the larger operations of the past. With units scattered throughout an area of operations, it was hard for the division to mass the fire support that had played such a decisive role in destroying Communist attacks before they could cause American casualties. General Hay recognized the situation: "Operations conducted in particularly thick jungle . . . require that the force be of sufficient size and strength to enable it to successfully fight an enemy of greater size for the period of time needed to reinforce the elements in contact."[62]

Busting Jungle: Operation Paul Bunyan

To deny the enemy jungle sanctuaries, the army developed equipment and methods to clear wide swaths of jungle along roads and near populated areas. The Agent Orange defoliant is the most famous of these tools, but bulldozers, tank dozers, and Rome plows were more commonly used by the 1st Infantry Division. Operation Paul Bunyan was the division's largest jungle clearing operation in 1967.

The 1st Engineer Battalion carried out Paul Bunyan from 19 July to 11 September. The 2nd Battalion, 2nd Infantry (M), provided security for the engineers as they cleared 15,000 acres of jungle north of Di An. The greatest risks the engineers faced were booby traps, mines, and an occasional sniper. Four Americans were killed and fifty wounded in the operation, while the Vietcong lost three men killed and one captured.[63]

Operation Paul Bunyan supported pacification efforts in several ways. The clearing of jungle denied the enemy sanctuaries and interdicted infiltration routes. The wood from the jungle was given to villagers to use as fuel and lumber. The South Vietnamese also established farms in the cleared areas, and refugees were resettled in new villages. Finally, Major General Hay believed that the removal of large sanctuaries forced the enemy to operate in smaller groups, making it possible for the South Vietnamese and Americans to use smaller units safely in their pacification efforts.[64]

Operation Portland: 12–21 August 1967

After Operation Billings, the Big Red One continued efforts to engage large Communist units. In Operation Portland, the division deployed battalions along Highway 13, from the Saigon River to the Song Be River, in mid-August 1967. Day after day, infantrymen slogged through the jungles, dug NDPs, and carried out airmobile operations. Most of the search effort hit empty jungle, with the major exception being when 1st Battalion, 18th Infantry, captured five Vietcong on 18 August. No Americans were killed or wounded.[65] The division returned to its base camps without incident on 21 August.

Intelligence officers interpreted the Communists' unwillingness to risk major battles as a sign that the war was going in the allies' favor. The heavy losses suffered by the *9th PLAF Division* in War Zone C during the spring certainly forced that unit to retreat to Cambodia to absorb replacements. But there was another reason for the lull in large-unit actions. The Communists were preparing an offensive across South Vietnam for which they were hoarding manpower and resources. This offensive was scheduled to occur during the Tet celebrations of the Vietnamese New Year, in January–February 1968. In one of the most successful intelligence security operations of the war, the Communists kept this information from the allies. Through the autumn, the war continued in its normal pattern of search and destroy and pacification missions by the allies and a steady level of Communist guerrilla activity.

On 1 September 1967, Major General Hay relocated the division headquarters to Lai Khe. The 9th Infantry Division assumed responsibility for the area north and west of Bien Hoa. The 1st Brigade continued to operate out of Phuoc Vinh, the 2nd Brigade carried out pacification efforts in southern Binh Duong Province, and the 3rd Brigade protected the engineers in Operation Paul Bunyan north of Lai Khe.

The division also established schools to train newly arrived soldiers in small-unit tactics, a move made necessary by the more than 80 percent turn-over in personnel during the summer. Each infantry battalion also received a fourth line company, designated Company D, to increase maneuver capability and to protect the battalion's NDP while the other three companies were out searching for the enemy.[66]

By the end of September, the Big Red One was ready to pursue the regiments of the *9th PLAF Division*, thought to be recuperating in the Long Nguyen Secret Zone. General Hay designated the nearly roadless jungle area as Area of Operations Shenandoah and named the operation Shenandoah II.

Shenandoah II: 29 September–19 November 1967

Intelligence reports indicated that the *271st PLAF Regiment* was in the Long Nguyen Secret Zone. The two other regiments of the *9th PLAF Division* (the *272nd* and the *273rd*) were reported to be near Loc Ninh, well to the north. Hay planned to leave two brigades in the Long Nguyen Secret Zone for an extended period of time and to rotate infantry battalions into the zone to find and destroy the *271st*. Hay committed the 1st Brigade to the northern half of the Long Nguyen and the 3rd Brigade to the southern portion.[67]

The operation commenced on 29 September when 1st Brigade units conducted air assaults into landing zones in the north. The next day, 3rd Brigade units moved by trucks and tracks to Ben Cat and then west along Route 240. As the battalions moved along the route, engineers cleared the jungle 100 meters on each side of the road. During the first four days, the division had only light contact. Artillery batteries established fire support bases to provide support for the infantrymen as they combed the jungles. As things progressed, the monsoons dumped rain on the troops and made air support problematic.

On 4 October, the 1st Battalion, 2nd Infantry, encountered a Vietcong force and called for fire support. Not knowing the size of the enemy unit, the Americans pulled back into the battalion's NDP while air strikes and artillery pounded the suspected enemy. During the action, three Americans were killed and twenty-seven were wounded. Later, a search of the area revealed twelve enemy bodies. As it appeared likely that a Vietcong battalion might have been involved, Hay inserted Cavazos's 1/18th Infantry into the area to cut off the enemy. Cavazos's men found nineteen Communist dead in a bunker complex near their landing zone, but the enemy refused to stay around to fight.[68]

During the next two days, the 1/2nd and 1/18th Infantry searched the area. On 5 October, Company B, 1/18th, destroyed a bunker complex, losing one man to sniper fire. The same day, the 1/2nd Infantry found another camp and killed three Vietcong. But the *271st* remained elusive. The next afternoon, the NDP of 1st Battalion, 18th Infantry, was hit by mortar rounds, indicating the enemy was planning a night assault. Air strikes were called in, and the Vanguards deployed ambush patrols around their perimeter. By 1800 hours, heavy rains and darkness made it impossible for helicopters to support Cavazos's battalion. Taking advantage of the poor weather and the isolation of the 1/18th Infantry, the *271st Regiment* attacked.

The action began at about 1855 when a patrol ambushed an unknown number of Vietcong and then withdrew into the perimeter. The enemy returned fire with machine guns, confirming Cavazos's view that a large force was present. During the next hour, the Vietcong hit the NDP with mortar, rifle, and machine-gun fire. Four batteries of artillery responded, allowing Cavazos's soldiers to conserve ammunition in case resupply could not reach them the next morning. When the enemy fire let up, a patrol left the NDP to search for a man missing from the ambush patrol. The patrol met heavy small-arms fire and quickly retreated. At about 2100 hours, the Vietcong resumed firing around the perimeter and at 2317 hours attacked on the eastern side. Protected by their DePuy-style bunkers, the men of the 1/18th Infantry placed accurate fire on the attackers, forcing them to retreat. Two US soldiers died and five were wounded, while the enemy lost fifty-nine men killed and sixty-seven wounded.[69]

The Vanguards tried to maintain contact with the *271st*, but no major action took place until 11 October. That day, Cavazos's men again encountered Vietcong willing to fight when Company B met an enemy company. Cavazos ordered Company B to pull back through Company C and to form a battalion perimeter. The Vietcong attempted to cut off Company B but failed as helicopter gunships added their firepower to the action. By 1515 hours, the Communists had retreated. The 1/18th lost one man killed and four wounded, and it found twenty-one enemy bodies in the area.[70]

While the 1st Brigade beat the jungle, the 3rd Brigade continued its jungle clearing and road repair efforts in the south. Infantry units made minor contact daily with the enemy and found numerous camps, but they did not encounter large units. Hay continued to rotate battalions from the field to base camps, giving the tired and wet infantrymen a chance to rest and dry out. By 16 October, it appeared that the *271st* had left the Long Nguyen Secret Zone and was possibly moving toward the Michelin Plantation. However, before ending the operation, Hay ordered Colonel George Newman's 1st Brigade to search once more along the Ong Thanh Stream. Lieutenant Colonel Terry Allen's 2nd Battalion, 28th Infantry, began the search with two companies of infantry near the Ong Thanh on the morning of 16 October.[71]

The 1st Division G3 Daily Journal for 16 October 1967 reflects "business as usual." The 2nd Brigade held a festival at Ben Cat for 1,500 Vietnamese, providing food, medical care, and entertainment as part of its pacification mission. Soldiers of the 3rd Brigade detained an "old woman without an ID card" and found a cache of rice, and Allen's 2/28th Infantry found an enemy base camp. After calling in air strikes and artillery, Company D entered the camp and triggered an ambush in which one US adviser was killed and five GIs were wounded.[72] Small groups of Vietcong were seen throughout the division's area of operations, and the day's losses included one US soldier killed and eleven wounded, with twenty-one enemy killed. It was a normal day.

The Battle of Ong Thanh: 17 October 1967

The 1st Brigade commander, Newman, was very interested in the contact made on 16 October by the 2nd Battalion, 28th Infantry. Two companies of the Black Lions had found an occupied camp. The Company D commander, Lieutenant Clark Welch, reported to Lieutenant Colonel Allen that there was evidence of many Vietcong in the area. Since the battalion had made its contact with the enemy in the afternoon, the S3, Major Jack Sloan, called in artillery and withdrew north to the NDP in accordance with division SOP not to start a battle late in the day. After discussions that afternoon, Newman and Allen agreed that the Black Lions would conduct a "reconnaissance in force" the next morning with two companies led by Allen.[73] Evidently, neither Newman nor Allen thought that the understrength battalion would need reinforcements, and there was no increase in the number of air strikes allocated. Allen planned the operation and decided that he would lead Companies A and D back to the point of contact while Company B and the Headquarters Company remained to protect the battalion's NDP.[74]

Allen's battalion was well below the authorized level of about 140 men per rifle company. When Allen and the column set out at 0800 hours, Welch's Company D had 73 men and Captain James George's Company A had 65 men present. Both companies left their mortar sections at the NDP. Allen and his command group brought the total strength of the column to about 150 soldiers. Company A led the advance with three understrength platoons in column; Company D followed with its platoons in column. Allen and the command group were behind the lead platoon of Welch's company.[75] The route of advance was due south from the battalion's NDP through fairly open jungle toward the enemy camp. Air strikes were brought in 1,000 meters east of the route, and artillery marking rounds advanced with the column, allowing forward observers to establish firing coordinates.[76]

The Black Lions moved cautiously, stopping frequently while the lead platoon sent sections forward in a cloverleaf pattern to clear the way. By 0956 hours, Company A had moved about 1,000 meters when its 1st Platoon discovered a trail that ran from the northeast to the southwest. The platoon also reported freshly cut brush, perhaps indicating the cutting of camouflage. The battalion column stopped while the lead platoon patrolled east and west of its position.[77]

George's lead squad soon spotted an enemy soldier west of the trail, but before it could set an ambush the Vietcong disappeared into the jungle. A few minutes later, as Captain George ordered the 1st Platoon leader to reinforce his lead element, Communists opened fire along the western flank of Company A. The 1st Platoon leader was hit and his men pinned down by fire coming from bunkers as near as 15 meters away. George sent his 2nd Platoon forward to reinforce the 1st, but the enemy fire intensified, forcing the 2nd Platoon to ground in front of a bunker. The two lead platoons lost radio contact with George, who then led his command group forward to re-establish control. When George reached the 2nd Platoon, he threw grenades into the bunker and set up a small perimeter. To this point in the battle, Allen knew little of what was happening, making it impossible for him to affect the action. By 1020, Company A had stuck its head into a Vietcong defensive position occupied by the *271st PLAF Regiment*.[78]

The battle intensified and spread as snipers fired on Company D's western flank. Welch's men quickly silenced them. Farther south, a Vietcong with a claymore rushed George's command group, detonating the weapon before he was shot. The blast blinded Captain George and wounded most of his command group. All officers in Company A were now casualties, and First Sergeant Jose Valdez took command. Communications within the company broke down, and many men fled to the east, away from the enemy fire (Map 30). Valdez was able to establish a new perimeter 100 meters east, where he rallied survivors before leading his group north toward the battalion's NDP. Many members of Alpha Company's 3rd Platoon joined Colonel Allen in a perimeter near a large anthill.[79]

When the seriousness of the contact became clear, Allen ordered George to pull his men back so he could call in artillery and air strikes. The breakdown in communications made this impossible, forcing Allen to call for fire close to Company A. The artillery fire covered the retreat of George's 3rd Platoon, but the air strikes did not arrive until 1100 because no fighter-bombers were in the area. When air force planes arrived, Colonel Newman, who was now overhead in a helicopter, ordered a check fire by the artillery so that the fighter-bombers could attack without interference. Newman believed the Vietcong were retreating, so he ordered the fighter-bombers to drop their ordnance 500 meters south of the initial contact. After the air strike, a lull ensued, at around 1120.[80]

During the first hour of the battle, most of the battalion command group, including Allen, his S2 (intelligence officer), Captain Jim Blackwell, and his radio operators, were hit by enemy fire. From this point on, hope of

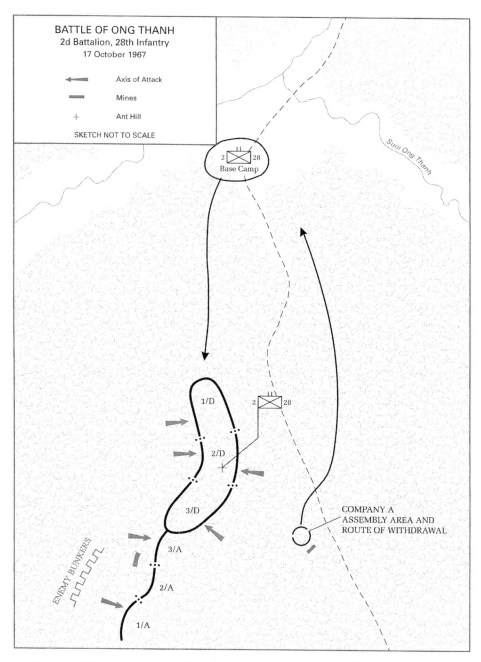

BATTLE OF ONG THANH
2d Battalion, 28th Infantry
17 October 1967

Axis of Attack

Mines

+   Ant Hill

SKETCH NOT TO SCALE

2 ⊠ 28
Base Camp

Suoi Ong Thanh

1/D

2 ⊠ 28

2/D

3/D

3/A

2/A

1/A

ENEMY BUNKERS

COMPANY A
ASSEMBLY AREA AND
ROUTE OF WITHDRAWAL

Map 30. The battle of Ong Thanh, 2nd Battalion, 28th Infantry, 17 October 1967. (George L. MacGarrigle, *Taking the Offensive, October 1966 to October 1967* [U.S. Army Center of Military History, 2000])

coordinating the action was gone. Lieutenant Welch moved part of his company into a perimeter around Allen, but his 3rd Platoon remained 50 meters south, in contact with the remnants of Company A. Meanwhile, the Vietcong realized that the American firepower was not being coordinated in the usual way and that there were gaps in the coverage. Capitalizing on this situation, the commander of the *271st Regiment* maneuvered his units around the beleaguered column, placing troops on three sides of the perimeter near an anthill. At 1135, the Communists renewed a heavy fire against Companies A and D. Badly outnumbered and outmaneuvered, the Black Lions lost the race to establish fire dominance. Welch was hit repeatedly, as was his first sergeant and Lieutenant Harold Durham, his artillery forward observer. By the time Newman turned on the artillery support again, it was too late for most of the command. By 1130, the Vietcong had accomplished their goal of destroying the two companies and had begun to withdraw.[81]

With Allen down, Colonel Newman landed at the Black Lions' NDP at about 1200 hours and took command. He ordered Company B to move south to provide sanctuary for the men fleeing from the action and Company C, 2nd Battalion, 28th Infantry, to be flown in. The company arrived at the battalion NDP at 1326. At 1211 hours, the division placed the 1st Battalion, 16th Infantry, on alert to reinforce the 2/28th. The Rangers arrived in mid-afternoon, but the fight was over. The reinforcements were harried by snipers, who killed Major Don Holleder as he started south from the NDP, but their main role was to search the battlefield for casualties and to help the survivors.[82]

The magnitude of the defeat of the Black Lions became clear as Company B moved into the battle area. Once Newman had the site surrounded, he created a perimeter and called for additional medical personnel to help with the casualties. The wounded were lifted out by helicopter before dark, but with the approaching dusk, Newman ended the search for bodies and pulled all troops back to the NDP. Artillery fire was placed around the battle site to deter the Vietcong from booby-trapping the dead. The next morning, the search resumed. By early afternoon, 18 October, the searchers had recovered fifty-six American bodies. Seventy-five Black Lions had been wounded and two were missing. The 2nd Battalion, 28th Infantry, moved to Lai Khe by helicopter the same day.[83] The battle of Ong Thanh was over.

The way in which the battle of Ong Thanh was conducted was quite different from the major battles during Cedar Falls and Junction City. When the reports came in on 16 October that the 2/28th had found a major Vietcong force, no action was taken to bring in additional forces. Instead, Newman spread his three infantry battalions across an area of about 20 square kilometers. No one beyond Captain Jim George and Lieutenant Clark Welch thought it possible that a large Communist unit might be waiting for a fight in fortified positions. When Allen set out he had no reserve and too few men. When the battle started, Captain George found his two lead platoons decisively engaged before he could pull them back and call for support. Once Company A was pinned down and Company D engaged, Allen lost the ability to maneuver his battalion. When the fighter-bombers arrived, Newman shut off the artillery rather than orchestrate the artillery, bombers, and helicopters simultaneously.

Among the dead was Terry Allen, son of the division commander of World War II. Both company commanders and all officers in the committed companies were killed or wounded. Lieutenant Harold Durham, the artillery forward observer, received the Medal of Honor posthumously for his actions in calling for fire and giving his own life while protecting wounded from the Vietcong. Although the division claimed that 106 Vietcong had died in the battle, there was no real doubt about who won. In a letter to General DePuy, on 27 October 1967, Major General Hay summed up Ong Thanh:

> Specifically, as to the action in which Terry was killed, it was a meeting engagement that so frequently happens on search and destroy missions. The paper [the *American Traveler*] talked about an ambush, but I can assure you it was no ambush. It was a sharp battle where a reinforced battalion of the 271st engaged two of our companies. . . . The battle lasted for about one hour when the enemy broke contact and the lead company (Alpha Company) began withdrawing through the second company in the column (Delta Company). . . . The high losses were due to two principal causes. The first was not moving the artillery in fast enough once the fire had broken out . . . and [second] later lifting artillery to bring in the air.[84]

The 2nd Battalion, 28th Infantry, returned to Lai Khe on 18 October. For the next month, Companies B and C performed local security missions while Alpha and Delta Companies reorganized and trained replacements. As soon as possible, the division committed the two companies to field operations.[85]

Shenandoah II Continued: 29 October–19 November 1967

The 1st Infantry Division inflicted a fair amount of damage on the *271st PLAF Regiment* in the Long Nguyen Secret Zone during phase one of Shenandoah II, which ended on 28 October. General Hay now turned the division's attention to the area between An Loc and Loc Ninh, on Highway 13. Intelligence reports and recent contacts indicated that the *9th PLAF Division*'s other two regiments were in the area and that possibly the *7th*

PAVN Division was also in the area. Operations began on 29 October when the 1st Battalion, 18th Infantry, flew from Quon Loi to conduct an air assault near a Special Forces camp that was under attack at Loc Ninh Airfield. The *1st* and *2nd Battalions, 273rd PLAF Regiment*, retreated into the jungle with the arrival of the reinforcements. Soon after the 1/18th established its NDP, Company C moved a kilometer north to help a South Vietnamese local defense company repel an attack. Company C made contact with Vietcong in trenches about 600 meters north of the battalion NDP. The company attacked and overran the enemy, killing nine Vietcong.

Thirty minutes later, the Communists counterattacked. The Company C commander shifted his platoons into a line facing east and called for artillery, air support, and reinforcements. Company D quickly moved north as artillery fire and helicopters hit the attackers. When the company arrived, it tied into Company C's right flank. Both companies and the local defense company then attacked, following a rolling barrage of artillery fire. The enemy fled into a draw where they were pummeled with fire before the survivors could get away. During the action, the 1/18th lost one man killed and nine wounded. The battalion found twenty-four enemy bodies and twelve weapons on the field.[86] The second phase of Shenandoah II was off to a quick start.

On 30 October, the 1st Battalion, 18th Infantry, again found the North Vietnamese when Company A encountered the *165th Regiment* in trenches north of Loc Ninh Airfield. The Communists tried to envelop Company A's flank, but the company commander shifted his 3rd Platoon to his left and stopped the enemy with small-arms and artillery fire. Meanwhile, hearing the engagement, Lieutenant Colonel Cavazos organized Company D and the local defense company into a task force to reinforce Company A. The relief force reached the action just as the enemy was trying to flank Company A. Together, the three allied companies gained fire superiority over the enemy and then pulled back 50 meters to allow artillery to hammer them. When fighter-bombers arrived, Cavazos shifted the artillery to the south and brought the air strikes on to the main enemy positions. At 1530, Cavazos ordered Company D to attack. Company D overran seven trench lines as the North Vietnamese Army troops (PAVN) retreated.[87]

During this engagement, Cavazos maneuvered his companies on the ground to foil the enemy's attempts to encircle Company A. He also orchestrated the simultaneous delivery of artillery fires and air strikes against the Communists and then followed up with an infantry assault. The results were impressive. US losses were four killed and five wounded, while the NVA lost eighty-three men killed and left thirty-two weapons on the battlefield. These results cinched Hay's decision to shift the 1st Brigade north to Quan Loi to control four battalions of infantry in their quest to destroy the *7th PAVN Division.*[88]

The Communists did not, however, flee. On the night of 31 October, two regiments of the *9th PLAF Division* attacked Loc Ninh Airfield and the Special Forces camp nearby. Company C, 2/28th, defended the airfield with the support of Battery A, 6th Battalion, 15th Artillery. At the height of the attack, the battery fired rounds directly down the runway at Vietcong trying to cross to attack the perimeter. Fighter-bombers finished the action. The Vietcong lost 110 men killed, while US and ARVN casualties totaled nine men killed and fifty wounded.[89]

Everything did not always go well for the division. On 5 November, the 1st Battalion, 26th infantry, conducted an air assault northwest of Loc Ninh near the Cambodian border. During the next two days, the Blue Spaders searched for the enemy. On 7 November, as the battalion was moving through a rubber plantation, it ran into an L-shaped ambush. As the after-action report notes, "The command group was hit directly with an unknown number of RPG-2 and RPG-7 rounds. Commanders and radio operators became primary targets. The Battalion Command Group sustained 100% casualties during the initial contact. The VC tried to encircle the Battalion on the west."[90]

The American company in the rear of the column foiled the enemy's attempt to outflank the battalion, and forward observers called for artillery fire and air strikes. Heavy artillery fire and twenty-seven sorties of tactical aircraft dropping cluster bombs disorganized and demoralized the Vietcong, giving the Blue Spaders time to establish a defensive perimeter. Colonel Newman also directed two companies of reinforcements to the action. After more than five hours the enemy retreated. US casualties were seventeen killed and twenty-one wounded, while the enemy lost an estimated 103 men. Lieutenant Colonel Arthur Stigall, who had commanded the battalion since 12 September, was one of those killed.[91]

The division had numerous small-scale contacts with the enemy around Loc Ninh and Quan Loi during the next twelve days, but the enemy chose not to launch another major attack. On 19 November, Major General Hay ended Shenandoah II. It is hard to see what was accomplished during the long operation. US losses totaled 106 men killed and 323 wounded, in exchange for 957 enemy killed and 15 prisoners. The Big Red One captured 104 weapons and destroyed a number of Communist base camps and storage facilities.[92] But the Communists soon replaced their losses and built new installations in nearby jungle.

Westmoreland Takes Stock: December 1967

As the big MACV operations came to an end in 1967, General Westmoreland assessed the results. "At the beginning of the year the enemy still enjoyed relative security in the huge War Zones in III Corps, and our use of the roads was generally restricted to Saigon and the immediate vicinity." One year later, American divisions had forced the enemy to retreat to Cambodia and had opened the roads in the more remote provinces. MACV estimated that more than 81,000 Communist soldiers had been killed and that enemy recruitment in South Vietnam had fallen to about 3,500 men per month. MACV also estimated that infiltration of replacements from the north had fallen from 9,000 to 6,000 men per month. Westmoreland believed that the Communist forces in South Vietnam had declined from 278,000 men in October 1966 to about 220,000 men a year later.[93]

American troop strength had grown to 459,700 soldiers, with more on the way. Westmoreland's ground strength had increased to 58 infantry battalions supported by 48 artillery battalions. Over 2,200 helicopters provided air mobility. Air support came from 400 fighter-bombers based in South Vietnam and from B-52 bombers operating from Guam.[94]

But, unfortunately, the Communists were not ready to quit. In Hanoi, the Communist leader, General Vo Nguyen Giap, wrote that "the situation has never been as favorable as it is now [September 1967]. The armed forces and the people have stood up to fight the enemy and are achieving one great victory after another." Giap believed that the American forces were stretched thin, and he believed that the United States "lacked the patience" to continue fighting a protracted war of attrition. While recognizing that American troops and firepower had inflicted grievous losses on their units in the south, Communist leaders decided to continue the war and to increase the costs for the Americans and their allies by launching a major offensive during the Tet holidays of 1968.[95]

16

Tet and the Light at the
End of the Tunnel

IN A SPEECH GIVEN ON 19 DECEMBER 1967, the army chief of staff, Harold K. Johnson, announced that the United States and its allies had made significant progress in the Vietnam War. According to Johnson, the enemy "is in trouble. Food and ammunition are critically short. . . . The Viet Cong and North Vietnamese Army units are being punished severely every time and place they attempt to confront or are found by the Free World Forces."[1]

Johnson's optimism reflected that of General Westmoreland, who believed the large-unit battles of 1967 had forced the Communists onto the defensive and opened the door to a more vigorous pacification effort. Consequently, the Big Red One and other American divisions in 1968–1969 were committed increasingly to pacification campaigns, such as Lam Son 67. Efforts to pacify the countryside, to win the loyalty of the population to an often-corrupt government, and to improve the fighting qualities of the ARVN were uphill struggles that by the end of 1967 had been less than successful.[2] Nonetheless, other than negotiations with the Communists, the achievement of such goals was the only way out of Vietnam for the United States.

Tet: 1968

The 1st Infantry Division shifted forces north in late 1967 to secure Highway 13 from Lai Khe to Loc Ninh and to cut Vietcong communications between War Zones C and D. The 1st Brigade moved to Quan Loi, northeast of An Loc, to direct operations from An Loc to the Cambodian border. In December, the division fought the *7th PAVN Division* and local Vietcong in places like Bu Dop, Hill 172, and Fire Support Base Caisson VI. These actions resulted in high casualties for the enemy, largely because American units were generally in NDPs or bases strongly supported by artillery, helicopters, and fighter-bombers.[3]

During the same period, the 2nd and 3rd Brigades took part in pacification efforts. The division's Lam Son operations supported South Vietnamese Revolutionary Development Programs (pacification). American infantry battalions helped to seal off villages while South Vietnamese officials moved in to interrogate the population and detain Vietcong suspects. The 1st Infantry

Division's Lam Son area of responsibility was between Lai Khe and Di An.[4] The 2nd Brigade secured Binh Duong and Bien Hoa Provinces from its base camp in Di An, and the 3rd Brigade kept Highway 13 and the nearby lateral roads open to traffic from its base in Lai Khe.[5]

From the division's perspective, things were going well as 1968 began. At the same time, the Communists finalized plans for an offensive to take place during the Tet holidays. Thousands of Communist replacements and tons of munitions and food had been sent to South Vietnam. General Giap's strategy had drawn most American divisions away from the population centers during the autumn. These deployments allowed Communist units closer to Saigon and other cities to move into position for the offensive without significant interference.[6]

The objectives of the 1968 Tet offensive were to force the United States to withdraw from Vietnam and to force the South Vietnamese to accept a coalition government that the Communists could dominate. The offensive was to feature major military attacks and a general uprising of the South Vietnamese people beginning on the night of 30 January. Those units not directly involved in the assaults on the cities were to engage American units to prevent them from reinforcing the allied forces in the population centers.[7]

American intelligence caught wind of enemy preparations in early January 1968. Lieutenant General Frederick Weyand, commanding general of II Field Force, pulled a number of combat battalions closer to the capital. Consequently, when the Tet offensive began, there were 27 rather than 14 American combat battalions within 30 miles of Saigon.[8] Nonetheless, no American or South Vietnamese leader envisioned the scope and audacity of the Communists' plans nor their determination. Although the South Vietnamese government shortened the holiday leave for its soldiers to thirty-six hours, this decision came too late to be widely disseminated. When the Communists struck, they found most ARVN and police units at 50 percent or less strength.[9]

Most Communists launched their attacks on the night of 30–31 January. In Saigon, nine local-force battalions, reinforced by the *2nd Sapper Battalion*, attacked major targets, including the American embassy, the ARVN headquarters, the Presidential Palace, and Tan San Nhut Air Base. The *5th PLAF Division*, which had been hiding in War Zone D, struck Bien Hoa and Long Binh, north of the capital. In the northern portion of the 1st Infantry Division's area of responsibility, the *7th PAVN Division* attacked Loc Ninh. Farther south, elements of the *9th PLAF Division* struck the 2nd Brigade.[10]

As the severity of the attacks in and around Saigon became evident, General Weyand ordered Hay to send a task force built around the 1st Battalion, 18th Infantry, and Troop A, 1st Squadron, 4th Cavalry, to Tan Son Nhut

Air Base. There it was to join the 2/27th Infantry and the 3rd Squadron, 4th Cavalry, to form Task Force Thebaud, under the command of Colonel Charles Thebaud. Task Force Thebaud's first task was to reinforce the 377th Air Force Security Detachment and several South Vietnamese police units at Gate 51, where three Vietcong battalions had penetrated the air base's perimeter. By 0430 hours, the Communist intrusion at Gate 51 had been contained in a 200-by-200-meter area. At 0500, two companies of the 8th ARVN Airborne Battalion counterattacked but failed to force the Communists back. Another determined frontal assault by a small force of ARVN and US Air Force personnel finally pushed the enemy back to a position just outside the gate, where the Vietcong dug in.[11]

By 1300 hours, 31 January, the 1st Battalion, 18th Infantry, had arrived at the air base, where it met the 3/4th Cavalry from Cu Chi. The two units attacked the Vietcong at Gate 51 but, even with support from artillery, helicopter gunships, and air force fighter-bombers, were unable to drive the enemy away. In fact, two Communist counterattacks had to be repulsed. At dark, the 1/18th Infantry and the 3/4th Cavalry fell back to the air base's perimeter and strengthened the defenses for the night. Tan Son Nhut had been saved, but there was hard work to be done the next morning.[12]

At 2300 hours, Troop A, 1/4th Cavalry, and the 2/27th Infantry arrived. Colonel Thebaud sent the cavalry troop and one infantry company into Saigon to secure American quarters there. The next morning, Task Force Thebaud renewed its attack against the Vietcong at Gate 51, finally driving them away. The 2/27th Infantry then cleared the enemy out of the nearby Vinatexco Textile Factory, finding 162 enemy bodies and 101 weapons in the process. During the afternoon of 1 February, Task Force Thebaud attacked Communists who were putting heavy pressure on the 1st South Vietnamese Marine Battle Group. Together, the allies cleared the enemy out of the ARVN Command headquarters.[13]

Early the next day, Troop A, 1/4th Cavalry, joined the 3/4th Cavalry and the 2/27th Infantry in a reconnaissance in force through the village of Ap Dong, north of Tan Son Nhut. After a bitter fight, the task force cleared the Vietcong out of the village, thus protecting Tan Son Nhut's northern perimeter.[14]

Over the next two days, the situation at Tan Son Nhut and within Saigon stabilized. The strongest enemy resistance was in Cholon, the Chinese quarter of Saigon, where it took ARVN units another month to clear out the Vietcong. On 2 February, the 1/18th Infantry moved by helicopter to Thu Duc to secure Saigon's water filtration and power plants and to protect the Thu Duc District Compound. Troop A, 1/4th Cavalry, joined the Vanguards in Thu Duc and became part of Task Force Tronsrue, under the command of the Vanguards' commander, Lieutenant Colonel George Tronsrue. Company A, from the 2nd Battalion, 16th Infantry, also secured the Binh Long Bridge over the Saigon River. On 7 February, the 1st Infantry Division assumed control of its units in Thu Duc District.[15]

The Tet Offensive in the Division's Area of Responsibility

On the first day of the Tet offensive, the division committed its forces to secure the towns and base camps in its sector. The 1st Battalion, 28th Infantry, moved from Quan Loi to Phu Loi, and the 1st Battalion, 2nd Infantry, returned from its field positions to Quan Loi, which was under artillery and rocket attack. 1st Brigade headquarters remained in Quan Loi and directed operations in An Loc, Loc Ninh, and along the northern portion of Highway 13. Quan Loi was hit repeatedly by 122mm rockets and mortar fire during the next two weeks. The initial barrage on 31 January destroyed one helicopter and one truck.[16]

2nd Brigade, in Di An, sent a task force to protect the Ben Loi Bridge while its two infantry battalions continued local search and destroy missions. The 3rd Brigade, in Lai Khe, came under heavy rocket attack. The brigade had sixty-two men wounded and four helicopters damaged by rockets and recoilless rifle rounds. The Lai Khe base was hit by seven additional rocket attacks on 31 January, although none of these caused much damage. The 3rd Brigade moved the 1/16th and the 2/28th back to Lai Khe during the day, while the 2nd Battalion, 2nd Infantry (M), continued security missions along Highway 13.[17]

Over the next few days, all four division base camps received rocket and mortar fire, but none were attacked by large units. The most serious engagement took place when a helicopter carrying a Xenon searchlight discovered an enemy force east of the village of An My, near Phu Loi. Company C, 1st Battalion, 28th Infantry, and a platoon of armored cavalry moved the next morning to An My to check on the sighting. As they approached the village, they received heavy RPG and small-arms fire from members of the *273rd PLAF Regiment*. American reinforcements arrived and joined an attack against the village. The Communists refused to back off, however, even when elements of the Quarterhorse joined the action with their ACAVs and .50-caliber machine guns. From about 1000 to 1830 hours, the cavalrymen and the 2/28th Black Lions received heavy fire from in and around the village.[18]

In a departure from their previous operations, the Communists remained throughout the day and turned An My into a fortified camp. From the volume of fire, it became clear that there were several Vietcong battalions in the village. After attempts by the cavalry and infantry failed to dislodge them, the acting division commander, Brigadier General Emil Eschenburg, received permission from South Vietnamese authorities to hammer the village with artillery and air strikes. Helicopter-borne psychological operations teams warned the civilians to flee before the fire commenced. Over the next twelve hours, Division Artillery fired over 4,500 rounds of artillery into An My and the air force delivered 7 tons of bombs and napalm. The barrages and air strikes caused more than thirty secondary explosions of Vietcong ammunition, but the enemy remained in place. As night fell, the Black Lions and the Quarterhorse surrounded the village to prevent an enemy retreat.[19]

The battle of An My resumed the next morning, 2 February. The Vietcong in the village stood their ground until midday, when they retreated. "After several hours of almost continuous artillery fire, a house to house search of the village was conducted." The Black Lions found 123 bodies that they believed were Vietcong. The division lost 5 men killed and 32 wounded. On 3 February, the 1st Engineers moved into An My with Rome plows and cleared 155 acres of debris, filling Vietcong spider holes and tunnels under the village.[20]

Often during the Tet offensive, the Communists positioned themselves in populated areas and used civilians as cover. On 3 February, the Vietcong attacked an ARVN post in the village of Tan Phuoc Khanh. At the request of the village chief, the 1st Infantry Division's artillery fired into the village. The next day, when the 2/16th Infantry and 1/4th Cavalry entered the village, they met heavy opposition, forcing them to call for artillery fire on the northern edge of the settlement. A sweep of the area later revealed twenty Vietcong bodies. In every case in which the 1st Infantry Division used artillery or air strikes against a village during Tet, a general officer was required to approve the strikes, and prior permission was sought for the action from South Vietnamese authorities.[21]

Early in the Tet offensive, the 2nd Battalion, 2nd Infantry (M), defeated Communist attempts to seize Ben Cat. On 8 February, the 2nd Battalion, 28th Infantry, defeated a Vietcong attempt to overrun its NDP, with 1 man killed and 12 wounded, while killing 27 enemy. Four days later, the Black Lions found a base camp that was 1 kilometer long. The battalion backed off and called for heavy air strikes and artillery fire before entering the camp unopposed.[22]

Because of such actions, the Communist offensive lost momentum by the end of its first week, although heavy fighting continued in Hue and in the Cholon District of Saigon. Officially, the offensive ended on 25 February. American forces and the ARVN prevented the enemy from taking control of most population centers and ensured that it did not retain those places it did capture. The biggest surprise of Tet may have been the solid combat performance of ARVN units. The ARVN carried the brunt of the fighting in Saigon. No South Vietnamese units collapsed, and none were routed. And the South Vietnamese people refused to heed the call for a general uprising, a critical part of the Communist plan. By March, the South Vietnamese armed forces, government, and people exhibited a new pride, in spite of the heavy losses they suffered. Communist atrocities also increased popular support for the Saigon government.[23]

II Field Force estimated that Communist losses in the III Corps area during Tet were 12,614 killed and 864 captured. A large portion of these personnel were local Vietcong. The loss of the local cadre, which normally provided guides for the North Vietnamese units, made it harder for the Communists to reinforce their troops in Saigon, Bien Hoa, and the Thu Duc District. "These losses have left the [Communist] infrastructure particularly vulnerable at the district and city level, where failure to replace cadre may result in the temporary breakdown of control in selected urban areas."[24]

II Field Force's conclusion about Tet was succinct: "Militarily it was a complete failure for the VC. Its political impact is both harder to judge and beyond the scope of this report. But it must be concluded that whatever political gains were made were bought at an enormous cost to both VC and NVA in terms of trained men and organized units. It was a price which neither North Vietnam nor the NFLA can afford for long."[25] In his personal after-action report, General Weyand observed correctly that "the enemy turned a decisive military defeat into a psychological gain. Despite heavy losses, he mounted an offensive of sizable proportions and demonstrated his capability to conduct coordinated attacks by fire and maneuver over widely dispersed locations. Politically he gained world-wide attention and may have enhanced his position at the current peace negotiations."[26]

The Tet offensive came shortly after Westmoreland had assured the American people that the war was going well. The scope of the offensive shocked the Johnson administration and the American people. The attack on the American embassy and the battles in Hue and Saigon made the Communists appear successful militarily.

The Johnson administration reevaluated its Vietnam policy and concluded that the United States had to disengage from the ground war. How to do so remained the question. Certainly, the burden of the war needed to be shifted to the ARVN, a process known as "Vietnamization." Johnson made these decisions clear when on 31 March he announced to a shocked nation that he would not seek a second term and that he was halting the bombing of North Vietnam except for those areas along the Demilitarized Zone.[27] He further offered to begin negotiations with Hanoi.

As American policy shifted, efforts were stepped up to reassure the South Vietnamese that the United States was not going to desert them. Modern weapons and equipment were provided to the ARVN. American adviser teams increased in size and competency, and thousands of South Vietnamese traveled to the United States to train. At the same time, MACV ordered American units to intensify pacification efforts. For the 1st Infantry Division, these changes meant a continuation of Lam Son 68 and increased efforts to help local defense forces fight the guerillas. The Big Red One also continued to be vigilant for operations by its old enemies, the *5th* and *9th PLAF* and the *7th PAVN Divisions*.

Operation Quyet Thang (Certain Victory): March–April 1968

Following Tet, the Communists in the Saigon area attempted to retreat to sanctuaries in War Zones C and D and in the Iron Triangle. On 11 March, the 1st Infantry Division joined Operation Quyet Thang to destroy the fleeing enemy. The 2nd and 3rd Brigades operated in Binh Duong Province, north of the Iron Triangle. The 2nd Brigade controlled battalion-level search and destroy missions in the southern portion of the Iron Triangle while the 3rd Brigade ran those in the north.[28]

On 11 March the division deployed five battalions to search for the enemy. The first major contact came on 13 March, when Company D, 1st Battalion, 26th Infantry, and a platoon from the Quarterhorse received claymore, small-arms, and RPG fire near the village of Chanh Luu. In the ensuing firefight, the infantrymen, supported by tanks, killed twenty-three enemy and captured nine weapons while losing one man killed and three wounded.[29]

The next day, the Blue Spaders and Troops B and C, 1/4th Cavalry, clashed with the enemy again. A three-hour fight followed. At 1700, the enemy broke contact, leaving thirty-four dead and eight weapons on the battlefield. Three other battalions in the division fought minor actions against smaller groups of the enemy that left six Vietcong dead and one American killed and twenty wounded.[30]

On 15 March, the 1st Battalion, 18th infantry (M), carried out Roadrunner operations with its M113s, while the 2nd Battalion, 16th Infantry, worked with two South Vietnamese regional companies in a seal and search mission of Tan Hiep Village. The Vanguards killed nine Vietcong while losing two men killed and eight wounded. The same day, the South Vietnamese and the Rangers captured ten Vietcong and five weapons in Tan Hiep while suffering no casualties. The 1st Battalion, 2nd Infantry (M), also discovered forty-two enemy bodies in an area where the 5th ARVN Division had fought three weeks earlier.[31]

By 22 March, intelligence indicated that a sizable Communist force was in the Iron Triangle. In response, the new 1st Infantry Division commander, Major General Keith Ware, massed three infantry battalions, two armored cavalry squadrons, and the 7th Squadron (Air), 1st Cavalry, for an assault into the Iron Triangle. Over the next sixteen days, task forces of infantry, armor, and air cavalry searched for the enemy west of Ben Cat. These forces did not make contact with any large units, although they encountered small groups of Vietcong daily. By the end of the operation, on 6 April, they had killed 119 Communist soldiers, destroyed 508 bunkers, and captured three prisoners.[32] The use of the newly arrived air cavalry squadron was a success, as the air cavalry platoons of Cobra gunships and OH-6 observation helicopters reinforced infantry and armor units in contact and made it harder for the enemy to escape.

Across III Corps, American and South Vietnamese troops hounded the retreating enemy. These operations were a good start for the Vietnamization program, as most ARVN units continued to fight well.[33] The division's casualties in Quyet Thang were 29 killed and 332 wounded, while the division killed at least 429 enemy and captured 150 weapons.[34]

American forces in general were able to withstand heavy casualties, thanks to a personnel pipeline fed by national conscription. Nonetheless, roughly half of the soldiers in Vietnam were volunteers who, for a variety of reasons, had chosen to enlist rather than be drafted. Troop strength, per se, was not a problem for the 1st Infantry Division. From January to April 1968, the division's authorized strength was 17,105 and its assigned strength was 17,706. During the period, 5,556 replacements joined the Big Red One, while 5,429 soldiers left, including the 240 men killed.[35]

Aggregate strength totals, however, masked a major problem faced by the US Army in 1968. In the words of the 1st Infantry Division operational report, "The shortage of middle grade NCO's, particularly in combat MOS [Military Occupational Specialties] continues to be acute. The further liberalization of promotion policies effective in January 1968 has not relieved this situation to the extent expected." There also was a shortage of captains, forcing commanders to place lieutenants in command of companies. The shortages in the midrange officer and noncommissioned officer ranks meant that squads, platoons, and companies were led by men lacking combat experience, maturity, and military education.[36] The root causes of this situation were the rapid expansion of the US Army from 1965 to 1968 and the significant increase in the number of career NCOs and officers who chose to leave the service.

The army did all it could to alleviate its shortage of junior leaders. A ninety-day program following basic training developed selected recruits into newly minted sergeants. New soldiers could also volunteer for Officer

Candidate School. Officer promotions accelerated dramatically. These inexperienced young officers and NCOs took charge of units upon their arrival in Vietnam. Although they did their best, they could not perform at the level of proficiency of the officers and NCOs in similar positions in 1965–1966.

There is no direct evidence that the 1st Infantry Division experienced more than its share of discipline problems. Court-martial rates were relatively high, as they were throughout the army, but that indicates that the division's leadership refused to lower standards of conduct. The officers and NCOs maintained discipline and cohesion in the middle of a difficult war against an elusive enemy who, although defeated during Tet, had not quit.

Operation Toan Thang I (Complete Victory): 8 April–31 May 1968

Operation Toan Thang I engaged the 1st Infantry Division in the northern half of Binh Duong Province to deny the enemy use of the area. The division also had the task of preventing Communist units from infiltrating back into the heavily populated areas around Saigon to carry out Tet-like attacks. Finally, Major General Ware was responsible for protecting the Special Forces camps and Vietnamese government and army installations in the area from Di An to Loc Ninh.[37]

To hinder movement by Communist forces through its area of operations and to protect its bases from rocket attacks, the 1st Infantry Division carried out jungle clearing operations. The 1st Engineer Battalion cleared over 2,000 acres of jungle and brush around Quan Loi and Lai Khe in April. On 3 May, the 27th and 86th Land Clearing Companies joined the 1st Engineers for Operation Giant Swath. Over the next two months, these companies cut a 300-meter-wide swath through the jungle from the Song Be River to the Michelin Plantation. The road was improved to allow mechanized units to deploy against enemy detected in the area. Rome plows also cut through the Michelin Plantation and carved a swath into the rocket belt around Lai Khe. The engineers cleared 13,895 acres by the end of June. In July, the 27th Land Clearing Company and the 1st Engineers cleared another 8,783 acres.[38]

In spite of the efforts of the engineers, infantrymen, and cavalrymen to prevent it, Communist units made their way back to the Saigon area and launched another offensive on 5 May. Although reflecting a much smaller operation than Tet, the Communist attacks of early May hit a number of cities in South Vietnam. Many of the NVA units moving in the 1st Infantry Division's area were intercepted and damaged so badly that they could not carry out their part of the "Second Tet" offensive.[39]

The first major encounter between the division and the enemy during Toan Thang I began on 4 May at the village of Tan Hiep. Company D,

1/18th Infantry, found a Communist unit while conducting a reconnaissance. As he began to enter Tan Hiep to check out reports of Vietcong activity, the company commander noticed that there were no civilians. At 0945 hours, as Company D moved cautiously from house to house, it was hit by rifle and RPG fire that wounded all three platoon leaders. Calling for fire support, the company commander pulled his men back to the edge of the village. Within ten minutes, artillery and helicopter gunship fire forced the Vietcong to ground. However, when Company D tried to move into Tan Hiep a second time, the Communists resumed a heavy fire.[40]

Colonel Norm Allen, 2nd Brigade commander, quickly reinforced Company D, believing that it may have cornered a major enemy unit. The 1/18th's Recon Platoon, mounted on the tracks of the Quarterhorse, arrived first. Company A, 1/18th Infantry, moved by foot from Di An toward the action, while Company B followed on trucks. Colonel Allen also sent the Headquarters and D Troops, 7/1st Air Cavalry, to block escape routes, while Troop B, 1/4th Cavalry, established a blocking position north of Tan Hiep. With this net in place, Allen ordered Companies B and D to pursue the enemy, who had retreated into the rice paddies east of Tan Hiep. The Vanguards caught up with many Vietcong who had taken cover in holes cut in an irrigation ditch berm. As the infantrymen advanced, they tossed grenades into the holes, forcing the Communists from their cover and into the gunsights of armed helicopters. A slaughter ensued, as the Vanguards opened fire with rifles and machine guns. When the engagement ended at 2045 hours, there were 260 soldiers from the *21st Battalion, 5th PLAF Division*, dead on the field. Another five enemy soldiers were captured, along with forty-nine weapons.[41]

The next day the 2nd Battalion, 28th Infantry, used dog tracking teams to sniff out the foe. At 1530 hours, the dogs led Company D into a large Communist camp. The Black Lions' commander, Lieutenant Colonel Louis Menetrey, reinforced Company D with armored elements of the 11th Cavalry and ordered it to attack. A fierce fight followed as the Vietcong prevented the Black Lions from entering. Calling for additional fire support, Menetrey launched another assault from the southwest. "The shock action of the mechanized force resulted in a successful sweep of the base camp. There were no US casualties. The contact resulted in 81 Vietcong KIA."[42] The Communists were from the *21st Infantry* and *22nd Artillery Battalions*, which had been hammered the day before by the Vanguards at Tan Hiep. These two engagements prevented those units from taking part in the renewed offensive to the east.

The next day, Troop B of the Quarterhorse, reinforced by Troop A, 7/1st Air Cavalry, and Company B, 1/18th, caught up with the North Vietnamese again. After running fights, the cavalrymen forced the Communists to ground in a base camp. An armor assault, supported by artillery and heli-copter gunships, overran the enemy bunkers. Five Americans died in the attack and twenty-one were wounded. The *165th NVA Regiment* lost 440 men during the two-day battle. For the next three days, the Quarterhorse searched the base complex, uncovering a hospital, tunnels, and significant amounts of ammunition and equipment. As a result of his unit's defeat, the regimental commander of the *165th* surrendered to ARVN forces, telling them that his unit had been prevented from moving to Saigon by the 1st Infantry Division.[43]

For the remainder of the summer, the 1st Infantry Division continued the search and destroy, jungle clearing, and pacification missions. Reinforced by the 11th Armored Cavalry Regiment, division task forces searched for Communist units from Thu Duc in the east to the "Trapezoid" in the west, near the Iron Triangle. Although there were few large contacts, the division hounded the enemy in his sanctuaries.

The division also ran five replacement training centers for newly arrived soldiers. Mobile training teams traveled throughout the division area to pro-vide training to twenty-five rifle companies and one artillery battery. And the Big Red One was responsible for providing "refresher" training to the twelve infantry battalions of the 5th ARVN Division as well. This process was slow, since only one ARVN battalion could be released from current operations each month.[44] The training of ARVN units and the pacification efforts in III Corps in 1968 were running against the clock. Peace talks had begun in Paris.

Westmoreland believed that MACV and ARVN were killing more enemy soldiers in the south than were coming in from North Vietnam. However, in August 1968, II Field Force intelligence estimated that 26,000 Communist soldiers had entered III Corps since the Tet offensive, replacing the 12,000 to 18,000 killed during Tet. The 1st Infantry Division's operational report for the period ending 31 July noted: "The known rates of infiltration in retrospect appear to have been adequate to maintain strength in III CTZ [Corps Tactical Zone] and to increase enemy strength in the 1st Division TAOI [tactical area of interest]."[45]

The tempo and intensity of the division's battles with the Communists in-creased in the second half of August when the *7th PAVN Division* launched a series of attacks against An Loc. On the morning of 18 August, the 2nd Squadron, 11th Armored Cavalry, operating under the 1st Infantry Division, encountered troops from the *165th NVA Regiment* near Quan Loi. Fight-ing continued until about 1530 hours. The enemy broke contact with dif-ficulty, losing seventeen men and fourteen weapons in the process. The next day, the Blackhorse (2nd Squadron, 11th Armored Cavalry, or 11th ACR) found the enemy again after G Troop was hit with mortar and RPG fire near Loc Ninh. The cavalry squadron moved into the area and carried out aggressive reconnaissance near Loc Ninh. During these maneuvers, the cavalrymen killed eighteen North Vietnamese Army (NVA) soldiers and captured another twenty, while losing one man wounded.[46]

The *165th Regiment* did not retreat from the area in spite of the pounding it was taking. On 20 August, two more fights developed, and General Ware sent the 1st Battalion, 2nd Infantry, by helicopter to Loc Ninh. For the next three days, "sporadic activity in the rubber tree area west of Loc Ninh continued with increasing intensity." The 2/11th Cavalry and the 1/2nd Infantry combed the area. During a series of small but violent encounters, the two units killed 85 NVA, while losing 5 men killed, 55 wounded, and 1 missing. Still, the enemy remained in the area, hoping to inflict heavy casualties on their American pursuers.[47]

The battles around Loc Ninh reached a peak on 24 August, when the 2/11th Cavalry and the 1/2nd Infantry engaged several NVA companies for seven hours east of Loc Ninh. The fighting subsided when the enemy retreated north to Cambodia. In all, 5 American soldiers died and 49 were wounded while the Communists left 106 dead in the area.[48] But the Communists remained firmly committed to their war effort and were willing to exchange losses at a highly unfavorable rate. The division after-action report noted that the *7th PAVN Division* "appeared to employ elements of two regiments, the *141st* to the north and the *32nd* to the east, attempting to draw friendly forces to the northeast. No more than one battalion was committed at one time, and companies appeared to have been alternated in order to sustain the contacts. The enemy units were able to fight effectively as independent entities down to squad size."[49]

In early September, the NVA avoided contact with large allied units while still attempting to interfere with pacification efforts. However, on 11 September, the *7th NVA Division* committed two regiments near Loc Ninh. The 1st Battalion, 2nd Infantry, found itself in a series of actions in the rubber plantations east of Loc Ninh. The next morning the tempo increased when the NVA attacked the 1/2nd—the Ramrods—as they moved out of their NDP. The fighting continued all day. To the north, the NVA also attacked the NDP of Company A, 1/28th Infantry. Troop E, 2/11th Cavalry, and Company B, 1/28th Infantry joined the fight, routing the attackers.

When the 1/28th Infantry then tried to drive the Communists from a nearby hill, on 13 and 14 September, they met a determined defense. Even after 113,000 pounds of ordnance of all types was dumped on the enemy, they refused to retreat until after dark. The 1st Battalion, 16th Infantry, arrived late on 13 September to cut the enemy's escape route. Over the next two days, the Rangers destroyed a number of carrying parties moving wounded to Cambodia.[50]

During the fighting in mid-September, Major General Keith Ware visited Loc Ninh often to ensure that the men on the ground had all necessary support. On 13 September, General Ware and a small command group that included Command Sergeant Major Joseph Venable and Lieutenant Colonel Henry Oliver, the division G3, took off from Loc Ninh and headed for Quan Loi. Five minutes after takeoff, Ware's helicopter was hit in the tail boom by NVA antiaircraft fire. The bullets weakened the tail boom, which then separated from the helicopter. The pilot lost control of the aircraft as it went into a steeply descending right turn. Although the pilot, Captain Gerald Plunkett, and his copilot, Chief Warrant Officer William Manzanares, directed the craft to a small clearing in the jungle, they were unable to stop the turn to the right or to slow the descent. During the crash that followed, all aboard were killed.[51]

The assistant division commander, Brigadier General Orwin Talbott, quickly flew to the site of the crash to oversee recovery operations. Armed helicopters of Troop D, 1/4th Cavalry, protected the wreckage until the troop's Aero Rifle Platoon arrived. By 1640, Quarterhorse troopers had evacuated all remains except those of one missing soldier, Specialist Raymond Lanter. Lanter had jumped from the aircraft before impact and his body was not found immediately.[52]

When Lieutenant General Walter Kerwin, the new II Field Force commander, was briefed, he radioed the following message to General Talbott: "I give you permanent command of the Division." Talbott acknowledged, saying, "I would have given anything, I say again, anything, to have had it been under other circumstances."[53] Throughout the Big Red One, the loss of General Ware, a Medal of Honor recipient in World War II, was deeply felt.

By 15 September, the action around Loc Ninh subsided as the NVA pulled back. The losses for the period 11 to 15 September were 33 Americans killed, 1 missing, and 126 wounded. The *7th PAVN Division* lost 216 men killed and 26 weapons. The decrease in the number of enemy weapons captured reflected its resilience as a disciplined opponent.[54]

The next major action took place in an area known as the Trapezoid, from 3 to 10 October. On 3 October, the 1st Brigade, with four infantry battalions, joined the 3rd Republic of Vietnam Marines in a search and destroy mission. Over the next seven days, the allies combed the jungle for enemy installations. Although there was not a great deal of fighting, the 2nd Battalion, 16th Infantry, discovered a camp one-half mile long and 300 meters wide containing a hospital and 3,000 pounds of medical supplies. At the end of the combined operation, US casualties totaled 14 dead and 80 wounded, in exchange for the captured medical supplies, 30 weapons, and 19 confirmed enemy dead.[55]

Major General Orwin Talbott and the Buck Up

For the most part, the division performed well in the summer of 1968, but there had been incidents during Toan Thang that concerned Major General Talbott and indicated that military fundamentals needed reemphasis. On 21 September 1968, Talbott issued "Commander's Notes #1 (Fundamentals)":

   a. *Professionalism*: There is nothing amateurish about this outfit, about the Big Red One, about our division. Nothing will be tolerated that is amateurish. We will be professional in every sense of the word and in all aspects of our business.
   b. *Standards ("Eyeballing")*: We all desire high standards. . . . But if you really want to know what the facts are, you have to see it for yourself. . . . And having identified the things that don't meet those standards, demand—not ask, not wish—*demand* that those standards are met.
   c. *Contacts*: When there is an enemy contact of any appreciable size at all, I want somebody up over it. . . . In a position to monitor . . . to help . . . to guide, whatever the case may be.
   d. *Hot LZ's*: We have been most fortunate during my time, and I gather some time before, on the subject of hot LZ's. We don't want any hot LZ's. . . . We want to find the enemy; we want to clobber him. But, we don't want him to clobber us. We want to stay in control of the situation.
   e. *"Pile ON"*: I won't paraphrase, I'll quote if I may some of the bywords of the 11th Cav: "Find the bastards then *Pile On*." If you have something worth piling on and run out of your own resources, we'll scrape up whatever we can out of the division until we just plain run out. And then we'll ask for more resources.[56]

General Talbott further explained that the division was going to move battalions from region to region rather than to leave them for a long time in a single area or assignment. This method of operations was meant to increase a sense of flexibility and aggressiveness within maneuver units. General Talbott's "Commander's Notes #1" was a reaction to problems in the division and to the changing nature of the war. Talbott told his senior leaders that "if the United States is ever going to be completely successful in Vietnam it will be because of the Vietnamese people, the Vietnamese government, the Vietnamese Armed Forces."

The Accelerated Pacification Campaign:
1 November 1968–17 February 1969

During the realignment of the division's area of responsibility, the 2/28th Infantry was inserted into Fire Support Base Rita as part of operations begun during October in the Tong Le Chon region. Early on the morning of 1 November, an NVA battalion attempted to overrun Fire Support Base Rita with human-wave assaults. The 1st Battalion, 5th Artillery, commanded by Lieutenant Colonel Charles Rogers, was on the base with the Black Lions and Troop B, 1/4th Cavalry, when the attack came. When the enemy broke through the perimeter, Rogers rushed to a threatened artillery battery to rally his gunners to open direct fire against the attackers. "Although knocked to the ground and wounded by an exploding round," Lieutenant Colonel Rogers got up and led a counterattack against a sapper squad in one of his positions. "Painfully wounded a second time, . . . he pressed the attack, killing several of the enemy and driving the remainder from their positions. Refusing medical treatment, Lt. Col. Rogers reestablished and reinforced the defensive positions." These and other actions forced the NVA to retreat, leaving 27 dead in the area after killing 12 and wounding 54 defenders.[57] Rogers received the Medal of Honor for his actions.

During the last two months of 1968 and into January 1969, 1st Infantry Division engagements with enemy units declined significantly.[58] In November, the 1st Infantry Division turned over control of the northern half of its area of operations to the 1st Cavalry Division, allowing better protection to the Saigon–Bien Hoa area. The new area of responsibility contained fewer than 5,000 Communist soldiers and no main force divisions. The Accelerated Pacification program was the focus of the division during this period. This program was part of an initiative to upgrade the security status of 250 hamlets in III Corps from a rating of D or lower to at least a C. These ratings were on a scale from A to E, highest to lowest. The Big Red One was responsible for sixty-one hamlets.[59]

From 1 November 1968 to 31 January 1969, the 1st Infantry Division committed most of its maneuver battalions to the Accelerated Pacification program. These units carried out 38 cordon and search operations, 3,713 ambush patrols, and 2,887 reconnaissance-in-forces missions. Most of these resulted in little action, although 69 Vietcong infiltrators were killed and 62 were captured. Equally important, the men of the Big Red One provided medical services to the local populations and took part in 287 village self-help projects. At the end of January, all hamlets assigned to the division were rated as C or better, and the division had helped the South Vietnamese government gain control of 111,928 civilians.[60]

The Accelerated Pacification program was a major departure in American operations to provide help to the South Vietnamese government to win its struggle for the hearts and minds of the people against the Communists. To succeed, American soldiers and leaders needed to be committed to, and believe in, its possibilities. Unfortunately, by 1968, many Americans in Vietnam had very negative attitudes about the South Vietnamese people. These attitudes were often reinforced by tactical leaders who dehumanized the enemy. Such a situation made it hard to maintain the professionalism and discipline needed to prevent American soldiers from crossing the line from civilization to barbarism.

Sound leadership was key to the division's proper attitude to its missions. In "Commander's Notes #2," dated 27 September 1968, Major General Talbott reminded the division that the indiscriminate operation of armored vehicles and trucks over cultivated fields badly affected South Vietnamese attitudes toward the US Army. In "Commander's Notes #5," dated 13 November, Talbott ordered commanders to exercise the utmost discretion during operations to avoid shooting friendly civilians or regional defense forces. This admonition was timely since one of the features of the Accelerated Pacification program was to arm and train local militias, known as Popular Forces and Regional Forces, to defend the hamlets from the Vietcong.[61]

Pacification remained the division's primary mission until mid-February 1969. At the same time, II Field Force ended the second phase of Operation Toan Thang and commenced Toan Thang III on 17 February, the start of the Vietnamese New Year. During Toan Thang III, the 1st Infantry Division engaged in large reconnaissance missions, often working with ARVN units, and increased night ambush operations against infiltrators. Engineers also continued extensive land clearing operations, removing trees and heavy brush from over 19,000 acres from February to the end of April 1969.[62]

Throughout 1969, ambush patrols were a key tool in denying the Communists free movement during the hours of darkness. Usually they were conducted by small infantry or cavalry units and resulted in few casualties. On 16 February, however, Company A, 1/28th Infantry, ambushed a company of NVA trying to infiltrate from Cambodia. After the ambush was sprung, Lieutenant Gary Miller led a patrol into the kill zone to search for bodies and equipment: "As the group advanced, they were attacked. 1st Lieutenant Miller was seriously wounded. As the patrol fought back, an enemy grenade landed in the midst of Miller's men. Miller threw himself on the grenade, absorbing the force and shrapnel of the explosion and saving his men from serious injury." The patrol then fought its way back to the company. For his action, Miller received the Medal of Honor posthumously.[63]

On 23 February, the NVA opened a series of artillery attacks and increased efforts to infiltrate forces toward the population centers. Rockets hit the 1st Infantry Division headquarters in Lai Khe, inflicting twelve casualties. A number of fire support bases and NDPs were hit over the next few days in an effort to divert attention from the enemy's movement of supplies and forces. Nonetheless, division units intercepted groups of infiltrators and inflicted a steady toll of casualties.[64]

In late March, the Quarterhorse returned to the Michelin Plantation to intercept an NVA unit trying to establish a base camp. After a series of engagements, the enemy retreated, leaving 79 dead and 24 weapons. The Quarterhorse, and an attached troop from the Blackhorse, lost 12 men killed and 19 wounded. Operation Atlas Wedge ended on 2 April, when the 1/4th Cavalry withdrew from the Michelin, leaving the 1st Battalion, 28th Infantry, in the plantation at Fire Support Base Picardy.[65]

For the remainder of April, the *COSVN* withheld its major units from operations and took stock of the results of its winter-spring offensive. A captured document indicates that *COSVN* viewed the offensive as a political success but with only limited military achievements. The main political gains, in the report's words, were to "encourage the anti-war movement in the U.S."[66] II Field Force intelligence agencies concluded that the Communists would continue to launch offensives aimed at causing American casualties.

Meanwhile, General Creighton Abrams reaffirmed that pacification was the "primary" concern of all US forces. The Big Red One used the Accelerated Pacification program of late 1968 as its model for its enlarged pacification responsibilities when MACV increased the division's jurisdiction in the program to 170 hamlets. For the remainder of its time in Vietnam, pacification was the 1st Infantry Division's most important mission.[67]

The Final Campaigns: 1 May 1969–31 January 1970

Throughout 1969, US military efforts focused on the Vietnamization and pacification programs. During this period, the new American president, Richard Nixon, worked to end the war through a negotiated settlement. Regardless of what agreement was reached, ultimately the Saigon government would survive only if its armed forces could prevent a Communist takeover and if it could win and retain the people's loyalty. Thus, the Big Red One's tactical operations continued to play a significant role in the strategic situation facing the United States.

Operation Toan Thang III continued through most of 1969, but operations shifted further away from large-unit maneuvers. The 1st Infantry Division continued to provide "an offensive-oriented, protective 'umbrella' in the northern area of the Division's Tactical Area of Interest (TAOI); conduct a vigorous pacification and security campaign in the central and southern TAOI; and assist ARVN and local GVN [Government of Vietnam] military units to improve their effectiveness."[68]

As the monsoon season approached, the division conducted reconnaissance operations and night ambush patrols. Attention was given to reconnaissance in the Saigon rocket belt and to pacification efforts in the hamlets assigned to the division. Although no major combat operations were undertaken from May through July, the 1st Engineers completed road clearing and improvement operations along the 87-kilometer route from Song Be to Dong Xoai, opening central Phuoc Long Province to road traffic. The 1st Infantry Division also carried out Operation Dong Tien (Progress Together), starting in June. Operation Dong Tien was undertaken to improve the capabilities of ARVN units through joint ARVN-US operations. The division continued to suffer losses, with an average of 50 men killed and 300 wounded each month.[69] Although these losses were lower than those suffered in 1968, they indicate that the Big Red One aggressively carried out its missions against a determined and dangerous foe.

During the spring of 1969, the Communists ended their unsuccessful winter-spring offensive. In late April, *COSVN* reoriented its operations and concentrated on sapper and rocket attacks against Saigon, Bien Hoa, and other allied installations. As the summer progressed, the NVA and Vietcong increased assaults against hamlets, South Vietnamese Regional and Popular Forces, resupply convoys, and isolated American bases. Hanoi's ultimate goal, as expressed in captured documents, "was to put political pressure on the Americans to withdraw from South Vietnam."[70]

Communist attacks against American bases and NDPs generally followed the scenario described in a 1st Infantry Division after-action report:

> The enemy initiated the action at [Fire Support Base] Buttons at 0330 hours, with an attack by 82mm mortar fire followed with a ground probe by an unknown-size force. The defenders, the 1/2nd Infantry Battalion, were supported by air and artillery until contact was broken at 0515 hours. The US suffered 2 WIA [wounded in action] in contrast to the 33 enemy KIA left on the battlefield along with much equipment.[71]

Enemy losses in the An Loc–Quan Loi area from 25 May to 22 June were 601 men killed and 29 taken prisoner. The 1st Infantry Division's casualties for June were 69 killed and 418 wounded. The Big Red One's total casualties during Toan Thang, from 17 February to 31 July, were 232 men killed and 1,811 wounded. The NVA and Vietcong lost 2,845 confirmed killed and possibly another 276. Over 5,000 replacements joined the 1st Infantry Division in this period, maintaining its strength at roughly 17,500 soldiers.[72] Clearly, the Communists were not winning the kill-ratio game, but the continued flow of American casualty lists from Vietnam worked in the enemy's favor on the domestic American political scene in 1969.

The same general pattern of missions and actions continued across the division area in the period August through October. The Big Red One placed renewed emphasis on interdicting the flow of enemy supplies and units toward Saigon. The shortage of captains continued to affect the experience level of the leadership of the infantry, armor, and artillery units, placing more pressure on senior and junior leaders. Partially in response to these problems, there was increased centralization of divisional assets such as engineer, aviation, and transport units.[73]

The division considered itself successful in its missions. Pressure against infiltration forced the enemy to operate in smaller groups to avoid detection. The pacification campaign proceeded in the populated regions in the central and southern area of operations. At the same time, the Big Red One worked closely with the 5th ARVN Infantry Division to sap "the dwindling Vietcong network and Communist local force units through systematic seal and search operations, centralization and coordination of intelligence data, rapid PW and rallier exploitation, and the extensive use of Mobile Resource Control Teams."[74] The division operations report also concluded: "Known enemy units within the Division TAOI have desperately tried to avoid contact and have often devoted their entire efforts to food, equipment and personnel resupply. Resupply has become their major mission. In order to conserve existing force levels, the enemy has abstained from large-scale attacks against allied installations. Combat operations have generally been limited to small unit sapper attacks and stand-off attacks by mortar and rocket fire."[75]

By the end of October, division intelligence officers believed that the Communists hoped to launch an offensive in November, but, due to logistical problems, probably would be unable to do so.[76] In this situation, the 1st Infantry Division casualties declined significantly from August to the end of October, with an average of fewer than 30 men killed and about 235 wounded per month.[77] On 12 January 1970, the division received orders to prepare to leave Vietnam and to reestablish its headquarters at Fort Riley, Kansas. As he conveyed this message to the division, the division commander, Major General A. E. Milloy, urged the troops to make their mark on the enemy as a parting gesture.[78]

During its last three or so months in Vietnam, the division increased the frequency and level of combined operations with the South Vietnamese armed forces and reduced its area of operations. The 1st Cavalry Division and the 5th ARVN Infantry Division began to take over responsibility for most of the Big Red One's sectors starting in January 1970, but until that time, the division continued its interdiction, pacification, and training missions. The division lost 65 men killed and 460 wounded in its final three months in Vietnam, while it killed 1,017 Communists and captured 96.[79]

Redeployment and the Results of the Vietnam War

When the time came to redeploy the division to Fort Riley, most of its soldiers remained in Vietnam. Only those soldiers with most of their one-year tour of duty completed were redeployed. When the division reached Fort Riley, it was redesignated the 1st Infantry Division (M), and it assumed the post, mission, and duties of the 24th Infantry Division (M), which was inactivated the same day.

The soldiers who survived their service in the 1st Infantry Division during the Vietnam War did not reflect on their combat experiences with the same sense of ultimate victory possessed by the veterans of World War I and World War II. Vietnam War veterans for the most part came home individually after completing their tours, or as casualties too badly injured to remain in the division. When the division redeployed from Vietnam in 1970, only a small group of veterans accompanied the colors to Fort Riley. There were no victory celebrations then or later.

What did the soldiers of the 1st Infantry Division accomplish in the Vietnam War? Were their sacrifices worthwhile? The first question is fairly easy to answer in tactical and operational terms, but the second question may never be adequately answered.

The Big Red One was one of the first divisions to deploy to Vietnam. During its first year of combat, the division stopped the deterioration of the South Vietnamese government and armed forces in the area north of Saigon and prevented the Communists from completing their conquest of South Vietnam in 1965. In 1966, the 1st Infantry Division was instrumental in successful efforts to push the Vietcong and North Vietnamese main force units away from the South Vietnamese capital.

In 1967, the soldiers of the Big Red One spearheaded multidivision offensives in III Corps. The division cleared the Vietcong out of the Iron Triangle, smashed the Communist bases in War Zone C, and soundly defeated the *5th* and *9th PLAF Divisions.* These successes proved to the enemy that they could not continue the war of attrition. As a result, the Communist leaders decided to gamble on a high-risk offensive against South Vietnamese population centers during the Tet holidays of January–February 1968.

During the 1968 Tet offensive, the Big Red One played an important part in the tactical defeat of the enemy. At the same time, the division showed remarkable flexibility in its response to the accelerated pacification efforts initiated that year. For the next two years, the division protected 170 hamlets while continuing its interdiction efforts. Because the 1st Infantry Division and other American and ARVN forces emasculated the Communist main force units before, during, and after Tet, the enemy pulled its large units back to border sanctuaries to rebuild and reequip. In this situation, the South Vietnamese government was given a two-year respite in which to establish control over the countryside and to earn the loyalty of its population.

When the 1st Infantry Division departed Vietnam in 1970, it left its area of operations more secure than it had been when the division arrived in 1965. The division did not win every battle, or always achieve all of its goals, but it did enhance the security of the population in its area of operations, giving the South Vietnamese government a chance to win their struggle against the Hanoi regime. The fact that the Saigon government eventually lost that struggle does not take away from the fact that the soldiers of the Big Red One once again met the exacting standards of their division's motto.

17

The Cold War to Desert Storm

WHEN THE FLAG OF THE BIG RED ONE WAS UNFURLED at Fort Riley, Kansas, in March 1970, the division opened a new era in its service to its nation. For the next twenty-nine years, the 1st Infantry Division (M) was an important part of the strategic reserve of the US Army in the Cold War struggle with the Soviet Union. The division headquarters, Division Artillery, and two maneuver brigades remained at Fort Riley throughout this period, prepared on short notice to reinforce American forces in Central Europe or to respond to crises around the globe. The third maneuver brigade of the division deployed to Germany to serve in the US Army, Europe (USAREUR), as part of NATO.

The Volunteer Army

The Vietnam War continued until 1975, five years after the Big Red One left Southeast Asia. For the American people and the soldiers in Vietnam, the war dragged on too long, and popular support declined. Racial tensions and incidents of poor discipline multiplied throughout the armed forces, even as President Richard Nixon found a way to force the North Vietnamese to conclude a peace settlement and the South Vietnamese to accept it. In late January 1973, the president announced an end of hostilities in Vietnam. During the next two months, prisoners of war from both sides were repatriated and American units in South Vietnam withdrew. Over the next two years, the North Vietnamese prepared to resume offensive operations in violation of the Paris Peace Accords. In the spring of 1975, the Communists launched an offensive that quickly destroyed the ARVN's will to resist. North Vietnamese divisions defeated the South Vietnamese armed forces and seized all of South Vietnam. Lacking support for intervention, the new president, Gerald Ford, was forced to watch as America's former ally collapsed. The Communist victory ended the Vietnam War.[1]

The Vietnam War badly eroded public support for the draft and the army. In 1971, in an attempt to defuse the antiwar movement, President Nixon announced that the administration would end conscription. By 1973, Congress had made the Selective Service a standby system requiring American males to enroll, but no longer calling them to active duty. At the same time, the armed forces declined from 3.4 million soldiers in 1968 to 2.1 million in 1975. The army was reduced to twelve active-duty divisions. However, since the United States was still faced with serious threats from the Soviet Union and Communist China, there remained the need to maintain a large active-duty military. Congress chose to rely on a volunteer system to man the armed forces. To recruit soldiers to fill a Regular Army of nearly 800,000 personnel, the US Army created the Volunteer Army Program (VOLAR). Pay scales and educational benefits were increased as incentives for volunteers to enlist. From 1973 through 1979, the army struggled to make the program work.[2]

VOLAR was characterized by a conscious effort to improve the conditions of service. Barracks with private rooms replaced the single-bay barracks. Food was improved and standards of personal appearance modified to allow soldiers to blend in with their civilian peers while off duty. From the perspective of many officers and NCOs, the inmates were given control of the institution. Increases in pay and benefits took place as Congress cut defense budgets. The army had insufficient funds to modernize equipment, support high standards of training, and replace aging base infrastructure.

The increased pay and laxer conditions of service failed to attract sufficient qualified enlistees to fill the ranks. Residual antimilitary sentiment and increasing racial tensions in the nation aggravated recruitment problems. As a result, the army accepted thousands of recruits who had failed to complete their high school educations. A substantial percentage of the enlistees scored in the bottom two categories of standardized aptitude tests. The results were predictable:

> The percentage of unauthorized absences, incomplete enlistments, and disciplinary actions were the worst in the history of the twentieth-century armed forces. . . . Drug- and race-related violence made barracks life an analogue of the worst of the adolescent culture, and the demoralization of the military's junior officers and NCOs made hard-line enforcement (the Marine Corps approach) and permissiveness (the Navy and Air Force approach) equally unproductive. Ominously, career officers and NCOs either left the service or sought duty away from ships at sea or troops in the field.[3]

Nonetheless, thousands of committed officers and NCOs remained in the service and dedicated themselves to army reform. For the next decade these soldiers rebuilt the US armed services. Even in those dark days a number of units, like the Big Red One, maintained traditions of service and combat proficiency in spite of austere budgets, VOLAR policies, and societal unrest. Leaders such as Lieutenant Colonel Don Watts, commander of the

2nd Battalion, 16th Infantry, in 1973–1974, made concerted efforts to re-build the officer and NCO corps. As Watts explained, "NCO prestige was increased; Platoon Leader Development Courses were held and corporals were required to attend before they were promoted to sergeant. The army invested in people and put responsibility right back at them."[4] The offi-cer corps went through three reductions in force in the 1970s. Although some good officers suffered as a result, the overall effect was to cull weaker-performing officers from the corps.

Efforts such as these took time to have wide effect, but by the end of the decade the army was clearly improving. In 1979–1980 changes in the national strategic situation and the public's appreciation of the need for a strong military were under way. Those professional soldiers who had re-mained in the services and had taken steps to reform the forces found their efforts adequately supported for the first time in over a decade. For the next ten years the US armed forces experienced the greatest renaissance in their peacetime history.

A New Strategic Environment

Shortly after taking office in 1969, the Nixon administration developed the Nixon Doctrine. As he sought to escape the Vietnam quagmire, Nixon an-nounced that the nation would concentrate on honoring its commitments to NATO and to its Asian allies. Other regional conflicts would have to be met by America's allies with limited American air and logistical support.

The reorganization of the 1st Infantry Division as a mechanized division and its commitment to NATO was an element of this strategic orientation. In 1970, while most of the Big Red One was stationed at Fort Riley, the division's 3rd Brigade was assigned to VII Corps in Germany, where it "re-flagged" a brigade of the 24th Infantry Division (M). The order directing this action stated that "the personnel and equipment assets of the inacti-vated 24th Infantry Division will be retained in place to be used to form the corresponding reorganized and activated 1st Infantry Division units."[5]

The major constituent units of the 1st Infantry Division (Forward), abbre-viated as 1IDF, included the 1st Battalion, 26th Infantry, the 1st Battalion, the 16th Infantry, the 4th Battalion, 73rd Armor, the 2nd Battalion, 33rd Field Artillery, and the 5th Battalion, 32nd Field Artillery. The brigade was rounded out by company-size support and combat support units. Over the next twenty-one years, the various units in the 1IDF would be reflagged a number of times, and the mix of the brigade would change. As a history of the 1IDF notes, there was "constant change in organization."[6]

The 1IDF was assigned to VII Corps and took part in numerous Return

of Forces to Germany (REFORGER) exercises from 1971 to 1989. It often
served with the 1st Infantry Division, which flew to Germany from Fort
Riley to take part. Lieutenant General Don Watts, commanding general of
the 1st Infantry Division (M) from 1984 to 1986 and now retired, noted that
"REFORGER allowed you to focus on what you needed to do to get ready
for war. It was an enhancement to training."[7] Since the Big Red One, both
at Fort Riley and in Bavaria, belonged to VII Corps for the NATO General
Deployment Plan (GDP), REFORGER deployments to Germany were an
integral part of the division's training from 1970 through 1991.

The Nixon Doctrine was not tested until the late 1970s, when it became
evident that a great nation cannot get by without a robust military organization if it wants to maintain its interests and influence around the world. The
real test came in the Middle East and South Asia.

In November 1979, revolution broke out in Iran. The shah was over-
thrown and his absolute monarchy replaced by an Islamic republic. In the
early stages of the revolution, Iranians seized the American embassy. During
the next year and a half, scores of embassy staff were held hostage. American attempts to rescue them with a military operation failed due in large part
to obsolete equipment. In December 1979, the Soviet Union tried to take
advantage of what it perceived as American weakness and invaded Afghanistan. These developments convinced most Americans that it was necessary
to increase military spending and to improve the quality and readiness of US
military forces. For the next ten years, the armed services—and especially
the US Army—underwent an incredible transformation.[8]

The increased military budgets approved by Congress from 1979 through
1989 paid for a complete reequipping of the army. New M1 Abrams tanks
and M2 Bradley Infantry Fighting Vehicles replaced the obsolete M60
tanks and the M113 Armored Personnel Carriers of the Vietnam era. AH-
64 Apache attack helicopters and UH-60 Blackhawk utility helicopters
replaced the AH-1 Cobra attack helicopters and many of the UH-1H Iro-
quois "Huey" utility helicopters, giving army aviation enhanced capabilities. Congress increased military pay, and a resurgence of national pride
and patriotism filled the ranks with qualified enlistees. Most important, the
educational quality of the men and women recruited to serve in the armed
forces increased significantly as it became possible for the army to insist that
all recruits must be high-school graduates. This directly affected personnel
retention. By the mid-1980s, statistics for the number or percentage of soldiers absent without leave had decreased so much that this offense was no
longer reported as a special-interest item in the army.

These developments allowed the armed forces to adopt a near-zero toler-
ance for drug use. The army gave the officer and NCO corps greater authority

to separate unsatisfactory soldiers. The army faced racial tensions head-on with a widespread education program. Those few soldiers who could not accept the new discipline and requirements were weeded out of the service. These policies and actions helped dedicated leaders transform the army.

As the personnel quality of the army improved, army leaders enhanced training standards, methods, and opportunities. General Bill DePuy, the Training and Doctrine Command (TRADOC) commander, and his deputy Paul Gorman oversaw the development of the National Training Center (NTC) in California where army maneuver battalions could train and be tested under simulated battlefield conditions. General Watts, as commander of the 1st Infantry Division from 1984 to 1986, initiated a battalion-level training system that stressed a "Mission Essential Task List" to bring focus to training. Watts considered the NTC as "the most important reason for the success [of the army] in the 1991 Gulf War."[9] In fact, the 1st Infantry Division sent the first brigade rotation to the NTC in 1982.

Throughout the 1980s, the quality of army personnel, training, and equipment steadily improved. The Big Red One focused its mission-essential task list on its NATO mission. The Cold War continued and provided all the armed forces with focus for their training and equipment development. The army's officer and NCO corps became incredibly professional and competent. As General Leonard Wishart, the division's commander from 1986 to 1988, noted, the division focused on "performance oriented training." Units were evaluated, and when they failed a task they "re-did the training event" until they got it right. Training, as Wishart explained, was "outcome oriented."[10]

The resolve of the United States to meet the Communist threat paid off. From 1989 to 1991, the Warsaw Pact and the Soviet Union dissolved under their own weight. Russia withdrew its armed forces from Central and Eastern Europe, and the Communist dictatorships in Russia and other East European states ended with minimal bloodshed. After the Berlin Wall fell in 1989, Brigadier General William Mullen, commanding general of 1IDF, led a contingent of Big Red One soldiers to Cheb, Czechoslovakia. There, for the first time since the late 1940s, members of the division could lay a wreath at the monument that was dedicated to members of the division who had fallen from January through May 1945. Mullen also oversaw efforts by the 1IDF to send soldiers to visit the battlefields and monuments of the division in the two world wars.[11]

By mid-1990, the US Army had begun to reduce its forces overall and to cut the size of the army in Germany. In this process, the 1IDF was one of the first major units to turn in its equipment in Europe and prepare for redeployment to the United States. However, on 2 August 1990, Iraq invaded neighboring Kuwait, putting any plans to pull forces from Germany on hold as the United States organized a coalition to meet and roll back Iraqi aggression in the Middle East.[12]

The Gulf War: The Army Graduation Exercise

Saddam Hussein, the brutal dictator of Iraq, created an international crisis with his unprovoked invasion of Kuwait. His move threatened Saudi Arabia as well, putting 20 percent of the world's oil supply at risk. The United States chose to take forceful action. The war that followed proved that the US armed forces had gotten past the malaise cast by the pall of the Vietnam War. In the process, the Big Red One again answered its nation's call to arms.

During the autumn of 1990, the United States and its allies assembled a coalition army of over 500,000 soldiers in Saudi Arabia. Working with allies, the administration of George H. W. Bush convinced the United Nations to sanction military action to eject the invaders from Kuwait. Thirty-eight nations sent troops to join the American-led Coalition. Over fifty nations contributed money and resources. The United States paid for most of its war costs, with over $50 billion in contributions from Middle East states, Japan, Korea, and Germany. The British and French sent armored divisions to the Gulf to join Syrian, Egyptian, Saudi, and American forces.[13] The military centerpiece of the Coalition, however, was the 500,000 American military personnel serving in the Middle East by early 1991.[14]

As it became clear by November that the Iraqi dictator had no intention of withdrawing his forces from Kuwait, President Bush authorized preparations for an air and ground war to eject the aggressors from Kuwait. The Fort Riley–based 1st Infantry Division moved to the desert and prepared to take part in Operation Desert Storm, the Coalition's offensive to defeat Iraq in Kuwait.[15]

In this crisis, the forward-deployed brigade of the Big Red One moved from Germany to Saudi Arabia to serve as stevedores, unloading the ships that carried the rest of the division from the United States and VII Corps from Germany. The brigade received this mission because it was scheduled for inactivation in May 1991 and had turned in most of its armored fighting vehicles. In December 1990 and January 1991, the soldiers of the brigade unloaded 50,000 pieces of equipment from 152 ships at the Saudi ports of Ad Dammam and Al Jubayl. The 1IDF also helped move over 100,000 soldiers through Saudi ports and airfields to frontline units.[16]

Once the 1IDF completed this mission, most of its senior leaders returned to Germany. Many soldiers of the brigade stayed in Saudi Arabia, however, and were organized into platoon-size replacement units in anticipation of potentially high losses during a ground campaign. The soldiers of the brigade contributed significantly to the eventual success of the operation in these ways. (After the Gulf War ended in 1991 with the defeat of Iraqi forces in Kuwait, the 1IDF was inactivated.)

The 1st Infantry Division (M) commander, Major General Thomas Rhame, had led the two maneuver brigades of the Big Red One from Fort Riley to Saudi Arabia in November 1990. The 2nd Armored Division (Forward), a brigade from northern Germany, joined the division to serve as its third maneuver brigade. The addition of the armor-heavy brigade from Germany made the 1st Infantry Division an "armored" division in reality, as there were more tank than infantry battalions in the division. Third Army assigned the 1st Infantry Division to VII Corps, commanded by Lieutenant General Frederick Franks.[17]

During January 1991, the four divisions of VII Corps trained for their role in the forthcoming offensive. On 17 January, coalition forces opened an air campaign to destroy Iraqi air defenses and to attrite the Iraqi forces in Kuwait. In the face of overwhelming air attacks, the aggressors remained in field fortifications as their leader gambled that the allies would not launch a ground assault due to their fear of suffering heavy casualties. This was a major blunder by Saddam Hussein. On 1 February, VII Corps and two other coalition corps moved into assembly areas for the opening of the ground war. By 10 February, the 1st Infantry Division was in the northwestern desert of Saudi Arabia near the town of Hafar al Batin. The 1st Squadron, 4th Cavalry, screened the Iraqi-Saudi border as the division waited to begin offensive operations.[18]

The air offensive took a dreadful toll on the Iraqi army. US Air Force estimates place the number of enemy tanks destroyed at 1,772, out of an initial force of 4,280. The Iraqis lost 948 armored personnel carriers and 1,474 of 3,100 artillery pieces to the air campaign as well. The coalition air forces flew over 100,000 sorties of all types and lost 38 aircraft. Iraqi air defenses were smashed and their command and control capability severely degraded.[19] Nonetheless, the fifty-six divisions of the Iraqi army possessed a substantial number of armored vehicles and artillery pieces to support its 500,000 soldiers in defensive positions in Kuwait and southern Iraq.

Coalition forces planned to launch the main attack from the Saudi Arabian desert west of Kuwait and drive east through northern Kuwait to the Euphrates River south of the Iraqi city of Basrah. This axis of advance would bypass the main Iraqi defenses and give the allies a chance to cut off the twenty Iraqi divisions in southern Kuwait. While an Arab corps and a US Marine–led corps attacked into Kuwait from the south to pin down the Iraqi divisions, the VII and XVII Corps were to swing nine allied divisions and two armored cavalry regiments through the desert northwest of the main Iraqi forces. Once in Kuwait, VII and XVIII Corps were to destroy Iraq's regular army and Republican Guard divisions.

The 1st Infantry Division's mission was to lead part of VII Corps through extensive barriers along the Saudi-Kuwaiti border (Map 31). The division was to cross the border, cut paths through a large berm of sand, bridge a ditch, and clear land mines and barbed wire from twenty-four lanes through the defenses. The division would then secure the breaches by establishing a defensive arc on the Iraqi side so that the British 1st Armoured Division and corps artillery units could move through and deploy on a wide front.[20]

During the first week of February, the 1st Squadron, 4th Cavalry, destroyed Iraqi radar and reconnaissance units along the border. When the Iraqis launched a cross-border raid near Khafji, General Rhame reinforced the Quarterhorse with an armor-infantry task force and created a screening force commanded by the assistant division commander, Brigadier General Bill Carter. This force screened the division's movement into its forward assembly areas on 13–14 February.[21]

With the Iraqis still refusing to retreat from Kuwait, the Central Command (CENTCOM) and Coalition Forces commander, General Norman Schwarzkopf, planned to set in motion the ground offensive on 25 February. The success of the air campaign, however, caused Schwarzkopf to launch the attack a day earlier than planned, on 24 February. The Big Red One moved forward on the evening of 23 February and penetrated the border defenses at 0545 hours, 24 February 1991.[22]

The division's advance was covered by heavy rains and wind that reduced visibility to 200 meters. Scouts of the 1/4th Cavalry crossed the border at 0507 hours, followed 40 minutes later by the tanks and Bradleys of the 1st and 2nd Brigades. From the onset of the offensive, the thermal imaging sights of the American armored vehicles enabled crews to see targets out to 3,000 meters in the dark. As the cavalrymen advanced, they encountered several hundred Iraqis from the *26th Infantry* and the *48th Armor Divisions* trying to surrender. These men were sent south to POW holding pens operated by military police.

When the scouts reached the berm, they found it smaller than anticipated and easier to cross than had been feared. The 1st and 2nd Brigades, moving abreast with Colonel Anthony Moreno's 2nd Brigade on the right and Colonel Lon Maggert's 1st Brigade on the left, caught up as the engineers cut the berm and cleared lanes through the barriers. On the division's left, Lieutenant Colonel Greg Fontenot's Task Force (TF) 2-34[23] Armor and Lieutenant Colonel Skip Baker's TF 5-16 Infantry moved through open lanes while Lieutenant Colonel Pat Ritter's 1st Battalion, 34th Armor, followed as an

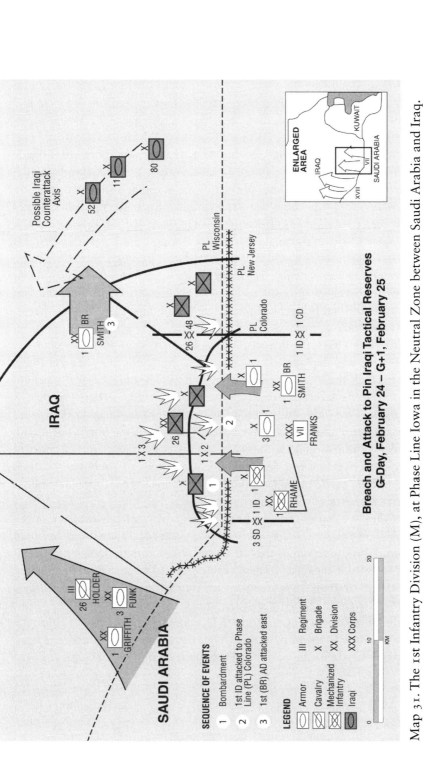

Map 31. The 1st Infantry Division (M), at Phase Line Iowa in the Neutral Zone between Saudi Arabia and Iraq. Corps initial attack, 24 February 1991, evening. (Stephen A. Bourque, *Jayhawk! The VII Corps in the Persian Gulf War* [U.S. Army Center of Military History, 2002])

exploitation force. In the 2nd Brigade's sector, TF 2-16 Infantry and TF 3-37 Armor cleared the way.[24]

By 1600 hours, the 1st Engineers and the tank-infantry task forces had cleared sixteen lanes and had advanced to a defensive arc 5 kilometers northeast of the border. By dark, the division had cleared twenty-four lanes and was ready to pass through the 2nd Armored Division (Forward) brigade (henceforth called the 3rd Brigade). General Franks, however, decided to delay the forward passage of lines of the follow-on forces until the next morning to avoid the risk of casualties due to friendly fire in the rainy darkness.[25]

Early on 25 February, Major General Rhame sent the 3rd Brigade and the 1st Infantry Division's artillery battalions through the breaches while VII Corps moved the 1st and 3rd Armored Divisions through passages cleared by the 2nd Armored Cavalry Regiment to the west of the 1st Infantry Division. In the afternoon and early evening the 1st Infantry Division resumed its advance to the final bridgehead phase line (Phase Line New Jersey), defeating several infantry brigades of the Iraqi *26th Infantry Division* it encountered. At 1000 hours, the British 1st Armoured Division passed through the Big Red One and deployed to the northeast. By 2400 hours, 25 February, VII Corps divisions had deployed on line and were heading northeast behind a reconnaissance screen provided by the 2nd Armored Cavalry Regiment.

Resistance was light, and the biggest challenges Rhame and the division faced were communications in the miserable weather, the need to deal with surrendering Iraqis, and the difficult task of passing massive amounts of fuel forward to refuel M1 Abrams tanks every four to six hours.[26] Losses were far fewer than anticipated, reflecting the qualitative superiority of the American forces over the Iraqi army.[27]

Once the 1st Infantry Division had breached the border defenses, it moved north behind the 2nd ACR screen to the right-rear of the 3rd Armored Division, where it served as the VII Corps reserve. As the cavalry regiment moved forward it engaged an enemy armor force. During a four-hour battle, the 2nd ACR destroyed over forty enemy tanks and personnel carriers from the *Tawakalna* and *12th Armored Divisions*. This action allowed VII Corps to maintain its forward momentum.[28] During the night of 26–27 February, the 1st Infantry Division passed through the cavalry screen and deployed two brigades on line. One historian labeled the night passage of lines "Fright Night":

The moon was up and provided some illumination of the battlefield. Visibility was obscured, however, by the haze from the many oil field fires set by Saddam's fleeing troops, and by the burning hulks left by the 2nd Cavalry in their initial fights with the *Tawakalna Division* at the 73 Easting. All these conditions combined to make this night a rather surrealistic experience and added to the anxiety of the troops of TF 5-16.[29]

After the 1st Infantry Division moved through the 2nd ACR, the VII Corps wheeled to the east with four divisions on line for the final drive to the Persian Gulf south of Safwan, Iraq.[30] (See Map 32.)

Around midnight, 26–27 February, the 1st Infantry Division slammed into the *Tawakalna Division*. During the next few hours, the Big Red One overwhelmed the Iraqi units in its path, with the 3rd Brigade alone destroying sixty tanks and thirty armored personnel carriers of the *18th Mechanized Brigade*.[31] The Iraqis attempted to reposition divisions to face the threat to their communications from Kuwait City to Basrah. However, as these units encountered VII Corps' armored phalanxes, they were unable to carry out tactical maneuvers that might have given them a chance against the coalition juggernaut. In addition, any Iraqi movement was rapidly attacked by air force fighter-bombers until the Iraqi units crossed the official Fire Coordination Line, at which time they were hammered by the massed fires of coalition artillery, attack helicopters, and surface-to-surface missiles. "In the main, the Iraqis surrendered or fought and were ground up."[32]

At 0135 hours, 27 February, Iraqi Radio announced that Saddam Hussein's forces were withdrawing from Kuwait. This message came as most of the Iraqi divisions in southern Kuwait disintegrated and thousands of leaderless Iraqis fled north.[33]

As the enemy forces disintegrated, VII Corps rolled east in a relentless attack. The 1st Infantry Division was, in the words of one historian, part of a "continuous, disciplined, and unforgiving progress through the Iraqi defensive barrier" that saw thousands of American and British armored vehicles overwhelm any Iraqi units that attempted to slow the advance. During the morning of 27 February, a brigade of the Big Red One helped the 3rd Armored Division overwhelm the *Medina Division* with long-range tank and Bradley fire, as the rest of the division destroyed a brigade of the *12th Armored Division*. Later in the day, word reached VII Corps that there was to be a cease-fire to take effect at 0500, 28 February. General Franks ordered the VII Corps divisions to stop in place and to rearm and refuel in case they needed to resume the offensive. The forward units of the Big Red One were well inside northern Kuwait, threatening to cut off the escape route from the south by interdicting the Basrah-Kuwait Highway.[34]

By this point in Desert Storm it was clear the Iraqi army was beaten. The news media reported that thousands of Iraqi soldiers were trying to escape in any vehicle they could commandeer. As they did so, coalition aircraft and artillery took a fearful toll along what became known as the Highway

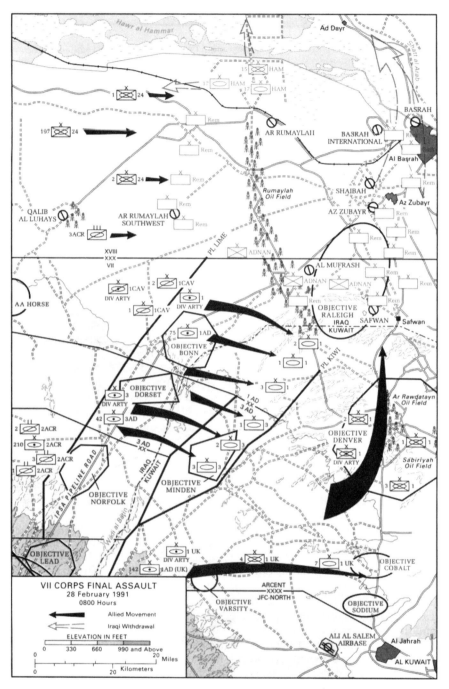

Map 32. The 1st Infantry Division (M) assault through the Kuwait oil fields and on to Safwan, Iraq. VII Corps final assault, 28 February 1991, 0800 hours. (Stephen A. Bourque, *Jayhawk! The VII Corps in the Persian Gulf War* [U.S. Army Center of Military History, 2002])

of Death near Basrah. Since it was impossible for the gunners or pilots to determine whether their targets were armed or not, President Bush became concerned that the possible slaughter of unarmed enemy soldiers along the highway might trigger adverse international publicity, caused in part by the news coverage of the sad events. Consequently, the decision was made to end the fighting as soon as the mission was accomplished to save further loss of life.

Around 0300, 28 February, General Franks learned that the cease-fire had been delayed, and Schwarzkopf ordered him to resume the advance to seize a road junction near Safwan, in northern Iraq. Franks ordered General Rhame to resume the attack at 1000 hours, 28 February. The 1st Infantry Division was to strike east to the highway and then turn north to Basrah, 45 kilometers away. The 1st Squadron, 4th Cavalry, prepared to screen the division's drive east by sending reconnaissance patrols across the Basrah Highway. The Quarterhorse was expected to seize a position at a crossroads south of Safwan as the rest of the division caught up.

Major General Rhame, however, had not received the message from Franks about turning the division north once it reached the highway so as to seize the Safwan crossroads.[35] The fog of war, the use of verbal orders, and general fatigue accounted for the misunderstanding between senior commanders. Consequently, General Franks assumed that the division would completely cut the Iraq army's escape route from Kuwait near Safwan, while the division commander planned to halt the Big Red One along the highway farther south, leaving the route open to the north.

By 0715, the division had accomplished the mission as Rhame understood it. At that point, General Franks was told that a cease-fire was then imminent and to hold his divisions in place. Generals Franks and Schwarzkopf evidently believed that the Basrah-Kuwait Highway was interdicted by the physical presence of VII Corps units, thus blocking the escape of Iraqi army divisions. In fact, the route had not been cut by ground forces but was interdicted by artillery fire and attack aircraft. At this point in the battle the 1st Infantry Division's units were on a line along the western edge of the Basrah Highway.

The mistake was discovered in the early hours of 1 March when a VII Corps staff officer asked the 1st Infantry Division duty officer if the division had secured the area around Safwan and the nearby airfield. The division duty officer said no. When this became clear to Franks, he ordered Rhame to conduct a reconnaissance up to the Safwan Airfield, "but to avoid becoming decisively engaged." Rhame ordered the Quarterhorse to move north to the airfield and the crossroads as soon as possible, but "to avoid combat."

The cavalry squadron moved north at 0615 and reached Safwan Airfield at 0700. The troopers found the airfield occupied by an Iraqi tank brigade.[36]

During the ensuing standoff, Colonel James Mowery, commander of the aviation brigade, skillfully bluffed the Iraqis into believing that they were willing to resume hostilities with the entire division. Rhame backed them up by sending Moreno's brigade to the airfield and by deploying the division's attack helicopters to the area. The Iraqis decided that discretion was the better part of valor and by noon had retreated, giving the division control of the Safwan Airfield and the crossroads.[37]

The 1st Infantry Division then occupied the airfield and secured the site selected for the armistice negotiation with the Iraqis, which was held on 3 March.[38] The Big Red One and VII Corps remained on a high state of alert and readiness in case talks broke down. Once final terms were agreed, the process of cleaning up the battlefield and sending the armies home commenced. For the next six weeks, the soldiers of the division destroyed abandoned enemy armored vehicles and artillery pieces and cleared Iraqi minefields. Finally, in mid-April, the division received orders to prepare its equipment for shipment to the United States. The soldiers moved their equipment from the desert to the port and then boarded aircraft for the flight home to Fort Riley, Kansas.[39] Upon their return, the soldiers were greeted by family and friends in a division ceremony. This welcome home was a stark contrast to that received by the soldiers who returned from the Vietnam War. The celebration symbolized the fundamental shift that had occurred in Americans' attitudes toward US military personnel from 1975 to 1991.

Successful Renaissance

The decisive coalition ground victory in a hundred hours vindicated the efforts by thousands of dedicated leaders and soldiers over the previous two decades to rebuild the fighting spirit of the US Army. The rearmament of the military forces provided for by Congress empowered the professional military to revitalize training, prune unsuitable soldiers from the ranks, and reaffirm essential military values. In a sense, the Gulf War was won in twenty years of preparation and four days of ground combat.

The Big Red One maintained its integrity and traditions throughout the post-Vietnam era. It played an important role in NATO deterrence strategy. Its participation in REFORGER exercises in Germany validated the Army's ability to reinforce USAREUR in Central Europe. The division trained rigorously at the National Training Center at Fort Irwin, California, to hone its combat skills. These years of preparation paid off in spades.

The conclusion of the Cold War and the 1991 Gulf War allowed the Bush administration to reduce the size of the armed forces. The US Army was reduced to fewer than 500,000 active-duty soldiers and ten divisions. The National Guard and Reserve were also reduced. During this process, the 1st Infantry Division (Forward) was returned to Fort Riley. American forces in Europe were reduced by roughly half.

Neither snow nor rain nor dark of night keeps Staff Sergeant Samuel T. Ngaropo from patrolling the Eagle Base internal perimeter with his scouts, 13 December 1996. (US Army Photo, McCormick Research Center Collections)

As Old Ironsides completes its mission enforcing the military aspects of the General Framework Agreement for Peace, the Big Red One covering force arrives to assure full capability through the end of IFOR's mandate, 20 December 1996. (US Army Photo, McCormick Research Center Collections)

Private First Class Shelli Stockstill and Sergeant A. G. Stockstill share their uniforms with two students at a school that received supplies from Pencils from Peace, 9 May 1997. (US Army Photo, McCormick Research Center Collections)

Staff Sergeant Johnny Lovell, of the Task Force 1-18 intelligence section, surveys some of a cache of confiscated weapons, 22 November 1996. (US Army Photo, McCormick Research Center Collections)

Private Benjamin L. Rider, Company C, 2nd Battalion, 2nd Infantry, scans
the nearby ruins of the town of Omerbegovaca from atop the watchtower at
Observation Post Nine, 11 April 1997. (US Army Photo, McCormick Research
Center Collections)

Members of 2nd Battalion, 2nd Infantry Regiment (M) roll across the Sava Bridge from Croatia into Bosnia and Herzegovina in their Bradley Fighting Vehicles, 8 March 1997. (US Army Photo, McCormick Research Center Collections)

First Sergeant Jon Meinholz, 1st Military Police Company, takes this photo while crossing Brcko Bridge to relieve 1AD for SFOR 1, in 1996. (Donation by Jon Meinholz, McCormick Research Center Collections)

Specialist Christopher Santos of Beckley, West Virginia, an artilleryman with
1st Battalion, 7th Artillery Regiment, 2nd Brigade Combat Team, 1st Infantry
Division, peers inside a parked vehicle for any illegal items on a street in the
Mutanabi neighborhood of Baghdad during a combined arms patrol, 7 May 2009.
(US Army Photo by Sergeant Jon Soles, MND-B PAO, McCormick Research
Center Collections)

Soldiers from 3rd Squad, 1st Platoon, 9th Engineer Battalion, attached to 1-77th
Armor, 2nd Brigade, 1st Infantry Division, move tactically through the front
gates of a house being searched in the early morning during a combat operation
in Samarra as part of Operation Iraqi Freedom. (Photo by Sergeant First Class
Johancharles Van Boers, 55th Signal Combat, Combat Camera, Fort Meade,
Maryland/Released for Public Use)

Captain Brad Bandy of G Company, 2nd Battalion, 32nd Field Artillery, 1st Infantry Division, on an IED overwatch in Baghdad, July 2007. (Donation by Captain Brad Bandy, McCormick Research Center Collections)

This photo was taken of Captain Patrick Tanner while patrolling in Baghdad in March 2009. The young Iraqi boy ran up to grab his hand and walk along with him for a few blocks. The man to the right of Captain Tanner is the assigned interpreter, Farouk (not a soldier, but he wears the BRO patch proudly). This photo was taken while Captain Patrick Tanner was assigned as the Brigade Adjutant in 2nd Heavy Brigade Combat Team, 1ID. (Donation by Captain Patrick Tanner, McCormick Research Center Collections)

An M1A1 Abrams from 2nd Tank Battalion attached to the 1st Battalion, 8th Marines, waits for personnel and vehicles (such as the M1114 High-Mobility Multipurpose Wheeled Vehicle [HMMWV] to its right) to move away before it fires on a suspected insurgent position in Fallujah. Both types of vehicles gave the 1st Marine Division the mobility and power needed to rapidly sweep across the city. (US Army Photo by Staff Sergeant Jonathon Knauth, McCormick Research Center Collections)

Captain Jodelle Schroder, Charlie Company, 101st Forward Support Battalion, 1st Brigade, 1ID, in Habbaniya as a part of Project School Nurse doing a health assessment on a local student, Iraq, 2004. (Donation by Jodelle Schroder, McCormick Research Center Collections)

Army Staff Sergeant Eric Winn and Sergeant First Class Jimmy Carswell from C Troop, 6th Squadron, 4th Cavalry Regiment, 3rd Brigade Combat Team, 1st Infantry Division, scan a mountain slope with their weapons before their troop departs on a patrol in Kunar Province. The patrol to search for caves and enemy passages was the first done in that region in more than two years. (US Army Photo by Staff Sergeant David Hopkins, McCormick Research Center Collections)

Second Lieutenant Michael Herndon and his squad provide overwatch security for workers below while they construct a bridge and improve a 3-mile stretch of road in the Lal Por District of Nangahar Province. Afghan National Security Forces also provided assistance in securing the area during the construction process. (Photo by US Army Captain Jay Bessey, McCormick Research Center Collections)

A US soldier assigned to 6th Squadron, 4th Cavalry Regiment, 3rd Brigade Combat Team, 1st Infantry Division, stands at the location of a new observation post at an undisclosed location in northeastern Afghanistan, 24 April 2009. The post will provide security for combat logistical patrols coming through the valley. (US Army Photo by Staff Sergeant Daniel Hopkins/Released, McCormick Research Center Collections)

Bravo Company, 1st Battalion, 26th Infantry Regiment, 1st Infantry Division, soldiers hike at elevations above 2,500 meters during Operation Viper Shake in the Korengal Valley, Afghanistan, 21 April 2009. (US Army Photo by Staff Sergeant Matthew Moeller, McCormick Research Center Collections)

US Army soldiers conduct a night raid mission during Emerald Warrior, near Hattiesburg, Mississippi, 5 March 2012. The primary purpose of Emerald Warrior was to exercise special operations components in urban and irregular warfare settings to support combatant commanders in theater campaigns. Emerald Warrior leveraged lessons from Operation Iraqi Freedom, Operation Enduring Freedom, and other historical lessons to provide better trained and ready forces to combatant commanders. (US Army Photo, McCormick Research Center Collections)

Headquarters Company, 1-178 Infantry Battalion (Task Force Bayonet), attached to 3-1 Task Force Duke at Forward Operating Base Mehtar Lam, Afghanistan, Lagman Province, RC East, 9 April 2009. (Coin/Afghanistan/2010.256 task force Bayonet/2010.256.60, 1-6 ARTY Apr. 9 2009)

US soldiers from 1-1 Kandak, 203rd Embedded Transition Team, Alpha Troop, 40th Cavalry Regiment, Explosive Ordnance Disposal, Provisional Reconstruction Team, members of the Afghan National Army, and Afghan National Police officers conduct a reconnaissance mission near Combat Outpost Zormat, Afghanistan, 26 March 2009. (US Army Photo by Private First Class Enoch Fleites/Released, McCormick Research Center Collections)

18

New Mission
Peacekeeping in the Balkans

FOLLOWING ITS RETURN TO FORT RILEY AFTER the 1991 Gulf War, the 1st Infantry Division maintained its combat capabilities and readiness during a period of declining budgets and significant reductions in the army's strength. The victory in Kuwait did not bring peace to the world. American forces were committed to action in places such as northern Iraq, Somalia, and Haiti. In the words of the official history, these deployments "reflected changing philosophies with respect to armed intervention on the part of both the United Nations and the United States. . . . By 1995, 80,000 [American] personnel were deployed on twenty peacekeeping operations."[1]

The new strategic environment still called for well-trained heavy forces. In March 1992, units of the Big Red One deployed to the National Training Center in California for tactical training. These deployments were structured so that the units went through a process that mimicked an overseas operation that the division might be called on to undertake.[2] Once at the NTC, the armor and mechanized infantry battalions trained with light infantry units from divisions like the 10th Mountain Division. At the completion of a rotation at the NTC, units practiced a redeployment process that would be used in the event of an overseas deployment. As it happened, the 1st Infantry Division was not called on to deploy overseas until 1996, but it took part in a major transformation of the army necessitated by the end of the Cold War and the attendant collapse of the Soviet threat in Europe.

In 1990, the George H. W. Bush administration reduced the number of active-duty divisions, with a planned reduction in personnel from 780,000 to 535,000 by 1995.[3] As divisions were inactivated, a wave of unit redesignations occurred. The Big Red One was affected in early 1996 when the army decided to replace the 3rd Infantry Division in Germany with the 1st Infantry Division from Fort Riley. The soldiers assigned to the division remained at Fort Riley, while the "flags" of the division and most of its major subordinate units were sent to Germany. There the Big Red One assumed the bases and missions of the 3rd Infantry Division, while the 1st Brigade, 1st Infantry Division, remained at Fort Riley. Officially, the 3rd Infantry Division was reflagged with the 1st Infantry Division's colors on 10 April

1996. Major General Montgomery C. Meigs, commander of the 3rd Infantry Division, became commanding general of the 1st Infantry Division with headquarters in Würzburg. The division arrived in Germany at a time when the stability of Southeast Europe was threatened by armed conflict and ethnic cleansing in the states of the former Yugoslavia.

The Disintegration of Yugoslavia and the Balkan Wars: 1990s

Yugoslavia was created at the end of World War I. From 1918 to 1941, Yugoslavia was a multinational state with a Serbian monarchy that included Serbs, Croats, Slovenes, Muslim Bosnians, and Albanians, plus smaller cohorts of other ethnic and national groups.[4] The territories of the new state had been ruled or dominated for centuries either by the Austrian Habsburgs or by the Ottoman Turks. From the early 1500s through the nineteenth century these two empires fought numerous wars for control of the Balkans (see Map 33), with the Ottomans dominant in the early half of this period and the Habsburgs ascendant in the latter half.[5]

Following the collapses of the Ottoman and the Habsburg empires in 1918, Serbia demanded, as one of the "victors" of the war, the creation of a greater Serbia, to include the former Habsburg lands south of Austria and Hungary.[6] The Croats, Slovenes, and Bosnian Muslims reluctantly accepted the establishment of a Yugoslavia ruled by a Serbian monarch. The 6 million Serbs outnumbered the 3.5 million Croats and the 1.1 million Slovenes, but those minorities hoped that the state would be a federal structure rather than a unitary state.[7]

Yugoslavia had twenty-four governments by 1929. "Most failed to deal with the state's dire problems and ended in turbulence or political deadlock. Major obstruction came from non-Serb political opponents, particularly the Croats."[8] In 1929, King Alexander seized control of the government. During the next decade, Croat nationalists became increasingly restive over their subordinate position within the state. Croat resistance became violent in 1934 when Croats murdered King Alexander. The Serb government responded with clumsily applied force against the minorities, making the country nearly ungovernable. In 1941, Nazi Germany put the government of Yugoslavia out of its misery by quickly conquering the country.[9]

"The story of the war years (1941–1945) is unbelievably complex."[10] Adolf Hitler and Benito Mussolini divided the country among Germany, Italy, Hungary, and Bulgaria and played the national groups against one another.

In the center they established the so-called "Independent State of Croatia" (NDH), which was ruled by about six hundred Ustasa [members of the revolutionary Ustase organization]. . . . These extremist Croat nationalists . . . planned to expel and destroy the Serbs, Jews and Roma. Of almost 40,000 Jews . . . in the territory, only about 9,000 survived the war. . . . The mass murders against the Serbs began in late April 1941. . . . Up to the end of World War II, about 330,000 Serbs died in the NDH state, about 200,000 murdered by the Ustasa.[11]

Resistance to the Germans, Italians, and their Ustase allies grew under the leadership of Draza Mihailovic, a Serb, and Josip Broz, a Croat-Slovene, known popularly as Tito. Mihailovic's Chetniks fought to reestablish a Serb-centered monarchy while Tito's Partisans fought to establish a Communist state. By 1943, the Chetniks were cooperating with the Germans and Italians, while the Partisans fought both the occupiers and their Chetnik and Ustase allies. Tito's Partisans defeated the Chetniks and Ustase and made life hell for the Germans. By early 1945 the Communists controlled the country and had proclaimed the Federal People's Republic of Yugoslavia.[12]

Tito's Communist state, encompassing six republics (Bosnia-Herzegovina, Croatia, Macedonia, Montenegro, Serbia, and Slovenia) and two autonomous regions within Serbia (Kosovo and Vojvodina), suffered enormous losses during the war. An estimated 1,027,000 people died, including 530,000 Serbs, 192,000 Croats, 103,000 Bosnian Muslims, 25,000 Slovenes, 57,000 Jews, and 18,000 Roma.[13] In light of these massive losses, it is not surprising that Tito's promise of a multinational state was not overtly resisted by national groups. Until his death in 1980, Tito ruled as a dictator of a Communist federal republic. Resistance to and criticism of the Yugoslav state were labeled as "remnants of bourgeois nationalism."[14]

During his lifetime, Tito "held his fractious state together through a complex system of rights and overlapping sovereignties," a system that minimized the chances of ethnic competition.[15] By the time Tito died, adjustments had been made in the governing relationships among the national groups. Until 1991, a committee representing the six republics and two autonomous regions held the country together. The presidency rotated among the nationalities to prevent any one group from dominating the state. However, as the Cold War ended, Slobodan Milosevic took control of Serbia's Communist Party and transformed it into a Serb nationalist movement. By 1989, he was telling the Serbian people that "Kosovo is Serbia, the Vojvodina is Serbia."[16] He quickly ended the autonomy of Kosovo and Vojvodina. In the case of Kosovo, Serbian police and army troops imposed martial law on a state that was over 80 percent ethnic Albanian and Muslim.

Milosevic's imposition of Serbian rule over Vojvodina and Kosovo prompted the Kosovars to agitate for independence. Milosevic's violent repression of Kosovo Muslims in 1989 triggered calls for independence by the Croats, Slovenes, Macedonians, and Bosnian Muslims and indirectly led to their secessions from Yugoslavia by the end of 1992.[17]

The progressive breakup of Yugoslavia commenced with the declaration by the Slovenes of an independent republic. The population of Slovenia was overwhelmingly Slovene, and its armed forces repulsed halfhearted attempts by Yugoslavia's Yugoslav People's Army (JNA) to repress the new state. "In 10 days the war was over. Deaths and casualties were minimal," and in October 1991 the JNA withdrew from Slovenia and a Slovene republic was recognized by the European Union and Serbia.[18] Western powers hoped that the breakup of Yugoslavia would take place with minimal conflict, and they had no desire to get involved.

During the same period, Croats voted to form an independent republic, and elections brought the Croatian Democratic Union (HDZ) to power. Croatia, unlike Slovenia, had a significant Serbian minority (540,000), which did not relish the idea of living in a Croat-dominated state.[19] Milosevic saw an opportunity to intervene in Croatia when Serbs in the Krajina area seceded from the Croat republic. When Croat police tried to stop them, Milosevic sent the JNA in to protect the Serbs.[20] As fighting broke out in March 1991 "between the Serbs and the Croat police, one of the latter and a Serbian fighter were killed. These were 'the first war victims in Croatia.'"[21]

Croat forces were no match for Yugoslavia's army, which quickly cut the nation in half and seized enclaves in the north and east. Civilian casualties were heavy, and the city of Dubrovnik, on the Adriatic Sea, was heavily damaged. More than 730,000 Croats and Serbs were displaced. The European Community tried repeatedly to establish a cease-fire, but only after the United Nations got involved was a truce established that November. Serbs controlled about one-third of the Croat republic's territory by that time. A UN peacekeeping force of 14,000 troops deployed to keep the warring parties separated.[22]

The European Union recognized Croatian independence in January 1992, and in February the majority of the population of Bosnia-Herzegovina voted for independence. In April, the United States recognized Croatia, Slovenia, and Bosnia-Herzegovina as sovereign states. In May, all three joined the United Nations. Serbia and Montenegro remained united and proclaimed the Federal Republic of Yugoslavia (FRY) on 27 April 1992. While the United States and the European powers sought to encourage stability in the former Yugoslavia, Croatian and Serbian interests turned to Bosnia-Herzegovina, where significant numbers of Croats and Serbs were living.

Serbs, especially, wanted to incorporate major portions of Bosnia into their newly proclaimed nation.[23]

The War in Bosnia-Herzegovina: 1992–1995

Bosnia-Herzegovina, with a population of 4.3 million, was the most ethnically diverse state in Yugoslavia, with roughly 43 percent Bosnian Muslim, 32 percent Serb, and 17 percent Croat.[24] All three groups were descended from Slavs who settled the region during the sixth and seventh centuries. Muslim Bosnians, often referred to as Bosniacs, were descendants of converts to Islam after the Ottoman Conquest, while Croats were Roman Catholic and the Serbs Eastern Orthodox. Under Tito, the rivalries among these groups had been suppressed.[25] In the 1990s, however, the rise of extremist Serbian and Croatian nationalism threatened to rip apart Bosnia-Herzegovina.

Bosnian leaders tried to oppose the breakup of Yugoslavia in 1991 because they believed if the breakup came to pass that the Serb and Croat states would covet control of Serbian and Croatian populations in Bosnia-Herzegovina.[26] As it turned out, events quickly spun beyond their control. Following the secession of Slovenia and Croatia, and the creation of the new Serbian state, Bosnian leaders held a referendum on independence in which the majority of the population voted in favor of forming a larger multiethnic state. The Serb minority in Bosnia rejected the referendum and, on 27 March 1992, declared their region of Bosnia to be the Serb Republic (Republika Srpska). Ten days later, war broke out as Serbs began military operations to conquer additional parts of Bosnia and to begin a process of "ethnic cleansing."[27]

The conflicts and recriminations within Bosnia festered for three years. Serbian forces were supplied by Serbia and received reinforcements from the JNA. Serbs concentrated attacks in eastern and northern Bosnia to create an arc of Serb-held territory linking ethnic Serbs in Bosnia and Croatia with those in Serbia. They also targeted the Bosnian capital of Sarajevo, hoping to make it their postwar headquarters. The Bosnian government, whose poorly equipped army was no match for Serb forces, appealed to the United Nations for assistance. "The UN responded by recognizing Bosnia-Herzegovina as an independent state on May 22." It followed up a week later with sanctions imposed on the Federal Republic of Yugoslavia (Serbia and Montenegro).[28]

In spite of UN actions, the war continued, and in the late summer and autumn of 1992 reports of concentration camps and crimes against civilians began to fill the media. That summer Bosnians fleeing "ethnic cleansing" and genocide

caused refugee numbers to swell, so that by November the figure for all national
groups reached 1.5 million. . . . When the International Red Cross obtained access to the camps, its investigators concluded that the Serbs were most to blame
for the human rights violations, including 20,000 rapes.[29]

During the next two years the European Union (EU) and the UN tried to end
the violence and protect innocent civilians. They deployed 6,000 UN peacekeepers in November 1992 to process refugees and prisoners of war. The
following year the UN declared a "no-fly zone" over Bosnia and established
six cities as "safe areas" (Sarajevo, Bihac, Gorazde, Srebrenica, Tuzla, and
Zepa). "For the most part, UN pronouncements were empty gestures that
were not enforced."[30]

Ethnic cleansing was ruthlessly applied in the Serb-dominated areas of
Bosnia. "The policy began in Muslim villages, where many of the inhabitants chose to flee. The less fortunate were tortured, raped, mutilated, and
murdered; their homes and other property were confiscated." In the fall of
1992, the Serbs extended ethnic cleansing to towns and cities where Muslim
cultural sites and facilities were destroyed. "Western governments and the
UN were aware of what was happening but chose not to act effectively to
stop the atrocities."[31]

While the UN and EU continued to treat Bosnia as a humanitarian crisis,
President Slobodan Milosevic of Serbia and his Bosnian henchmen orchestrated the Serb campaigns. The international community produced several
peace plans that would divide Bosnia-Herzegovina into two sovereign entities within a federal state, a proposal that was rejected by the Bosnian
government. The Serbs continued to expand and cleanse their territory in
Bosnia. By May 1993, two-thirds of Bosnia was Serb-controlled and Sarajevo was under siege.[32]

The Bosnian situation worsened and became more complex in 1993 when
Croatia's president, Franjo Tudjman, sent Croatian forces into Bosnia to
support the Croats. "The Croat-Muslim war was most vicious in the area of
Mostar." The city of Mostar was destroyed along with its famous sixteenth-
century bridge in November, and both sides ethnically cleansed areas under
their control.[33]

While the Croats were attacking in the southeast, the Bosnian Serbs
partially encircled Sarajevo and battered the city's population with sniper,
mortar, and artillery fire. In February 1994, an ABC News crew filmed a
particularly bloody massacre inflicted by artillery fire in the marketplace.
The news spread, and there was no longer any excuse for the EU and UN
to continue to dither in their efforts to end the atrocities. The EU turned
to NATO and asked the military alliance to enforce the no-fly zone over

Bosnia. NATO agreed and issued an ultimatum to the Serbs to vacate a 20-kilometer buffer zone around Sarajevo.[34]

The Serbs, however, decided to call NATO's bluff about the no-fly zone. In response, NATO aircraft shot down four Serbian jet fighters in late February. The major powers also organized the Contact Group made up of the United States, Germany, Russia, France, and the United Kingdom to deal with the crisis. The group convinced the Bosnian Muslims and Croats to end their conflict and to form a federation with a Croat president and a Muslim vice president. This action split the Croat-Serb alliance. NATO, however, used military force only to defend UN personnel in the country.[35]

The Bosnian Serbs denounced the Bosnian federation. Further, they violated Bosnia's safe areas, expelled journalists, abducted UN soldiers, "firebombed UN humanitarian relief offices (UNCHR) in Belgrade [Serbia], and in April shot down a British plane that was evacuating Muslim war victims for the Red Cross."[36] It was evident that only military force could make the Bosnian Serbs accept a compromise.

Meanwhile, UN economic sanctions on Serbia began to have effect. Inflation was rampant, and European markets were closed to the Serbs. Even their mentors, the Russians, supported the UN embargo and encouraged Milosevic to accept UN demands to cease supporting the Bosnian Serbs. In August 1994, Milosevic imposed an embargo on arms sales to Radovan Karadzic's forces and Serb newspapers openly criticized the Bosnian Serbs as "killers of civilians." (Karadzic was the president of Republika Srpska.) Unfortunately, Karadzic refused to stop his forces' campaign.[37]

The Bosnian Serbs continued to appear invincible. By December 1994, "Bosnia had been at war for 1,000 days. The estimated number of deaths was 200,000; there were 2 million refugees. . . . The Bosnian Serbs appeared to be the victors."[38] However, in early 1995 the situation began to change dramatically.

After its humiliating defeat in 1991, Croatia had embarked on a major effort to reequip and train its army. With the help of retired American military officers, the Croatian army became a competent and well-armed force. In the spring of 1995 the Croats reconquered most of their lost territories from the Serbs. As a result, roughly 170,000 Serbs fled from Croatia to Serbia.[39] The international community accepted the new situation in Croatia and looked on while the Croat army crossed in to the Bihac area of Bosnia and joined efforts by the Bosniacs to expel Serb forces. "The combined armies then quickly reduced Serb-held territory in Bosnia from 70 percent to about 50 percent of the country by mid-September."[40]

In spite of their defeats in western Bosnia, Bosnian Serbs continued to attack Muslim enclaves in eastern Bosnia and to besiege Sarajevo. In mid-July,

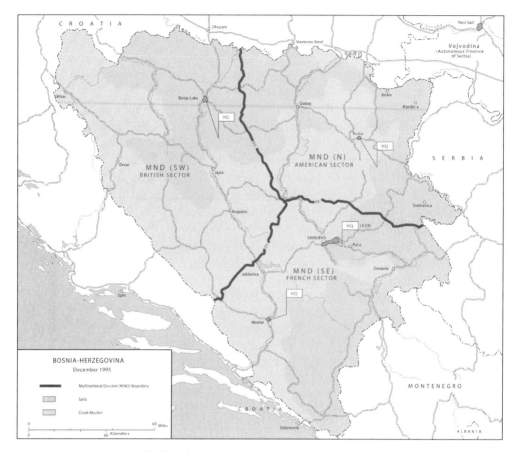

Map 33. Bosnia. (CMH Pub 70-97-1, 2005, US Government Printing Office, Washington, DC)

Bosnian Serbs captured the safe area of Srebrenica from UN peacekeepers. At least 8,000 Muslim men were murdered in the city by Serbs under the command of Ratko Mladic. These thugs then moved on to Zepa, another UN safe area.[41]

As the Serbs continued to commit atrocities, NATO escalated its air attacks against Serb positions. During August, NATO aircraft flew 3,315 sorties against Serb military installations.[42] By late summer, NATO attacks on ammunition and supply dumps near Sarajevo finally forced the Serbs to pull their heavy weapons back from around the Bosnian capital.[43]

As all sides in the war began to show signs of exhaustion, the United States sought a political solution to end the violence. The American ambassador, Richard Holbrooke, convinced the warring parties to agree to peace talks in September at Wright-Patterson Air Force Base, near Dayton, Ohio. The basic framework for the talks stipulated that Bosnia-Herzegovina would remain a federal union to consist of two parts: the Muslim-Croat federation that had been established in 1994 and the Serbian Republic known as Republika Srpska. With this framework, the Contact Group recognized the Bosnian Serb Republic for the first time.[44]

In late November an agreement was reached, and a signing ceremony was held in Paris on 14 December. The agreement, known as the Dayton Accords, confirmed the sovereignty of Bosnia-Herzegovina as a two-part state in which the Bosnian-Croat federation was to control about 51 percent of the territory and the Serbian republic the remaining 49 percent. "The Dayton agreement also spelled out a military settlement to be supervised by an Implementation Force (IFOR) headed by NATO and commanded by an American general."[45]

Implementation Force (IFOR)

During the spring of 1996, the 1st Infantry Division was in the midst of relocating from Fort Riley to Germany. Since the division was reflagging the 3rd Infantry Division in Bavaria, few leaders or soldiers moved from Kansas to Germany. In addition, the 1st Brigade remained at Fort Riley and retained its designation as 1st Brigade, 1st Infantry Division. The German-based forces included two maneuver brigades, the engineer brigade, an aviation brigade, and the Division Artillery. A number of battalions within the division were redesignated so that units like the 1st Squadron, 4th Cavalry, and the 1st Battalion, 26th Infantry, remained with the Big Red One. Major General Randolph House, the commanding general at Fort Riley, noted that "our plan was to ensure that the reorganization and subsequent movement of the division colors to Germany would be executed with minimal turbulence to our soldiers and their families and still maintain our warfighting capability for as long as possible."[46]

While the 1st Infantry Division was undergoing these changes, USAREUR (US Army, Europe), was ordered to provide a division-size force to serve in Bosnia as part of the Implementation Force (IFOR). The 1st Armored Division was selected for the mission and was to serve as part of Multinational Division North (MND-N). NATO designated its commanding general, Major General William Nash, as the commander of the Multinational Division North as well. MND-N was initially composed of the 1st Armored Division, one brigade each from Russia and Turkey, and a composite brigade of soldiers from Poland and the Nordic countries.[47] NATO established two other divisions in Bosnia to carry out its mission: MND Southwest, under British command, and MND Southeast, commanded by a French general. IFOR headquarters was established in Sarajevo.[48]

As the 1st Armored Division prepared to deploy, the 1st Infantry Division provided soldiers to fill vacancies in the armored division. Many of the maintenance personnel, aviation specialists, and military police were transferred from the Big Red One to the 1st Armored Division. As a result, the readiness of the 1st Infantry Division plummeted. However, since it was assumed at the time that the need to deploy units to Bosnia would last for only a year, the USAREUR commander assured Major General Meigs that there was little need to worry about the low readiness of the division and that if a crisis arose he would fill the division. Meigs noted that the division continued to train its soldiers and units to the highest standard possible.[49]

Under UN Security Council Resolution 1031, NATO was authorized to implement the military aspects of the peace. IFOR, consisting of 57,000 troops, 20,000 of them Americans, was to maintain the cease-fire, separate the warring forces, transfer territory between the two components of Bosnia, move heavy equipment and forces into designated sites, and control Bosnian airspace.[50] The United Nations transferred authority to enforce the peace agreement to NATO on 20 December 1995. The American-led division, with headquarters in Tuzla, was the first "out-of-sector" commitment of NATO forces in history, and the first time since World War II that Americans and Russians worked together. Designated Task Force Eagle, the MND-N was the lead element of IFOR to enter Bosnia.

The first challenge of IFOR was deploying its forces into the country. The first unit of MND-N to deploy was the 3rd Battalion, 325th Airborne Infantry, which parachuted into Tuzla to secure the town. The heavy forces of the 1st Armored Division came overland to a staging area near Taszar, Hungary, where they prepared to cross the Sava River on a pontoon bridge. Severe rain and snowstorms made the construction of the Sava Bridge a slow and dangerous task lasting ten days, but the army engineers prevailed and American forces crossed the Sava on 31 December and entered Croatia on their way to Bosnia.[51]

One of the first units to enter Bosnia was the 1st Squadron, 4th Cavalry, which was attached to the 1st Armored Division. Quarterhorse troopers led the advance into Bosnia on 3 January 1996 and assumed control of a sector along the Inter-Entity Boundary Line between Republika Srpska and the Bosnian federation. The route to the squadron's area of operations "was narrow, hazardous, and mine-laden. . . . Terrain and weather proved every bit as challenging as we had expected," noted the command historian Lieutenant Colonel Mark Viney.[52] It took the squadron twenty-three hours to reach Tuzla, but the only mishap was a vehicle accident involving several trucks. Fortunately, no one was injured. Viney was startled by the scale of the destruction of towns along the route of march. "Entire villages lay in rubble. . . . Fields were fallow and covered with trench lines."[53] Once the 2nd Brigade, 1st Armored Division, reached Tuzla, the Quarterhorse moved to its sector, which stretched from Banovice in the west to Zvornik in the east, with major population centers at Zivinice and Kalesija.[54]

IFOR settled in for a mission anticipated to last one year. The display of overwhelming air and land forces and the war-weariness of the opposing parties helped make the IFOR occupation peaceful. Bases were established throughout MND-N's sector to provide housing and decent living conditions for the troops. Civilian contractors and American engineers built the twenty-three camps required for MND-N, and contractors performed daily tasks like garbage disposal.[55]

The first step in IFOR's mission was to separate the warring parties. By 10 February, Quarterhorse troopers had succeeded in separating Serbian from Bosnian forces and establishing a 10-kilometer exclusion zone along the Inter-Entity Boundary Line. The troopers then oversaw the removal of weapons and equipment into designated storage sites.[56] The first casualties suffered by the cavalrymen occurred on 30 January, when a Bradley ran over an antitank mine. The crew was uninjured, but when several officers went to inspect the damage, First Lieutenant Bob Washburn stepped on a mine, which blew half of his foot off. Two other soldiers were slightly wounded. Mines were to remain one of the greatest dangers to the soldiers of IFOR.[57]

The Serbs and Bosnians occasionally tried to hide weapons and avoid inspections, but IFOR remained firm and vigilant. During the next eleven months IFOR kept the warring parties separated, "divided the disputed territory, and sent warring troops and heavy equipment to cantonment areas." IFOR also helped Bosnia hold national elections and "gave Bosnia its first year of peace since the civil war erupted in 1991."[58] IFOR ensured that military forces from outside the former Yugoslavia withdrew, and IFOR engineers helped repair bridges, roads, and airports and carried out numerous civil affairs projects.[59]

While IFOR accomplished its missions, Serbs and Bosnian Muslims remained unreconciled to coexistence. As a result, it became clear that if NATO forces were withdrawn in December 1996, as originally planned, warfare would resume.[60] Consequently, NATO established the Stabilization Force (SFOR) to replace IFOR and to enforce the Dayton Accords. Task Force Eagle remained the title for the US contingent in MND-N. The 1st Infantry Division was selected to replace the 1st Armored Division at the end of its eleven months in Bosnia.

SFOR1

Due to the success of IFOR in stabilizing Bosnia, only the 1st Infantry Division's 2nd Brigade, the aviation brigade, and division headquarters were to deploy to Bosnia. The American component of SFOR totaled 8,500 soldiers. Secretary of the Army William Perry noted that "physical presence is probably the single most important function they can perform in terms of war deterrence and in terms of maintaining [peace]."[61] It was anticipated that SFOR would last eighteen months, and the decision was made that "no soldier will serve in Bosnia-Herzegovina for more than a year."[62]

The 1st Infantry Division received little time to prepare for its deployment. General Meigs ensured, however, that every battalion assigned to SFOR received special training at the Combined Arms Training Center (CATC) at Hohenfels, Germany. Meigs and the division staff "certified" each battalion for peacekeeping upon the completion of its mission readiness exercise. At the same time, soldiers from the 3rd Brigade were transferred to the 2nd to fill vacancies that USAREUR or the army could not fill. The division also reorganized its maintenance, logistical, and aviation units to support both the units remaining in Germany and those going to the Balkans.[63]

General Meigs spent a month in Tuzla in September to "understudy" Major General Nash as commander of MND-N. Meigs decided to leave the division's G3 and chief of staff with the units remaining in Germany. This was a wise decision, since the 3rd Brigade had the major task of receiving replacements for the soldiers transferred to the 2nd Brigade and of preparing itself for potential deployment to Bosnia.[64]

In October 1996, 1st Infantry Division soldiers loaded their equipment and armored vehicles onto trains for the trip to the staging area at Taszar Air Base, Hungary. There they put ammunition into their vehicles and received briefings on the movement to Bosnia. The Taszar staging area included a "life support area" containing tents with shower facilities, a Post Exchange, dining facilities, and a gym. The USAREUR morale and welfare organization ran a phone tent where, in the age before cell phones, the soldiers could call their families. The chance to call home gave soldiers, like Sergeant Jimmy Van Pelt, a chance "to reassure my wife that I had arrived safely."[65]

From Hungary a covering force of over 1,000 soldiers moved to a staging area at Silavonski Brod, Croatia, for a short rest stop. From there, the covering force crossed the Sava River and rolled on to Tuzla, Bosnia, arriving on 20 October 1996. The covering force's mission was to provide security for the withdrawal of the 1st Armored Division.[66] "The journey from the Sava River to Eagle Base . . . showed the soldiers the clear effects that war had on this region."[67]

Sergeant First Class Rick Wissuchek, who rode in the lead vehicle of the division's headquarters company, described his initial impressions of Bosnia:

> Even though we encountered damaged buildings while driving through Croatia, the first town we entered in Bosnia on the southern edge of the Sava had been greatly damaged during the war. Houses with artillery shell holes and fire damage were literally lining the streets. . . . The one true highlight of this leg of the journey came when the convoy encountered children . . . and saw the look of hope in their eyes.[68]

The rest of the 2nd Brigade followed.

On 10 November, Major General Montgomery Meigs assumed command of Task Force Eagle, with his command post at Tuzla Airfield. The IFOR mandate ended on 20 December and NATO's Stabilization Force was officially established. SFOR's mission was to continue to enforce the provisions of the Dayton Accords.

Before the division took charge, Task Force 1-18 Infantry, which was part of the covering force, carried out its first operation. The action took place around the village of Celic, near TF 1-18 Infantry's Operating Base McGovern, on 14 November. Because of unrest in the area, IFOR declared Celic a "special zone of protection" and ordered the task force to move to the headquarters of the Bosnian 254th Reserve Mountain Infantry Brigade to seize weapons and munitions held there in violation of the peace settlement.[69]

Task Force 1-18 moved out of Operating Base McGovern at 0400 hours, 14 November, with Bradleys and 100 wheeled vehicles. They reached the Bosnian base without incident and loaded trucks with about 1,000 rifles and automatic weapons, 1,500 grenades, and 1,000 mortar rounds. Once loaded, the task force started its journey back to McGovern with two Bosnian armored personnel carriers in tow.[70] Things did not go smoothly on the way back, as Specialist William Young of Company A, 1/18th Infantry, related to a reporter from the division newspaper, *The Talon*:

> We were leaving in Bradleys and were somewhere in the middle of the convoy. We heard something hitting the side of the Bradley, and I guess we were right in front of the HEM-MTT [heavy cargo truck] that people were laying down in front of. We dismounted and pushed the crowd back and picked up the people on the ground. They spit on us and pushed us. . . . I got hit in the face with a shoe.[71]

Young and the other infantrymen then created a corridor through the crowd for the convoy. When the convoy passed through, they jumped on the last few vehicles and continued on their way.[72] The convoy got back to McGovern without further hindrance and with no losses. This operation of Task Force 1-18 was carried out without the soldiers harming any civilian protestors. Such a positive result was due to the training and discipline of the soldiers. When asked about his training, Specialist Young told the reporter that he had experience with crowd control from a previous mission and that his unit had trained at the CATC at Hohenfels: "We trained to do exactly what we did today."[73]

The local population's attitude was difficult for American soldiers to read. Remembering the early months of his first tour with IFOR, Specialist Malachi West noted that it was not uncommon for his MP unit to go through towns and not see many people on the streets. "The people we did encounter . . . had guns." Civilians often joined his convoy for safety as it traveled from village to village.[74] On his second tour in Bosnia, he saw progress in the civilian security situation.

Command Sergeant Major Robert Seiler noted that "it looks really different here the second time around. There's a lot more traffic on the roads; horse carts, tractors, and pedestrians." But the return of refugees was not going smoothly. "It's noticeable that they have tried to fix up their houses, but someone has gone back in there and blown them up."[75]

The soldiers of the Big Red One faced duty in a war-torn country with a population deeply divided. SFOR continued to enforce the military provisions of the peace accords, but emphasis was placed on protecting reconstruction efforts and providing support to civilian organizations.[76] As a consequence, units of the MND-N became involved in trying to protect Bosnian Muslims who were returning to their villages to rebuild their homes.

In cases where these villages had been occupied previously by Serb forces, there was a real danger that Serbs would sabotage the Bosnians' construction efforts. For example, in the village of Gajevi, northeast of Tuzla, Serbs blew up houses that Bosnian Muslims were rebuilding, and the Russian brigade was called on to investigate. In a bombing incident on 6 February, a Russian soldier was injured by a small bomb. The Russians, lacking bomb-detection means, called on the military police of Task Force Eagle to provide a bomb-sniffing dog.[77]

Throughout their mission in Bosnia, 1st Infantry Division soldiers had many opportunities to work with soldiers of other nations. One such opportunity was when the 1st Battalion, 7th Field Artillery, was given the mission to protect the dog team sent to help the Russians investigate the bombing in Gajevi. Military policeman Bradford Parker and his bomb dog worked with the Russians to find unexploded ordnance at the site, allowing investigators to determine where the munitions had been stored. According to navy explosive ordnance disposal (EOD) expert Lieutenant Tim Richardt, it was a dangerous mission as the team found two charges that had not detonated and another that had partially detonated. The mission was completed without any more casualties, as the soldiers involved followed the advice that "if you didn't put it there, don't pick it up."[78]

American and Russian soldiers also carried out joint reconnaissance missions. On one such mission, Russian soldiers traveled in BTR-80 armored vehicles along with men from the 1st Battalion, 26th Infantry, mounted in Humvees. "What villagers witnessed, in January 1997, was the first joint [Russian-American] patrol in their area." Blue Spader Lieutenant Nathan Wasser explained one important aspect of such joint patrols: "there's a perception in the eyes of some locals that there's a tension between U.S. and Russian forces. Operations like this show that SFOR is a multinational force, accomplishing the same goals."[79]

Another mission with Russian soldiers occurred when the 2nd Brigade, stationed in Brcko, assisted the Russians in the confiscation of a T-55 tank. The tank belonged to a Serb brigade whose commander lived in Brcko. The tank had been driven 80 meters outside of a weapon storage site and its movements had been observed by an American helicopter. According to 2nd Brigade's commander, Colonel Michael Thompson, "it was not a deliberate attempt to mobilize," but it was a violation of the peace accords. Consequently, the tank had to be confiscated and destroyed.[80]

Russian troops of SFOR controlled the area where the storage site was located, and their initial attempt to move the tank was blocked by a crowd of Serb civilians at the entrance. The Russian commander asked Colonel Thompson for support. Thompson contacted the Serb brigade commander in Brcko and drove with him to the site. Thompson related to a reporter that the crowd did not understand the situation until the Serb commander explained the rules to them. "By noon the crowd had been dispersed by senior Serb leaders and the SFOR soldiers were allowed to enter the site and confiscate the tank with no more incidents."[81]

The confiscated tank then was destroyed. However, the Serb brigade commander in the area complained to Major General Meigs that under the rules he had the right to see the tank destroyed. Meigs told him that it was too late since it was already done. The Serb remained adamant that he witness the event. At this point, Meigs's assistant division commander suggested that they reenact the destruction. Meigs agreed and the Serb colonel was allowed to witness the second "destruction" of the tank.[82]

American relations with the Russians sometimes were not much easier than those with the Serbs. The Russians considered themselves, historically, the "protectors" of the Serbs. In some cases, Russians in SFOR tipped off Serbs about operations to seize unauthorized weapons. When a joint Russian-American force arrived, they would find the arms site empty. The Russians also expected US soldiers to drink with them at night after patrol. Since American personnel were forbidden from drinking alcohol while in Bosnia, this caused a problem because the Russians considered it an insult not to drink together. Meigs found a solution to this problem by authorizing soldiers deployed with the Russians to drink one shot of vodka to make the Russians happy.[83]

The soldiers of the division also worked with Bosnian police and those of the Serb Republic. In February 1997, the 1st Battalion, 26th Infantry, provided security to Serb Republic police in the village of Malhala. Malhala was in a predominantly Muslim area before the war and had been seized by the Serbs. Under Dayton, Bosnian Muslims were allowed to return to their villages to rebuild homes. By the time the Blue Spaders arrived, Malhala was a shattered ruin, "with broken bricks and skeletal remains of homes." Nonetheless, some Muslim residents had returned and were in the process of rebuilding.[84]

Malhala was in Serbian-controlled Bosnia and the Serb Republic police were responsible for protecting the Muslim villagers. The SFOR troops were to provide security for the area as the police established their authority. The soldiers of Task Force 1-26 provided a show of force and presence. Specialist Raul Cardenas, of Company C, 1st Battalion, 26th Infantry, told a reporter that "we traveled the main road to the Inter Entity Boundary Line. So far it has been quiet."[85] American units had been active in the Malhala area since the fall of 1996. In February, a Russian team joined the Blue Spaders in their patrols, and members of the UN International Police Task Force arrived to train the Serbian police. The goal was to ensure that the Serb Republic police "evenhandedly maintain law and order." The Blue Spaders also continued to conduct twenty-four-hour patrols and searched for weapons in homes of Muslim villagers so they wouldn't "take law into their own hands."[86]

Staff Sergeant Richard Spry noted that "we only have influence while we are here [and that] once we go, it's up to them to make amends and get along." Spry emphasized to a *Talon* reporter, "We are doing what we set out to do. No one has been hurt. I plan to take everyone back home in the same condition they came."[87]

The joint work of the Blue Spaders and Russian troops to protect Muslims returning to homes in Serb-controlled areas never achieved the hoped-for results. The process of resettlement was very difficult because of the animosity of Serbs toward returning Muslims. For example, after months of negotiations, the Serb state approved the applications for resettlement in Gajevi; however, it required the presence of SFOR troops to make it safe for

Muslims to return. To protect Muslims, Russians and Blue Spaders established checkpoints on area roads.[88] Nonetheless, in villages like Gajevi and Jusici (located near the Posavina Corridor, which Serbs and Bosnians saw as a vital interest to control), Muslim attempts to resettle were defeated by mob violence and the hostility of the Serb police.[89]

In the disputed town of Brcko, soldiers of the 1st Battalion, 18th Infantry, worked with soldiers of the NORDPOL Brigade on routine patrols. The NORDPOL Brigade was a composite unit made up of soldiers from Scandinavian countries and Poland. Working with troops from another country helped break the monotony of patrolling, as 2nd Lieutenant John Colwell made clear: "Today is the second time we've worked with the Danish on a patrol. It's been great. They're real professional soldiers. A lot of their tactics and equipment are common to ours and they all speak good English."[90]

Joint patrols familiarized the Danes with important sites like the police headquarters, the Serb military compound, and the Brcko Bridge, over the river that divided the Serbian and Bosniac areas. "For soldiers in both contingents this was not the first time they had worked side-by-side with other nationalities." Private John Holm, a Danish soldier, told a reporter that he had worked with fellow Scandinavians "but said he's partial to Americans." He went on to say that "it's fun working with Americans. They're a lot different."[91]

One of the most dangerous and important tasks to be done in Bosnia was the removal of millions of land mines that had been sown along the former battle lines.[92] IFOR troops oversaw the removal of the mines, but the work was done by Serbs and Bosnians. The 1st Infantry Division was responsible for overseeing the demining process in its area of operations. A five-person Mine Action Center (MAC) was created in Tuzla to gather and analyze information about the locations of minefields. Sergeant Major Richard Jennings was the NCO in charge of the MAC in February 1997. His team's job was "to keep an accurate account of where the mine fields are located. To do this, they gather all mine records that are available from the former warring factions. They then compile them, make copies in English, plot the fields on a map, make maps available to all MND-North soldiers, and keep copies of all records."[93]

The MAC received reports from units whenever they discovered a minefield not previously plotted. The MAC then contacted the Bosnians and Serbs and asked for records on the field. The maps and records provided to the MAC by the factions did not directly correlate to the map grid system used by the US Army. Consequently, Jennings and his team had to "figure out exactly where that field is in relation to the terrain. We look for the name of a road or a town, match it up, and then draw it in."[94] Once the template was prepared, the engineers translated it to a map with the American grid system, and the draft was sent to Heidelberg, Germany, where it was re-created as a map. The maps produced in this manner were then made available to all SFOR units.[95]

The process of locating minefields on maps was tedious and far from complete in February 1997. In a number of cases, records had been destroyed, and in some cases minefields had been installed with no records. Once a minefield was mapped, it was the task of the responsible faction to remove the mines. The 1st Division engineers coordinated with local Bosnian or Serbian units to schedule the removal of minefields. SFOR troops observed the removal operation and updated MAC's database and its maps. According to the commander of the 9th Engineer Battalion, "we don't put any of our soldiers in the mine field, we simply observe them clearing it."[96]

Changing of the Guard: SFOR2

The soldiers of the division who served in SFOR from October 1996 to the spring of 1997 expected their tour of duty in Bosnia to last a full year, as had those of the soldiers of the 1st Armored Division. USAREUR, however, decided to reduce the tour length to six months for most units. Consequently, in March 1997, the division's 3rd Brigade, with the 2nd Battalion, 2nd Infantry, prepared to deploy to Bosnia as part of Operation Joint Guard. After the 3rd Brigade got settled in the American sector, 2nd Brigade, with the 1st Battalion, 26th Infantry, and the 1st Battalion, 18th Infantry, withdrew from Bosnia. The division's engineer brigade replaced the 9th Engineer Battalion with the 82nd Engineer Battalion at the same time. The 1st Battalion, 41st Infantry, was flown to Europe from Fort Riley to serve with 3rd Brigade. Similar rotations took place in the aviation brigade and the division artillery. The division headquarters remained in Tuzla, with soldiers from the staff sections rotating on an individual basis.

The units coming into Bosnia moved to the staging area at Taszar Air Base, Hungary, for final preparations. Units withdrawing from Bosnia reversed the process of entry by road, marching their equipment across Bosnia and the Sava River to Taszar Air Base. There, the departing units prepared their equipment for return to Germany. Soldiers turned in ammunition and sensitive items, washed their vehicles, and reconciled property books and inventories. Vehicles were inspected for plant and animal species that might be aboard. Then units were given documentation for movement by road convoys and rail shipments to home station.[97]

The Ramrods of the 2nd Battalion, 2nd Infantry, took over Camp Bedrock in March to provide security and checkpoints and to continue SFOR inspections of nearby weapon storage sites.[98] Assigned to the battalion's Medical Platoon was Private Shannon Oxford, one of the first three female soldiers assigned to the Ramrods. Private Oxford told a *Talon* reporter that her working relationships with the other soldiers were "nothing less than professional. I have no problem working with the male soldiers. They treat me like any other soldier, but they look out for me like a sister."[99]

Army policy did not allow for the assignment of women to infantry units, so Private Oxford was attached to the Ramrods' Medical Platoon. She was required to attend "extensive briefings and command meetings" before joining TF 2-2 Infantry. Oxford had joined the army nine months before arriving in Bosnia. The response from fellow soldiers was positive. "She is a soldier here just like the rest of us," according to Staff Sergeant Charles Miller, her platoon sergeant. Specialist Rob Lannom, a personnel specialist in the headquarters company, reported that she "gets a kick out of working in the infantry."[100]

Private Oxford told the *Talon* reporter that "the best feeling is when you help out a patient. You help them feel better and they come back later and compliment you on the job that you have done." Oxford also was the primary operator of the Medical Platoon's M577 armored personnel carrier. The tracked vehicle served as a clearing station for the unit when in the field. Oxford drove her M577 from Slavonski Brod, Croatia, to Camp Bedrock when the Ramrods deployed to Bosnia.[101] Once at Camp Bedrock, she and her unit settled down for its mission.

In 1997, the army was continuing a process begun in World War II of integrating women. Neither the Gulf War of 1991 nor the Bosnian mission halted that process. During the Gulf War, the 1st Infantry Division's support command was led by Colonel Rose Walker. And according to the division commander at the time, Lieutenant General Thomas Rhame, 13 percent of the division's soldiers in the Gulf War were women.[102] The fact that there is so little to report about problems with gender or racial integration in the missions of the 1990s demonstrates that the leaders and soldiers of the division attempted to treat all soldiers professionally and evenhandedly.

Setbacks in the Bosnia Mission

NATO and the UN hoped that the security and stability provided by IFOR and SFOR would foster a climate of opinion in which the Bosnian Croats, Muslims, and Serbs would accept a multiethnic state and live together peacefully. Provisions in the Dayton Accords for the return of refugees to their homes were designed to encourage reintegration. Unfortunately, the accords divided the Bosnian state into two sovereign nations (the Croat-Bosnian federation and the Serb republic in Bosnia). The failed attempts by refugees to rebuild in villages like Gajevi were typical. Unsuccessful attempts to foster integrated town life in places like Brcko and Mostar followed a similar pattern, as those places were effectively divided into ethnic enclaves.

The soldiers of SFOR and the 1st Infantry Division often found themselves in the middle of outbreaks of violence between ethnic groups. In the divided city of Brcko, a small patrol from Company D, 2nd Battalion, 2nd Infantry, was deployed to observe the Serbian police in their mission of protecting the UN Office of the High Representative (UNOHR) from a mob of Serbs armed with rocks and clubs. The mob was there to attack Bosnian Muslims who had come by bus to talk to the High Representative about resettlement in Brcko.[103]

The Muslims were refugees who had fled Brcko when the Serbs overran the town. Now they wanted to return. However, according to Major John Bryant, an American civil affairs officer in the town, "The majority of the population of Brcko right now is a lot of [Serbian] refugees who have lost family members, and who have moved several times in the area, and they are pretty upset about the fact that there were Bosniacs in the area." As the Muslims left the UNOHR building to return to their two buses, a group of Serbian women picked up rocks and moved toward the buses. The dozen or so Serbian police at the scene did nothing to stop the mob, and Major Bryant was unsuccessful in his attempts to get the women to drop their rocks.[104]

The Muslims, meanwhile, got onto their buses and started out of town. Bryant followed with his two vehicles. At the same time, Captain Kevin Hendricks and his patrol from the Ramrods moved toward the Brcko Bridge, which the buses would have to cross to get out of the Serb-dominated area. When Hendricks got to a point just south of the bridge, he observed groups of men armed with rocks. Hendricks dismounted and approached one of the groups, hoping to distract them from the approaching buses. However, before he could get to the group, the buses passed by. Hendricks related to a reporter that "as the buses came by they threw the rocks and then started chasing the buses, throwing rocks as they ran along beside them."[105]

Hendricks realized that his small patrol "couldn't stop them from throwing rocks, and they were not going to listen to me. The only thing I could really do was get my soldiers out of the way, observe what happened, and follow the buses through the rest of the town to ensure nothing more serious happened."[106] Nothing did, and when the Bosnian Muslims stopped to assess the damage, they found that no one was seriously injured, in spite of the shattered windows. Hendricks assessed the situation thus: "It could have been a lot worse had it not been for the professionalism of [my] men. . . . They controlled themselves very well, considering that rocks were thrown all around them."[107] However, the Serb police had done nothing to stop the violence, indicating a dim future for the return of refugees to Brcko.

Hendrick's Ramrods obeyed their rules of engagement, which restricted them from using lethal force against rioters except when their own lives were threatened. In such a situation, there was little more SFOR troops could do, since the security of the citizens rested with the local police and members of the International Police Task Force. Such situations were repeated across the region.

SFOR continued to enforce the disarmament rules under the peace accords during the summer of 1997. In mid-July, for example, Company B, 2-2 Infantry, rolled out in force to a storage site where a routine inventory revealed excess weapons. By moving with a full company of mechanized infantry in Bradleys, the Ramrods overawed anyone thinking of resisting. With helicopter gunships overhead, Company B and members of the 1st MP Company moved to the site and withdrew 180 rifles, several mortars, and some machine guns. These weapons were taken away for destruction. Such missions were always dangerous, and violence could escalate if they were not executed swiftly before a mob formed. In this case, rehearsals had prepared the task force for the operation and no one was injured.[108]

One of the stranger missions faced by the division was the removal of thirty-four World War II–vintage T-34 tanks from a weapon site in June 1997. Soldiers of Company C, 1st Battalion, 41st Infantry, provided security to the Heavy Equipment Transport System (HETS) Platoon of the 701st Transport Battalion for the operation. Serb possession of the tanks violated the peace accords, but Serbian forces did not have the means to move the heavy vehicles. The 701st provided HETS to move the tanks to a site near Sokolac for demilitarization. It took three days to move all the tanks, and during that time Task Force 1-41 maintained security patrols from a camp at the base of Mount Zeb. There was no interference to the mission, but the rain and "dense mud" of the road were major challenges to the HETS drivers. The NCO in charge of the HETS noted that "it was a challenge maneuvering [along the road] with all the cliffs and curves."[109] In the end, no one was hurt and the mission was accomplished.

The 1st Infantry Division had no combat casualties during its deployments in 1996 and 1997. A number of soldiers, however, were injured in accidents. The division safety officer, Lieutenant Colonel William Ramer, identified vehicle accidents as the most dangerous and described some of the contributing factors to them in a safety message in August 1997:

> The condition of the roads is enough to deal with! We could deal with the narrow roads, no berms, the poor drainage, the potholes, the lack of road signs, the

lack of lines on the roads, the [inadequate] bridges and don't forget the mines. Let's throw in the weather for a little excitement. . . . Peace has resulted in the onslaught of everything that Bosnia could pull, push, drag, or move to join our oversized vehicles [on the roads]. It gets worse. It's harvest season. . . . No, I didn't forget the horses and cattle, nor the pedestrians (both sides of the road). This isn't Germany. This isn't anything we've ever seen before.[110]

In July 1997, Major General Meigs turned over command of the division to Major General David Grange. General Grange, like Meigs, remained with the division headquarters in Bosnia. There the soldiers of the Big Red One continued to face a complicated and dangerous situation.

Although progress had been made by SFOR to stabilize and help rebuild the country, things still got out of hand on occasion as Serbs, Croats, and Bosniacs refused to live together in harmony. One of the major problems was the unwillingness of the special police brigade of Republika Srpska to treat Bosnians fairly. In fact, these police often acted like a small army. Consequently, SFOR instituted a policy that limited republic police "to ordinary civil police duties" and allowed the officers to carry sidearms only while on duty.[111]

In late August, Serbian resentment of SFOR led to mob violence aimed at 1st Infantry Division soldiers in Brcko. The violence began as a clash between rival police, paramilitary organizations, and local political factions that morphed into "orchestrated mob violence" directed at US soldiers. Early in the morning of 28 August, a patrol of about twenty soldiers from the 1st MP Company and Task Force 2-2 were in Brcko to secure a police station. At about 0400 air-raid sirens sounded and a crowd of Bosnian Serbs gathered outside the police station, where the executive officer of Company D, 2-2, was talking to the police. The Serbs began to throw rocks at the soldiers outside the station and tried to cut off the party inside. "They were definitely trying to hurt us," according to Sergeant Thomas Burnham of 2nd Platoon, 1st MP Company.[112]

The soldiers flanked the crowd to draw attention away from the police station's entrance, allowing the soldiers inside to escape and rejoin the column. The MPs then lined up in front of their vehicles to protect them from the mob. The platoon leader, Lieutenant Katita Ford, directed her soldiers on how to deal with the crowd: "Don't make any facial expression that will let them know you are getting upset. Don't touch them unless they hit you."[113] When the mob threw more rocks and bricks at her troops, Lieutenant Ford ordered her soldiers to mount their armored Humvees and reposition to the Brcko Bridge. The crowd did all it could to block the escape route to the bridge, but with the timely help of soldiers of Company D, 2-2, Ford and her vehicles got through the crowd and drove to the bridge, where they joined another patrol of Ramrods with two Bradleys.

About 100 American soldiers now formed a defensive perimeter around the bridge as about "1,200 people crowded in front of them and began throwing rocks, bottles, bricks, and Molotov Cocktails." The soldiers responded with tear gas and refused to back down or to fire at the crowd. The standoff lasted until the next day. "The crowd demanded that the soldiers leave town. The soldiers refused. Eventually the crowd began to die down and dispersed." First Sergeant Fernando Torres summed up the encounter: "It was a tricky situation. It felt really bad, just 100 of us hunkered down there. But we held our flag up; we defended our flag, and we held our ground."[114]

The Serb provocation in Brcko was not unique. The Brcko mob was part of a coordinated effort to intimidate SFOR in order to delay or prevent upcoming elections. A similar situation occurred at a checkpoint near the town of Zvornik, where soldiers from Company D, 1-41 Infantry, and military police were taunted, punched, and hit by flying debris during a ninety-minute melee. The checkpoint was maintained. "No soldier lost his cool," according to First Lieutenant Mark Siekman. In spite of provocations, the troops of the Big Red One maintained a disciplined posture and prevented the situation from deteriorating further. No one was killed, and stability was restored by the end of the day.[115]

General Grange assessed the situation and the performance of his troops in a message to the division:

> To the soldiers who were there on the Brcko bridge . . . [a] superb performance. To the soldiers who were tested by the crowds, you did not flinch. To the soldiers in reserve and those in the tactical operations centers and on the staff, you maintained incredible composure. . . . To the aviators, the record number of flight hours and your ability to surge when needed is indicative of your great capabilities. . . . The actions of our soldiers . . . have been extremely disciplined and highly professional.[116]

Although the peoples of Bosnia remained unreconciled to one another, SFOR maintained the peace. In September, SFOR provided security for municipal elections that previously had been postponed due to violence. The role of the 1st Infantry Division was to provide support and security for its area of responsibility. The Organization for Security and Cooperation in Europe was responsible for the actual polling.

During the elections, members of the 1st Military Police Company protected four polling stations south of Brcko. Soldiers of Task Force 2-2 delivered ballots and polling material to polling stations in the towns near Camp

Bedrock, and the 1st Battalion, 77th Armor, patrolled the streets of Tuzla, Zivinice, and other towns to maintain peace. In many instances, Big Red One soldiers provided drinking water and food for citizens waiting to vote. The elections went off without major problems. The civil affairs officer with Task Force 2-2 noted that "we're becoming a part of history in Bosnia."[117]

In October, shortly after the Bosnian municipal elections, the 1st Infantry Division was relieved from the SFOR mission by the 1st Armored Division and returned to Germany. Over the next few years, battalion task forces and individual replacements from the division continued to serve in Bosnia-Herzegovina and in Macedonia as part of Operation Able Sentry (discussed in the next section). But for most of the soldiers and families of the 1st Infantry Division, 1998 was, in General Grange's words, a year "to recharge our batteries and enjoy the blessings of being together with loved ones."[118] From 1998 to 2004, other divisions, including the National Guard 34th and 38th Infantry Divisions, provided the command and control elements for SFOR.

Throughout its yearlong deployment to Bosnia, the 1st Infantry Division worked to maintain proficiency for heavy combat operations as part of NATO. As a result, the tempo of operations remained high. The executive summary of the 1st Battalion, 26th Infantry, in the annual history report provides some idea of how busy the soldiers were:

> In the last year, 1st Battalion, 26th Infantry, was focused on conventional warfighting training after a successful peacekeeping operation, Operation Joint Guard in Bosnia-Herzegovina. In July, the Blue Spaders conducted and tested E[xpert] I[nfantryman] B[adge] training. From 4 to 12 July, D Company participated in a Partnership for Peace mission in Ukraine. The battalion deployed to Grafenwöhr Training Area to conduct an intensified gunnery rotation from 15 AUG to 15 SEP 97. In SEP 97, B Company was attached to 1-63 AR for rotation at the Combat Maneuver Training Center (CMTC) at Hohenfels Training Area. Task Force 1-26 executed gunnery and a high intensity rotation at CMTC from 15 OCT to 15 NOV 97. The task force was organized with A and C Companies, 1-26 IN, D Company 1-77 AR, and D Company 1-63 AR. The Blue Spaders were finally reorganized at garrison in Schweinfurt in NOV before I-26 Infantry was tasked with a United Nations' mission, Task Force Able [in Macedonia].[119]

The Blue Spaders' activities and missions were representative of all of the division's units.

SFOR operated in Bosnia until December 2004, when a European Union peacekeeping force took over the task of maintaining the status quo in the deeply divided country. By then, IFOR and SFOR had successfully demobilized the warring armies, reestablished civilian governments in the two states, and restored much of the region's infrastructure.[120] NATO soldiers had accomplished a great deal while taking few casualties and avoiding the shedding of civilian blood.

Macedonia Mission

Another important peacekeeping mission carried out by battalions from the 1st Infantry Division was Operation Able Sentry, a United Nations peacekeeping effort in Macedonia. When Slovenia and Croatia declared their "disassociation" from Yugoslavia in 1991, Macedonia followed suit. Due to pressure from Greece, the European nations recognized the new state as the Former Yugoslav Republic of Macedonia (FYROM). To prevent the spread of ethnic violence in 1992, the United Nations established a peacekeeping force to prevent Serb forces from crossing Macedonia's northern border from Kosovo.[121]

Macedonia was an extremely poor country with a mixed population. About a quarter of its two million people were Albanian Muslims, with most of the remainder Slavic Macedonians. Yet the state's leaders kept Macedonia out of the wars of the 1990s.[122] Operation Able Sentry lasted for six years as a UN mission, with a force of around 1,000 NATO soldiers at any one time rotating in for tours lasting six months. In April 1999, the UN declared its mission a success and turned Camp Able Sentry over to NATO.[123]

The 1st Battalion, 26th Infantry, was one of the Big Red One battalions to serve in Able Sentry. The Blue Spaders arrived in February 1998. They manned outposts along the Macedonian border to prevent armed Kosovars or Serbians from entering the country. Task Force 1-26 was accompanied by four UH-60 helicopters and crews from the 2nd Battalion, 1st Aviation, from Katterbach, Germany. The Blackhawk helicopters were painted white with UN markings, and the soldiers of Able Sentry wore the blue helmets and berets of UN peacekeepers.[124] The Blue Spaders were supported by elements from the 101st Military Intelligence Battalion, the 1st MP Company, and the 299th Forward Support Battalion.

The 1st Battalion, 18th Infantry, replaced the Blue Spaders in September 1998 as the eleventh rotation of troops in Macedonia. For the most part, service in Macedonia was uneventful, or even boring, when compared to duty in Bosnia. Nonetheless, the soldiers of Able Sentry played a crucial role in helping Macedonia's leaders maintain peace between their two largest ethnic populations. The only major threat to the survival of the Macedonian state came in 2000–2001, when Kosovar Albanians tried to ignite an Albanian insurrection. NATO forces reinforced Able Sentry, and the Macedonian government in Skopje responded by granting Albanians significant autonomy. These reforms prevented another Balkan civil war, but American and other NATO peacekeepers made the peaceful outcome possible.[125]

To this day, Macedonia is the one multiethnic state in the former Yugoslavia that appears to have a chance of surviving intact. As then–Secretary of Defense William Cohen stated, Macedonia became an "element of stability in a sea of instability."[126] However, its stability was threatened by the worsening situation in neighboring Kosovo in the late 1990s.

The Kosovo Mission: 1999

Kosovo had remained part of the Serbian state when Yugoslavia disintegrated. Kosovo is a landlocked country east of Albania, north of Macedonia, and southwest of Serbia. Its population is overwhelmingly Albanian Muslims, known as Kosovars, who, during Tito's rule, had been granted a great deal of autonomy. After Tito's death, Kosovars demanded recognition as a nation within Yugoslavia. The Belgrade government reacted by sending police and Yugoslav army units to crush demonstrations. In 1989, Serbian forces officially occupied Kosovo and declared it to be part of the Serbian state.[127] From then on, "Kosovo became a cauldron of injustice and anger, a vivid example of the dilemma of frustrated nationalism in a context of intercultural diversity that lies at the basis of the entire Balkan regional dilemma."[128]

In 1991, the Kosovar Albanian majority overwhelmingly voted in favor of independence, but Serbs continued to occupy the country. In response, Ibrahim Rugova, the leader of the Democratic League of Kosovo, adopted a pacifist approach to the Serb occupation believing that the Serbs were just waiting for a pretext to crush all resistance. During the wars in Croatia and Bosnia, Kosovo remained relatively quiet. The Kosovars boycotted Serbian elections, and the Serbs were too busy to take further steps to pacify or ethnically cleanse Kosovo. Kosovo was not on the agenda at the Dayton peace talks.[129]

Ibrahim Rugova's program of passive resistance yielded little fruit for Kosovar autonomy or independence. In 1993, frustrated Kosovars organized the Kosovo Liberation Army (KLA) around men who had fought in Bosnia. The KLA carried out a series of attacks against Serb police stations and military posts across Kosovo, culminating with the car bombing of the Serb head of Pristina University in 1997. In early 1998, Serb police attacked several Kosovar villages and in March killed 58 Kosovars, including 10 children and 18 women, in Donj Prekaz. In the wake of this atrocity, the KLA swelled to an estimated 20,000 fighters who seized control of large parts of the countryside. In June, the Yugoslav army counterattacked with 40,000 men backed by tanks, artillery, and helicopters.[130]

The United Nations passed a resolution calling on both sides to cease violence. Both sides ignored the UN resolution. In early 1999, fighting intensified in Kosovo, and a brutal attack by Serb forces against the village of Racak, where forty-five unarmed inhabitants were reportedly massacred, convinced NATO that armed intervention might be necessary.[131] In one last attempt to get the Serbs and Kosovars to end their war, the western powers held a peace conference at Rambouillet, near Paris. An agreement that would keep Kosovo within Serbia but also grant free elections and limited Kosovar autonomy was hammered out and reluctantly accepted by the Kosovar delegation. The Serb representatives refused, however, to accept the deal and walked out of the conference on 23 March.[132]

Meanwhile, the Serb police and military overran Kosovo, forcing as many as 200,000 Kosovars to flee. Fearing that the Kosovo war would destabilize Albania, Bosnia, and Macedonia, the western powers demanded that Serbia withdraw its forces from Kosovo.[133] Milosovic refused and escalated the Serbian campaign.

Western leaders were under pressure to end the conflict in Kosovo. *Time* magazine asked its readers a rhetorical question: "Why should we care?" *Time*'s answer: "In spreading hostilities, Serbs have killed thousands of Kosovars and uprooted hundreds of thousands more [of a population of 1 million]. This brutality could threaten European Security by enflaming passions in Albania, Macedonia, and Montenegro."[134] Elie Wiesel, the famous Holocaust survivor, wrote in *Newsweek* that "Slobodan Milosovic is a criminal. Those who believe that there are nonviolent ways to stop his inhuman actions against Albanians are naïve. They forget the nature of the century we live in."[135]

The United States and its allies, after the failure at Rambouillet, decided that military force had to be used.[136] From 24 March until 9 June, NATO aircraft carried out an air campaign against Serbian targets in Kosovo and Serbia. Over 1,100 aircraft from fourteen countries took part in the campaign, flying 38,000 sorties and dropping over 12,000 tons of munitions.[137] Although NATO aircraft attacked civilian targets in Serbia itself, the Serbs refused to give in, and, since NATO was unwilling to send in ground troops, the air war continued for seventy-seven days. In the end, Milosovic agreed to NATO's demands to withdraw his forces from Kosovo when it became clear that Russia would not stand with Serbia.[138] On 9 June Serbian forces began their withdrawal from Kosovo.

During the period of escalating violence in Kosovo the 1st Infantry Division continued to provide forces for Able Sentry in Macedonia and to support NATO operations in Bosnia. However, the focus of training for the division was on preparation for high intensity combat (HIC) operations in Europe and support for Partnership for Peace activities with former Warsaw Pact nations. In early 1999, the division G3 (operations officer) was planning training exercises and gunnery rotations "to prepare for the full spectrum of conflict," and the 3rd Brigade was scheduled to conduct an HIC rotation at the CMTC.[139] The 2nd Brigade was preparing to support the deployment of the 1st Battalion, 77th Armor, to Kuwait as part of Operation Intrinsic Action.[140] There was little thought given to peacekeeping operations in Kosovo.

The division was also undergoing a major reorganization to become a "Division XXI" structure. The division's strength was reduced by 250 soldiers, 42 M1A1 tanks, 42 M2A2 Bradleys, and a line company from each infantry and armor battalion. Each infantry platoon received an additional nine-man squad, and the Multiple Launch Rocket System battery became a three-battery battalion, while each brigade was assigned a reconnaissance troop. New high-tech equipment was promised sometime in the future.[141]

In early February 1999, however, the division received a warning order to prepare to send a brigade to Kosovo if called upon to enforce a peace deal. Major General Grange ordered the 3rd Brigade, under the command of Colonel Clinton Anderson, to prepare for the possible mission. In February and March, 3rd Brigade conducted mission readiness exercises for the 2nd Battalion, 2nd Infantry, and the 1st Battalion, 63rd Armor.[142] Preparations for the deployment of the Steel Tigers of TF 1-77 Armor to Kuwait continued in March, since the tank battalion was not slated for the possible Kosovo mission.[143]

On 1 April, the 2nd Brigade commander, Colonel Stephen Hicks, informed the battalion commander of the 1st Battalion, 77th Armor, that NATO had canceled the battalion's deployment to Kuwait because of the Kosovo situation.[144] The Steel Tigers' commander, Lieutenant Colonel Tim Reese, was disappointed but understood the reasoning behind the change of orders. The battalion resumed its normal training, believing that the 3rd Brigade would be the first to deploy to Kosovo if the air war was successful.

When Milosovic gave in on 9 June, the division was set to deploy forces to Kosovo. However, things did not work exactly as planned. For some reason, when the order came to deploy troops, General Grange decided to send the 2nd instead of the 3rd Brigade. This decision surprised Colonel Hicks and the rest of 2nd Brigade. Hicks was to lead his headquarters company, the Brigade Reconnaissance Troop, the 1-26 Infantry, the 1-77 Armor, the 9th Engineer Battalion, the 1-7 Field Artillery, and the 299th Forward Support

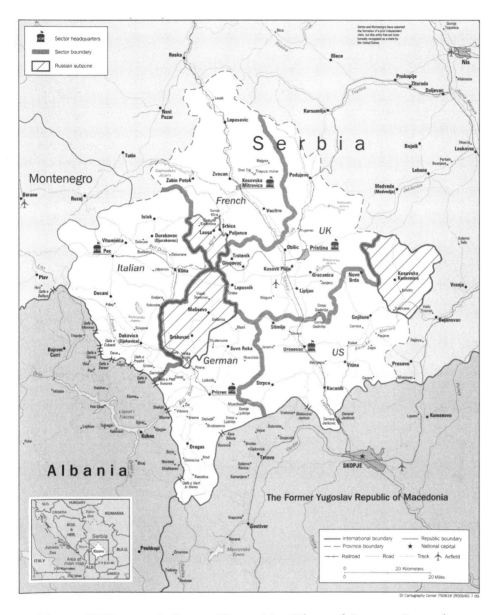

Map 34. KFOR sectors in Kosovo. (Kosovo Map, Library of Congress, Geography and Map Division)

Battalion to Kosovo to serve as the core force of Operation Joint Guardian, the NATO peacekeeping mission.[145]

NATO's deployment to Kosovo was approved by UN Security Council Resolution 1244 on 10 June. A Kosovo Force (KFOR) of roughly 42,000 troops would support the UN Mission in Kosovo (UNMIK) in its efforts to end the violence, disarm the KLA, ensure that Serbian forces evacuated the province, and allow the estimated 800,000 Albanian refugees to return to the country.[146] KFOR included troops from NATO and twelve non-NATO nations, including a Russian contingent. (See Map 34.)

The first elements of KFOR entered Kosovo on 12 June, and by 20 June all Serbian forces had left peacefully. The first Big Red One troops to deploy were soldiers of TF 1-26, who were airlifted from Germany to Macedonia. They joined a Marine unit in Task Force Hawk and crossed into Kosovo from Skopje, Macedonia, on 20 June. TF 1-26 included a tank platoon of four M1A1 tanks from 1-77 Armor and was "the first ever air deployment of an entire mechanized force."[147] The remaining units of 2nd Brigade moved their heavy equipment by rail to Bremerhaven, where it was loaded onto the transport *Bob Hope* bound for Thessaloniki, Greece. The equipment, including tanks, Bradleys, artillery pieces, and heavy support vehicles, arrived in Greece around 30 June and was moved to Skopje, where the soldiers had been airlifted from Germany.[148]

Colonel Hicks and the 2nd Brigade headquarters deployed to Kosovo to support Task Force Falcon, the American component of KFOR. The brigade set up operations in what became Camp Bondsteel and provided the command and control element for the commander of TF Falcon, Brigadier General John Craddock. Colonel Hicks served as the TF deputy commander. The 299th Forward Support Battalion provided support to the task forces that were deployed across the American sector to maintain the peace, disarm the KLA, and allow refugees to return.[149]

The surprise nature of the deployment to Kosovo made June a very hectic month for the 1-26 Infantry and 1-77 Armor. The Blue Spaders were headed to Hohenfels for training when they got word that they were going to deploy. Their Bradleys and other tracked vehicles were on trains to Hohenfels and had to be rerouted to Rhein Ordnance Barracks for air movement to Macedonia. While the battalion commander and staff stayed at Hohenfels for a training exercise, selected leaders returned to Schweinfurt to load essential equipment for shipment. The task force then was airlifted to Skopje Airfield and marched into Kosovo to its sector around the city of Gnjilane. There they established Camp Montieth at an old Serb barracks near the city.[150]

NATO forces divided Kosovo into five AOs, with the US areas of operations in the southeastern region of the country. Brigadier General Craddock divided his AO into three sectors, with the 2-505 Parachute Infantry, from the 82nd Airborne Division, in the west, TF 1-77 in the center, and TF 1-26 in the northeast, in the Gjilane and Novo Brdo Districts.[151] Responsibility for the Kamenica District, along the Serbian border, was assigned to a Russian airborne battalion that was part of KFOR. Major Steve Russell, of 1-26 Infantry, noted in a letter to *The Sentinel* that the Russians were "pretty disciplined . . . look sharp, their equipment is good, and they conduct themselves as any other professional force here."[152]

As the Blue Spaders provided a covering force, the rest of the US KFOR deployed. Task Force 1-77 joined its equipment in Thessaloniki in early July and, over a three-day period, drove its wheeled vehicles from there to Skopje. The Steel Tigers' tanks and other tracked vehicles traveled on heavy equipment transports. The task force waited four days for its turn to use the only paved road from Skopje, Macedonia, to Kosovo, as Task Force Falcon moved logistics, communications, engineer, and combat assets into Kosovo. General Craddock established his headquarters in Camp Bondsteel.[153] On 7 July, TF 1-77 drove the 114-kilometer-long road from Skopje to Camp Bondsteel, where it established its base.

Lieutenant Colonel Reese's initial impressions of the country were not flattering:

Choking dust and oppressive, humid heat combined with smoke to make moving about a chore. Temperatures regularly rose over 100 degrees between June and August. More than a few soldiers, burdened with flak jackets, Kevlar helmets and weapons succumbed to the heat and weight. . . . In August, every soldier in USKFOR would cheer when Falcon 6 [Brigadier General Craddock] lifted the requirement to wear full combat gear while on Camp Bondsteel.[154]

The soldiers of KFOR initially believed that their main task in Kosovo was to protect the Albanian Kosovars from violence by Serbs. Once the Serbian police and army had evacuated the country, however, a pattern developed in which the Kosovars, led by the KLA, launched a campaign of intimidation, arson, and murder to drive the Serb minority out. Reese noted that "this was unlike any operation I had done. . . . We were challenged to figure out what we were to 'do' on a day-to-day basis." In addition, the leaders of TF 1-77 had to figure out how to adapt tank tactics to peacekeeping.[155]

Reese found that the Steel Tigers' first days in Kosovo had an "Alice in Wonderland quality." NATO had bombed the Serbs into submission and now, Reese noted, US troops were taking over the task of protecting the Albanians, "only to find that it was the Serb civilians who needed our protection."[156] TF 1-77 assumed control of Vitina Opstina (county) in the middle of the American sector and experienced its first mass-casualty incident in its first week there. On 15 July, a bomb exploded in Vitina's marketplace, wounding over thirty civilians.

Soldiers from the Scout Platoon and Company A, 2-505 Airborne Infantry, which was part of TF 1-77, rushed to the scene, cordoned off the area, and aided the wounded. The Medical Platoon of 1-77 triaged the victims and called for medevac helicopters from Camp Bondsteel. When Reese arrived, he found wounded on the sidewalks "screaming for help. Parents were crying for us to treat their children. Soldiers and medics frantically ripped open treatment kits and applied bandages. . . . By some miracle the bomber killed no one and injured no soldiers."[157] Captain Sean MacFarland's airborne soldiers of Company A, 2-505, quickly established order and protected the evacuation process. They also searched the town unsuccessfully for the bomber, based on tips from Kosovars who blamed the carnage on Serbs.[158]

The Steel Tigers launched a number of initiatives to prevent another bombing. They searched people and vehicles coming into town every market day, banned parking in the town square, and stationed M1A1 tanks in the square "as a show of force and as a platform from which to survey the crowd." There were no more attacks in Vitina Opstina at any of the markets.[159]

While such measures seemed to work, some local Albanians believed that three Serb families in town were involved in the bombing. Searches of their houses found nothing suspicious, and their Kosovar neighbors defended them as "good Serbs." Nonetheless, the KLA members in the area were determined to drive out these Serbs. They left town for Serbia about a week later, despite the around-the-clock security of their homes provided by KFOR. After the Serbs left, their houses were burned to the ground in spite of the need for housing by returning Kosovar refugees.[160]

About two-thirds of the roughly 200,000 Serbs in Kosovo fled to Serbia in the first year of the KFOR mission.[161] Reese found that the majority of Serbs who remained in his AO "huddled in Serb-only villages or enclaves." Albanian revenge killings and burnings replaced Serb atrocities. Reese, as the senior officer in Vitina Opstina, imposed a countywide curfew between 2200 and 0600 hours, and his soldiers "spent a good deal of . . . time in the first weeks trying to catch the looters and arsonists."[162]

Lieutenant Colonel Randal Dragon's Blue Spaders found similar problems when they arrived in the Vitina area on 22 June. Soldiers of Company C patrolled the streets of Vitina until TF 1-77 arrived. "Violence was rampant with a pattern of nightly gunfire in the city and its outskirts. . . . The assailants—primarily Albanian but also Serb—engaged with automatic rifles and machine guns."[163] In the same period, TF 1-26 occupied the former Serb barracks near Gnjilane and protected the engineers and civilian contractors who built Camp Montieth. Amid these operations, Lieutenant Colonel Robert Scurlock assumed command of the Blue Spaders in a wheat field near Sojevo, on 29 June.[164]

On 10 July, TF 1-26 passed control of Vitina to TF 1-77 and relieved the 26th Marine Expeditionary Unit of its area of responsibility. The Blue Spaders then were responsible for the eastern half of the American sector. The month of July was characterized by widespread violence. "Homicide, looting and arson were epidemic initially."[165] The root of the problem was that the KLA (also known as the UCK) continued to operate in violation of its promise to disarm. In response, Serbs staged protests and frequently blocked the main roads into Gnjilane. The Blue Spaders carried out a number of search operations and found numerous illegal KLA training areas and arms caches. Continued violence by the Kosovars shaped the operations "and the attitudes of the soldiers of the task force."[166]

During July TF 1-26, which included Companies B and C of 1-26 Infantry, Company B, 1-77 Armor, Company B, 9th Engineers, Troop E, 1-4 Cavalry, and the 1st MP Company, carried out patrols, search and seizure operations, and roadblocks to dampen the violence and to confiscate illegal weapons. The dangerous environment and the constant threat of violence took a toll on men and equipment. On 18 July, during a mounted patrol by 1st Platoon, Company B, 9th Engineers, near the village of Donja Sisasnica, an M113 armored personnel carrier crashed into a ditch when a bushing failed and sheared the right track. The momentum of the vehicle caused it to roll over. Specialist Sherwood Brim and Sergeant William Wright were thrown halfway out of the track and crushed. Both were pronounced dead at the scene. The other three crew members received minor injuries. "The bodies of Brim and Wright were carried to the medical helicopter and flown to Camp Bondsteel." The Blue Spaders mourned their fellow comrades' loss while continuing the mission.[167]

Command, Control, and Support

The KFOR command structure placed American forces under the command of NATO. Brigadier General Craddock commanded the US forces and reported to a NATO major general whose headquarters was in Pristina. The 1st Infantry Division commander, Major General John Abazaid, however, spent a great deal of time in Kosovo visiting the division's units. Abazaid was concerned about the possibility of a Serbian army attack against KFOR and encouraged General Craddock to make plans for such an event. The 1st Battalion, 7th Field Artillery, prepared fire support plans for the American camps and stationed its firing batteries in locations from which their self-propelled howitzers could reach most of the American AO.[168]

Camp Bondsteel became the headquarters for the American KFOR. The 2nd Battalion, 1st Aviation Regiment, established its airfield on Bondsteel, which soon became the largest American forward operating base since the Vietnam War. Living conditions steadily improved as barracks, showers, mess halls, and maintenance facilities were built.

The 299th Forward Support Battalion supported KFOR units throughout the American AO. The battalion was augmented with an aviation maintenance company, a composite truck platoon, a mortuary affairs detachment, and a material management center. During its six months in Kosovo, the 299th distributed 1.3 million gallons of fuel and 1.2 million meals and processed 1,300 air-delivered pallets of supplies. In the process, the unit's trucks traveled over 250,000 miles and its maintenance companies completed 3,915 work orders for weapon and vehicle repairs.[169]

The soldiers of the 299th also supported efforts to restart civilized life in Kosovo by sponsoring two schools near Bondsteel. In partnership with their German host-nation community, the unit's soldiers and families collected over 2 tons of clothing, books, and school supplies in Germany for Kosovar children, enabling 300 children to resume their educations after nearly a year's interruption. The battalion's medical company provided over 300 medical assistance visits to Serbian and Albanian villages "where medical treatment had been virtually non-existent for years." The medical company treated over 3,900 civilian patients, "significantly raising the standard of health care . . . in the most rugged and remote areas of Kosovo."[170]

KFOR units also supported UN efforts to revitalize Kosovo's economy and to ease the return of refugees. The 1st Infantry Division's Staff Judge Advocate office contributed to the pretrial detention of Kosovar civilians suspected of criminal activity and ensured that diverse humanitarian assistance operations by nongovernmental organizations were lawful. Division lawyers also assisted war-crimes investigations and provided a full range of legal services to the soldiers in Kosovo, Macedonia, and Germany.[171]

Combat Operations during a "Peacekeeping Mission"

The biggest surprise for 1st Infantry Division soldiers in Kosovo was the violence carried out against the Serbian minority by the Kosovar Albanians. American soldiers quickly found themselves caught between the two factions and increasingly the target of KLA military action. For example, Blue

Spaders became involved in a firefight on 30 July as they attempted to protect a crowd at a funeral for two Serbian farmers who had been murdered. In order to prevent further violence, the Blue Spaders deployed a sniper team to overwatch the funeral. Shortly after the snipers were in place, shots were fired at the crowd and at the sniper team. Specialist Michael Epstein identified a man on a roof with a rifle aimed at the team and immediately opened fire, hitting the KLA sniper. The team then moved to its prearranged extraction point. As they did so, they received "large caliber, automatic weapons fire" and reported that they were also being pursued by men on foot.[172]

The TF 1-26 Tactical Operations Center quickly ordered its reaction force mounted in armored Humvees to move to the extraction point and requested AH-64 attack helicopter support from TF 2-1 Aviation. When the reaction force arrived at the extraction site, Kosovars opened fire from the surrounding hills. The American squad returned fire, forcing the Kosovars to back off and allowing the sniper team to join them. No Americans were injured, but such occurrences were far too common during the Blue Spaders' first two months in Kosovo.[173]

As the deadline for the KLA to disband approached, in September 1999, the level of violence in the towns of Cernica, Partes, and Pasjane increased. These villages in the Blue Spaders' sector had sizable Serb populations that were targets of militant Kosovars. On 7 September, KLA members drove up in front of a café and opened fire within 100 yards of the command post of 1st Platoon, Company A, 9th Engineers. The assailants quickly left and no one was injured. The engineers, who were attached to TF 1-26, secured the area and requested Company B, 1-77 Armor, to help cut off the fleeing Kosovars. The militants got away at the same time as Kosovars fired recoilless rifles at the village of Donja Budriga, west of Cernica. Although the task force scrambled its reaction force and called for attack helicopter support, no armed Kosovars were sighted.[174]

The same evening, Kosovar militants fired mortar rounds into the village of Donja Budriga. Six Serbs in the marketplace were hit: two were killed, including an 80-year-old woman who died instantly when a round "landed squarely on top of her." American patrols tried to track down the attackers, and Lieutenant Colonel Scurlock requested additional assets from Task Force Falcon in Camp Bondsteel. Reinforced with the 2nd Brigade Recon Troop, TF 1-26 sealed off the Serb villages and searched for arms and explosives. They found little, although the EOD team disarmed two unexploded mortar rounds that had been fired into Donja Budriga.[175]

KFOR failed to convince Serbs that they could remain safely in the country. Units such as Task Forces 1-77 and 1-26 worked diligently to protect the Serbs in their AOs and to get both sides to end the cycles of violence and revenge. KFOR also provided convoy escorts to Kosovo Serbs who periodically would drive to Serbia to buy supplies. Any time Serb civilians drove through an Albanian town there was a significant risk of violence. The added risks posed by the KLA made duty for the soldiers of 2nd Brigade dangerous and anything but boring.[176]

During the first six months of NATO's KFOR mission, the level of reported violence in the American-controlled sector of Kosovo declined from over 300 incidents per month to fewer than 50.[177] Although American commanders were frustrated that they could not get the Serbs and Albanians to live together peacefully, they did establish a safer environment in which, hopefully, the parties would find a political solution. After six months in the region, the soldiers of 2nd Brigade looked forward to the end of their deployment with some sense of success. As Lieutenant Colonel Reese concluded, "We saved many lives . . . delivered life-saving aid to tens of thousands of people, and did our best to get Serbs and Albanians, Catholics and Gypsies to work together for a brighter future in Kosovo. And for the first time in the lives of Kosovars, they experienced a conquering Army that did not loot, rape, and kill."[178]

The Changing of the Guard: 3rd Brigade Deploys to Kosovo

While the Division's 2nd Brigade worked to make Kosovo a safer place, the 3rd Brigade prepared to deploy to Kosovo from Germany. In late November, the advance parties of the brigade arrived. Meanwhile, USAREUR decided that the armored fighting vehicles in tank and infantry battalions in Kosovo would be transferred to the arriving units, reducing the costs of shipping equipment to and from Germany. Commanders of the returning units were appalled at this decision, since they believed that their soldiers took great pride in the maintenance of their tanks and Bradleys and that the vehicles they would take over from 3rd Brigade units would not be as well maintained. Nonetheless, the logic of the money saved prevailed.[179] In December 1999, 3rd Brigade took over the USKFOR and operations in the Multinational Division East. Brigadier General Ricardo Sanchez, 1st Division's assistant division commander, became the NATO commander of the MND-E, with headquarters in Camp Bondsteel.[180]

Colonel Clinton Anderson, the 3rd Brigade commander, issued guidance to his commanders that placed "force protection" as his first priority. He emphasized that the goal of KFOR was to eventually transfer the mission to local civilian leadership.[181] Anderson reflected the guidance from the Department of Defense to avoid American casualties, but the commanders on the ground in Kosovo continued to have flexibility to accomplish their daily missions. The 1st Infantry Division ensured that the rules of engagement for the use of force were clearly defined and that soldiers wore their protective gear and traveled in convoys of two or more vehicles and walked in squad-size patrols.[182]

By January 2000, the MND-E included Americans, Russians, Greeks, Canadians, and Italians, to name a few component elements. However, the 3rd Brigade's TF 2-2 Infantry, TF 1-63 Armor, 1-7 Field Artillery, and 82nd Engineer Battalion constituted the majority of the American-led force. The brigade concentrated its operations in the population centers of Gnjilane, Kacanik, Urosevac, and Kamenica. Conducting cordon and search tactics, units such as TF 2-2 and the 82nd Engineers found significant amounts of weapons and ammunition.[183] However, Albanian militants proved to be resilient foes who continued to murder civilians and destroy Serbian churches and homes.

A new threat to stability in the region also emerged early in the year 2000. Kosovar militants began to infiltrate a buffer zone in Serbia along that nation's border with Kosovo. In response, the 82nd Engineers built fortified checkpoints to search vehicles crossing the Serbian-Kosovo border. TF 1-63 provided the platoons to man these posts and was reinforced by an Austrian infantry company. On 14 April the Austrians stopped a convoy full of arms and ammunition destined for militants in Serbia. USKFOR also interdicted munitions and weapons crossing the Kosovo border with Albania.[184]

MND-E also developed tactics to turn the night into day in critical areas by using the Paladin 155mm howitzers of 1-6 Field Artillery to fire illumination rounds to support infantry patrols as they hunted for illegal activities. The three batteries of 1-6 Field Artillery fired 1,378 illumination rounds in sixteen separate "Bright Sky" missions. The artillery battalion also maintained "hot guns" ready to support American and allied forces in MND-E. Such operations hindered the militants' efforts to carry out atrocities or to move weapons and munitions at night.[185] In spite of such successes, an endemic level of violence, perpetrated mainly by Kosovars, continued.

In the first two weeks of June 2000, the 1st Infantry Division transferred authority for KFOR and MND-E to the 1st Armored Division. The soldiers of the Big Red One returned to Germany and began a 180-day-long process of "reintegration" into its NATO mission in the Central European Region. Major General John Abazaid complimented his returning soldiers in May, telling them that "your efforts to subdue the cycles of violence in the Balkans have been a testament to your professionalism. . . . As Big Red One soldiers, you have made a huge difference. You have given hope to people who have never had hope. . . . Well done. Duty First!"[186]

Beginning in the fall of 2001, US National Guard units provided most of the American contingent of KFOR. By 2005, KFOR's troop strength had been reduced to 17,000 troops. "Analysts consider the Kosovo operation to be the most successful operation of its kind in the Post-Cold War era. This success has been marked by the disarmament of the Albanian Kosovo Liberation Army, strong economic growth, and the implementation of local and regional elections."[187]

The ability of the 1st Infantry Division and other American units to rapidly transition from preparing to fight a major conventional war to executing the full spectrum of operations required in a mission such as KFOR validated the divisional structure once again.

The Way Ahead

The 1st Infantry Division spent the rest of 2000 reintegrating soldiers into their families, bases, and Germany. Training focused on preparation for high-intensity conflict. Partnership programs with German units and communities continued. The second half of 2000 was the first time since 1996 that none of the division's units were sent to the Balkans, although the division organized and trained an Immediate Reaction Force (IRF) to provide USAREUR a force that could be deployed within forty-eight hours. Over the next year, IRF units were sent on thirty-day missions in the Balkans to demonstrate NATO's continued capability to reinforce its units in Bosnia, Kosovo, and Macedonia.[188]

Were the peacekeeping operations in the Balkans successful? The answer is yes. NATO forces provided stability in the region and prevented the further spread of ethnic-based warfare. However, the missions did not end in 2000. In 2002 and 2003, the 1st Infantry Division returned to Kosovo to serve as KFOR4A and 4B.[189] By then, the focus of the American armed forces and nation had shifted to wars triggered by the attacks against the World Trade Center and the Pentagon on September 11, 2001.

19

Global Mission
The War on Terror

IN JANUARY 2000, THE 1ST INFANTRY DIVISION remained in Germany as part of the US Army, Europe (USAREUR), with the 1st Brigade stationed at Fort Riley, Kansas. The division continued to support NATO stability operations in the Balkans and to train for high-intensity combat in the European region.

The division's operations tempo remained high as units rotated through Kosovo. The 3rd Brigade Combat Team took over KFOR 1B in January 2000, relieving the 2nd BCT. In June 2000, the division passed the KFOR mission to the 1st Armored Division, allowing most units of the Big Red One to return to home stations for reintegration into their communities and training routines. During the year, the division staff was called upon to conduct "split operations" in Germany and Kosovo while planning and overseeing field training exercises in Central and Eastern Europe, CMTC mission rehearsals at Hohenfels, and gunnery training at Grafenwöhr.[1] Divisional units also took part in seventy-four partnership affiliation events with NATO allies.[2]

The Beginning of the War on Terror

As the century opened, the United States and its allies faced major threats from international terrorist organizations such as the radical Islamic group al-Qaeda. With the election of George W. Bush as president in 2000, a new Defense Department team entered office determined to defeat the terrorist threat and reshape the army. A central part of the Bush administration's defense strategy was to reduce the army's size and to make the remaining forces strategically more mobile so that they could move rapidly by air from bases in the United States to the next battlefield. Before this restructuring got under way, however, al-Qaeda struck the World Trade Center on 11 September 2001.

The United States responded to this challenge forcefully. Within two months American and British special operations forces defeated the Taliban allies of al-Qaeda in Afghanistan and drove them and the al-Qaeda high command into the rugged mountains of eastern Afghanistan. At the same time, the United States made it clear to Saddam Hussein, the brutal dictator of Iraq, that he had to give up all pretensions of developing weapons of mass destruction and submit to open and regular inspections by UN arms teams or face another war against the United States.[3]

In the words of the official army history, "With the Taliban removed from power and al Qaeda on the run in Afghanistan, President Bush turned his attention to Iraq. . . . The Bush administration deemed Saddam the next significant target in the GWOT. On 29 January 2002, President Bush . . . enunciated his policy of preemption: 'We'll be deliberate, yet time is not on our side. I will not wait on events, while dangers gather.'" In October 2003, Congress passed a joint resolution authorizing the administration to use force against Iraq if it deemed it necessary.[4]

Shortly after the September 2001 attacks, Secretary of Defense Donald Rumsfeld ordered the US military to prepare for an invasion of Iraq, even though there was no evidence that the Iraqis had anything to do with the 9/11 attacks. The Central Region Command (CENTCOM), led by General Thomas Franks, developed the invasion plans with direct guidance from Secretary Rumsfeld to keep the forces used to a minimum. Franks and his ground forces commander, Lieutenant General David McKiernan, were expected to destroy the Iraqi armed forces, overrun Iraq, and secure its cities and oil fields with fewer than 200,000 troops, compared to the 600,000 soldiers deployed in 1991 to liberate the much smaller country of Kuwait.[5] It was assumed by Rumsfeld that once Saddam's forces were defeated there would be little need for an extended occupation of Iraq.

While the invasion plans were being developed, American forces prepared for the invasion of Iraq. In November 2002, the 1st Infantry Division, commanded by Major General John Batiste, was alerted to deploy to Turkey to establish the line of communications to support the transit of the 4th Infantry Division across Turkey to the northern Iraqi border. The mission, known as Army Forces in Turkey (ARFORT-T), was to open three Turkish seaports and two airports for the debarkation of the 4th Infantry Division and to refurbish the road and rail routes running 500 miles across Turkey to a major assembly area just north of the Iraqi border.[6]

Beginning in early 2003, a 1st Infantry Division task force that included elements of the 1-26 Infantry, 1-4 Cavalry, 1-6 Artillery, 2-1 Aviation, the 9th Engineer Battalion, the DISCOM, and the 101st Military Intelligence Battalion, began deploying to Turkey. While waiting for an agreement with the Turkish government to allow the transit of the 4th Infantry Division, the task force opened the debarkation points, repaired highways and railroads, and readied support centers along the route from the port of Iskenderun to the town of Mardin, in eastern Turkey.[7]

As General Batiste noted, "We prepared to receive the 4th Infantry Division with enormous amounts of fuel, water, and food. Our plans called for robust maintenance and recovery capabilities along the entire distance of the approach march." Unfortunately, the Turkish parliament eventually voted to deny the United States permission to move combat forces across Turkey for an invasion of Iraq. In early April, ARFORT-T collapsed the line of communications it had built and withdrew its troops from Turkey.[8]

The 1st Infantry Division's units that deployed on short notice to Turkey were veterans of multiple deployments to the Balkans. As Wayne Grigsby, then a lieutenant colonel and commander of the Blue Spaders, recalled, "Our Balkans experience prepared us for this." The division carried out the ARFORT-T while also sustaining a brigade in Kosovo. Grigsby concluded that "we served as a deception force [if nothing else], forcing the Iraqis to look north and south at the same time."[9] General Batiste estimated that the presence of the Big Red One in Turkey "fixed up to thirteen Iraqi divisions in northern Iraq, reducing the enemy strength for the US V Corps fight in and around Baghdad."[10]

Faced with UN resolutions and a US ultimatum, Saddam Hussein badly underestimated American determination to accomplish its goals by force. After Hussein failed to provide credible and regular access to his country to weapons inspection teams, President Bush ordered the United States armed forces to invade Iraq and destroy the Baathist regime. The V Corps in Germany, under the command of Lieutenant General William S. Wallace, received the mission to lead the assault into Iraq from Kuwait. In the initial plans, the 3rd Infantry and 101st Airborne Divisions, along with a Marine expeditionary unit and a British armored division, made up the southern invasion force, while the 4th Infantry Division was to strike northern Iraq from Turkey. Because of the Turkish parliament's decision, the 4th Infantry Division had to be diverted by sea to Kuwait, where it served as a follow-on echelon of the V Corps offensive.

In a stunning campaign in March and April 2003, Lieutenant General Wallace led V Corps with two divisions to Baghdad and victory in a maneuver that carried his forces across the desert west of the Euphrates River. At the same time, the Marine expeditionary unit and the British armored division pushed into Iraq from the south and captured Basrah. The Iraqi army was "overwhelmed" by the onslaught of the coalition forces. However, instead of Iraqi resistance ending, V Corps found itself attacked by increasing numbers of Iraqi irregulars, including Fedayeen and Special Republican Guards.

These forces were lightly armed and often attacked in pickup trucks. Although American armored units quickly destroyed the attackers, their ferocity slowed the advance and showed that the coalition forces "would not be welcomed warmly by all Iraqis."[11] The fierce resistance of the Fedayeen led General Wallace to remark that the Iraqi irregulars were "not the enemy we war-gamed against."[12]

In spite of the fierce resistance of the Fedayeen, V Corps seized Baghdad on 7 April and coalition forces occupied all major Iraqi cities. Many Americans, including President Bush, perceived the swift and stunning victory as the end of hostilities. On 1 May, Bush announced that "major combat operations in Iraq have ended."[13]

The Occupation of Iraq and the Rise of the Sunni Insurgency:
2003–2004

Following the allied victory and the collapse of the Baathist regime, it appeared as if there was an opportunity for the establishment of a stable Iraqi government. Many Sunnis as well as the Kurds and Iraqi Shiites welcomed the fall of Saddam Hussein and looked to the coalition forces to provide security while a new government was established.[14] This period of hope was described by Colonel (later General) David Perkins, the commander of the 2nd Brigade Combat Team of the 3rd Infantry Division:

> Right after we got into Baghdad, there was a huge window of opportunity that if we had this well-defined plan and we were ready to come in with all these resources, we could have really grabbed ahold of the city and really started to push things forward [to a stable Iraq]. By the time we got a plan together to resource everything, the insurgents had closed the window of opportunity quickly. What we started doing in September was probably a good idea to have done in April 2003.[15]

Unfortunately, the Bush administration failed to allow the Joint Staff to plan for sufficient forces to occupy, secure, and rebuild Iraq after the initial fighting ended. Secretary of Defense Rumsfeld was tasked by Presidential Directive 24 to plan the postinvasion efforts. Bush "had taken office in 2001 having campaigned on his dislike for nation-building projects, such as those in the Balkans."[16] There were also some military theorists who believed that the American armed forces "existed to fight and win wars and should not have its strength dissipated in missions like SFOR and KFOR."[17] General Franks and CENTCOM concentrated their efforts on planning the invasion itself, and "Franks did not see postwar Iraq as his long-term responsibility.

He later wrote that he expected a huge infusion of civilian experts and other resources to come from the US government" to rebuild Iraq.[18]

Rumsfeld, believing there was no need for a large commitment of military resources after the defeat of Saddam's forces, rejected a plan presented by the Joint Staff, known as Phase IV, for the establishment of security in a postwar Iraq. Instead, Rumsfeld established the Office of Reconstruction and Humanitarian Assistance (ORHA) under retired Lieutenant General Jay Garner to plan for the postwar occupation. Garner had just sixty-one days to put together a multiagency staff and to plan for "Phase IV operations."[19] Meanwhile, Rumsfeld and Vice President Richard Cheney chastised the army chief of staff, General Eric Shinseki, for testifying to a congressional panel that the defeat and occupation of Iraq would require over 250,000 soldiers for a years-long occupation and reconstruction. Shinseki was soon mocked by administration supporters for disagreeing with Rumsfeld that a battlefield victory was all that was necessary in Iraq.[20]

The army was prepared for what is known as "Full Spectrum Operations." In this doctrinal concept there are four phases in a campaign like the one the Bush administration had ordered carried out in Iraq. The first three phases culminate with combat operations. In Iraq in 2003, the coalition forces did a superb job in their Phase III combat operations. The army was prevented, however, from properly planning for and resourcing Phase IV operations for security and stability. Iraq descended into anarchy as mobs looted palaces and bases and severely damaged the country's electrical system and oil infrastructure.

By the summer of 2003, American forces were in a war against enemies who used improvised explosive devices (IEDs) and ambushes against supply convoys and patrols. US bases came under frequent mortar and rocket attacks. The Iraqi insurgency that evolved in the spring of 2003 was extremely complex. No single Iraqi group coordinated the struggle, nor was there a single goal. Nonetheless, there was a religious core to the insurgency, with Shiites and Sunni seeing the coalition forces as "nonbelievers" who had come to fight Islam. "Between August 2003 and January 2005, the Iraqi insurgency continued to grow and diversify."[21]

Confusion in American policy exacerbated the situation when the Bush administration replaced General Jay Garner's ORHA after it was in Iraq for just three weeks. The new organization, known as the Coalition Provisional Authority (CPA), was under the direction of Ambassador Paul Bremer. Bremer "did not speak Arabic, although he had served in Kabul, Afghanistan, from 1966 to 1968, which was something. His most notable assignment had been as ambassador to the Netherlands."[22] Within days of his arrival, Bremer decided to disband the Iraqi army and to remove members of the Baath Party from government positions. These orders created a mass of unemployed men who became fertile recruiting grounds for insurgent organizations. Lieutenant General Wallace concluded that "the de-Baathification meant that the bureaucracy that made Iraq work was no longer allowed to help make Iraq work."[23]

The 1st Infantry Division in Iraq:
2003–2004

The first Big Red One combat unit to fight in Iraq was TF 1-63 Armor, which joined the 173rd Airborne Brigade in an air-insertion into northern Iraq in March 2003. The deployment of the armor task force from Germany was the largest operation of its kind in history, with air force C-17 aircraft flying the 68-ton M1A1 Abrams tanks from Ramstein Air Force Base to Kirkuk.[24] For the remainder of 2003, TF 1-63 served in Iraq while the rest of the division prepared to deploy to that country in early 2004.

The second major unit of the 1st Infantry Division to arrive in Iraq was the 1st Brigade, which departed Fort Riley, Kansas, in September 2003. The brigade joined the 82nd Airborne Division in the city of Ramadi, a clear indication of the need for additional forces to defeat the Iraqi insurgency. The 1st BCT received less than six weeks to prepare, indicating the serious situation in Iraq.[25] The 1st Battalion, 34th Armor, was allowed to take only one-third of its M1A1 tanks, forcing the unit to reorganize two of its companies as "dragoons," equipped with Humvees. Lieutenant Colonel John Nagl, the S3 (operations officer) of TF 1-34 Armor, later related that "we had next to no information on the enemy situation in Al Anbar Province, where we were deploying, and were limited in our ability to train the battalion staff for the intelligence support that would prove so essential once we were in the area of operations (AO)."[26]

Many in the 1st BCT felt they "were making it up as we went along." They certainly had very little time to get information from the 3rd Armored Cavalry Regiment, which they replaced so that the cavalry unit could concentrate its forces elsewhere in Anbar Province.[27] John Nagl described the situation the brigade found in its area of operations:

> We faced a very determined enemy in Khaldiyah—actually several different categories of enemy. The Sunni insurgency was quite strong and comprised the majority of the enemy we fought, but there were elements of al Qaeda in Iraq (AQI) north of Khaldiyah in the farmlands known as al-Jeezera. The Sunni insurgents fought us with IEDs and sniper fire because they saw us as supporting the Shi'a. AQI viewed the fight against us as part of the global struggle to form

the caliphate and their weapon of choice was the car bomb. We could practice classic counterinsurgency against the Sunni insurgents but AQI members had to be killed.[28]

The soldiers from Fort Riley adapted to their dangerous environment. It helped that they understood that the key to success in a counterinsurgency is not to create more insurgents than you kill or capture. This made it imperative to avoid accidentally killing noncombatants and "to use force as carefully and with as much discrimination as is possible."[29] Nagl believed that "many of the soldiers and junior officers in the task force understood the mission we were assigned in Iraq better because of their experiences . . . in Bosnia."[30]

The 1st Brigade's soldiers found themselves in combat while trying to train Iraqi security forces and, at the same time, working to revitalize the infrastructure and economy in their area of operations. The training of an Iraqi defense corps was controlled by the brigade headquarters from Ramadi. By the spring of 2004 several Iraqi battalions were ready to train with the brigade's units in active operations. The 1st BCT chose not to embed advisors in the Iraqi units because of the tenuous relationship between the Shiite battalions and the local Sunni population, "especially after the first battle of Fallujah in April 2004." (See Map 35.) American efforts to train Iraqi forces were made more difficult because the insurgents regularly assassinated Iraqis who cooperated. For example, the commander and S3 of the Iraqi battalion that TF 1-34 was training were both murdered in Fallujah because of their relationship with the coalition forces.[31]

The 1st BCT successfully performed its combat missions. During their first seven months in Iraq, soldiers of the 1st BCT detained more than 1,500 insurgents, killed 132, and wounded another 53. They also captured 47 mortars and 543 small arms and destroyed over 500 ammunition caches and IEDs. At the end of their year in Iraq, General Batiste took part in the ceremony awarding combat infantryman badges and combat medic badges to soldiers at Camp Junction City, near Ramadi.[32]

In September 2004, the Fort Riley brigade was replaced by the 1st Battalion, 506th Infantry. During the transfer of authority the 1st BCT provided a "well-coordinated and comprehensive right seat–left seat ride" for the incoming unit, "although they learned far too quickly how dangerous the AO was, suffering a KIA during the process." As TF 1-34's year ended, the insurgents gave them a "final gift" when their mortar fire hit the ammunition dump on Taqaddum Airfield. The task force's "flight schedule was completely disrupted," Nagl recalled, "and we spent several days waiting for new flights to be scheduled. It was one hell of a sound and light show, watching a division main ammunition dump go up in flames, but it wasn't worth the price of admission."[33]

The 1st Division's Deployment to Iraq from Germany: The Home Front

In late June 2003, the Department of Defense announced which units would replace the forces then in Iraq. The 1st Infantry Division was to deploy to an area of operations covering four Iraqi provinces north of Baghdad, beginning in January 2004.[34] This AO included the Sunni Triangle, where most Iraqi Sunnis lived. Major General John Batiste set in motion the plans and operations that had to be carried out to move Task Force Danger from Germany to Iraq and to prepare its soldiers for their mission in Operation Iraqi Freedom II.

One of the most important things that needed to be accomplished was to provide for the support of the division's home front. The Big Red One soldiers in Germany were accompanied by roughly 25,000 family members. One of General Batiste's first decisions was that when the division deployed, there would be a very capable rear detachment in Germany to care for the families and soldiers left behind. Deployments to the Balkans and Turkey had shown the importance of having strong support structures for families, and Batiste realized that the major benefit of a successful home-front operation was that it enabled the soldiers to focus on their mission without undue worry about family members.[35]

Batiste selected Lieutenant Colonel Chris Kolenda, incoming commanding officer designee of 1-4 Cavalry, to command the rear detachment (Rear D). During the second half of 2003, Batiste and the division's senior commanders held monthly meetings with Family Readiness Group (FRG) leaders, Area Support Group commanders, chaplains, and health providers to coordinate support for the families. Batiste hoped that the cohesive communities then in Germany would continue to function when the troops left. In the end, most families remained in Germany when the division departed.[36]

Lieutenant Colonel Kolenda arrived in Wurzburg in December. Kolenda found that solid Family Support Groups (FSGs) were already organized at the brigade and battalion levels and determined that the most important relationships for him and his staff were with group leaders. "Therefore," Kolenda noted, "I was to spend a lot of time with Michelle Batiste and Debbie Morgan, and with the FRG leaders and advisers."[37]

In previous deployments, some units had left weaker performers behind to command rear detachments. "This time, Batiste required high quality people to conduct rear detachment operations to a high standard."[38] Batiste personally approved the senior rear detachment commanders, noting later that "if it didn't hurt [the deploying unit], it was not the right person."[39]

The rear detachments established what Kolenda called "a routine battle rhythm." Kolenda and his staff held monthly "roundups" to discuss upcoming events, to build teamwork, and to provide training for Rear D leaders. They conducted monthly command and staff meetings to oversee the normal division functions such as in-processing of new soldiers and providing for the physical security of arms rooms, bases, and supply rooms. They also maintained good relationships with the German communities and helped coordinate medical, dental, and legal services for the families and those soldiers remaining in Germany.[40] The direct engagement with families occurred at the battalion and company levels. The FSGs provided reliable information about the units in Iraq to reduce misinformation. Units had "rumor boards" in the mailrooms, and the leaders understood that often the more outlandish rumors were the "most-believed."[41]

The Rear D also sent equipment and personnel from Germany to the division in Iraq. A dramatic example of this support occurred when Batiste ordered the rear detachment to ship twenty-eight M1A1 tanks from Ramstein to Tikrit. In less than ninety-six hours, the tanks were prepped, rail-loaded to Ramstein, put on C-17 aircraft, and flown to Iraq. The rear detachment also in-processed over a thousand replacements in Germany and sent them to the division.[42]

One of the most important missions of the rear detachments involved casualties in Iraq. In the case of fatalities, rear detachments "engaged fully, reached out to the families [of the casualties], provided notification, and . . . survivor assistance." Memorial services were a critical mission. Kolenda recalled that "there was work by the team to execute all of these to the highest standard: these helped healing and bonded communities while personalizing the possibility of death." These services "reaffirmed why the Rear D was there."[43]

Systems were put in place at the Wurzburg and Landstuhl military hospitals to care for the returning wounded and injured soldiers. A Big Red One liaison team served at the Landstuhl hospital where Captain Nancy McLaughlin, a physician assistant, and several division soldiers provided "incredibly caring" services. The liaison team provided communications between the doctors, the wounded, and the affected families. They met every medevac flight from Iraq, worked issues like finance and new uniforms, and wrapped their arms around every member of Task Force Danger, to include the soldiers from the National Guard and other units who were serving with the division in Iraq. Volunteers decorated the Fisher Houses in Landstuhl and Wurzburg, providing residences where family members could stay while their soldiers were in the hospital.[44]

Similar efforts were made at Walter Reed Hospital once it was determined that Big Red One soldiers were not getting the same level of "love and affection." A team led by Captain Rob Christie provided the services, while a "victory ward" was established by Colonel Clark for the rehabilitation of wounded and injured soldiers from Iraq.[45]

The Rear D also facilitated the division's Rest and Recuperation (R&R) program, which permitted soldiers in Iraq to take two weeks' leave in Germany. The R&R program allowed families to reunite. As General Batiste noted, "You need time to allow soldiers to get their heads back together" during an extended combat deployment.[46] According to Kolenda, the program was a "wonderful disruption" to the family's routine, although when the soldier returned to Iraq often some psychological issues were caused by another farewell and separation. The Rear D organized a media campaign that communicated that it was natural to have post-R&R blues. Chaplains, health providers, and FRG leaders got the word to the families that there was also stress on soldiers and families before the deployment or return from R&R.[47]

There was always the danger that volunteers and caregivers would burn out. Efforts were made to provide care for the caregivers "who put themselves on the line psychologically and emotionally" as they dealt with the families. Twice a year the division's Rear D put together meetings for volunteers and community leaders. These meetings, in Garmisch and Oberammergau, were "high pay off events" at which people could share ideas and the Rear D leaders could instill a sense of pride in the volunteers and soldiers.[48]

Kolenda stressed that "this is our mission for our division and our country." He told the soldiers in his command that "it was more important to do this job to a high standard than to go to Iraq." Kolenda noted that he would never forget "how our volunteers made our mission a success." He also communicated regularly with the commanding general and the chief of staff, keeping them informed of developments in Germany.[49] The rear detachment soldiers, professionals, and volunteers did a superb job in maintaining the morale of the families, thereby allowing the deployed soldiers to focus on their missions.

The 1st Division in Iraq: Deployment, 2004–2005

On 14 January 2004, five force packages of the 1st Infantry Division moved from their home bases to staging areas. During the next thirteen days, 7,500 pieces of equipment moved by rail, barge, and truck to the port of Antwerp, where they were loaded on ships bound for Kuwait. The division tactical (D TAC) headquarters equipment moved by truck to Ramstein Air Force Base and was flown directly to Iraq. There the D TAC established a forward command post while the Division Artillery (DIVARTY) headquarters and its equipment were flown to Kuwait to establish the command post there for reception assembly areas.[50]

Brigadier General Stephen Mundt, the assistant division commander for support, and his staff had planned for the deployment for six months. Although the move was a "laborious task," Mundt concluded that it was the safest he'd ever seen. "Did we ding any equipment? Yes. But no piece of equipment was destroyed and no soldier was injured."[51]

All of the equipment sent to Antwerp arrived on time, in spite of winter weather. After the ships departed, the soldiers had a few days with families before they moved by air to OIFII. The first group of key division staff members and DIVARTY arrived in Kuwait on 28 January 2004 to receive the main body, which began arriving on 6 February. DIVARTY personnel established command and control at the aerial and seaports of debarkation and at four camps in Kuwait. By the time the last ship arrived, on 23 February, the division had resolved the challenges inherent in such a large movement of troops and equipment. The arriving brigades and battalions were united with their equipment, and a short but intense training program was carried out to prepare them for their march into Iraq.[52]

Task Force Danger was joined by more than 7,000 soldiers once in Kuwait. The 2nd BCT, 25th Infantry Division, and the 30th Separate Infantry Brigade arrived from Hawaii and North Carolina, respectively. Task Force 2-108th Infantry, from the 42nd Infantry Division, and the 264th Engineer Group from Wisconsin, rounded out Task Force Danger. The 30th BCT, the 264th Engineer Group, and TF 2-108 were National Guard units, while 2nd BCT, 25th Infantry Division, was a Regular Army unit.

The infantry battalions of the 2nd BCT, 25th Infantry Division, were light battalions (i.e., with no armored vehicles). The division reallocated up-armored Humvees to the brigade and reinforced it with tanks and Bradleys whenever a mission called for it. General Batiste was very impressed with the professionalism of Colonel Milo Miles and his soldiers, noting they "did a great job inside Kirkuk."[53] The 1st Battalion, 14th Infantry, was part of the 2nd BCT, 1st Infantry Division, during the battle for Samarra in October, and Miles's artillery battalion was integrated into the 1st Infantry Division's artillery command.

The integration of the 264th Engineer Group and the 30th Separate BCT into Task Force Danger gave the division more resources to handle its enormous area of responsibility. The guardsmen performed magnificently, and Colonel Dan Hickman, the 30th BCT commander, became an integral part of the division's command team.[54] The attachment of so many nondivisional soldiers and units to the 1st Infantry Division was a harbinger of the way the US Army would provide forces for the wars in Iraq and Afghanistan.

The armor, artillery, and mechanized infantry battalions of Task Force Danger were not allowed by the Defense Department to bring their full complement of tanks, howitzers, and Bradleys. Each armor battalion was limited to fourteen M1A1 tanks, each artillery battalion to a single firing battery of four howitzers, and each mechanized infantry battalion to half of its Bradleys. General Batiste argued strongly that this was a mistake, but he was overruled. Events were quickly to prove Batiste right in his view that tanks and Bradleys were very effective in combat in Iraqi towns and cities, and as the insurgency spread he got permission to have twenty-eight tanks flown to Iraq from Germany.[55]

Batiste knew that the 1st Infantry Division was underresourced and was going to be short of infantry units to carry out its mission. Therefore, the 1st Battalion, 7th Artillery, and the 1st Battalion, 6th Artillery, were converted to motorized infantry units equipped with Humvees. The process of retraining the artillerymen began in Germany and continued in Kuwait. Each of the artillery battalions retained one firing battery, and during the division's year in Iraq those two batteries fired over 8,000 155mm rounds at the enemy. Because of the immense size of the division's AO, the firing batteries were moved frequently to wherever the action was heaviest. According to Batiste, the artillerymen in most cases embraced their new role, and many were awarded the Close Action Badge.[56]

While in Kuwait, Task Force Danger prepared for an approach march to its AO in northern Iraq. The National Guard soldiers and units were given the same training as the original members of the Big Red One. All soldiers underwent additional marksmanship training and practiced convoy procedures and security. Units focused on "fighting skills from sniper training to helicopter gunnery." Batiste expected that the division would face a "full spectrum mission," and therefore he emphasized Phase IV support and security operations training along with combat training. The Big Red One had a significant advantage in its preparations because most of the soldiers had been serving together for two years before their deployment due to stability measures taken after 9/11. "Our leaders all spoke the same [doctrinal] language."[57]

The intensive training in Kuwait paid off. Lieutenant Colonel Rex Roth's 701st Support Battalion conducted rehearsals for convoys, believing that every convoy in Iraq was a combat mission. This attitude and training paid off for the 701st, whose trucks drove tens of thousands of miles during the deployment without losing a single soldier.[58]

After several weeks of refresher training, Task Force Danger was ready:

> At 0400 hours on February 27, 2004, the lead elements of 1st ID departed Camp Udairi on their way to Convoy Support Center Navistar, and finally to start the long trek to Tikrit, Iraq. . . . Over the next nine days, 15,200 soldiers and 10,300 pieces of equipment, divided into 40-vehicle serials, would drive at least 850 kilometers from the Kuwait/Iraqi border to areas north of Baghdad. . . . 1st ID conducted the approach march . . . through hostile territory while only sustaining one [soldier] killed in action and four wounded in action.[59]

Another 7,400 Task Force Danger soldiers were airlifted into Iraq in groups of fifty on air force C-130 aircraft. These aircraft landed at Logistics Staging Area (LSA) Anaconda and, from there the soldiers were transported by helicopter or truck to their units at one of the division's twenty-eight Forward Operating Bases (FOBs). These operations continued until the last troops arrived, on 24 March 2004.[60]

The Big Red One assumed responsibility for four Iraqi provinces from the 4th Infantry Division. According to the division's experiences with Transfers of Authority (TOAs) in the Balkans, a TOA "is a very deliberate process" that normally should have taken about ten days. The outgoing unit is responsible for telling the incoming soldiers all it knows about the area of operations. A very important part of a TOA in Iraq was for the outgoing unit to pass on information about its relationships with local Iraqi leaders. It was key, according to Batiste, for the incoming unit "to find out who the local leaders were and where they stood, since the Iraqis are loyal to tribal leadership. These are details needed in stability and support operations."

General Batiste assigned a province to each of his brigade combat teams. 2nd BCT, 1st Infantry Division, took over Salah Ad Din Province, with its capital in Tikrit. The 3rd BCT assumed control of Diyala Province, which contained the major city of Baqubah. The 2nd BCT, 25th Infantry Division, moved into Kirkuk Province, and the 30th BCT assumed responsibility for Sulaymaniyah Province along the Iraq-Iran border. The aviation battalions and division Support Command operated from FOB Spiecher, north of Tikrit, to sustain the entire division area, which was roughly the size of the state of West Virginia.

The 264th Engineer Group and the 1st Engineer Battalion operated throughout the division's AO. They built and/or improved the FOBs and cleared and repaired roads. Road clearance was perhaps the most dangerous mission for the engineers. In March alone five soldiers of the 1st Engineer

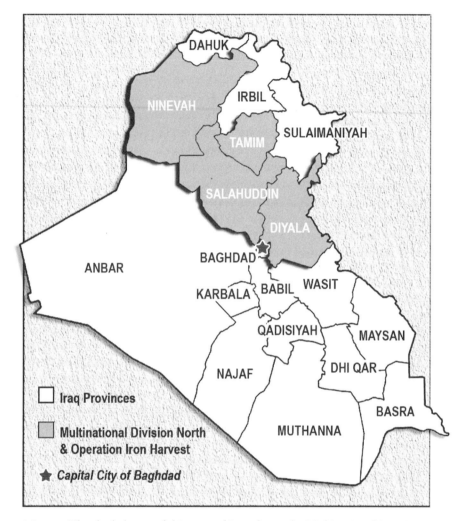

Map 35. The shaded area of this map of Iraq shows the Multinational Division North area of responsibility in the country. (American Forces Press Service map courtesy of Fred W. Baker III. [Dec. 2007], http://www.defense.gov/)

Battalion were killed by a roadside bomb. The 141st Engineer Battalion, 264th Engineer Group, was hit hard by IEDs and roadside bombs, losing a number of soldiers before the battalion received Unmanned Aerial Vehicles for route reconnaissance, as well as the Mercat and Buffalo vehicles for mine removal.[61]

The Coming of the Sunni Insurgency: April 2004

Immediately after settling in to their FOBs, the leaders of Task Force Danger began building relationships with local leaders and groups to create a climate of good governance. "Company commanders engaged village or neighborhood leaders and individual sheiks; battalion commanders engaged groups of sheiks, city councils, and mayors; brigade commanders engaged provincial governors, and governing and imam councils." Batiste met monthly with four provincial governors and convened a sheiks' council to gather the most important sheiks from across the division's AO. An Iraqi Senior Advisory Council composed of academics, doctors, former military officers, imams, and sheiks was also created to meet biweekly in order to help the division's leaders see the situation through Iraqi eyes.[62]

The Big Red One's mission included the task of organizing and training Iraqi police and security forces. General John Abizaid, the CENTCOM commander in 2004 and 1st Infantry Division commander from 1999 to 2001, noted that American forces alone could not defeat the Iraqi insurgency. They could at best assist the Iraqis. "I believe in my heart," Abizaid noted, "that the Iraqis must win this battle with our help."[63]

The division established training centers in Tikrit and Kirkuk, where Iraqi infantry and police battalions could be trained without insurgent interference. Task Force Danger also created twenty-one Joint Command Centers (JCCs) throughout its AO from which Iraqi police and security forces could operate and where coalition battalion and brigade commanders could work with Iraqi leaders.[64] These actions were part of the effort to enable Iraqi security forces to defend themselves and the villages, towns, and cities in the country.

Task Force Danger operated with a tiered command system. The main command post (D Main) planned and coordinated the long-term or "deep" battle. The tactical command post (D TAC), directed the "close-in fight," and the division rear command post (D Rear) conducted logistical, fire support, and aviation operations. The assistant division commander for maneuver (ADC, M), Brigadier General John Morgan, oversaw the D TAC. The ADC for support, Brigadier General Stephen Mundt, operated out of the D Rear, and the division's chief of staff ran the D Main.[65]

This command system supported the brigade combat teams that operated command posts in their respective provinces. Because he empowered his key senior leaders to carry out daily operations in the command posts, Major General Batiste was free to travel throughout the region. Batiste believed that leaders "have to be out there with the troops" to share the risks and to see what is happening: "a commander's place is not in the headquarters."

Batiste and Command Sergeant Major Cory McCarty traveled separately to visit the battalions and companies in the field. Batiste's goal was to visit a different battalion task force each day and to "get out on a mission with them."[66]

The Insurgency: 2004–2005

Shortly after taking over its area of operations, the 1st Infantry Division faced a major upsurge in enemy attacks with car bombs, IEDs, and ambushes.[67] Fourteen soldiers who deployed with the division from Germany were killed in March alone, ten by enemy action. By April it was clear that the Coalition faced a major Sunni insurgency. Since the division had one too few brigades for the size of its AO and the tasks at hand, Batiste and his staff found themselves "constantly task organizing to meet the changing threat."[68] At the same time, the Big Red One had to conduct support and stability operations if it was to achieve its ultimate mission of stabilizing Iraq.

The Coalition's military goal in 2004 was to establish security conditions in which an Iraqi Interim Government (IIG) could govern and national elections be held. In June, the UN Security Council endorsed the formation of an interim government and scheduled elections for a Transitional National Assembly to take place in late December 2004 or January 2005.[69] The rising insurgency posed a direct threat to the accomplishment of those goals.

On 31 March 2004, Sunni insurgents and al-Qaeda fighters seized the city of Fallujah, west of Baghdad, and murdered four American contractors. The insurgents dragged their bodies through the streets and hung their mutilated corpses from a bridge over the Tigris River. These barbarous actions were televised around the world. In response to the outcry at home, the Bush administration and the CPA ordered the 1st Marine Expeditionary Force (MEF), which had just taken over Anbar Province, to seize Fallujah. On 4 April the 1st MEF launched an assault into the city with two infantry battalions supported by artillery and aircraft.[70] (See Map 36.)

The insurgents in Fallujah fought back with a higher level of tactical skill than expected, and two additional Marine infantry battalions entered the fight. During the seven days of the first battle of Fallujah, both sides inflicted heavy damage on the city's infrastructure and the civilian population. By 9 April, Ambassador Bremer, under pressure from the Iraqi Interim Governing Council and the Bush administration to stop the bloodletting, ordered the Marines to halt their offensive and withdraw. An Iraqi unit, known as the Fallujah Brigade, moved into the city.[71]

During the Fallujah operation an Iraqi army battalion en route to Fallujah was stopped by a crowd of Iraqi civilians who convinced the Iraqi soldiers to refuse to fight.[72] The success of the insurgents in repelling the Marines in Fallujah and the refusal of the Iraqi unit to fight emboldened the insurgents. In Task Force Danger's AO, insurgent activity increased.[73]

As insurgent attacks intensified in Diyala Province, Colonel Dana Pittard's 3rd BCT found it necessary to secure the city of Baqubah before the Iraqi Interim Government assumed control of the country on 28 June. During the initial invasion of Iraq, Baqubah had been spared heavy fighting. In 2003 and early 2004, the 4th Infantry Division had worked with local Iraqi leaders to establish a city council and an Iraqi police force. The 4th Infantry Division also established a police academy in the city.[74] The 1st Infantry Division's 3rd BCT took over Diyala Province and Baqubah officially on 16 March. In April and May insurgent activity in the city increased. In June, Pittard ordered TF 2-63 Armor to set up observation posts around the city. The 1st Platoon, Company A, 2-63 Armor, led by First Lieutenant Neil Prakash, was part of this mission.[75]

On the morning of 24 June, Lieutenant Prakash was notified by his company commander, Captain Paul Fowler, that the police station was under siege and that the entire company "was going in." By 1030 hours the company was on its way with Prakash's tank platoon leading. The company's initial goal was to secure two bridges to prevent the insurgents from bringing reinforcements into the city. As it moved forward, the company was met by insurgent rocket-propelled grenade (RPG) teams and snipers on the rooftops. It took Prakash's platoon, with his tank leading, about "one hour to fight their way through the next one kilometer stretch of road. Official battle reports counted 23 IEDs and 20–25 RPG teams in that short distance, as well as multiple machine-gun nests and enemy dismounts armed with small arms and hand grenades."[76]

Prakash's tank took the brunt of the enemy fire. RPGs disabled his turret and blew off the navigation system. Prakash continued forward, using a map to navigate and firing his main gun and .50-caliber machine gun at the men on the rooftops. He later remembered thinking, "I hope these bullets don't go in this one inch of space around the partially opened hatch. . . . We just kept rolling, getting shot at from everywhere."[77] As enemy fire intensified, the company was ordered to pull back to a defensive position to allow maintenance crews to repair the damage to its vehicles. After his tank was repaired, Prakash again led his platoon toward its objective. This time the unit advanced without resistance and established a blocking position, which they held until relieved. During their fight, Prakash and his soldiers killed at least twenty-five insurgents, and Prakash personally "destroyed eight strong-points, one enemy supply vehicle, and multiple enemy dismounts."[78] For his leadership and bravery, Prakash was awarded the Silver Star.

Despite such actions, the insurgency continued in Baqubah. The situation came to a head on 28 July when insurgents detonated a car bomb outside a police station. More than seventy Iraqis were killed and another fifty-six wounded. The insurgents were most likely followers of the al-Qaeda leader Abu Musab a-Zargawi, and it was clear that Baqubah had to be cleared of insurgents.

The 3rd BCT had inherited Forward Operating Base Warhorse in the city from the 4th Infantry Division. This gave Pittard's soldiers a base from which to launch an offensive. At the same time, Batiste and Pittard planned to re-inforce the American presence in the city after the combat operations were completed and to intensify efforts to provide basic services to the populace. By early August, the soldiers of 3rd BCT had routed most insurgents from Baqubah, allowing Phase IV operations to continue. The Iraqi police and the city council resumed their work as well. According to General Batiste, "the division learned an important lesson" from Colonel Pittard's operations. "The Dukes never left Baqubah after major combat operations concluded; they maintained a strong, unobtrusive presence but responded forcefully to any enemy move," thereby emboldening the Iraqi security forces.[79] They also provided support to Iraqi police and to engineers and contractors who were working to rebuild the city's infrastructure.

Farther north, insurgents stepped up their efforts to take control of Samarra, in Salah Ad Din Province, where Colonel Randal Dragon's 2nd BCT operated. Dragon's BCT was stretched thin across the province, with TF 1-77 Armor on the northwestern side of Baghdad, in the Balad area, and TF 1-18 operating in Tikrit. TF 1-26 had just three companies in Samarra, a city of over 250,000 people. In April insurgent attacks in Samarra increased from five per week to fifteen per week, and Iraqi security forces began to desert in large numbers. In response to the increased level of attacks, TF 1-26 launched Operation Blue Spader to kill or capture insurgent leaders.

The Blue Spaders met heavy resistance from the hundreds of insurgents and foreign fighters in the city. As the security situation deteriorated, the city council president resigned and was replaced by a man sympathetic to the insurgency. Iraqi police reinforcements deserted as they arrived, and in June most of the men of the 202nd Iraqi National Guard Battalion deserted with their commander. "A local security vacuum quickly emerged."[80] In mid-July, a suicide bomber drove a vehicle filled with explosives into the headquarters of Patrol Base Razor, across the Tigris River Bridge west of the city. Five Blue Spaders were killed and twenty wounded.[81]

Colonel Dragon ordered the Tigris River Bridge closed to all Iraqi traffic, isolating the city from traffic from the west to bring economic pressure on the Samarra tribal leaders.[82] Batiste and Dragon concluded that the division would have to launch a major operation to reassert control over Samarra. But the key question for the division was: "What must be done to ensure long-term success?"[83]

Operation Baton Rouge

General Batiste and his staff realized that a strong military response by itself would not achieve long-term American goals. Consequently, they envisioned a full-spectrum operation with four phases that would often overlap. In the first phase, the coalition forces, including Iraqi units, would conduct reconnaissance missions to set the conditions for success. In the second phase, American forces were to isolate the area and conduct raids around the periphery of Samarra to force the insurgents to show themselves and their tactics. The third phase would include search and attack operations into the heart of the city to destroy the insurgent forces. The fourth, "decisive" phase was the transition to support and security operations.[84] This entire operation was code-named Operation Baton Rouge.

Since Bremer had passed control of Iraq from the CPA to the Iraqi Interim Government on 28 June, Batiste had to get permission from the IIG before launching the combat phase of the operation. While awaiting permission, the 2nd BCT began phase-one actions by conducting a series of "shaping operations."[85]

These operations were called Cajon Mousetraps One, Two, and Three. During Mousetrap One, on 5 August, Dragon sent four armored task forces to within 1.5 miles of the city to see what the enemy would do. On 13 August, the 2nd BCT launched Cajon Mousetrap Two in which TF 1-18 drove about a block into the city from the north, followed by TFs 1-77 and 1-4 Cav. "It was a very kinetic operation which resulted in a four to six hour firefight." At the same time, TF 1-26 pushed east across the Tigris bridge. On 14 August, Cajon Mousetrap Three was a "very concentrated effort." TF 1-77 Armor came from Balad, TF 1-26 crossed the Tigris bridge from the west, TF 1-18 came from the south along the east side of the Tigris, and TF 1-4 Cav operated on the south side of the city. According to Colonel Dragon, these operations "gave us a map of how the enemy would defend the city when we finally went in to really clear it."[86]

The Big Red One also trained Iraqi army and police units to take part in Baton Rouge. It was a critical component of Batiste's plan, since he wanted to ensure that the morning after the combat phase ended there would be Iraqi policemen on the streets and that any actions in the famous Golden

Mosque in Samarra would be carried out by Iraqis. The 2nd BCT trained the 202nd Iraqi Army Battalion (IAB) in a base specially built for the Iraqi unit by the 9th Engineer Battalion. The base included a mess hall, barracks, showers, and a rifle range. When the time came to enter Samarra, the retrained 202nd performed well. The 9th Engineers also built a base on the outskirts of the city for the 7th IAB, and the Support Command stockpiled equipment in a logistics base to use to equip Iraqi units.[87]

Without these supplies and bases, Batiste believed that "these Iraqi soldiers would have simply returned home." He further noted that Iraqi security forces' "participation was a critical element to success," especially since he counted on the Iraqi troops to clear the Golden Mosque and its sacred Muslim grounds.[88]

While preparing to seize and secure Samarra, the division continued to try to convince the tribal leaders in Samarra to help reestablish Iraqi government control. In late August, during a graduation ceremony for the retrained 202nd IAB, sheiks and local leaders from Samarra met with Batiste and Dragon to try to reopen the bridge. An agreement was made that allowed the bridge to reopen, while the coalition forces were to reestablish Iraqi police stations in the city. The 9th Engineer Battalion also prepared plans for a major reconstruction effort that included twenty-two "high-impact projects that would generate large numbers of jobs."[89]

By 10 September, Samarra leaders had seated a new city council and selected a police chief, and Iraqi and American patrols were operating in the city. "Regrettably, the halt in insurgent activity was short-lived." Between 10 and 19 September insurgents attacked coalition and Iraqi security forces eighty-three times.[90] Dragon again shut the Tigris River Bridge, and the Big Red One prepared to execute Baton Rouge.

The kinetic phase of Baton Rouge called for five American battalion task forces to spearhead the attack. Because 2nd BCT was spread over a large province, it was impossible for these units to stage for the operation near Samarra, with the exception of TF 1-26. If the task forces had been concentrated more than a day in advance, they would have had to leave their AOs uncovered, exposing Iraqis who had chosen to side with the coalition forces to the mercy of local insurgents. Furthermore, Batiste noted that if he pulled units out of their AOs "you would lose relationships with local leaders and no longer control local routes safely."[91]

By the end of September 2004, it was clear that Samarra could be secured only by force. Lieutenant General Ricardo Sanchez, V Corps commander and Batiste's boss, asked the Iraqi Interim Government for permission to launch phase three of Baton Rouge. On the evening of 29 September, the

Iraqi prime minister approved the operation. The next day, the five American task forces involved—TF 1-26, TF 1-77, TF 1-18, TF 1-4 Cav, and TF 1-14—moved from their AOs to their assigned positions around Samarra. Six IABs and the 36th Iraqi Commando Battalion also converged around the city.[92]

The attack commenced shortly after midnight on the morning of 1 October. American and Iraqi forces began "a well-rehearsed, deliberate, precise strike from multiple directions to kill or capture the enemy. By noon, key government and religious sites were under Iraqi Security Forces [ISF] control and the enemy largely defeated."[93] During the assault one American soldier was killed and eight wounded. Coalition forces killed 127 insurgents, wounded 60 more, and captured 128. Iraqi police were in possession of the city by 3 October:[94]

> Coalition forces and ISF now controlled the city, but the most difficult challenges still lay ahead. As expected, generating a police force was the long pole in the tent of transitioning to Iraqi control. Progress came slowly. On several occasions in November 2004, concurrent with [the Marines'] Operation Al Fajr in Fallujah, a number of insurgents returned to the city to target the police force, killing 15 policeman in one raid.[95]

Over the next two months, Samarra had six different police chiefs, and the Iraqi provincial governor failed to follow through on his promise to provide hundreds of policemen for Samarra. These developments forced Task Force Danger to take over responsibility for training a viable municipal police force. On 3 February 2005, the first 280 policemen began training at a division-run training camp in Tikrit. These men and a new police chief moved into Samarra in March 2005.

"Notwithstanding the rocky start in establishing the police force, other ISF operating in the city soon began exerting pressure on the remaining insurgents and criminals that once held Samarra hostage."[96] Coalition task forces and Iraqi Security Forces remained in the city and, notably, the Iraqi Ministry of the Interior's special commando unit continued to conduct "intelligence-driven" raids to seize insurgents' weapons and to capture or kill their leaders. These actions reduced the recruiting base for the insurgents and helped restore the trust of the citizens in their police and security forces. These actions allowed life in Samarra to return to some level of normalcy, with schools and businesses reopened and power and water services restored.[97]

The 1st Infantry Division staff and the 9th Engineers moved into Samarra with twenty-two projects ready to execute. These included water, electricity, and road projects for which the contracts were already signed.[98] These projects provided employment for Iraqis who otherwise would have been unemployed and thus might have become recruits for terrorist organizations. Four months after the swift combat phase of Baton Rouge, forty-six projects were completed, and another forty-four were in the works. These cost over $25 million. In November, the division received another $10 million "to maintain forward momentum in the city."[99] General Batiste concluded that "operations thus far appear to have validated the Army's doctrine of full-spectrum operations—kill or capture the enemy, change attitudes, and provide alternatives to insurgency."[100]

The Phase IV efforts in Samarra were representative of Task Force Danger's efforts throughout its AO to "improve the quality of life of the Iraqi people." The division spent about $850 million during its year in Iraq to train Iraqi police and army forces and to rebuild the infrastructure of the communities under its protection. Batiste noted that "successful units pile on the stability and support aspects of the mission in a big way."[101]

To facilitate reconstruction efforts, the division established an engineer group in its headquarters. Weekly meetings between division leaders and the provincial governors were held to decide where to spend reconstruction money. Batiste gave Iraqi leaders credit for the improvements to the infrastructure and the economy. Task Force 1-18 dispatched joint American and Iraqi survey patrols three times per week in Tikrit to decide priorities for reconstruction efforts. Colonel Dana Pittard's 3rd BCT stressed the importance of hiring locals for as many projects as possible. Through such measures, the division facilitated the repair of the Bayji power plant and many other projects.[102] Amid such efforts, however, the Big Red One never lost focus on its mission of defeating the insurgency.

The Second Battle of Fallujah: Joint Operations with the Marines

The insurgency threatened all major cities in non-Kurdish Iraq in the summer and fall of 2004. In Anbar Province—south of the 1st Infantry Division's AO and west of Baghdad—the city of Fallujah had become a sanctuary for Sunni insurgents, especially after the costly failure of the 1st Marine Division to secure the city in April. "By October 2004 intelligence estimates suggested that approximately 4,500 insurgents occupied the city."[103]

The Coalition and the Iraqi Interim Government realized that Fallujah had to be secured before the forthcoming elections. Consequently, the Multi-National Force–Iraq (MNF–I) planned Operation Al Fajr (known to US forces as Phantom Fury) to seize Fallujah with American and Iraqi forces.[104]

The plan for Operation Al Fajr was based on lessons from Operation Baton Rouge and from the failed attempt to take Fallujah in April 2004. The seizure of Samarra had been greatly facilitated by the use of army M1A1 tanks and Bradleys. The earlier Marine attack against Fallujah had relied primarily on light infantry, due in part to the fact that the 1st Marine Division had brought only sixteen tanks to Iraq.[105] The idea that urban warfare was not a good mission for tanks and Bradleys and that dismounted infantry was the best method to clear a city of insurgents had been found wanting and costly in lives. For the second battle of Fallujah, the Marines wanted the support of army armored task forces.[106]

The Iraqi government approved the operation and declared a state of emergency in November. American and Iraqi forces surrounded Fallujah and declared a curfew. Coalition forces sealed off the city and urged all noncombatants to leave, which most did.[107] Once the city was sealed off, the 1st Marine Division began combat operations. Two Marine regimental combat teams, each with an army armored task force, assaulted the city on 8 November 2004.[108] "For months the insurgents had been constructing extensive defenses . . . and these fortifications allowed the insurgents to resist coalition attack using small-arms fire, improvised explosive devices, and rocket-propelled grenades."[109]

The second Marine assault into Fallujah relied on the firepower and armor protection of the tanks and Bradleys of the army task forces. Task Force 2-2, from the Big Red One, and TF 2-7, from the 1st Cavalry Division, were pulled from their areas of operation to join the Marines. When Lieutenant Colonel Pete Newell's TF 2-2 moved south, it required a major effort by the 1st Infantry Division to support his force in Anbar Province. To limit the impact on his normally assigned AO, Newell took only his Company A of TF 2-2 to Fallujah, and 3rd BCT assigned Company A, 2/63rd Armor, to his task force. Colonel Pittard gave his brigade reconnaissance troop (F/4th Cav) to Newell, and the division reinforced TF 2-2 with two 155mm Paladin M109A6 howitzers and an engineer mine-clearing line charge (MCLIC). Task Force 2-2 moved to Fallujah in early November.[110]

The Marine plan for the seizure of Fallujah called for RCT7 and TF 2-2 to attack the city from the northeast while another Marine RCT, with TF 2-7, made the main effort to the west of RCT7. Other Marine and coalition forces isolated the city. The planning for Operation Al Fajr ensured the cooperation of the Marines and army units in the joint operation. After their planning sessions with the RCT7 commander, Colonel Craig Tucker, Newell and his officers believed that "they had been included as equal participants in planning for the upcoming battle."[111] (See Map 35.)

The assault into Fallujah began at 1900 hours, on 8 November 2004.

RCT7 attacked with three battalion task forces abreast, facing south, with TF 2-2 on the left (eastern) side of the regimental assault. The attackers' first task was to breach the defenses along the edge of the city. Captain Paul Fowler's Company A, 2/63rd Armor, crossed the line of departure at 1900 and took up positions to cover the assault of Company A, 2/2nd Infantry. The initial breach area was in a row of houses that the attached howitzers fired at. When the artillery rounds began to impact, Fowler ordered his tanks and Bradleys to fire three rounds in quick succession into the houses. Fowler recalled that "the results were exactly as we had hoped, creating massive casualties and chaos within the enemy ranks, disrupting their ability to defend against the breach."[112]

At 1915, Captain Sean Sims of Company A, 2/2nd Infantry, fired the MCLIC into the insurgent defenses. "The initial detonation produced numerous secondary explosions caused by IEDs that insurgents had placed around the city. 'When the big boom hit,' Major (Dr.) Lisa DeWitt, the TF 2-2 surgeon remembered, 'there were at least five daisy-chained IEDs that went off after that.'"[113]

Captain Sims's infantrymen with their Bradleys and supporting tanks opened a gap for the passage of Fowler's tanks. By 2013 hours, Fowler's company had secured its first objective and was moving south to its second objective (OBJ COYOTE). As the tanks moved they destroyed "enemy road blocks with 120-millimeter main gun rounds," crushing each obstacle in their path. "While under continuous fire, A/2-63 managed to call for pinpoint artillery strikes from the attached Paladins, while tank main gun rounds and 25-millimeter rounds from the Bradleys took out numerous vehicle borne improvised explosive devices (VBIEDs) and enemy fighting positions." The insurgents, not realizing that the tank and Bradley crews could see in the dark with their thermal imaging sights, attempted to move across streets and were cut down by machine-gun fire.[114]

Captain Kirk Mayfield's reconnaissance troop supported these operations from an overwatch position, using a long-range acquisition system to direct accurate artillery fire against insurgent positions. As the tanks and Bradleys moved south, Mayfield's soldiers displaced to positions from where they could continue to support the advance.[115]

After four hours of fighting, TF 2-2 had breached the defenses and "decimated insurgent forces in northeastern Fallujah." The task force's attack had been so rapid and powerful that it shattered the insurgents' command-and-control system, making enemy resistance ineffective. The Marines to the west, however, were barely able to move, having failed to breach the initial defenses.[116]

Task Force 2-2 continued to advance during the night of 8–9 November,

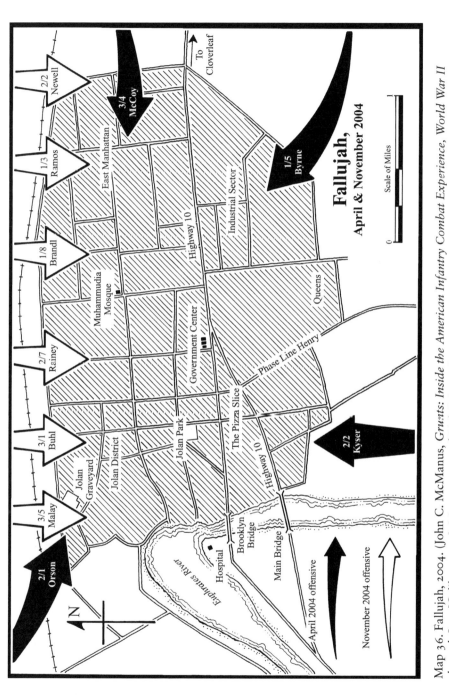

Map 36. Fallujah, 2004. (John C. McManus, *Grunts: Inside the American Infantry Combat Experience, World War II through Iraq* [Caliber, 2010]. Map courtesy of Rick Britton © 2010)

clearing the area around Phase Line (PL) Fran by mid-morning. "The TF 2-2 attack to PL Fran had been expeditious and violent killing scores of insurgents." During the action, Command Sergeant Major Steven Faulkenburg was killed by a sniper. At 1410 hours, on 9 November, Colonel Tucker ordered Newell to halt at PL Fran and to conduct search and attack missions northward because "the Marines were behind schedule."[117] In fact, the 1/3rd Marines were still close to the initial line of departure. This allowed the enemy to reoccupy some of the positions already cleared, and Fowler later noted that "we don't like to pay for ground more than once."[118]

For two days TF 2-2 held along PL Fran and cleared out pockets of insurgents from their rear. On 11 November, Newell turned over the area north of his task force to the Marines and prepared to resume TF 2-2's attack south. When TF 2-2 resumed its advance, it again outran the Marines, forcing another halt, on PL Heather. After this pause, Newell's tired soldiers resumed their assault, reaching their final limit of advance at 0600 hours, on 12 November. Unfortunately, at first light the task force was caught in an ambush during which Newell's executive officer was mortally wounded by a sniper.[119]

Task Force 2-2 held in place for two days, conducting "deliberate clearing operations." During this period, Captain Sean Sims, the A/2-2 commander, was killed when an RPG hit his Bradley. Sergeant James Mattheson was killed at the same time. On 13 November the task force pushed south to destroy the remaining enemy in its zone. That afternoon the task force withdrew to its logistical release point to refuel and rearm, with the help of the 1st Infantry Division's Support Command.[120]

Upon completion of its resupply operation, Task Force 2-2 was called upon by the RCT7 commander, Colonel Craig Tucker, to shift west to aid the 1st Battalion, 8th Marine Regiment, in efforts to breach the enemy defenses on the northern edge of the city. Newell suggested that TF 2-2 should pass through the Marines' front line and drive south. The Marine commanders were skeptical, with the 1/8th commander saying, "No way. We can't put tanks and Bradleys down there. It's impossible."[121] Newell insisted that it could be done, and at 1710 hours, on 13 November, TF 2-2 conducted a passage of lines through the Marines.

Captain Fowler recalled the movement:

So we all moved back to PL Isabella . . . into the 1st Battalion, 8th Marine sector: They had only cleared the first row of houses; everything south of that point was enemy-occupied territory. As we started to move into position, some Marine yelled at one of my tank commanders and said "that area's not clear, you guys can't go down there." My TC replied with a grin, "that's what we're here for!" . . . We began to deliberately open avenues of approach with well-placed main gun rounds, using our M88 recovery vehicle to assist in the reduction of the obstacles. . . . We moved quickly through the area, forcing the insurgents to flee ahead of us, and forcing them into the artillery that was falling to our south.[122]

The coordinated violence and speed of TF 2-2's advance broke the enemy's cohesion. According to Fowler, "they were in chaos." When the task force reached its limit of advance it halted and, after turning the cleared area over to the Marines, shifted east to its own sector. The soldiers of the Big Red One had created a hole in the defenses through which the Marines could advance.[123]

From 14 through 18 November, Newell's task force cleared its sector, breaking out on the south side of Fallujah on 20 November. In two weeks of fighting, TF 2-2 killed more than 304 enemy fighters and went from being the supporting effort of RCT7 to being the main effort. The task force lost four soldiers killed, with seventy-two wounded in action. No army soldiers were killed or wounded by friendly fire, thanks to careful control measures and coordination.[124]

Army Task Force 2-7, attached to the Marine RCT attacking into Fallujah from the south, had similar experiences assisting the Marines. TF 2-7 lost one soldier killed before they withdrew on 20 November. The actions of TFs 2-2 and 2-7 validated the US Army's use of tanks and Bradleys in urban combat. Both task forces often had to aid the more lightly equipped Marines. Sadly, the Marine Corps commandant did not draw the proper lessons from the battle, as his remarks to an audience in Quantico, Virginia, in 2005 indicated: "In my opinion, Fallujah is an example of what we're going to fight in the future. . . . It is about individual [M]arines with small arms going house to house, killing."[125]

Fallujah has remained a dangerous place for coalition forces. In 2005, six Marines were killed by a car bomb, and by 2006 the city was again controlled by insurgents and had to be retaken. And by 2013, fighters of the Islamic State in Iraq and the Levant (ISIL) had seized the city from Iraqi government troops and continued to control it until driven out in the summer of 2016.

The battles for Baqubah, Samarra, and Fallujah demonstrated the army's

ability to shift swiftly from low-level stability operations to a quickly-planned, large-scale combat operation. . . . As impressive was the Army's evolving capacity to look at a problem, such as the insurgent network in Samarra, in a holistic way, viewing combat operations as only one means of achieving objectives. In the case of Operation Baton Rouge, the 1st ID displayed a refined ability to plan deliberately and across the full-spectrum so as to avoid high-intensity urban combat. That operation [and Fallujah] also showed the division's lethal ability to conduct tough street fighting when the situation required.[126]

The Iraqi Elections of 2005 and the End of the Division's Iraqi Freedom Mission

The battles for Fallujah and Samarra were part of a strategy to prepare Iraq for free elections. When the CPA transferred authority to the interim government on 28 June 2004, it was with the understanding that the IIG would represent the three major groups in Iraq (Sunni, Shiite, and Kurd) and that fair and free elections would be held in late 2004 or early 2005. By December 2004, the security situation allowed for the election, and the Iraqi Security Forces seemed capable, with coalition help, of controlling the major population centers. Therefore, the elections were scheduled for 30 January 2005.[127]

The 1st Infantry Division and the Iraqi Security Forces deployed all available resources to disrupt insurgents' ability to interfere with the elections. These efforts included patrolling in and around the cities and villages within the division's AO and checkpoints on all major roads. The goal was to set an environment in which as many Iraqis as possible could vote in the Sunni areas, since their participation was essential to the appearance of validity in a nation that was 60 percent Shiite. American troops did all they could to keep a low profile, with Iraqi police and military providing as much of the security as possible in the days running up to the elections.[128]

In the two weeks prior to elections, the Big Red One stepped up its operational tempo. In Sulaymaniyah Province, Kurdish units worked with Colonel Dan Hickman's 30th BCT to protect polling stations. On 30 January 2005, the people of the province elected representatives to the Kurdistan National Assembly and to the Iraqi Transitional National Assembly. Voter turnout was higher than expected, and the success of the elections was largely attributed to the performance of the Iraqi police and troops, backed up by the National Guard soldiers from North Carolina.[129]

The division's 2nd BCT, in Salah Ad Din Province, hosted a three-day readiness exercise with Iraqi Security Forces. Iraqi police, army, and ministry representatives participated with coalition forces in the cities of Ash Shargat, Baji, Tikrit, Ad Dwar, Samarra, Balad, and Tuz to prepare for elections. Communications between Iraqi local and provincial organizations "were vastly improved," and the responsiveness of the emergency services increased. When the elections took place, Iraqi forces of all types successfully responded to insurgent threats and secured polling sites throughout the province.[130]

In Diyala Province, Pittard's 3rd BCT worked to convince Sunnis that they should take part in the election. Under the auspices of the 32nd Iraqi Army Brigade and the provincial governor, local sheiks, clerics, and former Baath Party members met in Baqubah on 18 January to discuss the elections. The religious leaders of Diyala read a fatwa (a religious decree) approving Sunni participation, and a local sheik and Colonel Dana Pittard shook hands as a symbol of goodwill. These efforts increased Sunni participation and offered a glimmer of hope for peace in the province.[131]

The Iraqi Security Forces were increasingly competent in their operations, reflecting that the division had done a good job in building relationships with the Iraqi people and in training Iraqi units. In January, search operations resulted in an estimated 19 anti-Iraqi insurgents killed and 779 detained, plus the capture of ammunition caches with more than 2,369 rocket, mortar, artillery, and tank rounds and 298 small arms, 37 RPGs, and hundreds of pounds of bomb-making ingredients. In Tikrit, soldiers of TF 1-112 Infantry and the 201st Iraqi Army Battalion foiled an insurgent attempt to plant an IED at a polling site. Such efforts paid off: more than 14 million Iraqis voted.[132]

By February 2005, the soldiers of Task Force Danger were looking forward to the end of their year-long tour in Iraq. The National Guard's 42nd Infantry Division was to take over the 1st Infantry Division's AO at the end of February. Leaders from the renowned Rainbow Division began "left-side, right-side" missions with their counterparts in January, and the 42nd Infantry Division's aviation brigade supported the First Division's aviation brigade during the transition and the Iraqi elections.[133]

Transfer of Authority and Return to Germany

The Big Red One began preparations for the transfer of authority for its area of operations to the 42nd Infantry Division in late 2004. General Batiste directed the staff to plan a transfer that mirrored the procedures used by USAREUR units in Bosnia and Kosovo. It was "a very deliberate process, rigorous, ten days' long." The division, as the outgoing unit, had the responsibility to plan and carry out the transfer. Commanders at every level ensured that the incoming troops were briefed on relationships with Iraqis, the dangers present in their areas of responsibility, and any other information that would allow the newcomers to carry on the mission.[134]

The Big Red One's soldiers did not relent in their efforts to defeat insurgents during their last month in Iraq. Units across Task Force Danger's four provinces continued full-spectrum operations, including "intelligence driven combat operations to kill or capture anti-Iraqi forces," while also continuing to rebuild the Iraqi infrastructure. The goal remained "to change Iraqi attitudes and provide Iraqis alternatives to the insurgency."[135]

The division's plan for redeployment to Germany was Operation Keystone Hawk. The move from Iraq was more complicated than the 2004 deployment into Iraq because Task Force Danger consisted of over 22,000 soldiers with 14,200 pieces of equipment, moving from one seaport to four seaports on two continents. Complicating the operation was the need to protect all convoys of the 1st and 42nd Infantry Divisions as they moved across Iraq. A special unit, named Task Force Vigilant Guard, was created with a cavalry troop from the 278th Armored Cavalry Regiment and sixty armored Humvees from the 1st Infantry Division. This unit organized fifteen teams to escort units from the Big Red One's FOBs in Iraq to a consolidated assembly area in Kuwait. On average, it took seven days to complete this move. After twenty-four hours of rest, the teams turned around and escorted convoys of the 42nd Division to their FOBs in northern Iraq. In this manner, the Big Red One began its journey home.[136]

Operation Keystone Hawk was successful. All of Task Force Danger's 22,600 soldiers and their equipment left Iraq safely. The majority of the Big Red One soldiers flew from Iraq to Germany aboard C-17 aircraft. The units from the United States flew home from Kuwait in chartered commercial aircraft. Most of the heavy equipment returned by sea, rail, and truck, although some in-country equipment was transferred to the 42nd Infantry Division to fill critical shortages and thus remained in the war zone. The official transfer of authority to the Rainbow Division took place in Tikrit on 14 February 2005.

General Batiste made the following remarks at a prayer breakfast on 8 February:

> Over the past year, I have been continually inspired by the resolve, courage, and determination of the American Soldier to hold to the higher standard—to denounce tyranny and repression as a way of life, and commit oneself to do something about it. We understand the meaning of sacrifice. We are committed to treating others with dignity and respect. Our soldiers are able to take decisive military action or render compassionate aid to schoolchildren, all in the same day. . . . The enemy has yet to figure out what we have known for a long, long time. You cannot build a society on fear, intimidation, and hatred.[137]

The soldiers and families of the Big Red One reunited in Germany in February 2005 and spent the next few months reintegrating soldiers, families, and spouses into their community. As of June, 193 soldiers, airmen, and Marines had died while serving in Task Force Danger in Iraq from 2003 to 2005. A memorial was dedicated at the division's headquarters in Wurzburg on 6 June. Family members of twenty-eight fallen soldiers attended the ceremony. In his remarks, General Batiste stated: "We grieve with you for your loss and at the same time are inspired by your indomitable spirit."[138] As the title of a recent book affirms, "They fought for each other" and for their comrades-in-arms who survived.[139]

Conclusion
The Long War Continues

THIS NARRATIVE OF THE US 1ST INFANTRY DIVISION reflects its profound impact on US military history during the modern era. However, in 2017—the centennial year of the Big Red One—facts on the ground cannot confirm or portend meaningful "victory" for the United States armed forces in Iraq and Afghanistan, or the defeat of radical Islamists beyond the homeland in Africa, the Middle East, and Southwest Asia. The US Army has endured sixteen years of combat, with no end in sight.[1] During this long war the army has redesigned its fundamental tactical organizations from company through division and transformed its organizational and tactical doctrines. As a result, the concept of a "division" has been altered dramatically.

The deployment of Task Force Danger to Iraq in 2004 was the last time the division fought with an organization structure similar to the divisions that fought in the two world wars and in the Vietnam War. It was also the last time that the Big Red One's headquarters deployed with most of its normally assigned units.

From 2006 to 2017, the division has been reorganized and transformed. Its brigades now fight as "modularized" teams, and its battalions have been reorganized as "combined arms battalions." These organizational changes have been made in response to the need for the army to carry out multiple types of missions, including counterinsurgency, peacekeeping, and heavy combat. Historic relationships and unit designations also have been changed significantly. Although soldiers of many combined arms battalions and brigade combat teams still wear the division patch, the concept that the Big Red One fights as a unified division no longer is reality, and it has not been since 2006.

The Big Red One Returns to Fort Riley: 2006

On New Year's Day 2006, the 1st Infantry Division was stationed in Germany with three of its four maneuver brigades. The 1st Brigade Combat Team remained at Fort Riley, Kansas, while the 2nd BCT (at Schweinfurt), the 3rd BCT (at Vilseck), and the 4th BCT (at Katterbach) continued to serve in USAREUR. Over 13,000 soldiers were with the division in Germany, counting those in the Division Artillery (at Bamberg) and the Division Support Command (at Kitzingen). The men and women in these organizations continued to train for high-intensity warfare and for counterinsurgency missions.

Changes in the American military posture in Central Europe continued to occur as the Bush administration reorganized the army and moved forces back to the United States. For example, the 1st Squadron, 4th Cavalry, was transformed from a mechanized cavalry squadron into a light airborne reconnaissance squadron and assigned to the separate 173rd Airborne Brigade. Lieutenant Colonel Chris Kolenda, the squadron commander, commented that "I can't imagine a more complex set of tasks than what this squadron's been asked to do." The mood among soldiers was a "mix of optimism and sadness."[2] In the same period, the 82nd Engineer Battalion was inactivated, and a number of its soldiers were reassigned to the 173rd Airborne Brigade.[3]

In July 2006, the 1st Infantry Division changed station from Germany to Fort Riley, Kansas, where it joined its 1st BCT and replaced the 24th Infantry Division (M). Before the division left Germany, the Division Artillery Brigade and the 1st Battalion, 6th Artillery, were inactivated for the first time since their creation in 1917. Each of the remaining artillery battalions in the division was assigned to a brigade combat team as part of the army's modular brigade structure. The 1st Battalion, 33rd Artillery, in Bamberg, Germany, became an airborne artillery unit assigned to the 173rd Airborne Brigade in Vicenza, Italy. The 1st Battalion, 7th Artillery, remained with the 1st Infantry Division's 2nd BCT.[4] Major General Kenneth Hunzeker brought the division back to Fort Riley and turned over command of the Big Red One to Major General Carter Ham on 1 August 2006.[5]

The relationship between the division and the civilian community around Fort Riley had been extremely close and amicable in the past, and General Ham noted that "Fort Riley's relationship with its surrounding communities was unlike anything he'd seen in his thirty years of service." Ham went on to say that the most important mission for the division was "to form, train, and prepare teams of advisors to deploy to Iraq and Afghanistan."[6]

After the division arrived in Fort Riley, its 1st Brigade assumed the mission of training Military Transition Teams (MiTTs) that the army organized to train Afghan and Iraqi forces. The soldiers in these teams wore the Big Red One patch, although they did not work for the division when deployed. In 2009, the army moved the MiTT training mission to Fort Polk, Louisiana, and the 1st BCT was reorganized as a deployable combat team.[7]

The 2nd Heavy Brigade Combat Team (HBCT) remained in Germany until its deployment to Iraq in August 2006, where it served until November

2007. During this fifteen-month-long deployment, sixty-one soldiers of the brigade died trying to defeat another insurgency. The brigade headquarters, TF 1-7 Artillery, the 299th Support Battalion, and the 9th Engineer Battalion were stationed at Camp Liberty, a sprawling encampment of over 30,000 Americans east of Baghdad International Airport. TF 1-26 operated in the Adhamiya district of Baghdad, TF 1-77 deployed to Ramadi, and TF 1-18 fought in the Al Rashid district of southwest Baghdad. The brigade served as part of a task force led by the headquarters of another division that was part of Multi-National Corps—Iraq. The Big Red One's battalions had little previous connection to the division headquarters they served under. Two books, Kelly Kennedy's *They Fought for Each Other*, and David Finkel's *The Good Soldiers*, tell the story from the soldiers' points of view.[8]

Big Red One soldiers continued to meet the demanding standards of the division's motto, but such service came with a cost. On 4 August 2006, the Blue Spaders arrived in Iraq. Company C, 1/26th Infantry, was assigned to Combat Outpost Apache, in northeast Baghdad, in an area that had lacked a US presence for eight months. It was an area characterized by "a lot of kidnappings, killings, and a lot of enemy activity," according to Staff Sergeant Ian Newland, a squad leader in the company.[9]

> In October, just two months into the deployment, Co. C had already lost two of its soldiers; Staff Sgt. Garth Sizemore to a sniper's bullet, and Sgt. Wilsun Mock in an IED explosion. In November, after Saddam Hussein was found guilty of crimes against humanity, the battalion fought a five hour battle against enemy insurgents who attacked the outpost. By December, the men of 1st Bn., 26th Inf. Regt., were battle hardened.[10]

The Blue Spaders worked to provide security for a Baghdad suburb while also helping to improve the quality of life of ordinary Iraqis. On 4 December 2006, 1st Platoon, Company C, was on a patrol to deliver a 250-kilowatt generator to provide increased electricity to the area. Shortly after the six-vehicle patrol left the outpost, an Iraqi threw a hand grenade into the last Humvee in the convoy. The explosion that followed blew the doors off the vehicle, but the vehicle remained drivable. Major Michael Baka, the company commander, had accompanied the platoon and quickly found a driver to get the damaged vehicle and its injured crew back to Outpost Apache.[11] When the convoy got back to Apache, Sergeant First Class Sean Thomas told Baka that Ross McGinnis "saved our lives today." It turned out that when the grenade entered the Humvee, McGinnis, the Humvee's machine gunner, alerted the crew inside about the grenade.

None of the crew could see the grenade, which was sitting on the radio.

McGinnis, who by SOP was to announce the grenade and then exit the vehicle, realized the situation and, "rather than leaping from the gunner's hatch to safety, Private McGinnis made the courageous decision to protect his crew. In a selfless act of bravery, in which he was mortally wounded, Private McGinnis covered the live grenade, pinning it between his body and the vehicle and absorbing most of the explosion."[12] McGinnis saved the lives of four fellow soldiers, while losing his own. For his unselfish act, Ross McGinnis received the Medal of Honor posthumously. He was the second soldier to receive the Medal of Honor in Operation Iraqi Freedom and the first Big Red One soldier to do so since the Vietnam War.

By the time the 2nd HBCT returned from Iraq to Germany, in November 2007, it had served a total of twenty-seven months cumulatively in Iraq and had sustained the greatest number of combat deaths for any European-based brigade. TF 1-26 lost twenty-seven soldiers killed, the most to date for any army battalion, and TF 1-18 lost another nineteen soldiers. A short while later, the administration authorized "the surge," a fifteen-month campaign in which American strength in Iraq was increased by 30,000 additional troops to fight the insurgencies. The 4th Infantry Brigade Combat Team (IBCT) deployed to southern Baghdad, led by Colonel Ricky Gibbs. The 2nd Battalion, 16th Infantry, however, served under the command of the 2nd Brigade, 2nd Infantry Division. The soldiers of TF 2-16 are the subject of David Finkel's book *The Good Soldiers*. Finkel, who was embedded in the battalion for most of a year, tells a depressing story of how the soldiers were, in effect, orphaned, since they served in a command with unfamiliar leaders and a different unit culture and identity.[13]

The initial results of the surge were hopeful, as the Sunni tribes decided to work with the coalition forces and to give the Shiite-dominated Iraqi government a chance to prove it was evenhanded in its treatment of all Iraqi citizens. Sadly, within a few years, the government demonstrated its antipathy to Kurds and Sunnis while favoring the majority Shiite population.

More Reorganization and "Transformation"

When the 2nd HBCT returned to Germany in November 2007 it became part of the 1st Armored Division. This transition ended the Big Red One's thirty-six-year association with Germany. The colors of the 2nd HBCT were unfurled at Fort Riley, Kansas, and the newly formed 2nd HBCT returned to Iraq for another year in September 2008. The brigade was responsible for the security of northwestern Baghdad, with the 1st Combined Arms Battalion (CAB), 18th Infantry, the 1st CAB 63rd Armor, and the 5th Squadron, 4th Cavalry, stationed in separate bases in the sprawling Iraqi capital. The

combined arms battalions were so named because they were battalion-size
units (around 700 soldiers) permanently organized with armor and infantry
companies in the battalion.

In September 2009, the First Division's 4th BCT deployed from Fort Riley
to Iraq for another tour of duty.[14] Two months later, the 1st Infantry Division's Combat Aviation Brigade returned from fifteen months in Iraq, where
it had operated in support of the Multi-National Corps—Iraq.[15] These were
two of the last deployments of combat brigades to Operation Iraqi Freedom.

While two of its assigned brigades were in northern Iraq, the 1st Division
headquarters moved to Iraq in 2010 to lead the US Multinational Division
South, with headquarters in Basrah. Major General Vincent Brooks, the
commanding general of Task Force Victory, had under his command the
3rd Brigade, 3rd Infantry Division; the 3rd Brigade, 4th Infantry Division;
the 4th Brigade, 1st Armored Division; the 12th Aviation Brigade; the 17th
Fires Brigade; and the 3rd Armored Cavalry Regiment. General Vincent and
his subordinate commanders operated in a professional manner, ensuring
the security of southern Iraq.

During the same period, the 1st Infantry Division's newly named "1st
Sustainment Brigade" and the 1st Combat Aviation Brigade arrived in Iraq
to support the drawdown of US forces and equipment as Operation Iraqi
Freedom transitioned into Operation New Dawn. The division headquarters
did not control the sustainment brigade or the other two combat brigades
then in Iraq (4th Stryker BCT or 4th Infantry BCT). In August and September, these two combat brigades returned to Fort Riley.

Meanwhile, the 1st HBCT deployed to Kirkuk as the "1st Advise and
Assist Brigade." Under Operation New Dawn, the American strategy was
to enable the Iraqi Security Forces to defend their country, and the "advise and assist" mission was best handled by modularized brigades task-
organized for their soldiers' roles as trainers. This is the current model for
deployed forces in the Middle East, Africa, and Asia. As the US mission in
Iraq changed, the division's 4th Stryker BCT, which crossed into Kuwait
from Iraq in August 2010, was supposedly the last major American combat
formation to leave Iraq.

The 2nd Advise and Assist Brigade arrived at Camp Liberty, west of Baghdad, in December 2011, with troops from the 1st CAB, 63rd Armor, the 1st
CAB, 7th Field Artillery, and the 5th Squadron, 4th Cavalry. The brigade
was under the control of the 1st Armored Division headquarters initially,
and then under the 25th Infantry Division. During their advise and assist
mission, the Big Red One's soldiers helped Iraqi Security Forces contain attacks by the Sadrist movement and other Iranian-backed militias in Baghdad
while protecting US bases and forces leaving Iraq. Nine members of the
brigade were killed in action before it departed in November 2011.

In 2012, the American military training mission in Iraq officially ended. There does not seem to be an end in sight for American deployments to Iraq in what one historian has called *America's War in the Greater Middle East.*[16] From 2014 to 2015, the 1st Infantry Division headquarters and commanding general served in northern Iraq to coordinate efforts by special operations forces and others to defeat the Islamic State.

The Big Red One in Afghanistan

The US war on terror (initially referred to as the "Global War on Terror," or GWOT, by the Bush administration) began with the American response to the cataclysmic events of 9/11. The leader of al-Qaeda, Osama bin Laden, coordinated the attack from Afghanistan. For the previous decade, the Afghan Taliban had given al-Qaeda sanctuary, believing that the western powers would not retaliate for terrorist operations around the world. The 9/11 attacks ended that situation when the United States decided to destroy al-Qaeda in Afghanistan and to end the rule of the Taliban.[17]

The American operation in Afghanistan, code-named Enduring Freedom, began on 7 October 2001 when US Navy fighter-bombers and air force B-1 and B-52 heavy bombers attacked Taliban and al-Qaeda installations throughout the country. These attacks were accompanied by cruise-missile strikes. Such aerial attacks in the past had failed to modify Taliban behavior, but the game changed when US and British special-operations teams joined the Afghan tribes of the Northern Coalition. The special-operations soldiers brought communications and target-designating systems to direct precision-guided munitions against enemy targets. Within a few days, eighteen Special Forces "A" Teams were on the ground, giving the anti-Taliban forces a decided edge. Few American soldiers were in Afghanistan initially, but roughly 50,000 airmen, sailors, and soldiers supported the effort from countries bordering Afghanistan. By January 2002, the Taliban and al-Qaeda forces had been driven into the rugged mountains of eastern Afghanistan, and all major cities in the country had been occupied by anti-Taliban forces and small numbers of American and British troops.[18]

During the same period, Afghan groups and tribes created a provisional government in Kabul with Hamid Karzai as interim leader. The United Nations recognized the transitional government and formed the International Security Assistance Force (ISAF), to secure Kabul. By May, the Karzai government was forming a new Afghan National Army, with help from various Western nations.[19]

During the first four months of the Afghan War a few hundred American special-operations soldiers and a handful of conventional army troops made it possible for anti-Taliban groups to seize most of the country. By

January 2002, about 5,000 US soldiers from the 10th Mountain and 101st Airmobile Divisions were conducting operations in the mountains of eastern Afghanistan to capture or kill Osama bin Laden. Unfortunately, there were too few American troops available to cut off the escape routes into Pakistan of the al-Qaeda leader and his followers. "Warfare in eastern Afghanistan [then] became a grim round of patrols and operations in the mountains to keep al Qaeda and Taliban remnants off balance and under pressure while a new Afghan army was equipped and trained, relief efforts stabilized the economy and society, and Karzai's government established a grip."[20]

During the next three years NATO worked to create effective Afghan army and police forces. By March 2003, the first two Afghan battalions had been raised, and in July Afghan units took part in their first combat actions. Over the next two years the Afghan army grew to 47,000 soldiers, with plans to increase its strength to 70,000.[21] As was the case in Iraq, it has been difficult to keep local forces from deserting whenever the fighting becomes particularly dangerous.

Realizing that the new Afghan government could not adequately defend the country from a resurgent Taliban and al-Qaeda, NATO continued ISAF, expanding its operations to the entire country. From 2003 to 2014, ISAF supported the Afghan National Army in its long struggle to keep the Taliban at bay. In 2014, ISAF ended its mission and was replaced by the American-led "Resolute Support" mission, which continues to this day.

The 1st Infantry Division's initial role in Afghanistan was its mission to train MiTTs. These teams worked closely with Afghan security forces to train them how to fight the Taliban successfully. The teams served in remote parts of the country while embedded in Afghan battalions. They faced constant danger from IEDs and sniper fire during their twelve- to fifteen-month-long deployments.

In 2008 the 1st Infantry Division's 3rd Brigade Combat Team deployed to Afghanistan from Fort Hood, Texas, to serve as part of Combined Joint Task Force–101 (CJTF-101). The brigade was responsible for four Afghan provinces (see Map 37), with missions to protect population centers such as Jalalabad and to help develop the local economy through the construction of roads. The brigade's Task Force 2-2 was stationed in Kandahar, where it served with another brigade of CJTF-101. During its year in Afghanistan, the troops of the 3rd BCT took part in over a thousand firefights in which they earned more than 400 Purple Hearts. These combat actions were significantly different than those in Iraq, as most took place in the rugged countryside rather than in the cities. The brigade returned to Fort Hood in July 2009.

The 3rd Infantry Brigade Combat Team again served in ISAF beginning

Map 37. Afghan provinces where the 1st Infantry Division deployed. (http://www
.mapresources.com/products/afghanistan-digital-vector-raster-country-map-afg-xx
-782375).

in January 2011, when it moved to Khost and Paktya Provinces in eastern
Afghanistan. The brigade's missions were to disrupt Taliban safe havens and
to protect Afghan government efforts to reach the people and improve their
lives. Big Red One soldiers fought in extremely remote mountainous regions
with few roads, forcing them to conduct dismounted operations to control
key terrain features. The 2nd CAB, 2nd Infantry, again served separately
when it was attached to a Polish brigade in Ghazni Province.

In January 2011, three combined arms battalions from the 1st HBCT deployed to Afghanistan from Fort Riley. The 1st CAB, 16th Infantry, was stationed in fifty-eight remote locations around the country, where its soldiers
conducted over 10,000 patrols as part of village stability operations to help
win the loyalty of the Afghan people to their government. The 2nd CAB,
34th Armor, fought in Kandahar Province along the Pakistan-Afghan border
to restrict Taliban crossborder operations, and 4th Squadron, 4th Cavalry,
deployed to Zhari District, the birthplace and homeland of the Taliban.

The 1st Infantry Division headquarters deployed to Afghanistan in April 2012 and was given responsibility for Regional Command East. The headquarters was designated CJTF-1 and controlled ISAF units around Kabul and the region along the Pakistan-Afghan border. During its year in Afghanistan, CJTF-1 oversaw the transition of authority in its area of operations to the Afghan army's 201st Corps north of Kabul and to the 203rd Corps south of Kabul.

In May 2012, the last Big Red One brigade to serve in ISAF arrived in eastern Afghanistan for a nine-month tour of duty. In February 2013, the 4th IBCT handed off its area of responsibility to the 1st BCT of the 10th Mountain Division and to the Afghan 203rd Corps. In 2016, over 8,000 American troops remained in Afghanistan, fighting to prevent the return of the Taliban and to prevent the spread of ISIS. Soldiers wearing the Big Red One will continue to serve in Afghanistan as needed to defeat the Taliban and the emerging ISIS threat.

The 1st Infantry Division in 2017

The 1st Infantry Division continues to serve the nation from its home station of Fort Riley, Kansas. Although it is unlikely that the division will deploy to a mission as a unified team in the near term, it will continue to oversee the training of its brigades and combined arms teams so that they can meet the military needs of the nation. For example, the division prepared its 2nd BCT and the 1st Sustainment Brigade for a deployment to Kuwait in 2016 in a deterrent/military assistance/counterterrorism role and its 1st HBCT for a deployment to Korea in 2016–2017, where it replaced a brigade from the 1st Cavalry Division. Army modularized brigades have proven to be the optimum self-sustaining tactical organization for such missions given their organic combat, combat support, and combat service support organizations. The division has been a valuable organization to help prepare them for missions ranging from counterinsurgency to traditional high-intensity combat.

The threats facing American armed forces around the world require military organizations to be smaller and more agile than the army divisions of the pre–9/11 world. The soldiers of the Big Red One serve all over the world in roles ranging from advisors to combat units fighting terrorists. While the army has reorganized itself for a wide range of missions, the retention of a division structure allows the nation, if necessary, to reassemble divisions to fight as unified teams.

No one knows for certain what military threats will face the nation and its army in the future. What is certain is this: the 1st Infantry Division's history is emblematic and representative of the history of the US Army since 1917. Often first to fight and last to leave, the Big Red One has led the way. There remains the intrinsic value and power of esprit and morale and of soldiers' beliefs that they are part of something greater than themselves. There remains no substitute for the message and power of the 1st Division's motto: No Mission too difficult. No Sacrifice too great. Duty First!

NOTES

Abbreviations Used in the Notes

AAR	after-action report
AEF	American Expeditionary Forces
AG	adjutant general
BG	brigadier general
CG	commanding general
CMH	Center of Military History, Washington, DC
CP	command post
CT	combat team
DSC	Distinguished Service Cross
Eisenhower Papers	A. Chandler et al., eds., *The Papers of Dwight David Eisenhower: The War Years*, 5 vols. (Baltimore, MD, 1970)
EUCOM	European Command
FA	Field Artillery
FO	Field Order
GHQ	General Headquarters
G3	operations officer of division, corps, or army
IG	inspector general
KIA	killed in action
Lewis Report	NA, RG407, AGO Decimal Files, Box 672, Lewis Board Report, 8 April 1919
LTG	Lieutenant General
MACV	United States Military Assistance Command
MG	machine gun
MHI	Military History Institute, Carlisle, PA
MRC	McCormick Research Center, Wheaton, IL
NA	National Archives, Washington, DC
ORLL	Operations Reports, lessons learned
PC	post of command (World War I)
RG	Record Group
USAREUR	US Army, Europe
USARV	US Army, Vietnam
USAWW	*United States Army in the World War, 1917–1919*, 17 vols. (Washington, DC, 1948; 1989 reprint)
WWR, 1st Division	*World War Records, 1st Division, A.E.F., Regular* (Washington, DC, 1928–1930)

1. Lafayette, We Are Here: Creation of the 1st Infantry Division

1. S. Clay, *Blood and Sacrifice: The History of the 16th Infantry Regiment* (Chicago, 2001), 12; D. Smythe, *Pershing, General of the Armies* (Bloomington, IN, 1986), 30.

2. G. Marshall, *Memoirs of My Service in the World War, 1917–1918* (Boston, 1976), 12; J. Pershing, *My Experiences in the World War*, 2 vols. (New York, 1931), 1:91–93.

3. Pershing, *My Experiences*, 1:93. Stanton was a member of Pershing's staff and an old army friend. Pershing spoke as well, but only briefly, and attributes the famous phrase to Stanton.

4. A. Taylor, *English History* (Oxford, 1965), 80–81; J. Keegan, *The First World War* (New York, 2000), 324–326.

5. Keegan, *The First World War*, 327–332; B. Schmitt and H. Vedeler, *The World in the Crucible, 1914–1919* (New York, 1988), 171–174; Smythe, *Pershing*, 21–23.

6. R. Weigley, *History of the United States Army* (New York, 1967), 352; E. Coffman, *The War to End All Wars: The American Military Experience in World War I* (New York, 1968), 8–9, 18–19, 32–33.

7. J. Wilson, *The Evolution of Divisions and Separate Brigades* (Washington, DC, 1998), 23–26.

8. E. Coffman, "John J. Pershing, General of the Armies," in *Essays in Some Dimensions of Military History*, vol. 4, ed. B. Cooling (US Army Military History Research Collection, Carlisle Barracks, PA, 1976), 51.

9. Coffman, *The War to End All Wars*, 42–45.

10. Weigley, *History of the United States Army*, 355–356; Coffman, *The War to End All Wars*, 42–44.

11. Pershing, *My Experiences*, 1:2–3, 38–40; Coffman, *The War to End All Wars*, 48–49.

12. A. Millett, *The General: Robert L. Bullard and Officership in the United States Army* (Westport, CT, 1975), 303 (for the logic behind his selection, see p. 307); Pershing, *My Experiences*, 1:1–4; Smythe, *Pershing*, 3–4; J. Eisenhower, *Yanks: The Epic Story of the American Army in World War I* (New York, 2001), 28–33; Coffman, "John J. Pershing," 48–51.

13. Society of the First Division, *History of the First Division during the World War, 1917–1919* (Philadelphia, 1922), 1–2.

14. Ibid.; J. Baumgartner, ed., *The Sixteenth Infantry Regiment, 1861–1946* (Bamberg, Germany, 1946; 1999 edition), 1–3; Clay, *Blood and Sacrifice*; P. Gorman, *Blue Spaders: The 26th Infantry Regiment, 1917–1967* (Wheaton, IL, 1996); Pershing, *My Experiences*, 1:88.

15. J. McKenney, *Field Artillery: Regular Army and Army Reserve*, The Army Lineage Series (Washington, DC, 1992), 67–71, 85–86, 103–106.

16. USAWW, 3:2:426, Letter from William Sibert, CG, 1st ID, to French General d'Armau de Pouydraguin, CG of 47th French Division, 18 July 1917.

17. Pershing, *My Experiences*, 1:88; J. Harbord, *The American Army in France, 1917–1919* (Boston, 1936), 99; Marshall, *Memoirs*, 245–246, nn. 5, 6.

18. Coffman, "John J. Pershing," 53; J. Cooke, *Pershing and His Generals: Command and Staff in the AEF* (Westport, CT, 1997), 61–73.

19. B. Buck, *Memories of Peace and War* (San Antonio, 1935), 169–170, President Theodore Roosevelt to BG B. Buck, 20 January 1918.

20. Marshall, *Memoirs*, 246, n. 11; R. Smith, *The Colonel: The Life and Legend of Robert R. McCormick, 1880–1955* (New York, 1997), 174–176, 188–200.

21. USAWW, 3:2:426, Sibert to CG of French 47th Division, 18 July 1917.

22. L. Ayres, *The War with Germany: A Statistical Summary* (Washington, DC, 1919 edition), 21–22.

23. Pershing, *My Experiences*, 1:154; Harold B. Fiske, *Report of the G5, AEF, Appendix 31, Divisional Training*, in Timberman-Fiske Family Papers (ca. 1919), MHI, 7–8.

24. A. Millett, "Cantigny," in *America's First Battles, 1776–1965*, ed. C. Haller and W. Stofft (Lawrence, KS, 1986), 159–162.

25. Ayres, *The War with Germany*, 73–84, especially 84, n. 12.

26. Ibid., 63–65.

27. Pershing, *My Experiences*, 1:131–132.

28. Ayres, *The War with Germany*, 65–68.

29. Society of the First Division, *History of the First Division*, 1–7; Marshall, *Memoirs*, 7–9.

30. Pershing, *My Experiences*, 1:38–40; Harbord, *The American Expeditionary Force*, 65–66.

31. Pershing, *My Experiences*, 1:38, Newton D. Baker to Major General John J. Pershing, 26 May 1917.

32. USAWW, 3:2:424–425, 1st ID War Diary, 15 and 16 July 1918.

33. MHI, WWI, Veterans' Surveys, 1st ID, 16th Infantry, Papers of Herbert L. McHenry, "Memoirs," 15.

34. Ibid.

35. MRC, memoir of Warren H. Mavity, 10.

36. MHI, WWI, Veterans' Surveys, 1st ID, 18th Infantry, Papers of Vern Baldwin.

37. L. Kennett, "The AEF through French Eyes," *Military Review* 52 (1972): 4–5.

38. Fiske, *Report of the G5*, app. 31, Divisional Training, 2, Memorandum attached to Pershing's telegram to War Department, 17 July 1917.

39. Ibid., 2.

40. Ibid., 3.

41. Ibid., 3–4.

42. Ibid., 5, 16. USAWW, 3:2:431, 1st ID War Diary, 24 July 1917, noted that BG Bullard and ten officers left for a month of detached duty at English and French schools; Millett, *The General*, 317–318.

43. USAWW, 3:2:56, 1st ID War Diary, 26 November 1917.

44. G. Duncan, "Reminiscences of the World War," unpublished typescript of George Duncan's memoirs, n.d., 19–20.

45. Ibid., 8, Training Memorandum, October 1917.

46. Pershing, *My Experiences*, 1:163–164.

47. Coffman, *The War to End All Wars*, 138.

48. Millett, *The General*, 320–324.

49. Ibid.

50. R. L. Bullard, *Personalities and Reminiscences of the War* (Garden City, NY, 1925), 93.

51. Coffman, "Pershing," 53.

52. Fiske, *Report of the G5*, 47.

53. Ibid., 15–17, Pershing message to the AG, War Department, 19 October 1917; J. Rainey, "Ambivalent Warfare: The Tactical Doctrine of the AEF in World War I," *Parameters* 13 (September 1983): 34–46.

54. USAWW, 3:2:426, Sibert to Pouydraguin, CG 47th French Division, 18 July 1917.

55. Ibid., 3:2:2, 4, David Lloyd George to Mr. Robertson, 2 December 1917.

56. Ibid., notes from a conversation between Joffre and Pershing, 26 January 1918.

57. Ibid., 29–34, notes from the Allied Conference at the Trianon Palace, 29 January 1918; T. Nenninger, "American Effectiveness," in *Military Effectiveness: The First World War*, ed. A Millett and W. Murray (Boston, 1988), 126, 129; M. Coffman, "American Command and Commanders in World War I," in *Essays in Some Dimensions of Military History*, vol. 3, ed. B. Cooling (US Army Military History Research Collection, Carlisle Barracks, PA, 1974), 32–33.

58. USAWW, 3:2:427, 1st Division Memorandum on Instruction and Training, 18 July 1917.

59. Ibid., 3:2:432, 1st Division Memorandum for Brigade and Regimental Commanders, 2 August 1917.

60. Ibid., 3:2:439–440, Sibert Memorandum for Brigade Commanders, 21 September 1917.

61. MHI, Hines Diary, entry for 28 October 1917; Clay, *Blood and Sacrifice*, 99.

62. Buck, *Memories*, 164–165.

63. USAWW, 3:2:440–441, 1st Division Memorandum for Brigade Commanders, 5 October 1917.

64. Marshall, *Memoirs*, 39–40.

65. MHI, Hines Diary, 31, entry for November–December. Hines had his aide make entries in his diary after he was promoted to brigadier general. I believe that those entries reflect Hines's view of things.

66. *Order of Battle of the United States Land Forces in the World War, American Expeditionary Forces, Divisions* (Washington, DC, 1931), 7.

67. USAWW, 3:2:441–442, Instructions from the French Military Mission to the AEF, 6 October 1917; ibid., 443–444, orders from the AEF Adjutant General to the 1st ID, 8 October 1917.

68. Ibid., 3:2:450, 1st ID War Diary, 23 October 1917.

69. Ibid.

70. Clay, *Blood and Sacrifice*, 99–100, claims that twelve prisoners were taken by the Germans; Society of the First Division, *History of the First Division*, 30–32, notes that the Germans captured ten Americans.

71. Bullard, *Personalities and Reminiscences*, 152.

72. Society of the First Division, *History of the First Division*, 35.

73. NA, RG120, War Diary Entry Ledger, AEF, GHQ, where pessimistic messages from Sibert to Pershing in October and November 1917 were regularly logged.

74. Duncan, "Reminiscences," 49–50.

75. Bullard, *Personalities and Reminiscences*, 93; for the quote, see Millett, *The General*, 321, 324.

76. Bullard, *Personalities and Reminiscences*, 91, entry for 3 December 1917.

This diary entry probably reflects Bullard's low morale in early December more than a thoughtful assessment of Pershing.

77. Millet, *The General*, 332.
78. Bullard, *Personalities and Reminiscences*, 111–114.
79. Millet, *The General*, 335.
80. Ibid., 332–335.
81. Bullard, *Personalities and Reminiscences*, 107–109.
82. Marshall, *Memoirs*, 52.
83. Bullard, *Personalities and Reminiscences*, 116.
84. USAWW, 3:2:456, 1st ID War Diary, 26 November 1917.
85. Marshall, *Memoirs*, 52–53.
86. Ibid., 53; USAWW, 3:2:457, 1st ID War Diary, 3 and 6 December 1917.
87. USAWW, 3:2:460, AEF G3 Memorandum for Coordination, 6 January 1918; Ibid., 463, 1st ID War Diary, 16 January 1918.
88. Duncan, "Reminiscences," 52.
89. Marshall, *Memoirs*, 58–59; Society of the First Division, *History of the First Division*, 43–45.
90. Society of the First Division, *History of the First Division*, 44–47; Marshall, *Memoirs*, 60–61.
91. Marshall, *Memoirs*, 62–64.
92. Ibid., 61–65.
93. Bullard, *Personalities and Reminiscences*, 137.
94. Marshall, *Memoirs*, 67–68.
95. Ibid., 68–70; Society of the First Division, *History of the First Division*, 56–58; Bullard, *Personalities and Reminiscences*, 142–143.

2. Cantigny to Soissons

1. J. Keegan, *The First World War* (New York, 2000), 332.
2. Ibid., 335–343.
3. M. Doubler, *I Am the Guard: A History of the Army National Guard, 1636–2000* (Washington, DC, 2001), 171.
4. Ibid., 176–177; E. Coffman, *The War to End All Wars*, 146–148.
5. *Some Accomplishments of the Services of Supply* (SOS Report, 1919), 22, in MHI.
6. Keegan, *The First World War*, 392–393.
7. *Some Accomplishments of the Services of Supply*, 15, 22.
8. Keegan, *The First World War*, 396–401.
9. USAWW, 3:275–277, 25 March 1918, Extract of Pétain and Pershing Conference.
10. Ibid., 3:287–289, 29 April 1918, Memorandum of Pétain's GHQ of the French Armies of the North and Northeast; 283–284, Pétain to Pershing, 10 April 1918; A. Millett, *The General*, 347, 351n44.
11. Pershing, *My Experiences*, 1:363–367.
12. MHI, J. Hines Diary, Hines Papers, 57–61, entries for 28–31 March 1918.
13. Millett, *The General*, 355–356.
14. Bullard, *Personalities and Reminiscences*, 174–175.
15. Marshall, *Memoirs*, 76–77.

16. Millett, *The General*, 356.

17. R. McLain, "Organization and Operations of the Division Trains, First Division, from December, 1917 to January, 1918," *Combat Studies*, 625–630, MHI.

18. USAWW, 3:261, 1st Division FO 13, 16 April 1918; Millett, "Cantigny," 164–165.

19. MHI, J. Hines Diary, Hines Papers, 68–69, entry for 16 April 1918.

20. Pershing, *My Experiences*, 1:392.

21. USAWW, 4:261, 1st Division FO 13, 20 April 1918; ibid., 263–264, 1st Division FO 14, 23 April 1918; ibid., 1st Division Operations Report, 27 April 1918; Marshall, *Memoirs*, 81–82; Millett, "Cantigny," 165–167.

22. Marshall, *Memoirs*, 83–86; Bullard, *Personalities and Reminiscences*, 185–191.

23. USAWW, 4:266, G3 Memo, 8 May 1918.

24. E. Savatier, "The American Doughboy Goes into Action," in *As They Saw Us*, ed., G. Viereck (Garden City, NJ, 1929), 81–83.

25. Bullard, *Personalities and Reminiscences*, 185, for the quote; Society of the First Division, *History of the First Division*, 97, for a casualty estimate.

26. Society of the First Division, *History of the First Division*, 72–75; Marshall, *Memoirs*, 84–85; Bullard, *Personalities and Reminiscences*, 184–187.

27. Marshall, *Memoirs*, 85.

28. Society of the First Division, *History of the First Division*, 271–336.

29. Keegan, *The First World War*, 405–407; A. Banks, *A Military Atlas of the First World War* (London, 1975), 180.

30. USAWW, 4:268, 1st Division FO 15, 10 May 1918, the plan for the X Corps attack; ibid., 4:270, French X Corps commander to First Army commander, 12 May 1918; Pershing, *My Experiences*, 2:54–55.

31. USAWW, 4:271, 13 May 1918, Bullard to Chief of Staff, AEF.

32. Ibid., 4:272–273, X Corps order, 15 May 1918; ibid., 4:275, X Corps order, 16 May 1918.

33. Buck, *Memories of Peace and War*, 172; Marshall, *Memoirs*, 89–91.

34. *World War Records, First Division*, 1st Division FO 18, 20 May 1918 (hereafter cited as WWR.)

35. Millett, "Cantigny," 169–170.

36. WWR, 1st ID, Annex 6 to FO 18, 22 May 1918.

37. Marshall, *Memoirs*, 91–94; USAWW, 4:288–289, 1st Division Relief Order 8, 26 May 1918; ibid., 1st Division G3 Memo, 26 May 1918.

38. Millett, "Cantigny," 170–171; Marshall, *Memoirs*, 92–93.

39. R. B. Asprey, *The German High Command at War: Hindenburg and Ludendorff Conduct World War I* (New York, 1991), 412–418; Pershing, *My Experiences*, 2:61–62; Keegan, *The First World War*, 406–407; B. Pitt, *1918: The Last Act* (New York, 1962), 163–167; B. Liddell Hart, *The Real War, 1914–1918* (Boston, 1930), 412–416.

40. USAWW, 4:321–322, Account by an Eyewitness, 29 May 1918.

41. USAWW, 4:300, Report from 26th Infantry PC to Division, 0916, 28 May 1918; ibid., Report from 28th Infantry PC to 1st Division, 0922, 28 May 1918.

42. USAWW, 4:300–301, a list of telephonic reports submitted to 1st Division, 28 May 1918.

43. Ibid., 301, Report from 28th Infantry PC to Division, 0922, 28 May 1918.

44. Bullard, *Personalities and Reminiscences*, 196–197; Millett, *The General*, 364–365.

45. USAWW, 4:307, 28th Infantry to 2nd Brigade PC, 1745, 28 May 1918;

ibid., Division Machine Gun Officer Major Frank Bowen to MG Barrage 2, 1750, 28 May 1918.

46. Ibid., 4:308, 2nd Brigade to 18th Infantry PC, 28 May 1918.

47. Ibid., 4:312, 1st Division to X Corps, 28 May 1918; ibid., 313, 1st Division G3 Operations Report, 29 May 1918. The G3's daily operations reports covered 10 a.m. to 10 a.m.

48. Millett, "Cantigny," 176–177.

49. USAWW, 4:314, G3 Memo, Reorganization of Cantigny Sector, 29 May 1918, 315–316; ibid., 1st Artillery Brigade Operations Order 59, 29 May 1918; Millett, "Cantigny," 178–179.

50. Millett, *The General*, 366–367; USAWW, 4:318–319, telephone messages about the course of the battle. At 2055 hours, on 29 May, Ely reported: "Front line pounded to hell and gone, and entire front line must be relieved tomorrow night and [or] he would not be responsible."

51. Society of the First Division, *History of the First Division*, 86.

52. Bullard, *Personalities and Reminiscences*, 197.

53. MRC, unpublished memoir of Alfred J. Buhl, n. d., 10.

54. Marshall, *Memoirs*, 98–99.

55. MHI, J. Hines Diary, Hines Papers, 76–87, entries for 2 May–4 June 1918.

56. USAWW, 4:742–790, for the period 4 June to 8 July 1918.

57. Society of the First Division, *History of the First Division*, 92–97.

58. Marshall, *Memoirs*, 102–105, for a very interesting exchange between Marshall and Bullard and the commander of the French division on the right flank of the 1st Division.

59. Ibid., 106–107; NA, RG120, AEF, GHQ Correspondence, Box 3158, Report by LTC Price, June 1918, Montdidier-Noyon Defensive, 1–2, 9.

60. NA, RG200, Harold Fiske Papers, Box 2, Divisional History Charts; Bullard, *Personalities and Reminiscences*, 210; Marshall, *Memoirs*, 113–116.

61. Millett, *The General*, 370, 381.

62. NA, RG200, Box 3, Pershing Papers, Pershing to AG War Department, 2 June 1918.

63. USAWW, 3:415–416, Order to Bullard to assume command of III Corps and to control 1st and 2nd Divisions as part of Tenth Army, 8 July 1918; D. Johnson II and R. Hillman, *Soissons, 1918* (College Station, TX, 1999), 10–14; J. Eisenhower, *Yanks*, 162–164; Coffman, *The War to End All Wars*, 235.

64. USAWW, 3:419–421.

65. USAWW, 5:33, I US Corps Daily Situation Report, 15–16 July 1918.

66. Coffman, *The War to End All Wars*, 234–238; WWR, 1st Division, vol. 25, French Documents, Mangin to CG, Group of Armies of the Reserve, 13 July 1918.

67. USAWW, 5:7–24; Asprey, *The German High Command at War*, 435–437.

68. Johnson and Hillman, *Soissons, 1918*, 39.

69. USAWW, 5:231–237.

70. Ibid., 5:276–277, Tenth Army Order 232, 14 July 1918.

71. WWR, 1st Division, FO 27, 16 July 1918.

72. Society of the First Division, *History of the First Division*, 99–100; NA, RG120, 1st Division papers, Box 61, 1st Brigade AAR, 4 August 1918; McLain, "Organization and Operations of the Division Trains," 627.

73. NA, RG120, 1st Division papers, Box 101, AAR, 6th Artillery, 1 August 1918; ibid., Box 104, AAR, 7th Artillery, 2 August 1918.

74. USAWW, 5:290–291, XX Corps Operations Order 227, 16 July 1918; ibid., 315, 1st Artillery Brigade Operations Order 180, 17 July 1918.

75. WWR, 1st Division, FO 27, 16 July 1918, paragraph 8.

76. Buck, *Memories of Peace and War*, 191.

77. USAWW, 5:323–327, 1st Division Report on Operations South of Soissons, 27 July 1918.

78. Ibid.

79. NA, RG120, 1st Division papers, Box 61, 1st Brigade AAR, 4 August 1918.

80. MRC, Buhl memoir, 13.

81. Buck, *Memories of Peace and War*, 194–195.

82. USAWW, 5:323–327, 1st Division Report, 27 July 1918; Buck, *Memories of Peace and War*, 194–195; Johnson and Hillman, *Soissons, 1918*, 45–48.

83. Medal of Honor citation for Captain Samuel I. Parker, in *First Division Notes*, 1937, in NA, RG319, micro, reel 2.

84. Johnson and Hillman, *Soissons, 1918*, 91.

85. NA, RG120, Box 61, 1st Brigade AAR, 4 August 1918.

86. USAWW, 5:325, 1st Division Report, 27 July 1918; NA, RG120, 1st Division papers, Box 61, 1st Brigade AAR, 4 August 1918; WWR, 1st ID, Operations Orders, G3 Memorandum 714, 18 July 1918.

87. USAWW, 5:325, 1st Division Report, 27 July 1918.

88. NA, RG120, 1st Division papers, Box 61, AAR of Co. A, 2nd MG Battalion, 27 July 1918.

89. NA, RG120, Box 62, AAR of 2nd MG Battalion, 2 August 1918.

90. MHI, WWI Veterans' Surveys, 1st Division, 16th Infantry, Herbert McHenry Memoir, 21–22. McHenry mentions that the company to which he was assigned as a replacement in August 1918 "had been shot down" in "the Soissons Drive, from ninety-six men [down] to thirty-five."

91. NA, RG120, AAR of 2nd MG Battalion, 2 August 1918.

92. WWR, 3:1st Division, G3 Memorandum 714, 18 July 1918.

93. USAWW, 5:325–326, 1st Division Report, 27 July 1918; Johnson and Hillman, *Soissons, 1918*, 88–91; Buck, *Memories of Peace and War*, 197.

94. NA, RG120, 1st Division papers, Box 61, AAR of 1st Brigade, 4 August 1918.

95. Buck, *Memories of Peace and War*, 197–198.

96. Society of the First Division, *History of the First Division*, 122–126.

97. Medal of Honor citation for Captain Samuel I. Parker.

98. NA, RG120, Box 101, AAR of 6th Field Artillery Regiment, 1 August 1918.

99. NA, RG120, Box 104, AARs of Batteries B and E, 7th Field Artillery, 2 August and 27 July 1918, respectively.

100. MRC, Mavity memoir, 16.

101. Coffman, *The War to End All Wars*, 242; Johnson and Hillman, *Soissons, 1918*, 111–113.

102. Johnson and Hillman, *Soissons, 1918*, 121–123.

103. USAWW, 5:317–318, 1st Division G3 Memorandum to Brigade Commanders, 19 July 1918.

104. Summerall quote, in Johnson and Hillman, *Soissons, 1918*, 123.

105. Society of the First Division, *History of the First Division*, 128–133.

106. MRC, Buhl memoir, 16.

107. Johnson and Hillman, *Soissons, 1918*, 124–127.

108. Ibid., 129–130; Society of the First Division, *History of the First Division*, 134–138.

109. Buck, *Memories of Peace and War*, 205–206; USAWW, 5:327, 1st Division Report, 27 July 1918.

110. NA, RG120, 1st Division papers, Box 11, Brief History of Operations of 1st Division, 21 December 1918.

111. USAWW, 5:327, 1st Division Report, 27 July 1918; Society of the First Division, *History of the First Division*, 139–141.

112. Asprey, *The German High Command at War*, 441; General Walther Reinhardt, Chief of Staff of the German Seventh Army, in Viereck, ed., *As They Saw Us*, 118–119.

3. Victory in Alsace-Lorraine: St. Mihiel and the Meuse Argonne

1. Asprey, *The German High Command at War*, 445–448; Keegan, *The First World War*, 410–412.

2. Keegan, *The First World War*, 408–409.

3. Ibid., 408, for British strength, which fell from 754,000 men in July 1918; Pershing, *My Experiences*, 2:192; see MHI, *Some Accomplishments of the Service of Supply, AEF* (1919), 14, for American strength.

4. For troop strength, see MHI, *Some Accomplishments of the Service of Supply*, 15. For corps activations, see Coffman, *The War to End All Wars*, 248, 171, 257, 275.

5. Pershing, *My Experiences*, 2:175–176.

6. MHI, *Some Accomplishments of the Service of Supply*, 105–121. There were 280,000 beds available in the AEF hospital system. Evacuation of casualties was accomplished using litters, ambulances, and hospital railway trains. Records indicate 236,766 men were treated for wounds and injuries, and 689,179 were treated for diseases. Fewer than 5.2 percent of the wounded and 2.6 percent of the ill patients died; 113,681 sick and wounded men were evacuated to the United States for care. For replacement numbers, see NA, RG200, Entry 19, Pershing's confidential messages, Box 3, message 1236-S, 3 June 1918.

7. NA, RG200, Entry 11, Harold Fiske Papers, Box 2, *Divisional History Charts, G3, AEF*, listing monthly losses and replacements for each division in the AEF during 1918; NA, RG120, 1st Division papers, Box 9, Reports in Strength of Infantry Companies, 18–21 August 1918, and Strength Report of Infantry Companies, 18 September 1918.

8. NA, RG120, 1st Division papers, Box 65, 2nd Brigade Memo, 7 August 1918.

9. WWR, 1st ID, 3: Memorandum, 25 August 1918, 1–5.

10. Society of the First Division, *History of the First Division*, 141, 145; WWR, 1st ID, Memoranda, 2nd Brigade, 25 July 1918.

11. WWR, 1st ID, Memorandum, 25 August 1918, 5–6.

12. NA, RG120, 1st Division papers, Box 11, Order of Battle, 1st Division; WWR, 1st ID, Memorandum, 29 August 1918.

13. WWR, 1st ID, 3: Memorandum, 29 August 1918, 1.

14. Ibid., 1st Division Memorandum, 1 September 1918, passing on verbatim

the First Army Memorandum, 1 September 1918. Emphasis of the underlined portion was in the original document.

15. Ibid., 3–4. Underlining is from original document.

16. Ibid., 3–5.

17. MHI, World War I, Veterans' Surveys, 1st Division, 16th Infantry, Herbert McHenry Memoir, 1–18.

18. Ibid., 17–19.

19. Ibid., 20–23.

20. Ibid., 23–24; NA, RG120, 1st Division papers, Box 15, Brief History of the Operations of the 1st Division, 21 December 1918.

21. MHI, World War I, Veterans' Surveys, McHenry Memoir, 24–25.

22. Ibid., 29.

23. Pershing, *My Experiences*, 2:207–225.

24. USAWW, 8:3–56, 173–181, for details of French support to First Army.

25. Pershing, *My Experiences*, 2:248–255; USAWW, 8:47, Conclusions of the Conference of 2 September 1918.

26. Marshall, *Memoirs*, 129–136.

27. NA, RG120, 1st Division papers, Box 61, Memorandum 64, 1st Brigade, 2 September 1918. The underlined words were underlined in the original document.

28. MHI, World War I, Veterans' Surveys, McHenry Memoir, 26–27.

29. WWR, 1st ID, 1: FO 36, 1 September 1918.

30. Ibid.

31. Ibid.; NA, RG120, 1st Division papers, Box 62, 1st Brigade Report on Operations, 19 September 1918, 1–3, for discussion of accompanying mortars, 37mm, and 75mm guns.

32. WWR, 1st ID, FO 36, 1 September 1918.

33. WWR, 1st ID, Orders, FO 36, 9 September 1918.

34. NA, RG120, 1st Division papers, Box 62, 1st Brigade Report on Operations of Sept. 12th-13th, in the Saint-Mihiel, 19 September 1918; Society of the First Division, *History of the First Division*, 156–163.

35. NA, RG120, 1st Division papers, 1st Brigade report, 19 September 1918; WWR, 1st ID, Intelligence Summaries, Summary of Intelligence, 12 September 1918; Society of the First Division, *History of the First Division*, 163–164.

36. Ibid.

37. MHI, World War I, Veterans' Surveys, McHenry Memoir, 35.

38. WWR, 1st ID, Intelligence Summaries, Information obtained from POWs, 12 September 1918.

39. Pershing, *My Experiences*, 2:269–270; Society of the First Division, *History of the First Division*, 166–168.

40. NA, RG120, 1st Division papers, Box 9, Strength Report of Infantry Companies, 18 September 1918, lists the nine or ten men from each rifle company that were on detached duty with the Bn. Intelligence Group. Ibid., Report of Strength of Infantry Companies, 18–21 August 1918, does not list such detachments from any company in the division. Society of the First Division, *History of the First Division*, 167, mentions a scout platoon from the 28th Infantry in Huttonville on 13 September.

41. WWR, 1st ID, Orders, Report of the Division Inspector General, 20 September 1918.

42. NA, RG200, Harold Fiske Papers, Box 1, Casualties reported by Consecutive

Dates to AEF, 11 September to 11 November 1918; Society of the First Division, *History of the First Division*, lists losses of 93 killed and 441 wounded. These figures are very close to the division's total reported losses for the period 11–24 September 1918 in the AEF report.

43. Society of the First Division, *History of the First Division*, 169–170.

44. Marshall, *Memoirs*, 138–142; L. Bland et al., eds., *The Papers of George Catlett Marshall*, 6 vols. (Baltimore, 1981), 1:160–161; Pershing, *My Experiences*, 2:285n1.

45. Pershing, *My Experiences*, 2:282–283; P. Braim, *The Test of Battle* (Shippensburg, PA, 1987), 74–75; J. Eisenhower, *Yanks*, 200–203.

46. Pershing, *My Experiences*, 2:292–293; USAWW, First Army Operations Order 20, 20 September 1918; J. J. Pershing, *Report of the First Army: American Expeditionary Forces* (Fort Leavenworth, KS, 1923), 47–49.

47. NA, RG120, Box 3382, Plans of Concentration for Argonne-Meuse, Drum Memorandum for Pershing, 4 September 1918; Braim, *Test of Battle*, 91–99.

48. Coffman, *The War to End All Wars*, 304–306.

49. NA, RG120, Box 3382, Memorandum to Pershing, 4 September 1918.

50. WWR, 1st ID, 3: FO 39, 19 September 1918, and FO 40, 23 September 1918.

51. WWR, 1st ID, FO 41, 27 September 1918.

52. A. Hartzell, *The Meuse-Argonne Battle, 26 September–11 November 1918* (prepared by Captain Hartzell for General Headquarters, AEF, March 1919), 22–26. This pamphlet was prepared for instructional purposes for officers visiting the battlefield; Braim, *Test of Battle*, 85–86; Pershing, *My Experiences*, 2:290–293.

53. Infantry School, *Infantry in Battle* (Washington, DC, 1939), 56–58.

54. Braim, *Test of Battle*, 87–90; Pershing, *Report of the First Army*, 50–51; Hartzell, *The Meuse-Argonne Battle*, 28.

55. Eisenhower, *Yanks*, 218–222; Braim, *Test of Battle*, 88–96.

56. Hartzell, *The Meuse-Argonne Battle*, 28; Eisenhower, *Yanks*, 222–223.

57. USAWW, 8: 82, Pétain to Foch, 30 September 1918.

58. Braim, *Test of Battle*, 102–103; Pershing, *My Experiences*, 2: 302–305.

59. NA, RG200, Fiske papers, Casualties Reported by Consecutive Dates, Box 1. The 35th Division lost 7,414 casualties during the offensive.

60. Pershing, *My Experiences*, 2:298–299; H. Liggett, *Commanding an American Army: Recollections of the World War* (New York, 1925), 81–83; Braim, *Test of Battle*, 89–90, 101–102; Eisenhower, *Yanks*, 214–215, 223.

61. NA, RG120, First Army Inspector General Reports, Box 5, Observations about 28th and 35th Divisions, 27–29 September 1918.

62. Ibid.

63. WWR, 1st ID, 3: FO 43, 30 September 1918.

64. NA, RG120, Box 3382, G3 First Army Memorandum, 29 September 1918; USAWW, 9: 181, I Corps Situation Report, 29–30 September 1918; Pershing, *Report of First Army*, 53–54; WWR, 1st ID, 13: Operations Reports, Division G3 Report, 1 October 1918.

65. MHI, World War I, Veterans' Surveys, McHenry Memoir, 46–49.

66. WWR, 1st ID, 3: FO 43 and 44, 30 September 1918.

67. R. Cochrane, "The 1st Division in the Meuse-Argonne, 1–12 October 1918," *Gas Warfare in the World War I*, Study Number 3 (Army Chemical Center, MD, 1957), 4–13.

68. Ibid., 15.

69. Ibid., 19; NA, RG120, Entry 1241, Box 15; NA, RG200, Fiske Papers, Box 1, Casualties Reported, 11 September to 11 November 1918.

70. WWR, 1st ID, 13: Operations Report, 2 October 1918.

71. WWR, 1st ID, 3: FO 47, 2 October 1918.

72. Ibid.

73. NA, RG200, Fiske Papers, Box 1, Casualties Reported by Consecutive Dates.

74. WWR, 1st ID, 13: Operations Report, 4 October 1918.

75. Ibid.

76. WWR, 1st ID, 3: G3 Memorandum 1064, 4 October 1918.

77. Ibid., 1066, 4 October 1918.

78. Pershing, *My Experiences*, 2:322–324; Braim, *Test of Battle*, 110–111.

79. WWR, 1st ID, 13: Field Hospital Reports, 5 October 1918.

80. Ibid., 3: FO 48, 5 October 1918.

81. Ibid., G3 Memorandum 1068, 4 October 1918.

82. Ibid., 13: Operations Report, 5 October 1918; ibid., Telegram, 1st Infantry Division to First Army, 6 October 1918.

83. Liggett, *Commanding an American Army*, 86–88.

84. WWR, 1st ID, 3: G3 Memoranda, 1073 and 1075, 5 and 6 October 1918.

85. Ibid., 13: Report 2543 from 1st Division to G3, I Corps, 6 October 1918.

86. Pershing, *My Experiences*, 2:330–331; Coffman, *The War to End All Wars*, 323–325; Center for Military History, *American Armies and Battlefields in Europe* (Washington, DC, 1995 edition), 177–178.

87. Pershing, *My Experiences*, 2:333.

88. WWR, 1st ID, 3: FO 49, 8 October 1918.

89. Ibid., G3 Warning Order, 7 October 1918.

90. Ibid., G3 Memoranda 1086–1088, to the 181st Brigade, 8–9 October 1918.

91. Ibid., Appendix I, FO 49, 8 October 1918.

92. WWR, 1st ID, 13: G3 Operations Report, as of noon, 9 October 1918; ibid., G3 Telegram to GHQ, AEF, 9 October 1918.

93. WWR, 1st ID, 3: G3 Memorandum, 9 October 1918; ibid., 13: Telegram to G3 V Corps, 10 October 1918; ibid., G3 Operations Report, as of noon, 10 October 1918.

94. MHI, World War I, Veterans' Surveys, McHenry Memoir, 65.

95. WWR, 1st ID, 13: G3 Operations Report, as of noon, 10 October 1918; ibid., G1 Memorandum, 11 October 1918; ibid., G2 Report for the period 4–12 October 1918, dated 16 October 1918; ibid., Operations Report, as of noon, 11 October 1918, which lists 9,056 casualties, including missing. This indicates the number not with their units, but not the final number of casualties, which fell as stragglers and lost soldiers returned to their units.

96. WWR, 1st ID, 3: FO 51, 11 October 1918.

97. Ibid., 70. Brigadier General Bamford was temporary commander for a week before Parker assumed command.

98. Pershing, *My Experiences*, 2:335–337; Marshall, *Memoirs*, 176–179; L. Ayres, *The War with Germany*, 103; MHI, *Some Accomplishments of the Services of Supply*, AEF, 17.

99. MHI, World War I, Veterans' Surveys, McHenry Memoir, 66.

100. WWR, 1st ID, 3: FO 53, 12 October 1918; ibid., FO 54, 12 October 1918; see Society of the First Division, *History of the First Division*, 212, for the quotes in the paragraph.

101. WWR, 1st ID, 13: Reports, Observations of Road Discipline, 16 October 1918.

102. Ibid., Report of Operations of the 1st Division, 17 October 1918.

103. Society of the First Division, *History of the First Division*, 212–213.

104. NA, RG200, Fiske Papers, Box 1, First Army Casualties Reported by Consecutive Dates.

105. NA, RG120, 1st Division papers, Box 16, Shortages in the 1st Division; NA, RG120, AEF Adjutant General's Central File, Box 9, Shortages by Week in the 1st Division.

106. NA, RG120, 1st Division papers, Box 15.

107. MHI, *Some Accomplishments of the Services of Supply, AEF*, 110; Ayres, *The War with Germany*, 119–130.

108. NA, RG120, 1st Division papers, Box 16, AEF G1 to I Corps G1, 1 June 1918.

109. WWR, 1st ID, 3: FO 55, 24 October 1918.

110. Hunter Liggett, *A. E. F., Ten Years Ago in France* (New York, 1928), 216–218.

111. Braim, *Test of Battle*, 130–132.

112. Ibid., 128–133; Liggett, *A. E. F.*, 206–212.

113. Liggett, Second Section, in Pershing, *Report of First Army*, 82–83.

114. Liggett, *A. E. F.*, 220–221.

115. Society of the First Division, *History of the First Division*, 221–222.

116. Ibid., 223–224; Liggett, Second Section, *Report of First Army*, 84–87.

117. WWR, 1st ID, 3: G3 Memorandum, 3 November 1918; ibid., FO 61, 5 November 1918.

118. Ibid., 3: FO 61, 5 November 1918.

119. Ibid., 13: Operations Report, 6 November 1918; ibid., 3: First Army Memorandum for I and V Corps, 5 November 1918; ibid., 13: Parker's "Report on the Operations of the First Division, 5–7 November 1918," to Summerall, 9 November 1918.

120. Pershing, *My Experiences*, 2:381–382.

121. WWR, 1st ID, 3: Memorandum from First Army to I and V Corps Commanders, 5 November 1918. A copy was furnished to 1st Division on 12 November 1918; Marshall, *Memoirs*, 189–190.

122. Marshall, *Memoirs*, 189–190.

123. WWR, 1st ID, 3: FO 62, 6 November 1918.

124. Society of the First Division, *History of the First Division*, 230.

125. Ibid., 232.

126. NA, RG200, Entry 11, Box 1, First Army Casualties Reported by Consecutive Date. The totals for 6–8 November 1918 for 1st Division were 53 killed, 409 wounded, and 113 missing.

127. Liggett, *A. E. F.*, 228–231.

128. Ayres, *The War with Germany*, 114–117.

4. Between the World Wars: The Twenty-Year Peace

1. USAWW, 11: 2–8, AEF General Order 198, 7 November 1918; ibid., Third Army General Order 1, 15 November 1918; ibid., Third Army FO 1, 15 November 1918.

2. Bland et al., eds., *The Papers of George Catlett Marshall*, 5 vols. (Baltimore, 1981), 1:168–169, First Army Memorandum, "Plan of Future Operations," 12 November 1918.

3. WWR, 1st Division, 13: Memorandum to the Members of the First Division, 8 November 1918.

4. Ibid.

5. NA, RG120, 1st Division papers, Box 61, 1st Division order, 22 September 1918.

6. J. Seidule, "Morale in the American Expeditionary Forces during World War I" (Ph.D. diss., Ohio State University, 1997), 15–23.

7. USAWW, 11:7, Third Army FO 1, 15 November 1918.

8. G. Marshall, *Memoirs of My Service*, 204–205.

9. WWR, 1st Division, 3: Third Army Memorandum, 13 November 1918; USAWW, 11: 7, Third Army FO 1, 15 November 1918. See USAWW 11:9, Map 131.

10. WWR, 1st Division, 3: 1st Division FO 68, 15 November 1918.

11. USAWW, 11: 23–25, Third Army Intelligence Summary, 22 November 1918; ibid., 27, Intelligence Summary, 23 November 1918.

12. USAWW, 11: 49–50, Third Army Strength Report, 1 December 1918.

13. WWR, 1st Division, 3: 1st Division FO 78–95, 20–30 November 1918.

14. USAWW, 11: 77–78.

15. Ibid., Third Army FO 11, 12 December 1918; ibid., 80, Operations Report, 13 December 1918; WWR, 1st Division FO 95, 12 December 1918; C. Coulter and H. O'Connor, *The Bridgehead Sentinel: A Souvenir of the Coblenz Bridgehead* (Montabaur, Germany, 1919).

16. NA, RG120, 1st Division papers, Division Memorandum 197, citing General Orders 218, AEF, 28 November 1918.

17. L. Hunt, *American Military Government of Occupied Germany, 1918–1920* (Washington, DC, 1943), 63–65. This report was written in 1920.

18. Ibid., 67.

19. NA, RG120, AEF IG Reports, Notes on Billeting in 1st Division, 16 February 1919.

20. NA, RG120, IG Reports, Box 9, Third Army IG to AEF IG, 12 February 1919.

21. NA, RG120, 1st Division papers, Division Memorandum 184, 28 November 1918.

22. Hunt, *American Military Government*, 95–97.

23. WWR, 1st Division, 3: Memorandum, 12 December 1918.

24. NA, RG200, Entry 23, Box 1, Report of Convictions in the AEF by General Court Martial.

25. Hunt, *American Military Government*, 212–214.

26. NA, RG120, Entry 590, Box 4, 1st Division IG Reports, 27 and 29 January 1919.

27. Hunt, *American Military Government*, 155.

28. NA, RG120, 1st Division papers Box 107, AEF IG Report, 16 February 1919 and AEF IG report of 19 February 1919 for loss percentages; ibid., Memorandum of 1st Division's Sanitary Trains Headquarters, 20 June 1919, for unit locations.

29. NA, RG120, Entry 290, Box 153, Third Army Memorandum 10, 1 December 1918.

30. *Some Accomplishments of the Services of Supply, AEF*, MHI, 105–114.

31. NA, RG120, AEF IG Report, Box 4, 10 January 1919.

32. Pershing, *My Experiences*, 1:177, 2:43–45; MHI, *Some Accomplishments of the Services of Supply, AEF*, MHI, 115.

33. NA, RG120, Entry 935, Box 153, Third Army Administrative Bulletin 29,

20 December 1918; RG120, 1st Division papers, Box 7, 1st Division Memorandum 127, 20 February 1919.

34. NA, RG120, 1st Division papers, Box 2, McGlachlin "To the Division," 28 April 1919.

35. Society of the First Division, *History of the First Division*, 36; NA, RG120, 1st Division papers, Box 2, Division Memorandum, 18 April 1919.

37. Society of the First Division, *History of the First Division*, 250–253.

38. NA, RG120, AEF General Correspondence, Box 3157, Study of Possible Advance of American Troops into Germany, 19 February 1919; F. Pogue, *George C. Marshall, Education of a General* (New York, 1963) 191–193.

39. G. Craig, *The Politics of the Prussian Army, 1640–1945* (New York, 1964), 364–373; Society of the First Division, *History of the First Division*, 255.

40. NA, RG407, Infantry Regimental Histories, Box 4; NA, RG120, 1st ID papers, Box 16, Demobilization Statistics, 12 September 1919.

41. M. Doubler, *I Am the Guard*, 182–187.

42. Ibid., 186–187; Weigley, *History of the United States Army*, 396–397; A. Millett and P. Maslowski, *For the Common Defense* (New York, 1984; 1994 edition), 385.

43. Millett and Maslowski, *For the Common Defense*, 271–274, 385; Weigley, *History of the United States Army*, 275–280, 336–340.

44. Weigley, *History of the United States Army*, 396–397.

45. Ibid., 397–398; Doubler, *I Am the Guard*, 187–188.

46. Bland et al., *The Papers of George Catlett Marshall*, 1:193–194, 199–201. Palmer and Marshall had become friends when they attended Leavenworth Staff College before the war. The debate over reorganization split the officer corps into two camps: March versus Pershing. Pershing's deep antipathy to March may have played a significant role in his decision to favor the retention of the citizen-soldier concept as central to army organization.

47. NA, RG200, Fiske papers, Box 3, Staff Manual for Combat Units, 1919.

48. Lewis Report, 3.

49. Ibid., 2–3.

50. Ibid., 12–27.

51. Ibid., 16–17.

52. J. Wilson, "Mobility versus Firepower: The Post–World War I Infantry Division," *Parameters* 13 (1983): 47–53; NA, RG165, AGO, Box 9, Report on Act of 1920 for CSA.

53. Lewis Report, 4–5.

54. Ibid., 6.

55. Ibid., 8.

56. See P. Mansoor, *The GI Offensive in Europe: The Triumph of American Infantry Divisions, 1941–45* (Lawrence, KS, 1999), for problems with infantry recruitment and replacement policies and the quality of infantrymen in World War II. R. Atkinson, *An Army at Dawn: The War in North Africa, 1942–1943* (New York, 2002), describes tactical problems faced by American units in North Africa that were the results of poor-quality training and poor organizational and tactical decisions.

57. NA, RG407, Box 1463, Memo to the division's Chief of Staff, 13 July 1920, explaining the organization and costs; NA, RG120, 1st Division papers, Box 8, 1st Division Memorandum 12, 29 March 1920, on organizing the circus.

58. NA, RG407, AGO Central Files, War Department Memorandum, 11

August 1920; ibid., 7 September 1920 report; ibid., War Department order, 2 October 1920, directing a telegram be sent to V Corps headquarters requesting that the remaining soldiers of the 1st ID at Camp Taylor be sent to Camp Dix.

59. R. Griffith, "Conscription and the All-Volunteer Army in Historical Perspective," *Parameters* 10, no. 3 (1980): 66.

60. NA, RG165, CSA Statistics, Box 7, Infantry Regiments, December 1920 to May 1921.

61. Griffith, "Conscription," 64–65.

62. Ibid., 65.

63. NA, RG159, Box 2, IG Reports for Fort Hamilton for the years 1929 through 1934.

64. NA, RG165, Special Reports for the Chief of Staff, 1920–1940, Boxes 4–14.

65. Pogue, *Marshall*, 2:210–212, 220.

66. NA, RG407, AGO Central Files, Box 1463, War Department Order, 6 December 1921; ibid., Letter from James Harbord, Deputy Chief of Staff to Assistant Chief of Staff, G3, 3 December 1921.

67. NA, RG159, IG Annual Inspections, 8 November 1924 report.

68. NA, RG407, AGO Central Files, Box 1463, CG, III Corps, to Army AG, 4 January 1922.

69. NA, RG407, AGO Central Data Files, Box 672, Chief of Infantry Memorandum, 4 April 1922; Pogue, *Marshall*, 2:220.

70. NA, RG120, 1st ID papers, Box 61, 1st Brigade Diaries, 1920s.

71. NA, RG407, Box 1442 for brigade histories, and Box 1485 for regimental histories.

72. NA, RG159, IG Reports, Box 2, concerning 1st ID headquarters and Fort Hamilton in the 1920s and 1930s.

73. NA, RG407, Box 1500, 16th Infantry report, 10 December 1924.

74. Ibid., 1st Brigade Diaries for 1922–1923.

75. NA, RG407, Box 1442, AGO Central Files, Record of Communication, 3 February 1939.

76. Millet and Maslowski, *For the Common Defense*, 386–387.

77. J. Votaw, "The Interwar Period: 1920–1941," in *Reference Guide to the United States Military History, 1919–1945*, ed. R Schrader (New York, 1994), 24–42; Pogue, *Marshall*, 1:249–251; Weigley, *History of the United States Army*, 395–420.

78. *Promotions and Retirement: Hearings before the Committee of Military Affairs*, House of Representatives (Washington, DC, 1927), 17–31.

79. NA, RG165, Box 6, Special Report 192, 20 October 1925.

80. NA, RG165, Boxes 4–10, Special Reports on officer performance from 1921 to 1941.

81. Pogue, *Marshall*, 1:271–274, 284.

82. NA, RG159, Box 2, Annual IG Reports for Fort Hamilton, 1933 and 1934.

83. Bland et al., *The Papers of George Catlett Marshall*, 1:662–663.

84. NA, RG159, Box 2, IG Report for Fort Hamilton, 21 March 1933.

85. Ibid., IG Report for Fort Hamilton, 14 May 1927.

86. Millett and Maslowski, *For the Common Defense*, 397–407; Weigley, *History of the United States Army*, 406–420.

87. NA, RG319, microfilm, reel 2, First Division Notes, 1938, 15, 20.

88. NA, RG407, Box 1485, AGO, Record of Communications, July 1935.

89. Pogue, *Marshall*, 1:274–279; NA, RG159, Box 2, IG Report for Fort Hamilton, 24 October 1933.

90. Pogue, *Marshall*, 1:274–277.

91. NA, RG407, Box 1485, AGO, 23 March 1933, a record of communication from the 1st ID to the AG requesting twenty-five copies of the pamphlet "Federal Aid in Domestic Disturbances."

92. NA, RG407, Box 672, Memorandum for the Deputy Chief of Staff, G1, 4 April 1922.

5. Mobilization for War: The Expansion and Training of the Big Red One, 1939 to November 1942

1. D. Kennedy, *Freedom from Fear: The American People in Depression and War, 1929–1945* (New York, 1999), 519–523.

2. Weigley, *History of the United States Army*, 430–436.

3. Millett and Maslowski, *For the Common Defense*, 397–404.

4. Clay, *Blood and Sacrifice*, 138.

5. Ibid., 142–143.

6. Ibid., 140.

7. Bland et al., *The Papers of George Catlett Marshall*, I: 409–411, Marshall to MG Stuart Heintzelman, 4 December 1933.

8. C. Gabel, *The U.S. Army GHQ Maneuvers of 1941* (Washington, DC, 1991), 12.

9. NA, RG319, Historical Records of the 1st ID, 1940–1945, 1st ID report on the Triangular Division, 25 May 1940, 1–2.

10. Ibid., 3; NA, RG319, Historical Records of the 1st ID, 5th Artillery Regiment Report on Triangular Division, 4 May 1940, 2–4.

11. Ibid., 3–4.

12. K. Greenfield, R. Palmer, and B. Wiley, *The Army Ground Forces: The Organization of Ground Combat Troops* (Washington, DC, 1947), table 1.

13. Clay, *Blood and Sacrifice*, 143–144; NA, RG165, Box 4, AGO CDF, Special Report 346, for troop strength in 1939.

14. Clay, *Blood and Sacrifice*, 144.

15. Gabel, *The U.S. Army GHQ Maneuvers*, 12; Weigley, *History of the United States Army*, 424.

16. Weigley, *History of the United States Army*, 424–428.

17. Greenfield et al., *The Army Ground Forces*, 11.

18. Ibid., 1–37, for the GHQ; P. Mansoor, *The GI Offensive in Europe: The Triumph of American Infantry Divisions, 1941–45* (Lawrence, KS, 1999), 21.

19. Greenfield et al., *The Army Ground Forces*, 37–38.

20. Clay, *Blood and Sacrifice*, 149.

21. Ibid., 149–150.

22. Greenfield et al., *The Army Ground Forces*, 86–90.

23. Ibid., 92; NA, RG407, Box 5965, Division order for amphibious exercises on Cape Cod, 23 June 1941; Clay, *Blood and Sacrifice*, 150–151.

24. MRC, S. Mason (Major General Retired), "Reminiscences and Anecdotes of World War II," Typescript prepared in Birmingham, AL, 1968, 13.

25. NA, RG407, Box 5964, Division order for amphibious exercises at New River, NC, 1 August 1941.

26. Clay, *Blood and Sacrifice*, 152; Gabel, *The U.S. Army GHQ Maneuvers*, 132–136; Greenfield et al., *The Army Ground Forces*, 90.

27. NA, RG407, Entry 427, Box 5663, 1st ID, Report on First Army Maneuvers, 1941.

28. Ibid., 132–135.

29. Clay, *Blood and Sacrifice*, 152; Gabel, *The U.S. Army GHQ Maneuvers*, 132–146.

30. Ibid., 187–188.

31. Clay, *Blood and Sacrifice*, 152–153.

32. Ibid., 153.

33. NA, RG319, Box 73, 1st ID papers, 1st Division Order, 9 February 1942.

34. Ibid., G3, copies of phone conversations between the advance party and division headquarters, 9–16 February 1942.

35. Ibid., Information Notes, 13 February 1942, 2.

36. Pogue, *Marshall*, 2:274–288; Millett and Maslowski, *For the Common Defense*, 417–420, 424–425.

37. Millett and Maslowski, *For the Common Defense*, 424–426.

38. NA, RG319, Box 73, 1st ID papers, Division movement order 2, 15 May 1942.

39. T. Dixon, "Terry Allen," *Army* (April 1978): 59; MRC, Mason, "Reminiscences," 14.

40. For a recent account of Allen's life and the division's history, see G. Astor, *Terrible Terry Allen: Combat General of World War I—The Life of an American Soldier* (New York, 2003); for Marshall's assessment of Allen and BG Roosevelt, see Bland et al., *The Papers of George Catlett Marshall*, 2:224.

41. NA, RG319, Box 73, 1st ID papers, 1st ID FO, 12 June 1942; MRC, Mason, "Reminiscences," 15, 23; Clay, *Blood and Sacrifice*, 154.

42. NA, RG319, Box 73, "Some Tips on England," 6 August 1942, 2.

43. Ibid.

44. MRC, Joe Dawson letter, 9 August 1942.

45. G. Howe, *Northwest Africa: Seizing the Initiative in the West* (Washington, DC, 1991), 10–14.

46. Ibid., 13–14.

47. Ibid., 15–17.

48. Ibid., 46–48.

49. Ibid., 22–25; R. Atkinson, *An Army at Dawn*, 26–27.

50. NA, Old RG319, Box 74, 1st ID papers, G3 Logs, 14–21 October 1942; Clay, *Blood and Sacrifice*, 154; Howe, *Northwest Africa*, 60–63; A. Heidenheimer, *Vanguard to Victory: History of the 18th Infantry Regiment* (Aschaffenburg, Germany, 1954), 1–2.

51. NA, Old RG319, Box 74, 1st ID papers, G3 Memorandum, 21 September 1942.

52. Ibid., 1st ID G3 Log, 25 October–7 November 1942. The division command group with Allen, Mason, and Cota, designated as Danger, was aboard the British ship *Reina del Pacifico*, while the rear command post with Andrus was aboard the *Warwick Castle*. Each CP maintained a log.

53. NA, Old RG319, Box 74, 1st ID FO 1, 10 October 1942; Howe, *North-west Africa*, 202–203.

54. NA, RG407, Entry 427, Box 5964, Combat Team 26, FO 1, 11 October 1942; NA, Old RG319, Box 74, 1st ID Memorandum, 1st ID Plan, 12 September 1942, 2.

55. 1st Division FO 1, 10 October 1942.

56. Howe, *Northwest Africa*, 185–187; NA, Old RG319, Box 74, 1st ID G3 Journal, 7 November 1942.

57. NA, RG407, Box 5662, II Corps, G2 Estimate of the Enemy Situation, 20 September 1942.

58. MRC, Mason, "Reminiscences," 25–26.

59. Howe, *Northwest Africa*, 195–199.

60. Ibid., 199.

61. Ibid., 199–200.

62. NA, RG407, Box 5899, 33rd FA AAR, 19 November 1942.

63. J. Kelly, *History of the 26th Infantry Regiment in the Present Struggle*, typescript in MRC, prepared 1943, thirteen parts, I:1–3.

64. NA, Old RG319, 1st ID Rear CP Journal, 10 November, attached Sequence of Events for CT26, 8–10 November 1942.

65. Ibid., 3; NA, RG407, Box 5899, 33rd FA AAR, Report of Action, 19 November 1942; Howe, *Northwest Africa*, 200–202.

66. Kelly, *History of the 26th Infantry*, I:3–4; NA, RG407, Box 5899, 33rd FA AAR, November 1942.

67. NA, Old RG319, 1st ID Rear CP Journal, 10 November, attached Sequence of Events for CT26, 8–10 November 1942.

68. Kelly, *History of the 26th Infantry*, I:4; NA, RG407, Box 5899, 33rd FA AAR, November 1942.

69. Ibid., 205–209.

70. NA, RG407, Box 5936, Combat Team 18's report, "Action against the Enemy in North African Operation," 19 November 1942, 2.

71. Ibid., 2.

72. Howe, *Northwest Africa*, 220–221, 224–225, and 220n24.

73. NA, RG407, Box 5936, CT18, Report after action, 19 November 1942, 3; 1st ID FO 2, 8 November 1942.

74. NA, RG407, Box 5908, CT16, Report after action, 21 November 1942, 1.

75. Ibid.

76. NA, RG407, Box 5883, 7th Field Artillery Report after action, 18 November 1942, 2.

77. Howe, *Northwest Africa*, 48–49.

78. Ibid., 209–212.

79. NA, Old RG319, 1st ID G3 Log, 9 November 1942.

80. NA, RG407, Box 5936, S1 Log of CT18, Entry 76, 9 November 1942.

81. NA, RG407, 1st ID FO 4, 9 November 1942, paragraph 4.

82. Bland et al., *The Papers of George Catlett Marshall*, 3:609–610.

83. NA, RG407, Box 5908, CT16, Report after action, 21 November 1942, 2–3; 1st Division G3 Journal, 10 November 1942, Entry 49.

84. NA, RG407, Box 5936, CT18 AAR, 19 November 1942, 2–3; ibid., Box 5885, 32nd Field Artillery Battle Report, 23 November 1942, 2.

85. Howe, *Northwest Africa*, 223.

86. Ibid., 224–225; NA, RG319, 1st ID Rear CP Journal, 10 November 1942, Sequence of Events, CT26.

87. Ibid., 223–224.

88. NA, RG407, Box 5936, CT, AAR, 19 November 1942; ibid., Box 5908, CT16, AAR, 21 November 1942; Kelly, *History of the 26th Infantry*, I:5.

89. Howe, *Northwest Africa*, 224.

90. NA, RG407, Box 5908, CT16, AAR; Box 5936, CT18 AAR; Box 5964, CT26, AAR; Box 5879, 5th FA, AAR; Box 5883, 7th FA, AAR; Box 5885, 32nd FA, AAR; Box 5899, 33rd FA, AAR; Box 5966, 1st Medical Battalion AAR, 20 November 1942.

6. Tunisia: The Division Comes of Age

1. G. Howe, *Northwest Africa*, 277–279.

2. Ibid., 278–279.

3. Ibid., 279–280.

4. Ibid.

5. Ibid., 255–260.

6. MRC, Dawson Letter, 26 November 1942.

7. Ibid., 283–288.

8. NA, RG407, Box 5879, 5th FA AAR, 13 November 1942–18 January 1943, 1; Atkinson, *An Army at Dawn*, 167–168; 1st ID, G3 Log, 17 November 1942, noting the initial alert for the move of 5th FA; ibid., Central Task Force order to move 5th FA, 19 November 1942.

9. Howe, *Northwest Africa*, 298–305.

10. NA, RG407, Box 5879, 5th FA AAR, 13 November 1942–18 January 1943, 1–2.

11. Ibid., 2.

12. Ibid.

13. Ibid., 3.

14. Howe, *Northwest Africa*, 304–309.

15. 1st ID G3 Report, 20 November 1942, attached to G3 Log for 20 November 1942.

16. Kelly, *History of the 26th Infantry*, 5:1.

17. 1st ID G3 Logs and Reports for 23, 27, 28, and 29 November 1942.

18. Kelly, *History of the 26th Infantry*, Part 5.

19. 1st ID G3 Log, reports and log entries for 7 and 8 December 1942.

20. NA, RG407, Box 5885, 32 FA AAR for 18 December 1942–8 April 1943, 30 April 1943; Heidenheimer, *Vanguard to Victory*, 20.

21. NA, RG407, Box 5936, 18th Infantry AAR of Engagement of 1/18th, 23–25 December 1942; Howe, *Northwest Africa*, 336–337.

22. Howe, *Northwest Africa*, 341.

23. Ibid., 338–344; NA, RG407, Box 5936, Engagement of 1st Battalion, 18th Infantry, 1–3; Atkinson, *An Army at Dawn*, 241–245, 253–255.

24. NA, RG407, Box 5936, Engagement of 1st Battalion, 18th Infantry, 2.

25. Atkinson, *An Army at Dawn*, 254; NA, RG407, Box 5885, 32nd FA AAR, 30 April 1943, entry for 25 December 1942.

26. NA, RG407, Box 5936, Engagement of 1st Battalion, 18th Infantry, 3; Howe, *Northwest Africa*, 342–343; Atkinson, *An Army at Dawn*, 255.

27. NA, RG407, Box 5662, 1st ID Summary of Activities, 8 March 1943.

28. Howe, *Northwest Africa*, 377.

29. Ibid., 377–378.

30. Ibid., 378–380.

31. Kelly, *History of the 26th Infantry*, 6:1–4.

32. Howe, *Northwest Africa*, 379–380.

33. Ibid., 380.

34. NA, RG407, Box 5899, 33rd FA AAR, 1 March 1943; Kelly, *History of the 26th Infantry*, 6:10–12.

35. Ibid., 6:14.

36. NA, RG407, Box 5899, 33rd FA AAR, 1 March 1943; *History of the 26th Infantry*, 6:14–19.

37. Clay, *Blood and Sacrifice*, 158–160; NA, RG319, Box 75, 1st ID G3 Log, Entry 13, 3 February 1943.

38. NA, RG319, Box 74, 1st ID G3 Log, Daily Situation Report, 29 January 1943; 1st ID FO 11, 30 January 1943; NA, RG407, Box 5662, 1st ID Summary of Activities, 8 March 1943.

39. NA, RG407, Box 5662, 1st ID Summary, 8 March 1943, 2.

40. NA, RG319, Box 74, 1st ID G3 Report, 2 February 1943; NA, RG407, Box 5662, Allen to Marshall, 10 March 1943. Allen updated the Chief of Staff.

41. NA, RG319, Box 75, 1st ID Memorandum, 2 February 1943, in G3 Log.

42. Ibid., 1st ID G3 Log, Allen to Fredendall, 4 February 1943, in 1st ID G3 Log.

43. Ibid., 1st ID G3 Log, message to the Commanding General, XIX Corps, 9 February 1943, 1st ID G3 Log, 9 February 1943.

44. MRC, Dawson Letter, 15 February 1943.

45. NA, RG319, Box 75, 1st ID G3 Log, letters from Allen to Karl Spaatz, General Koeltz, and General Anderson, 13 February 1943.

46. NA, RG407, 1st ID G3 Summary of Operations, 8 March 1943, 2.

47. Ibid., 2–3.

48. Howe, *Northwest Africa*, 390–392.

49. Kelly, *History of the 26th Infantry*, 7:1–4.

50. Ibid., 4; Howe, *Northwest Africa*, 390–392; The quote is from Atkinson, *An Army at Dawn*, 308.

51. Kelly, *History of the 26th Infantry*, 7:5–10; Howe, *Northwest Africa*, 245–248.

52. Howe, *Northwest Africa*, 403–405; M. Blumenson, "Kasserine," in *America's First Battles, 1776–1965* (Lawrence, KS, 1986), 245–248.

53. Howe, *Northwest Africa*, 410–413.

54. Atkinson, *An Army at Dawn*, 345.

55. Blumenson, "Kasserine," 248.

56. Ibid., 250–251; Howe, *Northwest Africa*, 419–422; Atkinson, *An Army at Dawn*, 350–353.

57. Blumenson, "Kasserine," 251–252; Atkinson, *An Army at Dawn*, 339–347.

58. Kelly, *History of the 26th Infantry*, 8:1–3.

59. Ibid., 8:15.

60. Atkinson, *An Army at Dawn*, 363–366; Howe, *Northwest Africa*, 433–437; NA, RG407, Box 5936, 18th Infantry AAR, 16 February–9 March 1943.

61. Kelly, *History of the 26th Infantry*, 8:14; NA, RG407, Box 5899, 33rd FA AAR, 1 March 1943, 11.

62. Atkinson, *An Army at Dawn*, 368.

63. NA, RG407, Box 5899, 33rd FA AAR, 1 March 1943, 11; Kelly, *History of the 26th Infantry*, 8:16–17.

64. Howe, *Northwest Africa*, 449–450.

65. NA, RG407, Box 5899, 33rd FA AAR, 1 March 1943, 11–12.

66. Ibid., 12.

67. Ibid.

68. Kelly, *History of the 26th Infantry*, 8:25.

69. Ibid., 8:25–28.

70. NA, Old RG319, Reel 75, 1st ID FO 13, 19 February 1943, and XIX Corps General Order 10, 19 February 1943; NA, RG407, Box 5662, Summary of Activities of 1st ID, 8 March 1943.

71. Clay, *Blood and Sacrifice*, 160–162.

72. Ibid., 160–162; NA, RG407, Box 5883, 7th FA AAR, 5 March 1943, 1–2; ibid., Box 5899, 33rd FA AAR, 1 March 1943, 14–15.

73. NA, RG407, Box 5662, Allen to Marshall, 10 March 1943, and the enclosed Summary of Activities of the 1st ID, 8 March 1943, 3.

74. Ibid.

75. Howe, *Northwest Africa*, 473–475.

76. Ibid., 477–477.

77. NA, RG407, Box 5662, Summary of Activities of the 1st ID, 8 March 1943, 4.

78. Howe, *Northwest Africa*, 477.

79. NA, RG407, Box 5662, Allen's memorandum to "All units in the 1st Infantry Division," 4 March 1943.

80. Kelly, *History of the 26th Infantry*, 9:12.

81. Quoted in Astor, *Terrible Terry Allen*, 156.

82. Howe, *Northwest Africa*, 487–488, 543–547; Atkinson, *An Army at Dawn*, 401–405.

83. M. Blumenson, *Patton* (New York, 1985), 183–185.

84. Howe, *Northwest Africa*, 501–509.

85. Kelly, *History of the 26th Infantry*, 8:4–6.

7. Offensive Operations: Gafsa to Victory in Africa

1. Kelly, *History of the 26th Infantry*, 9:15, Memorandum of the 26th Infantry, 14 March 1943.

2. Ibid., 9:8–9; NA, RG407, Box 5883, 7th FA AAR, 12 April 1943.

3. G. Howe, *Northwest Africa*, 543–546.

4. Ibid., 547–548; A. Towne, *Doctor Danger Forward: A World War II Memoir of a Combat Medical Aidman, First Infantry Division* (Jefferson, NC, 2000), 64–66.

5. NA, Old RG319, 1st ID G3 Log, microfilm, reel 76, 17 March 1943.

6. Ibid., memo from Allen to Darby, 17 March 1943.

7. Ibid., 18 March 1943, entry 14, and accompanying map overlay.

8. Kelly, *History of the 26th Infantry*, 9:31.

9. Howe, *Northwest Africa*, 530–534; R. Atkinson, *An Army at Dawn*, 417–425.

10. NA, Old RG319, 1st ID G3 Log, 20 March 1943, entry 28, and attached letter from Patton to Allen, 20 March 1943.

11. Howe, *Northwest Africa*, 550–552.

12. Mason, "Reminiscences," 50–51.

13. Ibid., 51.

14. NA, Old RG319, 1st ID G3 Log, 20 March 1943, entries 6 and 24.

15. NA, RG407, Box 5899, 33rd FA AAR, 10 April 1943, 1.

16. NA, Old RG319, 1st ID G3 Log, 21 March 1943, entries 33–43.

17. Ibid., 21 March 1943, entries 2, 8, 13, 18, 22, 26, 39.

18. Ibid., entries 33–43.

19. Kelly, *History of the 26th Infantry*, 9:46.

20. NA, Old RG319, 1st ID G3 Log, 21 March 1943; NA, RG407, Box 5885, 32nd FA AAR, 20 April 1943, 2.

21. Howe, *Northwest Africa*, 558–560.

22. NA, RG407, Box 5899, 33rd FA AAR, 10 April 1943, 1; NA, Old RG319, 1st ID G3 Log, 22 March 1943, entries 13, 28, 34, 64, 67, 77.

23. NA, Old RG319, 1st ID G3 Log, 22 March 1943, entries 17, 20, 36, 53, 61–63, 70.

24. Ibid., entry 58, at 1710 hours.

25. Ibid., entries 46, 72, 73.

26. NA, RG407, Box 5879, 5th FA AAR, 14 April 1943, 1–2.

27. NA, Old RG319, 1st ID G3 Log, 23 March 1943, entries 18, 21, 23, 24, 27, 35.

28. NA, RG407, Box 5883, 7th FA AAR, 12 April 1943, 1; ibid., Box 5899, 33rd FA AAR, 10 April 1943, 1.

29. Quoted in Atkinson, *An Army at Dawn*, 440.

30. Howe, *Northwest Africa*, 562.

31. Quoted in Atkinson, *An Army at Dawn*, 442.

32. NA, Old RG319, 1st ID G3 Log, 23 March 1943, entries 95–104.

33. MRC, Joe Dawson Letter, 26 March 1943.

34. NA, RG407, Box 5885, 32nd FA AAR, 20 April 1943, 2; ibid., Box 5883, 7th FA AAR, 12 April 1943, 1–2; ibid., Box 5899, 33rd FA AAR, 10 April 1943, 1–2.

35. Howe, *Northwest Africa*, 564–565.

36. NA, Old RG319, 1st ID G3 Log, 28 March 1943, entry 36.

37. Ibid., entries 56–60.

38. Howe, *Northwest Africa*, 567–568; Atkinson, *An Army at Dawn*, 453–457.

39. Kelly, *History of the 26th Infantry*, 9:67–75.

40. Ibid., 66–67.

41. NA, RG407, Box 5899, 33rd FA AAR, 10 April 1943, 2.

42. Quoted in Atkinson, *An Army at Dawn*, 461. The soldiers' psychological hardening to the process of killing is a major theme in Atkinson's book.

43. NA, Old RG319, 1st ID G3 Log, 29 March 1943, entries 2, 8, 9, 23, 30, 31.

44. Ibid., entry 54; G3 Periodic Report, 29 March 1943.

45. Howe, *Northwest Africa*, 569–570.

46. Ibid., 574, nn. 34 and 36; NA, Old RG319, 1st ID G3 Log, 1–2 April 1943; G3 Periodic Report, 2 April 1943.

47. NA, Old RG319, 1st ID G3 Log, 7 April 1943, entries 11–22.

48. Letter, Patton to Allen, 8 April 1943, quoted in Kelly, *History of the 26th Infantry*, 9:98.

49. A division order, 9 April 1943, in NA, Old RG319, 1st ID G3 Log, 9 April 1943.

50. Kelly, *History of the 26th Infantry*, 10:5.

51. Howe, *Northwest Africa*, 599–600.

52. Ibid., 609.

53. Ibid., 611–613.

54. Ibid., 613–614, 618–619.

55. Ibid., 621–623.

56. NA, Old RG319, 1st ID G3 Log, 23 April 1943, entries 13, 16, 24, 39, 36, and 53; Kelly, *History of the 26th Infantry*, 10:29–37.

57. NA, RG407, Box 5899, 33rd FA AAR, 18 May 1943, 1; ibid., Box 5879, 5th FA AAR, 22 May 1943, 1. The 5th FA fired 1,900 rounds against Hill 575 on 23 April.

58. Kelly, *History of the 26th Infantry*, 10:38.

59. NA, Old RG319, 1st ID G3 Log, 23 April 1943, entries 19, 28, 33, 37, 65, and 74.

60. Clay, *Blood and Sacrifice*, 27.

61. NA, Old RG319, 1st ID G3 Log, 23 April 1943, entries 15, 20, 27, 48–50; NA, RG407, Box 5937, personal account of LTC Ben Sternberg, n.d., 3; Heidenheimer, *Vanguard to Victory*, 51–52.

62. Howe, *Northwest Africa*, 623; Heidenheimer, *Vanguard to Victory*, 49–53.

63. NA, RG319, 1st ID G3 Log, 23 April 1943, entries 20, 27, 33, 36, 39, and 42.

64. Ibid., entry 2; ibid., 25 April 1943, entries 7, 18, 26, 68; ibid., 26 April 1943, entries 17, 35; NA, RG407, Box 5937, Record of Events of 1st Battalion, 18th Infantry, 21 April–8 May 1943, n.d., 1–2; Heidenheimer, *Vanguard to Victory*, 53–55.

65. Kelly, *History of the 26th Infantry*, 10:38–40.

66. NA, Old RG319, 1st ID G3 Log, 25 April 1943, entries 20 and 28; ibid., 25 April 1943, listing Taylor's call to Colonel Mason requesting additional litter bearers at 0430.

67. NA, RG407, Box 5937, Change Two to 1st ID FO 22, 25 April 1943; Howe, *Northwest Africa*, 625–626.

68. NA, RG407, Box 5937, Change Two to 1st ID FO 22, 27 April 1943; Howe, *Northwest Africa*, 628–631.

69. NA, Old RG319, 1st ID G3 Log, 28 April 1943, entries 3, 8, 11, 12, 13.

70. Ibid.; Howe, *Northwest Africa*, 632–634.

71. Howe, *Northwest Africa*, 632–635.

72. NA, Old RG319, 1st ID G3 Log, 30 April 1943, entries 3, 4, and 9.

73. Ibid., entries 40, 41, 48, 49.

74. Ibid., entries 50, 51, 54, 56, 58, 62, 73, and quote from 80.

75. NA, RG407, Box 5899, 33rd FA AAR, 18 May 1943, 2; Howe, *Northwest Africa*, 634–636.

76. NA, Old RG319, 1st ID G3 Log, 30 April 1943, entry 45.

77. Howe, *Northwest Africa*, 638–641.

78. NA, Old RG319, 1st ID G3 Log, 1–3 May 1943.

79. Ibid., 3 May 1943, entries 46, 51, 52,

80. Ibid., 5 May 1943, entry 49; ibid., 6 May 1943, entry 8; MRC, Mason, "Reminiscences," 148.

81. NA, RG407, Box 5937, 18th Infantry AAR for 21 April–8 May 1943.

82. Ibid., 6 May 1943, entries 2, 3, 12, 21, 22, 24.

83. Ibid., entry 32.

84. NA, RG407, Box 5899, 33rd FA AAR, 18 May 1943, 2.

85. NA, Old RG319, 1st ID G3 Log, 6 May 1943, 35–37.

86. Ibid., entries 71, 75.

87. Ibid., entry 79.

88. Ibid., entries 90–95.

89. Ibid., 7 May 1943, entry 2.

90. O. Bradley and C. Blair, *A General's Life* (New York, 1983), 158.

91. Quoted in Atkinson, *An Army at Dawn*, 520.

92. A. Chandler et al., eds., *The Papers of Dwight David Eisenhower: The War Years* (Baltimore, MD, 1970), 2:1090–1092, Eisenhower to Marshall, 16 April 1943.

93. Ibid., 2:1093–1094, Eisenhower to Bradley, 16 April 1943.

94. Ibid., 2:1104–1105, Eisenhower to Marshall, 30 April 1943.

95. Ibid., for example.

96. Bradley and Blair, *A General's Life*, 172–173.

97. MHI, WWII, Veterans' Surveys, LTC Donald V. Helgeson, 1st Battalion, 26th Infantry.

98. Atkinson, *An Army at Dawn*, 515–516.

99. Chandler et al., *Eisenhower Papers*, 2:1154–1156, Eisenhower to Marshall, 25 May 1943; ibid., 2:1159–11560, Eisenhower to Private Frank Sargent, 27 May 1943.

8. The Invasion of Sicily

1. A. Garland and H. Smyth, *Sicily and the Surrender of Italy* (Washington, DC, 2002), 1–10; Bland et al., *The Papers of George Catlett Marshall*, 3: 513–517; D. Porch, *The Path to Victory: The Mediterranean Theater in World War II* (New York, 2004), 3–29.

2. Towne, *Doctor Danger Forward*, 101–103; A. Heidenheimer, *Vanguard to Victory: History of the 18th Infantry Regiment* (Aschaffenburg, Germany, 1954), 57–58; Kelly, *History of the 26th Infantry*, 13:12.

3. Garland and Smyth, *Sicily*, 88–101.

4. NA, Old RG319, 1st ID G3 Log, 9 July 1943, entry 3; Garland and Smyth, *Sicily*, 111, 136–139.

5. MRC, Dawson Letter, 9 July 1943.

6. NA, RG407, 1st ID Report of Operation Husky, 3 September 1943, 4–5; Garland and Smyth, *Sicily*, 105–107.

7. NA, RG407, Box 5936, 1st ID FO 26, 20 June 1943.

8. MRC, Dawson Letter, 13 July 1943.

9. Kelly, *History of the 26th Infantry*, 13:1–13.

10. Garland and Smyth, *Sicily*, 136–139, 150–155.

11. NA, RG319, 1st Division G3 Log, 10 July 1943, Entry 17, microfilm of RG319; NA, RG407, Box 5909, 16th Regiment AAR, 18 August 1943, 2.

12. NA, RG319, 1st Division G3 Log, 10 July 1943, entries 21 and 23; NA, RG407, Box 5909, 16th Infantry AAR, 18 August 1943; Garland and Smyth, *Sicily*, 154.

13. NA, RG407, Box 5937, 18th Infantry AAR for the month of July 1943; Heidenheimer, *Vanguard to Victory*, 62–63.

14. Garland and Smyth, *Sicily*, 136–139, 163–165.

15. Kelly, *History of the 26th Infantry*, 13:17–20.

16. Ibid., 13:21.

17. Ibid., 13:21–24.

18. Garland and Smyth, *Sicily*, 170.

19. NA, RG319, 1st Division G3 Log, 11 July 1943, entries 13, 19; NA, RG407, Box 5909, 16th Infantry AAR, 18 August 1943, 5.

20. NA, RG319, 1st Division G3 Log, 11 July 1943, entries 13, 19.

21. Garland and Smyth, *Sicily*, 170.

22. Heidenheimer, *Vanguard to Victory*, 63.

23. Garland and Smyth, *Sicily*, 171, n. 21.

24. Ibid., 167, n. 12.

25. NA, RG319, 1st Division G3 Log, 10 July 1943, entries 24 and 25; 1st Division G3 Log, 11 July 1943, entry 30.

26. Garland and Smyth, *Sicily*, 175–181.

27. Ibid., 181–182.

28. C. D'Este, *Eisenhower: A Soldier's Life* (New York, 2002), 433.

29. Garland and Smyth, *Sicily*, 206–208.

30. NA, RG319, 1st Division G3 Log, 12 July 1943, entries 9, 14, 15, 18, 20.

31. Ibid., entries 12, 17, 24.

32. NA, RG407, Box 5937, 18th Infantry AAR for July 1943, no date, 2.

33. Garland and Smyth, *Sicily*, 210–216.

34. Kelly, *History of the 26th Infantry*, 13:36–37.

35. NA, RG319, 1st Division G3 Log, 14 July 1943, entries 35, 38, 47, 56, 58, 61; NA, RG407, Box 5937, 18th Infantry AAR for July 1943, no date, 2.

36. NA, RG319, 1st Division G3 Logs, 15 and 16 July 1943.

37. Kelly, *History of the 26th Infantry*, 13:42–43; NA, RG319, 1st Division G3 Log, 16 July 1943, entries 2, 15, 17.

38. NA, RG319, 1st Division G3 Log, 16 July 1943, entry 25.

39. Ibid., entry 36, 51; Kelly, *History of the 26th Infantry*, 13:43–47.

40. Kelly, *History of the 26th Infantry*, 13:45.

41. Ibid., 47–49; NA, RG319, 1st Division G3 Log, 16 July 1943, entries 58, 61, 62, 77, 79, 82.

42. NA, RG407, Box 5909, 16th Infantry AAR, 18 August 1943, 6; Garland and Smyth, *Sicily*, 232.

43. Garland and Smyth, *Sicily*, 233–234.

44. Ibid., 244–248.

45. NA, RG319, 1st Division G3 Log, 18 July 1943, entries 4, 7, 8, 11, 14, 27, 30; NA, RG407, Box 5909, 16th Infantry AAR, 18 August 1943, 7.

46. NA, RG319, 1st Division G3 Log, 18 July 1943.

47. Ibid., 19 July 1943, entries 24, 27, 39, 63; ibid., 20 July 1943, entries 2, 7; NA, RG407, Box 5937, 18th Infantry AAR for July 1943, no date, 3.

48. NA, RG407, Box 5909, 16th Infantry AAR, 18 August 1943, 7.

49. NA, RG319, 1st Division G3 Log, 21 July 1943, entries 6, 7, 11, 12, 29, 30; Kelly, *History of the 26th Infantry*, 13:58–59.

50. Kelly, *History of the 26th Infantry*, 13:59; NA, RG319, 1st Division G3 Log, 21 July 1943, entries 34, 42.

51. NA, RG319, 1st Division G3 Log, 21 July 1943, entry 49.

52. Ibid., 22 July 1943, entries 4, 6, 10, 18, 21, 23, 26, 32, 59, 60, 61, 68.

53. Ibid., 22 July 1943, entry 32.

54. Kelly, *History of the 26th Infantry*, 13:62–64.

55. Garland and Smyth, *Sicily*, 308–310.

56. NA, RG407, Box 5909, 16th Infantry AAR, 18 August 1943, 7–8; ibid., Box 5937, 18th Infantry Operations in July, no date, 3; ibid., Box 5879, 5th FA AAR, 15 August 1943, 2; ibid., Box 5883, 12 August 1943, 2; ibid., Box 5885, 32nd FA AAR, 12 August 1943, 4.

57. MRC, Dawson Letter, 23 July 1943.

58. Kelly, *History of the 26th Infantry*, 13:67–69; 1st Division G3 Log, 24 July 1943, entries 49, 58, 59, 67.

59. Kelly, *History of the 26th Infantry*, 13:70–71; NA, RG319, 1st Division G3 Log, 25 July 1943, entries 19, 23, 26.

60. Kelly, *History of the 26th Infantry*, 13:69–70; NA, RG319, 1st Division G3 Logs, 24 and 25 July 1943; NA, RG407, Box 5937, 18th Infantry Operations in July, no date, 3–4.

61. MRC, Dawson Letter, 30 July 1943.

62. NA, RG319, 1st Division G3 Log, 27 July 1943, entries 47, 48, 49, 53.

63. Ibid., entries 15, 23, 37; Kelly, *History of the 26th Infantry*, 13:80–82.

64. NA, RG407, Box 5909, 16th Infantry AAR, 18 August 1943, 7–8a.

65. NA, RG319, 1st Division G3 Log, 29 July 1943, entries 2, 6, 11.

66. NA, RG407, Box 5937, 18th Infantry Operations, July 1943, no date, 3–4.

67. Garland and Smyth, *Sicily*, 319–320.

68. MRC, Mason, "Reminiscences," 181.

69. Ibid., 329–332; NA, RG319, 1st Division G3 Log, 31 July 1943, entries 3, 9, 14, 19, 24.

70. NA, RG319, 1st Division G3 Log, 30 July 1943, entries 35, 73; ibid., 31 July 1943, entries 2, 5, 12, 18, 19.

71. Ibid., 1st Division G3 Log, 31 July 1943, entries 24, 28, 31, 32, 40, 45, 54.

72. Ibid., 1 August 1943, entries 9, 13, 31, 37, 56, 75, 76, 77; Garland and Smyth, *Sicily*, 337.

73. Garland and Smyth, *Sicily*, 336.

74. NA, RG319, 1st Division G3 Log, 2 August 1943, entries 5, 6, 8, 27, 43, 48.

75. Ibid., entry 27.

76. Garland and Smyth, *Sicily*, 339–340; NA, RG319, 1st Division G3 Log, 3 August 1943, entries 12, 22, 26, 57.

77. Baumgartner, ed., *The Sixteenth Infantry Regiment*, 58–59; Clay, *Blood and Sacrifice*, 177–178.

78. NA, RG319, 1st Division G3 Log, 3 August 1943; Kelly, *The History of the 26th Infantry*, 13:102–103; Baumgartner, *Sixteenth Infantry Regiment*, 59–60.

79. Garland and Smyth, *Sicily*, 341–342.

80. NA, RG319, 1st Division G3 Log, 4 August 1943, entries 6, 12, 17, 27.

81. Ibid., entries 8, 10, 11.

82. Ibid., entries 11, 18.

83. Ibid., entry 24; Baumgartner, *Sixteenth Infantry Regiment*, 61–62.

84. NA, RG407, Box 5938, 18th Infantry report for August 1943, 4 September 1943, 1.

85. NA, RG319, 1st Division G3 Log, 4 August 1943, entry 32.

86. Ibid., entry 53; ibid., 5 August 1943, entry 3.

87. Garland and Smyth, *Sicily*, 344–345.

88. Ibid., 343.

89. NA, RG319, 1st ID G3 Log, 5 August 1943, entries 15, 17, 22, 38.

90. Ibid., entry 25.

91. Ibid., 6 August 1943, entries 4, 6, 7, 10, 12, 14.

92. MRC, Mason, "Reminiscences," 182–184; Garland and Smyth, *Sicily,* 347.

93. MRC, Joe Dawson Letter, 6 August 1943.

94. Heidenheimer, *Vanguard to Victory*, 70–71; Garland and Smyth, *Sicily,* 379–387, 408–416.

9. Operation Overlord

1. M. Matloff, *Strategic Planning for Coalition Warfare, 1943–1944* (Washington, DC, 1959; 1994 edition).

2. Ibid., 227–234.

3. MRC, Dawson Letter, 22 August 1943.

4. MRC, S. Mason (Major General Retired), "Reminiscences and Anecdotes of World War II," typescript prepared in Birmingham, AL, 1968, 185.

5. Kelly, *History of the 26th Infantry*, 13:147, John Corley to MG Huebner, 10 August 1943.

6. Ibid., 148–149, Major J. W. Henderson to Colonel John Corley, 10 August 1943.

7. MHI, Army Ground Forces Report, 24 September 1943, "Subject: Observations on an infantry regiment in combat," 3.

8. NA, RG407, Box 5938, 18th Infantry AAR, 4 September 1943, 2; Heidenheimer, *Vanguard to Victory*, 72–73; Baumgartner, ed., *The Sixteenth Infantry Regiment*, 65–66; Kelly, *History of the 26th Infantry,* 125–152.

9. MRC, Mason, "Reminiscences," 190–199.

10. NA, RG407, Box 5966, 1st Medical Battalion AARs, August–October 1943.

11. MRC, Mason, "Reminiscences," 200.

12. NA, RG407, Box 5966, Embarkation Memorandum 3, 14 October 1943.

13. NA, RG407, Box 5938, 18th Infantry AARs for October and November 1943.

14. Ibid.; Baumgartner, *The Sixteenth Infantry Regiment*, 68.

15. MHI, WW II Veterans' Surveys, Lieutenant Jean Peltier, Battery A, 33rd Field Artillery.

16. Clay, *Blood and Sacrifice*, 179.

17. NA, RG407, Box 5938, 18th Infantry for November and December 1943.

18. NA, RG407, Box 5885, 32 FA AAR, 4 September 1943, Annex 1.

19. Clay, *Blood and Sacrifice,* 179; Heidenheimer, *Vanguard to Victory,* 73.

20. Heidenheimer, *Vanguard to Victory,* 73; Clay, *Blood and Sacrifice,* 179–180.

21. NA, RG407, Box 5938, 18th Infantry AAR for February 1944, 2;

G. Harrison, *Cross-Channel Attack* (Washington, DC, 1993), 162–164; Clay, *Blood and Sacrifice,* 179–180; Heidenheimer, *Vanguard to Victory,* 73. Harrison thought that only the 16th Infantry had trained at the center, but Heidenheimer notes that the 18th Infantry also trained there, and the 18th Infantry's AAR confirms this.

22. Clay, *Blood and Sacrifice,* 180.

23. NA, RG407, Box 5664, V Corps Operations Order L-44, for Operation Fox, 3 March 1944.

24. Ibid., 270–279, 352–369, 378–387; Harrison, *Cross-Channel Attack,* 114–127, 158; C. D'Este, *Eisenhower,* 466–467.

25. FDR, quoted in James Roosevelt, *My Parents: A Differing View* (Chicago, 1976), 176, quoted in D'Este, *Eisenhower,* 467.

26. Harrison, *Cross-Channel Attack,* 46–82.

27. Ibid., 114–118.

28. V Corps Historians' Office Files, Heidelberg, Germany, V Corps Operations Plan Neptune, 26 March 1944; D. Hogan, *A Command Post at War: First Army Headquarters in Europe, 1943–1945* (Washington, DC, 2000), 51–68.

29. C. Kirkpatrick, *V Corps Order of Battle, 1918–2002* (Heidelberg, Germany, 2002), 72–73; V Corps Operations Plan Neptune; MHI, The Provisional Engineer Brigade Group, "Operation Report Neptune" (London, 30 September 1944), 57–58.

30. Harrison, *Cross-Channel Attack,* 308–309.

31. MHI, The Provisional Engineer Brigade Group, "Operation Report Neptune" (London, 30 September 1944), 58–70.

32. Harrison, *Cross-Channel Attack,* 254–267.

33. NA, RG407, Box 5938, 18th Infantry AAR, 4 March 1944; C. Jones, "Neptune: Training for and Mounting the Operation, and the Artificial Ports," Part VI of *The Administrative and Logistical History of the E. T. O.* (Paris, 1946), 23–24; Harrison, *Cross-Channel Attack,* 191–192.

34. Harrison, *Cross-Channel Attack,* 192–193; Kirkpatrick, *V Corps Order of Battle,* 72–73.

35. Harrison, *Cross-Channel Attack,* 192, 309–314.

36. Baumgartner, *The Sixteenth Infantry Regiment,* 68–69.

37. MRC, Dawson Letter, 1 May 1943.

38. MHI, Lieutenant Colonel Derrill Daniel, "Landings at Oran, Gela, and Omaha Beaches: An Infantry Battalion Commander's Observations," Infantry School Paper, 1950, 21–22.

39. Harrison, *Cross-Channel Attack,* 270, n. 4; Clay, *Blood and Sacrifice,* 180; Kirkpatrick, *V Corps Order of Battle,* 72–73.

40. NA, RG407, Box 5910, 16th Infantry AAR, 9 July 1944; ibid., Box 5938, 18th Infantry AAR, 30 June 1944; ibid., Box 5944, 26th Infantry AAR, 7 August 1944; Clay, *Blood and Sacrifice,* 180; Heidenheimer, *Vanguard to Victory,* 73.

41. Harrison, *Cross-Channel Attack,* 188–190, 320–321.

42. D'Este, *Eisenhower,* 519–525.

43. Daniel, "Landings at Oran, Gela, and Omaha Beaches," 25, for the quote; Clay, *Blood and Sacrifice,* 184.

44. D'Este, *Eisenhower,* 496–499, 512–514. Eisenhower had to fight tooth and nail to force the United States Army Air Forces to conduct the operation known as the Transportation Plan. It was one of his most important contributions to the

victory in Normandy. In the process of crippling the German communications, the air forces lost 2,000 aircraft and 12,000 air crewmen killed from 1 April to 5 June 1944. The air forces also broke the back of the German fighter force; Harrison, *Cross-Channel Attack*, 300–301.

45. Harrison, *Cross-Channel Attack*, 278, 332–335.

46. Ibid., 301–302.

47. Ibid., 313–315.

48. S. Ambrose, *D-Day, June 6, 1944: The Climactic Battle of World War II* (New York, 1994), 323–331.

49. Ibid., 331.

50. Ibid.

51. Harrison, *Cross-Channel Attack*, 315.

52. NA, RG407, 16th Infantry AAR, 9 July 1944, 1.

53. Harrison, *Cross-Channel Attack*, 315.

54. NA, RG407, 16th Infantry AAR, 9 July 1944, 1.

55. "Operation Report Neptune," 86–95; Clay, *Blood and Sacrifice*, 187.

56. Harrison, *Cross-Channel Attack*, 316–317.

57. Ibid., 317–318.

58. Ibid., Ambrose, *D-Day*, 337–342.

59. Ambrose, *D-Day*, 339–340; Harrison, *Cross-Channel Attack*, 318–344.

60. NA, RG407, 16th Infantry AAR, 9 July 1944, 1.

61. Ambrose, *D-Day*, 355, quoting from an interview by Andy Rooney with Dawson, now in the Eisenhower Center.

62. MRC, Dawson Letter, 16 June 1944.

63. Baumgartner, *The Sixteenth Infantry Regiment*, 88–89.

64. Eisenhower Center, Interview with Lieutenant John Spaulding by M/Sgt F. C. Pogue and SSG J. M. Topete, 9 February 1945, 2–4; quote from Ambrose, *D-Day*, 351.

65. Baumgartner, *The Sixteenth Infantry Regiment*, 88–89.

66. Eisenhower Center, Spaulding interview with Pogue, 9 February 1945, 5.

67. NA, RG319, 1st Division G3 Report of Operations, 31 May–30 June 1944, 10.

68. Harrison, *Cross-Channel Attack*, 325; Baumgartner, *The Sixteenth Infantry Regiment*, 95–98.

69. Ambrose, *D-Day*, 356.

70. Harrison, *Cross-Channel Attack*, 320, n. 77.

71. Ibid., 322–327.

72. NA, RG407, Box 5910, 16th Infantry AAR, 9 July 1944, 1–2.

73. Ibid., 325–326.

74. 2nd Information and Historical Service, *Omaha Beach* (Washington, DC, 1945, 2001 edition), 97–98, 104–106.

75. NA, RG407, Box 5938, 18th Infantry AAR, 30 June 1944, 1–2; C. Kirkpatrick, *"It Will Be Done!" The Victory Corps, 1918–2002* (Heidelberg, Germany, 2002), 35.

76. NA, RG407, Box 5838, 18th Infantry AAR, 30 June 1944, 2; Kirkpatrick, *"It Will Be Done!"*, 35.

77. NA, RG407, Box 5883, 7th FA AAR, 1 July 1944, 1–2; for the organization of the artillery, see Annex 16 to the V Corps Operations Plan Neptune, paragraph 3.

78. Ibid., 2. Captain Woodward was recommended for the Distinguished Service Cross.

79. Ibid., 2.

80. Harrison, *Cross-Channel Attack,* 308–313.

81. NA, RG407, Box 5885, 32nd FA AAR, 1 July 1944, 1.

82. NA, RG407, Box 5900, 33rd FA AAR, 1 July 1944, 1; ibid., Box 5880, 5th FA AAR, Unit Journal for 6 and 7 June 1944.

83. Harrison, *Cross-Channel Attack,* 308–313.

84. Ibid., 328.

85. NA, RG407, Box 5938, 18th Infantry AAR, 30 June 1944, 2; Heidenheimer, *Vanguard to Victory,* 80–85.

86. NA, RG407, Box 5944, 26th Infantry AAR, 7 August 1944, 1; Harrison, *Cross-Channel Attack,* 328.

87. Harrison, *Cross-Channel Attack,* 329–330.

88. Ibid., 330n90; Kirkpatrick, *"It Will Be Done!",* 37.

89. NA, RG407, Box 5910, 16th Infantry AAR, and the attached Daily Casualty Reports for the period 6 June to 25 June 1944.

90. V Corps G1 Periodic Report 11, for the Period 6 to 10 June 1944, 1.

91. NA, RG407, Box 5966, 1st Medical Battalion AAR, 30 June 1944, 3.

92. G. Cosmas and A. Cowdry, *Medical Service in the European Theater of Operations* (Washington, DC, 1992), 210–213.

93. NA, RG407, Box 5910, 16th Infantry AAR, 7 August 1944, 1–4; Harrison, *Cross-Channel Attack,* 336.

94. 2nd Information and Historical Service, *Omaha Beach,* 114–115.

95. Harrison, *Cross-Channel Attack,* 332–335.

96. Ibid., 116.

97. NA, RG407, Box 5910, 16th Infantry AAR, 9 July 1944, 2; ibid., Box 5944, 26th Infantry AAR, 7 August 1944, 1; Society of the First Division, *History of the First Division,* 190–191; 2nd Information and Historical Service, *Omaha Beach,* 116–117.

98. Gorman, *Blue Spaders,* 55–56.

99. NA, RG407, Box 5938, 18th Infantry AAR, 30 June 1944, 2; 2nd Information and Historical Service, *Omaha Beach,* 117–118; Heidenheimer, *Vanguard to Victory,* 91–92.

100. 2nd Information and Historical Service, *Omaha Beach,* 122–127; Harrison, *Cross-Channel Attack,* 337–338.

101. Heidenheimer, *Vanguard to Victory,* 92–93; Harrison, *Cross-Channel Attack,* 368–369.

102. NA, RG407, Box 5944, 26th Infantry AAR, 9 August 1944, 2; ibid., Box 5900, 33rd FA AAR, 1 July 1944, 2; Gorman, *Blue Spaders,* 56–57; Harrison, *Cross-Channel Attack,* 339.

103. NA, RG407, Box 5944, 26th Infantry AAR, 9 August 1944, 2; Harrison, *Cross-Channel Attack,* 339–340; Gorman, *Blue Spaders,* 57–59.

104. NA, RG407, Box 5910, 16th Infantry AAR, 9 July 1944, which includes the daily strength reports of the regiment and attached units.

105. NA, RG407, Box 5938, 18th Infantry AAR, 30 June 1944, 2–3; ibid., Box 5944, 26th Infantry AAR, 9 August 1944, 2; ibid., Box 5885, 32nd FA AAR, 1 July 1944, 2; ibid., Box 5900, 33rd FA AAR, 1 July 1944, 1.

106. C. Kirkpatrick, *V Corps Remembers Its Heroes,* 18–19. Sergeant DeFranzo was awarded the Medal of Honor posthumously.

107. Ibid. By the end of June, five soldiers of the 1st Infantry Division had earned

the Medal of Honor: Carlton Barrett, Jimmie Monteith, and John Pinder, on 6 June; Walter Ehlers, on 9–10 June; and Arthur DeFranzo, on 10 June.

108. See ibid., for all units. Heidenheimer, *Vanguard to Victory*, 91–95; Gorman, *Blue Spaders*, 58–60.

109. C. D'Este, *Decision in Normandy* (Old Saybrook, CT, 1983; 1994 edition), 171–172.

110. NA, RG407, Box 5944, 26th Infantry AAR, 9 August 1944, 3; ibid., Box 5900, 33rd FA AAR, 1 July 1944, 2.

111. NA, RG407, Box 5938, 18th Infantry AAR, 30 June 1944, 3; Heidenheimer, *Vanguard to Victory*, 96.

112. NA, RG407, Box 5885, 32nd FA AAR, 1 July 1944, 2.

113. NA, RG407, Box 5944, 26th Infantry AAR, 9 August 1944, 3–4; ibid., Box 5938, 18th Infantry AAR, 30 June 1944, 3.

10. Crusade in Europe: The Drive to Germany

1. M. Blumenson, *Breakout and Pursuit* (Washington, DC, 2005), 10–13.

2. Ibid., 38.

3. MHI, WWII, Veterans' Surveys, 16th Infantry, Lieutenant William Dillon.

4. Heidenheimer, *Vanguard to Victory*, 97.

5. MHI, WWII, Veterans' Surveys, 18th Infantry, Sergeant Thomas McCann.

6. NA, RG407, Box 5938, 18th Infantry AAR, July 1944, 1.

7. Ibid., Box 5944, 26th Infantry AAR, 4 August 1944, 1.

8. MHI, WWII, Veterans' Surveys, 16th Infantry, Lieutenant William Dillon.

9. NA, RG407, Box 5966, 1st Medical Battalion AAR, June and July 1944.

10. MRC, Joe Dawson letter, 26 June 1944.

11. V Corps History Office, Heidelberg, G1 Log, 14 June 1944. The 16th and 116th Infantry Regiments, the 2nd and 5th Ranger Battalions, and the 741st and 743rd Tank Battalions were each to provide fifteen nominations for the DSC.

12. Society of the First Division, *Danger Forward* (Atlanta, 1947), 217–219.

13. A. Chandler et al., eds., *Eisenhower Papers, The War Years*, 3:1971–1972, Eisenhower to Marshall, 5 July 1944.

14. MRC, Papers of John A. Walker, 3rd Battalion, 16th Infantry, typescript of notes made by Walker in October 1944.

15. MRC, oral interview by author of Frank Murdoch, 7 April 2004.

16. V Corps History Office, G1 Papers, Memorandum of 29 June 1944; ibid., G1 Memorandum, 1 July 1944.

17. V Corps G1 Periodic Reports, 11 June to 8 July 1944.

18. V Corps History Office, G1 Papers, G1 Memorandum, 1 July 1944.

19. Ibid., Memorandum from Gerow to Huebner, 5 July 1944.

20. NA, RG407, Box 5910, 16th Infantry AAR, 9 July 1944.

21. V Corps History Office, G1 Papers, G1 Periodic Reports, 28 May to 8 July 1944.

22. Ibid., V Corps Memorandum, draft, August 1944.

23. Blumenson, *Breakout and Pursuit*, 55–77.

24. Ibid., 78–90.

25. Ibid., 90–118, 133–140.

26. A. Chandler et al., eds., *Eisenhower Papers, The War Years*, 3:1971, Eisenhower to Marshall, 5 July 1944.

27. Blumenson, *Breakout and Pursuit,* 175–176.

28. Ibid., 180–182.

29. Ibid., 185–187.

30. Ibid., 187.

31. Ibid., 215–217.

32. Ibid., 217–219.

33. NA, RG407, Box 5880, 1st Division Letter of Instruction, 13 July 1944.

34. NA, RG407, Box 5883, 7th FA AAR for July 1944; ibid., Box 5944, 26th Infantry AAR, 4 August 1944, 4; ibid., Box 5938, 18th Infantry AAR for July 1944.

35. NA, RG407, Box 5911, 16th Infantry AAR, 4 August 1944; Society of the First Division, *Danger Forward,* 413–414.

36. NA, RG407, Box 5944, 26th Infantry AAR, 4 August 1944, 4.

37. Bland et al., *The Papers of George Catlett Marshall,* 4:533–534, Marshall to the Army G1, 24 July 1944; ibid., 4:533 nn. 1 and 2.

38. 1st ID G3 Report of Operations for July 1944, 9–13; NA, RG407, Box 5880, 1st ID Movement Order 15, 19 July 1944; ibid., Box 5944, 26th Infantry AAR, 4 August 1944.

39. NA, RG407, Box 5880, 1st ID FO 38, 19 July 1944.

40. Blumenson, *Breakout and Pursuit,* 228–236.

41. Quoted in D'Este, *Decision in Normandy,* 402, and taken from a postwar interview.

42. Ibid., 238–241.

43. Ibid., 242–244; R. Weigley, *Eisenhower's Lieutenants* (Bloomington, IN, 1981; 1990 edition), 153–155.

44. MRC, 1st ID FO 39, 25 July 1944; 1st ID G3 Report of Operations for July 1944, 18; Blumenson, *Breakout and Pursuit,* 244–246; Weigley, *Eisenhower's Lieutenants,* 154–156.

45. Blumenson, *Breakout and Pursuit,* 251.

46. Heidenheimer, *Vanguard to Victory,* 106.

47. NA, RG407, Box 5938, 18th Infantry AAR for July 1944, 2; 1st ID WWII Combat Achievement Reports, Chapter 26, "The Rifle Company in Attack, The Battle of Marigny," 27 July 1944; 1st ID G3 Report of Operations, July 1944, 19–23; Heidenheimer, *Vanguard to Victory,* 106–108.

48. NA, RG407, Box 5911, 16th Infantry AAR, 4 August 1944, 3; Clay, *Blood and Sacrifice,* 206.

49. NA, RG407, Box 5880, 5th FA AAR, Unit Journal, 26–27 July 1944; ibid., Box 5883, 7th FA AAR for July 1944, 9–10; ibid., Box 5885, 32nd AAR, 1 August 1944, 4; ibid., Box 5900, 33rd FA AAR, July 1944, 12–13.

50. NA, RG407, Box 5944, 26th Infantry AAR, 4 August 1944, 6.

51. MRC, Colonel Walt Nechy, 3rd Battalion, 26th Infantry Regiment Journal, November 1942–May 1945, in Memory of BG John T. Corley, 53, entry for 28 July 1944.

52. Blumenson, *Breakout and Pursuit,* 260–263.

53. Ibid., 276–281.

54. NA, RG407, Box 5944, 26th Infantry AAR, 4 August 1944, 6; ibid., 3rd Battalion, 26th Infantry Journal, 54, entry for 30 July 1944; MRC, 1st Division G3 Report of Operations, 28–29, 29–30 July 1944.

55. Blumenson, *Breakout and Pursuit,* 305–308.

56. Ibid., 307–308; MRC, 1st ID G3 Report of Operations, 29, 30 July 1944.

57. MRC, 1st ID G3 Report of Operations, 29, 31 July 1944.

58. Blumenson, *Breakout and Pursuit*, 308–309; NA, RG407, Box 5911, 16th Infantry AAR, 4 August 1944, 3.

59. Blumenson, *Breakout and Pursuit*, 309.

60. Ibid., 309–322.

61. NA, RG407, Box 5966, 1st Medical Battalion AAR, 31 July 1944, app. B; ibid., 31 August 1944, app. B.

62. MRC, 1st ID G3 Report of Operations 32, 31 July 1944.

63. NA, RG407, Box 5938, 18th Infantry AAR for August 1944, 1; ibid., Box 5885, 32nd FA AAR, 3 September 1944, 1–2; ibid., Box 5944, 26th Infantry AAR, 5 September 1944, 2.

64. NA, RG407, Box 5938, 18th Infantry AAR for August 1944, 2; ibid., Box 5911, 16th Infantry AAR for August 1944, 2 September 1944, 2–3; ibid., Box 5944, 26th Infantry AAR, 5 September 1944, 6–7.

65. MRC, 3rd Battalion, 26th Infantry Journal, 56, entries for 12–14 August 1944.

66. NA, RG407, Box 5885, 32nd FA AAR, 3 September 1944, 2–3; ibid., Box 5938, 18th Infantry AAR, August 1944, 2.

67. MRC, 3rd Battalion, 26th Infantry Journal, 57–58, entries for 16–25 August 1944.

68. NA, RG407, Box 5900, 33rd FA AAR, 1 September 1944, 7; ibid., Box 5938, 18th Infantry AAR, August 1944, 2; ibid., Box 5944, 26th Infantry AAR, 5 September 1944, 6–8; ibid., Box 5911, 16th Infantry AAR, 2 September 1944, 2–3.

69. MRC, 3rd Battalion, 26th Infantry Journal, 58, entries for 28–30 August 1944.

70. Blumenson, *Breakout and Pursuit*, 553–558, 700.

71. NA, RG407, Box 5938, 18th Infantry AAR for August 1944, 2; MRC, 3rd Battalion, 26th Infantry Journal, 56–59, entries for late August 1944; Heidenheimer, *Vanguard to Victory*, 113–115.

72. MRC, 1st ID G3 Report of Operations for September 1944, 61–62; NA, RG407, Box 5938, 18th Infantry AAR for September 1944, 1; ibid., 3rd Battalion, 26th Infantry Journal, 58, entry for 1 September 1944.

73. NA, RG407, Box 5938, 18th Infantry AAR for September 1944, 1; ibid., Box 5911, 16th Infantry AAR, 3 October 1944, 1.

74. NA, RG407, Box 5955, 26th Infantry AAR, 30 September 1944, 2.

75. Ibid., 2–3; ibid., Box 5938, 18th Infantry AAR for September 1944, 1–2; ibid., Box 5911, 16th Infantry AAR, 3 October 1944, 1; MRC, 1st ID WWII Outstanding Combat Achievements, Chapter 29, "The Infantry Battalion in Offensive Action, 'Battle of Mons,'" 4 September 1944, 1–3.

76. Heidenheimer, *Vanguard to Victory*, 116.

77. Blumenson, *Breakout and Pursuit*, 682–684.

78. Ibid., 693–698; MRC, 1st ID WWII Outstanding Combat Achievements, "The Infantry Battalion in Offensive Action, 'Battle of Mons,'" 2–7; Clay, *Blood and Sacrifice*, 208–210.

79. NA, RG407, Box 5938, 18th Infantry AAR for September 1944, 2; ibid., Box 5955, 26th Infantry AAR, 30 September 1944, 4–5.

80. C. MacDonald, *The Siegfried Line Campaign* (Washington, DC, 1990), 4–6, 14–16. The Luftwaffe had approximately 4,500 aircraft total, with only 573

serviceable planes in the west to face 14,000 American and British aircraft of all types.

81. Ibid., 38, 41.

82. Ibid., 10–14.

83. MRC, 1st ID G3 Report of Operations for September 1944, 25; MacDonald, *The Siegfried Line Campaign*, 36–37, 66–68.

84. NA, RG407, Box 5664, 1st Division Report of Breaching the Siegfried Line, 2; ibid., Box 5911, 16th Infantry AAR, 3 October 1944, 2; ibid., Box 5938, 18th Infantry AAR for September 1944, 2.

85. MacDonald, *The Siegfried Line Campaign*, 67–68.

86. Gorman, *Blue Spaders*, 76–77.

11. The Battles of the German Frontier

1. MacDonald, *The Siegfried Line Campaign*, 71.

2. NA, RG407, Box 5938, 18th Infantry AAR for September 1944, 2; ibid., Box 5885, 32nd FA AAR, 23 September 1944, 5; NA, RG407, Box 5664, 1st Division Report of Breaching the Siegfried Line, 2.

3. NA, RG407, Box 5664, 1st Division Report of Breaching the Siegfried Line, 3.

4. NA, RG407, Box 5955, 26th Infantry AAR, 30 September 1944, 5–10; ibid., Box 5900, 33rd FA AAR, 1 October 1944, 1–8.

5. Gorman, *Blue Spaders*, 76–77; MacDonald, *The Siegfried Line Campaign*, 72–75.

6. P. Gorman, *Stolberg: Penetrating the Westwall, 1st Battalion, 26th Infantry, 13–22 September 1944* (Wheaton, IL, 1999), 11–12.

7. MacDonald, *The Siegfried Line Campaign*, 75–76.

8. NA, RG407, Box 5911, 16th Infantry AAR, 3 October 1944, 2–3.

9. MacDonald, *The Siegfried Line Campaign*, 77.

10. Ibid., 87–89.

11. Quoted in Gorman, *Blue Spaders*, 73. Captain Armand Levasseur monograph for the Advanced Infantry Officer Course, 1947–1948, "Operations of the 1/26th Infantry . . . 13–20 September 1944."

12. NA, RG407, Box 5664, 1st Division Report of Breaching the Siegfried Line, 4; MacDonald, *The Siegfried Line Campaign*, 77.

13. NA, RG407, Box 5885, 32nd FA AAR, 23 September 1944, 7; ibid., Box 5911, 16th Infantry AAR, 3 October 1944, 3; ibid., Box 5664, 1st Division Report of Breaching the Siegfried Line, 4; MacDonald, *The Siegfried Line Campaign*, 88.

14. NA, RG407, 1st Division Report of Breaching the Siegfried Line, 5–6; MacDonald, *The Siegfried Line Campaign*, 88–95; Gorman, *Stolberg*, 20–31.

15. MacDonald, *The Siegfried Line Campaign*, 252–260.

16. NA, RG40, Box 5885, 32nd FA AAR, 1 November 1944, 1.

17. MRC, "The Rifle Company in Attack: 'The Attack on Crucifix Hill,' 7–9 October 1944, Company C, 18th Infantry," 3.

18. MRC, "The Attack on Crucifix Hill," 3–4.

19. NA, RG407, Box 5955, 26th Infantry AAR, 30 September 1944, 6–9.

20. MRC, 1st ID WWII Outstanding Combat Achievements, "The Infantry Battalion in Offensive Action: 'Aachen,' 8–20 October 1944, Second Battalion, 26th Infantry," 1–3.

21. Ibid.; NA, RG407, Box 5955, 26th Infantry AAR, 1 November 1944, 1–4.

22. NA, RG407, Box 5912, 16th Infantry AAR, 2 November 1944, 1; ibid., Box 5883, 7th FA AAR, 1 November 1944, 1–2; ibid., Box 5664, 1st Division Report of Breaching the Siegfried Line, 6–7.

23. MacDonald, *The Siegfried Line Campaign,* 259–280.

24. MRC, "The Attack on Crucifix Hill," 7–8. A sketch of the hill's defenses is in the MRC.

25. NA, RG407, Box 5938, 18th Infantry AAR for October 1944, 2.

26. MacDonald, *The Siegfried Line Campaign,* 281–292.

27. NA, RG407, Box 5664, 1st Division Report of Breaching the Siegfried Line, 8.

28. NA, RG407, Box 5955, 26th Infantry AAR, 1 November, 7–9; MRC, 1st ID WWII Outstanding Combat Achievements, "The Infantry Battalion in Offensive Action, 'Farwick Park, Aachen,' Third Battalion, 26th Infantry," 1–4.

29. NA, RG407, Box 5955, 26th Infantry AAR, 9–10.

30. MacDonald, *The Siegfried Line Campaign,* 312–314.

31. Quoted in Clay, *Blood and Sacrifice,* 215.

32. Quote from MacDonald, *The Siegfried Line Campaign,* 291; see Baumgartner, *The Sixteenth Infantry Regiment,* 165–171, for extracts from the S3 Log of the 16th Infantry for 15 October 1944.

33. MacDonald, *The Siegfried Line Campaign,* 292.

34. MHI, WWII, Veterans' Surveys, 16th Infantry, Sergeant Joseph W. Pilck, Attachment A.

35. Baumgartner, *The Sixteenth Infantry Regiment,* 16–170.

36. Clay, *Blood and Sacrifice,* 216.

37. Quoted in Baumgartner, *The Sixteenth Infantry Regiment,* 171.

38. NA, RG407, Box 5912, 16th Infantry AAR, 2 November 1944, 2.

39. NA, RG407, Box 5883, 7th FA AAR, 1 November 1944, 6–7; ibid., Box 5880, 5th FA Operations Log for 14–18 October 1944; Weigley, *Eisenhower's Lieutenants,* 375–377.

40. MacDonald, *The Siegfried Line Campaign,* 287–289.

41. Ibid., 287 n. 14. Brown was wounded three times in the action and personally knocked out three pillboxes.

42. Weigley, *Eisenhower's Lieutenants,* 362–363.

43. NA, RG407, Box 5664, 1st Division Report of Breaching the Siegfried Line, 10–11.

44. MacDonald, *The Siegfried Line Campaign,* 316–317.

45. Ibid., 317–318.

46. NA, RG407, Box 5966, 1st Medical Battalion AAR, 31 October 1944, Appendix B.

47. Ibid., using the monthly summaries provided as appendices to each monthly report.

48. MRC, Joe Dawson Letter, 28 October 1944, 1.

49. MacDonald, *The Siegfried Line Campaign,* 377–389.

50. NA, RG407, Box 5880, 1st ID FO 53, 6 November 1944, 1.

51. MacDonald, *The Siegfried Line Campaign,* 413.

52. Clay, *Blood and Sacrifice,* 217–219; NA, RG407, Box 5912, 16th Infantry AAR, 1 December 1944, 2; ibid., Box 5883, 7th FA AAR, 1 December 1944, 3–4. The 7th Field Artillery fired 820 rounds on 16 November and another 1,437 on 17

November. The 5th Artillery fired over 980 rounds of 155mm in support of the 16th Infantry on 16 and 17 November. The 84th Field Artillery Battalion also supported the fires of the 7th Field Artillery.

53. Clay, *Blood and Sacrifice,* 218–219; NA, RG407, Box 5912, 16th Infantry AAR, 1 December 1944, 2.

54. Clay, *Blood and Sacrifice,* 219, 462 n. 304.

55. Heidenheimer, *Vanguard to Victory,* 165.

56. NA, RG407, Box 5955, 26th Infantry AAR, 4 December 1944, 2.

57. Ibid.

58. Ibid., 3.

59. Ibid.

60. NA, RG407, Box 5938, 18th Infantry AAR for November 1944, 2–3.

61. NA, RG407, Box 5938, 18th Infantry AARs for November and December 1944.

62. NA, RG407, Box 5955, 26th Infantry AAR, 4 December 1944, 4–5.

63. MRC, S. Miller, World War II Memoirs (27 November 1989), no pagination, last two sections.

64. Ibid., last page.

65. MRC, Comments by J. C. Hill at a breakfast panel, 11 March 1992, 3.

66. Ibid., 5.

67. NA, RG407, Box 5900, 33 FA AAR, 1 December 1944, 10–11.

68. NA, RG407, Box 5955, 26th Infantry AAR, 4 December 1944, 5.

69. Society of the First Division, *Danger Forward,* 295.

70. NA, RG407, Box 5912, 1 January 1944, 1.

71. MacDonald, *The Siegfried Line Campaign,* 492; NA, RG407, Box 5956, 26th Infantry AAR, 1 January 1945, 2.

72. NA, RG407, Box 5938, 18th Infantry AAR for December 1944, 1–2.

73. NA, RG407, Box 5966, 1st Medical Battalion AARs for November and December 1944, casualty annexes. The casualties treated in the Clearing Company included 653 neuropsychiatric patients, 1,540 disease casualties, and 2,760 wounded men for the period 16 November–6 December; for the regimental KIA and MIA, numbers, see MacDonald, *The Siegfried Line Campaign,* 492–493, p. 492, n. 49.

74. G. Cosmas and A. Cowdry, *Medical Service in the European Theater of Operations* (Washington, DC, 1992), 235–236; P. Kindsvatter, *American Soldiers: Ground Combat in the World Wars, Korea, and Vietnam* (Lawrence, KS, 2003), 168–172.

75. For example, the 16th Infantry's strength on 29 November was 3,181 officers and men, with an authorized strength of 3,118. NA, RG407, Box 5912, 16th Infantry AAR, 1 December 1944, Daily Casualty Report for 28–29 November 1944, which lists strength at the end of the period.

76. MacDonald, *The Siegfried Line Campaign,* 469–472; Roland Ruppenthal, *Logistical Support of the Armies,* 2 vols. (Washington, DC, 1995), 2:304–325.

77. H. Cole, *The Ardennes: The Battle of the Bulge* (Washington, DC, 1988), 48–74; Weigley, *Eisenhower's Lieutenants,* 457–464.

78. Kirkpatrick, *"It Will Be Done!",* 42–44; Cole, *The Ardennes,* 75–135; Charles MacDonald, *A Time for Trumpets* (New York, 1985), 160–183.

79. Weigley, *Eisenhower's Lieutenants,* 457–463.

80. NA, RG407, Box 5956, 26th Infantry AAR, 1 January 1945, 3; MRC, author's interview with General Frank Murdoch, 7 April 2004.

81. Gorman, *Blue Spaders*, 101–104.
82. Ibid., 128–130.
83. NA, RG407, Box 5938, 18th Infantry AAR for December 1944, 2–3.
84. NA, RG407, Box 5912, 16th Infantry AAR, 1 January 1945, 2; Clay, *Blood and Sacrifice*, 226.
85. NA, RG407, Box 5956, 26th Infantry AAR, 3–4; quote is from Gorman, *Blue Spaders*, 104.
86. NA, RG407, Box 5956, 26th Infantry AAR, 4.
87. Kirkpatrick, *V Corps*, 39–40, citation for Corporal Warner's Medal of Honor, posthumously awarded.
88. NA, RG407, Box 5956, 26th Infantry AAR, 1 January 1945, 4–5; ibid., Box 5900, 33rd FA AAR, 5.
89. NA, RG407, Box 5956, 26th Infantry AAR, 1 January 1945, 5.
90. Ibid., 9; Cole, *The Ardennes*, 132–133.
91. NA, RG407, Box 5912, 16th Infantry AAR, 1 January 1945, 2–3.
92. Ibid., 3.
93. NA, RG407, Box 5956, 26th Infantry AAR, 1 January 1945, 6.
94. NA, RG407, Box 5938, 18th Infantry AAR for December 1944, 3–4.
95. Ibid., 4.

12. *The Last Offensive against Germany: January to May 1945*

1. Cole, *The Ardennes*, 664, 666, 674; C. B. MacDonald, *The Last Offensive* (Washington, DC, 1950), 53.
2. MacDonald, *The Last Offensive*, 5–6.
3. Ibid., 27–31.
4. NA, RG407, Box 5956, 26th Infantry AAR, 2 February 1945, 6.
5. NA, RG407, Box 5966, 1st Medical Battalion AAR, 31 January 1945, 3.
6. Raymond Gantter, *Roll Me Over: An Infantryman's World War II* (New York, 1987), 97–98.
7. MacDonald, *The Last Offensive*, 46–48; NA, RG407, Box 5913, 16th Infantry AAR, 1 February 1945, 1–2; ibid., Box 5885, 32nd FA AAR, 2 February 1945, 2–3; ibid., Box 5956, 26th Infantry AAR, 2 February 1945, 1–6; Heidenheimer, *Vanguard to Victory*, 187.
8. Heidenheimer, *Vanguard to Victory*, 187–188.
9. MRC, 1st ID WWII Outstanding Combat Achievements, "The Infantry Battalion in Offensive Action, 'Operation Yukon,' 18 January 1945," 5–6.
10. NA, RG407, Box 5935, 18th Infantry AAR for January 1945, 2; ibid., Box 5885, 32nd FA AAR, 3–4; Heidenheimer, *Vanguard to Victory*, 188; MRC, 1st ID WWII Outstanding Combat Achievements, "The Infantry Battalion in Offensive Action, 'Operation Yukon,'" 7–9.
11. NA, RG407, Box 5913, 16th Infantry AAR, 1 February 1945, 2; Baumgartner, ed., *The Sixteenth Infantry Regiment*, 197–198.
12. NA, RG407, Box 5956, 26th Infantry AAR, 2 February 1945, 7–8; ibid., Box 5935, 18th Infantry AAR for January 1945, 2–3; Heidenheimer, *Vanguard to Victory*, 188; MRC, "The Rifle Company in the Attack, 'The Attack on Moderscheid,' 24 January 1945," 1–4.
13. Quoted in Gorman, *Blue Spaders*, 115–116.

14. Hogan, *A Command Post at War*, 239–241.

15. MacDonald, *Last Offensive*, 60–63; NA, RG407, Box 5935, 18th Infantry AAR for January 1945, 3; ibid., Box 5956, 26th Infantry AAR, 2 February 1945, 8–9.

16. NA, RG407, Box 5935, 18th Infantry AAR for January 1945, 8; ibid., Box 5885, 32nd FA AAR, 2 February 1945, 5. The 32nd fired 44 missions and 920 rounds.

17. NA, RG407, Box 5956, 26th Infantry AAR, 2 February 1945, 8–9.

18. Ibid., 9; ibid., Box 5879, 5th FA AAR, 4 February 1945, 1.

19. NA, RG407, Box 5805, 1st ID G3 Log, 30 January 1945, 3–7; ibid., XVIII Airborne Corps G3 Periodic Report for 30 January 1945, 3–4.

20. NA, RG407, Box 5805, 1st ID G3 Journal, 31 January 1945, 6–10.

21. NA, RG407, Box 5956, 26th Infantry AAR, 1 March 1945, 1.

22. NA, RG407, Box 5880, 5th FA AAR, Unit Journal for February 1945, 1; ibid., Box 5885, 32 FA AAR, 2 March 1945, 1.

23. NA, RG407, Box 5935, 18th Infantry AAR for February 1945, 1.

24. NA, RG407, Box 5956, 26th Infantry AAR, 1 March 1945, 1–2.

25. NA, RG407, Box 5966, 1st Medical Battalion AAR, 31 January 1945, Appendix B.

26. Towne, *Doctor Danger Forward*, 159–160.

27. NA, RG407, Box 5955, 18th Infantry AAR for February 1944, 2.

28. NA, RG407, Box 5880, 5th FA Unit Journal, February 1945.

29. NG, RG407, Box 5808, 1st Engineer Battalion plan, 12 February 1945, 1–4.

30. Heidenheimer, *Vanguard to Victory,* 196.

31. MacDonald, *The Last Offensive*, 145–162. The Ninth Army lost 92 men killed, 61 missing, and 913 wounded in four divisions, while VII Corps lost a total of 381 men. These low losses are largely attributable to weak German resistance.

32. Ibid., 191–193.

33. NA, RG407, Box 5913, 16th Infantry AAR, 1 March 1945, 3; ibid., Box 5883, 7th FA AAR, 1 March 1945, 1; ibid., Box 5956, 26th Infantry AAR, 1 March 1945, 3; Baumgartner, *The Sixteenth Infantry Regiment,* 209–211.

34. NA, RG407, Box 5913, 16th Infantry AAR, 1 March 1945, 4; ibid., Box 5956, 26th Infantry AAR, 1 March 1945, 3–4; ibid., Box 5880, 5th FA Unit Journal, 27–28 February 1945; MacDonald, *The Last Offensive,* 193–194.

35. MacDonald, *The Last Offensive,* 202–203.

36. NA, RG407, Box 5935, 18th Infantry AAR for February 1945, 2.

37. Ibid., 1.

38. NA, RG407, Box 5907, "The Attack on Bonn," 4; Baumgartner, *The Sixteenth Infantry Regiment,* 228–242.

39. NA, RG407, Box 5935, 18th Infantry AAR for March 1945, 1–2.

40. NA, RG407, Box 5957, 26th Infantry AAR, 1 April 1945, 3.

41. Ulysses Lee, *The Employment of Negro Troops* (Washington, DC, 1986); Morris MacGregor, *Integration of the Armed Forces, 1940–1965* (Washington, DC, 1981), 56.

42. Lee, *The Employment of Negro Troops,* 693–695.

43. MRC, Memoir of Major General Albert H. Smith, 3; Heidenheimer, *Vanguard to Victory,* 201; MRC, an article titled "K Company, History," 26th Infantry, 86; MRC, 1st ID AAR, 1 April 1945, 2, which lists 11 March 1945 as the date of

arrival of the platoons; MRC, AAR of 1st Battalion, 18th Infantry, January–May 1945, entries for March.

44. MRC, AAR of 1st Battalion, 18th Infantry, January–May 1945, entry for 19 March.

45. MRC, "K Company History," 93.

46. Quote from Wright's autobiography, *Black Robes, White Justice,* in G. Buckley, ed., *American Patriots: The Story of Blacks in the Military from the Revolution to Desert Storm* (New York, 2001), 324.

47. Buckley, *American Patriots,* 324–325.

48. Heidenheimer, *Vanguard to Victory,* 201.

49. A. Chandler et al., eds., *Eisenhower Papers, The War Years,* 4:2412–2413, Eisenhower to Marshall, 10 January 1945; Hogan, *A Command Post at War,* 239–250; MacDonald, *The Last Offensive,* 208–209.

50. MacDonald, *The Last Offensive,* 211–220.

51. Ibid., 221–222.

52. Ibid., 231–233.

53. NA, RG407, Box 5913, 16th Infantry AAR, 1 April 1945, 3; ibid., Box 5935, 18th Infantry AAR for March 1945, 2; ibid., Box 5957, 26th Infantry AAR, 1 April 1945, 2–3; ibid., Box 5881, 5th FA Unit Journal, 14–17 March 1945; ibid., Box 5883, 7th FA AAR, 1 April 1945, 1; ibid., Box 5885, 32nd FA AAR, 3 April 1945, 4.

54. MacDonald, *The Last Offensive,* 232–233.

55. NA, RG407, Box 5935, 18th Infantry AAR for March 1945, 2–3; ibid., Box 5957, 26th Infantry AAR, 1 April 1945, 4; MacDonald, *The Last Offensive,* 233–234.

56. NA, RG407, Box 5811, 1st ID FO 58, 24 March 1945, 1.

57. Ibid.

58. Heidenheimer, *Vanguard to Victory,* 192–193; NA, RG407, Box 5935, 18th Infantry AAR for March 1945, 2; ibid., Box 5957, 26th Infantry AAR, 1 April 1945, 5–6.

59. Baumgartner, *The Sixteenth Infantry Regiment,* 248–249.

60. NA, RG407, Box 5883, 7th FA AAR, 1 April 1945, 1; ibid., Box 5881, 5th FA Unit Journal, 22–26 March 1945.

61. NA, RG407, Box 5935, 18th Infantry AAR for March 1945, 3; MacDonald, *The Last Offensive,* 349–359.

62. MacDonald, *The Last Offensive,* 340–342.

63. NA, RG407, Box 5664, Battle Engagements, 1st Division, 1942–1945, 19–20; ibid., Box 5935, 16th Infantry AAR, 1 May 1945, 1–2; ibid., Box 5935, 18th Infantry AAR for April 1945, 2–3; ibid., Box 5957, 26th Infantry AAR, 1 May 1945, 1–3.

64. MacDonald, *The Last Offensive,* 380–381, 389–392.

65. NA, RG407, Box 5914, 16th Infantry AAR, 1 May 1945, 2–6; ibid., Box 5935, 18th Infantry AAR for April 1945, 3–4; ibid., Box 5957, 26th Infantry AAR, 1 May 1945, 3–5.

66. NA, RG407, Box 5879, 5th FA AAR, 3 May 1945, 1–3; ibid., Box 5883, 7th FA AAR, 2 May 1945, 1–2; ibid., Box 5885, 32nd FA AAR, 1 May 1945, 1–7.

67. Towne, *Doctor Danger Forward,* 406–407.

68. Ibid., 407–408.

13. The Occupation of Germany and the Cold War

1. NA, RG407, Box 5816, 1st ID G3 Journal, 7 May 1945, 2; ibid., Box 5935, 18th Infantry AAR for May 1945, p. 1 for the quote.

2. NA, RG407, Box 5816, 1st ID G3 Journal, 7 May 1945, 3.

3. Earl Ziemke, *The U.S. Army in the Occupation of Germany, 1944–1946* (Washington, DC; 1990 edition), 163–165.

4. NA, RG407, Box 5817, 1st ID G3 Journal, 9 May 1945, 1–6.

5. H. Potter, ed., and staff, *The First Year of the Occupation,* 3 vols. (Frankfurt, Germany, 1947), 1:62–69; Ziemke, *The U.S. Army in the Occupation of Germany,* 239, 240–242, 249–250, 284, 291.

6. NA, RG407, Box 5957, 26th Infantry AAR, Box 5957, 1 June 1945, 2–3.

7. NA, RG407, Box 5817, 1st Division G3 Journal, 9 May 1945, 1–5; ibid., Box 5935, 18th Infantry AAR for May 1945, 2.

8. NA, RG407, 1st Division G3 Journal, 9 May 1945, 2–3.

9. Ziemke, *The U.S. Army in the Occupation of Germany,* 291–293; Potter, *The First Year of the Occupation,* 1:61–62.

10. NA, RG407, Box 5817, 1st Division G3 Journal, 9 May 1945, 8.

11. Ibid., 12 May 1945, 3; ibid., 13 May 1945, 1.

12. Potter, *The First Year of the Occupation,* 1:62–64.

13. Ibid., 1:119–122; Ziemke, *The U.S. Army in the Occupation of Germany,* 380–395.

14. H. Potter, *American Military Occupation in Germany, 1945–1953* (Frankfurt, Germany, 1954), 97.

15. Ibid., 78–80, 91.

16. NA, RG407, Box 5885, 32 FA AAR, 1 June 1945, 2; ibid., Box 5935, 18th Infantry AAR for May 1945, 2.

17. NA, RG407, Box 5935, 18th Infantry AAR for May 1945, 2.

18. NA, RG407, Box 5957, 26th Infantry AAR, 1 June 1945, 3.

19. Ziemke, *The U.S. Army in the Occupation of Germany,* 328–329.

20. Quoted in ibid., 328.

21. Ibid., 329.

22. Potter, *The First Year of the Occupation,* 1:57–61.

23. Ibid., 1:52.

24. NA, RG407, Box 5879, 5th FA Report of Operations, October–December 1945, 2.

25. Potter, *The First Year of the Occupation,* 1:132–137.

26. Ibid., 1:48.

27. Ibid., 1:48, 133, 138, 142–143, 160.

28. Ziemke, *The U.S. Army in the Occupation of Germany,* 2–22, 93–94.

29. Ibid., 270–273.

30. NA, RG407, Box 5964, Troop List of 26th Infantry, 8 December 1945.

31. NA, RG407, Box 5938, 18th Infantry AAR for 1 October–31 December 1945, 2.

32. NA, RG407, Box 5914, 16th Infantry AAR, 8 May–30 September 1945, 1–2.

33. NA, RG407, Box 5958, 26th Infantry AAR, 8 January 1946, 1.

34. Ibid., 3.

35. Ibid., 3–5.

36. Ziemke, *The U.S. Army in the Occupation of Germany,* 160, 321–327; Potter, *The First Year of the Occupation,* 2:81–93.

37. Potter, *The First Year of the Occupation,* 2:86–93.

38. Ziemke, *The U.S. Army in the Occupation of Germany,* 332.

39. Ibid., 324–327; Potter, *The First Year of the Occupation,* 2:91–95.

40. NA, RG407, Box 5914, 16th Infantry AAR, 8 May–30 September 1945, 3; see Ziemke, *The U.S. Army in the Occupation of Germany,* 250–252, for the small incidence of looting by Germans; see ibid., 351–353, for rations and malnutrition.

41. Ziemke, *The U.S. Army in the Occupation of Germany,* 355–358; see NA, RG407, Box 5958, 26th Infantry AAR, 8 January 1945, for the period 1 October–31 December 1945, 5.

42. Ziemke, *The U.S. Army in the Occupation of Germany,* 422–423; Potter, *The First Year of the Occupation,* 2:157.

43. NA, RG407, Box 5958, 26th Infantry AARs for January–March 1946, 1; ibid., 26th Infantry AAR for April–June 1946, 1.

44. NA, RG407, Box 5879, 5th FA AAR, April–June 1946, 1–2.

45. NA, RG407, Box 5938, 18th Infantry AAR for July–September 1946, 6.

46. Ibid., 8–9; ibid., Box 5958, 26th Infantry AAR, January–March 1946, 1.

47. NA, RG407, Box 5958, 26th Infantry AAR for April–June 1946, 1.

48. Ziemke, *The U.S. Army in the Occupation of Germany;* Potter, *The First Year of the Occupation,* vols. 2 and 3; Potter, *American Military Occupation in Germany, 1945–1953.*

49. NA, RG407, Box 5939, 18th Infantry AAR for October–December 1946, paragraph 14.

50. Ibid.

51. Potter, *The First Year of the Occupation,* 2:95–96.

52. Ibid., 2:95–101.

53. Discussion at lunch with Major General and Mrs. Frank Murdoch, 6 April 2004.

54. Potter, *The First Year of the Occupation,* 1:93–94, 105–106, 111.

55. NA, RG407, Box 5939, 18th Infantry AAR for October–December 1946, paragraph 8.

56. Ibid., paragraph 94.

57. Ibid., paragraphs 11 and 94.

58. NA, RG337, Box 85, "Major Causes of Dissatisfaction within the Army, 1947 and 1948." This record summarizes the results of a survey ordered by General Jacob Devers, commanding general of the Army Ground Forces Command. Major problems included personnel turmoil, low pay, poor billets, too much guard duty, and too little meaningful tactical training.

59. NA, RG407, Box 5959, 26th Infantry AAR, April–June 1947, 1; ibid., Box 5959, Training Directive Number 1, Headquarters, First Military District, 5 April 1947; H. Potter, ed., and staff, *The Third Year of the Occupation,* 3 vols. (Frankfurt, Germany, 1947), 3:4–6.

60. NA, RG407, Box 5879, 5th FA Report for April–June 1947, 2–3; ibid., Box 5939, 18th Infantry AAR for April–June 1947; ibid., 18th Infantry AAR for July–September 1947.

61. NA, RG407, Box 5959, 26th Infantry AAR, April–June 1947, 2–3; ibid., Quarterly Report of the 1st Battalion, 26th Infantry, April–June 1947.

62. Potter, *The Third Year of the Occupation,* 5–6.

63. Ibid., 6–7.

64. Ibid., 7–9.

65. Weigley, *History of the United States Army,* 501–502; Michael Doubler, *I Am the Guard: A History of the Army National Guard, 1636–2000* (Washington, DC, 2001), 227–231.

66. NA, RG337, Box 6, Memorandum for the Army Chief of Staff, 23 January 1947; Potter, *The Third Year of the Occupation,* 10; A. Millett and P. Maslowski, *For the Common Defense* (New York, 1984; 1994 edition), 500–502; Weigley, *History of the United States Army,* 501–504.

67. *American Traveler* (the division's news journal), 3 June 1947, 5. The regimental headquarters and the 2nd Battalion, 16th Infantry, moved to Salzburg, the 1st Battalion moved to Vienna, and the 3rd Battalion deployed to Berlin.

68. NA, RG407, Box 5962, Historical Narrative of the 16th Infantry, 1 October 1948, 1–6; *Bridgehead Sentinel* 7 (April 1949): 8–9.

69. NA, RG337, Box 6, Recapitulation of Army and Army Air Force Strength, 30 June 1947.

70. Andrew Bacevich, *The Pentomic Era: The U.S. Army between Korea and Vietnam* (Washington, DC, 1986).

71. Millett and Maslowski, *For the Common Defense,* 506.

72. Heidenheimer, *Vanguard to Victory,* 201; 18th Infantry Regiment AAR, January–May 1945; MRC, "K Company History, 26th Infantry, March–April 1945"; U. Lee, *The Employment of Negro Troops* (Washington, DC, 1986), 693–698.

73. EUCOM Historical Division, *Negro Personnel in the European Command, 1 January 1946–30 June 1950* (Karlsruhe, Germany, 1952), 191–192.

74. Ibid, 3.

75. MacGregor, *Integration of the Armed Forces, 1940–1965,* 216–218.

76. Ibid., 5–7.

77. Millett and Maslowski, *For the Common Defense,* 506; Historical Division, USAREUR, *Integration of Negro and White Troops in the U.S. Army, Europe, 1952–54* (Karlsruhe, Germany, 1956), 10.

78. EUCOM Historical Division, *Negro Personnel in the European Command,* 44, 88–89, 191–192.

79. EUCOM Historical Division, *EUCOM Annual Narrative Report, 1949* (Karlsruhe, Germany, 1950), 1–26.

80. NA, RG407, Box 5825, EUCOM Order, 29 September 1948.

81. Ibid., 1st ID Station List, 20 October 1948, 1–4.

82. Ibid., 176–177.

83. Ibid., 176.

84. NA, RG407, Box 5879, 5th Field Artillery Historical Reports for September–December 1948, 1–3.

85. Ibid., 3–4.

86. Headquarters USAREUR, *Annual Narrative Report, 1 January–31 December 1950* (Karlsruhe, Germany, 1951), 4–10.

87. NA, RG337, Box 25, Army Field Forces Inspection of the United States Army Troops, European Command, 3 November 1950, Tab H, summations of quarterly training, 1950.

88. Ibid., 16.

89. Ibid., 63–64, 76–78.

90. EUCOM Historical Division, *Command Report, European Command, 1951* (Karlsruhe, Germany, 1952), 3–4, 49–54.

91. Ibid., 137–142.

92. Headquarters USAREUR, *Annual Narrative Report, 1 January–31 December 1950,* 105–106.

93. Ibid., 106.

94. Ibid., 46, 56–63, 72–75.

95. Ibid., 73.

96. Ibid., 74.

97. *Annual Historical Report, Headquarters, US Army, Europe, 1 January 1953–30 June 1954* (Karlsruhe, Germany, 1955), 60.

98. Historical Division, USAREUR, *Integration of Negro and White Troops in the U.S. Army,* 36–38, quote on page 36.

99. NA, RG500, Box 46, Headquarters, 1st ID, AG Records, Division Station List, 1955, 1–5; *Annual Historical Report, Headquarters, US Army, Europe, 1 July 1954–30 June 1955,* 1–2.

100. USAREUR, *Operation Gyroscope in the United States Army, Europe* (6 September 1957), 1, 9–11.

101. Ibid., 1–5.

102. Bacevich, *The Pentomic Era,* 5.

103. *Bridgehead Sentinel* (Summer 1957): 1.

104. *Bridgehead Sentinel* (October 1956): 10–11.

105. Ibid., 44–52.

106. *Bridgehead Sentinel* (Fall 1958): 21.

107. *Bridgehead Sentinel* (Winter 1960): 2, 20, 24.

108. Ibid., 15–18.

109. Ibid., 134.

110. *Bridgehead Sentinel* (Fall 1961), cover, 1–2.

14. The Vietnam War and the Big Red One: Deployment and First Battles

1. J. Carland, *Stemming the Tide, May 1965 to October 1966* (Washington, DC, 2000), 3.

2. Ibid., 11–14; for a detailed account of the decision-making process that got the United States committed to a land war in Asia, see H. McMaster, *Dereliction of Duty: Lyndon Johnson, Robert McNamara, the Joint Chiefs of Staff, and the Lies That Led to Vietnam* (New York, 1997; 1998 paper edition).

3. A. Langguth, *Our Vietnam: The War, 1954–1975* (New York, 2000), 351–353; McMaster, *Dereliction of Duty,* 290.

4. Carland, *Stemming the Tide,* 17, citing a memo from General Johnson to Robert McNamara, "Report on the Military Situation in Vietnam [5–12 March 1965]," 15.

5. Carland, *Stemming the Tide,* 24–25.

6. Ibid., 46, citing Westmoreland's message to CINCPAC and the JCS, 7 June 1965.

7. McMaster, *Dereliction of Duty,* 298.

8. Carland, *Stemming the Tide,* 46–61.

9. NA, RG472, 1st ID Organizational Histories, Box 1, 2nd Brigade, annual history, 1965, n.d.

10. Carland, *Stemming the Tide,* 33. Carland cites an interview with General Seaman on 10 September 1970, 6–9, in CMH Historians files.

11. Carland, *Stemming the Tide,* 34; NA, RG472, 1st ID Organizational Histories, Box 1, 2nd Brigade, annual history, 1965, n.d., 2–3.

12. See Carland, *Stemming the Tide,* 34, for the 2nd Brigade's assignments; ibid., 49, for a quote from a message from William Westmoreland to Admiral Ulysses Sharp, Commander in Chief, Pacific, 24 June 1965, in which Westmoreland told his superiors that he envisioned "a war of attrition" in Vietnam.

13. Ibid., 34–35.

14. Ibid., 35, citing NA, RG334, Box 1, 68A/1507, 2nd Brigade Quarterly Command Report, 1 July–30 September 1965, 2–3.

15. Carland, *Stemming the Tide,* 65.

16. NA, RG472, Box 1, 2nd Brigade, 1st ID Unit History, 1965, 1.

17. Carland, *Stemming the Tide,* 63–64.

18. NA, RG472, 1st ID Organizational Histories, Box 2, Re-Organization of the 1st Infantry Division, 1965, 30 September 1965.

19. D. Starry, *Mounted Combat in Vietnam* (Washington, DC, 1973; 2002 edition), 38–39.

20. Historical Report of 1st Battalion, 26th Infantry, 1 July to 31 December 1965, 2, from the *Vietnam Chronology of the 1st Battalion, 26th Infantry, 1965–1970.*

21. NA, RG472, 1st ID Organizational Histories, Box 2, Division History, 1917–1965, 7.

22. Bradfield, as quoted in P. Gorman, *Blue Spaders: The 26th Infantry Regiment, 1917–1967* (Wheaton, IL, 1996), 127.

23. Carland, *Stemming the Tide,* 73–74, citing an intelligence estimate on III CTZ, Asst CofS, J-2 [Intel], MACV, 23 May 1966, 1–3.

24. Carland, *Stemming the Tide,* 75–76.

25. Ibid., 75.

26. Ibid., 76–80.

27. NA, RG472, 1st ID Organizational Histories, Box 2, Division History, 1917–1965, 8–9.

28. Carland, *Stemming the Tide,* 81–83.

29. NA, RG472, 1st ID Annual Historical Summaries, Box 2, Operation Bloodhound/Bushmaster I AAR, 3rd Brigade, 1st Division, annex B, 2.

30. Ibid.

31. Ibid. The enemy claimed to have inflicted 2,000 American casualties.

32. 1st ID Quarterly Command Report, 1 October–31 December 1965, 15.

33. NA, RG472, 1st ID Organizational Histories, Box 7, 3rd Brigade, Bloodhound/Bushmaster II AAR, 30 December 1965, 4–5.

34. NA, RG472, 1st ID Organizational Histories, Box 7, 3rd Brigade, Operation Bloodhound/Bushmaster II AAR, 30 December 1965, 2–4.

35. NA, RG472, 1st ID Organizational Histories, Box 2, Division History, 8–9; Carland, *Stemming the Tide,* citing the 1st ID Press Release, 20 February 1967.

36. NA, RG472, 1st ID Organizational Histories, Box 7, 3rd Brigade, Bloodhound/Bushmaster II AAR, 30 December 1965, 6–7.

37. Quote in Carland, *Stemming the Tide,* 151.

38. Ibid., 152–155.

39. Ibid., 165–166.

40. Ibid., 166.

41. Ibid., 169–171; NA, RG472, 1st ID Annual Historical Summaries, Box 2, 3rd Brigade AAR for Operation Crimp, 7–12 January 1966, n.d.

42. NA, RG472, 1st ID Annual Historical Summaries, Box 2, 3rd Brigade AAR for Operation Buckskin, 12–31 January 1969.

43. Carland, *Stemming the Tide,* 167–168, citing Tom Mangold and John Pennygate, *The Tunnels of Cu Chi* (New York, 1985), 202–213, 263–264.

44. NA, RG472, 1st Division AARs, Box 1, Operation Mastiff, n.d., 7.

45. Ibid., 16–17; Carland, *Stemming the Tide,* 173–175.

46. NA, RG472, 1st ID Annual Historical Summaries, Box 2, 3rd Brigade AAR for Operation Mastiff, 21–27 February 1966.

47. NA, RG472, 1st ID AARs, Box 1, Operation Rolling Stone, 7 February–2 March 1966, 12 March 1966, 1–11.

48. Ibid., 1–12; Gorman, *Blue Spaders,* 131–133.

49. Carland, *Stemming the Tide,* 180–181, citing S. Pennygate, *The Tunnels Support of the US Army in Vietnam, 1965–1970* (Washington, DC, 1973), 164–165.

50. Carland, *Stemming the Tide,* 176–177; NA, RG472, 1st ID Organizational Histories, Box 4, 2nd Battalion, 28th Infantry Annual Historical Summary, 1966, app. B, ii; Medal of Honor Citation for Robert Hibbs, in G. Lang, R. Collins, and G. White, eds., *Medal of Honor Recipients, 1863–1994* (New York, 1995), 693–694.

51. Carland, *Stemming the Tide,* 175–178, citing Annual Historical Summary, 1966, 2nd Battalion, 28th Infantry, n.d., app. B, ii.

52. Carland, *Stemming the Tide,* 305–306.

53. Quoted in ibid., 305, citing *Newsweek,* 5 December 1966, 53.

54. Interview by the author with General (retired) Paul F. Gorman, 6–8 April 2004, 9–12. The interview is on file with the First Division Museum, Wheaton, Illinois.

55. General Gorman notes to the author, January 2006.

56. Observation by General Gorman to the author in December 2005.

57. Ibid.; Gorman, *Blue Spaders,* 133–135.

58. DePuy, quoted in Gorman, *Blue Spaders,* 133–134; also Gorman interview, 6–8 April 2004, 10.

59. Gorman interview, 6–17.

60. Ibid., 28–29.

61. Ibid., 4–5.

62. Ibid., 17.

63. Ibid., 17–18.

64. Ibid., 29–30.

65. Ibid., 34–35.

66. NA, RG472, 1st ID AARs, Box 1, Operation Birmingham, 24 April–17 May 1966, n.d., 3–4.

67. Ibid., 12–14.

68. Ibid., 16.

69. Ibid., 30–31.

70. Ibid., 37.

71. Carland, *Stemming the Tide,* 308–309.

72. NA, RG472, 1st ID AARs, Box 1, Operation El Paso I, 19–26 May 1966, 26 June 1966, 1–2.

73. Ibid., 7–9.

74. NA, RG472, 1st ID AARs, Box 1, Operation Lexington III, 21 May–9 June 1966, 20 June 1966, 1–8.

75. Ibid., 11.

76. Gorman interview, 6–8 April 2004; Gorman, *Blue Spaders,* 138–139.

77. NA, RG472, 1st ID O[perations] L[essons] L[earned], 2nd Brigade, 16 May 1966, 7.

78. NA, RG472, USARV Historian Files, Box 2, The Battle of Ap Tau O, 5 July 1966, 2.

79. Ibid., 1–5.

80. Ibid., 3–4.

81. NA, RG472, 1st ID AARs, Box 1, Operation El Paso II/III, 2 June–3 September 1966, n.d., 1–3.

82. Ibid., 3; ibid., Annex B to El Paso II/III, "Battle of Loc Ninh Rubber Plantation," B-1 to B-3; Carland, *Stemming the Tide,* 314.

83. NA, RG472, 1st ID AARs, Box 1, Narrative of the Battle of Srok Dong, 30 June 1966, 9 August 1966, 1–2.

84. Ibid., 3.

85. Ibid., 3–4.

86. Ibid., 4–5.

87. Ibid., 5–9.

88. NA, RG472, 1st ID AARs, Box 1, Annex C to El Paso II/III AAR, "Battle of Minh Thanh Road," C-1 to C-8.

89. Ibid., C-1.

90. Ibid., C-3 to C-4.

91. Ibid., C-4.

92. Ibid., C-4 to C-6.

93. Ibid., C-6 to C-7.

94. NA, RG472, 1st ID AARs, Box 1, El Paso II/III, n.d., 30–43, and 48 for DePuy's assessment.

95. NA, RG472, 1st ID Organizational Histories, Box 3, 1st Brigade Annual Supplement, 1966, 2.

96. NA, RG472, 1st ID G3 Daily Journals, Box 3, 25 August 1966, items 6–30.

97. Ibid., item 43.

98. Carland, *Stemming the Tide,* 330.

99. NA, RG472, 1st ID G3 Daily Journals, Box 3, 25 August 1966, items 39–44.

100. NA, RG472, 1st ID, G3 Daily Journals, Box 3, 25 August 1966, items 63–68; Gorman interview, 6–8 April 2004; Gorman, *Blue Spaders,* 159–164.

101. NA, RG472, 1st ID Situation Reports, Box 2, 26 August 1966, 1; ibid., 1st ID G3 Daily Journals, Box 3, 25 and 26 August 1966; Gorman, *Blue Spaders,* 169–170.

102. Carland, *Stemming the Tide,* 332–333; see NA, RG472, 1st ID G3 Daily Journals, 26 August 1966, item 85, where the II Field Force was notified that the friendly casualties from the napalm included twenty-two killed and thirty-six wounded; the G3 Daily Journal for 27 August 1966, item 15, indicates that twenty-two Americans were killed by the napalm and another thirty-seven were wounded. Six Vietcong were listed as casualties in the incident; see also Gorman, *Blue Spaders,* 170.

103. Carland, *Stemming the Tide,* 333.

104. Quoted in Gorman, *Blue Spaders,* 174.

105. NA, RG472, 1st ID AARs, Box 2, Operations Tulsa and Shenandoah, 26 March 1967, 1–8.

106. Ibid., 6–7.

107. 1st Battalion, 26th Infantry, *Vietnam Chronology,* "Operation Shenandoah, 16–30 October 1966," C-22 to C-23; NA, RG472, 1st ID AARs, Box 2, 1st Brigade Combat Operations AAR, 5 January 1967, 5; ibid., 1st ID AARs, Box 2, Operations Tulsa and Shenandoah, 9–10.

108. 1st Battalion, 26th Infantry, *Vietnam Chronology,* C-23; Gorman, *Blue Spaders,* 183–185.

109. NA, RG472, 1st Division AARs, Box 2, Operations Tulsa and Shenandoah, 9–10.

110. Ibid., 10–11.

111. G. MacGarrigle, *Taking the Offensive, October 1966 to October 1967* (Washington, DC, 1998), 34.

112. Ibid., 38.

113. Ibid., 38–39. The *PAVN* was part of the *PLAF.*

114. Ibid., 39–42; NA, RG472, USARV Command Historian AARs, Box 2, Operation Attleboro/Battle Creek, 6 April 1967, 1–3.

115. NA, RG472, USARV Command Historians AARs, Box 2, Operation Attleboro/Battle Creek, 9–10.

116. Ibid., 10–11.

117. Ibid., 11–15.

15. The Year of Decision? The 1st Infantry Division in Vietnam, 1967

1. MacGarrigle, *Taking the Offensive,* 3, 11–12.

2. Ibid., 3–11, 17–23; Carland, *Stemming the Tide,* 356, for American strength in October 1966.

3. Carland, *Stemming the Tide,* 360.

4. MacGarrigle, *Taking the Offensive,* 95–96; B. Rogers, *Cedar Falls–Junction City: A Turning Point* (Washington, DC, 1974), 15–19.

5. Rogers, *Cedar Falls–Junction City,* 19–20.

6. Ibid., 25–27.

7. Ibid., 30–34.

8. Ibid., 37–39.

9. Ibid., 74.

10. Ibid., 60.

11. Ibid., 61–66.

12. MRC, Hay Collection, letter dated 27 January 1967, "Results of Operation Cedar Falls," 3.

13. Ibid., 91–94.

14. NA, RG472, 1st ID AARs, Box 2, Operation Tucson (14–21 February 1967), 26 March 1967, 1–4.

15. Ibid., 3–5.

16. Ibid., 3–8.

17. NA, RG472, 1st ID AARs, Box 2, Operation Junction City (22 February–15

April 1967), 8 May 1967, 1–3; see Rogers, *Cedar Falls–Junction City,* 96–111, for the first phase.

18. MacGarrigle, *Taking the Offensive,* 113–122.

19. Ibid., 118–120.

20. NA, RG472, 1st ID AARs, Box 2, Operation Junction City, 2.

21. MacGarrigle, *Taking the Offensive,* 121–122.

22. Rogers, *Cedar Falls–Junction City,* 113–115; NA, RG472, 1st ID AARs, Box 2, Operation Junction City, 3.

23. NA, RG472, 1st ID AARs, Box 2, Operation Junction City, 3; Rogers, *Cedar Falls–Junction City,* 114–116.

24. NA, RG472, 1st ID AARs, Box 2, Operation Junction City, 4–6.

25. NA, RG472, 1st ID AARs, Box 2, Operation Junction City, 5; Rogers, *Cedar Falls–Junction City,* 117–125.

26. NA, RG472, 1st ID AARs, Box 2, Operation Junction City, 7.

27. NA, RG472, USARV Command Historians AARs, Box 1, Battle of Ap Bau Bang (19–20 March 1967), 1 May 1967, 3–6.

28. Ibid.

29. Ibid.

30. Ibid.

31. Ibid., 8–12; NA, RG472, 1st ID AARs, Box 2, Operation Junction City, 4–5.

32. MacGarrigle, *Taking the Offensive,* 136–137; Gorman, *Blue Spaders: The 26th Infantry Regiment, 1917–1967* (Wheaton, IL, 1996), 210–211.

33. NA, RG472, 1st ID AARs, Box 2, Operation Junction City, 9–10; NA, RG472, 1st ID G3 Daily Journals, Box 4, 30 March 1967, items 17 and 20. Some very good accounts of the Battle of Ap Gu are found in the following sources: D. Puckett, *The Blue Spaders at the Battle of Ap Gu, 31 March–1 April 1967* (Wheaton, IL, 1997); Gorman, *Blue Spaders,* 210–220; MacGarrigle, *Taking the Offensive,* 136–140.

34. NA, RG472, 1st ID G3 Daily Journals, Box 4, 31 March 1967, item 41; Puckett, *Battle of Ap Gu,* 8–10; author's interview with General Paul Gorman, 6–8 April 2004; author's interview with General George Joulwan, 30 September 2004.

35. NA, RG472, 1st ID G3 Daily Journals, Box 4, 31 March 1967, items 46–49.

36. Author's interview with Colonel Rudy Egersdorfer, 7 April 2004; Joulwan interview, 30 September 2004; Puckett, *The Blue Spaders at the Battle of Ap Gu,* 10–11; NA, RG472, 1st ID Daily Situation Reports, Box 3, 31 March 1967, 2.

37. NA, RG472, 1st ID G3 Daily Journals, Box 4, 31 March 1967, items 57, 61, 63, 67–69.

38. Gorman interview, 6–7 April 2004, 13.

39. Author's interview with First Sergeant Al Cooper, 7 April 2004.

40. Puckett, *The Blue Spaders at the Battle of Ap Gu,* 21.

41. MacGarrigle, *Taking the Offensive,* 140–143.

42. NA, RG472, 1st ID AARs, Box 2, Operation Junction City, 8 May 1967, 10; NA, RG472, 1st ID G3 Journal, 1 April 1967, item 71, where initial reports were received that American casualties were eleven dead and seventy-seven wounded.

43. NA, RG472, USARV Command Historian Reports, Box 15, II Field Force AAR for Operation Junction City, 9 August 1967, 8–9.

44. MRC, Hay Collection, Lieutenant Colonel Paul Gorman, "Report by the 1st Infantry Division on Revolutionary Development," 21 March 1967, 1–2.

45. Ibid., 3–6.

46. Ibid., 8–9.

47. J. Shelton, *The Beast Was Out There: The 28th Infantry Black Lions and the Battle of Ong Thanh Vietnam, October 1967* (Chicago, 2002), 18–19.

48. Ibid., 19.

49. Ibid., 19–20.

50. NA, RG472, 1st ID AARs, Box 2, Operation Manhattan, 23 April–11 May 1967, 12 June 1967, 1–3.

51. Ibid., 3–9.

52. MacGarrigle, *Taking the Offensive*, 331–336.

53. Ibid., 336–337.

54. NA, RG472, 1st ID AARs, Box 2, Operation Dallas, 17–25 May 1966, 28 June 1967, 1–9.

55. NA, RG472, 1st ID AARs, Box 2, Operation Billings, 12–26 June 1967, 26 July 1967, 1.

56. Ibid., 2–3.

57. Ibid., 3–7.

58. NA, RG472, 1st ID AARs, Box 2, Operation Billings, 3.

59. Ibid., 3–5; MacGarrigle, *Taking the Offensive*, 345–347.

60. Ibid., 7.

61. Shelton, *The Beast Was Out There*, 19.

62. NA, RG472, 1st ID AARs, Box 2, Operation Billings, 7.

63. NA, RG472, 1st ID AARs, Box 3, Operation Paul Bunyan, 19 July–11 September 1967, 9 November 1967, 1–7.

64. Ibid., 7–8.

65. NA, RG472, 1st ID AARs, Operation Portland, 6–9.

66. Ibid., 3–7.

67. NA, RG472, 1st ID AARs, Box 3, Operation Shenandoah II, 29 September–19 November 1967, 12 April 1968, 1–5.

68. Ibid., 6–7.

69. Ibid., 3–4.

70. Ibid., 10.

71. Ibid., 13; MacGarrigle, *Taking the Offensive*, 352–353.

72. NA, RG472, 1st ID G3 Daily Journals, Box 6, 16 October 1967, items 10, 29, 30, and 34.

73. Shelton, *The Beast Was Out There*, 124–128.

74. NA, RG472, 1st ID AARs, Box 3, Operation Shenandoah II, 13–14; MacGarrigle, *Taking the Offensive*, 353–361. See NA, RG472, 1st ID AARs, Combat After Action Interview Report, 31 March 1967, which provides a superb summary of the action. For a detailed analysis of the Battle of Ong Thanh, see Shelton, *The Beast Was Out There*. I was also present at an oral interview by the McCormick Research Center with Welch in August 2002.

75. MacGarrigle, *Taking the Offensive*, 355.

76. NA, RG472, 1st ID AARs, Box 3, Operation Shenandoah II, 13.

77. Ibid.

78. Ibid., NA, RG472, 1st ID Situation Report for 17 October 1967, 1; MacGarrigle, *Taking the Offensive*, 355–356; Shelton, *The Beast Was Out There*,

128–129, where Shelton provides a copy of the battalion's G3 Log for 17 October 1967.

79. NA, RG472, 1st ID AARs, Box 3, Operation Shenandoah II, 13–14.

80. 2nd Battalion, 28th Infantry Log, in Shelton, *The Beast Was Out There,* 128–129.

81. Ibid.; NA, RG472, 1st ID Situation Report for 17 October 1967, 1–2.

82. Ibid., 1–3.

83. NA, RG472, 1st ID AARs, Box 3, Operation Shenandoah II, 13–14.

84. MRC, Hay Collection, Hay to Major General William DePuy, 27 October 1967.

85. Author's interview with Colonel (retired) James George, 8 February 2005.

86. NA, RG472, 1st ID AARs, Box 3, Operation Shenandoah, 17–18.

87. Ibid., 18–19.

88. Ibid., 19.

89. Ibid.

90. Ibid., 22.

91. Ibid.; *1st Battalion, 26th Infantry, Vietnam Chronology,* 11–12; *First Infantry Division in Vietnam,* 1:93–94.

92. NA, RG472, 1st ID AARs, Box 3, Shenandoah II, 25–28.

93. MacGarrigle, *Taking the Offensive,* 431–432.

94. Ibid., 432–434.

95. Ibid., 439–440.

16. Tet and the Light at the End of the Tunnel

1. MRC, Hay Collection, Address by Harold K. Johnson, 19 December 1967, 6.

2. J. J. Clarke, *Advice and Support: The Final Years, 1965–1973* (Washington, DC, 1998), 245–254.

3. *The First Division in Vietnam, 1965–1970* (Paducah, KY, 1993), 55. This is a consolidation of the three volumes of the 1st Division yearbooks published from 1965 to 1968.

4. MRC, 1st ID Operational Report for the Period Ending 30 April 1968, 27 May 1968, 1.

5. NA, RG472, 1st ID ORLL, Box 2, 3rd Brigade ORLL, 8 February 1968, 1–3.

6. S. Tucker, *Encyclopedia of the Vietnam War: A Political, Social, and Military History* (New York, 2000), 133–135.

7. NA, RG472, USARV Historians File, Box 33, Combat Operations After Action Report for Tet, n.d., 6–7.

8. Ibid., 1–4.

9. Tucker, *Encyclopedia of the Vietnam War,* 136–138; A. Langguth, *Our Vietnam: The War, 1954–1975* (New York, 2000), 468–471.

10. NA, RG472, USARV Historians File, Box 33, Tet AAR, 7–9; ibid., 1st ID AARs, Box 4, 2nd Brigade Combat Operations After Action Report, Lam Son 68, 3 May 1968, 1–3.

11. NA, RG472, 1st ID AARs, Box 3, Combat Operations AAR of Task Force Ware, 31 January–18 February 1968, n.d., 1–2.

12. Ibid., 2; D. Starry, *Mounted Combat in Vietnam* (Washington, DC, 2002), 118–123.

13. NA, RG472, 1st ID AARs, Box 3, Task Force Ware, 3–4.

14. Starry, *Mounted Combat in Vietnam,* 122–123.

15. NA, RG472, 1st ID AARs, Task Force Ware, 3–5.

16. NA, RG472, 1st ID G3 Situation Reports, Box 5, 31 January 1968, 1.

17. Ibid., 2–4.

18. MRC, 1st ID Operational Report for the Period Ending 30 April 1968, 5–6.

19. Ibid., 5–6; NA, RG472, 1st ID Situation Reports, Box 5, 1 February 1968, 3; NA, RG472, 1st ID AARs, Box 4, 2nd Brigade Combat After Action Report, Lam Son 68, 3 May 1968, 1–2.

20. NA, RG472, 1st ID Situation Reports, Box 5, 1 and 2 February 1968; NA, RG472, 1st ID AARs, Box 4, 2nd Brigade Combat After Action Report, Lam Son 68, 3 May 1968, 2–6.

21. NA, RG472, 1st ID AARs, Box 4, 2nd Brigade Combat AAR, Lam Son 68, 3 May 1968, 3; MRC, 1st ID Operational Report for the Period Ending 30 April 1968, 5–9.

22. NA, RG472, 1st ID ORLLs, Box 2, 3rd Brigade ORLL for the period ending 30 April 1968, 1.

23. Tucker, *Encyclopedia of the Vietnam War,* 138–140; Langguth, *Our Vietnam,* 474–481.

24. NA, RG472, USARV Command Historian Files, Box 33, II Field Force Combat Operations AAR for Tet, n.d., 26.

25. Ibid., 27.

26. Ibid., 28.

27. A. Millett and P. Maslowski, *For the Common Defense* (New York, 1984; 1994 edition), 588–589; Tucker, *Encyclopedia of the Vietnam War,* 140–143; Langguth, *Our Vietnam,* 486–493.

28. MRC, 1st ID Operations Report for the Period Ending 30 April 1968, 8; NA, RG472, 1st ID AARs, Box 4, Operation Quyet Thang, 11 March–7 April 1968, 30 July 1968, 1.

29. MRC, 1st ID Operations Report for the Period Ending 30 April 1968, 8; NA, RG472, 1st ID AARs, Box 4, Operation Quyet Thang, 11 March to 7 April 1968, 30 July 1968, 2–6.

30. MRC, 1st ID Operations Report Ending 30 April 1968, 27 May 1968, 8; NA, RG472, 1st ID AARs, Box 4, Operation Quyet Thang, 6–8.

31. NA, RG472, 1st ID AARs, Box 4, Operation Quyet Thang, 8.

32. MRC, 1st ID Operations Report for the Period Ending 30 April 1968, 8–9.

33. NA, RG472, 1st ID AARs, Box 4, Operation Quyet Thang, 17–18.

34. Ibid., 19.

35. MRC, 1st ID Operational Report for the Period Ending 30 April 1968, 1–2; see Millett and Maslowski, *For the Common Defense,* 587–589, for a discussion of the characteristics of the US Army in 1968.

36. MRC, 1st ID Operational Report for the Period Ending 30 April 1968, 2–3.

37. Ibid., 9; ibid., 1st ID Operations Report for the Period Ending 31 July 1968, 1.

38. Ibid., 4.

39. Ibid., 4–7; Tucker, *Encyclopedia of the Vietnam War,* 144–145.

40. MRC, 1st ID Operational Report for the Period Ending 31 July 1968, 5.

41. Ibid., 5–6.

42. Ibid., 6.

43. Ibid., 7.

44. Ibid., 13–14.

45. Ibid., 15.

46. Ibid., 6.

47. Ibid., 6 and 15.

48. Ibid., 6–7.

49. Ibid., 15.

50. Ibid., 7–9.

51. Ibid., 8; NA, RG472, 1st ID Organizational Histories, Box 9, Report of Investigation of the Facts and Circumstances Surrounding the Death of Major General Ware and Others on 13 September 68 Near Loc Ninh, Republic of Vietnam, 49–52.

52. Ibid., 51.

53. Ibid., 52.

54. MRC, 1st ID Operations Report for the Period Ending 31 October 1968, 8.

55. Ibid., 9.

56. Ibid., Inclosure 13, Commander's Notes #1, 21 September 1968.

57. Ibid., 5; Medal of Honor Citation, G.O. Number 29, 5 June 1970, in G. Lang, R. Collins, and G. White, eds., *Medal of Honor Recipients, 1863–1994* (New York, 1995), 738.

58. MRC, 1st ID Operational Report for the Period Ending 31 January 1969, 5–6.

59. Ibid., 14–15.

60. Ibid.

61. Ibid., 54.

62. MRC, 1st ID Operational Report for the Period Ending 30 April 1969, 15 May 1969, 3–4.

63. Medal of Honor Citation, G.O. Number 29, 5 June 1970, in Lang, Collins, and White, *Medal of Honor Recipients, 1863–1994, 721.*

64. MRC, 1st ID Operations Report for the Period Ending 30 April 1969, 8–10.

65. Ibid., 10.

66. Ibid.

67. Ibid., 18–19; MRC, 1st ID Operational Report for the Period Ending 31 October 1969, 1 December 1969; MRC, 1st ID Operational Report for the Period Ending 31 January 1970, 10 March 1970.

68. MRC, 1st ID Operational Report for the Period Ending 31 July 1969, 29 August 1969, 4.

69. See ibid., 4–5, for operations. Monthly casualty figures are listed at the beginning of each quarterly report for 1968 and 1969. They match closely the casualty figures found in NA, RG472, USARV Command Historian Files, Boxes 7 and 8, USARV Periodic Reports for 1968 and 1969.

70. MRC, 1st ID Operational Report for the Period Ending 31 July 1969, 6–7.

71. Ibid., 7.

72. Ibid., 3, 9, 11.

73. MRC, 1st ID Operational Report for the Period Ending 31 October 1969, 1–3.

74. Ibid., 8.

75. Ibid., 8–9.

76. Ibid., 9.

77. Ibid., 4.

78. *American Traveler,* 26 January 1970, 1.

79. MRC, 1st ID Operational Report for the Period Ending 31 January 1970, 1–8.

17. The Cold War to Desert Storm

1. Millett and Maslowski, *For the Common Defense,* 599–601.

2. Ibid., 597–598.

3. Ibid.

4. MRC, Oral Interview with LTG (R) Donald L. Watts, conducted 7 November 2014, 2.

5. 1st Infantry Division (Fwd) Public Affairs Staff, *History of the 1IDF: April 1970–August 1991* (Goeppingen, Germany, 1991), 9.

6. Ibid., 12, 26, 30–31, 47, and 50 for examples of reflagging.

7. MRC, LTG Donald Watts Oral Interview, 7 November 2014, 5.

8. Millett and Maslowski, *For the Common Defense,* 613–614.

9. MRC, LTG Donald Watts Oral Interview, 7 November 2014, 3–4.

10. MRC, Oral Interview with LTG (Ret.) Leonard P. Wishart, 8 November 2014, 2.

11. *History of the 1IDF, April 1970–August 1991,* 52–54.

12. Department of Defense, *Conduct of the Persian Gulf War: Final Report* (Washington, DC, 1992), 18–20.

13. Ibid.; Millett and Maslowski, *For the Common Defense,* 633–634.

14. *Conduct of the Persian Gulf War,* 18–25, 487–521.

15. R. Swain, *"Lucky War": Third Army in Desert Storm* (Washington, DC, 1993), 163.

16. *History of the 1IDF, April 1970–August 1991,* 58–63; S. Gehring, *From Fulda Gap to Kuwait, US Army, Europe and the Gulf War* (Washington, DC, 1998), 155.

17. Ibid., 163, 197.

18. Ibid., 197, 199.

19. Department of Defense, *Conduct of the Persian Gulf War,* xiii–xiv, 140.

20. Clay, *Blood and Sacrifice,* 352–357.

21. Swain, *Lucky War,* 198–199.

22. Ibid., 210, 227, 229, 232.

23. The US Army changed its naming conventions for unit designations three times between 1990 and 2010, beginning with the Gulf War. If a tactical situation called for companies to be swapped between two battalions ("cross-attachment"), Task Forces were formed at battalion level. A similar system organizes Teams at company level when cross-attaching platoons. These temporary task organizations became so common that today they are permanent. The chapters on the Gulf War, the Balkans campaign, and Iraq and Afghanistan post–9/11, as well as the Conclusion, reflect these naming conventions. Numbered units are typically abbreviated with a hyphen (TF 1-63 Armor, for example).

Since 2010, the army has reorganized to form permanent Combined Arms Battalions (CABs). In the modern nomenclature a battalion might be referred to as the

1st Battalion, 63rd Armor for purposes of tradition (shortened to 1/63rd under the old system) but is actually a CAB, permanently organized into two tank companies and two infantry companies. Task Forces would not be shown on any permanent tables of organization, just as pure battalions. The cross-attachment would be noted on the order for the operation, and the troop list on that order would show, for example, TF 1-63 Armor (1st Battalion, 63rd Armor), task-organized with one or more infantry companies.

24. S. Bourque, *Jayhawk! The VII Corps in the Persian Gulf War* (Washington, DC, 2002), 223–225.

25. Ibid., 232–239; Gehring, *From Fulda Gap to Kuwait*, 193; Clay, *Blood and Sacrifice*, 352–354.

26. Swain, *"Lucky War,"* 246; *Conduct of the Persian Gulf War*, 262, 264, 272.

27. Swain, *"Lucky War,"* 241.

28. *Conduct of the Persian Gulf War*, 279.

29. Clay, *Blood and Sacrifice*, 357.

30. Swain, *"Lucky War,"* 247–248.

31. Bourque, *Jayhawk!*, 332–337.

32. Swain, *"Lucky War,"* 244.

33. Ibid., 250.

34. Ibid., 259.

35. Ibid., 282, 295–300.

36. Bourque, *Jayhawk!*, 399–403.

37. Ibid., 403–405.

38. Clay, *Blood and Sacrifice*, 357–358.

39. Ibid., 358–359.

18. New Mission: Peacekeeping in the Balkans

1. Richard Stewart, ed., *The United States Army in a Global Era, 1917–2003* (Washington, DC, 2005), 436–438. This is volume two of *American Military History* and is hereafter cited as Stewart, *The United States Army in a Global Era*.

2. Ibid., 423–426.

3. Ibid., 403.

4. Arnold Suppan, "Yugoslavism versus Serbian, Croatian, and Slovene Nationalism," in Norman M. Naimark and Holly Case, eds., *Yugoslavia and Its Historians: Understanding the Balkan Wars of the 1990s* (Stanford, CA, 2003), 116–119.

5. Carole Rogel, *The Breakup of Yugoslavia and its Aftermath* (Westport, CT, 2004), 1–2.

6. Ibid., 6–7.

7. Suppan, "Yugoslavism," 117–119; Rogel, *The Breakup of Yugoslavia*, 6–7.

8. Rogel, *The Breakup of Yugoslavia*, 8.

9. Ibid., 8–9.

10. Ibid., 9.

11. Suppan, "Yugoslavism," 129.

12. Ibid., 130.

13. Ibid., 129–130.

14. Ibid., 131.

15. Steven Metz, *The American Army in the Balkans: Strategic Alternatives and Implications* (Carlisle, PA, 2001), 3.

16. Suppan, "Yugoslavism," 132–33 for the quote; Rogel, *The Breakup of Yugoslavia*, 17–19.

17. Metz, *The American Army in the Balkans*, 3–4; Rogel, *The Breakup of Yugoslavia*, 18–25.

18. Rogel, *The Breakup of Yugoslavia*, 23.

19. Ibid., 18–19; Suppan, "Yugoslavism," 134–135.

20. Rogel, *The Breakup of Yugoslavia*, 21–22;

21. Suppan, "Yugoslavism," 134–135.

22. Rogel, *The Breakup of Yugoslavia*, 23–24.

23. R. Craig Nation, *War in the Balkans, 1991–2002* (Carlisle, PA, 2003), 122–123.

24. Ibid., 149; Rogel, *The Breakup of Yugoslavia*, 26.

25. Ibid., 26–27.

26. John Fine, "Heretical Thoughts about the Postcommunist Transition in the Once and Future Yugoslavia," in Naimark, ed., *Yugoslavia and Its Historians*, 185; Metz, *The American Army in the Balkans*, 4.

27. Rogel, *The Breakup of Yugoslavia*, 29–32.

28. Ibid., 30–31; Nation, *War in the Balkans*, 153.

29. Rogel, *The Breakup of Yugoslavia*, 29–32.

30. Ibid., 31; Nation, *War in the Balkans*, 171, 174.

31. Rogel, *The Breakup of Yugoslavia*, 31–32.

32. Ibid., 32–33.

33. Ibid., 33; Fine, "Heretical Thoughts about the Postcommunist Transition," 185–186.

34. Rogel, *The Breakup of Yugoslavia*, 33–34; Nation, *War in the Balkans*, 179–180.

35. Rogel, *The Breakup of Yugoslavia*, 34.

36. Ibid.

37. Ibid., 34–35.

38. Ibid., 35.

39. Metz, *The American Army in the Balkans*, 4; Rogel, *The Breakup of Yugoslavia*, 35–36; Nation, *War in the Balkans*, 190–191.

40. Rogel, *The Breakup of Yugoslavia*, 36.

41. Nation, *War in the Balkans*, 188–190.

42. Ibid., 191.

43. Rogel, *The Breakup of Yugoslavia*, 36–37.

44. Ibid., 37.

45. Ibid., 38; Metz, *The American Army in the Balkans*, 5.

46. McCormick Research Center, First Division Museum, "1996 Information Paper." Battalions with regimental affiliations in the First Division after the reorganization included units from the 4th Cavalry, the 2nd, 16th, 18th, and 26th Infantry, the 5th, 6th, 7th, and 33rd Artillery, and the 1st Engineer Battalion.

47. Metz, *The American Army in the Balkans*, 5; MRC, *Talon*, Vols. 2, 4, 25 October 1996.

48. Stewart, *The United States Army in a Global Era*, 441–446; "IFOR Deployment," www.globalsecurity.org.

49. Telephone interview with General (Ret.) Montgomery C. Meigs by the author, 6 April 2015, 1. Hereafter cited as Meigs OH, 6 April 2015. A copy of the interview is available at the McCormick Research Center, First Division Museum.

50. Metz, *The American Army in the Balkans*, 5; Stewart, *The United States Army in a Global Era*, 441; Nation, *War in the Balkans*, 195.

51. Stewart, *The United States Army in a Global Era*, 442.

52. Mark Viney, "Quarterhorse in Bosnia: A Case Study of American Stability Operations in the Post-Cold War Era" (a presentation at the 43rd Annual Seminar Series of the US Army Heritage and Education Center, Carlisle Barracks, PA, 19 January 2011), 13.

53. Ibid., 13.

54. Ibid., 14–15.

55. Stewart, *The United States Army in a Global Era*, 442.

56. Viney, "Quarterhorse in Bosnia," 21.

57. Ibid., 27.

58. MRC, *Talon*, 13 December 1996, 6.

59. Nation, *War in the Balkans*, 196.

60. MRC, *Talon*, 27 December 1996, 1; Stewart, *The United States Army in a Global Era*, 443.

61. MRC, *Talon*, 27 December 1996, 1 and 12.

62. Ibid., 12.

63. Meigs OH, 6 April 2015, 1.

64. Ibid.

65. MRC, *Danger Forward*, Winter 1996, 8–9.

66. MRC, *Talon*, 25 October 1996, 2 and 12.

67. MRC, *Danger Forward*, Winter 1996, 9.

68. Ibid.

69. "Operation Joint Endeavor," 2, www.GlobalSecurity.org; MRC, *Talon*, 22 November 1996, 6 and 12.

70. MRC, *Talon*, 22 November 1996, 6 and 12.

71. Ibid.

72. Ibid., 12.

73. Ibid.

74. MRC, *Talon*, 6 December 1996, 4.

75. Ibid.

76. MRC, *Talon*, 1 January 1997, 3.

77. MRC, *Talon*, 14 February 1997, 1.

78. Ibid., 12.

79. MRC, *Talon*, 3 January 1997, 9.

80. MRC, *Talon*, 21 February 1997, 12.

81. Ibid.

82. Meigs OH, 6 April 2015, 3.

83. Ibid.

84. MRC, *Talon*, 14 February 1997, 4.

85. Ibid.

86. Ibid.

87. Ibid.

88. Ibid., 5.

89. Nation, *War in the Balkans,* 201; MRC, *Talon,* 7 March 1997, 5.

90. MRC, *Danger Forward,* Spring 1997, 30; MRC, *Talon,* 7 February 1997, 1.

91. MRC, *Talon,* 12.

92. Ibid., 202.

93. MRC, *Talon,* 14 February 1997, 5.

94. Ibid.

95. Ibid.

96. Ibid.

97. MRC, *Talon,* 25 October 1996, 6 and 7.

98. MRC, *Talon,* 28 March 1997, 1.

99. MRC, *Talon,* 30 May 1997, 4.

100. Ibid.

101. Ibid.

102. Author's discussion with Lieutenant General Rhame, 21 June 2015, at the First Division Museum.

103. MRC, *Talon,* 9 May 1997, 10–12.

104. Ibid., 10.

105. Ibid.

106. Ibid.

107. Ibid.

108. MRC, *Talon,* 25 July 1997, 7.

109. MRC, *Talon,* 27 June 1997, 3.

110. MRC, *Talon,* 1 August 1997, 2.

111. MRC, *Talon,* 15 August 1997, 3.

112. MRC, *Talon,* 5 September 1997, 4.

113. Ibid., 5–6.

114. MRC, *Talon,* 5–6.

115. Ibid., 3.

116. Ibid.

117. MRC, *Talon,* 19 September 1997, 6–7.

118. MRC, *Duty First,* January 1998, 3.

119. CMH, 1st Infantry Division Historical Review, 1997, 54.

120. John McGrath, *Boots on the Ground: Troop Density in Contingency Operations* (Fort Leavenworth, KS, 2006), 46–48.

121. Stewart, *The United States Army in a Global Era,* 441; Rogel, *The Breakup of Yugoslavia,* 64–65; Nation, *War in the Balkans,* 334.

122. Nation, *War in the Balkans,* 333; Rogel, *The Breakup of Yugoslavia,* 91.

123. MRC, *The Sentinel,* 20 April 1999, 3.

124. MRC, *The Sentinel,* 26 November 1998, 4; MRC, The Sentinel, 24 April 1998, 2.

125. Nation, *War in the Balkans,* 335–339.

126. MRC, *The Sentinel,* 22 October 1998, 7.

127. Rogel, *The Breakup of Yugoslavia,* 69–70.

128. Nation, *War in the Balkans,* 223–224.

129. Rogel, *The Breakup of Yugoslavia,* 75–77; Nation, *War in the Balkans,* 225–226.

130. Nation, *War in the Balkans,* 226–227.

131. Ibid., 240–241.

132. Rogel, *The Breakup of Yugoslavia,* 79–80; Nation, *War in the Balkans,* 242–243.

133. Nation, *War in the Balkans,* 231–233, 239; McGrath, *Boots on the Ground,* 52–54.

134. *Time,* 5 April 1999.

135. *Newsweek,* 12 April 1999, 37.

136. R. Craig Nation believes that the means to achieve NATO's goals were debatable, since "NATO had launched an attack against a sovereign state engaged in suppressing a domestic insurgency without a convincing international mandate." Nation, *War in the Balkans,* 244.

137. William Arkin, "Operation Allied Force," in Andrew J. Bacevich, ed., *War over Kosovo: Politics and Strategy in a Global Age* (New York, 2001), 21.

138. Ibid.

139. CMH, 1st Infantry Division Annual History, 1999, 17.

140. Ibid., 50.

141. MRC, *Duty First,* December 1998, 3, "Restructuring the Force for the Next Century."

142. 1st Infantry Division Historical Review, 1999, 17.

143. Lieutenant Colonel Timothy R. Reese, "The TF 1–77 Armor 'Steel Tigers' in Kosovo" (Carlisle Barracks, PA, 2001), 1.

144. Ibid., 1–2.

145. 1st Infantry Division Historical Review, 1999, 17 and 50; Reese, "Steel Tigers," 2.

146. Rogel, *The Breakup of Yugoslavia,* 82–83.

147. MRC, TF 1–26 "Combat Awards Packet for Service in Kosovo, 16 June 1999 to December 1999," 1.

148. Reese, "Steel Tigers," 5–6, 10–12.

149. 1st Infantry Division Historical Review, 1999, 17 and 50;

150. Ibid., 58–59.

151. Reese, "Steel Tigers," 12; McGrath, *Boots on the Ground,* 52–53.

152. MRC, *The Sentinel,* "Letter from Kosovo, 30 July 1999."

153. Reese, "Steel Tigers," 11–12.

154. Ibid., 9.

155. Ibid., 11.

156. Ibid., 22.

157. Ibid., 20.

158. Ibid., 21.

159. Ibid.

160. Ibid., 22.

161. Nation, *War in the Balkans,* 263; McGrath, *Boots on the Ground,* 54. McGrath estimates that half of about 137,000 Serbs living in Kosovo fled to Serbia when the Serbian army withdrew in June.

162. Reese, "Steel Tigers," 22.

163. MRC, TF 1–26 "Combat Awards Packet," 2.

164. Ibid., 1–2.

165. Ibid., 3, "July 1999 Summary of Operations."

166. Ibid.

167. Ibid., 7–9.
168. Reese, "Steel Tigers," 33.
169. 1st Infantry Division Historical Review, 1999, 139–140.
170. Ibid., 140.
171. Reese, "Steel Tigers," 32.
172. MRC, TF 1–26 "Combat Awards Packet," 10.
173. Ibid.
174. Ibid., 11.
175. Ibid., 12.
176. Reese, "Steel Tigers," 80–81.
177. Ibid., 59.
178. Ibid., 96.
179. Ibid., 93–94.
180. 1st Infantry Division Historical Review, 2000, 75.
181. Ibid., 76.
182. Reese, "Steel Tigers," 61.
183. 1st Infantry Division Historical Review, 2000, 77–82.
184. Ibid., 82–85.
185. Ibid., 112.
186. MRC, *Duty First,* July 2000, 5. The headline read, "Big Red One Finally Returns Home."
187. McGrath, *Boots on the Ground,* 53–54.
188. MRC, *Duty First,* September 2000, "IRF Deploys to Kosovo"; 1st Infantry Division Historical Review, 2000, 54–67;
189. McGrath, *Boots on the Ground,* 182.

19. Global Mission: The War on Terror

1. 1st Infantry Division Annual History, 2000, 17, 21.
2. Ibid., 28–29.
3. Stewart, *The United States Army in a Global Era,* 459–476.
4. Donald Wright and Timothy Reese, *On Point II: Transition to a New Campaign, The United States Army in Operation Iraqi Freedom, May 2003–January 2005* (Fort Leavenworth, KS, 2008), 12–13.
5. Stewart, *The United States Army in a Global Era,* 477.
6. MRC, *Duty First,* Summer 2003, 2, John Batiste, "Division Delivers for the Nation."
7. Ibid.
8. Ibid.
9. MRC, LTC Wayne Grigsby OH, 5 December 2005, 1. The original audio of all oral histories cited in this chapter are in the MRC along with a transcript.
10. MRC, *Duty First,* Summer 2003, 2.
11. Wright and Reese, *On Point II,* 15; Stewart, *The United States Army in a Global Era,* 482–483.
12. Stewart, *The United States Army in a Global Era,* 483.
13. Wright and Reese, *On Point* II, 9.
14. Ibid., 89.
15. Ibid.
16. Ibid., 70.

17. Ibid.
18. Ibid.; Daniel Bolger, *Why We Lost: A General's Inside Account of the Iraq and Afghanistan Wars* (New York, 2014), 118–119, 161.
19. Wright and Reese, *On Point II,* 71.
20. Andrew J. Bacevich, *The Limits of Power* (New York, 2008), 98.
21. Wright and Reese, *On Point II,* 99–100.
22. Bolger, *Why We Lost,* 161.
23. Wright and Reese, *On Point II,* 92–94, and 96.
24. MRC, Major General John Batiste OH, 7–8 December 2005, 1; Major Michael Smith, "A Lesson in Deploying the Modern Army: 1st Infantry Division's Deployment to Operation Iraqi Freedom II," 1; Stewart, *The United States Army in a Global Era,* 485.
25. CSI, "Interview with LTC John A Nagl," (Fort Leavenworth, KS: Operational Leadership Experiences, 9 January 2007), 3.
26. Ibid., 4.
27. Ibid., 5.
28. Ibid.
29. Ibid., 8.
30. Ibid., 4.
31. Ibid., 6–7.
32. MRC, *Danger Forward,* May 2004, np.
33. CSI, "Interview with LTC John A. Nagl," 8.
34. Smith, "1st Infantry Division's Deployment," 1.
35. MRC, Batiste OH, 4; MRC, *Duty First,* Winter 2003, 5.
36. MRC, Batiste OH, 4.
37. MRC, LTC Chris Kolenda OH, 6 July 2006, 1.
38. Ibid.
39. MRC, Batiste OH, 4.
40. About 1,000 soldiers of TF 1–63 Armor returned from Iraq as the rest of the Division deployed.
41. MRC, Kolenda OH, 2.
42. Ibid., 2–3.
43. Ibid., 2.
44. Ibid., 3.
45. Ibid.
46. Batiste OH, 8.
47. MRC, Kolenda OH, 3.
48. Ibid., 3–4.
49. Ibid., 4.
50. Smith, "A Lesson in Deploying the Modern Army," 8.
51. MRC, *Danger Forward,* April 2004, 8.
52. Ibid., 10.
53. MRC, Batiste OH, 2.
54. Ibid.
55. Ibid.
56. Ibid., 3.
57. Ibid., 2.
58. Ibid., 3.
59. Smith, "A Lesson in Deploying the Modern Army," 10.

60. Ibid., 11.

61. MRC, Batiste OH, 2.

62. MG John Batiste and LTC Paul Daniels, "The Fight for Samarra: Full Spectrum Operations in Modern Warfare," *Military Review* (May–June 2005), 16.

63. General Abizaid quoted in Bolger, *Why We Lost,* 164.

64. MRC, Batiste OH, 5–6.

65. Ibid., 6.

66. Ibid., 7.

67. Wright and Reese, *On Point II,* 38–41.

68. Ibid., 3; MRC, Colonel Randy Dragon, CO, 2nd BCT, 1st ID, Oral History, 29 November 2005, 1. Dragon's 2nd BCT took over Salah Ad Din Province from two brigades of the 4th Infantry Division.

69. Wright and Reese, *On Point II,* 418.

70. Ibid., 38–39.

71. Ibid., 39.

72. Ibid.

73. Batiste and Daniels, "The Fight for Samarra," 15.

74. Wright and Reese, *On Point II,* 121–122, 419.

75. MRC, "1st Division News," 20 January 2005, 1; *Danger Forward,* April 2004, 10–11.

76. MRC, "1st Division News," 20 January 2005, 2.

77. Ibid.

78. Ibid., 2–3.

79. Batiste and Daniels, "The Fight for Samarra," 19.

80. Ibid., 15.

81. Ibid.

82. MRC, Dragon OH, 3.

83. Ibid.

84. Ibid.

85. Batiste and Daniels, "The Fight for Samarra," 19.

86. MRC, Dragon OH, 4.

87. Ibid.

88. Batiste and Daniels, "The Fight for Samarra," 20; MRC, *Danger Forward,* October 2004, 24.

89. MRC, *Danger Forward,* October 2004, 24; Batiste and Daniels, "The Fight for Samarra," 18.

90. Batiste and Daniels, "The Fight for Samarra," 19.

91. MRC, Batiste OH, 4.

92. Ibid.; MRC, *Danger Forward,* October 2004, 24; Batiste and Daniels, "The Fight for Samarra,"

93. Batiste and Daniels, "The Fight for Samarra," 20; *Danger Forward,* October 2004, 24.

94. MRC, Batiste OH, 4.

95. Batiste and Daniels, "The Fight for Samarra," 20.

96. Ibid., 21.

97. Ibid.

98. MRC, Dragon OH, 4–5.

99. Batiste and Daniels, "The Fight for Samarra," 25; MRC, *Danger Forward,* October 2004, 24.

100. Batiste and Daniels, "The Fight for Samarra," 21.
101. MRC, Batiste OH, 6–7.
102. Wright and Reese, *On Point II*, 382.
103. Ibid., 44.
104. Ibid.
105. Matt Matthews, *Operation AL FAJR: A Study in Army and Marine Corps Joint Operations* (Fort Leavenworth, KS, 2006), 10.
106. Ibid., 14–15.
107. Wright and Reese, *On Point II*, 344–352.
108. Ibid., 44.
109. Ibid.
110. Matthews, *Operation AL FAJR*, 18–20.
111. Ibid., 15–17.
112. Ibid., 42.
113. Ibid., 43–45.
114. Ibid., 45.
115. Ibid.
116. Ibid., 47.
117. Ibid., 48.
118. Ibid.
119. Ibid., 50–52.
120. Ibid., 52–54.
121. Ibid., 54.
122. Ibid., 55.
123. Ibid.
124. Ibid., 60.
125. Ibid., 74. The Marine Commandant's quote came from Thomas Rick's book, *Fiasco* (New York, 2006), 405.
126. Wright and Reese, *On Point II*, 358.
127. Ibid., 45–46.
128. Ibid., 45.
129. MRC, 1st Infantry Division Press Release, 3 February 2005, 1.
130. Ibid., 2.
131. Ibid., 2–3.
132. Ibid., 1.
133. Ibid., 6.
134. MRC, Batiste, OH, 2.
135. 1st Infantry Division Press Release, 3 February 2005, 3.
136. Smith, "A Lesson in Deploying the Modern Army," 13–14.
137. MRC, "Relief in Place Prayer Breakfast," 8 February 2005, 1–2.
138. MRC, "Fallen Soldier Memorial Dedication," 6 June 2005, 1.
139. Kelly Kennedy, *They Fought for Each Other* (New York, 2010).

Conclusion: The Long War Continues

1. Andrew Bacevich, *America's War for the Greater Middle East* (New York, 2016).
2. MRC, 1st Infantry Division News, 10 February 2006, 1.
3. MRC, 1st Infantry Division News, 4 April 2006, 1.

4. MRC, 1st Infantry Division News, 24 February 2006.

5. MRC, 1st Infantry Division News, 29 August 2006, 1.

6. Ibid., 3.

7. MRC, *Army Times*, 10 February 2006.

8. Kennedy, *They Fought for Each Other*; David Finkel, *The Good Soldiers* (New York, 2009).

9. MRC, *Duty First,* June 2007, 5–6.

10. Ibid., 6–7.

11. Ibid., 7.

12. Ibid., 6.

13. Finkel, *The Good Soldiers*; The Combat Aviation Brigade also joined the surge, serving under the command of Multinational Division-North. The 1st Infantry Division headquarters remained at Fort Riley.

14. MRC, 1st Infantry Division News, 25 September 2009.

15. MRC, 1st Infantry Division News, 4 November 2009.

16. Bacevich, *America's War for the Greater Middle East* (2016).

17. Stewart, *The United States Army in a Global Era*, 464–465.

18. Ibid., 464–468.

19. Ibid., 466–470; Ludwig Adamec and Parvez Dewan, *Historical Dictionary of Afghan Wars, Revolutions, and Insurgencies* (New York, 2005), lxxv–lxxix.

20. Stewart, *The United States Army in a Global Era*, 474.

21. Adamec and Dewan, *Historical Dictionary of Afghan Wars,* lxxxii–lxxxv, 27–28.

INDEX